INTRODUCTION TO INFORMATION SYSTEMS

Sharon G. Skinner

Chapter 7: Electronic Business Systems
* Salesforce.com and Others: Challenges of Customer Relationship Management Systems
* GE Power Systems and Corporate Express: The Business Case for Enterprise Application Integration
* Welch's, Straightline, Skyworks, and Pella: The Business Value of Supply Chain Management
* Lowe Worldwide and HP: The Business Case for Swarming Collaboration

Chapter 8: Electronic Commerce Systems
* eBay Inc.: Managing Success in a Dynamic Online Marketplace
* Corporate Express: The Business Value of Integrating Customer and Supplier Procurement Systems
* E-Trade and Wells Fargo: The Business Case for Clicks and Bricks e-Commerce
* Providence Washington Insurance and Tharco: The Business Value of an Online Customer Interface

Chapter 9: Decision Support Systems
* Ben & Jerry's and GE Plastics: The Business Value of Business Intelligence
* Wal-Mart, BankFinancial, and HP: The Business Value of AI
* Proctor & Gamble and Others: Using Agent-Based Modeling for Supply Chain Management
* Boehringer Ingelheim: Using Web-based Tools for Financial Analysis and Reporting

Chapter 10: Developing Business/IT Solutions
* Blue Cross, AT&T Wireless and CitiStreet: Development Challenges of Self-Service Web Systems
* InterContinental Hotels, Del Taco, and Cardinal Health: Implementation Strategies
* Du Pont and Southwire: Implementing Successful Enterprise Information Portals
* Wyndham International and Amazon.com: Cost-Effective IT

Chapter 11: Security and Ethical Challenges
* F-Secure, Microsoft, GM, and Verizon: The Business Challenge of Computer Viruses
* Geisinger Health Systems and Du Pont: Security Management
* Banner Health, Arlington County and Others: Security Management of Windows Software
* Online Resources, Lehman Brothers and Others: Managing Network Security Systems

Chapter 12: Enterprise and Global Management of Information Technology
* Chicago Board of Trade: From Failure to Success in Managing Information Technology
* Global Exchange Services and Allstate: Challenges and Solutions in Offshore Systems Development
* Bio-ERA and Burlington Northern Santa Fe: The Business Case for Global Collaborative Development
* Avon Products and Guardian Life Insurance: Successful Management of IT Projects

INTRODUCTION TO INFORMATION SYSTEMS

Twelfth Edition

James A. O'Brien

College of Business Administration
Northern Arizona University

McGraw-Hill
Irwin

Boston   Burr Ridge, IL   Dubuque, IA   Madison, WI   New York   San Francisco   St. Louis
Bangkok   Bogotá   Caracas   Kuala Lumpur   Lisbon   London   Madrid   Mexico City
Milan   Montreal   New Delhi   Santiago   Seoul   Singapore   Sydney   Taipei   Toronto

McGraw-Hill
Irwin

INTRODUCTION TO INFORMATION SYSTEMS
Published by McGraw-Hill/Irwin, a business unit of The McGraw-Hill Companies, Inc.,
1221 Avenue of the Americas, New York, NY 10020. Copyright © 2005, 2003, 2001, 2000,
1997, 1994, 1991, 1988, 1985, 1982, 1978, 1975, by The McGraw-Hill Companies, Inc.

Some ancillaries, including electronic and print components, may not be available to customers
outside the United States.

This book is printed on acid-free paper.

domestic   1 2 3 4 5 6 7 8 9 0 VNH/VNH 0 9 8 7 6 5 4
international 1 2 3 4 5 6 7 8 9 0 VNH/VNH 0 9 8 7 6 5 4

ISBN 0-07-289042-8

Publisher: *Stewart Mattson*
Senior sponsoring editor: *Paul Ducham*
Editorial assistant: *Jennifer Wisnowski*
Senior marketing manager: *Greta Kleinert*
Media producer: *Greg Bates*
Senior project manager: *Jean Lou Hess*
Senior production supervisor: *Michael R. McCormick*
Designer: *Adam Rooke*
Photo research coordinator: *Judy Kausal*
Photo researcher: *Judy Mason*
Supplement producer: *Matthew Perry*
Senior digital content specialist: *Brian Nacik*
Cover design: *Adam Rook*
Interior design: *Adam Rook*
Typeface: *10/12 Janson*
Compositor *GTS–Los Angeles, CA Campus*
Printer: *Von Hoffman Corporation*

Library of Congress Control Number: 2003116665

INTERNATIONAL EDITION ISBN 0-07-111212-X

www.mhhe.com

To your love, happiness, and success

James A. O'Brien is an adjunct professor of Computer Information Systems in the College of Business Administration at Northern Arizona University. He completed his undergraduate studies at the University of Hawaii and Gonzaga University and earned an M.S. and Ph.D. in Business Administration from the University of Oregon. He has been professor and coordinator of the CIS area at Northern Arizona University, professor of Finance and Management Information Systems and chairman of the Department of Management at Eastern Washington University, and a visiting professor at the University of Alberta, the University of Hawaii, and Central Washington University.

Dr. O'Brien's business experience includes working in the Marketing Management Program of the IBM Corporation, as well as serving as a financial analyst for the General Electric Company. He is a graduate of General Electric's Financial Management Program. He has also served as an information systems consultant to several banks and computer services firms.

Jim's research interests lie in developing and testing basic conceptual frameworks used in information systems development and management. He has written eight books, including several that have been published in multiple editions, as well as in Chinese, Dutch, French, Japanese, or Spanish translations. He has also contributed to the field of information systems through the publication of many articles in business and academic journals, as well as through his participation in academic and industry associations in the field of information systems.

Preface

A Business and Managerial Perspective

Strategic, International, and Ethical Coverage

Realistic Coverage of e-Business and e-Commerce

This new Twelfth Edition is an introduction systems and information technology for business students who are or who will soon become business professionals in the fast changing business world of today. The goal of this text is to help business students learn how to use and manage information technologies to revitalize business processes, improve business decision making, and gain competitive advantage. Thus it places a major emphasis on up-to-date coverage of the essential role of Internet technologies in providing a platform for business, commerce, and collaboration processes among all business stakeholders in today's networked enterprises and global markets.

This is the business and managerial perspective that this text brings to the study of information systems. Of course, as in all my texts, this edition:

- Loads the text with real world cases, examples, and exercises about real people and companies in the business world.
- Organizes the text around a simple five-area framework that emphasizes the IS knowledge a business professional needs to know.
- Places a major emphasis on the strategic role of information technology in providing business professionals with tools and resources for managing business operations, supporting decision making, enabling enterprise collaboration, and gaining competitive advantage.

This edition also contains substantial text material and real world cases and examples reflecting strategic issues and uses of information technology for competitive advantage (Chapter 2), ethical and security issues and challenges (Chapter 11), and international and global business issues and practices (Chapter 12). These chapters demonstrate the strategic and ethical challenges of managing information technology for competitive advantage in today's dynamic global business markets.

> Recently coined, yet already clichéd, the expression "e-business is business" speaks the truth . . .
>
> Contrary to popular opinion, e-business is not synonymous with e-commerce. E-business is much broader in scope, going beyond transactions to signify use of the Net, in combination with other network technologies and forms of electronic communication, to enable any type of business activity [1].

Today, businesses of all sizes and types are using Internet technologies to enable all kinds of business activities. That's what e-business really is. The new Twelfth Edition recognizes that Internet-enabled business processes are becoming so fundamentally pervasive in business that the term "e-business" is becoming redundant in many instances. Therefore this edition has significantly reduced its use of that term, while concentrating the e-business coverage that today's business students need into one chapter on e-business applications and one chapter on e-commerce. The text material and real world cases and examples in these chapters provide students with a solid e-

The O'Brien Method

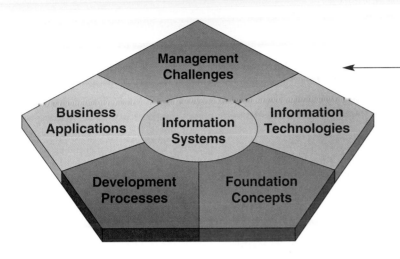

An Information Systems Framework

O'Brien uses a five-area IS framework to reduce the complexity of MIS. On each chapter opener the appropriate area is highlighted depending on what is being covered in that chapter.

This text reduces the complexity of a course in management information systems by using a conceptual framework that organizes the knowledge needed by business students into five major areas:

- **Foundation Concepts.** Fundamental business information systems concepts including trends, components, and roles of information systems (Chapter 1) and competitive advantage concepts and applications (Chapter 2). Other behavioral, managerial, and technical concepts are presented where appropriate in selected chapters.
- **Information Technologies.** Includes major concepts, developments, and managerial issues involved in computer hardware, software, telecommunications network and data resource management technologies (Chapters 3, 4, 5, and 6). Other technologies used in business information systems are discussed where appropriate in selected chapters.
- **Business Applications.** How businesses use Internet and other information technologies to support their business processes, e-business and e-commerce initiatives, and business decision making (Chapters 7, 8, and 9).
- **Development Processes.** Developing and implementing business/IT strategies and systems using several strategic planning and application development approaches (Chapters 10).
- **Management Challenges.** The challenges of business/IT technologies and strategies, including security and ethical challenges and global IT management (discussed in many chapters, but emphasized in Chapters 11 and 12).

Modular Structure of the Text

The text is organized into modules that reflect the five major areas of the framework for information systems knowledge mentioned earlier. Also, each chapter is organized into two distinct sections. This is done to avoid proliferation of chapters, as well as to provide better conceptual organization of the text and each chapter. This organization increases instructor flexibility in assigning course material since it structures the text into modular levels (i.e., modules, chapters, and sections) while reducing the number of chapters that need to be covered.

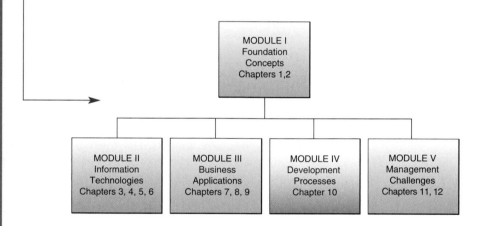

Changes to this Edition

Besides providing all new real world cases, the Twelfth Edition includes significant changes to the Eleventh Edition's content which update and improve its coverage, many of them suggested by an extensive faculty review process. Highlights of the key changes in this edition include:

- Chapter 1 now starts with an introduction to the fundamental roles of information systems in business and an overview of the managerial challenges of IT in Section I. The more conceptual material on the components of information systems is then covered in Section II.
- Introductory coverage of competitive advantage issues in Chapter 2 has been further simplified at the urging of reviewers by removing several topics previously covered, including Internet value chains, e-business/e-commerce strategy development, and total quality management.
- Chapter 4 on Computer Software has been strengthened with new material on business application software, application service providers, XML and Java, and Web services.
- Chapter 5 on Data Resource Management has been restructured to improve its sequence of topics and improved with the addition of material on database software and traditional file processing, which has returned at the urging of reviewers to contrast it with the modern database management approach.
- Coverage of customer relationship management, enterprise resource planning, and supply chain management has been significantly expanded in Section I of Chapter 7 on Electronic Business Systems, emphasizing their role in essential business processes and the challenges they pose, as well as the benefits they can provide to a business. Coverage of functional business systems in Section II has been streamlined to emphasize a few key examples in each functional area of business.
- The content of Section I of Chapter 12 on Enterprise and Global Management of Information Technology has been revised to focus primarily on the management of information technology by expanding coverage of topics on the key management processes and challenges involved, and by moving some of the conceptual material on the impact of IT on managers and organizations to other chapters.
- All other chapters have been updated with new text material, and most in-text real world examples that illustrate topics throughout the text have been replaced with more current examples. In addition, most of the photos and software screen shots in the text have been replaced with updated content.

Solving Problems with Information Systems

Real World Cases

Each chapter includes four case studies of actual (and recent) situations faced by some of the most widely recognized organizations in the world.

O'Brien set the standard for bringing corporate reality into the information systems classroom.

REAL WORLD CASE 1 — Argosy Gaming Co.: Challenges in Building a Data Warehouse

When you've got half a dozen riverboat gambling operations, it's important that everyone plays by the same rules. Argosy Gaming Co., with headquarters in Alton, Illinois, and a fleet of six Mississippi riverboat casinos, had decided that bringing all customer data together would enhance management's view of operations and potentially help strengthen customer relationships. To accomplish those goals, though, the company needed to access a variety of databases and develop an extract, transform, and load (ETL) system to help construct and maintain a central data warehouse.

Jason Fortenberry, a data-warehousing analyst, came aboard at Argosy just as the company's data warehouse project started in 2001. His job was made easier, he says, by the adoption of Hummingbird Ltd.'s Genio ETL software tool, which helped bridge systems and automate processes. But like others going through such projects, he learned the hard way that preparing for the ETL process is just as important as having the right software.

The riverboats each had unique and incompatible ways of defining a host of operational activities and customer characteristics—in essence, the floating casinos were each playing the same game but with different rules. But those problems remained hidden until reports from the company's data warehouse began to turn up inconsistent or troubling data. That's when Fortenberry and his staff discovered conflicting definitions for a wide range of data types—problems he wishes he had identified much earlier. Fortenberry's troubles—and his successes—are typical of ETL, the complex and often expensive prelude to data warehouse success.

ETL is often problematic because of its inherent complexity and underlying business challenges, such as making sure you plan adequately and have quality data to process. Analysts, users, and even vendors say all bets are off if you don't have a clear understanding of your data resources and what you want to achieve with them. Then there are choices, like whether to go for a centralized architecture—the simplest and most common configuration—or a distributed system, with ETL processing spread across various software tools, system utilities, and target databases, which is sometimes a necessity in larger, more complicated data warehouses. Even if you navigate those waters successfully, you still need to ensure that the ETL foundation you build for your data warehouse can meet growing data streams and future information demands.

As the term implies, ETL involves extracting data from various sources, transforming it, (usually the trickiest part), and loading it into the data warehouse. A transformation could be as simple as reordering the fields of a record from a source system. But, as Philip Russom, a Giga Information Group analyst explains, a data warehouse often contains data values and data structures that never existed in a source system. Since many analytical questions a business user would ask of a data warehouse can be answered only with calculated values (like averages, rankings or metrics), the ETL tool must calculate these from various data sources and load them into the warehouse. Similarly, notes Russom, a data warehouse typically contains "time-series" data. The average operational application keeps track of the current state of a value such as a bank account balance. It's the job of the ETL tool to regularly add new states of a value to the series.

For his yearlong ETL project, Argosy's Fortenberry says Hummingbird's Genio Suite, a data integration and ETL tool, quickly became the project's "central nervous system," coordinating the process for extracting source data and loading the warehouse.

But for Argosy, getting all that data into the warehouse didn't produce immediate usable and dependable results. "The lesson was that people thought that they were talking about the same thing, but they actually were not," says Fortenberry. For example, he explains, riverboats calculated visits differently. One riverboat casino would credit a customer with a visit only if he actually played at a slot machine or table. Another had an expanded definition and credited customers with visits when they redeemed coupons, even if they didn't play. So identical customer activity might have one riverboat reporting 4 player visits and another reporting 10. "This type of discovery was repeated for everything from defining what a 'player' is to calculating a player's profitability," says Fortenberry.

IT played a lead role in identifying problems and helping to hammer out a consensus among the business units about how to define and use many categories of data, he says. Now, the data warehouse is running smoothly and producing dependable results for business analysis and management reporting, so the number of problem-resolution meetings has dropped dramatically. Still, Fortenberry reckons that three-quarters of the meetings he attends nowadays have a business focus. "For our part, we now know better what questions to ask business users as we continue with the data warehouse development process," he says.

Case Study Questions

1. What is the business value of a data warehouse? Use Argosy Gaming as an example.

2. Why did Argosy use an ETL software tool? What benefits and problems arose? How were they solved?

3. What are some of the major responsibilities that business professionals and managers have in data warehouse development? Use Argosy Gaming as an example.

Source: Adapted from Alan Earls, "ETL: Preparation Is the Best Bet," *Computerworld*, August 25, 2003, pp. 27–28.

FIGURE 6.9 Extranets connect the internetworked enterprise to consumers, business customers, suppliers, and other business partners.

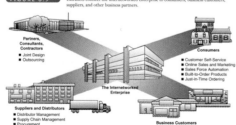

Partners, Consultants, Contractors
- Joint Design
- Outsourcing

The Internetworked Enterprise

Consumers
- Customer Self-Service
- Online Sales and Marketing
- Sales Force Automation
- Built-to-Order Products
- Just-in-Time Ordering

Suppliers and Distributors
- Distributor Management
- Supply Chain Management
- Procurement

Business Customers

business can build and strengthen strategic relationships with its customers and suppliers. Also, extranets can enable and improve collaboration by a business with its customers and other business partners. Extranets facilitate an online, interactive product development, marketing, and customer-focused process that can bring better-designed products to market faster.

Countrywide and Snap-on: Extranet Examples

Countrywide Home Loans has created an extranet called Platinum Lender Access for its lending partners and brokers. About 500 banks and mortgage brokers can access Countrywide's intranet and selected financial databases. The extranet gives them access to their account and transaction information, status of loans, and company announcements. Each lender or broker is automatically identified by the extranet and provided with customized information on premium rates, discounts, and any special business arrangements they have negotiated with Countrywide [2].

Snap-on Incorporated spent $300,000 to create an extranet link to their intranet called the Franchise Information Network. The extranet lets Snap-on's 4,000 independent franchises for automotive tools access a secured intranet website for customized information and interactive communications with Snap-on employees and other franchisees. Franchisers can get information on sales plus marketing updates. Tips and training programs about managing a franchise operation and discussion forums for employees and franchisees to share ideas and best practices are also provided by the extranet. Finally, the Franchise Information Network provides interactive news and information on car racing and other special events sponsored by Snap-on, as well as corporate stock prices, business strategies, and other financial information [17].

Real Examples

The frequent use of real examples illustrates how companies apply the specific information systems concepts.

Analysis Exercises

1. **Application Service Provider Marketplace**
The traditional ASP definition includes web interface (or thin client) and external, Internet based, server-side processing and data storage. However, the business world hasn't always felt constrained by these definitions. Microsoft, McAfee, QuickBooks, and others are providing Internet based application services without meeting these exact criteria.

   Microsoft provides automatic Internet based application maintenance as part of its one-time licensing fee. Through "automatic updates," Microsoft provides updates, fixes, and security patches to its software without IT staff involvement and minimal end user inconvenience.

   McAfee, on the other hand, charges an annual maintenance fee that includes daily application and virus definition updates. McAfee provides it for one year as part of its license. After the first year license holders may continue to use the software, but they must pay a subscription fee if they want updates. Customers tend to pay for this subscription service in order to protect themselves from new virus threats.

   a. Would you use or recommend any of Intuit's online application services (www.intuit.com) to a small business? Why or why not?

   b. America Online provides a free instant messaging service (AIM). This service enables instant messaging, file sharing, and voice and video conferencing through a free application anyone can download and install. Is AOL operating as an ASP? How so?

   c. Visit AOL's "Enterprise AIM services" website (enterprise aim com). What additional features does AOL provide to enterprises? Why do you suppose AOL moved away from the ASP model for their enterprise solution?

2. **eWork Exchange and eLance.com: Online Job Matching and Auctions**
Many opportunities await those who troll the big job boards, the free-agent sites, the auction services where applicants bid for projects, and the niche sites for specialized jobs and skills. Examples of top job matching and auction sites are eWorkExchange and eLance.com.

   eWorkExchange (www.eworkexchange.com). No more sifting through irrelevant search results; fill out a list of your skills and let eWork Exchange's proprietary technology find the most suitable projects for you—no bidding required.

   eLance.com (www.elance.com). This global auction marketplace covers more than just IT jobs; it runs the gamut from astrology and medicine to corporate work and cooking projects. Register a description of your services or go straight to browsing the listings of open projects—and then start bidding. A feedback section lets both employers and freelancers rate one another.

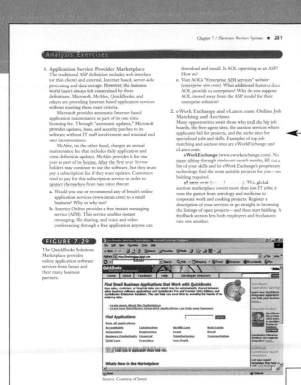

FIGURE 7.29
The QuickBooks Solutions Marketplace provides online application software services from Intuit and their many business partners.

Source: Courtesy of Intuit

Problem-solving, analysis, and critical thinking are important skills. Students hone these skills through a variety of thought-provoking questions and creative exercises.

Analysis Exercises

Each chapter concludes with exercises that challenge students to analyze data from a variety of perspectives. Each innovative scenario inspires them to combine their newly acquired knowledge with analytical, Web-based, spreadsheet, and database skills to solve business problems.

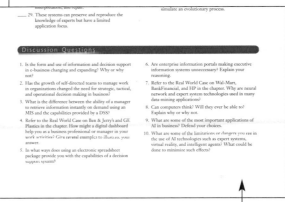

interpretation, and repair.

simulate an evolutionary process.

____ 29. These systems can preserve and reproduce the knowledge of experts but have a limited application focus.

Discussion Questions

1. Is the form and use of information and decision support in e-business changing and expanding? Why or why not?

2. Has the growth of self-directed teams to manage work in organizations changed the need for strategic, tactical, and operational decision making in business?

3. What is the difference between the ability of a manager to retrieve information instantly on demand using an MIS and the capabilities provided by a DSS?

4. Refer to the Real World Case on Ben & Jerry's and GE Plastics in the chapter. How might a digital dashboard help you as a business professional or manager in your work activities? Give several examples to illustrate your answer.

5. In what ways does using an electronic spreadsheet package provide you with the capabilities of a decision support system?

6. Are enterprise information portals making executive information systems unnecessary? Explain your reasoning.

7. Refer to the Real World Case on Wal-Mart, BankFinancial, and HP in the chapter. Why are neural network and expert system technologies used in many data-mining applications?

8. Can computers think? Will they ever be able to? Explain why or why not.

9. What are some of the most important applications of AI in business? Defend your choices.

10. What are some of the limitations or dangers you see in the use of AI technologies such as expert systems, virtual reality, and intelligent agents? What could be done to minimize such effects?

Discussion Questions

Whether assigned as homework or used for in-class discussion, these insightful questions develop critical thinking skills.

Software Skills & Computer Concepts

MISource provides animated tutorials and simulated practice of the core skills in Microsoft Excel, Access and PowerPoint. MISource also animates forty-seven important computer concepts.

Spend less time reviewing software skills and computer literacy. Each text includes a copy of MISource.

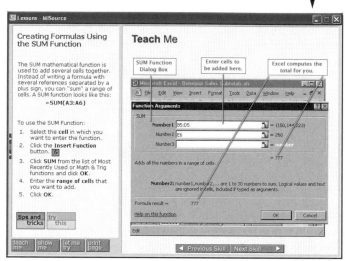

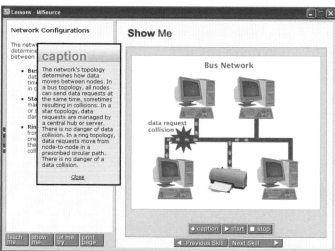

MIS Practice and Principles

MISource includes three video vignettes about the problems and opportunities facing a growing beverage company. Use the questions that follow each vignette as homework assignments or for discussion. Animated presentations of data mining, online transaction processing, and the systems development life cycle give students more perspective.

Empowered Instruction

Classroom Performance System

Engage students and assess real-time lecture retention with this simple yet powerful wireless application. You can even deliver tests that instantly grade themselves.

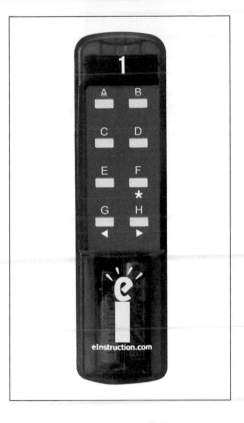

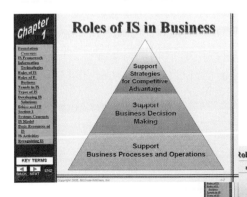

Instructor Resource CD

Everything you need on one CD: PowerPoint slides, Test Item File (in Word and Diploma format), Solutions to end-of-chapter exercises and real world case questions, and much more.

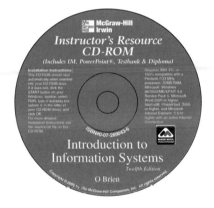

PowerPoint Presentation

Robust, detailed, and designed to keep students engaged.

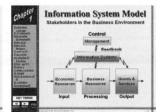

Problem Solving Video Vignettes

Three separate segments show how a growing beverage company comes to terms with problems and opportunities that can be addressed with database systems, telecommunications technology, and system development. Use the questions that follow each segment to inspire discussion or test students' critical thinking skills.

PowerWeb

PowerWeb is dynamic and easy to use. It automatically finds and delivers newly published supplemental MIS-specific content. PowerWeb is the first online supplement to offer your students access to . . .

- Course-specific current articles refereed by content experts
- Course-specific real-time news
- Weekly course updates
- Interactive exercises and assessment tools
- Student study tips
- Web research tips and exercises
- Refereed and updated research links
- Daily news
- Access to the Northernlight.com Special Collection™ of journals and articles

MBA MIS Cases

Developed by Richard Perle of Loyola Marymount University, these fourteen comprehensive cases allow you to add MBA-level analysis to your course. Visit our website to review a sample case.

Application Cases for MIS

Looking for a more substantial hands-on component? The Fifth Edition of Application Cases in MIS (ISBN 0072933631) by James Morgan is the proven answer.

Online Learning Center

Visit www.mhhe.com/obrien for additional instructor and student resources.

Online Courses

Content for the Twelfth Edition is available in WebCT, Blackboard, and PageOut formats to accommodate virtually any online delivery platform.

Acknowledgments

The new Twelfth Edition represents an ongoing effort to improve and adapt this text to meet the needs of students and instructors. For this revision, we received the guidance of sixty-nine reviewers. I thank every one of them for their insight and advice.

Adeyemi Adekoya, *Virginia State University*

Kamal Nayan Agarwal, *Howard University*

Ralph Annina, *Keller Graduate School of Management*

Abdelhaleem Ashqar, *Howard University*

James P. Borden, *Villanova University*

Kevin Brennan, *The University of Rochester*

Ralph Caputo, *Manhattan College*

Carl J. Case, *St. Bonaventure University*

Chandrashekar D. Challa, *Virginia State University*

Robert Chi, *California State University–Long Beach*

Rosann W. Collins, *The University of South Florida*

Samuel Coppage, *Old Dominion University*

Andy Curran, *The University of Cincinnati–Clermont College*

Joanna DeFranco-Tommarello, *New Jersey Institute of Technology*

Gayle DeGennaro, *Franklin University*

Kevin Lee Elder, *Ohio University*

Kurt Engemann, *Iona College*

Roger Finnegan, *Metropolitan State University*

Morris Firebaugh, *The University of Wisconsin–Parkside*

Fred Fisher, *Florida State University–Tallahassee*

Gary Fisher, *Angelo State University*

Thomas Franza, *Dowling College*

Carl Friedman, *The University of the District of Columbia*

Blaine Garfolo, *San Francisco State University*

Norman Garrett, *Eastern Illinois University*

Kemal Gersoy, *Long Island University–Brooklyn*

Ginny Gibson, *The University of Maine*

Rajni Goel, *Howard University*

Vipul Gupta, *St. Joseph's University*

James He, *Fairfield University*

Sam Hicks, *Virginia Polytechnic Institute*

Jeanne Johnson, *Culver–Stockton College*

Donald Kalmey, *Indiana University Southeast*

Kathy Kegley, *Clemson University*

Ranjan Kini, *Indiana University Northwest*

Ronald Kizior, *Loyola University*

Gerald Klonarides, *Florida International University*

Ravindra Krovi, *The University of Akron*

Linda Lau, *Longwood University*

David Lewis, *The University of Massachusetts–Lowell*

Stan Lewis, *The University of Southern Mississippi–Hattiesburg*

Weiqi Li, *The University of Michigan–Flint*

Shin-jeng Lin, *Le Moyne College*

Marneice Liput, *Slippery Rock University of Pennsylvania*

Carla Lowery, *Mississippi University for Women*

Rashmi Malhotra, *St. Joseph's Unversity*

Farrokh Mamaghani, *St. John Fisher College*

Philip Musa, *The University of Alabama at Birmingham*

Janet T. Nilsen, *Metropolitan State University*

Robert Plant, *The University of Miami*

John E. Powell, *The University of South Dakota*

Leonard Presby, *William Patterson University*

Mahesh (Mike) Raisinghani, *The University of Dallas*

Arthur Rutledge, *Mercer University–Atlanta*

Mark B. Schmidt, *Mississippi State University*

Ganesan Shankaranarayanan, *Boston University*

Betsy Page Sigman, *Georgetown University*

Thomas Slivinski, *American University*

Changsoo Sohn, *St. Cloud State University*

Richard W. Srch, *Illinois Institute of Technology*

Gerhard Steinki, *Seattle Pacific University*

Stephen W. Thorpe, *Neumann College*

Kent VanCleave, *The University of Tennessee*

Sameer Verma, *San Francisco State University*

Therese Viscelli, *Georgia State University*

Linda Wallace, *Virginia Polytechnic Institute and State University*

Robert Wurm, *Nassau Community College*

Mario Yanez, Jr., *The University of Miami*

Don Yates, *The University of South Carolina–Spartanburg*

My thanks also go to Robert Lawton of Western Illinois University for his contribution to the analysis exercises, Mary Carol Hollingsworth of Georgia Perimeter College for her work on the PowerPoint slides, Stan Lewis of Southern Mississippi University for his work on the real world case solutions, Queen Booker of the University of Arizona for writing the test questions, Beverly Amer of Northern Arizona University for producing the new problem-solving video cases, Ginny Gibson of the University of Maine for developing transition notes, Toni Sommers of Wayne State University for piloting and creating content for the Classroom Performance System, Karen Forcht of James Madison University for adding instructor resources, Richard Perle of Loyola Marymount University for his MBA cases, and James Morgan of Northern Arizona University for his Application Cases in the MIS book that so many instructors use in conjunction with this text.

Much credit should go to several individuals who played significant roles in this project. Thus, special thanks go to the editorial and production team at Irwin/ McGraw-Hill, Paul Ducham, senior sponsoring editor; Greta Kleinert, senior marketing manager; Jean Lou Hess, senior project manager; and Adam Rooke, designer. Their ideas and hard work were invaluable contributions to the successful completion of the project. The contributions of many authors, publishers, and firms in the computer industry that contributed case material, ideas, illustrations, and photographs used in this text are also thankfully acknowledged.

Acknowledging the Real World of Business

The unique contribution of the hundreds of business firms and other computer-using organizations that are the subject of the real world cases, exercises, and examples in this text is gratefully acknowledged. The real-life situations faced by these firms and organizations provide the readers of this text with a valuable demonstration of the benefits and limitations of using the Internet and other information technologies to enable electronic business and commerce, and enterprise communications and collaboration in support of the business processes, managerial decision making, and strategic advantage of the modern business enterprise.

James A. O'Brien

Brief Contents

Module I Foundation Concepts

1 Foundations of Information Systems in Business 3

SECTION I: Foundation Concepts: Information Systems in Business 4

SECTION II: Foundation Concepts: The Components of Information Systems 20

2 Competing with Information Technology 37

SECTION I: Fundamentals of Strategic Advantage 38

SECTION II: Using Information Technology for Strategic Advantage 46

Module II Information Technologies

3 Computer Hardware 65

SECTION I: Computer Systems: End User and Enterprise Computing 66

SECTION II: Computer Peripherals: Input, Output, and Storage Technologies 78

4 Computer Software 101

SECTION I: Application Software: End User Applications 102

SECTION II: System Software: Computer System Management 115

5 Data Resource Management 137

SECTION I: Managing Data Resources 138

SECTION II: Technical Foundations of Database Management 153

6 Telecommunications and Networks 169

SECTION I: The Networked Enterprise 170

SECTION II: Telecommunications Network Alternatives 182

Module III Business Applications

7 Electronic Business Systems 211

SECTION I: Enterprise Business Systems 212

SECTION II: Functional Business Systems 234

8 Electronic Commerce Systems 255

SECTION I: Electronic Commerce Fundamentals 256

SECTION II: e-Commerce Applications and Issues 268

9 Decision Support Systems 291

SECTION I: Decision Support in Business 292

SECTION II: Artificial Intelligence Technologies in Business 315

Module IV   Development Processes

10 Developing Business/IT Solutions 339

   SECTION I: Developing Business Systems 340

   SECTION II: Implementing Business
Systems 356

Module V   Management Challenges

11 Security and Ethical Challenges 377

   SECTION I: Security, Ethical, and Societal
Challenges of IT 378

   SECTION II: Security Management of
Information Technology 398

**12 Enterprise and Global Management
of Information Technology 419**

   SECTION I: Managing Information
Technology 420

   SECTION II: Managing Global IT 432

Review Quiz Answers RQ-1

Selected References R-1

Glossary for Business
Professionals G-1

Name Index I-1

Company Index I-5

Subject Index I-9

Contents

Module I   FOUNDATION CONCEPTS

Chapter 1

Foundations of Information Systems in Business   3

SECTION I   Foundation Concepts: Information Systems in Business   4

Introduction   4

The Real World of Information Systems   4

   Analyzing Amazon.com   4

Real World Case: Amazon.com: Success with Information Technology   5

What Is an Information System?   6

   Information Technologies   6

What You Need to Know   6

   An IS Framework for Business Professionals   6

The Fundamental Roles of IS in Business   6

The Role of e-Business in Business   6

Trends in Information Systems   10

Types of Information Systems   12

   Operation Support Systems   12

   Management Support Systems   13

   Other Classifications of Information Systems   14

Managerial Challenges of Information Technology   15

   Success and Failure with IT   16

   Developing IS Solutions   16

   Challenges of Ethics and IT   18

   Challenges of IT Careers   18

   The IS Function   19

SECTION II   Foundation Concepts: The Components of Information Systems   20

System Concepts: A Foundation   20

   Analyzing Kodak, HP, and Amersham Biosciences   20

Real World Case: Kodak, HP, and Amersham Biosciences: Information Systems for Sales   21

   What Is a System?   22

   Feedback and Control   22

   Other System Characteristics   23

Components of an Information System   24

Information System Resources   25

   People Resources   25

   Hardware Resources   25

   Software Resources   26

   Data Resources   26

   Network Resources   27

Information System Activities   27

   Input of Data Resources   27

   Processing of Data into Information   28

   Output of Information Products   28

   Storage of Data Resources   28

   Control of System Performance   28

Recognizing Information Systems   29

   Analyzing Kodak and HP's Information Systems   29

Real World Case: Aviall Inc.: From Failure to Success with Information Technology   35

Real World Case: Pacific Gas and Electric Co.: Developing Customer Service Information Systems   36

Chapter 2

Competing with Information Technology   37

SECTION I   Fundamentals of Strategic Advantage   38

Strategic IT   38

   Analyzing GE, Dell, Intel, and Others   38

Real World Case: GE, Dell, Intel, and Others: The Competitive Advantage of Information Technology   39

Competitive Strategy Concepts   40

   Competitive Forces and Strategies   40

Strategic Uses of Information Technology   41

Other Competitive Strategies 42

The Value Chain and Strategic IS 44

Value Chain Examples 44

SECTION II Using Information Technology for Strategic Advantage 46

Strategic Uses of IT 46

Analyzing Intec Engineering 46

Real World Case: Intec Engineering: The Strategic Value of Knowledge Management Systems 47

Building a Customer-Focused Business 48

Reengineering Business Processes 50

The Role of Information Technology 50

Becoming an Agile Company 52

Creating a Virtual Company 54

Virtual Company Strategies 55

Building a Knowledge-Creating Company 56

Knowledge Management Systems 56

Real World Case: Progressive, Yellow, JetBlue, and Gentex: Using Information Technology for Competitive Advantage 62

Real World Case: CDW and Harrah's Entertainment: Developing Strategic Customer-Loyalty Systems 63

Module II   INFORMATION TECHNOLOGIES

Chapter 3

Computer Hardware 65

SECTION I   Computer Systems: End User and Enterprise Computing 66

Analyzing Progressive Insurance and UniFirst 66

Real World Case: Progressive Insurance and UniFirst Corp.: The Business Case for Mobile Computing Systems 67

Types of Computer Systems 68

Microcomputer Systems 68

Network Computers 71

Information Appliances 71

Computer Terminals 71

Midrange Systems 72

Mainframe Computer Systems 73

Supercomputer Systems 73

Technical Note: The Computer System Concept 75

Computer Processing Speeds 77

SECTION II   Computer Peripherals: Input, Output, and Storage Technologies 78

Analyzing Delta and Northwest Airlines 78

Real World Case: Delta and Northwest Airlines: The Business Value of Customer Self-Service Kiosks 79

Peripherals 80

Input Technologies 80

Pointing Devices 80

Pen-Based Computing 81

Speech Recognition Systems 82

Optical Scanning 84

Other Input Technologies 85

Output Technologies 86

Video Output 86

Printed Output 87

Storage Trade-Offs 87

Computer Storage Fundamentals 88

Direct and Sequential Access 89

Semiconductor Memory 89

Magnetic Disks 90

Types of Magnetic Disks 91

RAID Storage 92

Magnetic Tape 92

Optical Disks 93

Business Applications 94

Real World Case: Nappi Distributors and Old Dominion Freight Line: The Business Value of Wireless Handhelds 99

Real World Case: Wisconsin Physicians Service and Winnebago: Moving to Linux on the Mainframe 100

Chapter 4

Computer Software 101

SECTION I   Application Software: End User Applications 102

Introduction to Software 102

Analyzing Intuit and Lone Star Doughnuts 102

Types of Software 102

Real World Case: Intuit and Lone Star Doughnuts: The Small Business Software Challenge 103

Application Software for End Users 104

Business Application Software 104

Software Suites and Integrated Packages 106

Web Browsers and More 107

Electronic Mail and Instant Messaging 107

Word Processing and Desktop Publishing 109

Electronic Spreadsheets   109

Presentation Graphics   110

Personal Information Managers   111

Groupware   112

Software Alternatives   112

    Application Service Providers   112

SECTION II   System Software: Computer System Management   115

System Software Overview   115

    Analyzing Wells Fargo and Others   115

    Overview   115

Real World Case: Wells Fargo and Others: Business Applications of Web Services   116

Operating Systems   117

    Operating System Functions   117

    Microsoft Windows   119

    UNIX   120

    Linux   120

    Mac OS X   120

Other System Management Programs   121

Programming Languages   123

    Machine Languages   123

    Assembler Languages   123

    High-Level Languages   124

    Fourth-Generation Languages   124

    Object-Oriented Languages   124

Web Languages and Services   125

    HTML   125

    XML   126

    Java   127

    Web Services   128

Programming Software   130

    Language Translator Programs   130

    Programming Tools   130

Real World Case: Merrill Lynch and Others: The Growth of Linux in Business   135

Real World Case: Mark's Work Wearhouse and Others: Using Java in Business   136

Chapter 5

Data Resource Management   137

SECTION I   Managing Data Resources   138

Data Resource Management   138

    Analyzing Argosy Gaming Co.   138

Real World Case: Argosy Gaming Co.: Challenges in Building a Data Warehouse   139

Foundation Data Concepts   140

    Character   140

    Field   140

    Record   141

    File   141

    Database   141

Types of Databases   141

    Operational Databases   141

    Distributed Databases   142

    External Databases   143

    Hypermedia Databases   143

Data Warehouses and Data Mining   143

    Data Mining   145

Traditional File Processing   146

    Problems of File Processing   147

The Database Management Approach   148

    Database Management Software   149

    Database Interrogation   149

    Database Maintenance   151

    Application Development   151

SECTION II   Technical Foundations of Database Management   153

Database Management   153

    Analyzing Owens & Minor and Vivendi Universal   153

Real World Case: Owens & Minor and Vivendi Universal: Protecting Strategic Data Resources   154

Database Structures   155

    Hierarchical Structure   155

    Network Structure   156

    Relational Structure   156

    Multidimensional Structure   156

    Object-Oriented Structure   157

    Evaluation of Database Structures   158

Database Development   160

    Data Planning and Database Design   161

Real World Case: Henry Schein Inc.: The Business Value of a Data Warehouse   167

Real World Case: Anadarko Petroleum and Prudential Financial: Challenges of Data Resource Management   168

Chapter 6

Telecommunications and Networks   169

SECTION I   The Networked Enterprise   170

Networking the Enterprise   170

Analyzing Celanese Chemicals and Others   170

Real World Case: Celanese Chemicals and Others:
Wireless Business Applications   171

Trends in Communications   172

   Industry Trends   172

   Technology Trends   173

   Business Application Trends   174

The Business Value of Telecommunications Networks   174

The Internet Revolution   175

   Internet Applications   175

Business Use of the Internet   176

The Business Value of the Internet   177

The Role of Intranets   178

   The Business Value of Intranets   178

The Role of Extranets   180

   Business Value of Extranets   180

SECTION II   Telecommunications Network Alternatives   182

Telecommunications Alternatives   182

   Analyzing Con-Way NOW and Trimble Navigation   182

Real World Case: Con-Way NOW and Trimble
Navigation: The Business Value of GPS Satellite
Networks   183

A Telecommunications Network Model   184

Types of Telecommunications Networks   185

   Wide Area Networks   185

   Local Area Networks   185

   Virtual Private Networks   186

   Client/Server Networks   188

   Network Computing   188

Peer-to-Peer Networks   188

Telecommunications Media   190

   Twisted-Pair Wire   190

   Coaxial Cable   190

   Fiber Optics   190

Wireless Technologies   191

   Terrestrial Microwave   191

   Communications Satellites   191

   Cellular and PCS Systems   193

   Wireless LANs   193

   The Wireless Web   193

Telecommunications Processors   194

   Modems   194

   Multiplexers   195

   Internetwork Processors   195

Telecommunications Software   196

   Network Management   197

Network Topologies   198

Network Achitectures and Protocols   199

   The OSI Model   199

   The Internet's TCP/IP   199

Bandwidth Alternatives   200

Switching Alternatives   200

Real World Case: UPS, Wells Dairy, Novell, and GM:
The Business Value and Challenges of Wi-Fi
Networks   208

Real World Case: Grant Thornton and Others: Return on
Investment Challenges of Internet Phone Systems   209

Module III   BUSINESS APPLICATIONS

Chapter 7

Electronic Business Systems   211

SECTION I   Enterprise Business Systems   212

Introduction   212

   Analyzing Salesforce.com and Others   212

Real World Case: Salesforce.com and Others: Challenges
of Customer Relationship Management Systems   213

Cross-Functional Enterprise Applications   214

   Enterprise Application Architecture   214

ERP: The Business Backbone   216

   Benefits of ERP   217

   Failures in ERP   218

   Causes of ERP Failures   219

CRM: The Business Focus   219

   Contact and Account Management   219

   Sales   220

   Marketing and Fulfillment   221

   Customer Service and Support   221

   Retention and Loyalty Programs   221

Benefits and Challenges of CRM   222

   CRM Failures   222

SCM: The Business Network   223

Benefits and Challenges of SCM   225

Enterprise Application Integration   227

Transaction Processing Systems   228

   The Transaction Processing Cycle   229

Enterprise Collaboration Systems   231

   Tools for Enterprise Collaboration   231

SECTION II Functional Business Systems 234

Introduction 234

Analyzing GE Power and Corporate Express 234

Real World Case: GE Power Systems and Corporate Express: The Business Case for Enterprise Application Integration 235

IT in Business 236

Marketing Systems 236

Interactive Marketing 237

Targeted Marketing 237

Sales Force Automation 238

Manufacturing Systems 240

Computer-Integrated Manufacturing 240

Human Resource Systems 242

HRM and the Internet 242

HRM and Corporate Intranets 242

Accounting Systems 244

Online Accounting Systems 245

Financial Management Systems 246

Real World Case: Welch's, Straightline, Skyworks, and Pella: The Business Value of Supply Chain Management 253

Real World Case: Lowe and HP: The Business Case for Swarming Collaboration 254

Chapter 8

Electronic Commerce Systems 255

SECTION I Electronic Commerce Fundamentals 256

Introduction to e-Commerce 256

Analyzing eBay 256

Real World Case: eBay Inc.: Managing Success in a Dynamic Online Marketplace 257

The Scope of e-Commerce 258

Electronic Commerce Technologies 258

Categories of e-Commerce 258

Essential e-Commerce Processes 260

Access Control and Security 260

Profiling and Personalizing 261

Search Management 262

Content and Catalog Management 262

Workflow Management 263

Event Notification 264

Collaboration and Trading 265

Electronic Payment Processes 265

Web Payment Processes 265

Electronic Funds Transfer 265

Secure Electronic Payments 266

SECTION II e-Commerce Applications and Issues 268

e-Commerce Application Trends 268

Analyzing Corporate Express 268

Real World Case: Corporate Express: The Business Value of Integrating Customer and Supplier Procurement Systems 269

e-Commerce Trends 270

Business-to-Consumer e-Commerce 271

e-Commerce Success Factors 271

Web Store Requirements 274

Developing a Web Store 274

Serving Your Customers 276

Managing a Web Store 276

Business-to-Business e-Commerce 277

e-Commerce Marketplaces 278

Electronic Data Interchange 280

Clicks and Bricks in e-Commerce 281

e-Commerce Integration 281

Other Clicks and Bricks Strategies 282

e-Commerce Channel Choices 282

Real World Case: E-Trade and Wells Fargo: The Business Case for Clicks and Bricks e-Commerce 289

Real World Case: Providence Washington Insurance and Tharco: The Business Value of an Online Customer Interface 290

Chapter 9

Decision Support Systems 291

SECTION I Decision Support in Business 292

Introduction 292

Analyzing Ben & Jerry's and GE Plastics 292

Real World Case: Ben & Jerry's and GE Plastics: The Business Value of Business Intelligence 293

Information, Decisions, and Management 294

Information Quality 294

Decision Structure 295

Decision Support Trends 296

Management Information Systems 298

Management Reporting Alternatives 298

Online Analytical Processing 300

Decision Support Systems 301

DSS Components 302

Geographic Information and Data Visualization Systems 303

Using Decision Support Systems   304
   What-If Analysis   305
   Sensitivity Analysis   305
   Goal-Seeking Analysis   305
   Optimization Analysis   306
   Data Mining for Decision Support   307
Executive Information Systems   308
   Features of an EIS   308
Enterprise Portals and Decision Support   309
   Enterprise Information Portals   310
Knowledge Management Systems   312

SECTION II   Artificial Intelligence Technologies in Business   314

Business and AI   314
   Analyzing Wal-Mart, BankFinancial, and HP   314
Real World Case: Wal-Mart, BankFinancial, and HP: The Business Value of AI   315
An Overview of Artificial Intelligence   316
   The Domains of Artificial Intelligence   316

Neural Networks   319
Fuzzy Logic Systems   320
   Fuzzy Logic in Business   321
Genetic Algorithms   321
Virtual Reality   321
   VR Applications   323
Intelligent Agents   323
Expert Systems   325
   Components of an Expert System   325
   Expert System Applications   325
   Benefits of Expert Systems   327
   Limitations of Expert Systems   327
Developing Expert Systems   329
   Knowledge Engineering   330
Real World Case: Procter & Gamble and Others: Using Agent-Based Modeling for Supply Chain Management   336
Real World Case: Boehringer Ingelheim: Using Web-Based Tools for Financial Analysis and Reporting   337

Module IV   DEVELOPMENT PROCESSES

Chapter 10

Developing Business/IT Solutions   339

SECTION I   Developing Business Systems   340

IS Development   340
   Analyzing Blue Cross, AT&T Wireless, and CitiStreet   340
Real World Case: Blue Cross, AT&T Wireless, and CitiStreet: Development Challenges of Self-Service Web Systems   341
The Systems Approach   342
   Systems Thinking   342
The Systems Development Cycle   343
Prototyping   343
   The Prototyping Process   344
Starting the Systems Development Process   346
   Feasibility Studies   346
Systems Analysis   348
   Organizational Analysis   348
   Analysis of the Present System   348
   Functional Requirements Analysis   350
Systems Design   350
   User Interface Design   351
   System Specifications   353

End User Development   353
   Focus on IS Activities   353
   Doing End User Development   354

SECTION II   Implementing Business Systems   356

Implementation   356
   Analyzing InterContinental, Del Taco, and Cardinal Health   356
Implementing New Systems   356
Real World Case: InterContinental Hotels, Del Taco, and Cardinal Health: Implementation Strategies   357
Evaluating Hardware, Software, and Services   358
   Hardware Evaluation Factors   360
   Software Evaluation Factors   361
   Evaluating IS Services   361
Other Implementation Activities   363
   Testing   363
   Data Conversion   363
   Documentation   363
   Training   363
   Conversion Methods   364
   IS Maintenance   365
Managing Organizational Change   366
   End User Resistance and Involvement   366
   Change Management   368

Real World Case: Du Pont and Southwire: Implementing Successful Enterprise Information Portals   374

Real World Case: Wyndham International and Amazon.com: Cost-Effective IT   375

Module V   MANAGEMENT CHALLENGES

Chapter 11

Security and Ethical Challenges   377

SECTION I   Security, Ethical, and Societal Challenges of IT   378

Introduction   378

   Analyzing F-Secure, Microsoft, GM, and Verizon   378

   Business/IT Security, Ethics, and Society   378

Real World Case: F-Secure, Microsoft, GM, and Verizon: The Business Challenge of Computer Viruses   379

Ethical Responsibility of Business Professionals   380

   Business Ethics   380

   Technology Ethics   381

   Ethical Guidelines   382

Computer Crime   383

   Hacking   385

   Cyber Theft   385

   Unauthorized Use at Work   387

   Software Piracy   389

   Piracy of Intellectual Property   389

   Computer Viruses and Worms   390

Privacy Issues   391

   Privacy on the Internet   391

   Computer Matching   392

   Privacy Laws   393

   Computer Libel and Censorship   393

Other Challenges   393

   Employment Challenges   393

   Computer Monitoring   394

   Challenges in Working Conditions   395

   Challenges to Individuality   395

Health Issues   395

   Ergonomics   396

Societal Solutions   397

SECTION II   Security Management of Information Technology   398

Introduction   398

   Analyzing Geisinger Health Systems and Du Pont   398

Real World Case: Geisinger Health Systems and Du Pont: Security Management   399

Tools of Security Management   400

Internetworked Security Defenses   401

   Encryption   401

   Firewalls   402

   Denial of Service Defenses   404

   e-Mail Monitoring   405

   Virus Defenses   406

Other Security Measures   407

   Security Codes   407

   Backup Files   407

   Security Monitors   408

   Biometric Security   408

   Computer Failure Controls   408

   Fault Tolerant Systems   409

   Disaster Recovery   410

System Controls and Audits   410

   Information System Controls   410

   Auditing IT Security   411

Real World Case: Banner Health, Arlington County, and Others: Security Management of Windows Software   417

Real World Case: Online Resources, Lehman Brothers, and Others: Managing Network Security Systems   418

Chapter 12

Enterprise and Global Management of Information Technology   419

SECTION I   Managing Information Technology   420

Business and IT   420

   Analyzing The Chicago Board of Trade   420

Real World Case: Chicago Board of Trade: From Failure to Success in Managing Information Technology   421

Managing Information Technology   422

Business/IT Planning   423

   Information Technology Architecture   424

Managing the IS Function   425
   Organizing IT   425
   Managing Application Development   427
   Managing IS Operations   427
   Human Resource Management of IT   428
   The CIO and Other IT Executives   428
   Technology Management   429
   Managing User Services   429
Failures in IT Management   429
   Management Involvement and Governance   430

SECTION II   Managing Global IT   432
The International Dimension   432
   Analyzing Global Exchange Services and Allstate   432
Real World Case: Global Exchange Services and Allstate: Challenges and Solutions in Offshore Systems Development   433
Global IT Management   434
Cultural, Political, and Geoeconomic Challenges   435
Global Business/IT Strategies   436
Global Business/IT Applications   436

Global IT Platforms   439
   The Internet as a Global IT Platform   440
Global Data Access Issues   441
   Internet Access Issues   442
Global Systems Development   443
   Systems Development Strategies   444
Real World Case: Bio-ERA and Burlington Northern Santa Fe: The Business Case for Global Collaborative Development   451
Real World Case: Avon Products and Guardian Life Insurance: Successful Management of IT Projects   452

Review Quiz Answers   RQ-1
Selected References   R-1
Glossary for Business Professionals   G-1
Name Index   I-1
Company Index   I-5
Subject Index   I-9

INTRODUCTION TO
INFORMATION
SYSTEMS

MODULE I

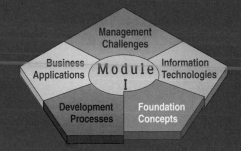

FOUNDATION CONCEPTS

hy study information systems? Why do businesses need information technology? What do you need to know about the use and management of information technologies in business? The introductory chapters of Module I are designed to answer these fundamental questions about the role of information systems in business.

- **Chapter 1: Foundations of Information Systems in Business** presents an overview of the five basic areas of information systems knowledge needed by business professionals, including the conceptual system components and major types of information systems.

- **Chapter 2: Competing with Information Technology** introduces fundamental concepts of competitive advantage through information technology, and illustrates major strategic applications of information systems.

Completing these chapters will prepare you to move on to study chapters on information technologies (Module II), business applications (Module III), systems development processes (Module IV), and the management challenges of information systems (Module V).

CHAPTER 1

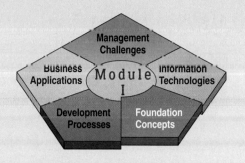

FOUNDATIONS OF INFORMATION SYSTEMS IN BUSINESS

Chapter Highlights

Section I
Foundation Concepts: Information Systems in Business

Introduction
The Real World of Information Systems
Real World Case: Amazon.com: Success with Information Technology
What You Need to Know
An IS Framework for Business Professionals
The Fundamental Roles of IS in Business
The Role of e-Business in Business
Trends in Information Systems
Types of Information Systems
Managerial Challenges of Information Technology
Success and Failure with IT
Developing IS Solutions
Challenges of Ethics and IT
Challenges of IT Careers

Section II
Foundation Concepts: The Components of Information Systems

Real World Case: Kodak, HP, and Amersham Biosciences: Information Systems for Sales Support
System Concepts: A Foundation
Components of an Information System
Information System Resources
Information System Activities
Recognizing Information Systems
Real World Case: Aviall Inc.: From Failure to Success with Information Technology
Real World Case: Pacific Gas and Electric Co.: Developing Customer Service Information Systems

Learning Objectives

After reading and studying this chapter, you should be able to:

1. Explain why knowledge of information systems is important for business professionals and identify five areas of information systems knowledge they need.

2. Give examples to illustrate how the business applications of information systems can support a firm's business processes, managerial decision making, and strategies for competitive advantage.

3. Provide examples of several major types of information systems from your experiences with business organizations in the real world.

4. Identify several challenges that a business manager might face in managing the successful and ethical development and use of information technology in a business.

5. Provide examples of the components of real world information systems. Illustrate that in an information system, people use hardware, software, data, and networks as resources to perform input, processing, output, storage, and control activities that transform data resources into information products.

SECTION I	Foundation Concepts: Information Systems in Business

Introduction

Why study information systems and information technology? That's the same as asking why anyone should study accounting, finance, operations management, marketing, human resource management, or any other major business function. Information systems and technologies have become a vital component of successful businesses and organizations. They thus constitute an essential field of study in business administration and management. That's why most business majors must take a course in information systems. Since you probably intend to be a manager, entrepreneur, or business professional, it is just as important to have a basic understanding of information systems as it is to understand any other functional area in business.

Information technologies, including Internet-based information systems, are playing a vital and expanding role in business. Information technology can help all kinds of businesses improve the efficiency and effectiveness of their business processes, managerial decision making, and workgroup collaboration and thus strengthen their competitive positions in a rapidly changing marketplace. This is true whether information technology is used to support product development teams, customer support processes, electronic commerce transactions, or any other business activity. Internet-based information technologies and systems are fast becoming a necessary ingredient for business success in today's dynamic global environment.

The Real World of Information Systems

Let's take a moment to bring the real world into our discussion of the importance of information systems (IS) and information technology (IT). Read the Real World Case on Amazon.com on the next page. Then let's analyze it together. See Figure 1.1.

Analyzing Amazon.com

This case demonstrates the vital importance of information technology to the success of Amazon.com. But Jeff Bezos's declaration about the importance of "technology, technology, technology" to his company's success, also rings true for the

FIGURE 1.1

Founder and CEO Jeff Bezos has relied on information technology to help him lead Amazon.com to business success by emphasizing peerless Web-based customer sales and service, superior inventory and back-office systems, and business data-based decision making.

Source: John Froschauer

REAL WORLD CASE 1

Amazon.com: Success with Information Technology

Jeff Bezos, CEO of Amazon.com, Inc. (www. amazon.com) has a point about information technology, one he's been making since he started Amazon, but that people are only now starting to believe. "In the physical world, it's the old saw: location, location, location," he says. "The three most important things for us are technology, technology, technology."

Visit one of Amazon's six warehouses today, and it becomes clear why Bezos believes in information technology. They are models of GE-like efficiency. The Fernley, Nevada, site sits about 35 miles east of Reno and hundreds of miles from just about anything else. It doesn't look like much at first. Just three million books, CDs, toys, and housewares in a building a quarter-mile long by 200 yards wide. But here's where the Bezos commitment to numbers and technology pays off: The place is completely computerized. Amazon's warehouses are so high tech that they require as many lines of code to run as Amazon's website does. Computers start the process by sending signals to workers' wireless receivers, telling them what items to pick off the shelves; then they crunch everything, from which item gets plucked first to whether the weight is right for sending.

Along the way the computers generate reams of data on everything from misboxed items to chute backup times—and managers are expected to study the information. In response, the managers sweat every last drop of productivity out of the warehouses. For example, by redesigning a bottleneck where workers transfer orders arriving in green plastic bins to a conveyor belt that automatically drops them into the appropriate chutes, Amazon has been able to increase the capacity of the Fernley warehouse by 40 percent. Today, Amazon's warehouses can handle three times the volume they could in 1999, and in the past three years the cost of operating them has fallen from nearly 20 percent of Amazon's revenues to less than 10 percent. The company doesn't believe it will even have to think about building a new warehouse for another year.

The warehouses are so efficient that Amazon turns over its inventory 20 times a year. Virtually every other retailer's turnover is under 15. Indeed, one of the fastest-growing and most profitable parts of Amazon's business today is its use of its warehouses, and sometimes its entire back end, to run the e-commerce business of other retailers, such as Toys "R" Us and Target.

Call it the Amazon way: Project an image of fun, but inside, hire smart, drive fast, and above all, bet on the numbers. How's customer service doing? Bezos isn't interested in a qualitative answer. He wants to know average customer contacts per order, average time per contact, the breakdown of e-mail versus telephone contacts, and the total cost to the company of each. Jeff Wilke, who runs customer service and Amazon's warehouse and distribution operations, says he looks at about 300 charts a week for his division alone. The boss makes no apologies for his love of data. "With most decisions, you can do the math and figure out the right answer, and math-based decisions always trump opinion and judgment," he says. "The trouble with most corporations is that they make judgment-based decisions when data-based decisions could be made." Says public relations director Bill Curry: "I've seen Jeff end discussions by saying, 'We don't need to debate this, because this is data we can get.'"

Amazon spent big on software development, but now its platform requires little additional investment. Thanks largely to its conversions to the free Linux operating system, technology and content expenses are down 20 percent in the past two years. "There just aren't other companies that let a consumer order two out of what are millions of products in a warehouse and then quickly and efficiently, at low cost, get those two things into a single box," Bezos says.

Bezos has outfoxed other retailers, too, by welcoming competitors instead of fighting them. Alongside its own wares, Amazon now sells other retailers' products, as well as used items. They are all on the same Web page. "This sounded suicidal when Bezos first proposed the idea in early 2001, but he saw eBay as an emerging threat, and he saw this as an opportunity to overtake them," says an ex-Amazonian. Now selling partners' used and new goods next to Amazon's own has become a cornerstone of its offerings. Amazon can do this because its warehouse operations are so efficient. Amazon earns about the same profit margins selling on commission as it does selling retail. In addition, the company doesn't have to advertise that its prices are lower, because consumers themselves can now compare prices from Amazon and other vendors.

Sure this saves money, but it also breeds loyalty, Bezos says. "Giving people the choice to buy new and used side by side is good for customers," he says. "Give them the choice. They're not going to hurt themselves with that choice. The data we have tell us that customers who buy used books from us go on to buy more new books than they have ever bought before."

Case Study Questions

1. Could Amazon.com achieve business success without information technology? Why or why not?

2. Can any business today succeed without information technology? Why or why not?

3. Jeff Bezos says, "The trouble with most corporations is that they make judgment-based decisions, when data-based decisions could be made." Do you agree or not? Explain.

Source: Adapted from Fred Vogelstein, "Mighty Amazon." *Fortune*, May 26, 2003, pp. 60–74.

opportunities for success of many other companies and business ventures today. Like Amazon, a lot of companies now depend on their Internet websites to attract, sell to, and service many of their customers. And like Amazon, the majority of businesses, large and small, depend on information technology to empower many of their basic business processes—from back-office accounting systems, to warehouse inventory systems, to frontline sales and customer support systems. And like Amazon, many business managers and professionals today use the data and information they derive from their information systems to help them make successful business decisions—for example, like Bezos's decision to place competitors' new and used products on the same Web page as Amazon's own products. It is that kind of success that dramatizes the power and the promise of the use of information technology in business today.

What Is an Information System?

Let's begin with a simple definition of an information system, which we will expand later in the chapter. An **information system** can be any organized combination of people, hardware, software, communications networks, and data resources that collects, transforms, and disseminates information in an organization. People have relied on information systems to communicate with each other using a variety of physical devices *(hardware)*, information processing instructions and procedures *(software)*, communications channels *(networks)*, and stored data *(data resources)* since the dawn of civilization.

Information Technologies

Business professionals rely on many types of information systems that use a variety of **information technologies.** For example, some information systems use simple manual (paper-and-pencil) hardware devices and informal (word-of-mouth) communications channels. However, in this text, we will concentrate on *computer-based information systems* and their use of the following information technologies:

- **Computer hardware technologies,** including microcomputers, midsize servers, and large mainframe systems, and the input, output, and storage devices that support them.
- **Computer software technologies,** including operating system software, Web browsers, software productivity suites, and software for business applications like customer relationship management and supply chain management.
- **Telecommunications network technologies,** including the telecommunications media, processors, and software needed to provide wire-based and wireless access and support for the Internet and private Internet-based networks such as intranets and extranets.
- **Data resource management technologies,** including database management system software for the development, access, and maintenance of the databases of an organization.

What You Need to Know

There is no longer any distinction between an IT project and a business initiative. IT at Marriott is a key component of the products and services that we provide to our customers and guests at our properties. As such, there's very little that goes on within the company that either I personally or one of my top executives is not involved in [5].

Those are the words of Carl Wilson, executive vice-president and CIO of the Marriott International chain of hotels. So even top executives and managers must learn how to apply information systems and technologies to their unique business situations. In fact, business firms depend on all of their managers and employees to help them apply and manage their use of information technologies. So the important question for any business professional or manager is: What do you need to know in order to help manage the hardware, software, data, and network resources of your business, so they are used for the strategic success of your company?

This framework outlines the major areas of information systems knowledge needed by business professionals.

An IS Framework for Business Professionals

The field of information systems encompasses many complex technologies, abstract behavioral concepts, and specialized applications in countless business and nonbusiness areas. As a manager or business professional you do not have to absorb all of this knowledge. Figure 1.2 illustrates a useful conceptual framework that organizes the knowledge presented in this text and outlines what you need to know about information systems. It emphasizes that you should concentrate your efforts in the following five areas of IS knowledge:

- **Foundation Concepts.** Fundamental behavioral, technical, business, and managerial concepts about the components and roles of information systems. Examples include basic information system concepts derived from general systems theory, or competitive strategy concepts used to develop business applications of information technology for competitive advantage. Chapters 1 and 2 and other chapters of the text support this area of knowledge.

- **Information Technologies.** Major concepts, developments, and management issues in information technology—that is, hardware, software, networks, data management, and many Internet-based technologies. Chapters 3 and 4 provide an overview of computer hardware and software technologies, while Chapters 5 and 6 provide coverage of key data resource management and telecommunications network technologies for business.

- **Business Applications.** The major uses of information systems for the operations, management, and competitive advantage of a business. Thus, Chapter 7 covers applications of information technology in the functional areas of business like marketing, manufacturing, and accounting, and cross-functional enterprise applications like customer relationship management and enterprise resource planning. Chapter 8 focuses on electronic commerce applications that most companies are using to buy and sell products on the Internet, while Chapter 9 covers the use of information systems and technologies to support decision making in business.

- **Development Processes.** How business professionals and information specialists plan, develop, and implement information systems to meet business opportunities. Several developmental methodologies are explored in Chapter 10, including the systems development life cycle and prototyping approaches to business application development. Chapter 10 also helps you gain an appreciation of the business issues involved in IS development.

- **Management Challenges.** The challenges of effectively and ethically managing information technology at the end user, enterprise, and global levels of a business. Thus, Chapter 11 focuses on security challenges and security management issues in the use of information technology, while Chapter 12 covers some of the key methods business managers can use to manage the information systems function in a company with global business operations.

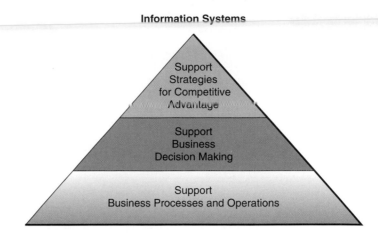

The three major roles of the business applications of information systems. Information systems provide an organization with support for business processes and operations, decision making, and competitive advantage.

The Fundamental Roles of IS in Business

There are three fundamental reasons for all business applications of information technology. They are found in the three vital roles that information systems can perform for a business enterprise.

- Support of its business processes and operations.
- Support of decision making by its employees and managers.
- Support of its strategies for competitive advantage.

Figure 1.3 illustrates the three major roles of the business applications of information systems. Let's look at a retail store as a good example of how these three fundamental roles can be implemented by a business.

The Major Roles of IS: Examples

Support Business Processes. As a consumer, you have to deal regularly with the information systems that support the business processes and operations at the many retail stores where you shop. For example, most retail stores now use computer-based information systems to help them record customer purchases, keep track of inventory, pay employees, buy new merchandise, and evaluate sales trends. Store operations would grind to a halt without the support of such information systems.

Support Decision Making. Information systems also help store managers and other business professionals make better decisions. For example, decisions on what lines of merchandise need to be added or discontinued, or on what kind of investment they require, are typically made after an analysis provided by computer-based information systems. This not only supports the decision making of store managers, buyers, and others, but also helps them look for ways to gain an advantage over other retailers in the competition for customers.

Support Competitive Advantage. Gaining a strategic advantage over competitors requires innovative use of information technology. For example, store management might make a decision to install touch-screen kiosks in all of their stores, with links to their e-commerce website for online shopping. This might attract new customers and build customer loyalty because of the ease of shopping and buying merchandise provided by such information systems. Thus, strategic information systems can help provide products and services that give a business a comparative advantage over its competitors.

The Role of e-Business in Business

The Internet and related technologies and applications have changed the way businesses are operated and people work, and how information systems support business processes, decision making, and competitive advantage. Thus, many businesses today are using Internet technologies to Web-enable business processes and create innovative *e-business* applications. See Figure 1.4.

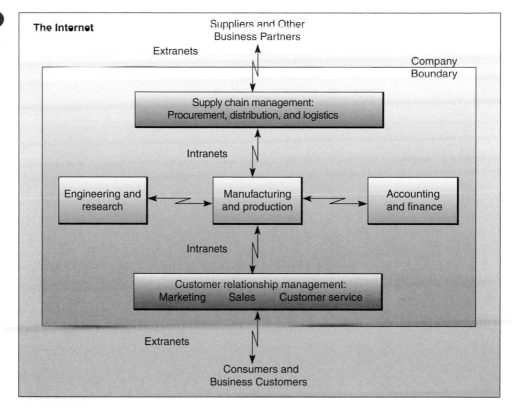

In this text, we define **e-business** as the use of Internet technologies to internetwork and empower business processes, electronic commerce, and enterprise collaboration within a company and with its customers, suppliers, and other business stakeholders. The Internet and Internet-like networks—inside the enterprise **(intranets),** and between an enterprise and its trading partners **(extranets)**—have become the primary information technology infrastructure that supports the e-business applications of many companies. These companies rely on e-business applications to (1) reengineer internal business processes, (2) implement electronic commerce systems with their customers and suppliers, and (3) promote enterprise collaboration among business teams and workgroups.

Enterprise collaboration systems involve the use of software tools to support communication, coordination, and collaboration among the members of networked teams and workgroups. A business may use intranets, the Internet, extranets, and other networks to implement such systems. For example, employees and external consultants may form a *virtual team* that uses a corporate intranet and the Internet for electronic mail, videoconferencing, electronic discussion groups, and Web pages of work-in-progress information to collaborate on business projects.

Electronic commerce is the buying and selling, and marketing and servicing of products, services, and information over a variety of computer networks. Many businesses now use the Internet, intranets, extranets, and other networks to support every step of the commercial process. This might include everything from advertising, sales, and customer support on the World Wide Web, to Internet security and payment mechanisms that ensure completion of delivery and payment processes. For example, electronic commerce systems include Internet websites for online sales, extranet access of inventory databases by large customers, and the use of corporate intranets by sales reps to access customer records for customer relationship management. Now let's look in more detail at how one company is using the Internet for e-business applications.

WESCO International: e-Business Sales and Supplier System

WESCO International, Inc. (www.wescodist.com), a $3.9 billion Pittsburgh-based company, through its WESCO Distribution subsidiary, is one of the largest distributors of electrical products and other MRO (maintenance, repair, and operating) supplies to large companies. WESCO has over 6,000 employees working out of five distribution centers in the U.S. and Canada, and about 360 branches, mainly in the U.S. and also in Canada, Mexico, Nigeria, Singapore, the U.K., and Venezuela, to serve over 100,000 global customers. Major markets served by WESCO include commercial and industrial construction, industrial processes and discrete manufacturers, large OEMs (original equipment manufacturers), data communications and electric utilities, institutions, and government agencies.

Until recently, when WESCO sales representatives received orders for nonstocked items, they had to call the manufacturers directly or check their websites for pricing and availability. That information was then relayed back to the customer in a separate phone call. Although orders for nonstocked items account for only 20 percent of WESCO's business, gathering information on those purchases for customers took 40 percent of the sales force's time, says Russ Lambert, WESCO's director of e-commerce.

To address the problem, the company developed a new e-business system to connect its customer ordering system and inventory systems to the inventory systems of its major suppliers. WESCO had to develop a standard way to query and pull information from a variety of supplier systems over the Web and into its own 20-year-old proprietary, mainframe "legacy" systems. That was the most difficult part of the project, Lambert says.

Since the new system became operational, about 1,000 salespeople in over 400 locations have been able to access the finished goods inventory systems of major suppliers directly. Now, while a customer requesting nonstocked items is still on the line, a salesperson can send a query over the Web to the supplier's inventory system with a one-button application, receive an answer in about 30 seconds, and communicate that to the customer.

WESCO's new Web-based procurement system has resulted in increased sales of nonstock items and cut phone costs by reducing the duration of each call by at least six minutes. It has also saved an enormous amount of time for salespeople, Lambert says. He estimates that the company can save nearly $12 million annually if the new system saves 1,000 salespeople just three hours per week [8].

Trends in Information Systems

The business applications of information systems have expanded significantly over the years. Figure 1.5 summarizes these changes.

Until the 1960s, the role of most information systems was simple: transaction processing, record-keeping, accounting, and other *electronic data processing* (EDP) applications. Then another role was added, as the concept of *management information systems* (MIS) was conceived. This new role focused on developing business applications that provided managerial end users with predefined management reports that would give managers the information they needed for decision-making purposes.

By the 1970s, it was evident that the prespecified information products produced by such management information systems were not adequately meeting many of the decision-making needs of management. So the concept of *decision support systems* (DSS) was born. The new role for information systems was to provide managerial end users with ad hoc and interactive support of their decision-making processes. This support would be tailored to the unique decision-making styles of managers as they confronted specific types of problems in the real world.

In the 1980s, several new roles for information systems appeared. First, the rapid development of microcomputer processing power, application software packages, and telecommunications networks gave birth to the phenomenon of *end user computing*. End

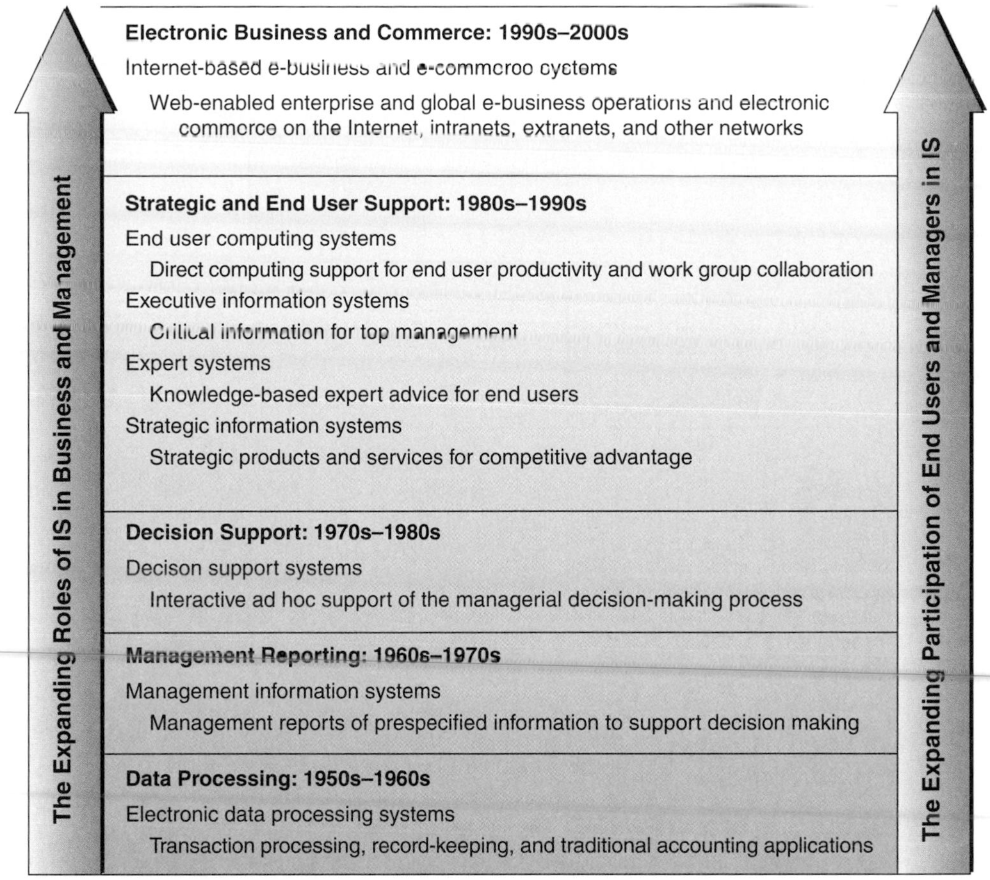

FIGURE 1.5

The expanding roles of the business applications of information systems. Note how the roles of computer-based information systems have expanded over time. Also, note the impact of these changes on the end users and managers of an organization.

The Expanding Roles of IS in Business and Management / **The Expanding Participation of End Users and Managers in IS**

Electronic Business and Commerce: 1990s–2000s
Internet-based e-business and e-commerce systems
Web-enabled enterprise and global e-business operations and electronic commerce on the Internet, intranets, extranets, and other networks

Strategic and End User Support: 1980s–1990s
End user computing systems
Direct computing support for end user productivity and work group collaboration
Executive information systems
Critical information for top management
Expert systems
Knowledge-based expert advice for end users
Strategic information systems
Strategic products and services for competitive advantage

Decision Support: 1970s–1980s
Decison support systems
Interactive ad hoc support of the managerial decision-making process

Management Reporting: 1960s–1970s
Management information systems
Management reports of prespecified information to support decision making

Data Processing: 1950s–1960s
Electronic data processing systems
Transaction processing, record-keeping, and traditional accounting applications

users could now use their own computing resources to support their job requirements instead of waiting for the indirect support of centralized corporate information services departments.

Second, it became evident that most top corporate executives did not directly use either the reports of management information systems or the analytical modeling capabilities of decision support systems, so the concept of *executive information systems* (EIS) was developed. These information systems were created to give top executives an easy way to get the critical information they want, when they want it, tailored to the formats they prefer.

Third, breakthroughs occurred in the development and application of artificial intelligence (AI) techniques to business information systems. *Expert systems* (ES) and other *knowledge-based systems* forged a new role for information systems. Today, expert systems can serve as consultants to users by providing expert advice in limited subject areas.

An important new role for information systems appeared in the 1980s and continued through the 1990s. This is the concept of a strategic role for information systems, sometimes called *strategic information systems* (SIS). In this concept, information technology becomes an integral component of business processes, products, and services that help a company gain a competitive advantage in the global marketplace.

Finally, the rapid growth of the Internet, intranets, extranets, and other interconnected global networks in the 1990s dramatically changed the capabilities of information systems in business at the beginning of the twenty-first century. Internet-based and Web-enabled enterprise and global electronic business and commerce systems are becoming commonplace in the operations and management of today's business enterprises.

FIGURE 1.6

Operations and management classifications of information systems. Note how this conceptual overview emphasizes the main purposes of information systems that support business operations and managerial decision making.

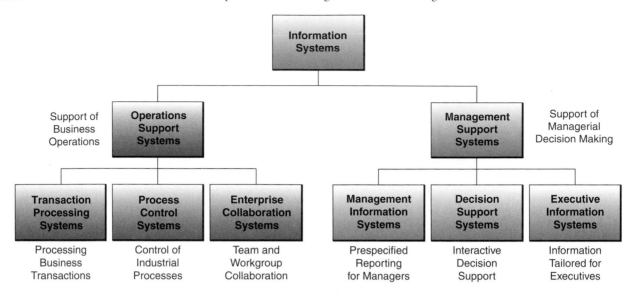

Types of Information Systems

Conceptually, the applications of information systems that are implemented in today's business world can be classified in several different ways. For example, several types of information systems can be classified as either operations or management information systems. Figure 1.6 illustrates this conceptual classification of information systems applications. Information systems are categorized this way to spotlight the major roles each plays in the operations and management of a business. Let's look briefly at some examples of such information systems categories.

Operations Support Systems

Information systems have always been needed to process data generated by, and used in, business operations. Such **operations support systems** produce a variety of information products for internal and external use. However, they do not emphasize producing the specific information products that can best be used by managers. Further processing by management information systems is usually required. The role of a business firm's operations support systems is to efficiently process business transactions, control industrial processes, support enterprise communications and collaboration, and update corporate databases. See Figure 1.7.

Transaction processing systems are an important example of operations support systems that record and process data resulting from business transactions. They process transactions in two basic ways. In *batch processing*, transactions data are accumulated over a period of time and processed periodically. In *real-time* (or online) processing, data are processed immediately after a transaction occurs. For example, point-of-sale (POS)

FIGURE 1.7

A summary of operations support systems with examples.

Operations Support Systems
● **Transaction processing systems.** Process data resulting from business transactions, update operational databases, and produce business documents. Examples: sales and inventory processing and accounting systems.
● **Process control systems.** Monitor and control industrial processes. Examples: petroleum refining, power generation, and steel production systems.
● **Enterprise collaboration systems.** Support team, workgroup, and enterprise communications and collaboration. Examples: e-mail, chat, and videoconferencing groupware systems.

FIGURE 1.8

QuickBooks is a popular accounting package that automates small business accounting transaction processing while providing business owners with management reports.

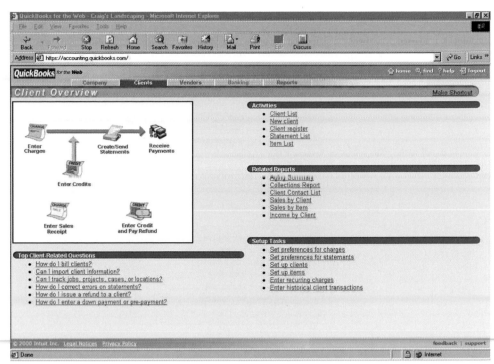

Source: Courtesy of QuickBooks.

systems at many retail stores use electronic cash register terminals to electronically capture and transmit sales data over telecommunications links to regional computer centers for immediate (real-time) or nightly (batch) processing. Figure 1.8 is an example of software that automates accounting transaction processing.

Process control systems monitor and control physical processes. For example, a petroleum refinery uses electronic sensors linked to computers to continually monitor chemical processes and make instant (real-time) adjustments that control the refinery process. **Enterprise collaboration systems** enhance team and workgroup communications and productivity, and include applications that are sometimes called *office automation systems.* For example, knowledge workers in a project team may use electronic mail to send and receive electronic messages, and videoconferencing to hold electronic meetings to coordinate their activities.

Management Support Systems

When information system applications focus on providing information and support for effective decision making by managers, they are called **management support systems.** Providing information and support for decision making by all types of managers and business professionals is a complex task. Conceptually, several major types of information systems support a variety of decision-making responsibilities: (1) management information systems, (2) decision support systems, and (3) executive information systems. See Figure 1.9.

FIGURE 1.9

A summary of management support systems with examples.

Management Support Systems
• **Management information systems.** Provide information in the form of prespecified reports and displays to support business decision making. Examples: sales analysis, production performance, and cost trend reporting systems.
• **Decision support systems.** Provide interactive ad hoc support for the decision-making processes of managers and other business professionals. Examples: product pricing, profitability forecasting, and risk analysis systems.
• **Executive information systems.** Provide critical information from MIS, DSS and other sources tailored to the information needs of executives. Examples: systems for easy access to analyses of business performance, actions of competitors, and economic developments to support strategic planning.

FIGURE 1.10

Management information systems provide information to business professionals in a variety of easy-to-use formats.

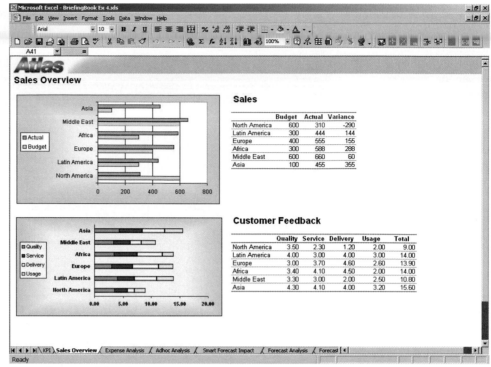

Source: Courtesy of Comshare.

Management information systems provide information in the form of reports and displays to managers and many business professionals. For example, sales managers may use their networked computers and Web browsers to get instantaneous displays about the sales results of their products and to access their corporate intranet for daily sales analysis reports that evaluate sales made by each salesperson. **Decision support systems** give direct computer support to managers during the decision-making process. For example, advertising managers may use an electronic spreadsheet program to do what-if analysis as they test the impact of alternative advertising budgets on the forecasted sales of new products. **Executive information systems** provide critical information from a wide variety of internal and external sources in easy-to-use displays to executives and managers. For example, top executives may use touchscreen terminals to instantly view text and graphics displays that highlight key areas of organizational and competitive performance. Figure 1.10 is an example of an MIS report display.

Other Classifications of Information Systems

Several other categories of information systems can support either operations or management applications. For example, **expert systems** can provide expert advice for operational chores like equipment diagnostics, or managerial decisions such as loan portfolio management. **Knowledge management systems** are knowledge-based information systems that support the creation, organization, and dissemination of business knowledge to employees and managers throughout a company. Information systems that focus on operational and managerial applications in support of basic business functions such as accounting or marketing are known as **functional business systems.** Finally, **strategic information systems** apply information technology to a firm's products, services, or business processes to help it gain a strategic advantage over its competitors. See Figure 1.11.

It is also important to realize that business applications of information systems in the real world are typically integrated combinations of the several types of information systems we have just mentioned. That's because conceptual classifications of information systems are designed to emphasize the many different roles of information systems. In practice, these roles are combined into integrated or **cross-functional informational**

FIGURE 1.11   A summary of other categories of information systems with examples.

Other Categories of Information Systems

- **Expert systems.** Knowledge-based systems that provide expert advice and act as expert consultants to users. Examples: credit application advisor, process monitor, and diagnostic maintenance systems.
- **Knowledge management systems.** Knowledge-based systems that support the creation, organization, and dissemination of business knowledge within the enterprise. Examples: intranet access to best business practices, sales proposal strategies, and customer problem resolution systems.
- **Strategic information systems.** Support operations or management processes that provide a firm with strategic products, services, and capabilities for competitive advantage. Examples: online stock trading, shipment tracking, and e-commerce Web systems.
- **Functional business systems.** Support a variety of operational and managerial applications of the basic business functions of a company. Examples: information systems that support applications in accounting, finance, marketing, operations management, and human resource management.

systems that provide a variety of functions. Thus, most information systems are designed to produce information and support decision making for various levels of management and business functions, as well as do record-keeping and transaction processing chores. So whenever you analyze an information system, you will probably see that it provides information for a variety of managerial levels and business functions.

Managerial Challenges of Information Technology

Figure 1.12 illustrates the scope of the challenges and opportunities facing business managers and professionals in effectively managing information systems and technologies. Success in today's dynamic business environment depends heavily on maximizing the use of Internet-based technologies and Web-enabled information systems to meet the competitive requirements of customers, suppliers, and other business partners in a global marketplace. Figure 1.12 also emphasizes that information systems and their technologies must be managed to support the business strategies, business processes, and organizational structures and culture of a business enterprise. That's because computer-based information systems, though heavily dependent on information technologies, are designed, operated, and used by people in a variety of organizational settings and business

FIGURE 1.12   Examples of the challenges and opportunities that business managers face in managing information systems and technologies to meet business goals.

Business / IT Challenges

- Speed and flexibility requirements of product development, manufacturing, and delivery cycles
- Reengineering and cross-functional integration of business processes using Internet technologies
- Intergration of e-business and e-commerce into the organization's strategies, processes, structure, and culture

Business / IT Developments

- Use of the Internet, intranets, extranets, and the Web as the primary IT infrastructure
- Diffusion of Web technology to internetwork employees, customers, and suppliers
- Global networked computing, collaboration, and decision support systems

Business / IT Goals

- Give customers what they want, when and how they want it, at the lowest cost
- Coordination of manufacturing and business processes with suppliers and customers
- Marketing channel partnerships with suppliers and distributors

environments. The goal of many companies today is to maximize their customer and business value by using information technology to support their employees in implementing cooperative business processes with customers, suppliers, and others.

Success and Failure with IT

Therefore, the success of an information system should not be measured only by its *efficiency* in terms of minimizing costs, time, and the use of information resources. Success should also be measured by the *effectiveness* of information technology in supporting an organization's business strategies, enabling its business processes, enhancing its organizational structures and culture, and increasing the customer and business value of the enterprise.

However, it is important that you realize that information technology and information systems can be mismanaged and misapplied so that IS performance problems create both technological and business failure. Let's look at an example of how information technology contributed to business failure and success at a major corporation.

Hershey Foods: Failure and Success with IT

Hershey Foods Corp. (www.hersheys.com) ran into major problems when it deployed SAP AG's enterprise resource planning (ERP) software and other business applications in 1999. But the candy maker had better luck with a major upgrade to the Web-enabled version of the ERP software (that supports information processing for key business processes) that was completed in 2002.

A $112 million ERP project blew up in the face of Hershey back then while it struggled to fix order-processing problems that hampered its ability to ship candy and other products to retailers. Analysts and sources in the industry said the Hershey, Pennsylvania, manufacturer appeared to have lost a gamble when it installed a wide swath of SAP AG's R/3 enterprise resource planning applications, plus companion packages from two other vendors simultaneously, during one of its busiest shipping seasons. Hershey squeezed what was originally envisioned as a four-year project into just 30 months before going live with the full ERP system in July of 1999. That's when retailers began ordering large amounts of candy for back-to-school and Halloween sales.

On the other hand, Hershey says the recent upgrade of its enterprise resource planning (ERP) system to a new R/3 version was completed 20 percent under budget and without any of the order processing and product-shipment disruptions that marred the initial $112 million rollout in 1999. The upgrade began in July 2001 and was finished in May 2002, the Hershey, Pennsylvania–based company said.

Hershey said it was able to make more than 30 improvements to its core business processes within 60 days of going live with R/3 4.6, which is part of SAP's mySAP.com e-business product line. The company cited enhancements such as the automation of pick-list processing and materials management invoice verification, plus credit processing for distributors to military customers.

Those improvements have helped reduce costs and speed up processing times, Hershey said in a statement. The company added that it has also "achieved a near-zero-defect production environment" with R/3 4.6 and is using SAP's business analysis tools to measure the impact of sales and marketing programs as they happen. In the statement, Joe Zakutney, director of the SAP upgrade program, said Hershey's IT staff was able to exceed its delivery commitments for the project because of "strong program management and executive leadership, diligent planning and . . . an extensive testing and training plan" [7, 10].

Developing IS Solutions

Developing successful information system solutions to business problems is a major challenge for business managers and professionals today. As a business professional, you will be responsible for proposing or developing new or improved uses of information technologies for your company. As a business manager, you will also frequently manage the development efforts of information systems specialists and other business end users.

FIGURE 1.13

Developing information systems solutions to business problems can be implemented and managed as a multistep process or cycle.

Most computer-based information systems are conceived, designed, and implemented using some form of systematic development process. Figure 1.13 shows that several major activities must be accomplished and managed in a complete IS development cycle. In this development process, end users and information specialists *design* information system applications based on an *analysis* of the business requirements of an organization. Examples of other activities include *investigating* the economic or technical feasibility of a proposed application, acquiring and learning how to use the software required to *implement* the new system, and making improvements to *maintain* the business value of a system.

We will discuss the details of the information systems development process in Chapter 10. Many of the business and managerial challenges that arise in developing and implementing new uses of information technology will be explored in Chapters 11 and 12. Now let's look at an example of the challenges faced and overcome by a company that developed and installed a major new information system application. This example emphasizes how important good systems development practices are to a business.

A-DEC Inc.: Challenges in Systems Development

After turning on Baan Co.'s enterprise resource planning (ERP) suite of business software, A-DEC expected it to automate much of their manufacturing, distribution, and financial information processing. But they soon fell behind on processing orders, building products, and then shipping the goods to dealers. "We lost a lot of business," said CIO Keith Bearden, who was brought in to manage A-DEC's information systems three months into the rollout. To get by, the Newberg, Oregon, dental equipment maker even had to fill some orders outside the system "because workers didn't understand it, and the performance was so bad," he said. At A-DEC, business changes initially were fought, Bearden said. End-user training also fell short at first, he said, and the IT department underestimated the processing power that Baan's software required.

After Bearden was hired, he pulled together a stabilization team from all parts of the company. It took about six months of systems development work to fix the performance issues by changing databases and upgrading A-DEC's servers and network. Another six months were spent redesigning business processes and training users. All that work basically doubled the cost of the project, Bearden said. "We spent a lot of money just cleaning up problems," he said. Even now, 50-plus key users spend 20 percent of their work time looking for ways to improve A-DEC's use of the software.

But the company now is getting some of the benefits it expected, Bearden said. For example, inventory levels have been cut by about 30 percent since the new system was put into use. And one of A-DEC's four product lines has been switched to a fast turnaround modular manufacturing approach that wasn't feasible before [6].

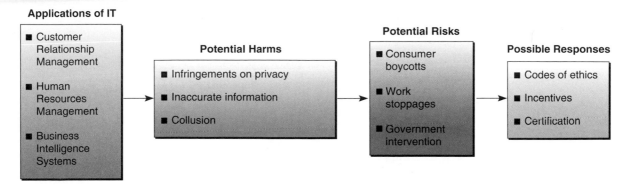

FIGURE 1.14 Examples of some of the ethical challenges that must be faced by business managers who implement major applications of information technology.

Challenges of Ethics and IT

As a prospective manager, business professional, and knowledge worker, you will be challenged by the **ethical responsibilities** generated by the use of information technology. For example, what uses of information technology might be considered improper, irresponsible, or harmful to other individuals or to society? What is the proper business use of the Internet and an organization's IT resources? What does it take to be a **responsible end user** of information technology? How can you protect yourself from computer crime and other risks of information technology? These are some of the questions that outline the ethical dimensions of information systems that we will discuss and illustrate with Real World Cases in Chapter 11 and other chapters of this text. Figure 1.14 outlines some of the ethical risks that may arise in the use of several major applications of information technology. The following example illustrates some of the security and ethical challenges in the use of business resources to access the Internet.

Link Staffing: Network Security and Ethical Use

Antivirus and e-mail filtering tools are being supplemented in many companies with new measures aimed at reducing the risk of attacks on their company networks. "E-mail, to me, is always the weakest link, because you are open to just about anything and everything that comes over the Web," says George Gualda, CIO at Link Staffing Services Inc. (www.linkstaffing.com) in Houston.

Link prohibits attachments of certain types and sizes on its network. All Internet-based chatting is banned, and users aren't allowed to download and install software. Scripting functions are disabled to prevent unauthorized scripts from wreaking havoc, says Gualda. Link Staffing uses a secure virtual private network (VPN) service from OpenReach Inc. to connect its 45 remote sites. The OpenReach VPN provides firewall and encryption services, but Link placed an extra firewall in front of the VPN anyway.

Augmenting physical and electronic security measures with IT security and ethical use policies that are clearly articulated and enforced is also crucial, Gualda says. Link Staffing has a tough IT and Internet usage policy that employees must abide by. Failure to comply can result in termination, says Gualda, who has fired two employees for unethical use in the past. To enforce the policy, the company uses network monitoring and auditing software tools to inventory employee computer usage [9].

Challenges of IT Careers

Information technology and its uses in information systems have created interesting, highly paid, and challenging career opportunities for millions of men and women. So learning more about information technology may help you decide if you want to pursue an IT-related career. Employment opportunities in the field of information systems are excellent, as organizations continue to expand their use of information technology. However, this poses a resource management challenge to many companies, since there frequently are shortages of qualified information systems personnel in a variety of job categories. Also, job requirements in information systems are continually changing due to dynamic developments in business and information technology.

One major recruiter is the IT industry itself. Thousands of companies develop, manufacture, market, and service computer hardware, software, data, and network products and services, or provide e-business and commerce applications and services, end user training, or business systems consulting. However, the biggest need for qualified people comes from the millions of businesses, government agencies, and other organizations that use information technology. They need many types of IS professionals such as systems analysts, software developers, and network managers to help them plan, develop, implement, and manage today's Internet-based and Web-enabled business/IT applications. Let's take a look at IT career challenges at a leading Web company.

Amazon.com: IT Career Challenges	John Vlastelca is the technical recruiting manager of Amazon.com Inc. in Seattle. He says: "We have a huge demand for software developers and systems analysts who have experience building systems that support relationships with customers online—people who bring together a retailing background and some IT background. We hire smart folks, and they are working their butts off. There is a heavy dose of informality. People aren't title-centric; the best idea wins and the career path is often a vertical crossover to management or content areas.

"The one thing that drives us is an obsession with the customer. What helps us make our selection decision is the question, 'Is this a technical person who views technology as a means to an end, where the end is the customer? Or does this person define him or herself as just a Java programmer?'

"But the bar is incredibly high here. It is really hard for my team to find the combination of skills—the software engineer who really understands the customer and the business. So half don't make it because they are not strong enough technically. Other reasons have to do with soft skills—being open to ideas, just raw smarts, and not being passionate enough. The problem space we operate in is unexplored territory" [3].

The IS Function

In summary, successful management of information systems and technologies presents major challenges to business managers and professionals. Thus, the information systems function represents:

- A major functional area of business that is as important to business success as the functions of accounting, finance, operations management, marketing, and human resources management.

- An important contributor to operational efficiency, employee productivity and morale, and customer service and satisfaction.

- A major source of information and support needed to promote effective decision making by managers and business professionals.

- A vital ingredient in developing competitive products and services that give an organization a strategic advantage in the global marketplace.

- A dynamic, rewarding, and challenging career opportunity for millions of men and women.

- A key component of the resources, infrastructure, and capabilities of today's networked business enterprises.

SECTION II Foundation Concepts: The Components of Information Systems

System Concepts: A Foundation

System concepts underlie all business processes and the field of information systems. That's why we need to discuss how generic system concepts apply to business firms and the components and activities of information systems. Understanding system concepts will help you understand many other concepts in the technology, applications, development, and management of information systems that we will cover in this text. For example, system concepts help you understand:

- **Technology.** That computer networks are systems of information processing components that use a variety of hardware, software, data management, and telecommunications network technologies.

- **Applications.** That electronic business and commerce applications involve interconnected business information systems.

- **Development.** That developing ways to use information technology in business includes designing the basic components of information systems.

- **Management.** That managing information technology emphasizes the quality, strategic business value, and security of an organization's information systems.

Analyzing Kodak, HP, and Amersham Biosciences

Read the Real World Case on Kodak, HP, and Amersham Biosciences on the next page. We can learn a lot from this case about the use of information technology to empower and support business professionals today. See Figure 1.15.

Kodak and Hewlett-Packard had a problem. Their marketing departments were producing a lot of information in a variety of media about their products, customers, orders, and sales and promotion strategies, but they were failing to make them easily accessible to their sales forces scattered across the globe. The solution was to install a Web-based software tool that could capture, update, and manage such multimedia

FIGURE 1.15

Kodak and HP implemented sales readiness systems that provide their global salesforces with Web-based access to sales and marketing materials.

Source: Corbis

REAL WORLD CASE 2

Kodak, HP, and Amersham Biosciences: Information Systems for Sales Support

Call it a classic case of silo syndrome. Every month, corporate marketing departments spend hundreds of hours and tens of thousands of dollars conducting research, preparing reports, and developing promotional materials designed to help their companies' salespeople sell more products and services. The problem is that salespeople often have no easy way to access these gold mines of information.

"Like a lot of companies, Kodak was good at collecting data but not very good at sharing and updating that data," says James Sanford, senior manager of sales communication and strategy development at Eastman Kodak Co.'s (www.kodak.com) consumer imaging unit in Atlanta. The upshot was that a lot of scattered but valuable marketing information and other intellectual property, such as details about customer preferences and orders, was going untapped by the Rochester, N.Y.–based company's sales force.

That's the business challenge Eloquent Inc. (www.eloquent.com) is addressing with its LaunchForce content production and navigation software, which enables Kodak, Hewlett-Packard Co., and several other big companies to deliver a full range of product information—including text, synchronized video, graphics, audio and search capabilities—to globally dispersed sales organizations. Eloquent says the software is a "sales readiness tool" that can give salespeople instant access to information about new products, pricing, and special promotions, all of which can be critical to sealing a deal and boosting sales.

In August, Kodak deployed Eloquent's software as a means of establishing a central Web-based repository for all product information and collateral marketing materials. The results so far have been "very positive," Sanford says. But, he adds, "I don't think you can say it increases sales. What it has really done is allow people to get more done and spend more face time with customers as opposed to calling around for information on the phone."

At HP's Nonstop Enterprise Division in Cupertino, California, program manager Tom Hill says the Eloquent system has delivered a tenfold return on investment since its deployment in November 2001. Hill says HP (www.hp.com) is in the process of "closing the loop on sales readiness" by tapping the Eloquent software's capability to track and report on how frequently people actually use the system and to measure what they learn from it.

For example, Hill says he can provide a sales manager in California with information on how a sales and support engineer in El Salvador performs on an online test about a particular product. "We're finally taking learning content and integrating it with sales," Hill says. "When we have additional product lines and salespeople, it will probably add up to a ten- to twentyfold ROI on the system."

At $1 billion Amersham Biosciences Corp. (www.amershambiosciences.com), the business issue wasn't getting information to salespeople, but rather paying them accurately for what they had already sold, says Dan Eldridge, manager of business operations at the Piscataway, New Jersey–based company. Again, information silos—in the form of dozens of Microsoft Excel spreadsheets with data downloaded from Oracle Corp. databases—were to blame.

"We were managing incentive compensation for 150 to 160 employees via Excel spreadsheets, which was a very manual process, very labor-intensive, and fraught with error," Eldridge says. "Our sales reps had no confidence in our ability to produce accurate sales reports and accurate incentive payments. The financial quarter would end, and we'd begin calculating incentives, and then it would take us six weeks to pay. After that, we'd spend the next four weeks putting out fires, making corrections. So we'd spend 12 weeks out of every quarter paying incentives."

The issue came to a head when Amersham named a new president who spent his first weeks in office getting an earful from disgruntled salespeople. Eldridge evaluated payment software from several vendors. Ultimately, he opted to deploy Synygy Inc.'s compensation software. Amersham electronically transfers its sales data to Synygy once a week, and compensation payments are calculated and paid on an ongoing basis. Amersham pays Synygy a monthly fee that Eldridge declined to disclose, but he says the ROI has already been positive.

"To calculate ROI, I looked at things like 'shadow accounting,' which is how much time sales reps were spending analyzing their reports for mistakes rather than spending it out in the field selling," Eldridge says. He was also able to reduce his department's head count by one full-time worker. The bottom line from Eldridge: "We used to spend four weeks after we paid salespeople fixing problems. Now, we don't even spend a week because very few salespeople have problems with their payments."

Case Study Questions

1. What is the business challenge facing companies like Kodak and HP in supporting their global sales forces? How successfully is the Eloquent software tool helping these two companies meet this challenge? Explain.

2. Why was Amersham Biosciences' Excel-based system a business and IT failure? How successfully is the Synygy software solving the business and IT problems involved? Explain.

3. How else could IT be used to support a global sales force? Give several examples.

information and make it available anytime, anywhere, via the Internet to their global sales forces to support their selling and customer service needs. In addition, they are now using this sales support information system to provide and manage sales training materials and learning processes for their sales professionals.

Amersham Biosciences had a different problem. The incentive compensation system for their sales professionals utilized a spreadsheet-based system that was woefully inadequate for the job. Amersham replaced their slow, error prone, and morale busting system with the specialized software and services of a company that does the sales incentive compensation management job for them. Results of the new system have been positive, both in terms of the morale of the company's sales force and the return on investment of the new system.

What Is a System?

What is a *system*? A system can be most simply defined as a group of interrelated or interacting elements forming a unified whole. Many examples of systems can be found in the physical and biological sciences, in modern technology, and in human society. Thus, we can talk of the physical system of the sun and its planets, the biological system of the human body, the technological system of an oil refinery, and the socioeconomic system of a business organization.

However, the following generic system concept provides a more appropriate foundation concept for the field of information systems: a **system** is a group of interrelated components working together toward a common goal by accepting inputs and producing outputs in an organized transformation process.

Such a system (sometimes called a *dynamic* system) has three basic interacting components or functions:

- **Input** involves capturing and assembling elements that enter the system to be processed. For example, raw materials, energy, data, and human effort must be secured and organized for processing.
- **Processing** involves transformation processes that convert input into output. Examples are a manufacturing process, the human breathing process, or mathematical calculations.
- **Output** involves transferring elements that have been produced by a transformation process to their ultimate destination. For example, finished products, human services, and management information must be transmitted to their human users.

Example. A manufacturing system accepts raw materials as input and produces finished goods as output. An information system is a system that accepts resources (data) as input and processes them into products (information) as output. A business organization is a system where economic resources are transformed by various business processes into goods and services.

Feedback and Control

The system concept becomes even more useful by including two additional components: feedback and control. A system with feedback and control components is sometimes called a *cybernetic* system, that is, a self-monitoring, self-regulating system.

- **Feedback** is data about the performance of a system. For example, data about sales performance is feedback to a sales manager.
- **Control** involves monitoring and evaluating feedback to determine whether a system is moving toward the achievement of its goal. The control function then makes necessary adjustments to a system's input and processing components to ensure that it produces proper output. For example, a sales manager exercises control when reassigning salespersons to new sales territories after evaluating feedback about their sales performance.

Example. A familiar example of a self-monitoring, self-regulating system is the thermostat-controlled heating system found in many homes; it automatically monitors

FIGURE 1.16

A business is an example of an organizational system where economic resources (input) are transformed by various business processes (processing) into goods and services (output). Information systems provide information (feedback) on the operations of the system to management for the direction and maintenance of the system (control) as it exchanges inputs and outputs with its environment.

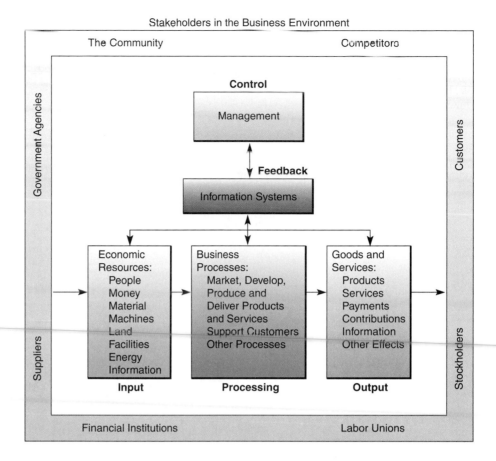

and regulates itself to maintain a desired temperature. Another example is the human body, which can be regarded as a cybernetic system that automatically monitors and adjusts many of its functions, such as temperature, heartbeat, and breathing. A business also has many control activities. For example, computers may monitor and control manufacturing processes, accounting procedures help control financial systems, data entry displays provide control of data entry activities, and sales quotas and sales bonuses attempt to control sales performance.

Other System Characteristics

Figure 1.16 uses a business organization to illustrate the fundamental components of a system, as well as several other system characteristics. Note that a system does not exist in a vacuum, rather, it exists and functions in an *environment* containing other systems. If a system is one of the components of a larger system, it is a *subsystem*, and the larger system is its environment.

Several systems may share the same environment. Some of these systems may be connected to one another by means of a shared boundary, or *interface*. Figure 1.16 also illustrates the concept of an *open system;* that is, a system that interacts with other systems in its environment. In this diagram, the system exchanges inputs and outputs with its environment. Thus, we could say that it is connected to its environment by input and output interfaces. Finally, a system that has the ability to change itself or its environment in order to survive is an *adaptive system.*

Example. Organizations such as businesses and government agencies are good examples of the systems in society, which is their environment. Society contains a multitude of such systems, including individuals and their social, political, and economic institutions. Organizations themselves consist of many subsystems, such as departments, divisions, process teams, and other workgroups. Organizations are examples of open

FIGURE 1.17

The components of an information system. All information systems use people, hardware, software, data, and network resources to perform input, processing, output, storage, and control activities that transform data resources into information products.

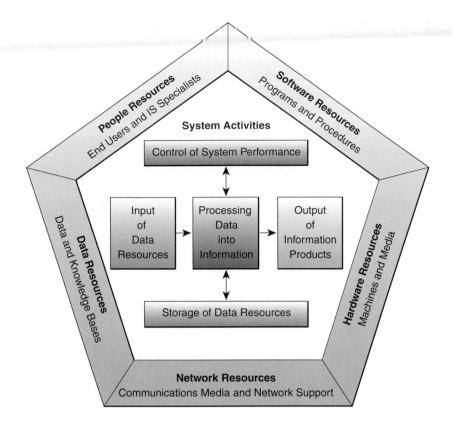

Components of an Information System

systems because they interface and interact with other systems in their environment. Finally, organizations are examples of adaptive systems, since they can modify themselves to meet the demands of a changing environment.

We are now ready to apply the system concepts we have learned to help us better understand how an information system works. For example, we have said that an information system is a system that accepts data resources as input and processes them into information products as output. How does an information system accomplish this? What system components and activities are involved?

Figure 1.17 illustrates an **information system model** that expresses a fundamental conceptual framework for the major components and activities of information systems. An information system depends on the resources of people (end users and IS specialists), hardware (machines and media), software (programs and procedures), data (data and knowledge bases), and networks (communications media and network support) to perform input, processing, output, storage, and control activities that convert data resources into information products.

This information system model highlights the relationships among the components and activities of information systems. It provides a framework that emphasizes four major concepts that can be applied to all types of information systems:

- People, hardware, software, data, and networks are the five basic resources of information systems.
- People resources include end users and IS specialists, hardware resources consist of machines and media, software resources include both programs and procedures, data resources can include data and knowledge bases, and network resources include communications media and networks.
- Data resources are transformed by information processing activities into a variety of information products for end users.
- Information processing consists of the system activities of input, processing, output, storage, and control.

FIGURE 1.18

Examples of information system resources and products.

Information Systems Resources and Products
People Resources Specialists—systems analysts, software developers, system operators. End Users—anyone else who uses information systems.
Hardware Resources Machines—computers, video monitors, magnetic disk drives, printers, optical scanners. Media—floppy disks, magnetic tape, optical disks, plastic cards, paper forms.
Software Resources Programs—operating system programs, spreadsheet programs, word processing programs, payroll programs. Procedures—data entry procedures, error correction procedures, paycheck distribution procedures.
Data Resources Product descriptions, customer records, employee files, inventory databases.
Network Resources Communications media, communications processors, network access and control software.
Information Products Management reports and business documents using text and graphics displays, audio responses, and paper forms.

Information System Resources

Our basic IS model shows that an information system consists of five major resources: people, hardware, software, data, and networks. Let's briefly discuss several basic concepts and examples of the roles these resources play as the fundamental components of information systems. You should be able to recognize these five components at work in any type of information system you encounter in the real world. Figure 1.18 outlines several examples of typical information system resources and products.

People Resources

People are required for the operation of all information systems. These people resources include end users and IS specialists.

- **End users** (also called users or clients) are people who use an information system or the information it produces. They can be customers, salespersons, engineers, clerks, accountants, or managers. Most of us are information system end users. And most end users in business are **knowledge workers,** that is, people who spend most of their time communicating and collaborating in teams and workgroups and creating, using, and distributing information.

- **IS specialists** are people who develop and operate information systems. They include systems analysts, software developers, system operators, and other managerial, technical, and clerical IS personnel. Briefly, systems analysts design information systems based on the information requirements of end users, software developers create computer programs based on the specifications of systems analysts, and system operators help to monitor and operate large computer systems and networks.

Hardware Resources

The concept of **hardware resources** includes all physical devices and materials used in information processing. Specifically, it includes not only **machines,** such as computers and other equipment, but also all data **media,** that is, tangible objects on which data are recorded, from sheets of paper to magnetic or optical disks. Examples of hardware in computer-based information systems are:

- **Computer systems,** which consist of central processing units containing microprocessors, and a variety of interconnected peripheral devices. Examples are hand-held, laptop, or desktop microcomputer systems, midrange computer systems, and large mainframe computer systems.

- **Computer peripherals,** which are devices such as a keyboard or electronic mouse for input of data and commands, a video screen or printer for output of information, and magnetic or optical disks for storage of data resources.

Software Resources

The concept of **software resources** includes all sets of information processing instructions. This generic concept of software includes not only the sets of operating instructions called **programs,** which direct and control computer hardware, but also the sets of information processing instructions called **procedures** that people need.

It is important to understand that even information systems that don't use computers have a software resource component. This is true even for the information systems of ancient times, or the manual and machine-supported information systems still used in the world today. They all require software resources in the form of information processing instructions and procedures in order to properly capture, process, and disseminate information to their users.

The following are examples of software resources:

- **System software,** such as an operating system program, which controls and supports the operations of a computer system.
- **Application software,** which are programs that direct processing for a particular use of computers by end users. Examples are a sales analysis program, a payroll program, and a word processing program.
- **Procedures,** which are operating instructions for the people who will use an information system. Examples are instructions for filling out a paper form or using a software package.

Data Resources

Data are more than the raw material of information systems. The concept of data resources has been broadened by managers and information systems professionals. They realize that data constitute valuable organizational resources. Thus, you should view data as **data resources** that must be managed effectively to benefit all end users in an organization.

Data can take many forms, including traditional alphanumeric data, composed of numbers and alphabetical and other characters that describe business transactions and other events and entities. Text data, consisting of sentences and paragraphs used in written communications; image data, such as graphic shapes and figures, and photographic and video images; and audio data, the human voice and other sounds, are also important forms of data.

The data resources of information systems are typically organized, stored, and accessed by a variety of data resource management technologies into:

- Databases that hold processed and organized data.
- Knowledge bases that hold knowledge in a variety of forms such as facts, rules, and case examples about successful business practices.

For example, data about sales transactions may be accumulated, processed, and stored in a Web-enabled sales database that can be accessed for sales analysis reports by managers and marketing professionals. Knowledge bases are used by knowledge management systems and expert systems to share knowledge or give expert advice on specific subjects. We will explore these concepts further in later chapters.

Data versus Information. The word **data** is the plural of *datum*, though data commonly represents both singular and plural forms. Data are raw facts or observations, typically about physical phenomena or business transactions. For example, a spacecraft launch or the sale of an automobile would generate a lot of data describing those events. More specifically, data are objective measurements of the *attributes* (the characteristics) of *entities* (such as people, places, things, and events).

Example. Business transactions such as buying a car or an airline ticket can produce a lot of data. Just think of the hundreds of facts needed to describe the characteristics of the car you want and its financing, or the details for even the simplest airline reservation.

People often use the terms *data* and *information* interchangeably. However, it is better to view data as raw material resources that are processed into finished information products. Then we can define **information** as data that have been converted into a meaningful and useful context for specific end users. Thus, data are usually subjected to a value-added process (we call *data processing* or *information processing*) where (1) its form is aggregated, manipulated, and organized; (2) its content is analyzed and evaluated; and (3) it is placed in a proper context for a human user. So you should view information as processed data placed in a context that gives it value for specific end users.

Example. Names, quantities, and dollar amounts recorded on sales forms represent data about sales transactions. However, a sales manager may not regard these as information. Only after such facts are properly organized and manipulated can meaningful sales information be furnished, specifying, for example, the amount of sales by product type, sales territory, or salesperson.

Network Resources

Telecommunications technologies and networks like the Internet, intranets, and extranets have become essential to the successful electronic business and commerce operations of all types of organizations and their computer-based information systems. Telecommunications networks consist of computers, communications processors, and other devices interconnected by communications media and controlled by communications software. The concept of **network resources** emphasizes that communications technologies and networks are a fundamental resource component of all information systems. Network resources include:

- **Communications media.** Examples include twisted-pair wire, coaxial cable, and fiber-optic cable; and microwave, cellular, and satellite wireless technologies.
- **Network support.** This generic category emphasizes that many hardware, software, and data technologies are needed to support the operation and use of a communications network. Examples include communications processors such as modems and internetwork processors, and communications control software such as network operating systems and Internet browser packages.

Information System Activities

Let's take a closer look now at each of the basic **information processing** (or **data processing**) activities that occur in information systems. You should be able to recognize input, processing, output, storage, and control activities taking place in any information system you are studying. Figure 1.19 lists business examples that illustrate each of these information system activities.

Input of Data Resources

Data about business transactions and other events must be captured and prepared for processing by the **input** activity. Input typically takes the form of *data entry* activities such as recording and editing. End users typically enter data directly into a computer

FIGURE 1.19

Business examples of the basic activities of information systems.

Information System Activities
● **Input.** Optical scanning of bar-coded tags on merchandise.
● **Processing.** Calculating employee pay, taxes, and other payroll deductions.
● **Output.** Producing reports and displays about sales performance.
● **Storage.** Maintaining records on customers, employees, and products.
● **Control.** Generating audible signals to indicate proper entry of sales data.

system, or record data about transactions on some type of physical medium such as a paper form. This usually includes a variety of editing activities to ensure that they have recorded data correctly. Once entered, data may be transferred onto a machine-readable medium such as a magnetic disk until needed for processing.

For example, data about sales transactions can be recorded on source documents such as paper sales order forms. (A **source document** is the original formal record of a transaction.) Alternately, salespersons can capture sales data using computer keyboards or optical scanning devices; they are visually prompted to enter data correctly by video displays. This provides them with a more convenient and efficient **user interface,** that is, methods of end user input and output with a computer system. Methods such as optical scanning and displays of menus, prompts, and fill-in-the-blanks formats make it easier for end users to enter data correctly into an information system.

Processing of Data into Information

Data are typically subjected to **processing** activities such as calculating, comparing, sorting, classifying, and summarizing. These activities organize, analyze, and manipulate data, thus converting them into information for end users. The quality of any data stored in an information system must also be maintained by a continual process of correcting and updating activities.

Example. Data received about a purchase can be (1) *added* to a running total of sales results, (2) *compared* to a standard to determine eligibility for a sales discount, (3) *sorted* in numerical order based on product identification numbers, (4) *classified* into product categories (such as food and nonfood items), (5) *summarized* to provide a sales manager with information about various product categories, and, finally, (6) used to *update* sales records.

Output of Information Products

Information in various forms is transmitted to end users and made available to them in the **output** activity. The goal of information systems is the production of appropriate **information products** for end users. Common information products include messages, reports, forms, and graphic images, which may be provided by video displays, audio responses, paper products, and multimedia. We routinely use the information provided by these products as we work in organizations and live in society. For example, a sales manager may view a video display to check on the performance of a salesperson, accept a computer-produced voice message by telephone, and receive a printout of monthly sales results.

Storage of Data Resources

Storage is a basic system component of information systems. Storage is the information system activity in which data and information are retained in an organized manner for later use. For example, just as written text material is organized into words, sentences, paragraphs, and documents, stored data are commonly organized into a variety of data elements and databases. This facilitates its later use in processing or its retrieval as output when needed by users of a system. Such data elements and databases are discussed further in Chapter 5, Data Resource Management.

Control of System Performance

An important information system activity is the **control** of system performance. An information system should produce feedback about its input, processing, output, and storage activities. This feedback must be monitored and evaluated to determine if the system is meeting established performance standards. Then appropriate system activities must be adjusted so that proper information products are produced for end users.

For example, a manager may discover that subtotals of sales amounts in a sales report do not add up to total sales. This might mean that data entry or processing procedures need to be corrected. Then changes would have to be made to ensure that all sales transactions would be properly captured and processed by a sales information system.

Recognizing Information Systems

As a business professional, you should be able to recognize the fundamental components of information systems you encounter in the real world. This means that you should be able to identify:

- The people, hardware, software, data, and network resources they use.
- The types of information products they produce.
- The way they perform input, processing, output, storage, and control activities.

This kind of understanding will help you be a better user, developer, and manager of information systems. And that, as we have pointed out in this chapter, is important to your future success as a manager, entrepreneur, or professional in business.

Analyzing Kodak and HP's Information Systems

Refer back to the Real World Case on Kodak, HP, and Amersham Biosciences on page 21. Now, let's try to recognize or visualize the resources used, activities performed, and information products produced by some of their information systems.

IS Resources. People resources include end users like the salespeople in Kodak's and HP's global sales forces, and IS specialists like program manager Tom Hill of Hewlett-Packard's Nonstop Enterprise Division. Hardware resources include the thousands of PCs, servers, and other computers that the sales and other professionals at both companies must be using. Software resources include everything from Web browsers to operating systems, and especially the Eloquent Web-based software tool. You can just visualize all of the communications media and network support components that are part of Kodak and HP's Internet-based systems. Finally, both companies undoubtedly have substantial data resources in the form of databases of business information about customers, employees, and products, as well as sales and marketing activities.

Information Products. The information products we can most easily visualize are the displays on the networked PCs of sales and other business professionals at both companies that provide Web-based multimedia displays of information about customers, products, orders, and sales and marketing strategies. You can get an idea of some of these displays at the business and enterprise links at www.kodak.com and www.hp.com.

IS Activities. Some of the input activities we can visualize are the input of website navigation clicks, and product, customer, order, and sales and marketing data entries and selections made by the sales and other business professionals of both companies. Processing activities are accomplished whenever any of the computer systems of both companies we identified previously execute the programs that are part of the Eloquent and other software resources involved. Output activities primarily involve the display or printing of the information products we identified earlier. Storage activities take place whenever business data is stored and managed in the files and databases stored on the disk drives and other storage media of both companies' computer systems. Finally, we can visualize several control activities, including the use of passwords and other security codes by the business professionals involved for entry into secure company websites, and access to company databases and knowledge bases.

So you see, analyzing an information system to identify its basic components is not a difficult task. Just identify the resources that the information system uses, the information processing activities it performs, and the information products it produces. Then you will be better able to identify ways to improve these components, and thus the performance of the information system itself. That's a goal that every business professional should strive to attain.

Summary

- **An IS Framework for Business Professionals.** The IS knowledge that a business manager or professional needs to know is illustrated in Figure 1.2 and covered in this chapter and text. This includes (1) *foundation concepts:* fundamental behavioral, technical, business, and managerial concepts like system components and functions, or competitive strategies; (2) *information technologies:* concepts, developments, or management issues regarding hardware, software, data management, networks, and other technologies; (3) *business applications:* major uses of IT for business processes, operations, decision making, and strategic/competitive advantage; (4) *development processes:* how end users and IS specialists develop and implement business/IT solutions to problems and opportunities arising in business; and (5) *management challenges:* how to effectively and ethically manage the IS function and IT resources to achieve top performance and business value in support of the business strategies of the enterprise.

- **Business Roles of Information Systems.** Information systems perform three vital roles in business firms. Business applications of IS support an organization's business processes and operations, business decision making, and strategic competitive advantage. Major application categories of information systems include operations support systems, such as transaction processing systems, process control systems, and enterprise collaboration systems, and management support systems, such as management information systems, decision support systems, and executive information systems. Other major categories are expert systems, knowledge management systems, strategic information systems, and functional business systems. However, in the real world most application categories are combined into cross-functional information systems that provide information and support for decision making and also perform operational information processing activities. Refer to Figures 1.7, 1.9, and 1.11 for summaries of the major application categories of information systems.

- **System Concepts.** A system is a group of interrelated components working toward the attainment of a common goal by accepting inputs and producing outputs in an organized transformation process. Feedback is data about the performance of a system. Control is the component that monitors and evaluates feedback and makes any necessary adjustments to the input and processing components to ensure that proper output is produced.

- **An Information System Model.** An information system uses the resources of people, hardware, software, data, and networks to perform input, processing, output, storage, and control activities that convert data resources into information products. Data are first collected and converted to a form that is suitable for processing (input). Then the data are manipulated and converted into information (processing), stored for future use (storage), or communicated to their ultimate user (output) according to correct processing procedures (control).

- **IS Resources and Products.** Hardware resources include machines and media used in information processing. Software resources include computerized instructions (programs) and instructions for people (procedures). People resources include information systems specialists and users. Data resources include alphanumeric, text, image, video, audio, and other forms of data. Network resources include communications media and network support. Information products produced by an information system can take a variety of forms, including paper reports, visual displays, multimedia documents, electronic messages, graphics images, and audio responses.

Key Terms and Concepts

These are the key terms and concepts of this chapter. The page number of their first explanation is in parentheses.

1. Computer-based information system (6)
2. Control (22)
3. Data (26)
4. Data or information processing (27)
5. Data resources (26)
6. Developing business/IT solutions (16)
7. E-business (9)
8. E-business role in business (8)
9. Electronic commerce (9)
10. End user (25)
11. Enterprise collaboration systems (9)
12. Extranet (9)
13. Feedback (22)
14. Hardware resources (25)
    a. Machines (25)
    b. Media (25)
15. Information (27)
    a. Products (28)
16. Information system (6)
17. Information system activities (27)
    a. Input (27)
    b. Processing (28)
    c. Output (28)
    d. Storage (28)
    e. Control (28)
18. Information system model (24)
19. Information technology (IT) (6)
20. Intranet (9)
21. IS knowledge needed by business professionals (7)
22. Knowledge workers (25)

23. Management challenges of IS (15)

   a. Ethics and IT (18)

   b. IT career challenges (18)

   c. IT success and failure (16)

24. Network resources (27)

25. People resources (25)

   a. IS specialists (25)

   b. End users (25)

26. Roles of IS in business (8)

   a. Support of business processes and operations (8)

   b. Support of business decision making (8)

   c. Support of strategies for competitive advantage (8)

27. Software resources (26)

   a. Programs (26)

   b. Procedures (26)

28. System (22)

29. Trends in information systems (10)

30. Types of information systems (12)

   a. Cross-functional systems (14)

   b. Management support systems (13)

   c. Operations support systems (12)

Review Quiz

Match one of the previous key terms and concepts with one of the following brief examples or definitions. Look for the best fit for answers that seem to fit more than one key term or concept. Defend your choices.

_____ 1. You should know some fundamental concepts about information systems and their technologies, development processes, business applications, and management challenges.

_____ 2. People who spend most of their workday creating, using, and distributing information.

_____ 3. Computer hardware and software, networks, data management, and other technologies.

_____ 4. Information systems support an organization's business processes, operations, decision making, and strategies for competitive advantage.

_____ 5. Using IT to reengineer business processes to support e-business operations.

_____ 6. Using Web-based decision support systems to support sales managers.

_____ 7. Using information technology for electronic commerce to gain a strategic advantage over competitors.

_____ 8. A system that uses people, hardware, software, and network resources to collect, transform, and disseminate information within an organization.

_____ 9. An information system that uses computers and their hardware and software.

_____ 10. Anyone who uses an information system or the information it produces.

_____ 11. Businesses today are using the Internet, corporate intranets, and interorganizational extranets for electronic business operations, e-commerce, and enterprise collaboration.

_____ 12. The buying, selling, marketing, and servicing of products over the Internet and other networks.

_____ 13. The use of groupware tools to support collaboration among networked teams.

_____ 14. A group of interrelated components working together toward the attainment of a common goal.

_____ 15. Data about a system's performance.

_____ 16. Making adjustments to a system's components so that it operates properly.

_____ 17. Facts or observations.

_____ 18. Data that have been placed into a meaningful context for an end user.

_____ 19. The act of converting data into information.

_____ 20. An information system uses people, hardware, software, network, and data resources to perform input, processing, output, storage, and control activities that transform data resources into information products.

_____ 21. Machines and media.

_____ 22. Computers, disk drives, video monitors, and printers are examples.

_____ 23. Magnetic disks, optical disks, and paper forms are examples.

_____ 24. Programs and procedures.

_____ 25. A set of instructions for a computer.

_____ 26. A set of instructions for people.

_____ 27. End users and information systems professionals.

_____ 28. Using the keyboard of a computer to enter data.

_____ 29. Computing loan payments.

_____ 30. Printing a letter you wrote using a computer.

_____ 31. Saving a copy of the letter on a magnetic disk.

_____ 32. Having a sales receipt as proof of a purchase.

_____ 33. Information systems can be classified into operations, management, and other categories.

_____ 34. Includes transaction processing, process control, and end user collaboration systems.

_____ 35. Includes management information, decision support, and executive information systems.

_____ 36. Information systems that perform transaction processing and provide information to managers across the boundaries of functional business areas.

_____ 37. Information systems have evolved from a data processing orientation to the support of strategic decision making, end user collaboration, and electronic business and commerce.

_____ 38. Internet-like networks and websites inside a company.

_____ 39. Interorganizational Internet-like networks among trading partners.

_____ 40. You need to be a responsible end user of IT resources in your company.

_____ 41. Managing the IT resources of a company effectively and ethically to improve its business performance and value.

_____ 42. Using the Internet, intranets, and extranets to empower internal business operations, electronic commerce, and enterprise collaboration.

Discussion Questions

1. How can information technology support a company's business processes and decision making, and give it a competitive advantage? Give examples to illustrate your answer.

2. How does the use of the Internet, intranets, and extranets by companies today support their business processes and activities?

3. Refer to the Real World Case on Amazon.com in the chapter. What advice could you give Jeff Bezos about the business use of information technology at Amazon that might help them continue to prosper during the next five years? Explain your recommendations.

4. Why do big companies still fail in their use of information technology? What should they be doing differently?

5. How can a manager demonstrate that he or she is a responsible end user of information systems? Give several examples.

6. Refer to the Real World Case on Kodak, HP, and Amersham Biosciences in the chapter. What

challenges in salesperson morale, performance, and management might arise in the use of Web-based sales support and training systems like the Eloquent system used by Kodak and HP? What solutions could you suggest?

7. What are some of the toughest management challenges in developing IT solutions to solve business problems and meet new business opportunities?

8. Why are there so many conceptual classifications of information systems? Why are they typically integrated in the information systems found in the real world?

9. In what major ways have information systems in business changed during the last 40 years? What is one major change you think will happen in the next 10 years? Refer to Figure 1.5 to help you answer.

10. Refer to the real world example of Hershey Foods in the chapter. Are the failure and success described due to managerial or technological challenges? Explain.

Analysis Exercises

Complete the following exercises as individual or group projects that apply chapter concepts to real world business situations.

1. **Using PowerWeb Resources**
   Visit the McGraw-Hill PowerWeb website for Management Information Systems, which is available for users of this text at http://www.dushkin.com/powerweb/
   As you will see, PowerWeb is a great online resource for self-study resources on MIS topics covered in this text, Web research tips and links, MIS periodicals, and current news on information technology topics. For example, click on the *Current News* link and search for and read a few current news articles o an MIS topic you are interested in, such as cyber crime or e-commerce.

   a. Prepare a one or two page summary describing the *Current News* articles you found most interesting and relevant as a business professional.

   b. End your paper with a few sentences describing one thing you have learned from your reading that might help you in your future career.

2. **Career Research**
   Select a job title that you would like to pursue as a summer intern or new graduate. Use your favorite job search websites or access the McGraw-Hill PowerWeb website for links to several job listing search engines. Use these resources to look up four different job postings for your desired job title.

   a. Select several job listings most relevant to your desired job title. List the degrees, training, experience, and/or certifications these job postings shared in common.

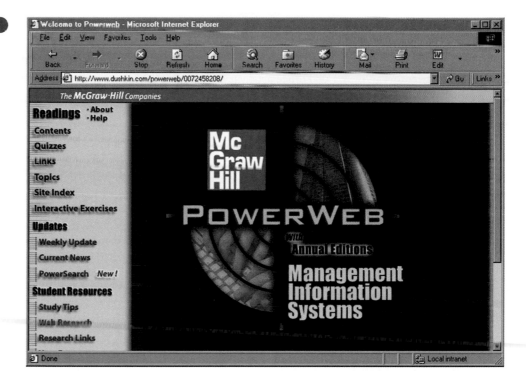

FIGURE 1.20

The McGraw-Hill PowerWeb home page for management information systems.

b. Outline your plan for obtaining any requirements that you do not *currently* have.

c. Which website did you find most useful? Describe the attributes you found most important in making this determination.

3. Skydive Chicago: Recognizing IS Components
Skydive Chicago (www.SkydiveChicago.com) is one of the United State's premier skydiving resorts. In 2002, Skydive Chicago welcomed over one hundred new skydivers who made well over one thousand training jumps through its advanced training program. To support this enterprise, Skydive Chicago founder Roger Nelson, 1982 Olympic Skydiving Team captain and six-time world record holder, developed an innovative training program far exceeding the specifications set forth by the United States Parachute Association (USPA) (www.uspa.org).

Each student in Skydive Chicago's training program makes a series of progressive training jumps under the direct supervision of a USPA rated jumpmaster. The training program gears each jump in the series toward teaching one or two new skills. Nelson's training innovations included mounting a video camera to the helmet of each jumpmaster. After each training jump, the jumpmaster debriefs the student using the tape for illustration. Jumpmasters also copy well executed student skydives to the facility's tape library. Using this video library, students can stop by the dropzone's training room and watch video clips to prepare for their next jump in the training series. By video taping each student jump, the training program gains numerous benefits:

- Students learn more quickly
- Jumpmasters can identify and correct even subtle bad habits
- Students require less jumpmaster time to brief and debrief
- The dropzone's chief trainer can frequently assess current training techniques' effectiveness
- Jumpmasters can easily replace the video library's dated clips with new clips reflecting any training program changes
- Whenever new safety issues arise, the dropzone's Safety & Training Advisor can provide the USPA with video documentation supporting recommendations to modify the organization's Basic Safety Requirements

Aside from the initial capital expense for video cameras, helmets, and TV/VCRs, this process adds no appreciable variable costs. However, both dropzone and student significantly benefit. By increased training efficiency, the dropzone can train more students per instructor. The student can also see and more easily recall their skydives. Lastly, skydivers often enjoy sharing their training triumphs and "bloopers" with their friends long after they've earned their skydiving license.

a. What are the inputs, processes, outputs, and storage devices associated with this information system?

b. Briefly describe each "process" associated with this information system.

c. How might Skydive Chicago combine Internet technologies and student video to their advantage?

d. What other products or services might Skydive Chicago provide using Internet technologies?

4. **Office Products Corporation: Recognizing IS Components**

Office Products Corporation receives more than 10,000 customer orders a month, drawing on a combined inventory of over 1,000 office products stocked at the company's warehouse. About 60 PCs are installed at Office Product's headquarters and connect in a local area network to several IBM Netfinity servers. Orders are received by phone or mail and entered into the system by customer representatives at network computers, or they are entered directly by customers who have shopped at the electronic commerce website developed by Office Products. Formatted screens help users follow data entry procedures. Netfinity servers store these orders on magnetic disks.

As the order is entered, a server checks the availability of the parts, allocates the stock, and updates customer and part databases stored on its magnetic disks. It then sends the order pick list to the warehouse printer, where warehouse personnel use the printout to fill the order. The company president has a networked PC workstation in her office and so do the controller, sales manager, inventory manager, and other executives. They use simple database management inquiry commands to get responses and reports concerning sales orders, customers, and inventory, and to review product demand and service trends.

Make an outline that identifies the information system components in Office Product's order processing system.

a. Identify the people, hardware, software, data, and network resources and the information products of this information system.
b. Identify the input, processing, output, storage, and control activities that occurred.

5. **Western Chemical Corporation: Recognizing the Types and Roles of Information Systems**

Western Chemical uses the Internet and an electronic commerce website to connect to its customers and suppliers, and to capture data and share information about sales orders and purchases. Sales and order data are processed immediately, and inventory and other databases are updated. Videoconferencing and electronic mail services are also provided. Data generated by a chemical refinery process are captured by sensors and processed by a computer that also suggests answers to a complex refinery problem posed by an engineer. Managers and business professionals access reports on a periodic, exception, and demand basis, and use computers to interactively assess the possible results of alternative decisions. Finally, top management can access text summaries and graphics displays that identify key elements of organizational performance and compare them to industry and competitor performance.

Western Chemical Corporation has started forming business alliances and using intranets, extranets, and the Internet to build a global electronic commerce website to offer their customers worldwide products and services. Western Chemical is in the midst of making fundamental changes to their computer-based systems to increase the efficiency of their e-business operations and their managers' ability to react quickly to changing business conditions.

a. Make an outline that identifies how information systems support (1) business operations, (2) business decision making, (3) strategic advantage, (4) an e-business enterprise, and (5) electronic commerce at Western Chemical.
b. There are many different types of information systems at Western Chemical. Identify as many as you can in the preceding scenario. Explain the reasons for your choices.

REAL WORLD CASE 3

Aviall Inc.: From Failure to Success with Information Technology

Joseph Lacik, Jr., doesn't try to measure the return on investment of his company's e-business website. The fact that Dallas-based Aviall Inc. (www.aviall.com) was saved from financial disaster by a controversial multimillion-dollar IT project that included developing the website as one key element is all the return he needs to see. That investment, in the words of Larry DeBoever, chief strategy officer at the IT consulting firm Experio Solutions Corp. in Dallas, "Turned Aviall from a catalog business into a full-scale logistics business" that hundreds of aviation parts manufacturers and airlines large and small depend on for ordering, inventory control, and demand forecasting. He says the new approach ties Aviall more tightly to customers such as Rolls-Royce PLC. "Aviall is now the logistics back end for the aviation firms," says DeBoever, whose company was retained to help with portions of Aviall's systems integration work. "And they did it even though the airline industry shrank over the last three years."

In early 2000, with quarterly sales dropping and Aviall on the ropes, "We invested $30 million to $40 million to build this infrastructure." says Lacik, vice president of information services at Aviall Services, a unit of Aviall. "Our competitors thought we were insane. Some investors asked for my resignation." But the results of the project have been extremely successful and represent a huge comeback from Aviall's recent business/IT problems, which sprang from a failed enterprise resource planning (ERP) system that had been designed to automate and integrate the company's order processing, inventory control, financial accounting, and human resources business systems. However, there were major problems in implementing the new ERP system that resulted in Aviall's inventory getting out of control.

When Lacik joined the company in early 2000, "You couldn't properly order or ship things. My job was to bring back operational stability," he says. To do so, he implemented the CEO's vision of transforming Aviall into a provider of supply chain management services through the integration of a range of Web-enabled e-business software systems. Aviall bought and installed a BroadVision online purchasing system, Siebel Systems sales force automation and order entry software, a Lawson Software financial system, a Catalyst Manufacturing Services inventory control and warehouse management system, and Xelus product allocation, inventory management, and purchasing forecasting software. All of these systems were integrated by using common business databases managed by database software from Sybase, Inc.

Of course, even with planning, some of the systems integration was more difficult than expected. One major reason was the sheer size of the project. The new combined system has to properly access and deal with customized pricing charts for 17,000 customers who receive various types of discounts, and with an inventory of 380,000 different aerospace parts.

The development of Aviall.com was one of the least expensive parts of the project, at a cost of about $3 million, Lacik says. But it provides big benefits. When customers order products on the Aviall website, it costs the company about 39 cents per order, compared with $9 per transaction if an Aviall employee takes the order over the phone, he says. New supply chain functions are also possible, such as the ability for customers to transfer their orders from an Excel spreadsheet directly to the website. Customers can also receive price and availability information on aerospace parts in less than five seconds—a real-time feature that hadn't been available before the BroadVision system was installed, Lacik says.

The process also frees the company's sales force from routine order taking and follow-up, thus allowing them to spend more time developing relationships with customers. What's more, the website helps Aviall build relationships with suppliers by providing them with customer ordering data that enables them to better match production with demand. The website now generates $60 million of the company's $800 million in annual revenue, or 7.5 percent, up from less than 2 percent a year ago. "Over the next three to five years, it could become more than 30 percent." Lacik says.

Case Study Questions

1. Why do you think that Aviall failed in their implementation of an enterprise resource planning system? What could they have done differently?

2. How has information technology brought new business success to Aviall? How did IT change Aviall's business model?

3. How could other companies use Aviall's approach to the use of IT to improve their business success? Give several examples.

REAL WORLD CASE 4

Pacific Gas and Electric Co.: Developing Customer Service Information Systems

Pacific Gas and Electric Co. (www.pge.com) has completed a three-year-plus effort to replace its legacy customer information system (CIS) with off-the-shelf technology, a project that one analyst described as the largest implementation of packaged CIS software in the energy industry thus far.

The new system, which went live late in 2002, required a total investment of $204 million, said Roger Gray, CIO at San Francisco–based PG&E. That covered the cost of hardware, software, and consulting services and 11 months of operational testing and parallel billing runs on the new system and the one it replaced, he said. PG&E built the new system around CorDaptix, a set of customer management applications developed by Morristown, New Jersey–based SPL WorldGroup (www.splwg.com). Gray said the project was launched in response to the deregulation of California's power industry, which created a need for utilities such as PG&E to meet new customer service requirements in a more competitive environment.

PG&E's homegrown mainframe-based CIS system "was 37 years old, had exhausted its useful life, and wasn't flexible enough to handle deregulation," he added. The CorDaptix software runs on an IBM mainframe, like the homegrown system did. But it's considerably more feature-rich than the older technology, said Tracy Harizal, director of CIS at PG&E. For example, Harizal said CorDaptix works in real time so that when a customer service representative fields a call, information in the system is automatically updated. Before, PG&E employees had to wait a few days for customer accounts to be updated following mainframe batch-processing jobs. In addition, the new software is more fully integrated with applications such as PG&E's metering and rate-calculation systems, making data from those systems more readily available to customer service workers, Harizal said.

Because the CIS project was driven by deregulation, PG&E didn't conduct an up-front analysis of potential returns on investment, Harizal said. But despite the size of the project—which included the conversion of 30 billion rows of data from the legacy system—the company managed to complete the work on time at a cost that was 10 percent below its original budget, she said.

Zarko Sumic, a Bellevue, Washington-based analyst at Meta Group, Inc., said he isn't aware of any off-the-shelf CIS software installations within the energy industry that have been larger than the one done by PG&E, which provides natural gas and electricity in a 70,000-square-mile area of northern and central California. Sumic said that since the 1999 deregulation of California's energy market, the state has established some of the most complex formats in North America for setting the billing rates that different utility customers are charged. PG&E needed a CIS system that could handle that kind of complexity, he said. In addition, the lack of integration between PG&E's old IBM mainframe systems and other applications resulted in lag time for its customer service workers when they tried to access data from multiple systems, Sumic said.

Harizal said that PG&E faced a number of onerous technical challenges, including the need to convert its historical customer data as well as information from other systems that was required to set up interfaces to the new CIS software. To ensure success in that area, the utility conducted more than 50 trial runs of the data conversion routines it developed before it felt ready to begin the implementation of the new customer information system, she said.

Case Study Questions

1. Why has deregulation of the electric power industry increased the need for new approaches to provide better customer service and management by utility companies?

2. What are the business benefits and costs of PG&E's new customer information system? Also, visit the PG&E website and evaluate how well it helps the company provide better customer service.

3. How can new customer information systems like CorDaptix help companies like PG&E compete in their new deregulated markets? Visit the SPL WorldGroup website and evaluate their claims for companies that use CorDaptix.

CHAPTER 2

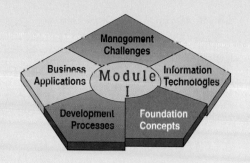

COMPETING WITH INFORMATION TECHNOLOGY

Chapter Highlights

Section I
Fundamentals of Strategic Advantage

Strategic IT

Real World Case: GE, Dell, Intel, and Others: The Competitive Advantage of Information Technology

Competitive Strategy Concepts

Strategic Uses of Information Technology

The Value Chain and Strategic IS

Section II
Using Information Technology for Strategic Advantage

Strategic Uses of IT

Real World Case: Intec Engineering: The Strategic Value of Knowledge Management Systems

Building a Customer-Focused Business

Reengineering Business Processes

Becoming an Agile Company

Creating a Virtual Company

Building a Knowledge-Creating Company

Real World Case: Progressive, Yellow, JetBlue, and Gentex: Using Information Technology for Competitive Advantage

Real World Case: CDW and Harrah's Entertainment: Developing Strategic Customer-Loyalty Systems

Learning Objectives

After reading and studying this chapter, you should be able to:

1. Identify several basic competitive strategies and explain how they can use information technologies to confront the competitive forces faced by a business.

2. Identify several strategic uses of Internet technologies and give examples of how they give competitive advantages to a business.

3. Give examples of how business process reengineering frequently involves the strategic use of Internet technologies.

4. Identify the business value of using Internet technologies to become an agile competitor or to form a virtual company.

5. Explain how knowledge management systems can help a business gain strategic advantages.

SECTION I	Fundamentals of Strategic Advantage

Strategic IT

Technology is no longer an afterthought in forming business strategy, but the actual cause and driver [17].

This chapter will show you that it is important that you view information systems as more than a set of technologies that support efficient business operations, workgroup and enterprise collaboration, or effective business decision making. Information technology can change the way businesses compete. So you should also view information systems strategically, that is, as vital competitive networks, as a means of organizational renewal, and as a necessary investment in technologies that help a company adopt strategies and business processes that enable it to reengineer or reinvent itself in order to survive and succeed in today's dynamic business environment.

Section I of this chapter introduces fundamental competitive strategy concepts that underlie the strategic use of information systems. Section II then discusses several major strategic applications of information technology used by many companies today.

Analyzing GE, Dell, Intel, and Others

Read the Real World Case on GE, Dell, Intel, and Others on the next page. We can learn a lot about the strategic business uses of information technologies from this case. See Figure 2.1.

This case confronts a highly publicized assertion that "IT doesn't matter" anymore in terms of helping a business gain capabilities that give it a competitive advantage. The statements and examples from top executives of GE, Dell, Intel, and other companies make it plain that investing in information technology is absolutely vital in providing them with the capabilities they need to compete successfully in business today. The executives make two other major points. First, that the real business and competitive value of information technology lies in the capabilities of the software and value of the information a business acquires and uses, and not in the infrastructure of hardware, networks, and other IT facilities that is commonly used

FIGURE 2.1

Michael Dell (left), CEO of Dell Computer, and Jeff Immelt, CEO of General Electric, make it plain that the skillful management and use of their investments in information technology give their firms a competitive advantage.

Source: Mario Tama/Getty Images

REAL WORLD CASE 1

GE, Dell, Intel, and Others: The Competitive Advantage of Information Technology

There's nothing like a punchy headline to get an article some attention. A recent piece in the *Harvard Business Review* (May 2003), shockingly labeled "IT Doesn't Matter" has garnered the magazine more buzz than at any time since the Jack Welch affair. The article has been approvingly cited in the *New York Times*, analyzed in Wall Street reports, and e-mailed around the world. But without such a dramatic and reckless title, I doubt the article would have been much noticed. It's a sloppy mix of ersatz history, conventional wisdom, moderate insight, and unsupportable assertions. And it is dangerously wrong.

Author Nicholas Carr's main point is that information technology is nothing more than the infrastructure of modern business, similar to railroads, electricity, or the internal combustion engineering advances that have become too commonplace for any company to wangle a strategic advantage from them. Once-innovative applications of information technology have now become merely a necessary cost. Thus Carr thinks today's main risk is not underusing IT but overspending on it.

But before we get any further, let's have a reality check. First, let's ask Jeff Immelt, the CEO of General Electric Co., one of the premier business corporations in the world, this question: "How important is information technology to GE?" Here's his answer: "It's a business imperative. We're primarily a service-oriented company, and the lifeblood for productivity is more about tech than it is about investing in plants and equipment. We tend to get a 20 percent return on tech investments, and we tend to invest about $2.5 billion to $3 billion a year."

Then let's ask Dell Corporation CEO, Michael Dell: "What's your take on Nick Carr's thesis that technology no longer gives corporate buyers a competitive advantage?" Here's his answer: "Just about anything in business can be either a sinkhole or a competitive advantage if you do it really, really bad or you do it really, really well. And information technology is an often misunderstood field. You've got a lot of people who don't know what they're doing and don't do it very well. For us, IT is a huge advantage. For Wal-Mart, GE, and many other companies, technology is a huge advantage and will continue to be. Does that mean that you just pour money in and gold comes out? No, you can screw it up really bad."

Finally, let's ask Andy Grove, former CEO and now Chairman of Intel Corporation, a direct question about IT: "Nicholas Carr's recent *Harvard Business Review* article says: "IT Doesn't Matter." Is information technology so pervasive that it no longer offers companies a competitive advantage?" Andy says. "In any field, you can find segments that are close to maturation and draw a conclusion that the field is homogeneous. Carr is saying commercial-transaction processing in the United States and some parts of Europe has reached the top parts of an S-curve. But instead of talking about that segment, he put a provocative spin on it—that information technology doesn't matter—and suddenly the statement is

grossly wrong. It couldn't be further from the truth. It's like saying: I have an old three-speed bike, and Lance Armstrong has a bike. So why should he have a competitive advantage?"

So basically, Carr misunderstands what information technology is. He thinks it's merely a bunch of networks and computers. He notes, properly, that the price of those has plummeted and that companies bought way too much in recent years. He's also right that the hardware infrastructure of business is rapidly becoming commoditized and, even more important, standardized. Computers and networks per se are just infrastructure. However, one of the article's most glaring flaws is its complete disregard for the centrality of software and that human knowledge or information can be mediated and managed by software.

Charles Fitzgerald, Microsoft's general manager for platform strategy, says that Carr doesn't put enough emphasis on the "I" in IT. "The source of competitive advantage in business is what you do with the information that technology gives you access to. How do you apply that to some particular business problem?" To say IT doesn't matter is tantamount to saying that companies have enough information about their operations, customers, and employees. I have never heard a company make such a claim."

Paul Strassman, who has spent 42 years as a CIO—at General Foods, Xerox, the Pentagon, and most recently NASA—was more emphatic. "The hardware—the stuff everybody's fascinated with—isn't worth a damn," he says. "It's just disposable. Information technology today is a knowledge-capital issue. It's basically a huge amount of labor and software." Says he: "Look at the business powers—most of all Wal-Mart, but also companies like Pfizer or FedEx. They're all waging information warfare."

Case Study Questions

1. Do you agree with the argument made by Nick Carr to support his position that IT no longer gives companies a competitive advantage? Why or why not?

2. Do you agree with the argument made by the business leaders in this case in support of the competitive advantage that IT can provide to a business? Why or why not?

3. What are several ways that IT could provide a competitive advantage to a business? Use some of the companies mentioned in this case as examples. Visit their websites to gather more information to help you answer.

Source: Adapted from David Kirkpatrick, "Stupid-Journal Alert. Why HBR's View of Tech Is Dangerous," *Fortune*, June 9, 2003, p. 190; Robert Hoff, "Andy Grove: We Can't Even Glimpse the Potential," *Business Week*, August 25, 2003, pp. 86–88; and "Speaking Out: View from the Top," *Business Week*, August 25, 2003, pp. 108–13.

by many companies. Second, that the strategic advantage of information technology can only be gained by its proper use and management. Mismanaged IT can lead to business failure; skillfully managed IT can indeed lead to competitive advantage.

Competitive Strategy Concepts

In Chapter 1, we emphasized that a major role of information systems applications in business was to provide effective support of a company's strategies for gaining competitive advantage. This strategic role of information systems involves using information technology to develop products, services, and capabilities that give a company major advantages over the competitive forces it faces in the global marketplace.

This creates **strategic information systems,** information systems that support or shape the competitive position and strategies of a business enterprise. So a strategic information system can be any kind of information system (TPS, MIS, DSS, etc.) that uses information technology to help an organization gain a competitive advantage, reduce a competitive disadvantage, or meet other strategic enterprise objectives [21]. Let's look at several basic concepts that define the role of such strategic information systems.

Competitive Forces and Strategies

How should a business professional think about competitive strategies? How can competitive strategies be applied to the use of information systems by a business? Figure 2.2 illustrates an important conceptual framework for understanding and applying competitive strategies.

A company can survive and succeed in the long run only if it successfully develops strategies to confront five **competitive forces** that shape the structure of competition in its industry. In Michael Porter's classic model of competitive strategy, any business that wants to survive and succeed must develop and implement strategies to effectively counter (1) the rivalry of competitors within its industry, (2) the threat of new entrants into an industry and its markets, (3) the threat posed by substitute products which might capture market share, (4) the bargaining power of customers, and (5) the bargaining power of suppliers [23].

FIGURE 2.2

Businesses can develop competitive strategies to counter the actions of the competitive forces they confront in the marketplace.

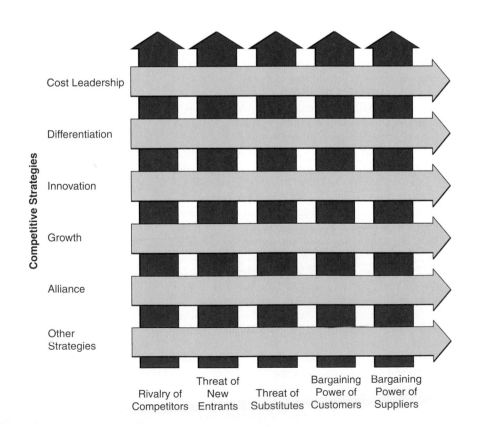

Competitive Forces

Figure 2.2 also illustrates that businesses can counter the threats of competitive forces that they face by implementing five basic **competitive strategies** [21].

- **Cost Leadership Strategy.** Becoming a low-cost producer of products and services in the industry. Also, a firm can find ways to help its suppliers or customers reduce their costs or to increase the costs of their competitors.
- **Differentiation Strategy.** Developing ways to differentiate a firm's products and services from its competitors' or reduce the differentiation advantages of competitors. This may allow a firm to focus its products or services to give it an advantage in particular segments or niches of a market.
- **Innovation Strategy.** Finding new ways of doing business. This may involve the development of unique products and services, or entry into unique markets or market niches. It may also involve making radical changes to the business processes for producing or distributing products and services that are so different from the way a business has been conducted that they alter the fundamental structure of an industry.
- **Growth Strategies.** Significantly expanding a company's capacity to produce goods and services, expanding into global markets, diversifying into new products and services, or integrating into related products and services.
- **Alliance Strategies.** Establishing new business linkages and alliances with customers, suppliers, competitors, consultants, and other companies. These linkages may include mergers, acquisitions, joint ventures, forming of "virtual companies," or other marketing, manufacturing, or distribution agreements between a business and its trading partners.

Strategic Uses of Information Technology

How can business managers use investments in information technology to directly support a firm's competitive strategies? Figure 2.3 answers that question with a summary of the many ways that information technology can help a business implement the five basic competitive strategies. Figure 2.4 provides examples of how specific companies have

FIGURE 2.3

A summary of how information technology can be used to implement the five basic competitive strategies. Many companies are using Internet technologies as the foundation for such strategies.

Basic Strategies in the Business Use of Information Technology

Lower Costs
- Use IT to substantially reduce the cost of business processes.
- Use IT to lower the costs of customers or suppliers.

Differentiate
- Develop new IT features to differentiate products and services.
- Use IT features to reduce the differentiation advantages of competitors.
- Use IT features to focus products and services at selected market niches.

Innovate
- Create new products and services that include IT components.
- Develop unique new markets or market niches with the help of IT.
- Make radical changes to business processes with IT that dramatically cut costs, improve quality, efficiency, or customer service, or shorten time to market.

Promote Growth
- Use IT to manage regional and global business expansion.
- Use IT to diversify and integrate into other products and services.

Develop Alliances
- Use IT to create virtual organizations of business partners.
- Develop interenterprise information systems linked by the Internet and extranets that support strategic business relationships with customers, suppliers, subcontractors, and others.

FIGURE 2.4 Examples of how companies have used information technology to implement five competitive strategies for strategic advantage.

Strategy	Company	Strategic Use of Information Technology	Business Benefit
Cost Leadership	Dell Computer	Online build to order	Lowest cost producer
	Priceline.com	Online seller bidding	Buyer-set pricing
	eBay.com	Online auctions	Auction-set prices
Differentiation	AVNET Marshall	Customer/supplier e-commerce	Increase in market share
	Moen Inc.	Online customer design	Increase in market share
	Consolidated Freightways	Customer online shipment tracking	Increase in market share
Innovation	Charles Schwab & Co.	Online discount stock trading	Market leadership
	Federal Express	Online package tracking and flight management	Market leadership
	Amazon.com	Online full service customer systems	Market leadership
Growth	Citicorp	Global intranet	Increase in global market
	Wal-Mart	Merchandise ordering by global satellite network	Market leadership
	Toys 'Я' Us Inc.	POS inventory tracking	Market leadership
Alliance	Wal-Mart/Procter & Gamble	Automatic inventory replenishment by supplier	Reduced inventory cost/increased sales
	Cisco Systems	Virtual manufacturing alliances	Agile market leadership
	Staples Inc. and Partners	Online one-stop shopping with partners	Increase in market share

used strategic information systems to implement each of these five basic strategies for competitive advantage. Note the major use of Internet technologies for electronic business and commerce applications. In the rest of this chapter, we will discuss and provide examples of many strategic uses of information technology.

Other Competitive Strategies

There are many other competitive strategies in addition to the five basic strategies of cost leadership, differentiation, innovation, growth, and alliance. Let's look at several key strategies that are also implemented with information technology. They are: locking in customers or suppliers, building switching costs, raising barriers to entry, and leveraging investment in information technology.

Investments in information technology can allow a business to **lock in customers and suppliers** (and lock out competitors) by building valuable new relationships with them. These business relationships can become so valuable to customers or suppliers that it deters them from abandoning a company for its competitors, or intimidating it into accepting less-profitable business arrangements. Early attempts to use information systems technology in these relationships focused on significantly improving the quality of service to customers and suppliers in a firm's distribution, marketing, sales, and service activities. Then businesses moved to more innovative uses of information technology.

Wal-Mart and Others

For example, Wal-Mart built an elaborate satellite network linking the point-of-sale terminals in all of its stores. The network was designed to provide managers, buyers, and sales associates with up-to-date sales and inventory status information to improve product buying, inventories, and store management. Then Wal-Mart began to use the operational efficiency of such information systems to offer lower cost, better-quality products and services, and differentiate itself from its competitors.

Companies like Wal-Mart began to extend their networks to their customers and suppliers in order to build innovative continuous inventory replenishment systems that would lock in their business. This creates **interenterprise information systems** in which the Internet and other networks electronically link the business processes of a company with their customers and suppliers, resulting in internet worked business systems that form new business alliances and partnerships. Extranets between businesses and their suppliers are prime examples of such strategic linkages. An even stronger e-business link is formed by *stockless* inventory replenishment systems such as those between Wal-Mart and Procter & Gamble. In that system, Procter & Gamble automatically replenishes Wal-Mart's stock of Procter & Gamble products [18].

A major emphasis in strategic information systems has been to find ways to build **switching costs** into the relationships between a firm and its customers or suppliers. That is, investments in information systems technology, such as those mentioned in the Wal-Mart example, can make customers or suppliers dependent on the continued use of innovative, mutually beneficial interenterprise information systems. Then, they become reluctant to pay the costs in time, money, effort, and inconvenience that it would take to switch to a company's competitors.

By making investments in information technology to improve its operations or promote innovation, a firm could also erect **barriers to entry** that would discourage or delay other companies from entering a market. Typically, this happens by increasing the amount of investment or the complexity of the technology required to compete in an industry or a market segment. Such actions would tend to discourage firms already in the industry and deter external firms from entering the industry.

Investing in information technology enables a firm to build strategic IT capabilities that allow it to take advantage of strategic opportunities when they arise. In many cases, this results when a company invests in advanced computer-based information systems to improve the efficiency of its own business processes. Then, armed with this strategic technology platform, the firm can **leverage investment in information technology** by developing new products and services that would not be possible without a strong IT capability. An important current example is the development of corporate intranets and extranets by many companies, which enables them to leverage their previous investments in Internet browsers, PCs, servers, and client/server networks. Figure 2.5 summarizes the additional strategic uses of IT we have just discussed.

FIGURE 2.5   Additional ways that information technology can be used to implement competitive strategies.

Other Strategic Uses of Information Technology
• Develop interenterprise information systems whose convenience and efficiency create switching costs that lock in customers or suppliers.
• Make major investments in advanced IT applications that build barriers to entry against industry competitors or outsiders.
• Include IT components in products and services to make substitution of competing products or services more difficult.
• Leverage investment in IS people, hardware, software, databases, and networks from operational uses into strategic applications.

Merrill Lynch and Charles Schwab	Merrill Lynch is a classic example of the use of several competitive strategies. By making large investments in information technology, along with a groundbreaking alliance with BancOne, they became the first securities brokers to offer a credit line, checking account, Visa credit card, and automatic investment in a money market fund, all in one account. This gave them a major competitive advantage for several years before their rivals could develop the IT capability to offer similar services on their own [21]. However, Merrill is still playing catch-up in online discount securities trading with Charles Schwab, e-Trade, and others. Schwab is now the leading online securities company, far surpassing Merrill's online statistics. Thus, large investments in IT can make the stakes too high for some present or prospective players in an industry, but can evaporate over time as new technologies are employed by competitors [20].

The Value Chain and Strategic IS

Let's look at another important concept that can help you identify opportunities for strategic information systems. The value chain concept was developed by Michael Porter [23] and is illustrated in Figure 2.6. It views a firm as a series, chain, or network of basic activities that add value to its products and services, and thus add a margin of value to the firm. In the value chain conceptual framework, some business activities are primary processes; others are support processes. This framework can highlight where competitive strategies can best be applied in a business. That is, managers and business professionals should try to develop a variety of strategic uses of Internet and other technologies for those basic processes that add the most value to a company's products or services, and thus to the overall business value of the company.

Value Chain Examples

Figure 2.6 provides examples of how and where information technologies can be applied to basic business processes using the value chain framework. For example, Figure 2.6 emphasizes that collaborative workflow intranets can increase the communications and collaboration needed to dramatically improve administrative coordination and support services. An employee benefits intranet can help the human resources management function provide employees with easy self-service access to their benefits

---

FIGURE 2.6 The value chain of a firm. Note the examples of the variety of strategic information systems that can be applied to a firm's basic business processes for competitive advantage.

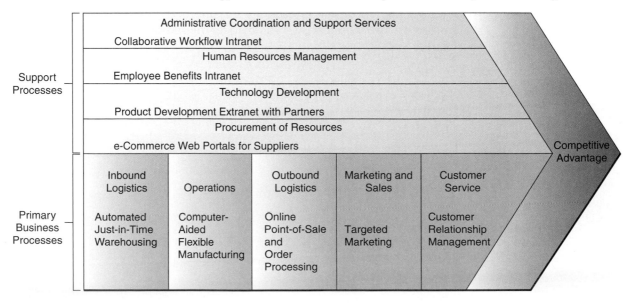

information. Extranets enable a company and its global business partners to use the Web to jointly design products and processes. Finally, e-commerce Web portals can dramatically improve procurement of resources by providing online marketplaces for a firm's suppliers.

Other examples of strategic applications of information systems technology to primary business processes are identified by the value chain model in Figure 2.6. These include automated just-in-time warehousing systems to support inbound logistic processes involving storage of inventory, computer-aided flexible manufacturing (CAM) systems for manufacturing operations, and online point-of-sale and order processing systems to improve outbound logistics processes that process customer orders. Information systems can also support marketing and sales processes by developing an interactive targeted marketing capability on the Internet and the Web. Finally, customer service can be dramatically improved by a coordinated and integrated customer relationship management system.

Thus, the value chain concept can help you analyze where and how to apply the strategic capabilities of information technology. It shows how various types of information technologies might be applied to specific business processes to help a firm gain competitive advantages in the marketplace.

SECTION II — Using Information Technology for Strategic Advantage

Strategic Uses of IT

There are many ways that organizations may view and use information technology. For example, companies may choose to use information systems strategically, or they may be content to use IT to support efficient everyday operations. But if a company emphasized strategic business uses of information technology, its management would view IT as a major competitive differentiator. They would then devise business strategies that would use IT to develop products, services, and capabilities that would give the company major advantages in the markets in which it competes. In this section, we will provide many examples of such strategic business applications of information technology.

Analyzing Intec Engineering

Read the Real World Case on Intec Engineering on the next page. We can learn a lot about the competitive advantage of knowledge management systems. See Figure 2.7.

Intec Engineering has a culture of collaboration and information sharing but found that as the company grew, it was becoming more difficult to keep track of and access information. So the company acquired a knowledge management software tool and integrated it with their repositories of information to create a Web-based knowledge management system that is used by their engineers on work assignments all over the world. The new system has demonstrated significant savings in the time needed by engineers to research and access information they need in their work. It has also shown its ability to gather important information from Intec's engineers worldwide that is vital for the success of their customer's engineering projects, as well as helping to support sales situations with information needed by prospective clients. Thus the new knowledge management system has significantly improved Intec's competitive position in satisfying their present clients and gaining new customers.

FIGURE 2.7

Fran Steele, chief information officer of Intec Engineering, emphasizes the capability of their knowledge management system to significantly improve Intec's engineers' ability to satisfy present and prospective clients.

Source: Scott F. Kohn

REAL WORLD CASE 2

Intec Engineering: The Strategic Value of Knowledge Management Systems

It's hard to put a value on knowledge management systems. Their ability to generate income is often measured indirectly; their links to cost savings frequently seem tenuous. The return on investment is hard to quantify. Too often, the case for implementing a system to leverage intellectual capital and expertise rests mainly on intuition.

But intuition wasn't nearly enough to sell executives at Intec Engineering Partnership Ltd. (www.intecengineering.com), a company whose dedication to thrift is exceeded only by its passion for sharing knowledge. Intec is based in Houston and has offices in Argentina, Chile, Bolivia, England, the Netherlands, Malaysia, and Australia. The privately held, $80 million engineering and project management company serves the international oil and gas industry. Its 500-plus employees specialize in marine pipelines, terminals, and facilities. Clients include BP PLC, ExxonMobil Corp., and ChevronTexaco Corp.

CIO Fran Steele says Intec's culture is "extremely collaborative. It's a culture of sharing information, with a strong bias against bureaucracy and anything that might constrain creativity," she says. During 2002, as Intec grew through expansion and international acquisitions, it was becoming more difficult to keep track of and access information.

Early last year, a group of Intec engineers, later dubbed the Learning Team, volunteered to work on the problem of how to better capture lessons learned and share knowledge among Intec engineers. The Learning Team decided that any technology to assist this process had to integrate existing knowledge resources, automatically find experts, capture results for reuse, facilitate the identification of best practices, and provide a quick and easy user interface. Administration had to be minimal.

The Learning Team shopped around and selected software from AskMe Corp. as the product most likely to facilitate Intec's problem-solving model. AskMe agreed to customize a three-month, large-scale pilot project of the system for 250 engineers. The actual cost of Intec's system is proprietary, but Dan Wright, vice president of field operations at AskMe, says the average system includes 750 users at a cost of more than $100,000. There is also an 18 percent annual maintenance fee.

AskMe integrated its Web-based software and search engine with Intec's information repositories including 75,000 technical documents, skills and certification databases, and files of individuals' names, titles, locations, e-mail addresses, and photos. The team agreed that qualitatively, knowledge management is about sharing knowledge, but quantitatively, it's about saving time. So ROI would be about time saved and putting a value on it. The pilot, called AskIntec, began in May 2002. Three months later, it had exceeded all the performance and user metrics, and ROI calculations projected an annual return of 133 percent.

Actual savings are higher than the ROI figures indicate, adds Steele. An answered question, for example, often turns out to be worth much more than the Learning Team's estimate of saving 30 minutes, as senior project engineer David Raby demonstrated while working in Perth, Australia. Raby had an esoteric question about deep-water pipelines. Before AskIntec, getting an answer would have required accessing the library in Houston, ordering materials and having them sent through the mail. "I might have got the wrong stuff or needed additional stuff, and it could have gone back and forth for weeks," he says. "And I still wouldn't necessarily have the information I was looking for." Using AskIntec, he got 10 answers in a day, saving about three weeks' worth of effort, he says.

"Some of the return on information is not quantified just by how quickly you can do something, but by the fact that you can do it at all," emphasizes Steele. For example, during an engagement last year in Beijing, senior project manager Julio Daneri found that Chinese pipeline codes specified certain design parameters that his client didn't want to use. Daneri used AskIntec to query colleagues on cases where companies had successfully circumvented national specifications. Quick replies from engineers on three continents enabled him to build a case for using different specifications, without which his client wouldn't have been able to compete for the project.

The system is also improving Intec's sales process. Timmermans recounts that a prospective customer in Australia was skeptical about the local office's ability to draw on Intec's expertise all over the world. Intec invited him to pose a difficult question, which the Intec engineer put into the system. "The next morning they had four very relevant answers," Timmermans recalls. "We dazzled the client."

In the end, customers profit from Intec's knowledge management investment, Steele says, explaining that a typical oil facility can produce millions of dollars per day in revenue. "If we can cut weeks off a project and help them get their facility ready earlier, they can get to market sooner and get that revenue earlier," she says. "That's the ultimate value."

Case Study Questions

1. What is the potential value for competitive advantage that a business might gain from knowledge management systems? Why might this value be difficult to measure?

2. Do you approve of how Intec Engineering is measuring the value of their KMS? Why or why not? How else could the strategic value of their KMS be measured?

3. Does Intec's knowledge management system give them a competitive advantage? Give several examples from the case to support your answer.

Building a Customer-Focused Business

The driving force behind world economic growth has changed from manufacturing volume to improving customer value. As a result, the key success factor for many firms is maximizing customer value [5].

For many companies, the chief business value of becoming a **customer-focused business** lies in its ability to help them keep customers loyal, anticipate their future needs, respond to customer concerns, and provide top-quality customer service. This strategic focus on **customer value** recognizes that quality, rather than prices, has become the primary determinant in a customer's perception of value. From a customer's point of view, companies that consistently offer the best value are able to keep track of their customers' individual preferences, keep up with market trends, supply products, services, and information anytime, anywhere, and provide customer services tailored to individual needs [5]. And so Internet technologies have created a strategic opportunity for companies, large and small, to offer fast, responsive, high-quality products and services tailored to individual customer preferences.

Internet technologies can make customers the focal point of customer relationship management (CRM) and other e-business applications. CRM systems and Internet, intranet, and extranet websites create new channels for interactive communications within a company, with customers, and with the suppliers, business partners, and others in the external environment. This enables continual interaction with customers by most business functions and encourages cross-functional collaboration with customers in product development, marketing, delivery, service, and technical support [5]. We will discuss CRM systems in Chapter 7.

Typically, customers use the Internet to ask questions, air complaints, evaluate products, request support, and make and report their purchases. Using the Internet and corporate intranets, specialists in business functions throughout the enterprise can contribute to an effective response. This encourages the creation of cross-functional discussion groups and problem-solving teams dedicated to customer involvement, service, and support. Even the Internet and extranet links to suppliers and business partners can be used to enlist them in a way of doing business that ensures prompt delivery of quality components and services to meet a company's commitments to its customers [13]. This is how a business demonstrates its focus on customer value.

Figure 2.8 illustrates the interrelationships in a customer-focused business. Intranets, extranets, e-commerce websites, and web-enabled internal business processes form the invisible IT platform that supports this e-business model. This enables the business to focus on targeting the kinds of customers it really wants, and "owning" the customer's total business experience with the company. A successful business streamlines all business processes that impact their customers, and develops customer management relationship systems that provide its employees with a complete view of each customer, so they have the information they need to offer their customers top-quality personalized service. A customer-focused business helps their e-commerce customers to help themselves, while also helping them do their jobs. Finally, a successful business nurtures an online community of customers, employees, and business partners that builds great customer loyalty, while fostering cooperation to provide an outstanding customer experience [26]. Let's review a real world example.

Hilton Hotels: Customer-Focused e-Business Systems

Hilton Hotels, via Hilton.com, has one of the fastest reservation services in the world: The average time to complete a reservation is less than two minutes. Frequent guests have services automatically tailored to their last visit, and meeting planners access the website for group reservations and floor plans of venues. Bruce Rosenberg, Hilton's vice president of market distribution, says, "The Web opened up people's eyes about how we can and should do business. We looked at all the business models—every customer segment from the business traveler, the tourist, the meeting planner, the travel agent—and identified an e-business way of doing business with them."

Hilton's e-business initiative required information from multiple business units, interactivity among the customer, Hilton.com, and Hilton's existing back-end reservation

FIGURE 2.8 How a customer-focused business builds customer value and loyalty using Internet technologies.

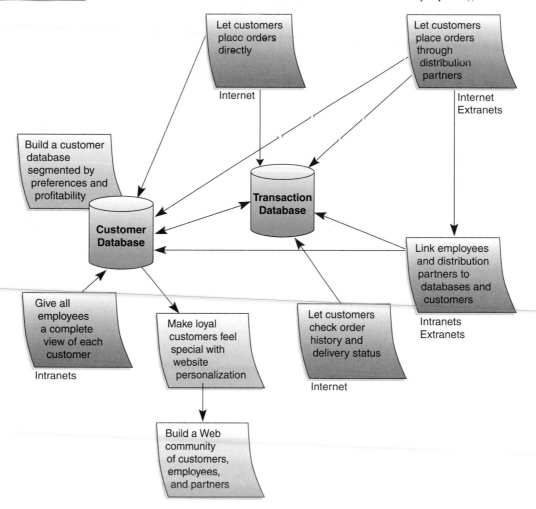

systems, and a high level of personalization. "We want profiles on the customers, their history with us and what they like and don't like, accessible no matter where they touch us in the world," Rosenberg says. Hilton has very good profiles of members of HHonors (the Hilton frequent-customer loyalty program), but not so good profiles, Rosenberg notes, for the tens of millions of customers that only occasionally stay with Hilton. "The new systems we are building will allow us to have a larger number of profiles and a finer segmentation of our customer base. The Web will enable us to reach them cost effectively and develop a deeper personal relationship. We just couldn't do this before by mailing material to them. The budgets weren't there to support it."

Hilton is implementing a direct-to-customer business model via the Web channel, targeting the frequent-traveler segment and providing a single point of contact. All customer segments can use the Web channel, including both individuals and travel agents—with some travel agents bypassed when individuals contact Hilton directly. To implement this e-business initiative, Hilton integrates workflows, reservation systems, call centers, and business processes with the common goal of obtaining more finely segmented customer data. The initiative required a strong e-business vision, many negotiations across business units within Hilton, alliances with other firms, investment in IT infrastructure, and integration of an Internet-based application with a large database of segmented customer profiles and various existing reservation systems [30].

FIGURE 2.9

Some of the key ways that business process reengineering differs from business improvement.

	Business Improvement	Business Process Reengineering
Level of Change	Incremental	Radical
Process Change	Improved new version of process	Brand new process
Starting Point	Existing processes	Clean slate
Frequency of Change	One-time or continuous	Periodic one-time change
Time Required	Short	Long
Typical Scope	Narrow, within functions	Broad, cross functional
Horizon	Past and present	Future
Participation	Bottom-up	Top-down
Path to Execution	Cultural	Cultural, structural
Primary Enabler	Statistical control	Information technology
Risk	Moderate	High

Source: Adapted from Howard Smith and Peter Fingar, *Business Process Management: The Third Wave.* Tampa, FL: Meghan-Kiffer Press, 2003, p. 118.

Reengineering Business Processes

One of the most important implementations of competitive strategies is **business process reengineering** (BPR), most often simply called reengineering. Reengineering is a fundamental rethinking and radical redesign of business processes to achieve dramatic improvements in cost, quality, speed, and service. So BPR combines a strategy of promoting business innovation with a strategy of making major improvements to business processes so that a company can become a much stronger and more successful competitor in the marketplace.

However, Figure 2.9 points out that while the potential payback of reengineering is high, so is its risk of failure and level of disruption to the organizational environment [10]. Making radical changes to business processes to dramatically improve efficiency and effectiveness is not an easy task. For example, many companies have used cross-functional enterprise resource planning (ERP) software to reengineer, automate, and integrate their manufacturing, distribution, finance, and human resource business processes. While many companies have reported impressive gains with such ERP reengineering projects, many others have experienced dramatic failures or have failed to achieve the improvements they sought (as we saw in the Real World Examples of Hershey Foods and A-DEC in Chapter 1).

Many companies have found that *organizational redesign* approaches are an important enabler of reengineering, along with the use of information technology. For example, one common approach is the use of self-directed cross-functional or multidisciplinary *process teams*. Employees from several departments or specialties including engineering, marketing, customer service, and manufacturing may work as a team on the product development process. Another example is the use of *case managers*, who handle almost all tasks in a business process, instead of splitting tasks among many different specialists.

The Role of Information Technology

Information technology plays a major role in reengineering most business processes. The speed, information processing capabilities, and connectivity of computers and Internet technologies can substantially increase the efficiency of

FIGURE 2.10 The order management process consists of several business processes and crosses the boundaries of traditional business functions.

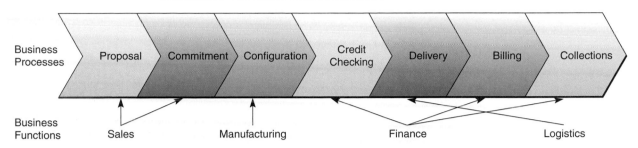

business processes, as well as communications and collaboration among the people responsible for their operation and management. For example, the order management process illustrated in Figure 2.10 is vital to the success of most companies [6]. Many of them are reengineering this process with enterprise resource planning software and Web-enabled electronic business and commerce systems, as outlined in Figure 2.11. Now, let's take a look at examples from Johnson Controls and Agilent Technologies.

Johnson Controls: Success with Reengineering

Collaborate or die. That's the unspoken motto at Johnson Controls Inc. (JCI). It permeates nearly everything from product design to delivery within the company's automotive supply division. So it comes as no surprise that Johnson Controls (www.jci.com) is well along in a Web-based reengineering project that has turned collaboration into something far more than a motto.

"Collaboration connects blue sky with solid ground," says John Waraniak, executive director of e-business at the Milwaukee manufacturer. The automotive division where he works delivered $13.6 billion of JCI's $18.4 billion in revenue last year and is a supplier of car and truck cockpits, which include the dashboard, seats, and other interior parts. JCI builds almost half of the cockpits used in the approximately 50 million vehicles manufactured by the world's major automakers each year.

Waraniak says, to avoid costly mistakes, product ideas must be analyzed in the early design stages by those most affected. Fixing a problem during engineering design, for example, costs one-tenth of what it would cost once a product reaches the prototype stage. If the product reaches the field, the cost can easily top 1,000 times what it would have taken to correct the problem on the assembly line. Waraniak says that Web-based collaboration reengineering at JCI has saved the company a whopping 80 percent on research and development investments. "Sixty percent of our work is engineer-to-order. We conceive and then we build," he says. "That means we depend on tribal knowledge for insight into the product and the process for making it."

For Waraniak, progress from the reengineering project is tangible. Collaboration on 2003 and 2004 model-year automobiles has yielded big gains in efficiency. He says engineers have used collaborative online design to reduce costs by $20 million in JCI's "core products portfolio," primarily by reducing the number of discrete parts in each cockpit component. Collaboration cuts time out of component design, Waraniak says. What once took days as overnight express packages went back and forth takes "a few hours on the Web," he says, which is critical when there are as many as 5,000 distinct parts in a vehicle [14].

FIGURE 2.11

Examples of information technologies that support reengineering the order management processes.

Reengineering Order Management
● Customer relationship management systems using corporate intranets and the Internet.
● Supplier managed inventory systems using the Internet and extranets.
● Cross-functional ERP software for integrating manufacturing, distribution, finance, and human resource processes.
● Customer-accessible e-commerce websites for order entry, status checking, payment, and service.
● Customer, product, and order status databases accessed via intranets and extranets by employees and suppliers.

Agilent Technologies: Failure in Reengineering

The good news is that Agilent Technologies Inc. (www.agilent.com) says its enterprise resource planning applications are stable. The bad news is they got that way only after a rocky ERP reengineering project that cost the company $105 million in revenue and $70 million in profits.

In mid-August 2002, the multinational communications and life sciences company, formerly a part of Hewlett-Packard Co., said problems with the ERP components in Oracle's newly installed e-Business Suite software froze production for the equivalent of a week, leading to the massive losses. The Oracle system, part of which went live in June, handles about half of the company's worldwide production of test, measurement, and monitoring products and almost all of its financial operations, as well as functions such as order handling and shipping.

In a statement, Agilent president and CEO Ned Barnholt said the disruptions to the business after implementing the ERP system were "more extensive than we expected." An Agilent spokeswoman said the issue wasn't the quality of the Oracle application, but rather the "very complex nature of the enterprise resource planning implementation."

Agilent also had a take-away lesson that they should have learned before beginning the major ERP reengineering project. "Enterprise resource planning implementations are a lot more than software packages," the company said in a statement. "They are a fundamental transformation of a company's business processes. People, processes, policies, and the company's culture are all factors that should be taken into consideration when implementing a major enterprise system." [29].

Becoming an Agile Company

We are changing from a competitive environment in which mass-market products and services were standardized, long-lived, information-poor, and exchanged in one-time transactions, to an environment in which companies compete globally with niche market products and services that are individualized, short-lived, information-rich, and exchanged on an ongoing basis with customers [12].

Agility in business performance is the ability of a company to prosper in rapidly changing, continually fragmenting global markets for high-quality, high-performance, customer-configured products and services. An **agile company** can make a profit in markets with broad product ranges and short model lifetimes, and can produce orders individually and in arbitrary lot sizes. It supports *mass customization* by offering individualized products while maintaining high volumes of production. Agile companies depend heavily on Internet technologies to integrate and manage business processes, while providing the information processing power to treat masses of customers as individuals.

To be an agile company, a business must implement four basic strategies. First, customers of an agile company perceive products or services as solutions to their

FIGURE 2.12 How information technology can help a company be an agile competitor with the help of customers and business partners.

Type of Agility	Description	Role of IT	Example
Customer	Ability to co-opt customers in the exploitation of innovation opportunities • as sources of innovation ideas • as cocreators of innovation • as users in testing ideas or helping other users learn about the idea	Technologies for building and enhancing virtual customer communities for product design, feedback, and testing	eBay customers are its defacto product development team because they post an average of 10,000 messages each week to share tips, point out glitches, and lobby for changes.
Partnering	Ability to leverage assets, knowledge, and competencies of suppliers, distributors, contract manufacturers and logistics providers in the exploration and exploitation of innovation opportunities	Technologies facilitating inter-firm collaboration, such as collaborative platforms and portals, supply-chain systems, etc.	Yahoo! has accomplished a significant transformation of its service from a search engine into a portal by initiating numerous partnerships to provide content and other media related services from its website.
Operational	Ability to accomplish speed, accuracy, and cost economy in the exploitation of innovation opportunities	Technologies for modularization and integration of business processes	Ingram Micro, a global wholesaler has deployed an integrated trading system allowing its customers and suppliers to connect directly to its procurement and ERP systems.

Source: Adapted from V. Sambamurthy, Anandhi Bhaharadwaj, and Varun Grover. "Shaping Agility Through Digital Options: Reconceptualizing the Role of Information Technology in Contemporary Firms." *MIS Quarterly*, June 2003, p. 246.

individual problems. Thus, products can be priced based on their value as solutions, not on their cost to produce. Second, an agile company cooperates with customers, suppliers, and other companies, and even with competitors. This allows a business to bring products to market as rapidly and cost-effectively as possible, no matter where resources are located and who owns them. Third, an agile company organizes so that it thrives on change and uncertainty. It uses flexible organizational structures keyed to the requirements of different and constantly changing customer opportunities. Finally, an agile company leverages the impact of its people and the knowledge they possess. By nurturing an entrepreneurial spirit, an agile company provides powerful incentives for employee responsibility, adaptability, and innovation [12].

Figure 2.12 summarizes another useful way to think about agility in business. This framework emphasizes the roles that customers, business partners, and information technology can play in developing and maintaining the strategic agility of a company. Notice how information technology can enable a company to develop relationships with its customers in virtual communities that help it be an agile innovator. And as we will see repeatedly throughout this text, information technologies enable a company to partner with its suppliers, distributors, contract manufacturers, and others via collaborative portals and other Web-based supply chain systems that significantly improve its agility in exploiting innovative business opportunities [25]. Now let's look at a real world example.

Dell Inc.: Agility in Action

Dell Inc. is the world's leading maker of personal computer systems and a premier user of Internet technology. Dell is widely recognized as an outstanding example of an agile, customer-focused company and champion of mass customization and the build-to-order business model. Customers across the globe can order customized systems from the dell.com website and only after the order is placed, is the system built in a Dell factory.

You can see it in action inside the Topfer Manufacturing Center, a squat, white factory a few miles south of Dell Computer's headquarters campus in Round Rock, Texas. The newest of Dell's seven plants worldwide, it is cavernous—big enough to enclose five and one-half football fields—and a blur of activity: market domination in motion.

Boxes of Intel microchips and electronic components from Taiwan and Korea skitter by on double-decker conveyor belts. Workers read orders off a monitor and assemble a new Dell OptiPlex desktop computer every three to five minutes. The finished boxes, more than 25,000 on a typical day, then trundle off on other conveyors to be shipped directly to customers. The whole fandango is choreographed so tightly by supply chain management software and Web links to suppliers that the factory rarely needs more than two hours' worth of parts inventory [16].

Creating a Virtual Company

In today's dynamic global business environment, forming a **virtual company** can be one of the most important strategic uses of information technology. A virtual company (also called a *virtual corporation* or *virtual organization*) is an organization that uses information technology to link people, organizations, assets, and ideas.

FIGURE 2.13 A virtual company uses the Internet, intranets, and extranets to form virtual workgroups and support alliances with business partners.

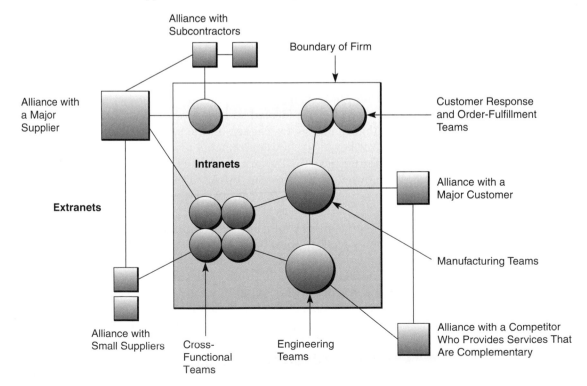

FIGURE 2.14

The basic business
strategies of virtual
companies.

Strategies of Virtual Companies
● Share infrastructure and risk with alliance partners.
● Link complementary core competencies.
● Reduce concept-to-cash time through sharing.
● Increase facilities and market coverage.
● Gain access to new markets and share market or customer loyalty.
● Migrate from selling products to selling solutions.

Figure 2.13 illustrates that virtual companies typically form virtual workgroups and alliances with business partners that are interlinked by the Internet, intranets, and extranets. Notice that this company has organized internally into clusters of process and cross-functional teams linked by intranets. It has also developed alliances and extranet links that form **interenterprise information systems** with suppliers, customers, subcontractors, and competitors. Thus, virtual companies create flexible and adaptable virtual workgroups and alliances keyed to exploit fast-changing business opportunities [1].

Virtual Company Strategies

Why are people forming virtual companies? Several major reasons stand out and are summarized in Figure 2.14. People and corporations are forming virtual companies as the best way to implement key business strategies and alliances that promise to ensure success in today's turbulent business climate.

For example, in order to quickly exploit a new market opportunity, a business may not have the time or resources to develop the manufacturing and distribution infrastructure, people competencies, and information technologies needed. Only by quickly forming a virtual company through a strategic alliance of all-star partners can it assemble the components it needs to provide a world-class solution for customers and capture the market opportunity. Of course, today, the Internet, intranets, extranets, and a variety of other Internet technologies are vital components in creating such successful solutions.

Cisco Systems: Virtual Manufacturing Alliances

Cisco Systems is the world's largest manufacturer of telecommunications products. Jabil Circuit is a leader in the electronics contract manufacturing industry, with annual sales exceeding $3.5 billion in 2002. Cisco has a *virtual manufacturing company* arrangement with Jabil and Hamilton Standard, a major electronics parts supplier and division of United Technologies Corporation. Let's look at an example of how these three companies are involved in a typical business transaction.

An order placed for a Cisco router (communications processor used to interconnect telecommunications networks) arrives simultaneously at Cisco in San Jose, California, and Jabil in St. Petersburg, Florida. Jabil immediately starts to build the router by drawing parts from three on-site inventories: Jabil's, one belonging to Cisco, and one owned and controlled by Hamilton. When completed, the router is tested and checked against the order in St. Petersburg by computers in San Jose, then shipped directly to the customer by Jabil. That triggers a Cisco invoice to the customer and electronic billings from Jabil and Hamilton to Cisco in San Jose. Thus, Cisco's virtual manufacturing company alliance with Jabil Circuit and Hamilton Standard gives them an agile, build-to-order capability in the fiercely competitive telecommunications equipment industry [28].

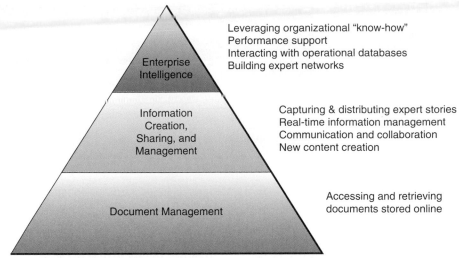

Source: Adapted from Marc Rosenberg, *e-Learning: Strategies for Delivering Knowledge in the Digital Age* (New York, McGraw-Hill, 2001), p. 70.

FIGURE 2.15

Knowledge management can be viewed as three levels of techniques, technologies, and systems that promote the collection, organization, access, sharing, and use of workplace and enterprise knowledge.

Building a Knowledge-Creating Company

In an economy where the only certainty is uncertainty, the one sure source of lasting competitive advantage is knowledge. When markets shift, technologies proliferate, competitors multiply, and products become obsolete almost overnight, successful companies are those that consistently create new knowledge, disseminate it widely throughout the organization, and quickly embody it in new technologies and products. These activities define the "knowledge-creating" company, whose sole business is continuous innovation [22].

To many companies today, lasting competitive advantage can only be theirs if they become **knowledge-creating companies** or *learning organizations*. That means consistently creating new business knowledge, disseminating it widely throughout the company, and quickly building the new knowledge into their products and services.

Knowledge-creating companies exploit two kinds of knowledge. One is *explicit knowledge*—data, documents, things written down or stored on computers. The other kind is *tacit knowledge*—the "how-tos" of knowledge, which reside in workers. As illustrated in Figure 2.15, successful **knowledge management** creates techniques, technologies, systems, and rewards for getting employees to share what they know and to make better use of accumulated workplace and enterprise knowledge. In that way, employees of a company are leveraging knowledge as they do their jobs [22].

Knowledge Management Systems

Making personal knowledge available to others is the central activity of the knowledge-creating company. It takes place continuously and at all levels of the organization [22].

Knowledge management has thus become one of the major strategic uses of information technology. Many companies are building **knowledge management systems** (KMS) to manage organizational learning and business know-how. The goal of such systems is to help knowledge workers create, organize, and make available important business knowledge, wherever and whenever it's needed in an organization. This includes processes, procedures, patents, reference works, formulas, "best practices," forecasts, and fixes. As you will see in Chapter 9, Internet and intranet websites, groupware, data mining, knowledge bases, and online discussion groups are some of the key technologies that may be used by a KMS.

Knowledge management systems facilitate organizational learning and knowledge creation. They are designed to provide rapid feedback to knowledge workers, encourage behavior changes by employees, and significantly improve business performance. As the organizational learning process continues and its knowledge base expands, the knowledge-creating company works to integrate its knowledge into its business processes, products, and services. This helps the company become a more innovative and agile provider of high-quality products and customer services, and a formidable competitor in the marketplace [24]. Now let's close this chapter with an example of knowledge management strategies from the real world.

Siemens AG: Global Knowledge Management System	Joachim Doring is a Siemens vice president in charge of creating a high-tech solution to the age-old problem of getting employees to stop hoarding their know-how. His grand plan: Use the Internet to spread the knowledge of 461,000 coworkers around the globe so that people could build off one another's expertise. At the heart of his vision is a website called ShareNet. The site combines elements of a chat room, a database, and a search engine. An online entry form lets employees store information they think might be useful to colleagues—anything from a description of a successful project to a PowerPoint presentation. Other Siemens workers can search or browse by topic, then contact the authors via e-mail for more information.

So far, the payoff has been a dandy: In the two years since its inception, ShareNet has been put to the test by nearly 12,000 salespeople in Siemens' $10.5 billion Information & Communications Networks Groups, which provides telecom equipment and services. The tool, which cost only $7.8 million, has added $122 million in sales. For example, it was crucial to landing a $3 million contract to build a pilot broadband network for Telecom Malaysia. The local salespeople did not have enough expertise to put together a proposal, but through ShareNet they discovered a team in Denmark that had done a nearly identical project. Using the Denmark group's expertise, the Malaysia team won the job.

Better yet, the system lets staffers post an alert when they need help fast. In Switzerland, Siemens won a $460,000 contract to build a telecommunications network for two hospitals even though its bid was 30 percent higher than a competitor's. The clincher: Via ShareNet, colleagues in the Netherlands provided technical data to help the sales rep prove that Siemens' system would be substantially more reliable [9].

Summary

- **Strategic Uses of Information Technology.** Information technologies can support many competitive strategies. They can help a business cut costs, differentiate and innovate in its products and services, promote growth, develop alliances, lock in customers and suppliers, create switching costs, raise barriers to entry, and leverage its investment in IT resources. Thus, information technology can help a business gain a competitive advantage in its relationships with customers, suppliers, competitors, new entrants, and producers of substitute products. Refer to Figures 2.3 and 2.5 for summaries of the uses of information technology for strategic advantage.

- **Building a Customer-Focused Business.** A key strategic use of Internet technologies is to build a company that develops its business value by making customer value its strategic focus. Customer-focused companies use Internet, intranet, and extranet e-commerce websites and services to keep track of their customers' preferences; supply products, services, and information anytime, anywhere; and provide services tailored to the individual needs of their customers.

- **Reengineering Business Processes.** Information technology is a key ingredient in reengineering business operations by enabling radical changes to business processes that dramatically improve their efficiency and effectiveness. Internet technologies can play a major role in supporting innovative changes in the design of workflows, job requirements, and organizational structures in a company.

- **Becoming an Agile Company.** A business can use information technology to help it become an agile company. Then it can prosper in rapidly changing markets with broad product ranges and short model lifetimes in which it must process orders in arbitrary lot sizes, and can offer its customers customized products while maintaining high volumes of production. An agile company depends heavily on Internet technologies to help it be responsive to its customers with customized solutions to their needs and cooperate with its customers, suppliers, and other businesses to bring products to market as rapidly and cost-effectively as possible.

- **Creating a Virtual Company.** Forming virtual companies has become an important competitive strategy in today's dynamic global markets. Internet and other information technologies play an important role in providing computing and telecommunications resources to support the communications, coordination, and information flows needed. Managers of a virtual company depend on IT to help them manage a network of people, knowledge, financial, and physical resources provided by many business partners to quickly take advantage of rapidly changing market opportunities.

- **Building a Knowledge-Creating Company.** Lasting competitive advantage today can only come from innovative use and management of organizational knowledge by knowledge-creating companies and learning organizations. Internet technologies are widely used in knowledge management systems to support the creation and dissemination of business knowledge and its integration into new products, services, and business processes.

Key Terms and Concepts

These are the key terms and concepts of this chapter. The page number of their first explanation is in parentheses.

1. Agile company (52)
2. Business process reengineering (50)
3. Competitive forces (40)
4. Competitive strategies (41)
5. Creating switching costs (43)
6. Customer-focused business (48)
7. Interenterprise information systems (43)
8. Knowledge-creating company (56)
9. Knowledge management system (56)
10. Leveraging investment in IT (43)
11. Locking in customers and suppliers (42)
12. Raising barriers to entry (43)
13. Strategic information systems (40)
14. Strategic uses of information technology (46)
15. Strategic uses of Internet technologies (41)
16. Value chain (44)
17. Virtual company (54)

Review Quiz

Match one of the key terms and concepts listed previously with one of the brief examples or definitions that follow. Try to find the best fit for answers that seem to fit more than one term or concept. Defend your choices.

_____ 1. A business must deal with customers, suppliers, competitors, new entrants, and substitutes.

_____ 2. Cost leadership, differentiation of products, and new product innovation are examples.

_____ 3. Using investment in technology to keep firms out of an industry.

_____ 4. Making it unattractive for a firm's customers or suppliers to switch to its competitors.

_____ 5. Time, money, and effort needed for customers or suppliers to change to a firm's competitors.

_____ 6. Information systems that reengineer business processes or promote business innovation are examples.

_____ 7. Internet technologies enable a company to emphasize customer value as its strategic focus.

_____ 8. Highlights how strategic information systems can be applied to a firm's business processes and support activities for competitive advantage.

_____ 9. A business can find strategic uses for the computing and telecommunications capabilities it has developed to run its operations.

_____ 10. A business can use information systems to build barriers to entry, promote innovation, create switching costs, and so on.

_____ 11. Information technology can help a business make radical improvements in business processes.

_____ 12. A business can prosper in rapidly changing markets while offering its customers individualized solutions to their needs.

_____ 13. A network of business partners formed to take advantage of rapidly changing market opportunities.

_____ 14. Many companies use the Internet, intranets, and extranets to achieve strategic gains in their competitive position.

_____ 15. Learning organizations that focus on creating, disseminating, and managing business knowledge.

_____ 16. Information systems that manage the creation and dissemination of organizational knowledge.

_____ 17. Using the Internet and extranets to link a company's information systems to those of its customers and suppliers.

Discussion Questions

1. Suppose you are a manager being asked to develop e-business and e-commerce applications to gain a competitive advantage in an important market for your company. What reservations might you have about doing so? Why?

2. How could a business use information technology to increase switching costs and lock in its customers and suppliers? Use business examples to support your answers.

3. How could a business leverage its investment in information technology to build strategic IT capabilities that serve as a barrier to entry by new entrants into its markets?

4. Refer to the Real World Case on GE, Dell, Intel, and Others in the chapter. Can information technology give a competitive advantage to a small business? Why or why not? Use an example to illustrate your answer.

5. What strategic role can information play in business process reengineering?

6. How can Internet technologies help a business form strategic alliances with its customers, suppliers, and others?

7. How could a business use Internet technologies to form a virtual company or become an agile competitor?

8. Refer to the Real World Case on Intec Engineering in the chapter. Will Intec's knowledge management system help them become a knowledge-creating company? A learning organization? Why or why not?

9. Information technology can't really give a company a strategic advantage, because most competitive advantages don't last more than a few years and soon become strategic necessities that just raise the stakes of the game. Discuss.

10. MIS author and consultant Peter Keen says: "We have learned that it is not technology that creates a competitive edge, but the management process that exploits technology." What does he mean? Do you agree or disagree? Why?

Analysis Exercises

1. **Customer Focused Business**
   Visit the top-rated websites of Dell Computer (www.dell.com) and Hilton Hotels (www.hilton.com), which are highlighted in the chapter as examples of customer-focused companies. Check out many of their website features and e-commerce services.

   a. Which site provided you with the best quality of service as a prospective customer? Explain.

   b. How could these companies improve their website design and marketing to offer even better services to their customers and prospective customers?

2. **Sabre's Travelocity and American Airlines: Competing for e-Travel Services**
   Visit the top-rated websites of Travelocity (www.travelocity.com), which is 70% owned by Sabre and American Airlines (www.aa.com), the former corporate owner of Sabre. Check out their website features and e-commerce services.

   a. How do their e-commerce websites and business models seem to differ?

   b. Refer to the summaries of strategic uses of IT in Figures 2.3 and 2.5. Which strategies can you see each company using? Explain.

   c. How has the new entrant to this market, Orbitz (www.orbitz.com), sought to gain a competitive advantage among its well-established competitors?

   d. What strategies might traditional travel agents adopt in order to compete?

3. **Assessing Strategy and Business Performance**
   Recent annual figures for eBay.com's net revenue, stock price, and earnings per share at the time of publication of this book are shown in Table 2.1. eBay™ is one of the firms identified in Figure 2.4 as following a cost

Table 2.1 eBay's Financial Performance

Year	Net Revenue (in millions)	Earnings per Share (basic)	Stock Price (at year end)
1998	86.129	.07	40.21
1999	224.724	.04	62.60
2000	431.424	.19	33.00
2001	748.821	.34	66.90
2002	1,214.100	.87	67.82

Stock price source: *Yahoo Finance*

leadership strategy. Update the data for eBay™ if more recent annual figures are available and get comparable data for at least one other firm from the set of firms listed in Figure 2.4. (You can get financial data about most companies by looking on their website for a link called investor relations or about the company. If necessary search the index or site map.)

   a. Create a spreadsheet based on these data. Your spreadsheet should include measures of percentage change in revenues, earnings per share, and stock price. You should also compute the price/earnings (PE) ratio, which is stock price divided by earnings per share. Note that some companies may have no earning for a particular year so that the PE ratio cannot be computed for that year. Rather than display "DIV/0" in the calculated cell when this happens, savvy spreadsheet developers will write a formula to display a text message such as "No Earnings" instead.

   b. Create appropriate graphs highlighting trends in the performance of each company.

   c. Write a brief (1-page) report addressing how successful each company appears to be in maintaining strategic advantage. How important were general market conditions in affecting the financial performance of your companies?

4. **Just-in-Time Inventory Systems for Pinnacle Manufacturing**
   Pinnacle Manufacturing is evaluating a proposal for the development of a new inventory management system that will allow it to use just-in-time techniques to manage the inventories of key raw materials. It is estimated that the new system will allow Pinnacle to operate with inventory levels for gadgets, widgets, and sprockets equaling 10 days of production and with inventories equaling only 5 days of production for cams and gizmos.

   In order to estimate the inventory cost savings from this system, you have been asked to gather information about current inventory levels at all of Pinnacle's production facilities. You have received estimates of the current inventory level of each raw material used in a typical production day and the average dollar value of a unit of each raw material. These estimates are shown in Table 2.2.

Table 2.2 Pinnacle's inventory estimates

Item	Inventory (units)	Units Used per Day	Cost per Unit
Gadget	2,437,250	97,645	$2.25
Widget	3,687,450	105,530	0.85
Sprocket	1,287,230	29,632	3.25
Cam	2,850,963	92,732	1.28
Gizmo	6,490,325	242,318	2.60

   a. Create a spreadsheet based on Table 2.2. Your spreadsheet should include a column showing the number of days of inventory of each raw material currently held (inventory value divided by inventory used per production day). It should also include columns showing the inventory needed under the new system (inventory used per day times 10 or 5) and the reduction in inventory under the new system for each raw material. Finally you should include columns showing the dollar value of existing inventories, the dollar value of inventories under the new system, and the reduction in dollar value of the inventories held.

   b. Assume that the annual cost of holding inventory is 10 percent times the level of inventory held. Add a summary column showing the overall annual savings for the new system.

5. **Knowledge Management**
   Within large organizations, employees often receive a great deal of unstructured information in the form of e-mails. For example, employees may receive policies, announcements, and daily operational information via e-mail. However, e-mail systems typically make poor

enterprise-wide knowledge management systems. New employees don't have access to e-mails predating their start date. Employees typically aren't permitted to search others' e-mail files for needed information. Organizations lose productivity when each employee spends time reviewing and organizing their e-mail files. Lastly, the same information may find itself saved across thousands of different e-mail files thereby ballooning e-mail file storage space requirements.

Microsoft's Exchange server, IBM's Domino server, and iManage's WorkSite, along with a wide variety of open-standard web-based products aim to address an organization's need to share unstructured information. These products provide common repositories for various categories of unstructured information. For example, management may use a "Policy" folder in Microsoft Exchange to store all their policy decisions. Likewise, sales representatives may use a "Competitive Intelligence" folder to store information obtained during the sales process about competing products, prices, or marketplace rumors. WorkSite users categorize and store all their electronic documents in a large, searchable, secured common repository.

Organizations using these systems can secure them, manage them, and make them available to the appropriate personnel. Managers can also appoint a few, specific employees requiring little technical experience to manage the content.

However, these systems cannot benefit an organization if its employees fail to contribute their knowledge, if they fail to use the system to retrieve information, or if the system simply isn't available where and when needed. To help managers better understand how employees use these systems, knowledge management systems include usage statistics such as date/time, user name, reads, writes, and even specific document access information.

a. What steps might a manager take to encourage his or her employees to use their organization's knowledge management system?

b. Should managers set minimum quotas for system usage for each employee? Why or why not?

c. Aside from employee quotas, how else might an organization benefit from usage statistics?

Progressive, Yellow, JetBlue, and Gentex: Using Information Technology for Competitive Advantage

It's easy to think of examples of technology-based companies that have figured out ways to use information technology to stay ahead of rivals. Just think of Dell Inc. and how its pioneering Web-driven build-to-order system propelled it to first place in PCs. Or eBay Inc., which dominates the online auction market with 1 billion product listings.

But companies outside of the technology sector are also using information technology to claim a competitive advantage for themselves and their stockholders. These companies aren't tech fetishists. They just make information technology work to accomplish their business strategies. Instead of big, bet-the-farm investments, they use IT to chip away at business problems, looking for incremental improvements year after year that add up to a major advantage.

It's a long-term commitment that typically comes from the top. For example, the CEOs of insurer Progressive, trucker Yellow, and auto-equipment maker Gentex have long stressed information technology and have kept IT spending steady even during the downturn. The formula is working. In the past three years, these three stocks are up an average of 110 percent versus a 31 percent drop in the Standard & Poor's 500 Stock Index.

Progressive Corp. (www.progressive.com), has spent years using information technology to raise the bar in car insurance. In 1997, the company pioneered selling online and using digital cameras and wireless Net links from their mobile claims adjusters to process accident claims—sometimes writing checks in under 20 minutes. It built a website for its 30,000 independent agents that dishes up sophisticated pricing tools, paperless filing, and policy updates to improve productivity and loyalty. Since starting its Net initiatives, Progressive's revenues have jumped from $3.4 billion in 1996 to $9.5 billion in 2002—an average increase of almost 20 percent annually, versus 5 percent for the overall auto-insurance industry. Analysts expect revenues to hit $11.8 billion by the end of 2003.

Using information technology effectively often means being more demanding than the average customer. William D. Zollars, Yellow Corp.'s (www.yellowcorp.com), CEO, set tough standards for tech projects in 1997: They couldn't take longer than a year to implement, and had to have a 15 percent rate of return. Such guiding principles have helped the 325 employees in the company's Yellow Technologies lab automate most of the trucker's operations—quickly and profitably. For example, two years ago, the $2.6 billion company installed software that lets Yellow change staffing on its loading docks daily based on predictions of labor demand. The result? The staff averages 90 workers per week, down from 100 before, even as the number of shipments has increased.

Even in industries with many technology-adept players, it's possible to stand out. JetBlue Airways Corp., (www.jetblue.com), which only started operating in 2000, was the first airline to allow pilots to carry laptops that automatically update flight manuals. And it was the first to have a virtual call center, with 700 reservation agents working from home in Salt Lake City. Meantime, 72 percent of its tickets are booked through JetBlue's own website, saving on agent commissions and other travel sites' fees. Add it all up, and in the second quarter, ended June 30, 2003, JetBlue posted 19 percent operating margins, versus Southwest Airlines Co.'s 12 percent. And its stock? Shares have surged 156 percent since the company's initial public offering in April 2002.

Small companies often use information technology to offset the economies of scale of bigger rivals. For example, Gentex Corp. (www.gentex.com), is the pacesetter in car mirrors. It has achieved 40 percent gross margins by cutting costs 4 percent to 5 percent annually through IT. Gentex keeps adding more automation and monitoring systems in its factories that pinpoint problems before too many faulty products are made. That has upped manufacturing yield 30 percent in the past three years. Gentex's revenue is expected to jump 19.5 percent, to $472 million this year, says analyst Alexander P. Paris of Barrington Research Associates Inc.

Investors looking for promising companies, and a lot of other companies fighting for survival and success out there could learn a lesson from these companies: A long-term commitment to information technology can mean a long-term strategic advantage over the competition.

Case Study Questions

Note: Refer to the competitive strategies outlined in Figures 2.3 and 2.5 to help you answer the following questions.

1. What strategies in the use of IT for competitive advantage are being used by each of the companies in this case? Explain your choices.

2. Visit the website of one these companies for more information on their business. What other competitive strategies could you recommend for this company? Explain your recommendations.

3. How could other companies apply the competitive strategies being used by the companies in this case? Use examples from both a large and a small business perspective to illustrate your answer.

Source: Adapted from Heather Green, "Companies That Really Get It," *Business Week*, August 25, 2003, p. 144.

REAL WORLD CASE 4

CDW and Harrah's Entertainment: Developing Strategic Customer-Loyalty Systems

Customer satisfaction is good, but customer loyalty is even better. "A satisfied customer is one who sees you as meeting expectations," says John Samuels, a senior manager in the marketing department at CDW Corp., (www.cdw.com), a direct marketer of more than 50,000 hardware and software products, with net sales of $4.3 billion. "A loyal customer, on the other hand, wants to do business with you again and will recommend you to others."

CRM packages may help measure satisfaction, but not all of them can be used to benchmark loyalty, and the link is tenuous. A good loyalty program, according to Bob Chatham, an analyst at Forrester Research, Inc., in Cambridge, Massachusetts, combines customer feedback and business information with sophisticated analytics to produce actionable results. This is why IT has to take the lead in loyalty. "IT is just about the only department that can coordinate among business processes, vendors of data analysis software and services, and the executives who can translate output into action," says Chatham.

Five years ago, CDW started working with Walker Information, Inc., a 64-year-old market research firm in Indianapolis that focuses on customer loyalty, to gather customer experience data. "Initially, these were phone surveys with cycle times of two months that were used to generate reports," says Samuels. Then CDW replaced the phone surveys with Walker's SmartLoyalty service, which includes an e-mail solicitation that directs willing customers to a website that Walker co-hosts with CDW. It dramatically reduced survey cycle times, and some reports are even generated in real time.

"It's not that difficult to do Web surveys," says Harry Watkins, a research director at Aberdeen Group, Inc., in Boston. "Walker's real value is that they have built validated, multivariate measures of loyalty into their software. As an ASP, Walker also acts as a consultant, helping companies determine the causal variables that determine loyalty."

SmartLoyalty divides customers into four "buckets," or categories, commonly used for analyzing customer loyalty. CDW compared a customer's purchasing behavior with his bucket and then in further testing saw that all the buckets lined up very well with customers' behavior. "In other words," says Samuels, "we proved that the software-generated model was very predictive."

In response, executives sought sales improvements. For example, the model told them that customers wanted more out of the website and from account managers. So CDW's CEO directed the CIO to develop a response plan, which led to a new search engine and a website that delivers more product information. "And now our account managers are trained to provide more than just 'speeds and feeds,'" says Samuels. "For example, they are trained in areas such as security and disaster recovery." These changes are paying off, he says, adding, "Each year that we have used SmartLoyalty, we have seen the percentage of truly loyal customers increase."

At Harrah's Entertainment Inc. (www.harrahs.com), in Las Vegas, CIO Tim Stanley says focusing on loyalty has helped push the casino chain's numbers in the right direction. In 1997, Harrah's launched a new IT-driven loyalty program that pulled all customer data into a centralized data warehouse and provided sophisticated data mining analytics. "We wanted to better understand the value of the investments we make in our customers," says Stanley. But this analysis came at a price. "Back then, we used Informix running on NCR for both our operational and analytic systems," he explains. "When we converted to the centralized warehouse, the analytic system was a real dog, far too slow." So in 1999, Stanley offloaded the analytics to Teradata, the NCR Corp. database designed for large data sets and parallel architectures. "And the performance improvement was stunning," he says. Harrah's now does near-real-time analysis: As customers interact with slot machines, check into casinos, or buy meals, they receive reward offers based on the predictive analyses.

The data revealed other trends as well. For example, Stanley says Harrah's previously focused mostly on high rollers. But as executives further studied the analyses and reports, they realized that the person who visits a casino once or twice a week and spends modestly is a great investment. "This was a big 'Aha!' for us," Stanley says. The result was a new rewards program tailored to low rollers. "We have seen consistent growth in revenue and profits every quarter since 1999, when we implemented the new loyalty program," says Stanley. "By cross-correlating questionnaire analysis with our revenue numbers, we estimate a steady 60 percent ROI year after year on our investment in customer loyalty."

When CDW began using SmartLoyalty, Samuels already had a rich source of market research reports. "The problem was that all this information was on thousands of sheets of paper, and there was no way to get it quickly to the right decision makers," he explains. That's where IT closes the loop. Aberdeen's Watkins puts it this way: "With good customer loyalty technology, IT can wire the voice of the customer back into the enterprise."

Case Study Questions

1. Does CDW's customer loyalty program give them a competitive advantage? Why or why not?

2. What is the strategic value of Harrah's approach to determining and rewarding customer loyalty?

3. What else could CDW and Harrah's do to truly become customer-focused businesses? Visit their websites to help you suggest several alternatives.

Source: Adapted from Mark Leon, "Catering to True-Blue Customers," *Computerworld*, August 11, 2003, p. 37. Copyright © 2003 by Computerworld, Inc. Framingham, MA 01701. All rights reserved.

MODULE II

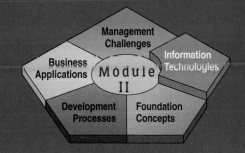

Management Challenges

Information Technologies

Business Applications

Module II

Development Processes

Foundation Concepts

INFORMATION TECHNOLOGIES

What challenges do information system technologies pose for business professionals? What basic knowledge should you possess about information technology? The four chapters of this module give you an overview of the hardware, software, and data resource management and telecommunications network technologies used in information systems and their implications for business managers and professionals.

- **Chapter 3: Computer Hardware,** reviews trends and developments in microcomputer, midrange, and mainframe computer systems; basic computer system concepts; and the major types of technologies used in peripheral devices for computer input, output, and storage.

- **Chapter 4: Computer Software,** reviews the basic features and trends in the major types of application software and system software used to support enterprise and end user computing.

- **Chapter 5: Data Resource Management,** emphasizes management of the data resources of computer-using organizations. This chapter reviews key database management concepts and applications in business information systems.

- **Chapter 6: Telecommunications and Networks,** presents an overview of the Internet and other telecommunications networks, business applications, and trends, and reviews technical telecommunications alternatives.

CHAPTER 3

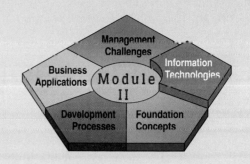

COMPUTER HARDWARE

Chapter Highlights

Section I

Computer Systems: End User and Enterprise Computing

Real World Case: Progressive Insurance and UniFirst Corp.: The Business Case for Mobile Computing Systems

Types of Computer Systems

Microcomputer Systems

Midrange Systems

Mainframe Systems

Technical Note: The Computer System Concept

Section II

Computer Peripherals: Input, Output, and Storage Technologies

Real World Case: Delta and Northwest Airlines: The Business Value of Customer Self-Service Kiosks

Peripherals

Input Technologies

Pointing Devices

Pen-Based Computing

Speech Recognition Systems

Optical Scanning

Other Input Technologies

Output Technologies

Video Output

Printed Output

Storage Trade-Offs

Semiconductor Memory

Magnetic Disks

Magnetic Tape

Optical Disks

Real World Case: Nappi Distributors and Old Dominion Freight Line: The Business Value of Wireless Handhelds

Real World Case: Wisconsin Physicians Service and Winnebago: Moving to Linux on the Mainframe

Learning Objectives

After reading and studying this chapter, you should be able to:

1. Identify the major types and uses of microcomputer, midrange, and mainframe computer systems.

2. Outline the major technologies and uses of computer peripherals for input, output, and storage.

3. Identify and give examples of the components and functions of a computer system.

4. Identify the computer systems and peripherals you would acquire or recommend for a business of your choice, and explain the reasons for your selections.

SECTION I Computer Systems: End User and Enterprise Computing

All computers are systems of input, processing, output, storage, and control components. In this section, we will discuss the trends, applications, and some basic concepts of the many types of computer systems in use today. In Section II, we will cover the changing technologies for input, output, and storage that are provided by the peripheral devices that are part of modern computer systems.

Analyzing Progressive Insurance and UniFirst

Read the Real World Case on Progressive Insurance and UniFirst on the next page. We can learn a lot about the business use of mobile computing devices from this case. See Figure 3.1.

Progressive Insurance is a great example of a company that capitalizes on a variety of computer hardware components and microprocessor-powered and wireless-enabled devices to give themselves a competitive edge in the fierce competition for customers that marks the auto insurance business. Of course, these devices are available to all companies, but it is Progressive's investment and commitment to their IRV (immediate response vehicle) program that enables them to provide the fast claims service that distinguishes their business performance. The UniFirst example demonstrates that even simple PDAs (personal digital assistants) can serve as powerful special-purpose microcomputer devices that can provide sales professionals and managers in the field with the information they need to support their sales and service activities, as well as cutting costs and increasing revenues for the company.

FIGURE 3.1

Progressive Insurance adjuster Micah Long depends on the computer-empowered devices in his IRV (immediate response vehicle) to give him a competitive edge in providing fast claims service.

Source: Markham Johnson

> ## REAL WORLD
> ## CASE 1

Progressive Insurance and UniFirst Corp.: The Business Case for Mobile Computing Systems

I f you've ever been in a fender bender car accident, you know how it feels to wait for your claim payment to arrive. Insurance companies love to hold the money as long as possible to wring out every penny of interest. Progressive Insurance (www.progressive.com) in Mayfield Village, Ohio, is the notable exception to the industry rule: It tries to unload payments as quickly as it can—by getting its claims adjusters out of the office and onto the street, where they rub elbows with clients and commiserate about the jerk who was driving the other car. The logic behind such a radical notion? Happier customers and more productive claims reps will more than make up for the lost interest revenue.

At Progressive, that radical notion is spelled IRV. The acronym stands for "immediate response vehicles," a fleet of Ford Explorers and Escapes loaded with enough communications gear—laptops, printers, and cell phones—to allow adjusters to settle claims right at the scene of an accident. That's a big improvement over the scenario that still pervades the industry: Wait a week to see the car and make handwritten notes, snap Polaroids, drive back to the office, type it all into the mainframe, and issue a request for a check.

Ten years ago, the IRV project involved just 10 adjusters in Florida. Today more than 11,000 mobile claims reps share a fleet of 2,600 IRVs. Not only did the program help improve customer retention by 20 percent last year, it has helped Progressive shave labor costs: San Francisco claims manager Hellen Greenway, who oversees more than 100 reps, says Progressive's mobile adjusters can handle nearly twice the workload they could a decade ago. Progressive also credits the fleet of Fords with helping company revenues climb from $1.8 billion to more than $9 billion during that period. And, for the record, the ultrabusy Progressive agents aren't contributing to accidents. Adjusters are strictly prohibited from talking on their cell phones when they're behind the wheel.

A wireless-ready laptop provides around-the-clock access to Progressive's mainframe. An adjuster can type a claim while sitting in a body shop and go over it with the policyholder right on the screen. The laptops also let agents use fax machines around the country as printer surrogates when a satellite office needs a hard copy instead of e-mail.

Agents spend hours every day talking to clients, auto shops, and other adjusters on their cell phones, but it's the two-way radio feature that gets the most use. Dispatchers keep tabs on agents' whereabouts, sending the closest adjuster to investigate a scene. Digital cameras let agents snap as many pictures as they need, upload them to Progressive's servers for storage, and share them with managers if necessary. Some adjusters even film short movies, which are used to document traffic patterns at accident-prone intersections.

Finally, each IRV includes an ink-jet printer to spit out hard copies of estimates, claims, and, of course, checks. Adjusters carry around reams of blanks; the printer adds everything from the Progressive logo to routing numbers.

UniFirst Corp. With 400 salespeople, 90 sales managers, and 145 locations in the U.S. and Canada, UniFirst is the third-largest uniform maker in the United States. UniFirst (www.unifirst.com) is moving from a form-based system that's updated once a month to a responsive CRM system that's updated daily to bolster sales calls, assist follow-ups, and get technology to people who often shun the stuff. Now, instead of a monthly mainframe-produced paper printout that probably got left in the car, sales reps can see the latest information on their PDAs using a new mobile CRM application.

UniFirst uses software from SalesLogix, a division of Best Software. UniFirst worked with Vaultus Mobile Technologies to get a Java-based PC application linked to an application server that shares data with the corporate sales database. As a result, UniFirst has lower costs. Gone: $55,000 a year for paper, $40,000 for planners and calendars, and $100,000 for FedEx service. And, of course, the company no longer needs data entry people.

And this is before the sales rep even meets with the client. At that point, there are more opportunities to save money, and to make more money. For example, the UniFirst test has shown a reduction in past-due invoices. Moreover, managers now can get their hands on data they can use to create calendars, prioritize accounts, and help the reps sell.

The daily downloads take three minutes on a link established via a toll-free number. Sales reps in six locations tested the system on H-P Jornada and iPaq PDA devices for several months, before the mobile computing initiative was expanded to include all 400 reps during the fall of 2003.

Case Study Questions

1. What are the business benefits and limitations of Progressive's IRV system and the UniFirst PDA system?

2. What computer system technologies could Progressive add to improve the business value of its IRV program? Why?

3. Should UniFirst switch from PDAs to laptop PCs or tablet PCs? Why or why not? Check out websites like www.cnet.com or www.pcworld.com for the latest product reviews to help you answer.

Source: Adapted from Christopher Null, "The Check Is in the Car," *Business 2.0*, July 2003, pp. 44–45, and Pimm Fox, "Power in the Field," *Computerworld*, August 11, 2003, pp. 20–21.

FIGURE 3.2 Examples of computer system categories.

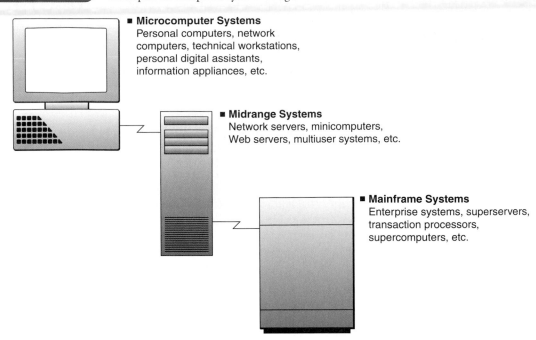

■ **Microcomputer Systems**
Personal computers, network computers, technical workstations, personal digital assistants, information appliances, etc.

■ **Midrange Systems**
Network servers, minicomputers, Web servers, multiuser systems, etc.

■ **Mainframe Systems**
Enterprise systems, superservers, transaction processors, supercomputers, etc.

Types of Computer Systems

Today's computer systems come in a variety of sizes, shapes, and computing capabilities. Rapid hardware and software developments and changing end user needs continue to drive the emergence of new models of computers, from the smallest hand-held personal digital assistant/cell phone combinations to the largest multiple-CPU mainframe for the enterprise. See Figure 3.2.

Categories such as *mainframe*, *midrange*, and *microcomputer* systems are still used to help us express the relative processing power and number of end users that can be supported by different types of computers. But these are not precise classifications, and they do overlap each other. Thus, other names are commonly given to highlight the major uses of particular types of computers. Examples include personal computers, network servers, network computers, and technical workstations.

In addition, experts continue to predict the merging or disappearance of several computer categories. They feel, for example, that many midrange and mainframe systems have been made obsolete by the power and versatility of *client/server* networks of end user microcomputers and servers. Other industry experts have predicted that the emergence of network computers and *information appliances* for applications on the Internet and corporate intranets will replace many personal computers, especially in large organizations and in the home computer market. Only time will tell whether such predictions will equal the expectations of industry forecasters.

Microcomputer Systems

The entire center of gravity in computing has shifted. For millions of consumers and business users, the main function of desktop PCs is as a window to the Internet. Computers are now communications devices, and consumers want them to be as cheap as possible [4].

Microcomputers are the most important category of computer systems for businesspeople and consumers. Though usually called a *personal computer*, or PC, a microcomputer is much more than a small computer for use by an individual. The computing power of microcomputers now exceeds that of the mainframes of previous computer generations at a fraction of their cost. Thus, they have become powerful networked *professional workstations* for business professionals.

FIGURE 3.3   Examples of microcomputer systems

a. A notebook microcomputer.
Source: Courtesy of Hewlett-Packard.

b. The microcomputer as a professional workstation.
Source: Peter Kornicker/Corbis.

c. The microcomputer as a technical workstation.
Source: Richard T. Nowitz/Corbis.

Microcomputers come in a variety of sizes and shapes for a variety of purposes, as Figure 3.3 illustrates. For example, PCs are available as hand-held, notebook, laptop, portable, desktop, and floor-standing models. Or, based on their use, they include home, personal, professional, workstation, and multiuser systems. Most microcomputers are *desktops* designed to fit on an office desk, or **laptops** for those who want a small, portable PC for their work activities. Figure 3.4 offers advice on some of the key features you should consider in acquiring a high-end professional workstation, multimedia PC, or beginner's system. This should give you some idea of the range of features available in today's microcomputers.

Some microcomputers are powerful **workstation computers** (technical workstations) that support applications with heavy mathematical computing and graphics display demands such as computer-aided design (CAD) in engineering, or investment and portfolio analysis in the securities industry. Other microcomputers are used as **network servers.** They are usually more powerful microcomputers that coordinate telecommunications and resource sharing in small local area networks (LANs), and Internet and intranet websites.

FIGURE 3.4 Examples of recommended features for the three types of PC users.

Business Pro	Multimedia Heavy	Newcomer
To track your products, customers, and performance, you'll need more than just a fast machine:	Media pros and dedicated amateurs will want at least a Mac G4 or a 2–3GHz Intel chip, and:	Save money with a Celeron processor in the 1–2GHz range. Also look for:
● 2–3 Gigahertz processor	● 512MB RAM	● 256MB RAM
● 512MB RAM	● 80GB hard drive or more	● 40GB hard drive
● 80GB hard drive	● 18-inch or larger CRT, flat-panel LCD, or plasma display	● Internal 56K modem
● 18-inch flat-panel display	● High-end color printer	● CD–RW/DVD drive
● CD–RW/DVD drive or portable hard drives for backup	● CD–RW/DVD+RW drive	● 17-inch CRT or 15-inch flat panel LCD
	● Deluxe speaker system	● Basic inkjet printer

Note: www.dell.com and www.gateway.com are good sources for the latest PC features available.

Boeing, Monster.com, and Others: Corporate PC Criteria

What do you look for in a new PC system? A big, bright screen? Zippy new processor? Capacious hard drive? Acres of RAM? Sorry, none of these is a top concern for corporate PC buyers. Numerous studies have shown that the price of a new computer is only a small part of the total cost of ownership (TCO). Support, maintenance, and other intangibles contribute far more heavily to the sum. Let's take a look at three top criteria.

Solid performance at a reasonable price. Corporate buyers know that their users probably aren't mapping the human genome or plotting trajectories to Saturn. They're doing word processing, order entry, sales contact management, and other essential business tasks. They need a solid, competent machine at a reasonable price, not the latest whiz-bang. "Mainstream machines from respected vendors are going to do the job fine," says Bob Jorgenson, a spokesman for The Boeing Co. in Seattle.

Operating system ready. "A change in an operating system is the most disruptive upgrade an enterprise has to face," says Paul Neilson, vice president of technical support at Monster.com, an online job-placement service in Maynard, Massachusetts. That's why many corporate buyers want their machines to be able to handle current operating systems and anticipated new ones. While some enterprises still use Windows 9x or NT, they must be able to make a possible transition to Windows XP soon, and even OS versions expected three to five years out. Primarily, that means deciding what hard disk space and RAM will be sufficient.

Connectivity. Networked machines are a given in corporate life, and Internet-ready machines are becoming a given. Buyers need machines equipped with reliable network interface cards or even wireless LAN capabilities. "With fewer cables to worry about, wireless LANs, especially when combined with laptop PCs, contribute to the flexibility of the workplace and the simplicity of PC deployment," says Matt Heller, vice president of operations at GoTo.com Inc. in Pasadena, California, which provides online search services to tens of thousands of affiliate companies. Many organizations are planning for Internet-based applications and need machines ready to make fast, reliable, and secure connections. "Connection performance and ports are prime factors for us," says Chris Carrara, IT manager at Sartorious AG, a global lab technology manufacturer in Goettingen, Germany [5].

FIGURE 3.5

An example of a network computer: the Sun Ray I enterprise appliance.

Source: Courtesy of Sun Microsystems Inc.

Network Computers

Network computers (NCs) are a microcomputer category designed primarily for use with the Internet and corporate intranets by clerical workers, operational employees, and knowledge workers with specialized or limited computing applications. NCs are low-cost, sealed, networked microcomputers with no or minimal disk storage. Users of NCs depend primarily on Internet and intranet servers for their operating system and Web browser, application software, and data access and storage.

One of the main attractions of network computers is their lower cost of purchase, upgrades, maintenance, and support compared to full-featured PCs. Other benefits to business include ease of software distribution and licensing, computing platform standardization, reduced end user support requirements, and improved manageability through centralized management and enterprise-wide control of computer network resources [4]. See Figure 3.5.

Information Appliances

PCs aren't the only option: A host of smart gadgets and information appliances—from cellular phones and pagers to hand-held PCs and Web-based game machines—promise Internet access and the ability to perform basic computational chores [4].

Hand-held microcomputer devices known as **personal digital assistants** (PDAs) are some of the most popular devices in the **information appliance** category. Web-enabled PDAs use touch screens, pen-based handwriting recognition, or keypads so mobile workers can send and receive e-mail, access the Web, and exchange information such as appointments, to-do lists, and sales contacts with their desktop PCs or Web servers.

Information appliances may also take the form of video-game consoles and other devices that connect to your home TV set. These devices enable you to surf the World Wide Web or send and receive e-mail and watch TV programs or play video games at the same time. Other information appliances include wireless PDAs and Internet-enabled cellular and PCS phones, and wired telephone-based home appliances that can send and receive e-mail and access the Web.

Computer Terminals

Computer terminals are undergoing a major conversion to networked computer devices. *Dumb terminals*, which are keyboard/video monitor devices with limited processing capabilities, are being replaced by *intelligent terminals*, which are modified networked PCs or network computers. Also included are **network terminals,** which may be *Windows terminals*, that are dependent on network servers for Windows software, processing power, and storage, or *Internet terminals*, which depend on Internet or intranet website servers for their operating systems and application software.

Intelligent terminals take many forms and can perform data entry and some information processing tasks independently. This includes the widespread use of **transaction terminals** in banks, retail stores, factories, and other work sites. Examples are automated teller machines (ATMs), factory production recorders, and retail point-of-sale (POS) terminals. These intelligent terminals use keypads, touch screens, bar code scanners, and other input methods to capture data and interact with end users during a transaction, while relying on servers or other computers in the network for further transaction processing.

Midrange Systems

Midrange systems are primarily high-end network servers and other types of servers that can handle the processing of many business applications. Though not as powerful as mainframe computers, they are less costly to buy, operate, and maintain than mainframe systems, and thus meet the computing needs of many organizations. See Figure 3.6.

> *Burgeoning data warehouses and related applications such as data mining and online analytical processing are forcing IT shops into higher and higher levels of server configurations. Similarly, Internet-based applications, such as Web servers and electronic commerce, are forcing IT managers to push the envelope of processing speed and storage capacity and other [business] applications, fueling the growth of high-end servers* [14].

Midrange systems have become popular as powerful **network servers** to help manage large Internet websites, corporate intranets and extranets, and other networks. Electronic commerce and other business uses of the Internet are popular high-end server applications, as are integrated enterprise-wide manufacturing, distribution, and financial applications. Other applications, like data warehouse management, data mining, and online analytical processing (which we discuss in Chapters 5 and 9), are contributing to the growth of high-end server systems [14].

Midrange systems first became popular as **minicomputers** for scientific research, instrumentation systems, engineering analysis, and industrial process monitoring and control. Minicomputers could easily handle such uses because these applications are narrow in scope and do not demand the processing versatility of mainframe systems. Today, midrange systems include servers used in industrial process-control and manufacturing plants, and play a major role in computer-aided manufacturing (CAM). They

Source: Courtesy of IBM.

can also take the form of powerful technical workstations for computer-aided design (CAD) and other computation-intensive and graphics intensive applications. Midrange systems are also used as *front-end servers* to assist mainframe computers in telecommunications processing and network management.

Los Alamos Laboratory and Others: Moving to Blade Servers	Los Alamos National Laboratory and Washington-based e-learning software and application service provider (ASP) Blackboard Inc. (www.blackboard.com) are finding that blade servers cost 30 to 50 percent less than traditional rack-mounted servers, with the biggest savings derived from their smaller size, low power-consumption costs, and the reduced costs of cabling, power supply management, and integrated telecom switching. Dollar Rent A Car Inc. (www.dollar.com) began using HP blade servers in 2002 to help speed the deployment of new Unix-based Web and data center applications while keeping costs down, and expanded their use in 2003. Meanwhile, AOL (www.aol.com) began testing IBM BladeCenter servers running Linux in 2002, as part of their goal of reducing IT costs by 30 percent in 2003. Freed of the physical bulk and componentry of traditional servers, blade servers slide into slots on racks. In most cases, blade servers consist of microcomputer processing and storage assemblies that fit into slots in a rack unit that provides a common backplane, cooling fan, cabling, and network and external storage connections, reducing both cabling and space requirements. Analysts say cost savings increase the longer these systems are used. "Blade servers take up less space, generate less heat, use less power, and don't need the environment requirements of air conditioning or raised flooring, as larger servers require," says Tom Manter, research director at Aberdeen Group. The primary caveat in trying to achieve quick ROI on blade servers largely rests on how well the processing, networking, and storage features are integrated. "Any cost savings can quickly be eaten away if maintaining blade servers becomes complex and time-consuming," says John Humphreys, an analyst at IDC [13].

Mainframe Computer Systems

Several years after dire pronouncements that the mainframe was dead, quite the opposite is true: Mainframe usage is actually on the rise. And it's not just a short-term blip. One factor that's been driving mainframe sales is cost reductions [of 35 percent or more]. Price reductions aren't the only factor fueling mainframe acquisitions. IS organizations are teaching the old dog new tricks by putting mainframes at the center stage of emerging applications such as data mining and warehousing, decision support, and a variety of Internet-based applications, most notably electronic commerce [14].

Mainframe systems are large, fast, and powerful computer systems. For example, mainframes can process thousands of million instructions per second (MIPS). Mainframes also have large primary storage capacities. Their main memory capacity can range from hundreds of megabytes to many gigabytes of primary storage. And mainframes have slimmed down drastically in the last few years, dramatically reducing their air-conditioning needs, electrical power consumption, and floor space requirements, and thus their acquisition and operating costs. Most of these improvements are the result of a move from water-cooled mainframes to a newer air-cooled technology for mainframe systems [11]. See Figure 3.7.

Thus, mainframe computers continue to handle the information processing needs of major corporations and government agencies with high transaction processing volumes or complex computational problems. For example, major international banks, airlines, oil companies, and other large corporations process millions of sales transactions and customer inquiries each day with the help of large mainframe systems. Mainframes are still used for computation-intensive applications such as analyzing seismic data from oil field explorations or simulating flight conditions in designing aircraft. Mainframes are also widely used as *superservers* for the large client/server networks and

FIGURE 3.7

Mainframe computer systems are the heavy lifters of corporate computing.

Source: Corbis.

high-volume Internet websites of large companies. And as previously mentioned, mainframes are becoming a popular business computing platform for data mining and warehousing, and electronic commerce applications [11].

Supercomputer Systems

Supercomputers have now become "scalable servers" at the top end of the product lines that start with desktop workstations. Market-driven companies, like Silicon Graphics, Hewlett-Packard, and IBM, have a much broader focus than just building the world's fastest computer, and the software of the desktop computer has a much greater overlap with that of the supercomputer than it used to, because both are built from the same cache-based microprocessors [9].

The term **supercomputer** describes a category of extremely powerful computer systems specifically designed for scientific, engineering, and business applications requiring extremely high speeds for massive numeric computations. The market for supercomputers includes government research agencies, large universities, and major corporations. They use supercomputers for applications such as global weather forecasting, military defense systems, computational cosmology and astronomy, microprocessor research and design, large-scale data mining, and so on.

Supercomputers use *parallel processing* architectures of interconnected microprocessors (which can execute many instructions at the same time in parallel). They can easily perform arithmetic calculations at speeds of billions of floating-point operations per second *(gigaflops)*. Supercomputers that can calculate in *teraflops* (trillions of floating-point operations per second), which use massively parallel processing (MPP) designs of thousands of microprocessors, are now in use. Purchase prices for large supercomputers are in the $5 million to $50 million range.

However, the use of symmetric multiprocessing (SMP) and distributed shared memory (DSM) designs of smaller numbers of interconnected microprocessors has spawned a breed of *minisupercomputers* with prices that start in the hundreds of thousands of dollars. For example IBM's RS/6000 SP starts at $150,000 for a one-processing-node SMP computer. However, it can be expanded to hundreds of processing nodes, which drives its price into the tens of millions of dollars.

FIGURE 3.8

The ASCI White supercomputer system at Lawrence Livermore National Laboratory in Livermore, California.

Source: Courtesy of IBM.

The ASCI White supercomputer system shown in Figure 3.8, consists of three IBM RS/6000 SP systems: White, Frost, and Ice. White, the largest of these systems, is a 512-node, 16-way symmetric multiprocessor (SMP) supercomputer with a peak performance of 12.3 teraflops. Frost is a 68-node, 16-way SMP system, and Ice is a 28-node, 16-way SMP system [15]. Supercomputers like these continue to advance the state of the art for the entire computer industry.

Technical Note: The Computer System Concept

As a business professional, you do not need a detailed technical knowledge of computers. However, you do need to understand some basic concepts about computer systems. This should help you be an informed and productive user of computer system resources.

A computer is more than a high-powered collection of electronic devices performing a variety of information processing chores. A computer is a *system*, an interrelated combination of components that performs the basic system functions of input, processing, output, storage, and control, thus providing end users with a powerful information processing tool. Understanding the computer as a **computer system** is vital to the effective use and management of computers. You should be able to visualize any computer this way, from the smallest microcomputer device, to a large computer network whose components are interconnected by telecommunications network links throughout a building complex or geographic area.

Figure 3.9 illustrates that a computer is a system of hardware devices organized according to the following system functions:

- **Input.** The input devices of a computer system include computer keyboards, touch screens, pens, electronic mouses, optical scanners, and so on. They convert data into electronic form for direct entry or through a telecommunications network into a computer system.

- **Processing.** The **central processing unit** (CPU) is the main processing component of a computer system. (In microcomputers, it is the **main microprocessor.** See Figure 3.10.) Conceptually, the circuitry of a CPU can be subdivided into two major subunits: the arithmetic-logic unit and the control unit. It is the electronic circuits (known as *registers*) of the **arithmetic-logic** unit that perform the arithmetic and logic functions required to execute software instructions.

FIGURE 3.9   The computer system concept. A computer is a system of hardware components and functions.

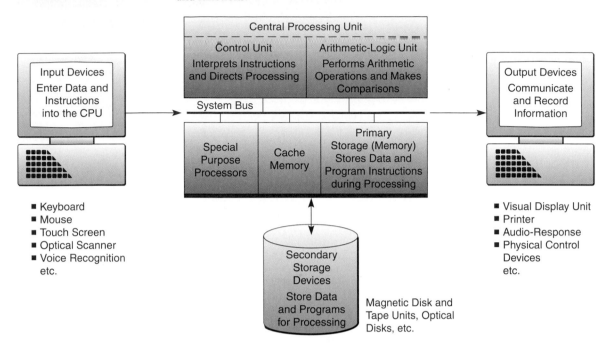

- **Output.** The output devices of a computer system include video display units, printers, audio response units, and so on. They convert electronic information produced by the computer system into human-intelligible form for presentation to end users.

- **Storage.** The storage function of a computer system takes place in the storage circuits of the computer's **primary storage unit,** or *memory*, supported by

FIGURE 3.10

This Intel Mobile Pentium 4-M microprocessor operates at 3 GHz clock speeds to bring desktop power to laptop PCs.

Source: Courtesy of Intel Corporation.

secondary storage devices such as magnetic disk and optical disk drives. These devices store data and software instructions needed for processing. Computer processors may also include storage circuitry called *cache memory* for high-speed, temporary storage of instruction and data elements.

- **Control.** The control unit of a CPU is the control component of a computer system. Its registers and other circuits interpret software instructions and transmit directions that control the activities of the other components of the computer system.

Computer Processing Speeds

How fast are computer systems? Early computer operating speeds were measured in **milliseconds** (thousandths of a second) and **microseconds** (millionths of a second). Now computers operate in the **nanosecond** (billionth of a second) range, with **picosecond** (trillionth of a second) speed being attained by some computers. Such speeds seem almost incomprehensible. For example, an average person taking one step each nanosecond would circle the earth about 20 times in one second!

We have already mentioned the *teraflop* speeds of some supercomputers. However, most computers can now process program instructions at *million instructions per second* (MIPS) speeds. Another measure of processing speed is *megahertz* (MHz), or millions of cycles per second, and *gigahertz* (GHz), or billions of cycles per second. This rating is commonly called the *clock speed* of a microprocessor, since it is used to rate microprocessors by the speed of their timing circuits or internal clock.

However, such ratings can be misleading indicators of the effective processing speed of microprocessors, and their *throughput*, or ability to perform useful computation or data processing assignments during a given period of time. That's because processing speed depends on a variety of factors including the size of circuitry paths, or *buses* that interconnect microprocessor components; the capacity of instruction processing *registers*; the use of high-speed cache memory; and the use of specialized microprocessors such as a math coprocessor to do arithmetic calculations faster.

<table>
<tr><td>SECTION II</td><td># Computer Peripherals: Input, Output, and Storage Technologies</td></tr>
</table>

SECTION II

Computer Peripherals: Input, Output, and Storage Technologies

The right peripherals can make all the difference in your computing experience. A top-quality monitor will be easier on your eyes—and may change the way you work. A scanner can edge you closer to that ever-elusive goal—the paperless office. Backup-storage systems can offer bank-vault security against losing your work. CD and DVD drives have become essential for many applications. Thus, the right choice of peripherals can make a big difference [7].

Analyzing Delta and Northwest Airlines

Read the Real World Case on Delta and Northwest Airlines on the next page. We can learn a lot about the business value of consolidating computer operations and systems from this case. See Figure 3.11.

Delta Air Lines is playing catch-up with other airlines like Northwest that have been making big investments in information technology in the form of self-service check-in services on company websites and networked microcomputer-based kiosks in airport terminals. The airport kiosks support a variety of self-service applications for airline travelers, especially check-in services that help travelers avoid some of the delays caused by long airport waiting lines. Thus, Northwest reports that more passengers are using their Web and kiosk self-service check-in alternatives than their traditional airport check-in process. But Delta plans to finish installing over 800 self-service kiosks in the United States in 2003, with more being installed internationally. The kiosks obviously offer a more convenient but less costly check-in alternative for the airlines. Thus, Delta reports an "enormous" payback on their investment in kiosk technology, as millions of their passengers are increasingly choosing to use this check-in alternative.

FIGURE 3.11

Mike Childress, senior vice-president of development at Delta Technology, leads the project that is installing hundreds of self-service kiosks in airports for Delta Air Lines.

Source: Ann States.

REAL WORLD CASE 2

Delta and Northwest Airlines: The Business Value of Customer Self-Service Kiosks

For travelers, the best trips are fast and hassle-free, with limited time spent at the airport. That's why Atlanta-based Delta Air Lines Inc. (www.delta.com) teamed up with its technology subsidiary, Delta Technology Inc., to deploy hundreds of self-service check-in kiosks at airports across the country, with a goal of speeding travelers to their destinations.

Mike Childress, senior vice president of development at Delta Technology and the project's leader, says there are now 449 kiosks installed at airports in 81 U.S. cities. The kiosks had been part of Delta's multiyear business plan, but when airports increased security in the wake of the Sept. 11 terrorist attacks—and the amount of time customers spent waiting in line grew longer—the airline decided to accelerate the project. Delta acknowledges that it had been trailing some other carriers' kiosk initiatives before Sept. 11.

For example, Northwest Airlines (www.nwa.com) had embraced self-service airport kiosks in a big way before Delta. Northwest had over 650 e-Service Center check-in kiosks in over 150 airports, more than any other airline, and will have added over 100 more kiosks by the end of 2003. In fact, more of Northwest's customers are using self-service check-ins by checking in online on the Web at nwa.com, or through one of their e-Service Center check-in kiosks, than through traditional check-in methods.

Thus, beginning in May 2003, more than half of eligible customers chose one of Northwest's self-service check-in options, a record high. At the carrier's Detroit World Gateway and Minneapolis/St. Paul airport hubs, usage averaged 70 percent. Systemwide usage has continued to soar over the last three years. "On May 1, our Minneapolis/St. Paul hub achieved a record 74 percent of check-in transactions performed through one of our convenient self-service check-in options," said Al Lenza, vice president of e-commerce and distribution. "With the rapid growth we are experiencing, by the end of the year we expect that at least 70 percent of our customers, systemwide, will be choosing nwa.com online check-in or an e-Service Center kiosk for their check-in needs," said Lenza.

Rob Maruster, Delta Air Lines' director of airport strategy and service, says the kiosks help customers shave 5 to 15 minutes off the time they have to stand in line. Passengers can use the kiosks to check in for their flights, get boarding passes for originating or connecting flights, select or change seats, request to stand by for an upgrade, check baggage, change flights, and initiate multiparty check-ins.

This year, Delta plans to add more than 400 kiosks and enhance functionality to include international check-in and fee collection. With this change, Delta will offer customers more than 800 kiosks in airports nationwide. "From the business side, the kiosks are the cornerstone of a broader airport strategy to offer customers more control," Maruster says.

Since the project was launched in November 2001, the airline has spent $5 million to $7 million on customer-service initiatives, including the kiosks, he says. Maruster says the payback has been enormous, but he declines to give financial details. Delta checked in approximately 1 million travelers via the kiosks in October and 1.4 million in January. "For 2002, our goal was to check in 5 million customers, but we actually checked in 7.4 million, and we're on track to check in 13 million to 14 million people this year," Maruster says.

Delta Technology purchased the self-service check-in kiosks from Kinetics USA (www.kineticsusa.com), the dominant supplier of self-service kiosks in the airline industry, with six of the top ten airlines in the world using Kinetics self-service technology. The self-service kiosks are really networked special-purpose microcomputer terminals, featuring video touchscreens as the primary user interface, a built-in high-speed thermal printer for printing flight itineraries and boarding passes, and a magnetic stripe card reader to read customers' airline and credit cards.

Childress says an internal application-development team integrated the kiosk functionality with Delta's Digital Nervous System, the network that communicates with every part of the Delta organization. "Last year we deployed over 300 kiosks in 81 cities," Childress says. "From start to finish, it took six months, and we were checking in half a million people per month. We wouldn't have been able to do it without the infrastructure." Childress says he learned how important it is to have the application and business teams work together. "Having a team that knows what they want to achieve from a strategy and business perspective enables the technology team to drive a solution as soon as possible."

Case Study Questions

1. What computer system technologies and functions are included in self-service kiosks? What other technologies should be provided? Why? Visit the Kinetics USA website for more details.

2. What is the customer value of self-service kiosks for airline check-ins? What other services should be provided? Take the demo tour of the Delta check-in kiosk at www.delta.com/travel/trav_serv/kiosk to help you answer.

3. What is the business value of self-service kiosks in the airline industry? Do self-service kiosks give airlines a competitive advantage? Why or why not?

Source: Adapted from Linda Rosencrance, "Self-Service Check-In Kiosks Give Travelers More Control," *Computerworld*, February 24, 2003, p. 48; and Kinetics Inc., "Touch Your World," www.kinetics.tv, August 25, 2003.

Peripherals Checklist

- **Monitors.** Bigger is better for computer screens. Consider a high-definition 19-inch or 21-inch flat screen CRT monitor, or LCD flat panel display. That gives you much more room to display spreadsheets, Web pages, lines of text, open windows, etc.

- **Printers.** Your choice is between laser printers or color inkjet printers. Lasers are better suited for high-volume business use. Moderately priced color inkjets provide high-quality images and are well suited for reproducing photographs. Per-page costs are higher than for laser printers.

- **Scanners.** You'll have to decide between a compact, sheetfed scanner or a flatbed model. Sheetfed scanners will save desktop space, while bulkier flatbed models provide higher speed and resolution.

- **Hard Disk Drives.** Bigger is better; as with closet space, you can always use the extra capacity. So go for 40 gigabytes at the minimum to 80 gigabytes and more.

- **CD and DVD Drives.** CD and DVD drives are a necessity for software installation and multimedia applications. Common today is a built-in CD-RW/DVD drive that both reads and writes CDs and plays DVDs.

- **Backup Systems.** Essential. Don't compute without them. Removable mag disk drives and even CD-RW and DVD-RW drives are convenient and versatile for backing up your hard drive's contents.

Peripherals

A computer is just a high-powered "processing box" without peripherals. **Peripherals** is the generic name given to all input, output, and secondary storage devices that are part of a computer system, but are not part of the CPU. Peripherals depend on direct connections or telecommunications links to the central processing unit of a computer system. Thus, all peripherals are **online** devices; that is, they are separate from, but can be electronically connected to and controlled by, a CPU. (This is the opposite of **off-line** devices that are separate from and not under the control of the CPU.) The major types of peripherals and media that can be part of a computer system are discussed in this section. See Figure 3.12.

Input Technologies

Input technologies now provide a more **natural user interface** for computer users. You can enter data and commands directly and easily into a computer system through pointing devices like electronic mice and touch pads, and technologies like optical scanning, handwriting recognition, and voice recognition. These developments have made it unnecessary to always record data on paper *source documents* (such as sales order forms, for example) and then keyboard the data into a computer in an additional data entry step. Further improvements in voice recognition and other technologies should enable an even more natural user interface in the future.

Pointing Devices

Keyboards are still the most widely used devices for entering data and text into computer systems. However, **pointing devices** are a better alternative for issuing commands, making choices, and responding to prompts displayed on your video screen. They work with your operating system's **graphical user interface** (GUI), which presents you with icons, menus, windows, buttons, bars, and so on, for your selection. For example, pointing devices such as electronic mouses and touchpads allow you to easily choose from menu selections and icon displays using point-and-click or point-and-drag methods. See Figure 3.13.

The **electronic mouse** is the most popular pointing device used to move the cursor on the screen, as well as to issue commands and make icon and menu selections. By moving the mouse on a desktop or pad, you can move the cursor onto an icon

FIGURE 3.13

The touchpad is a popular pointing device in laptop PCs.

Source: Pedro Coll/Age fotostock.

displayed on the screen. Pressing buttons on the mouse activates various activities represented by the icon selected.

The trackball, pointing stick, and touchpad are other pointing devices most often used in place of the mouse. A **trackball** is a stationary device related to the mouse. You turn a roller ball with only its top exposed outside its case to move the cursor on the screen. A **pointing stick** (also called a *trackpoint*) is a small button-like device, sometimes likened to the eraserhead of a pencil. It is usually centered one row above the space bar of a keyboard. The cursor moves in the direction of the pressure you place on the stick. The **touchpad** is a small rectangular touch-sensitive surface usually placed below the keyboard. The cursor moves in the direction your finger moves on the pad. Trackballs, pointing sticks, and touchpads are easier to use than a mouse for portable computer users and are thus built into most notebook computer keyboards.

Touch screens are devices that allow you to use a computer by touching the surface of its video display screen. Some touch screens emit a grid of infrared beams, sound waves, or a slight electric current that is broken when the screen is touched. The computer senses the point in the grid where the break occurs and responds with an appropriate action. For example, you can indicate your selection on a menu display by just touching the screen next to that menu item.

Pen-Based Computing

Handwriting-recognition systems convert script into text quickly and are friendly to shaky hands as well as those of block-printing draftsmen. The pen is more powerful than the keyboard in many vertical markets, as evidenced by the popularity of pen-based devices in the utilities, service, and medical trades [10].

FIGURE 3.14

Many PDAs accept pen-based input.

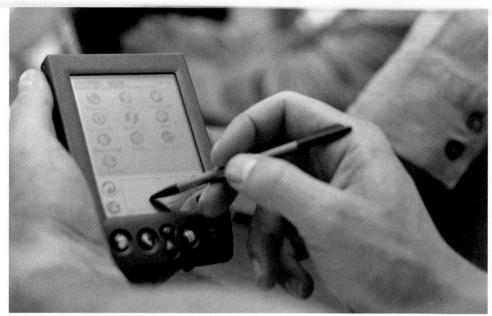

Source: RNT Productions/Corbis.

Pen-based computing technologies are being used in many hand-held computers and personal digital assistants. *Tablet* PCs and PDAs contain fast processors and software that recognizes and digitizes handwriting, handprinting, and hand drawing. They have a pressure-sensitive layer like a graphics pad under their slatelike liquid crystal display (LCD) screen. So instead of writing on a paper form fastened to a clipboard or using a keyboard device, you can use a pen to make selections, send e-mail, and enter handwritten data directly into a computer. See Figure 3.14.

A variety of other penlike devices are available. One example is the *digitizer pen* and *graphics tablet*. You can use the digitizer pen as a pointing device, or use it to draw or write on the pressure-sensitive surface of the graphics tablet. Your handwriting or drawing is digitized by the computer, accepted as input, displayed on its video screen, and entered into your application.

Speech Recognition Systems

Speech recognition is gaining popularity in the corporate world among nontypists, people with disabilities, and business travelers, and is most frequently used for dictation, screen navigation, and Web browsing [3].

Speech recognition promises to be the easiest method for data entry, word processing, and conversational computing, since speech is the easiest, most natural means of human communication. Speech input has now become technologically and economically feasible for a variety of applications. Early speech recognition products used *discrete speech recognition*, where you had to pause between each spoken word. New *continuous speech recognition* (CSR) software recognizes continuous, conversationally-paced speech. See Figure 3.15.

Speech recognition systems digitize, analyze, and classify your speech and its sound patterns. The software compares your speech patterns to a database of sound patterns in its vocabulary and passes recognized words to your application software. Typically, speech recognition systems require training the computer to recognize your voice and its unique sound patterns in order to achieve a high degree of accuracy. Training such systems involves repeating a variety of words and phrases in a training session, as well as using the system extensively.

FIGURE 3.15

Using speech recognition technology for word processing.

Source: Courtesy of Plantronics, Inc.

Continuous speech recognition software products like Dragon NaturallySpeaking and ViaVoice by IBM have up to 300,000-word vocabularies. Training to 95 percent accuracy may take several hours. Longer use, faster processors, and more memory make 99 percent accuracy possible. In addition, Microsoft Office 2000, XP, and 2003 have built-in speech recognition for dictation and voice commands of software processes.

Speech recognition devices in work situations allow operators to perform data entry without using their hands to key in data or instructions and to provide faster and more accurate input. For example, manufacturers use speech recognition systems for the inspection, inventory, and quality control of a variety of products; and airlines and parcel delivery companies use them for voice-directed sorting of baggage and parcels. Speech recognition can also help you operate your computer's operating systems and software packages through voice input of data and commands. For example, such software can be voice-enabled so you can send e-mail and surf the World Wide Web.

Speaker-independent voice recognition systems, which allow a computer to understand a few words from a voice it has never heard before, are being built into products and used in a growing number of applications. Examples include *voice-messaging computers*, which use speech recognition and voice response software to verbally guide an end user through the steps of a task in many kinds of activities. Typically, they enable computers to respond to verbal and Touch-Tone input over the telephone. Examples of applications include computerized telephone call switching, telemarketing surveys, bank pay-by-phone bill-paying services, stock quotation services, university registration systems, and customer credit and account balance inquiries.

FIGURE 3.16

This multifunction unit serves as an optical scanner, copier, fax, and printer.

Source: Courtesy of Hewlett-Packard.

Optical Scanning

Few people understand how much scanners can improve a computer system and make your work easier. Their function is to get documents into your computer with a minimum of time and hassle, transforming just about anything on paper—a letter, a logo, or a photograph—into the digital format that your PC can make sense of. Scanners can be a big help in getting loads of paper off your desk and into your PC [7].

Optical scanning devices read text or graphics and convert them into digital input for your computer. Thus, optical scanning enables the direct entry of data from source documents into a computer system. For example, you can use a compact desktop scanner to scan pages of text and graphics into your computer for desktop publishing and Web publishing applications. Or you can scan documents of all kinds into your system and organize them into folders as part of a *document management* library system for easy reference or retrieval. See Figure 3.16.

There are many types of optical scanners, but they all employ photoelectric devices to scan the characters being read. Reflected light patterns of the data are converted into electronic impulses that are then accepted as input into the computer system. Compact desktop scanners have become very popular due to their low cost and ease of use with personal computer systems. However, larger, more expensive *flatbed scanners* are faster and provide higher resolution color scanning.

Another optical scanning technology is called **optical character recognition** (OCR). OCR scanners can read the OCR characters and codes on merchandise tags, product labels, credit card receipts, utility bills, insurance premiums, airline tickets, and other documents. OCR scanners are also used to automatically sort mail, score tests, and process a wide variety of forms in business and government.

Devices such as hand-held optical scanning **wands** are frequently used to read OCR coding on merchandise tags, product labels, and other media. Many business applications involve reading *bar coding*, a code that utilizes bars to represent characters. One common example is the Universal Product Code (UPC) bar coding that you see on product labels, product packaging, and merchandise tags. For example, the automated checkout scanners found in supermarkets read UPC bar coding. Supermarket scanners emit laser beams that are reflected off a UPC bar code. The reflected image is converted to electronic impulses that are sent to the in-store computer, where they are matched with pricing information. Pricing information is returned to the terminal, visually displayed, and printed on a receipt for the customer. See Figure 3.17.

Using an optical scanning wand to read bar coding of inventory data.

Source: Getty Images

Other Input Technologies

Magnetic stripe technology is a familiar form of data entry that helps computers read credit cards. The iron oxide coating of the magnetic stripe on the back of such cards can hold about 200 bytes of information. Customer account numbers can be recorded on the mag stripe so it can be read by bank ATMs, credit card authorization terminals, and many other types of magnetic stripe readers.

Smart cards that embed a microprocessor chip and several kilobytes of memory into debit, credit, and other cards are popular in Europe, and becoming available in the United States. One example is in Holland, where millions of smart debit cards have been issued by Dutch banks. Smart debit cards enable you to store a cash balance on the card and electronically transfer some of it to others to pay for small items and services. The balance on the card can be replenished in ATMs or other terminals.

The smart debit cards used in Holland feature a microprocessor and either 8 or 16 kilobytes of memory, plus the usual magnetic stripe. The smart cards are widely used to make payments in parking meters, vending machines, newsstands, pay telephones, and retail stores [6].

Digital cameras represent another fast-growing set of input technologies. Digital still cameras and digital video cameras (digital camcorders) enable you to shoot, store, and download still photos or full motion video with audio into your PC. Then you can use image-editing software to edit and enhance the digitized images and include them in newsletters, reports, multimedia presentations, and Web pages.

The computer systems of the banking industry can magnetically read checks and deposit slips using **magnetic ink character recognition** (MICR) technology. Computers can thus sort and post checks to the proper checking accounts. Such processing is possible because the identification numbers of the bank and the customer's account are preprinted on the bottom of the checks with an iron oxide-based ink. The first bank receiving a check after it has been written must encode the amount of the check in magnetic ink on the check's lower right-hand corner. The MICR system uses 14 characters (the 10 decimal digits and 4 special symbols) of a standardized design. Equipment known as *reader-sorters* read a check by first magnetizing the magnetic ink characters and then sensing the signal induced by each character as it passes a reading head. In this way, data are electronically captured by the bank's computer systems.

Output Technologies

Computers provide information to you in a variety of forms. Video displays and printed documents have been, and still are, the most common forms of output from computer systems. But other natural and attractive output technologies such as **voice response** systems and multimedia output are increasingly found along with video displays in business applications.

For example, you have probably experienced the voice and audio output generated by speech and audio microprocessors in a variety of consumer products. Voice messaging software enables PCs and servers in voice mail and messaging systems to interact with you through voice responses. And of course, multimedia output is common on the websites of the Internet and corporate intranets.

Video Output

Of all the peripherals you can purchase for your system, a [video] monitor is the one addition that can make the biggest difference. Forget about faster processors, bigger hard drives, and the like. The fact is, the monitor is the part of your system you spend the most time interacting with . . . Invest in a quality monitor, and you'll be thankful every time you turn on your computer [7].

Video displays are the most common type of computer output. Many desktop computers still rely on **video monitors** that use a *cathode ray tube* (CRT) technology similar to the picture tubes used in home TV sets. Usually, the clarity of the video display depends on the type of video monitor you use and the graphics circuit board installed in your computer. These can provide a variety of graphics modes of increasing capability. A high-resolution, flicker-free monitor is especially important if you spend a lot of time viewing multimedia on CDs or the Web, or the complex graphical displays of many software packages.

The biggest use of **liquid crystal displays** (LCDs) has been to provide a visual display capability for portable microcomputers and PDAs. However, the use of "flat panel" LCD video monitors for desktop PC systems has become common as their cost becomes more affordable. See Figure 3.18. LCD displays need significantly less electric current and provide a thin, flat display. Advances in technology such as *active matrix* and *dual scan* capabilities have improved the color and clarity of LCD displays. In

---

FIGURE 3.18

Using a flat panel LCD video monitor for a desktop PC system.

Source: Index Stock/Picture Quest.

FIGURE 3.19

This mobile inkjet printer produces high-quality color output.

Source: Courtesy of Hewlett-Packard.

addition, high-clarity flat panel TVs and monitors using *plasma* display technologies are becoming popular for large-screen (42 to 60-inch) viewing.

Printed Output

Printing information on paper is still the most common form of output after video displays. Thus, most personal computer systems rely on an inkjet or laser printer to produce permanent (hard copy) output in high-quality printed form. Printed output is still a common form of business communications, and is frequently required for legal documentation. Thus, computers can produce printed reports and correspondence, documents such as sales invoices, payroll checks, bank statements, and printed versions of graphic displays. See Figure 3.19.

Inkjet printers, which spray ink onto a page, have become the most popular, low-cost printers for microcomputer systems. They are quiet, produce several pages per minute of high-quality output, and can print both black-and-white and high-quality color graphics. **Laser printers** use an electrostatic process similar to a photocopying machine to produce many pages per minute of high-quality black-and-white output. More expensive color laser printers and multifunction inkjet and laser models that print, fax, scan, and copy are other popular choices for business offices.

Storage Trade-Offs

Data and information must be stored until needed using a variety of storage methods. For example, many people and organizations still rely on paper documents stored in filing cabinets as a major form of storage media. However, you and other computer users are more likely to depend on the memory circuits and secondary storage devices of computer systems to meet your storage requirements. Progress in very-large-scale integration (VLSI), which packs millions of memory circuit elements on tiny semiconductor memory chips, is responsible for continuing increases in the main-memory capacity of computers. Secondary storage capacities are also escalating into the billions and trillions of characters, due to advances in magnetic and optical media.

There are many types of storage media and devices. Figure 3.20 illustrates the speed, capacity, and cost relationships of several alternative primary and secondary storage media. Note the cost/speed/capacity trade-offs as one moves from semiconductor memories to magnetic disks, to optical disks, and to magnetic tape. High-

FIGURE 3.20

Storage media cost, speed, and capacity trade-offs. Note how cost increases with faster access speeds, but decreases with the increased capacity of storage media.

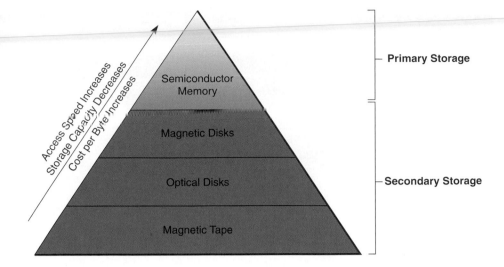

speed storage media cost more per byte and provide lower capacities. Large-capacity storage media cost less per byte but are slower. This is why we have different kinds of storage media.

However, all storage media, especially memory chips and magnetic disks, continue to increase in speed and capacity and decrease in cost. Developments like automated high-speed cartridge assemblies have given faster access times to magnetic tape, and the speed of optical disk drives continues to increase.

Note in Figure 3.20 that semiconductor memories are used mainly for primary storage, though they are sometimes used as high-speed secondary storage devices. Magnetic disk and tape and optical disk devices, on the other hand, are used as secondary storage devices to greatly enlarge the storage capacity of computer systems. Also, since most primary storage circuits use RAM (random access memory) chips, which lose their contents when electrical power is interrupted, secondary storage devices provide a more permanent type of storage media.

Computer Storage Fundamentals

Data are processed and stored in a computer system through the presence or absence of electronic or magnetic signals in the computer's circuitry or in the media it uses. This is called a "two-state" or **binary representation** of data, since the computer and the media can exhibit only two possible states or conditions. For example, transistors and other semiconductor circuits are either in a conducting or nonconducting state. Media such as magnetic disks and tapes indicate these two states by having magnetized spots whose magnetic fields have one of two different directions, or polarities. This binary characteristic of computer circuitry and media is what makes the binary number system the basis for representing data in computers. Thus, for electronic circuits, the conducting (ON) state represents the number one, while the nonconducting (OFF) state represents the number zero. For magnetic media, the magnetic field of a magnetized spot in one direction represents a one, while magnetism in the other direction represents a zero.

The smallest element of data is called a **bit,** or binary digit, which can have a value of either zero or one. The capacity of memory chips is usually expressed in terms of bits. A **byte** is a basic grouping of bits that the computer operates as a single unit. Typically, it consists of eight bits and represents one character of data in most computer coding schemes. Thus, the capacity of a computer's memory and secondary storage devices is usually expressed in terms of bytes. Computer codes such as ASCII (American Standard Code for Information Interchange) use various arrangements of bits to form bytes that represent the numbers zero through nine, the letters of the alphabet, and many other characters. See Figure 3.21.

FIGURE 3.21

Examples of the ASCII computer code that computers use to represent numbers and the letters of the alphabet.

Character	ASCII Code	Character	ASCII Code	Character	ASCII Code
0	00110000	A	01000001	N	01001110
1	00110001	B	01000010	O	01001111
2	00110010	C	01000011	P	01010000
3	00110011	D	01000100	Q	01010001
4	00110100	E	01000101	R	01010010
5	00110101	F	01000110	S	01010011
6	00110110	G	01000111	T	01010100
7	00110111	H	01001000	U	01010101
8	00111000	I	01001001	V	01010110
9	00111001	J	01001010	W	01010111
		K	01001011	X	01011000
		L	01001100	Y	01011001
		M	01001101	Z	01011010

Storage capacities are frequently measured in **kilobytes** (KB), **megabytes** (MB), **gigabytes** (GB), or **terabytes** (TB). Although kilo means 1,000 in the metric system, the computer industry uses K to represent 1,024 (or 2^{10}) storage positions. Therefore, a capacity of 10 megabytes, for example, is really 10,485,760 storage positions, rather than 10 million positions. However, such differences are frequently disregarded in order to simplify descriptions of storage capacity. Thus, a megabyte is roughly 1 million bytes of storage, a gigabyte is roughly 1 billion bytes and a terabyte represents about 1 trillion bytes, while a **petabyte** is over 1 quadrillion bytes.

Direct and Sequential Access

Primary storage media such as semiconductor memory chips are called **direct access** or random access memories (RAM). Magnetic disk devices are frequently called direct access storage devices (DASDs). On the other hand, media such as magnetic tape cartridges are known as **sequential access** devices.

The terms *direct access* and *random access* describe the same concept. They mean that an element of data or instructions (such as a byte or word) can be directly stored and retrieved by selecting and using any of the locations on the storage media. They also mean that each storage position (1) has a unique address and (2) can be individually accessed in approximately the same length of time without having to search through other storage positions. For example, each memory cell on a microelectronic semiconductor RAM chip can be individually sensed or changed in the same length of time. Also any data record stored on a magnetic or optical disk can be accessed directly in approximately the same time period. See Figure 3.22.

Sequential access storage media such as magnetic tape do not have unique storage addresses that can be directly addressed. Instead, data must be stored and retrieved using a sequential or serial process. Data are recorded one after another in a predetermined sequence (such as in numeric order) on a storage medium. Locating an individual item of data requires searching the recorded data on the tape until the desired item is located.

Semiconductor Memory

Memory is the coalman to the CPU's locomotive: For maximum PC performance, it must keep the processor constantly stoked with instructions. Faster CPUs call for larger and faster memories, both in the cache where data and instructions are stored temporarily, and in the main memory [7].

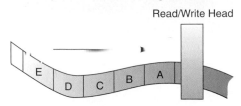

FIGURE 3.22 Sequential versus direct access storage. Magnetic tape is a typical sequential access medium. Magnetic disks are typical direct access storage devices.

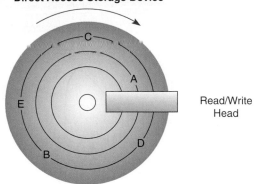

The primary storage (main memory) of your computer consists of microelectronic **semiconductor memory** chips. It provides you with the working storage your computer needs to process your applications. Plug-in memory circuit boards containing 256 megabytes or more of memory chips can be added to your PC to increase its memory capacity. Specialized memory can help improve your computer's performance. Examples include external cache memory of 512 kilobytes to help your microprocessor work faster, or a video graphics accelerator card with 64 megabytes of RAM for faster and clearer video performance. Removable credit-card-size and smaller "flash memory" RAM cards can also provide hundreds of megabytes of erasable direct access storage for PDAs or digital cameras.

Some of the major attractions of semiconductor memory are its small size, great speed, and shock and temperature resistance. One major disadvantage of most semiconductor memory is its **volatility.** Uninterrupted electric power must be supplied or the contents of memory will be lost. Therefore, emergency transfer to other devices or standby electrical power (through battery packs or emergency generators) is required if data are to be saved. Another alternative is to permanently "burn in" the contents of semiconductor devices so that they cannot be erased by a loss of power.

Thus, there are two basic types of semiconductor memory: random access memory (RAM) and read only memory (ROM).

- **RAM: random access memory.** These memory chips are the most widely used primary storage medium. Each memory position can be both sensed (read) and changed (written), so it is also called read/write memory. This is a volatile memory.

- **ROM: read only memory.** Nonvolatile random access memory chips are used for permanent storage. ROM can be read but not erased or overwritten. Frequently used control instructions in the control unit and programs in primary storage (such as parts of the operating system) can be permanently burned in to the storage cells during manufacture. This is sometimes called *firmware.* Variations include PROM (programmable read only memory) and EPROM (erasable programmable read only memory), which can be permanently or temporarily programmed after manufacture.

Magnetic Disks

Multigigabyte magnetic disk drives aren't extravagant, considering that full-motion video files, sound tracks, and photo-quality images can consume colossal amounts of disk space in a blink [7].

FIGURE 3.23   Magnetic disk media: A hard magnetic disk drive and a 3 1/2-inch floppy disk.

Source: Corbis.

Source: Quantum.

Magnetic disks are the most common form of secondary storage for your computer system. That's because they provide fast access and high storage capacities at a reasonable cost. Magnetic disk drives contain metal disks that are coated on both sides with an iron oxide recording material. Several disks are mounted together on a vertical shaft, which typically rotates the disks at speeds of 3,600 to 7,600 revolutions per minute (rpm). Electromagnetic read/write heads are positioned by access arms between the slightly separated disks to read and write data on concentric, circular tracks. Data are recorded on tracks in the form of tiny magnetized spots to form the binary digits of common computer codes. Thousands of bytes can be recorded on each track, and there are several hundred data tracks on each disk surface, thus providing you with billions of storage positions for your software and data. See Figure 3.23.

Types of Magnetic Disks

There are several types of magnetic disk arrangements, including removable disk cartridges as well as fixed disk units. Removable disk devices are popular because they are transportable and can be used to store backup copies of your data offline for convenience and security.

- **Floppy disks,** or magnetic diskettes, consist of polyester film disks covered with an iron oxide compound. A single disk is mounted and rotates freely inside a protective flexible or hard plastic jacket, which has access openings to accommodate the read/write head of a disk drive unit. The 3 1/2-inch floppy disk, with capacities of 1.44 megabytes, is the most widely used version, with a Superdisk technology offering 120 megabytes of storage. Zip drives use a floppy-like technology to provide up to 750 MB of portable disk storage.

- **Hard disk drives** combine magnetic disks, access arms, and read/write heads into a sealed module. This allows higher speeds, greater data recording densities, and closer tolerances within a sealed, more stable environment. Fixed or removable disk cartridge versions are available. Capacities of hard drives range from several hundred megabytes to many gigabytes of storage.

RAID Storage

RAID computer storage equipment—big, refrigerator-size boxes full of dozens of interlinked magnetic disk drives that can store the equivalent of 100 million tax returns—hardly gets the blood rushing. But it should. Just as speedy and reliable networking opened the floodgates to cyberspace and e-commerce, ever-more-turbocharged data storage is a key building block of the Internet [8].

Disk arrays of interconnected microcomputer hard disk drives have replaced large-capacity mainframe disk drives to provide many gigabytes of online storage. Known as **RAID** (redundant arrays of independent disks), they combine from 6 to more than 100 small hard disk drives and their control microprocessors into a single unit. RAID units provide large capacities with high access speeds since data are accessed in parallel over multiple paths from many disks. RAID units also provide a *fault tolerant* capacity, since their redundant design offers multiple copies of data on several disks. If one disk fails, data can be recovered from backup copies automatically stored on other disks. *Storage area networks* (SANs) are high-speed *fiber channel* local area networks that can interconnect many RAID units and thus share their combined capacity through network servers with many users.

Magnetic Tape

Tape storage is moving beyond backup. Disk subsystems provide the fastest response time for mission-critical data. But the sheer amount of data users need to access these days as part of huge enterprise applications, such as data warehouses, requires affordable [magnetic tape] storage [12].

Magnetic tape is still being used as a secondary storage medium in business applications. The read/write heads of magnetic tape drives record data in the form of magnetized spots on the iron oxide coating of the plastic tape. Magnetic tape devices include tape reels and cartridges in mainframes and midrange systems, and small cassettes or cartridges for PCs. Magnetic tape cartridges have replaced tape reels in many applications and can hold over 200 megabytes.

One growing business application of magnetic tape involves the use of high-speed 36-track magnetic tape cartridges in robotic automated drive assemblies that can directly access hundreds of cartridges. These devices provide lower-cost storage to supplement magnetic disks to meet massive data warehouse and other online business storage requirements. Other major applications for magnetic tape include long-term *archival* storage and backup storage for PCs and other systems [12].

Optical Disks

Optical disk technology has become a necessity. Most software companies now distribute their elephantine programs on CD-ROMs. Many corporations are now rolling their own CDs to distribute product and corporate information that once filled bookshelves [7].

Optical disks are a fast-growing storage media, that uses several major alternative technologies. See Figure 3.24. One version is called **CD-ROM** (compact disk–read only memory). CD-ROM technology uses 12-centimeter (4.7 inch) compact disks (CDs) similar to those used in stereo music systems. Each disk can store more than 600 megabytes. That's the equivalent of over 400 1.44 megabyte floppy disks or more than 300,000 double-spaced pages of text. A laser records data by burning permanent microscopic pits in a spiral track on a master disk from which compact disks can be mass-produced. Then CD-ROM disk drives use a laser device to read the binary codes formed by those pits.

CD-R (compact disk–recordable) is another popular optical disk technology. CD-R drives or CD *burners* are commonly used to permanently record digital music tracks or digital photo images on CDs. The major limitation of CD-ROM and CD-R disks is that recorded data cannot be erased. However, **CD-RW** (CD-rewritable) drives have now become available that record and erase data by using a laser to heat a micro-

FIGURE 3.24

Comparing the capabilities of optical disk drives.

Optical Disk Drive Capabilities
● **CD-ROM**   A CD-ROM drive provides a low cost way to read data files and load software onto your computer, as well as play music CDs.
● **CD-RW**   A CD-RW drive allows you to easily create your own custom data CDs for data backup or data transfer purposes. It will also allow you to store and share video files, large data files, digital photos, and other large files with other people that have access to a CD-ROM drive. This drive will also do anything your CD-ROM drive will do. It reads all your existing CD-ROMs, Audio CDs, and CDs that you have created with your CD burner.
● **CD-RW/DVD**   A CD-RW/DVD combination drive brings all the advantages of CD-RW, CD-ROM, and DVD-ROM to a single drive. With a CD-RW/DVD combo drive, you can read DVD-ROM disks, read CD-ROM disks, and create your own custom CDs.
● **DVD-ROM**   A DVD-ROM drive allows you to enjoy the crystal clear color, picture, and sound clarity of DVD video on your PC. It will also prepare you for future software and large data files that will be released on DVD-ROM. A DVD-ROM drive can also read CD-ROM disks effectively providing users with full optical read capability in one device.
● **DVD+RW/+R with CD-RW**   A DVD-RW/R with CD-RW drive is a great all-in-one drive, allowing you to burn DVD-RW or DVD-R disks, burn CDs, and read DVDs and CDs. It enables you to create DVDs to back-up and archive up to 4.7GB of data files (that's up to 7 times the capacity of a standard 650MB CD) and store up to to 2 hours of MPEG2 digital video.

Source: Adapted from "Learn More–Optical Drives," www.dell.com.

scopic point on the disk's surface. In CD-RW versions using magneto-optical technology, a magnetic coil changes the spot's reflective properties from one direction to another, thus recording a binary one or zero. A laser device can then read the binary codes on the disk by sensing the direction of reflected light.

DVD technologies have dramatically increased optical disk capacities and capabilities. **DVD** (digital video disk or digital versatile disk) optical disks can hold from 3.0 to 8.5 gigabytes of multimedia data on each side. The large capacities and high-quality images and sound of DVD technology are expected to replace CD technologies for data storage, and promise to accelerate the use of DVD drives for multimedia products that can be used in both computers and home entertainment systems. Thus, **DVD-ROM** disks are increasingly replacing magnetic tape video-cassettes for movies and other multimedia products, while **DVD-RW** disks are being used for backup and archival storage of large data and multimedia files. See Figure 3.25.

Business Applications

One of the major uses of optical disks in mainframe and midrange systems is in **image processing,** where long-term archival storage of historical files of document images must be maintained. Financial institutions, among others, are using optical scanners to capture digitized document images and store them on *WORM* (write once, read many) versions of such optical disks as an alternative to microfilm media.

One of the major business uses of CD-ROM disks for personal computers is to provide a publishing medium for fast access to reference materials in a convenient, compact form. This includes catalogs, directories, manuals, periodical abstracts, part

FIGURE 3.25

Optical disk storage
includes CD and DVD
technologies.

Source: PhotoDisc.

listings, and statistical databases of business and economic activity. Interactive multi-media applications in business, education, and entertainment are another major use of optical disks. The large storage capacities of CD and DVD disks are a natural choice for computer video games, educational videos, multimedia encyclopedias, and advertising presentations.

Summary

- **Computer Systems.** Major types of computer systems are summarized in Figure 3.2. Microcomputers are used as personal computers, network computers, personal digital assistants, technical workstations, and information appliances. Midrange systems are increasingly used as powerful network servers, and for many multiuser business data processing and scientific applications. Mainframe computers are larger and more powerful than most midsize systems. They are usually faster, have more memory capacity, and can support more network users and peripheral devices. They are designed to handle the information processing needs of large organizations with high volumes of transaction processing, or with complex computational problems. Supercomputers are a special category of extremely powerful mainframe computer systems designed for massive computational assignments.

- **The Computer Systems Concept.** A computer is a system of information processing components that perform input, processing, output, storage, and control functions. Its hardware components include input and output devices, a central processing unit (CPU), and primary and secondary storage devices. The major functions and hardware in a computer system are summarized in Figure 3.9.

- **Peripheral Devices.** Refer to Figures 3.12 and 3.20 to review the capabilities of peripheral devices for input, output, and storage discussed in this chapter.

Key Terms and Concepts

These are the key terms and concepts of this chapter. The page number of their first explanation is given in parentheses.

1. Binary representation (88)
2. Central processing unit (75)
3. Computer system (75)
4. Computer terminal (71)
5. Digital cameras (85)
6. Direct access (89)
7. Information appliance (71)
8. Laptop computer (69)
9. Liquid crystal displays (86)
10. Magnetic disks (91)
    - *a.* Floppy disk (91)
    - *b.* Hard disk (91)
    - *c.* RAID (92)
11. Magnetic ink character recognition (85)
12. Magnetic stripe (85)
13. Magnetic tape (92)
14. Mainframe system (73)
15. Microcomputer (68)
16. Microprocessor (75)
17. Midrange system (72)
18. Minicomputer (72)
19. Network computer (71)
20. Network server (69)
21. Network terminal (71)

22. Offline (80)
23. Online (80)
24. Optical character recognition (84)
25. Optical disks (92)
    - *a.* CD-ROM (92)
    - *b.* CD-R (92)
    - *c.* CD-RW (92)
    - *d.* DVD-ROM (93)
    - *e.* DVD-R (93)
    - *f.* DVD-RW (93)
26. Optical scanning (84)
27. Pen-based computing (82)
28. Peripheral devices (80)
29. Personal digital assistant (71)
30. Pointing devices (80)
    - *a.* Electronic mouse (80)
    - *b.* Pointing stick (81)
    - *c.* Touchpad (81)
    - *d.* Trackball (81)
31. Primary storage (76)
32. Printers (87)
33. Secondary storage (77)
34. Semiconductor memory (90)
    - *a.* RAM (90)
    - *b.* ROM (90)
35. Sequential access (89)

36. Smart cards (85)
37. Speech recognition (82)
38. Storage capacity elements (88)
    - *a.* Bit (88)
    - *b.* Byte (88)
    - *c.* Kilobyte (89)
    - *d.* Megabyte (89)
    - *e.* Gigabyte (89)
    - *f.* Terabyte (89)
39. Storage media trade-offs (87)
40. Supercomputer (74)
41. Time elements (77)
    - *a.* Millisecond (77)
    - *b.* Microsecond (77)
    - *c.* Nanosecond (77)
    - *d.* Picosecond (77)
42. Touch screen (81)
43. Transaction terminals (72)
44. Video output (86)
45. Volatility (90)
46. Wand (84)
47. Workstation (69)

Review Quiz

Match one of the previous key terms and concepts with one of the following brief examples or definitions. Try to find the best fit for answers that seem to fit more than one term or concept. Defend your choices.

_____ 1. A computer is a combination of components that perform input, processing, output, storage, and control functions.

_____ 2. The main processing component of a computer system.

_____ 3. A small, portable PC.

_____ 4. Devices for consumers to access the Internet.

_____ 5. The memory of a computer.

_____ 6. Magnetic disks and tape and optical disks perform this function.

_____ 7. Input/output and secondary storage devices for a computer system.

_____ 8. Connected to and controlled by a CPU.

_____ 9. Separate from and not controlled by a CPU.

_____ 10. Results from the presence or absence or change in direction of electric current, magnetic fields, or light rays in computer circuits and media.

_____ 11. The central processing unit of a microcomputer.

_____ 12. Can be a desktop/laptop, or hand-held computer.

_____ 13. A computer category between microcomputers and mainframes.

_____ 14. A computer that can handle the information processing needs of large organizations.

_____ 15. Hand-held microcomputers for communications and personal information management.

_____ 16. Low-cost microcomputers for use with the Internet and corporate intranets.

_____ 17. Point-of-sale (POS) terminals in retail stores and bank ATMs are examples.

_____ 18. A terminal that depends on network servers for its software and processing power.

_____ 19. A computer that manages network communications and resources.

_____ 20. The most powerful type of computer.

_____ 21. A magnetic tape technology for credit cards.

_____ 22. One billionth of a second.

_____ 23. Roughly one billion characters of storage.

_____ 24. Includes electronic mouses, trackballs, pointing sticks, and touchpads.

_____ 25. You can write on the pressure-sensitive LCD screen of hand-held microcomputers with a pen.

_____ 26. Moving this along your desktop moves the cursor on the screen.

_____ 27. You can communicate with a computer by touching its display.

_____ 28. Produces hard copy output such as paper documents and reports.

_____ 29. Promises to be the easiest, most natural way to communicate with computers.

_____ 30. Capturing data by processing light reflected from images.

_____ 31. Optical scanning of bar codes and other characters.

_____ 32. Bank check processing uses this technology.

_____ 33. A debit card with an embedded microprocessor and memory is an example.

_____ 34. A device with a keyboard and a video display networked to a computer is a typical example.

_____ 35. Photos or video can be captured and downloaded to your PC for image processing.

_____ 36. A video output technology.

_____ 37. A hand-held device that reads bar coding.

_____ 38. Storage media cost, speed, and capacity differences.

_____ 39. You cannot erase the contents of these storage circuits.

_____ 40. The memory of most computers consists of these storage circuits.

_____ 41. The property that determines whether data are lost or retained when power fails.

_____ 42. Each position of storage can be accessed in approximately the same time.

_____ 43. Each position of storage can be accessed according to a predetermined order.

_____ 44. Microelectronic storage circuits on silicon chips.

_____ 45. Uses magnetic spots on metal or plastic disks.

_____ 46. Uses magnetic spots on plastic tape.

_____ 47. Uses a laser to read microscopic points on plastic disks.

_____ 48. Vastly increases the storage capacity and image and sound quality of permanently recorded optical disks compared to videocassettes.

Discussion Questions

1. What trends are occurring in the development and use of the major types of computer systems?

2. Will the convergence of PDAs, sub-notebook PCs, and cell phones produce an information appliance that will make all of those categories obsolete? Why or why not?

3. Refer to the Real World Case on Progressive Insurance and UniFirst in the chapter. Should Progressive replace much of their IRV hardware devices with a combination cell phone, PDA, and digital camera? Why or why not?

4. Do you think that information appliances like PDAs will replace personal computers (PCs) in business applications? Explain.

5. Are networks of PCs and servers making mainframe computers obsolete? Explain.

6. Refer to the Real World Case on Delta and Northwest airlines in the chapter. What are several other present or potential business applications for self-service networked kiosks? What are their business benefits and limitations? Give several examples.

7. What are several trends that are occurring in computer peripheral devices? How do these trends affect business uses of computers?

8. What are several important computer hardware developments that you expect to happen in the next ten years? How will these affect the business use of computers?

9. What processor, memory, magnetic disk storage, and video display capabilities would you require for a personal computer that you would use for business purposes? Explain your choices.

10. What other peripheral devices and capabilities would you want to have for your business PC? Explain your choices.

Analysis Exercises

1. **Determining Computer Hardware Specifications**

   Your manager would like you to determine the appropriate specifications for a new computer. The marketing department will use this computer to create multimedia presentations for your organization's sales force. The marketing department will make these presentations available to users both on the Internet and through DVDs.

   Your manager has also informed you that your information technology (IT) department will support only PC-based computers and the Adobe® Premiere® Pro video editing DVD designing software package. Your manager insists that your specifications conform to these standards in order to minimize long-term training and support costs.

   a. Given that these machines need to support video editing, look up on the Internet the *minimum* hardware specifications you will need to support your business needs for the following attributes:

   - Number of CPUs
   - CPU speed
   - RAM capacity
   - Hard Drive storage space
   - Input/Output devices (other than video cameras)

   b. Would you recommend Adobe's minimum hardware specifications to your manager? Why or why not?

   c. Describe how the business needs shaped the hardware needs in this problem.

2. **Purchasing Computer Systems for Your Workgroup**

   You have been asked to get pricing information for a potential purchase of PCs for the members of your workgroup. Go to the Internet to get prices for these units from at least two prominent PC suppliers.

   The list below shows the specifications for the basic system you have been asked to price and potential upgrades to each feature. You will want to get a price for the basic system described below and a separate price for each of the upgrades shown.

	Basic Unit	Upgrade
CPU (gigahertz)	2+	3+
Hard Drive (gigabytes)	40	160
RAM (megabytes)	256	512
Removable media storage	CD-R/RW, DVD Player	CD-R/RW, DVD-R/RW
Monitor	17 inch CRT	17 inch flat screen

   Network cards and modems will not be purchased with these systems. These features will be added from stock already owned by the company. Select the standard software licenses; your IT department will install the necessary software for your workgroup. Take a two-year warranty and servicing coverage offered by each supplier. If a two-year warranty is not available, simply note any differences in the coverage with the closest match.

a. Prepare a spreadsheet summarizing this pricing information and showing the cost, from each supplier of the following options: **a.** units with the basic configuration, **b.** the incremental cost of each upgrade separately, and **c.** the cost of a fully upgraded unit. If you cannot find features that exactly match the requirements, then use the next higher standard for comparison and make a note of the difference.

b. Prepare a set of PowerPoint slides or similar presentation materials summarizing your results. Include a discussion of the warranty and servicing contract options offered by each supplier.

3. **Can Computers Think Like People?—The Turing Test**

The "Turing Test" is a hypothetical test to determine whether or not a computer system reaches the level of "artificial intelligence." If the computer can fool a person into thinking it is another person, then it is has "artificial intelligence." Except in very narrow areas, no computer has passed the "Turing Test."

Free e-mail account providers such as Hotmail or Yahoo take advantage of this fact. They need to distinguish between new account registrations generated by a person and registrations generated by spammers' software. Why? Spammers burn through thousands of e-mail accounts in order to send millions of e-mails. To help them, spammers need automated tools to generate these accounts. Hotmail fights this practice by requiring registrants to correctly enter an alphanumeric code hidden within a small picture. Spammer's programs have trouble correctly reading the code, but most humans do not. With this Turing test, Hotmail can distinguish between person and program and allow only humans to register. As a result, spammers must look elsewhere for free accounts.

a. In what applications other than ISP registration might businesses find it useful to distinguish between a human and a computer?

b. Describe a Turing test that a visually impaired person but not a computer might pass.

c. Use the Internet to read more about this topic and determine whether or not commercial Internet sites have a legal obligation in the U.S. to provide access to Americans with disabilities. List several arguments both for and against.

4. **Price and Performance Trends for Computer Hardware**

The table below shows a set of price and capacity figures for common components of personal computers. Typical prices for Microprocessors, Random Access Memory (RAM), and Hard Disk storage prices are shown. The performance of typical components has increased substantially over time, so the speed (for the microprocessor) or the capacity (for the storage devices) is also listed. Although there have been improvements in these components that are not reflected in these capacity measures, it is interesting to examine trends in these measurable characteristics.

a. Create a spreadsheet based on the figures below and include a new row for each component showing the price per unit of capacity (cost per megahertz of speed for microprocessors and cost per megabyte of storage for RAM and hard disk devices).

b. Create a set of graphs highlighting your results and illustrating trends in price per unit of performance (speed) or capacity.

c. Write a short paper discussing the trends you found. How long do you expect these trends to continue? Why?

	1991	1993	1995	1997	1999	2001	2003
Microprocessor Speed (Megahertz)	25	33	100	125	350	1000	3,000
Cost	$180	$125	$275	$250	$300	$251	$395[1]
RAM Chip Megabytes per Chip	1	4	4	16	64	256	512
Cost	$55	$140	$120	$97	$125	$90	$59
Hard Disk Device Megabytes per disk	105	250	540	2,000	8,000	40,000	160,000
Cost	$480	$375	$220	$250	$220	$138	$114

1 http://www.pricewatch.com/

REAL WORLD CASE 3

Nappi Distributors and Old Dominion Freight Line: The Business Value of Wireless Handhelds

Nappi Distributors (www.nappidist.com) salespeople used to work in a fashion familiar to all twentieth century road warriors: They would visit a customer, such as a liquor store, write down order information, then call the orders in from a cell phone or pay phone. Back at headquarters in Portland, Maine, a representative would take the orders, enter them into Nappi's back-office systems (which run on an IBM AS/400 midrange system) and print them out. Warehouse pickers used the printouts to fill orders for the next day's shipments.

As familiar as the process was, there was much that could go wrong. For starters, it wasn't unusual for Nappi's sales reps to overwhelm headquarters with calls. This resulted in lots of waiting around, which meant salespeople either cooled their heels at pay phones rather than hitting the road and visiting other customers or sat on hold on cell phones to the tune of 6.5 cents per minute.

One day, a frustrated sales rep came into the office of Peter Paglio, Nappi's IT director, and said he had heard that another distributor in the area was using wireless computers to enter orders. Paglio says "He had a number for Vermont Information Processing (VIP), so I checked it out." Like many of the companies favored by second-generation wireless adopters, VIP is highly specialized: Its services are just for beverage wholesalers.

Paglio says his first move was to make sure Nappi's sales territory was served by a carrier using the Cellular Digital Packet Data specification, which allows Internet digital communications traffic to run on top of analog phone service. Nappi was in luck: AT&T Corp. offered the specification in "99.9 percent of our territory," Paglio says.

Nappi uses Symbol Technologies (www.symbol.com) hand-held computers with bar code scanners running the Palm OS operating system. However, the handhelds communicate with headquarters over the AT&T phone network at only 9.6Kbit/sec. But VIP is tweaking its software to nearly triple that speed.

Sales reps now key in orders on the fly and send them straight to Nappi's IBM AS/400, where the next day's loads and schedules are determined automatically and sent to the warehouse for picking. Sales reps no longer call from pay phones, and office workers don't spend time keying in orders. Paglio says the wireless system costs Nappi $800 per month to support all 32 of its sales reps. Previously, the company paid $600 per month for 15 cell phones, plus toll calls from pay phones for the salespeople who didn't have phones of their own.

According to Paglio, the system has a few drawbacks. "It goes wacky around radar" near airports and a local Naval base. And some sales reps aren't crazy about a recent upgrade that offers more features but is harder to learn.

Old Dominion. Old Dominion has garnered numerous benefits from its $3 million wireless/handheld application, including increased customer satisfaction, improved driver efficiency, and a decrease in loading errors, says senior application development manager Barry Craver. He describes Old Dominion as a "superregional" carrier, meaning that although the bulk of the company's freight is hauled in the Southeast, it has outposts nationwide.

But according to Craver, simply being equipped with 1,000 Symbol Technologies wireless hand-held computers running the Windows CE operating system has increased the status of Old Dominion's drivers when they arrive at their stops. And that alone boosts efficiency. "The service centers and shippers know which trucking lines have computers," Craver says. "That makes a difference—we've been bumped up in some places." That bump means less waiting in line, which translates into more stops per day.

When it came to navigating the crazy quilt of U.S. wireless networks, Old Dominion turned to Aether Systems, which offers middleware and services that lets companies outsource all or part of their wireless needs. For example, while Old Dominion's application sends and receives transmissions between trucks and headquarters, Aether manages connections to the various wireless providers and is the entity billed by those providers. In addition, Aether manages the overnight synchronization of drivers' handhelds. This saves money; Old Dominion uses the proprietary Ardis network which charges by the character. The idea is to use real-time communication only where it adds value, as in proof-of-delivery messages. Old Dominion is deploying another 1,000 handheld PCs, but doesn't expect all of its drivers to applaud. In an unexpected benefit, the company has noticed a reduction in miles between stops among wireless-equipped truckers. "We think maybe they got more efficient because there's a little more accountability there," Craver says.

Case Study Questions

1. What are the business benefits and limitations of the use of wireless handheld computers by Nappi Distributors? How could their mobile sales application be improved? Defend your proposals.

2. What are the business benefits and limitations of the use of wireless hand-held computers by Old Dominion Freight Lines? How could their mobile freight management application be improved? Defend your proposals.

3. Would you recommend the use of wireless laptop or tablet PCs to either Nappi or Old Dominion? Why or why not? Visit the Symbol Technologies website to help you answer.

Source: Adapted from Steve Ulfelder, "On the Heels of the Pioneers," *Computerworld*, May 5, 2003, pp. 44–46. Copyright © 2003 by Computerworld, Inc. Framingham, MA 01701. All rights reserved.

Wisconsin Physicians Service and Winnebago: Moving to Linux on the Mainframe

The attraction of Linux on the mainframe isn't so much the low cost of licensing Linux or the fact that users can modify it and rely on a community of developers to fix bugs, users say. Instead, the big draw is the ability to combine Linux with the mainframe's proven reliability, speed, and management tools to drive down the cost of running critical applications. "We're not interested in just getting the least expensive thing on the market," says Randy Lengyel, senior vice president of MIS at Wisconsin Physicians Service Insurance Corp. (WPS), a health insurer in Madison, Wisconsin. "We want something that is reliable, functional and has great customer service from the vendor."

The sweet spot for mainframe Linux today is server consolidation—replacing dozens or even hundreds of separate Intel-based Linux or Windows servers with a partition on the mainframe that dedicates a single processor, memory, and other system sources to running Linux. For example, WPS created a virtual Linux Server running on one 250-MIPS processor that was available within an IBM eServer zSeries 900 mainframe and did it at 40 percent of the cost of ordering, installing, and configuring a new Intel-based server, says Lengyel. A virtual server can be created within two to three minutes and deliver as much as nine times the throughput of a stand-alone server, he says. WPS, a longtime mainframe user, was drawn to running Linux on the mainframe as a way to leverage the mainframe's reliability and to keep support costs low.

The instability of its Windows NT servers was one reason why recreational vehicle manufacturer, Winnebago Industries Inc., implemented a Bynari InsightServer groupware application for Linux on an IBM zSeries mainframe. Dave Ennen, technical support manager at the Forest City, Iowa–based company, says he had to reboot his Windows NT servers once a week in an effort to improve their stability. But, "On the mainframe, everything is geared to staying up 24 hours a day, seven days a week," he says.

Winnebago already had a mainframe (an IBM S/390 Multiprise 3000 Enterprise Server) and a staff skilled in IBM's z/VM, an operating system that can divide each partition in a mainframe into multiple software-based virtual machines, each running its own operating system and applications. Rather than go through the expense of training his staff for the upgrade from Windows NT to Windows 2000 and Windows Exchange Server 2000, Ennen says it was more cost-effective to use part of his existing mainframe capacity and his staff's mainframe skills to run its Linux-based e-mail system. However, "If you were going to go out and buy a mainframe just to run Linux," he says, "it's going to be a little hard to justify."

Many observers say users should be running at least 20 to 25 servers before even considering consolidation into a mainframe Linux environment. Some of the best candidates for consolidation are infrastructure applications such as file and print services, e-mail, domain name servers, and Web servers. But not every application is a natural for mainframe Linux. Windows applications are a poor choice, since they don't run on Linux, although Linux equivalents are available in many cases. And applications that have complex graphical user interfaces or that perform complicated data analysis can use so much processing power that it's more cost-effective to keep running them on stand-alone servers.

Users have also been reluctant to move complex applications such as SAP R/3, which can take years to implement on distributed servers, onto a new environment. Although SAP AG has been among the first vendors to support Linux with its flagship products, Linux will represent only about 10 percent of new installations in 2003, says Manfred Stem, product manager for Linux Lab and Unix platforms at SAP.

Once you've identified applications to run on the mainframe, users and analysts recommend migrating them first to stand-alone servers running Linux. That's a good way to get support staff familiar with Linux before tackling the additional complexity of the mainframe, they say. Training Unix veterans in mainframe Linux skills—or Linux veterans in Unix skills—can be one of the biggest challenges. Many organizations have one support organization for mainframes and another for Windows and Unix servers, says John Kogel, vice president of the systems and service management group at Candle Corporation of America. These groups must work together and learn new terms for familiar concepts, he adds. For example, since beginning its move to mainframe Linux in January 2002, WPS cross-trained two mainframe and two Unix staffers in the combined Linux/mainframe environment. Each employee then took his knowledge back to his respective group.

Case Study Questions

1. How can a mainframe use Linux to replace the equivalent of hundreds of Unix or Windows servers?

2. What are the business benefits and challenges of using Linux on a mainframe to replace Windows or Unix servers? Use WPS and Winnebago to illustrate your answer.

3. What business applications are best suited to servers? To mainframes? Explain your reasoning.

CHAPTER 4

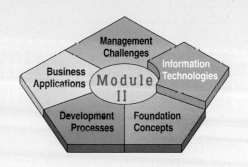

COMPUTER SOFTWARE

Chapter Highlights

Section I
Application Software: End User Applications

Introduction to Software

Real World Case: Intuit and Lone Star Doughnuts: The Small Business Software Challenge

Business Application Software

Software Suites and Integrated Packages

Web Browsers and More

Electronic Mail and Instant Messaging

Word Processing and Desktop Publishing

Electronic Spreadsheets

Presentation Graphics

Personal Information Managers

Groupware

Software Alternatives

Section II
System Software: Computer System Management

System Software Overview

Real World Case: Wells Fargo and Others: Business Applications of Web Services

Operating Systems

Other System Management Programs

Programming Languages

Web Languages and Services

Programming Software

Real World Case: Merrill Lynch and Others: The Growth of Linux in Business

Real World Case: Mark's Wearhouse and Others: Using Java in Business

Learning Objectives

After reading and studying this chapter, you should be able to:

1. Describe several important trends occurring in computer software.

2. Give examples of several major types of application and system software.

3. Explain the purpose of several popular software packages for end user productivity and collaborative computing.

4. Outline the functions of an operating system.

5. Describe the main uses of computer programming software, tools, and languages.

SECTION I	Application Software: End User Applications

Introduction to Software

This chapter presents an overview of the major types of software you depend on as you work with computers and access computer networks. It discusses their characteristics and purposes and gives examples of their uses. Before we begin, let's look at an example of the changing world of software in business.

Analyzing Intuit and Lone Star Doughnuts

Read the Real World Case on Intuit and Lone Star Doughnuts on the next page. We can learn a lot about the challenges and opportunities in the small business software market from this example. See Figure 4.1.

Intuit has regained its dynamic sales growth and profitability under new CEO Steve Bennet and is rapidly expanding its QuickBooks line of small business accounting software under the direction of Executive VP Lorrie Norrington. Intuit is parlaying its dominant market share positions in personal finance, income tax preparation, and small business accounting software into the development of a broad range of specialized accounting and other business application software and online services to meet the competitive threats to their small business markets of Microsoft, SAP, and Oracle. For example, QuickBooks is being expanded into a line of 25 small business accounting software products to serve specific industry and professional markets, as well as larger small businesses with up to 250 employees. In addition, Bennet and Norrington have been acquiring small companies that make integrated suites of business application software for specific industries, as another part of their strategy for making Intuit the dominant provider of software for small business.

Types of Software

Let's begin our analysis of software by looking at an overview of the major types and functions of **application software** and **system software** available to computer users, shown

FIGURE 4.1

Lorrie Norrington is executive vice president of Intuit and leader of their strategy to expand their product line of small business accounting and other software.

Source: Thomas Broening.

REAL WORLD CASE 1

Intuit and Lone Star Doughnuts: The Small Business Software Challenge

The software company that new CEO Steve Bennett inherited in January 2000 had a lot of problems, and was stalling into a slow sales growth mode, just as software giant Microsoft was starting an all out assault on the small business software market. But Intuit Inc. (www.intuit.com), came with two important strengths: a fiercely loyal customer base and three of the most powerful brands in retail software. Quicken, the personal finance program that is all but synonymous with Intuit, has 15 million active users and owns 73 percent of its market. TurboTax holds 81 percent of its market. And QuickBooks, the accounting program for small businesses, has an 84 percent share.

But Intuit desperately needed to start growing again, and Bennett had a plan. The evidence, as it happened, had been staring Intuit in its customer-focused face: The standard version of QuickBooks is designed for companies with fewer than 20 employees, yet 5 to 10 percent of its most loyal users were larger—some had as many as 200 employees. In fact, more of them used QuickBooks than brands of software intended for companies their size.

As Bennett looked closer, he realized there was room for more than just an expanded version of QuickBooks. Many small businesses are still run with pencil and paper, and of those that embrace PCs, few have moved beyond spreadsheets or simple accounting programs. Intuit estimates that North American small businesses, which it defines as companies with fewer than 250 employees, will buy $7 billion in business software and $11 billion in related services this year. Analysts expect double-digit growth for years to come. In an era when corporate IT budgets have been squeezed dry, this was a rare thing: an expanding market for business software.

Even so, by mid-2001, Intuit had made no move to capitalize on it. The executives of the small business group argued over the business model, organizational design, partnerships, and so on—even as Microsoft, Oracle, and SAP announced that they were entering the market. Losing patience, Bennett went looking for a replacement to run the group. He soon found one in a former colleague, 20-year GE veteran Lorrie Norrington, whom he lured away with the help of a $750,000 signing bonus and a $5 million interest-free relocation loan.

In her new job, Norrington essentially announced that Intuit intended to become the SAP or Oracle of small business. The company would offer software and services for a wide variety of enterprises, from the smallest shops to those with a couple hundred employees. Intuit would help not just with accounting but also with payroll and benefits, keeping track of customers, and managing computer systems. It would also customize its software for specific kinds of businesses, like accountancies or construction firms.

Norrington first turned her attention to QuickBooks. With nearly 3 million users, the accounting program was the obvious beachhead for a push deeper into the small-business market. Bennett had already ordered up a new version—QuickBooks Enterprise Solutions—for businesses with more than 20 employees. Within 18 months, Norrington added 13 more "flavors," and by the end of 2003, QuickBooks will have sliced the accounting market 25 ways, with special editions for the smallest small companies and larger small companies, and specific versions for retailers, distributors, contractors, and nonprofits.

To serve the largest and richest companies in their target audience, Bennett and Norrington have begun acquiring small companies that make fully integrated suites of business applications for specific industries. The packages, which Intuit sells for as much as $100,000 per customer, now cover property management, the public sector, construction, and distribution, and there are plans to buy as many as six more.

Microsoft, however remains Intuit's most formidable competitor. The $1.1 billion acquisition in 2001 of Great Plains Software (www.greatplains.com), which caters to businesses with up to 1,000 employees, shows just how serious Microsoft is. On the other hand, Bennett has turned Intuit into a serious competitor itself.

To understand why, consider Lone Star Doughnuts, Ltd., a Houston company that runs seven Krispy Kreme donut shops and distributes to 350 hospitals, grocery stores, and other outlets. As it expanded, it outgrew its QuickBooks software a couple of years ago, and went looking for something new.

At that time, says Jason Gordon, Lone Star's CFO, Great Plains accounting software seemed his best choice, since it easily handled the number crunching. But it cost $85,000, required consultants to install, and would force Lone Star to retrain the six people who would have to use it. Then, just before signing the purchase order, Gordon heard that Intuit was about to introduce a heavier-duty version of QuickBooks known as Enterprise Solutions. As soon as it was ready, he bought it. "I just plugged it in and was ready to go." No consultants, no retraining. And it cost just $3,500. Proving once again, that in this arena, Intuit's brands remain the ones to beat.

Case Study Questions

1. Why does Intuit dominate its present software markets? Visit its website and review its software products and services to help you answer.

2. How successful will Microsoft be in competing with Intuit in the small business software market? Why? Visit the Great Plains Software website and review their software products and services to help you answer.

3. Do you agree with Intuit's strategy to capitalize on the opportunities in small business software, and the threat posed by competition from Microsoft, SAP, and Oracle? Why or why not? What else could they do? Explain.

Source: Adapted from Eric Nee, "The Hottest CEO in Tech," *Business 2.0*, June 2003, pp. 86–92.

FIGURE 4.2   An overview of computer software. Note the major types and examples of application and system software.

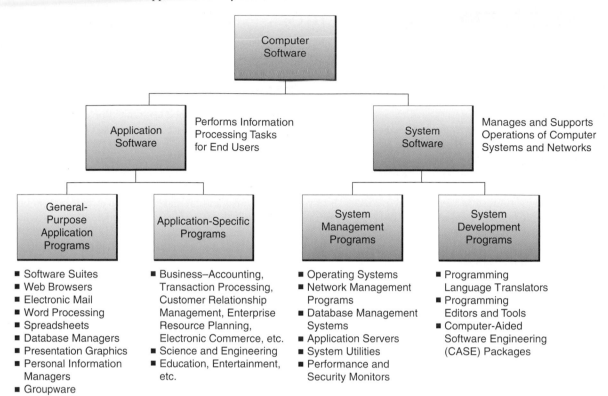

in Figure 4.2. This figure summarizes the major categories of system and application software we will discuss in this chapter. Of course, this is a conceptual illustration. The types of software you will encounter depend primarily on the types of computers and networks you use, and on what specific tasks you want to accomplish. We will discuss application software in this section and the major types of system software in Section II.

Application Software for End Users

Figure 4.2 shows that application software includes a variety of programs that can be subdivided into general-purpose and application-specific categories. **General-purpose** application programs are programs that perform common information processing jobs for end users. For example, word processing programs, spreadsheet programs, database management programs, and graphics programs are popular with microcomputer users for home, education, business, scientific, and many other purposes. Because they significantly increase the productivity of end users, they are sometimes known as *productivity packages*. Other examples include Web browsers, electronic mail, and *groupware*, which help support communication and collaboration among workgroups and teams.

Business Application Software

Thousands of **application-specific** software packages are available to support specific applications of end users in business and other fields. For example, business application software supports the reengineering and automation of business processes with strategic e-business applications like customer relationship management, enterprise resource planning, and supply chain management. Other examples are software packages that Web-enable applications in electronic commerce, or in the functional areas of business like human resource management and accounting and finance. Still other software empowers managers and business professionals with decision support tools like data mining, enterprise information portals, or knowledge management systems.

We will not discuss these applications here, but in upcoming chapters that go into more detail about these business software tools and applications. For example, data warehousing and data mining are discussed in Chapters 5 and 9; accounting, marketing,

FIGURE 4.3   The business applications in Oracle's E-Business Suite software product illustrate some of the many types of business application software being used today.

ORACLE E-BUSINESS SUITE

Advanced Planning	Business Intelligence	Contracts
e-Commerce	Enterprise Asset Management	Exchanges
Financials	Human Resources	Interaction Center
Manufacturing	Marketing	Order Fulfillment
Procurement	Product Development	Professional Services Automation
Projects	Sales	Service
Training	Treasury	

Source: Adapted from Oracle Corporation, "E-Business Suite: Manage by Fact with Complete Automation and Complete Information," Oracle.com, 2002.

manufacturing, human resource management, and financial management applications are covered in Chapter 7, as are customer relationship management, enterprise resource planning, and supply chain management. Electronic commerce is the focus of Chapter 8, and decision support and data analysis applications are explored in Chapter 9. Figure 4.3 illustrates some of the many types of business application software that are available today. These particular applications are integrated in the Oracle E-Business Suite software product of the Oracle Corporation.

Visa International: Implementing an e-Business Suite

Despite the innovations brought to global commerce by Visa's sophisticated consumer payments processing system, Visa International had surprisingly outdated systems managing some of its most critical internal business processes. "KPMG did an analysis of our business and found that our internal systems were becoming a risk to our organization," said Gretchen McCoy, senior vice president of Visa International. "We were in the red zone."

McCoy found that Visa's internal systems were unnecessarily complex and utilized few of the advantages that technology can bring to an enterprise. The financial management infrastructure was fragmented, complex, and costly to maintain. Data were not standardized, resulting in many different databases making disparate interpretations of business data. Corporate purchasing, accounts payable, and asset management were managed manually, resulting in time-consuming delays and discrepancies. Fragmented internal systems are not unusual in a company that experiences rapid growth. Visa experienced double digit growth for eleven consecutive years. Visa chose the Oracle E-Business Suite of business application software to remedy the problems that come with a complex and inefficient back office.

The resulting implementation turned Visa's cumbersome, outdated desktop procedures into Web-based e-business solutions that met Visa's demands for all roles and processes. For example, Oracle Financials automated Visa's old organization and created a more agile system capable of accounting for the impact of financial activities on a global scale. Accounts payable was transformed from a cumbersome manual process into a streamlined system that automatically checks invoices against outgoing payments and requests review of any discrepancies via e-mail. And Oracle iProcurement helped automate Visa's requisitioning and purchasing system by streamlining the entire purchasing process and implementing a self-service model to increase processing efficiency, said McCoy [7].

FIGURE 4.4   The basic program components of the top four software suites. Other programs may be included, depending on the suite edition selected.

Programs	Microsoft Office	Lotus SmartSuite	Corel WordPerfect Office	Sun StarOffice
Word Processor	Word	WordPro	WordPerfect	StarWriter
Spreadsheet	Excel	1–2–3	Quattro Pro	StarCalc
Presentation Graphics	PowerPoint	Freelance	Presentations	StarImpress
Database Manager	Access	Approach	Paradox	StarBase
Personal Information Manager	Outlook	Organizer	Corel Central	StarSchedule

Software Suites and Integrated Packages

Let's begin our discussion of popular general-purpose application software by looking at **software suites.** That's because the most widely used productivity packages come bundled together as software suites such as Microsoft Office, Lotus SmartSuite, Corel WordPerfect Office, and Sun's StarOffice. Examining their components gives us an overview of the important software tools that you can use to increase your productivity.

Figure 4.4 compares the basic programs that make up the top four software suites. Notice that each suite integrates software packages for word processing, spreadsheets, presentation graphics, database management, and personal information management. Microsoft, Lotus, Corel, and Sun bundle several other programs in each suite, depending on the version you select. Examples include programs for Internet access, e-mail, Web publishing, desktop publishing, voice recognition, financial management, electronic encyclopedias, and so on.

A software suite costs a lot less than the total cost of buying its individual packages separately. Another advantage is that all programs use a similar **graphical user interface** (GUI) of icons, tool and status bars, menus, and so on, which gives them the same look and feel, and makes them easier to learn and use. Software suites also share common tools such as spell checkers and help wizards to increase their efficiency. Another big advantage of suites is that their programs are designed to work together seamlessly and import each other's files easily, no matter which program you are using at the time. These capabilities make them more efficient and easier to use than using a variety of individual package versions.

Of course, putting so many programs and features together in one super-size package does have some disadvantages. Industry critics argue that many software suite features are never used by most end users. The suites take up a lot of disk space, from over 100 megabytes to over 150 megabytes, depending on which version or functions you install. So such software is sometimes derisively called *bloatware* by its critics. The cost of suites can vary from as low as $100 for a competitive upgrade to over $700 for a full version of some editions of the suites.

These drawbacks are one reason for the continued use of **integrated packages** like Microsoft Works, Lotus eSuite WorkPlace, AppleWorks, and so on. Integrated packages combine some of the functions of several programs—word processing, spreadsheets, presentation graphics, database management, and so on—into one software package.

Because Works programs leave out many features and functions that are in individual packages and software suites, they cannot do as much as those packages do. However, they use a lot less disk space (less than 10 megabytes), cost less than a hundred dollars, and are frequently pre-installed on many low-end microcomputer systems. So integrated packages have proven that they offer enough functions and features for many computer users, while providing some of the advantages of software suites in a smaller package.

FIGURE 4.5

Using the Microsoft Internet Explorer browser to access Google and other search engines on the Netscape.com website.

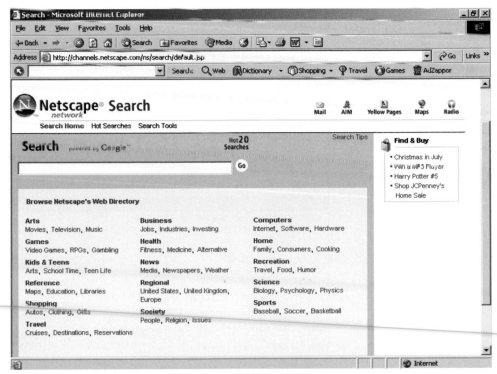

Source: Courtesy of Netscape.

Web Browsers and More

The most important software component for many computer users today is the once simple and limited, but now powerful and feature-rich, **Web browser.** A browser like Microsoft Explorer or Netscape Navigator is the key software interface you use to point and click your way through the hyperlinked resources of the World Wide Web and the rest of the Internet, as well as corporate intranets and extranets. Once limited to surfing the Web, browsers are becoming the universal software platform on which end users launch into information searches, e-mail, multimedia file transfer, discussion groups, and many other Internet applications.

Figure 4.5 illustrates using the Microsoft Internet Explorer browser to access the search engines on the Netscape.com website. Netscape uses top-rated Google as its default search engine, but also provides links to other popular search tools including Ask Jeeves, Look Smart, Lycos, and Overture. Using search engines to find information has become an indispensable part of business, and personal Internet, intranet, and extranet applications.

Industry experts are predicting that the Web browser will be the model for how most people will use networked computers in the future. So now, whether you want to watch a video, make a phone call, download some software, hold a videoconference, check your e-mail, or work on a spreadsheet of your team's business plan, you can use your browser to launch and host such applications. That's why browsers are sometimes called the *universal client*, that is, the software component installed on all of the networked computing and communications devices of the clients (users) throughout an enterprise.

Electronic Mail and Instant Messaging

The first thing many people do at work all over the world is check their e-mail. **Electronic mail** has changed the way people work and communicate. Millions of end users now depend on e-mail software to communicate with each other by sending and receiving electronic messages and file attachments via the Internet or their

FIGURE 4.6

Using the e-mail features of the ICQ instant messaging system.

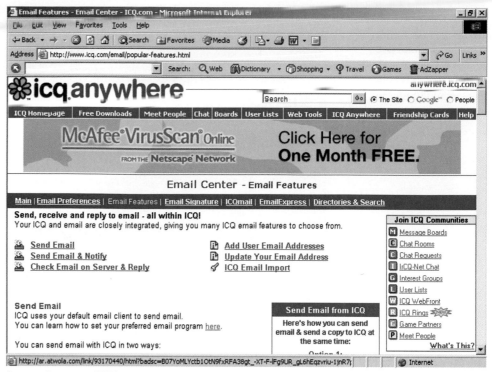

Source: Courtesy of ICQ.com.

organizations' intranets or extranets. E-mail is stored on network servers until you are ready. Whenever you want to, you can read your e-mail by displaying it on your workstations. So, with only a few minutes of effort (and a few microseconds or minutes of transmission time), a message to one or many individuals can be composed, sent, and received.

As we mentioned earlier, e-mail software is now a component of top software suites and Web browsers. Free e-mail packages like Microsoft HotMail and Netscape WebMail are available to Internet users from online services and Internet service providers. Most e-mail software like Microsoft Outlook Express or Netscape Messenger can route messages to multiple end users based on predefined mailing lists and provide password security, automatic message forwarding, and remote user access. They also allow you to store messages in folders and make it easy to add document and Web file attachments to e-mail messages. E-mail packages also enable you to edit and send graphics and multimedia files as well as text, and provide computer conferencing capabilities. Finally, your e-mail software may automatically filter and sort incoming messages (even news items from online services) and route them to appropriate user mailboxes and folders.

Instant messaging (IM) is an e-mail/computer conferencing hybrid technology that has grown so rapidly that it has become a standard method of electronic messaging for millions of Internet users worldwide. By using instant messaging, groups of business professionals or friends and associates can send and receive electronic messages instantly, and thus communicate and collaborate in real time in a near-conversational mode. Messages pop up instantly in an IM window on the computer screens of everyone who is part of your business workgroup or circle of friends who are members of your IM "buddy list," if they are online, no matter what other tasks they are working on at that moment. Instant messaging software can be downloaded and IM services implemented by subscribing to many popular IM systems, including AOL's Instant Messenger and ICQ, MSN Messenger, and Yahoo Messenger. See Figure 4.6.

FIGURE 4.7

Using the Microsoft Word word processing package. Note the insertion of a table in the document.

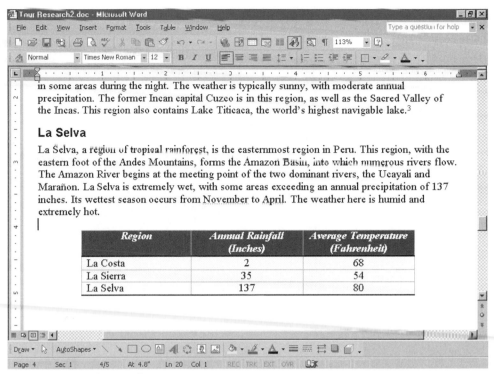

In some areas during the night. The weather is typically sunny, with moderate annual precipitation. The former Incan capital Cuzco is in this region, as well as the Sacred Valley of the Incas. This region also contains Lake Titicaca, the world's highest navigable lake.[3]

La Selva

La Selva, a region of tropical rainforest, is the easternmost region in Peru. This region, with the eastern foot of the Andes Mountains, forms the Amazon Basin, into which numerous rivers flow. The Amazon River begins at the meeting point of the two dominant rivers, the Ucayali and Marañón. La Selva is extremely wet, with some areas exceeding an annual precipitation of 137 inches. Its wettest season occurs from November to April. The weather here is humid and extremely hot.

Region	Annual Rainfall (Inches)	Average Temperature (Fahrenheit)
La Costa	2	68
La Sierra	35	54
La Selva	137	80

Source: Courtesy of Microsoft Corporation.

Word Processing and Desktop Publishing

Software for **word processing** has transformed the process of writing. Word processing packages computerize the creation, editing, revision, and printing of *documents* (such as letters, memos, and reports) by electronically processing your *text data* (words, phrases, sentences, and paragraphs). Top word processing packages like Microsoft Word, Lotus WordPro, and Corel WordPerfect can provide a wide variety of attractively printed documents with their desktop publishing capabilities. These packages can also convert all documents to HTML format for publication as Web pages on corporate intranets or the World Wide Web.

Word processing packages also provide other helpful features. For example, a spelling checker capability can identify and correct spelling errors, and a thesaurus feature helps you find a better choice of words to express ideas. You can also identify and correct grammar and punctuation errors, as well as suggest possible improvements in your writing style, with grammar and style checker functions. Besides converting documents to HTML format, you can also use the top packages to design and create Web pages from scratch for an Internet or intranet website. See Figure 4.7.

End users and organizations can use **desktop publishing** (DTP) software to produce their own printed materials that look professionally published. That is, they can design and print their own newsletters, brochures, manuals, and books with several type styles, graphics, photos, and colors on each page. Word processing packages and desktop publishing packages like Adobe PageMaker and QuarkXPress are used to do desktop publishing. Typically, text material and graphics can be generated by word processing and graphics packages and imported as text and graphics files. Optical scanners may be used to input text and graphics from printed material. You can also use files of *clip art*, which are predrawn graphic illustrations provided by the software package or available from other sources.

Electronic Spreadsheets

Electronic spreadsheet packages like Lotus 1-2-3, Microsoft Excel, and Corel QuattroPro are used for business analysis, planning, and modeling. They help you develop an *electronic spreadsheet*, which is a worksheet of rows and columns that can be stored on

FIGURE 4.8

Using an electronic spreadsheet package, Microsoft Excel. Note the use of graphics.

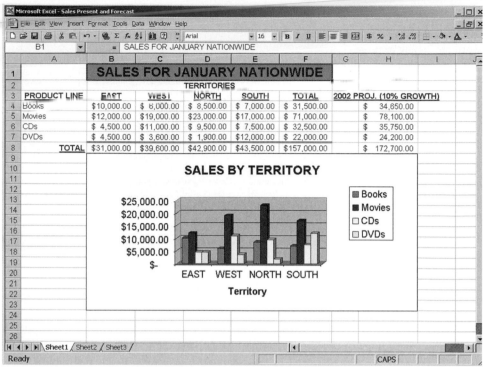

Source: Courtesy of Microsoft Corporation.

your PC or a network server, or converted to HTML format and stored as a Web page or *websheet* on the World Wide Web. Developing a spreadsheet involves designing its format and developing the relationships (formulas) that will be used in the worksheet. In response to your input, the computer performs necessary calculations based on the formulas you defined in the spreadsheet, and displays results immediately, whether at your workstation or website. Most packages also help you develop graphic displays of spreadsheet results. See Figure 4.8.

For example, you could develop a spreadsheet to record and analyze past and present advertising performance for a business. You could also develop hyperlinks to a similar websheet at your marketing team's intranet website. Now you have a decision support tool to help you answer *what-if questions* you may have about advertising. For example, "What would happen to market share if advertising expense increased by 10 percent?" To answer this question, you would simply change the advertising expense formula on the advertising performance worksheet you developed. The computer would recalculate the affected figures, producing new market share figures and graphics. You would then have a better insight into the effect of advertising decisions on market share. Then you could share this insight with a note on the websheet at your team's intranet website.

Presentation Graphics

Presentation graphics packages help you convert numeric data into graphics displays such as line charts, bar graphs, pie charts, and many other types of graphics. Most of the top packages also help you prepare multimedia presentations of graphics, photos, animation, and video clips, including publishing to the World Wide Web. Not only are graphics and multimedia displays easier to comprehend and communicate than numeric data but multiple-color and multiple-media displays also can more easily emphasize key points, strategic differences, and important trends in the data. Presentation graphics has proved to be much more effective than tabular presentations of numeric data for reporting and communicating in advertising media, management reports, or other business presentations. See Figure 4.9.

Using the slide preview feature of a presentation graphics package, Microsoft PowerPoint.

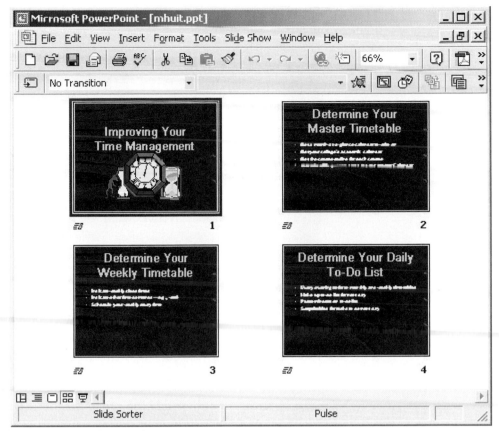

Source: Courtesy of Microsoft Corporation.

Presentation graphics software packages like Microsoft PowerPoint, Lotus Freelance, or Corel Presentations give you many easy-to-use capabilities that encourage the use of graphics presentations. For example, most packages help you design and manage computer-generated and -orchestrated *slide shows* containing many integrated graphics and multimedia displays. Or you can select from a variety of predesigned *templates* of business presentations, prepare and edit the outline and notes for a presentation, and manage the use of multimedia files of graphics, photos, sounds, and video clips. And of course, the top packages help you tailor your graphics and multimedia presentation for transfer in HTML format to websites on corporate intranets or the World Wide Web.

Personal Information Managers

The **personal information manager** (PIM) is a popular software package for end user productivity and collaboration, and is a popular application for personal digital assistant (PDA) hand-held devices. PIMs such as Lotus Organizer and Microsoft Outlook help end users store, organize, and retrieve information about customers, clients, and prospects, or schedule and manage appointments, meetings, and tasks. The PIM package will organize data you enter and retrieve information in a variety of forms, depending on the style and structure of the PIM and the information you want. For example, information can be retrieved as an electronic calendar or list of appointments, meetings, or other things to do; the timetable for a project; or a display of key facts and financial data about customers, clients, or sales prospects. Most PIMs now include the ability to access the World Wide Web and provide e-mail capability. Also, some PIMs use Internet and e-mail features to support team collaboration by sharing information such as contact lists, task lists, and schedules with other networked PIM users. See Figure 4.10.

FIGURE 4.10

Using a personal
information manager
(PIM): Microsoft Outlook.

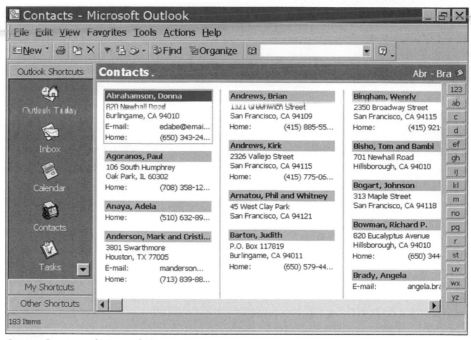

Source: Courtesy of Microsoft Corporation.

Groupware

Groupware is *collaboration software*, that is, software that helps workgroups and
teams work together to accomplish group assignments. Groupware is a category of
general-purpose application software that combines a variety of software features and
functions to facilitate collaboration. For example, groupware products like Lotus
Notes, Novell GroupWise, and Microsoft Exchange support collaboration through
electronic mail, discussion groups and databases, scheduling, task management, data,
audio and videoconferencing, and so on.

Groupware products rely on the Internet and corporate intranets and extranets to
make collaboration possible on a global scale by *virtual teams* located anywhere in the
world. For example, team members might use the Internet for global e-mail, project
discussion forums, and joint Web page development. Or they might use corporate intranets to publish project news and progress reports, and work jointly on documents
stored on Web servers. See Figure 4.11.

Collaborative capabilities are also being added to other software to give them
groupware features. For example, in the Microsoft Office software suite, Microsoft
Word keeps track of who made revisions to each document, Excel tracks all changes
made to a spreadsheet, and Outlook lets you keep track of tasks you delegate to other
team members.

Software Alternatives

Many businesses are finding alternatives to acquiring, installing, and maintaining business application software purchased from software vendors or developing and maintaining their own software in-house with their own software developer employees. For
example, as we will discuss further in Chapter 12, many large companies are *outsourcing* the development and maintenance of software they need to *contract programming*
firms and other software development companies, including the use of *offshore* software
developers in foreign countries, and using the Internet to communicate, collaborate,
and manage their software development projects.

Application Service Providers

But a large and fast-growing number of companies are turning to **application service
providers** (ASPs), instead of developing or purchasing the application software they
need to run their businesses. Application service providers are companies that own,
operate, and maintain application software and the computer system resources

FIGURE 4.11

Lotus Sametime enables
workgroups and project
teams to share spreadsheets
and other work documents
in an interactive online
collaboration process.

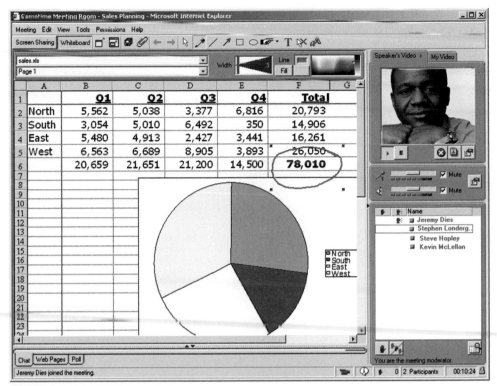

Source: Courtesy of IBM Lotus Software.

(servers, system software, networks, and IT personnel) required to offer the use of the application software for a fee as a service over the Internet. The ASP bills their customers on a per use basis, or on a monthly or annual fee basis.

Businesses are using an ASP instead of owning and maintaining their own software for many reasons. One of the biggest advantages is the low cost of initial investment, and in many cases, the short time needed to get the Web-based application set up and running. The ASP's pay-as-you-go fee structure is usually significantly less expensive than the cost of developing or purchasing, as well as running and maintaining the application software. And using an ASP eliminates or drastically reduces the need for much of the IT infrastructure (servers, system software, and IT personnel) that would be needed to acquire and support the application software, including the continual challenges of distributing and managing companywide software patches and upgrades. Consequently, the use of ASPs by businesses and other organizations is expected to accelerate in the coming years [12]. See Figure 4.12.

Fujitsu Technical Solutions: Using an ASP

A salesforce.com customer for over two years, Fujitsu Technology Solutions Inc. estimates that salesforce.com has saved it $75,000 per year on application costs alone because the Web-based sales management application requires no software or hardware, and eliminates lengthy implementations, cumbersome upgrades, and costly maintenance. Salesforce.com also allowed Fujitsu to save $415,000 a year by drastically reducing the number of hours required to maintain the system, allowing redeployment of those hours towards more core sales activities. Fujitsu has also saved $640,000 annually on time and resources formerly spent on sales data gathering and maintenance.

"Investing in salesforce.com has been a smart decision on the part of management, and it has enhanced our sales pipeline, especially that of UNIX servers and

Salesforce.com is a leading application service provider of Web-based sales management and customer relationship management services to both large and small businesses.

Source: Courtesy of SalesForce.com.

managed services," said Ken Mason, vice-president of marketing at Fujitsu Technology Solutions. "The system is robust and intuitive, yet requires no outside IT support. New users have been extremely satisfied with the flexibility of salesforce.com."

"We deployed a majority of our salespeople in less than a month for the total implementation. That initiated a flow of requests for additional access internally. In less than a year, we have tripled the user base and currently have employees in sales, marketing, finance, and management using the sales management application for their diverse functions," he continued [8].

SECTION II System Software: Computer System Management

System Software Overview

System software consists of programs that manage and support a computer system and its information processing activities. For example, operating systems and network management programs serve as a vital *software interface* between computer networks and hardware and the application programs of end users.

Analyzing Wells Fargo and Others

Read the Real World Case on Wells Fargo and Others on the next page. We can learn a lot about the business value of Web services technology from this example. See Figure 4.13.

Wells Fargo is using Web services software to transform payments data that it receives in a variety of formats from its largest corporate customers into a common format for processing by its internal banking systems. Things Remembered developed Web services software to connect their order entry systems to the Web site of their online partner 1-800 Flowers. In addition, they are planning to use Web services to connect the point of sale systems in their retail stores to the corporate inventory systems. However, connecting to Things Remembered's other online business partners has been put on hold until adequate security for Web services-based systems between them and their business partners is assured. And Providence Health System is using Web services software to tie internal systems together and develop small customer relationship management applications, including the development of Web portals that give patients and health professionals access to patient information. All of the companies in this case report that their Web services applications have generated considerable savings in time and money both in their development and business uses.

Overview

Figure 4.14 shows that we can group system software into two major categories:

- **System management programs.** Programs that manage the hardware, software, network, and data resources of computer systems during the execution of

FIGURE 4.13

Steve Ellis is executive vice president of the wholesale banking services group of Wells Fargo and leads the business planning for their first Web services applications.

Source: Seth Affoumado.

Wells Fargo and Others: Business Applications of Web Services

Wells Fargo. For years, Wells Fargo & Co.'s wholesale banking operations dealt with many diverse methods for handling wire transfers and interbank electronic payments for its 100 largest corporate customers. Those customers sent payment instructions in formats such as EDI, flat files, and XML, which forced Wells Fargo (www.wellsfargo.com) to build separate channels to tie each customer's data into the bank's back-end systems. No longer. The bank's ePayment Manager Web services module now transforms payment data in a wide variety of formats and sends it to Wells Fargo's back-end systems, where payments are processed and customer acknowledgments are sent.

Rather than build a custom setup for each customer, existing Web service modules are snapped together in Lego-like fashion. "Using Web services reduces account setup times by 30 to 50 percent for each new customer we add," says Steve Ellis, executive vice president of the Wells Fargo wholesale services group in San Francisco. The bank saves development time and money, and customers don't have to spend time and money altering their data formats. The bank started work in April 2002, using WebMethods Inc.'s Integration Platform development tools, and the system was in operation by November of that year.

Things Remembered. At Things Remembered, Inc. (www.thingsremembered.com), the largest personalized gift retailer in the United States, Web services are helping to speed up deliveries to customers. Before the Web services technology was in place, when a customer ordered a monogrammed vase from Things Remembered's online partner 1-800-Flowers.com, the gift retailer had to pull that order manually from the florist's website. That process took time and didn't tie the order into Things Remembered's real-time inventory system.

To solve the problem, parent company Cole National Corp. (www.colenational.com) built a Web services module with IBM's WebSphere development tools that directly ties the 1-800-Flowers.com site to the Things Remembered order-entry systems. Now that the company has built a basic tool kit of Web services objects, it will reuse them as part of a larger Web services initiative, says Mark Fodor, director of e-business at Cole National. That initiative will include integrating with other online business partners, he says. However, that will depend on how soon adequate Web services security software tools for interenterprise Web services are developed by software providers.

In addition, Web services will eventually be used at point-of-sale systems in the 760 Things Remembered retail stores, says Fodor. Currently, managers must dial into the Cole internal network to check on inventory. The stores also connect to the Internet through an Internet service provider. But because a Web services application has already been built that ties into the inventory system, the Internet connection will eventually be used to check on inventory. That

will save telecommunications costs and reduce the time it takes to confirm customer orders, Fodor says.

Providence Health. With an enormous amount of data and disparate computing systems, the health care industry is a natural fit for Web services. Providence Health System (www.providence.org), a $3.3 billion health care provider in Seattle, is a case in point. It uses Web services for enterprise application integration and to build small CRM systems. As a result, Providence has cut its development costs, decreased the amount of time it takes to bring a new service for customers to market by 30 to 50 percent, and now provides patients and health care workers immediate access to patient information.

Mike Reagin, Providence's director of research and development, says the company "is very distributed, and so we have many in-house legacy systems, from old mainframe systems to new Microsoft ones, and we needed a consistent way of aggregating data from all of them." The company started development work on Web services last spring using Infravio, Inc.'s Web Services Management System and had its first module working within four weeks—a far faster turnaround time than for projects using other types of technology, Reagin says.

Patients can now look up benefits information online and use a portal for transactions. Providence has relationships with WebMD.com and Wellmed.com, so when patients log on to those websites, all their personal information (height, weight, date of birth) is already populated via Web services modules that link to Providence's back-end systems. Similarly, doctors can connect to a portal that aggregates patient information from all of Providence's clinics, hospitals, and offices. The portal "improves clinical care and patient care, and hopefully reduces costs and increases efficiencies," Reagin says.

Reagin recommends getting the right tool set and management platform in place before launching. "Going into development we were worried, 'What if we have a hundred Web services out there, how would we manage them all? Would it get chaotic?'" he says. By first choosing the Infravio Web services management platform, he says he's been able to keep track of all the Web services modules and reuse existing ones.

Case Study Questions

1. What are the purpose and business value of Web services?

2. What are the benefits of Web services for Wells Fargo, Things Remembered, and Providence Health?

3. What are the business challenges of Web services? Visit the Web services websites of BEA (www.bea.com/products/webservices), IBM (www.ibm.com/solutions/webservices), and Microsoft (www.microsoft.com/webservices), to help you answer.

FIGURE 4.14

The system and application
software interface between
end users and computer
hardware.

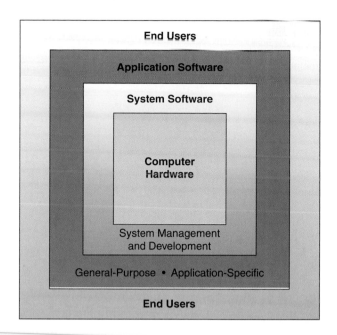

the various information processing jobs of users. Examples of important system management programs are operating systems, network management programs, database management systems, and system utilities.

- **System development programs.** Programs that help users develop information system programs and procedures and prepare user programs for computer processing. Major software development programs are programming language translators and editors, and a variety of CASE (computer-aided software engineering) and other programming tools.

Operating Systems

The most important system software package for any computer is its operating system. An **operating system** is an integrated system of programs that manages the operations of the CPU, controls the input/output and storage resources and activities of the computer system, and provides various support services as the computer executes the application programs of users.

The primary purpose of an operating system is to maximize the productivity of a computer system by operating it in the most efficient manner. An operating system minimizes the amount of human intervention required during processing. It helps your application programs perform common operations such as accessing a network, entering data, saving and retrieving files, and printing or displaying output. If you have any hands-on experience on a computer, you know that the operating system must be loaded and activated before you can accomplish other tasks. This emphasizes the fact that operating systems are the most indispensable components of the software interface between users and the hardware of their computer systems.

Operating System Functions

An operating system performs five basic functions in the operation of a computer system: providing a user interface, resource management, task management, file management, and utilities and support services. See Figure 4.15.

The User Interface. The **user interface** is the part of the operating system that allows you to communicate with it so you can load programs, access files, and accomplish other tasks. Three main types of user interfaces are the *command-driven*, *menu-driven*, and *graphical user interfaces*. The trend in user interfaces for operating systems and other software is moving away from the entry of brief end user commands, or even

FIGURE 4.15

The basic functions of an operating system include a user interface, resource management, task management, file management, and utilities and other functions.

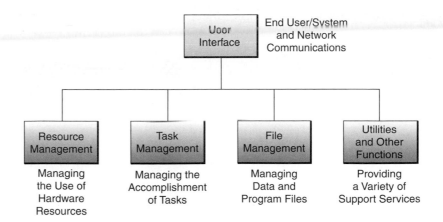

the selection of choices from menus of options. Instead, most software provides an easy-to-use **graphical user interface** (GUI) that uses icons, bars, buttons, boxes, and other images. GUIs rely on pointing devices like the electronic mouse or touchpad to make selections that help you get things done. See Figure 4.16.

Resource Management. An operating system uses a variety of **resource management** programs to manage the hardware and networking resources of a computer system, including its CPU, memory, secondary storage devices, telecommunications processors, and input/output peripherals. For example, memory management programs keep track of where data and programs are stored. They may also subdivide memory into a number of sections and swap parts of programs and data between memory and magnetic disks or other secondary storage devices. This can provide a computer system with a **virtual memory** capability that is significantly larger than the real memory capacity of its primary storage circuits. So, a computer with a virtual memory capability can process large programs and greater amounts of data than the capacity of its memory chips would normally allow.

File Management. An operating system contains **file management** programs that control the creation, deletion, and access of files of data and programs. File management also involves keeping track of the physical location of files on magnetic disks and other secondary storage devices. So operating systems maintain directories of information about the location and characteristics of files stored on a computer system's secondary storage devices.

Task Management. The **task management** programs of an operating system manage the accomplishment of the computing tasks of end users. They give each task a slice of a CPU's time and interrupt the CPU operations to substitute other tasks. Task management may involve a **multitasking** capability where several computing tasks can occur at the same time. Multitasking may take the form of *multiprogramming*, where the CPU can process the tasks of several programs at the same time, or *timesharing*, where the computing tasks of several users can be processed at the same time. The efficiency of multitasking operations depends on the processing power of a CPU and the virtual memory and multitasking capabilities of the operating system it uses.

Most microcomputer, midrange, and mainframe operating systems provide a multitasking capability. With multitasking, end users can do two or more operations (e.g., keyboarding and printing) or applications (e.g., word processing and financial analysis) concurrently, that is, at the same time. Multitasking on microcomputers has also been made possible by the development of more powerful microprocessors and their ability to directly address much larger memory capacities (up to 4 gigabytes). This allows an

The graphical user interface of Microsoft's Windows XP operating system.

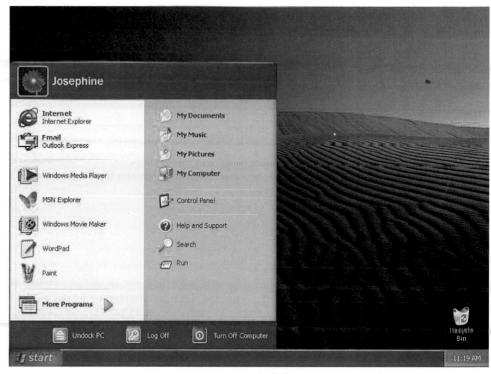

Source: Courtesy of Microsoft Corporation.

operating system to subdivide primary storage into several large partitions, each of which can be used by a different application program.

In effect, a single computer can act as if it were several computers, or *virtual machines*, since each application program is running independently at the same time. The number of programs that can be run concurrently depends on the amount of memory that is available and the amount of processing each job demands. That's because a microprocessor (or CPU) can become overloaded with too many jobs and provide unacceptably slow response times. However, if memory and processing capacities are adequate, multitasking allows end users to easily switch from one application to another, share data files among applications, and process some applications in a *background* mode. Typically, background tasks include large printing jobs, extensive mathematical computation, or unattended telecommunications sessions.

Microsoft Windows

For many years, MS-DOS (Microsoft Disk Operating System) was the most widely used microcomputer operating system. It is a single-user, single-tasking operating system, but was given a graphical user interface and limited multitasking capabilities by combining it with Microsoft **Windows.** Microsoft began replacing its DOS/Windows combination in 1995 with the Windows 95 operating system, featuring a graphical user interface, true multitasking, networking, multimedia, and many other capabilities. Microsoft introduced an enhanced Windows 98 version during 1998, and a Windows ME (Millennium Edition) consumer PC system in 2000.

Microsoft introduced its **Windows NT** (New Technology) operating system in 1995. Windows NT is a powerful, multitasking, multiuser operating system that was installed on many network servers to manage client/server networks and on PCs with high-performance computing requirements. New Server and Workstation versions were introduced in 1997. Microsoft substantially enhanced its Windows NT products with the **Windows 2000** operating system during the year 2000.

Late in 2001 Microsoft introduced **Windows XP** Home Edition and Professional versions, and thus formally merged its two Windows operating system lines for consumer and business users, uniting them around the Windows NT and Windows 2000

FIGURE 4.17 Comparing the purposes of the four versions of the Microsoft Windows Server 2003 operating system.

Microsoft Windows Server 2003 Comparisons
● **Windows Server 2003, Standard Edition** For smaller server applications, including file and print sharing, Internet and intranet connectivity, and centralized desktop application deployment.
● **Windows Server 2003, Enterprise Edition** For larger business applications, XML Web services, enterprise collaboration, and enterprise network support.
● **Windows Server 2003, Datacenter Edition** For business-critical and mission-critical applications demanding the highest levels of scalability and availability.
● **Windows Server 2003, Web Edition** For Web serving and hosting, providing a platform for developing and deploying Web services and applications.

code base. With Windows XP, consumers and home users finally received an enhanced Windows operating system with the performance and stability features that business users had in Windows 2000, and continue to have in Windows XP Professional. Microsoft also introduced four new **Windows Server 2003** versions in 2003, which are summarized and compared in Figure 4.17 [6].

UNIX

Originally developed by AT&T, **UNIX** now is also offered by other vendors, including Solaris by Sun Microsystems and AIX by IBM. UNIX is a multitasking, multiuser, network-managing operating system whose portability allows it to run on mainframes, midrange computers, and microcomputers. UNIX is still a popular choice for Web and other network servers.

Linux

Linux is a low-cost, powerful, and reliable UNIX-like operating system that is rapidly gaining market share from UNIX and Windows servers as a high-performance operating system for network servers and Web servers in both small and large networks. Linux was developed as free or low-cost *shareware* or *open-source software* over the Internet in the 1990s by Linus Torvald of Finland and millions of programmers around the world. Linux is still being enhanced in this way, but is sold with extra features and support services by software vendors such as Red Hat, Caldera, and SUSE Linux. PC versions are also available, which support office software suites, Web browsers, and other application software.

Mac OS X

The **Mac OS X** is the latest operating system from Apple for the iMac and other Macintosh microcomputers. The Mac OS X version 10.2 Jaguar, has an advanced graphical user interface and multitasking and multimedia capabilities, along with an integrated Web browser, e-mail, instant messaging, search engine, digital media player, and many other features.

Orbitz and E* Trade: Switching to Linux

Chicago-based Orbitz Inc. (www.orbitz.com) is sold on the cost savings and enhanced processing power and speed afforded by Linux. The transaction-intensive online travel reservation company is going a step further with Linux by replacing its 50 Sun Microsystems Java application servers running the Solaris Unix operating system. These heavy-lifting systems feed the company's 700 Web servers—already running Linux—which dish up the screens customers interact with when they make airline, hotel, and vacation reservations online.

Orbitz benchmarked several vendors' latest operating systems including Linux on Intel servers, and the results were compelling. "To maintain the same capacity in terms of the number of users on our site, we were able to move from the Unix servers to the Linux systems for about one-tenth the cost," says Roger Liew, vice president of technology development. "We also increased the speed in moving into a more efficient hardware and software environment," adds Liew, referring to the faster response times of the Intel environment. As for the Web servers, Liew especially appreciates Linux's ease of maintenance, which requires a single administrator for the 700 machines. "Everything is automated. It's probably one of the most reliable aspects of our system," he says.

For some companies, the gains from converting to Linux are so large that CIOs get giddy talking about it. Take E*Trade Financial (www.etrade.com). In 1999, it paid $12 million for 60 Sun machines to run its online trading website. CIO Josh Levine just finished replacing those machines in 2002 with 80 Intel-based servers running Linux for a mere $320,000. That has let E*Trade bring its tech budget down 30 percent, from $330 million in 2000 to $200 million in 2002—a big reason the company has stayed alive despite the carnage in its business. "It's remarkable," he says. "On top of all that, website response time has improved by 30 percent" [11].

Other System Management Programs

There are many other types of important system management software besides operating systems. These include *database management systems*, which we will cover in Chapter 5, and *network management programs*, which we will cover in Chapter 6. Figure 4.18 compares several types of system software offered by IBM and its competitors.

Several other types of system management software are marketed as separate programs or are included as part of an operating system. Utility programs, or **utilities,** are an important example. Programs like Norton Utilities perform miscellaneous housekeeping and file conversion functions. Examples include data backup, data recovery, virus protection, data compression, and file defragmentation. Most operating systems also provide many utilities that perform a variety of helpful chores for computer users.

Other examples of system support programs include performance monitors and security monitors. **Performance monitors** are programs that monitor and adjust the

FIGURE 4.18 Comparing system software offered by IBM and its main competitors.

Software Category	What It Does	IBM Product	Customers	Main Competitor	Customers
Network management	Monitors networks to keep them up and running.	**Tivoli**	T. Rowe Price uses it to safeguard customer records.	**HP OpenView**	Amazon.com uses it to monitor its servers.
Application server	Shuttles data between business apps and the Web.	**WebSphere**	REI uses it to serve up its website and distribute data.	**BEA WebLogic**	Washingtonpost.com builds news pages with it.
Database manager	Provides digital storehouses for business data.	**DB2**	Mikasa uses it to help customers find its products online.	**Oracle 9i**	It runs Southwest Airlines's frequent-flyer program.
Collaboration tools	Powers everything from e-mail to electronic calendars.	**Lotus**	Retailer Sephora uses it to coordinate store maintenance.	**Microsoft Exchange**	Time Inc. uses it to provide e-mail to its employees.
Development tools	Allows programmers to craft software code quickly.	**Rational**	Merrill Lynch used it to build code for online trading.	**Microsoft Visual Studio .Net**	Used to develop Allstate's policy management system.

Source: Adapted from Susan Orenstein, Erik Schonfeld, and Scott Herhold. "The Toughest Guy in Software." *Business 2.0*, April 2003, p. 82.

performance and usage of one or more computer systems to keep them running efficiently. **Security monitors** are packages that monitor and control the use of computer systems and provide warning messages and record evidence of unauthorized use of computer resources. A recent trend is to merge both types of programs into operating systems like Microsoft's Windows 2003 Datacenter Server, or into system management software like Computer Associates' CA-Unicenter, which can manage both mainframe systems and servers in a data center.

Another important software trend is the use of system software known as **application servers,** which provide a *middleware* interface between an operating system and the application programs of users. **Middleware** is software that helps diverse software applications and networked computer systems exchange data and work together more efficiently. Examples include application servers, Web servers, and enterprise application integration (EAI) software. Thus, for example, application servers like BEA's WebLogic and IBM's WebSphere help Web-based e-business and e-commerce applications run much faster and more efficiently on computers using Windows, UNIX, and other operating systems.

TravelNow: Converting to an Application Server	When Chris Kuhn became the chief information officer at TravelNow, he realized that the online travel agency's website was headed for expensive trouble. Hotel and airline bookings had been growing rapidly and showed no signs of slowing. He knew the site would start crashing if he didn't expand its capacity. Until recently that would have meant buying additional Web server hardware, networking those machines together, and hiring more employees to manage it all. But Kuhn decided to try another, potentially far less costly route: an application server, a software technology that promised to greatly expand the site's capacity—without buying any new machines or enlarging the staff—and add lots of flexibility in the bargain.

Application servers essentially make a website's important work—running search engines, verifying a user's credit-card number, serving up news articles, and so forth—much faster and more efficient. An application server amounts to a layer of software inserted between a server's operating system (Windows, Linux, Sun's Solaris, IBM's zOS, or another) and all those search engines and credit-card verifiers. It handles the heavy demands of serving up Web pages, accessing databases, and hooking into back-office servers. Think of it as a kind of automatic transmission for your e-business; a super agile intermediary between your website's applications and the raw power of the server's CPU and operating system.

Another nice thing about an application server is that it greatly simplifies the procedure for adding new functions to your website. Most application servers use Sun's Java programming language, and unlike older programs written for a specific set of hardware and software, Java programs can work unchanged on almost any system. So if you suddenly realize that your website needs a function that, say, allows customers to see their previous purchases, adding that function is a matter of simply dropping in a bit of code.

Off-the-shelf applications written in Java—content management software and personalization routines, for example—can easily be added to the collection of software on your application server. And most of these servers run on multiple hardware and software configurations, so moving from low-end Windows or Linux machines to higher powered Unix servers doesn't require a painful process of "porting," or rewriting, all of your code.

So it should come as no surprise that TravelNow's Kuhn eventually settled on BEA's WebLogic Server, which cost about $90,000 but allowed him to reduce his hardware from 22 servers to just three. There was a catch: It took almost six months to rewrite the site's applications in Java, with consulting fees of more than $500,000. But now that his programmers can add new functions and rewrite old ones much more easily than before, Kuhn doesn't expect to go through another rewrite anytime soon. He's glad he made the switch to an application server. "Our growth rate has been faster and harder than all the other years combined," he says. "There's no way the old system could have handled it" [10].

Programming Languages

To understand computer software, you need a basic knowledge of the role that programming languages play in the development of computer programs. A **programming language** allows a programmer to develop the sets of instructions that constitute a computer program. Many different programming languages have been developed, each with its own unique vocabulary, grammar, and uses.

Machine Languages

Machine languages (or *first-generation languages*) are the most basic level of programming languages. In the early stages of computer development, all program instructions had to be written using binary codes unique to each computer. This type of programming involves the difficult task of writing instructions in the form of strings of binary digits (ones and zeros) or other number systems. Programmers must have a detailed knowledge of the internal operations of the specific type of CPU they are using. They must write long series of detailed instructions to accomplish even simple processing tasks. Programming in machine language requires specifying the storage locations for every instruction and item of data used. Instructions must be included for every switch and indicator used by the program. These requirements make machine language programming a difficult and error-prone task. A machine language program to add two numbers together in the CPU of a specific computer and store the result might take the form shown in Figure 4.19.

Assembler Languages

Assembler languages (or *second-generation languages*) are the next level of programming languages. They were developed to reduce the difficulties in writing machine language programs. The use of assembler languages requires language translator programs called *assemblers* that allow a computer to convert the instructions of such language into machine instructions. Assembler languages are frequently called symbolic languages because symbols are used to represent operation codes and storage locations. Convenient alphabetic abbreviations called *mnemonics* (memory aids) and other symbols represent operation codes, storage locations, and data elements. For example, the computation X = Y + Z in an assembler language might take the form shown in Figure 4.19.

Assembler languages are still used as a method of programming a computer in a machine-oriented language. Most computer manufacturers provide an assembler language that reflects the unique machine language instruction set of a particular line of

FIGURE 4.19

Examples of four levels of programming languages. These programming language instructions might be used to compute the sum of two numbers as expressed by the formula X = Y + Z.

Four Levels of Programming Languages	
● **Machine Languages:** Use binary coded instructions 1010 11001 1011 11010 1100 11011	● **High-Level Languages:** Use brief statements or arithmetic notations BASIC: X = Y + Z COBOL: COMPUTE X = Y + Z
● **Assembler Languages:** Use symbolic coded instructions LOD Y ADD Z STR X	● **Fourth-Generation Languages:** Use natural and nonprocedural statements SUM THE FOLLOWING NUMBERS

computers. This feature is particularly desirable to *system programmers*, who program system software (as opposed to application programmers, who program application software), since it provides them with greater control and flexibility in designing a program for a particular computer. They can then produce more efficient software, that is, programs that require a minimum of instructions, storage, and CPU time to perform a specific processing assignment.

High-Level Languages

High-level languages (or *third-generation languages*) use instructions, which are called *statements*, that use brief statements or arithmetic expressions. Individual high-level language statements are actually *macroinstructions*; that is, each individual statement generates several machine instructions when translated into machine language by high-level language translator programs called *compilers* or *interpreters*. High-level language statements resemble the phrases or mathematical expressions required to express the problem or procedure being programmed. The *syntax* (vocabulary, punctuation, and grammatical rules) and the *semantics* (meanings) of such statements do not reflect the internal code of any particular computer. For example, the computation $X = Y + Z$ would be programmed in the high-level languages of BASIC and COBOL as shown in Figure 4.19.

High-level languages like BASIC, COBOL, and FORTRAN are easier to learn and program than an assembler language, since they have less-rigid rules, forms, and syntaxes. However, high-level language programs are usually less efficient than assembler language programs and require a greater amount of computer time for translation into machine instructions. Since most high-level languages are machine independent, programs written in a high-level language do not have to be reprogrammed when a new computer is installed, and programmers do not have to learn a different language for each type of computer.

Fourth-Generation Languages

The term **fourth-generation language** describes a variety of programming languages that are more nonprocedural and conversational than prior languages. These languages are called fourth-generation languages (4GLs) to differentiate them from machine languages (first generation), assembler languages (second generation), and high-level languages (third generation).

Most fourth-generation languages are *nonprocedural languages* that encourage users and programmers to specify the results they want, while the computer determines the sequence of instructions that will accomplish those results. Thus, fourth-generation languages have helped simplify the programming process. **Natural languages** are sometimes considered to be *fifth-generation* languages (5GLs), and are very close to English or other human languages. Research and development activity in artificial intelligence (AI) is developing programming languages that are as easy to use as ordinary conversation in one's native tongue. For example, INTELLECT, a natural language, would use a statement like, "What are the average exam scores in MIS 200?" to program a simple average exam score task.

The ease of use of 4GLs is gained at the expense of some loss in flexibility. It is frequently difficult to override some of the prespecified formats or procedures of 4GLs. Also, the machine language code generated by a program developed by a 4GL is frequently much less efficient (in terms of processing speed and amount of storage capacity needed) than a program written in a language like COBOL. Thus, some large transaction processing applications programmed in a 4GL have not provided reasonable response times when faced with a large amount of real-time transaction processing and end user inquiries. However, 4GLs have shown great success in business applications that do not have a high volume of transaction processing.

Object-Oriented Languages

Object-oriented programming (OOP) languages like Visual Basic, C++, and Java are also considered to be fifth-generation languages and have become major tools of software development. Briefly, while most other programming languages separate data elements from the procedures or actions that will be performed upon them, OOP

FIGURE 4.20

An example of a bank savings account object. This object consists of data about a customer's account balance and the basic operations that can be performed on those data.

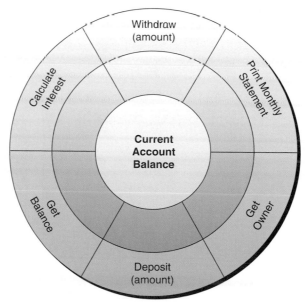

Savings Account Object

languages tie them together into **objects.** Thus, an object consists of data and the actions that can be performed on the data. For example, an object could be a set of data about a bank customer's savings account, and the operations (such as interest calculations) that might be performed upon the data. Or an object could be data in graphic form such as a video display window, plus the display actions that might be used upon it. See Figure 4.20.

In procedural languages, a program consists of procedures to perform actions on each data element. However, in object-oriented systems, objects tell other objects to perform actions on themselves. For example, to open a window on a computer video display, a beginning menu object could send a window object a message to open and a window will appear on the screen. That's because the window object contains the program code for opening itself.

Object-oriented languages are easier to use and more efficient for programming the graphics-oriented user interfaces required by many applications. Therefore, they are the most widely used programming languages for software development today. Also, once objects are programmed, they are reusable. Therefore, reusability of objects is a major benefit of object-oriented programming. For example, programmers can construct a user interface for a new program by assembling standard objects such as windows, bars, boxes, buttons, and icons. Therefore, most object-oriented programming packages provide a GUI that supports a "point and click," "drag and drop" visual assembly of objects known as *visual programming*. Figure 4.21 shows a display of the Visual Basic object-oriented programming environment. Object-oriented technology is discussed further in the coverage of object-oriented databases in Chapter 5.

Web Languages and Services

HTML, XML, and Java are three programming languages that are important tools for building multimedia Web pages, websites, and Web-based applications. In addition, XML and Java have become strategic components of the software technologies that are supporting many Web services initiatives in business.

HTML

HTML (Hypertext Markup Language) is a page description language that creates hypertext or hypermedia documents. HTML inserts control codes within a document at points you can specify that create links (*hyperlinks*) to other parts of the document or to other documents anywhere on the World Wide Web. HTML embeds control

FIGURE 4.21 The Visual Basic object-oriented programming environment.

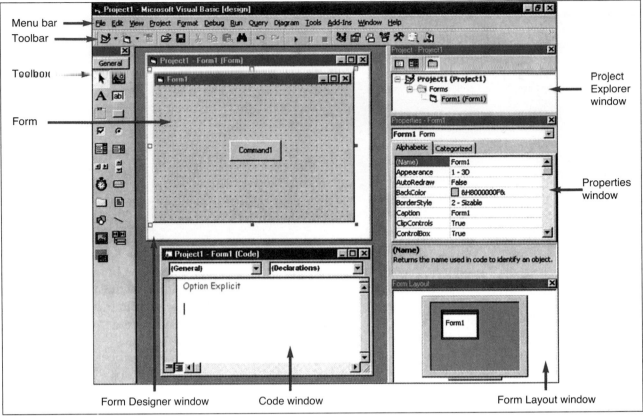

Menu bar
Toolbar
Toolbox
Form

Project Explorer window

Properties window

Form Designer window   Code window   Form Layout window

Source: Courtesy of Microsoft.

codes in the ASCII text of a document that designate titles, headings, graphics, and multimedia components, as well as hyperlinks within the document.

As we mentioned earlier, several of the programs in the top software suites will automatically convert documents into HTML formats. These include Web browsers, word processing and spreadsheet programs, database managers, and presentation graphics packages. These and other specialized *Web publishing* programs like Microsoft FrontPage and Lotus FastSite provide a range of features to help you design and create multimedia Web pages without formal HTML programming.

XML

XML (eXtensible Markup Language) is not a Web page format description language like HTML. Instead, XML describes the contents of Web pages (including business documents designed for use on the Web) by applying identifying tags or *contextual labels* to the data in Web documents. For example, a travel agency Web page with airline names and flight times would use hidden XML tags like "airline name" and "flight time" to categorize each of the airline flight times on that page. Or product inventory data available at a website could be labeled with tags like "brand," "price," and "size." By classifying data in this way, XML makes website information a lot more searchable, sortable, and easier to analyze.

For example, XML-enabled search software could easily find the exact product you specify if the product data at a website had been labeled with identifying XML tags. And a website that used XML could more easily determine what Web page features its customers used and what products they investigated. Thus XML promises to make electronic business and commerce processes a lot easier and more efficient by supporting the automatic electronic exchange of business data between companies and their customers, suppliers, and other business partners.

FIGURE 4.22 The benefits and limitations of the Java2 Enterprise Edition (J2EE) and Microsoft .Net software development platforms.

J2EE		.NET	
PROS	**CONS**	**PROS**	**CONS**
• Runs on any operating system and application server (may need adjustments). • Handles complex, high-volume, high-transaction applications. • Has more enterprise features for session management, fail-over, load balancing, and application integration. • Is favored by experienced enterprise vendors such as IBM, BEA, SAP, and Oracle. • Offers a wide range of vendor choices for tools and application servers. • Has a proven track record.	• Has a complex application development environment. • Tools can be difficult to use. • Java Swing environment's ability to build graphical user interfaces has limitations. • May cost more to build, deploy, and manage applications. • Lacks built-in support for Web services standards. • Is difficult to use for quick-turnaround, low-cost, and mass-market projects.	• Easy-to-use tools may increase programmer productivity. • Has a strong framework for building rich graphical user interfaces. • Gives developers choice of working in more than 20 programming languages. • Is tightly integrated with Microsoft's operating system and enterprise server software. • May cost less, due in part to built-in application server in Windows, unified management, less expensive tools. • Has built-in support for Web service standards.	• Framework runs only on Windows, restricting vendor choice. • Users of prior Microsoft tools and technology face a potentially steep learning curve. • New runtime infrastructure lacks maturity. • Questions persist about the scalability and transaction capability of the Windows platform. • Choice of integrated development environments is limited. • Getting older applications to run in new .Net environment may require effort.

Source: Carol Sliwa, ".Net vs. Java," *Computerworld*, May 20, 2002, p. 31.

Java

Java is an object-oriented programming language created by Sun Microsystems that is revolutionizing the programming of applications for the World Wide Web and corporate intranets and extranets. Java is related to the C++ and Objective C programming languages, but is much simpler and more secure, and is computing platform independent. Java is also specifically designed for real-time, interactive, Web-based network applications. Java applications consisting of small application programs, called *applets*, can be executed by any computer and any operating system anywhere in a network.

The ease of creating Java applets and distributing them from network servers to client PCs and network computers is one of the major reasons for Java's popularity. Applets can be small special-purpose application programs or small modules of larger Java application programs. Java programs are platform independent too—they can run on Windows, UNIX, and Macintosh systems without modification. The latest version of Java is Java2 Enterprise Edition (J2EE), which has become the primary alternative to Microsoft's .Net software development platform for many organizations intent on capitalizing on the business potential of Web-based applications and Web services. Figure 4.22 compares the pros and cons of using J2EE and .Net for software development.

Fidelity Investments: Converting to XML

Fidelity Investments recently completed a retrofit of its corporate data to an XML format in an effort that has already allowed it to eliminate a significant amount of hardware, proprietary databases, and Web and transactional protocols.

Two years ago, Fidelity started looking for a way to simplify communications between consumer Web applications and back-end systems. During the past decade, the Boston-based mutual funds giant had installed a plethora of proprietary messaging formats, remote procedure calls, interfaces, and commercial middleware applications, such as Sybase Enterprise Connect, to support its various e-commerce and e-business iniatives. By using XML as its core communications connection to translate data among its website, its UNIX and Windows NT servers, and its back-office mainframes, Fidelity was able to eliminate a glut of translation protocols and message buffers and 75 of its 85 mid-tier network servers.

Bill Stangel, XML team leader and an enterprise architect at Fidelity, said a common language has also allowed the company's IT managers to redeploy programmers who were tied up writing interfaces to work on more important business functions. The conversion should also improve time to market for applications, he said. "It's simplified our environment significantly," Stangel said. "Instead of us having to invent our own messaging, we can now use XML as the common language" [5].

Web Services

Web services are software components that are based on a framework of Web and object-oriented standards and technologies for using the Web to electronically link the applications of different users and different computing platforms [4]. Thus, Web services can link key business functions for the exchange of data in realtime within the Web-based applications a business might share with its customers, suppliers, and other business partners. For example, Web services would enable the purchasing application of a business to use the Web to quickly check the inventory of a supplier before placing a large order, while the sales application of the supplier could use Web services to automatically check the credit rating of the business with a credit-reporting agency before approving the purchase. Therefore, among both business and IT professionals, the term "Web services" is commonly used to describe the Web-based business and computing functions or "services" accomplished by Web services software technologies and standards.

Figure 4.23 illustrates how Web services works and identifies some of the key technologies and standards that are involved. The XML language is one of the key technologies that enable Web services to make applications work between different computing platforms. Also important are UDDI (Universal Description and Discovery Integration), the "yellow pages" directory of all Web services and how to locate and use them, and SOAP (Simple Object Access Protocol), an XML-based protocol of specifications for connecting applications to the data that they need [4].

Web services promise to be the key software technology for automating the access to data and application functions between a business and its trading partners. As companies increasingly move to doing business over the Web, Web services will become essential for the development of the easy and efficient e-business and e-commerce applications that will be required. The flexibility and interoperability of Web services will also be essential for coping with the fast changing relationships between a company and its business partners that are commonplace in today's dynamic global business environment.

Dollar Rent A Car: Developing Web Services

The term "Web services" is used to describe a collection of technologies—an alphabet soup of Web-based technical standards and communication protocols—such as XML, Universal Description Discovery and Integration (UDDI), and Simple Object Access Protocol (SOAP)—that link applications running on different computer platforms. Unlike present application integration approaches that require custom coding or expensive middleware to link individual applications, Web services aim to expose and link key functions within applications (such as the ability to see the balance in your checking account or to place an order from a factory) to other applications that need them to complete business processes.

FIGURE 4.23

The basic steps in accomplishing a Web services application.

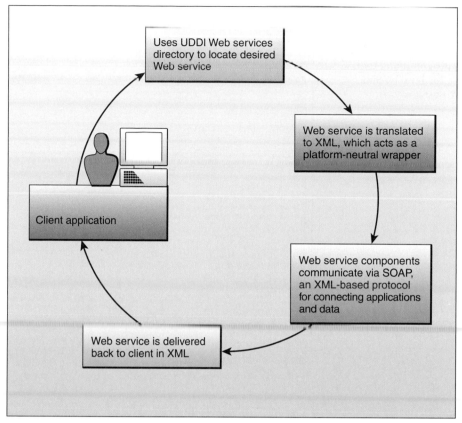

Source: Adapted from Bala Iyer, Jim Freedman, Mark Gaynor, and George Wyner, "Web Services: Enabling Dynamic Business Networks," *Communications of the Association for Information Systems*, Volume 11, 2003, p. 543.

Still confused? A few businesses have already started using Web services technology from BEA Systems, IBM, Microsoft, and others. Seeing it in action is probably the easiest way to understand what all this buzz is about.

Peter Osbourne, group manager of the advanced technology group at Dollar Rent A Car (www.dollar.com) in Tulsa, Oklahoma, is one of the first to successfully implement Web services using Microsoft's ".Net" technology. Osbourne built a system that lets travelers book car reservations with Dollar while buying tickets on the Southwest Airlines website. Instead of struggling to get Dollar's reservation system to share information with other companies' machines, Dollar used Microsoft's technology as an intermediary. Reservations from outside partners are translated into Web services protocols—which are then translated back into formats that Dollar's computers can understand.

The advantage of Web services is that they provide a standard way for Dollar's computers to talk to even more outsiders in the future. Osbourne has already used Microsoft's Web services to build direct machine-to-machine links to a small tour operator and a sprawling travel reservation system. He has also rolled out a wireless website for use on mobile phones and PDAs. Web services protocols are making all of this relatively easy to do, which in turn makes it more convenient for Dollar customers to reserve cars. "The potential for reuse was the real key for me," Osbourne says [3].

Programming Software

A variety of software packages are available to help programmers develop computer programs. For example, *programming language translators* are programs that translate other programs into machine language instruction codes that computers can execute. Other software packages, such as programming language editors, are called *programming tools*

FIGURE 4.24

Using the graphical programming interface of a Java programming tool, Forte for Java, by Sun Microsystems.

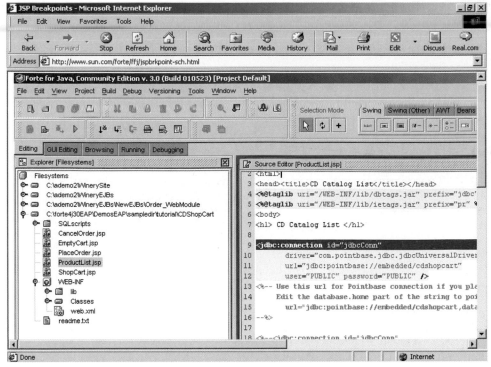

Source: Courtsey of Sun Microsystems.

because they help programmers write programs by providing a variety of program creation and editing capabilities. See Figure 4.24.

Language Translator Programs

Computer programs consist of sets of instructions written in programming languages that must be translated by a **language translator** into the computer's own machine language before they can be processed, or executed, by the CPU. Programming language translator programs (or *language processors*) are known by a variety of names. An **assembler** translates the symbolic instruction codes of programs written in an assembler language into machine language instructions, while a **compiler** translates high-level language statements.

An **interpreter** is a special type of compiler that translates and executes each statement in a program one at a time, instead of first producing a complete machine language program, as compilers and assemblers do. Java is an example of an interpreted language. Thus, the program instructions in Java applets are interpreted and executed *on-the-fly* as the applet is being executed by a client PC.

Programming Tools

Software development and the computer programming process have been enhanced by adding *graphical programming interfaces* and a variety of built-in development capabilities. Language translators have always provided some editing and diagnostic capabilities to identify programming errors or *bugs.* However, most software development programs now include powerful graphics-oriented *programming editors* and *debuggers.* These **programmining tools** help programmers identify and minimize errors while they are programming. Such programming tools provide a computer-aided programming environment. This decreases the drudgery of programming while increasing the efficiency and productivity of software developers. Other programming tools include diagramming packages, code generators, libraries of reusable objects and program code, and prototyping tools. All of these programming tools are an essential part of widely used programming languages like Visual Basic, C++, and Java.

Summary

- **Software.** Computer software consists of two major types of programs: (1) application software that directs the performance of a particular use, or application, of computers to meet the information processing needs of users, and (2) system software that controls and supports the operations of a computer system as it performs various information processing tasks. Refer to Figure 4.2 for an overview of the major types of software.

- **Application Software.** Application software includes a variety of programs that can be segregated into general-purpose and application-specific categories. General-purpose application programs perform common information processing jobs for end users. Examples are word processing, electronic spreadsheet, and presentation graphics programs. Application-specific programs accomplish information processing tasks that support specific business functions or processes, scientific or engineering applications, and other computer applications in society.

- **System Software.** System software can be subdivided into system management programs and system development programs. System management programs manage the hardware, software, network, and data resources of a computer system during its execution of information processing jobs. Examples of system management programs are operating systems, network management programs, database management systems, system utilities, application servers, and performance and security monitors. Network management programs support and manage telecommunications activities and network performance telecommunications networks. Database management systems control

the development, integration, and maintenance of databases. Utilities are programs that perform routine computing functions, such as backing up data or copying files, as part of an operating system or as a separate package. System development programs like language translators and programming editors help IS specialists develop computer programs to support business processes.

- **Operating Systems.** An operating system is an integrated system of programs that supervises the operation of the CPU, controls the input/output storage functions of the computer system, and provides various support services. An operating system performs five basic functions: (1) a user interface for system and network communications with users, (2) resource management for managing the hardware resources of a computer system, (3) file management for managing files of data and programs, (4) task management for managing the tasks a computer must accomplish, and (5) utilities and other functions that provide miscellaneous support services.

- **Programming Languages.** Programming languages are a major category of system software. They require the use of a variety of programming packages to help programmers develop computer programs, and language translator programs to convert programming language instructions into machine language instruction codes. The five major levels of programming languages are machine languages, assembler languages, high-level languages, fourth-generation languages, and object-oriented languages. Object-oriented languages like Java and special-purpose languages like HTML and XML are being widely used for Web-based business applications and services.

Key Terms and Concepts

These are the key terms and concepts of this chapter. The page number of their first explanation is given in parentheses.

1. Application server (122)
2. Application software (104)
3. Application-specific programs (104)
4. Assembler language (123)
5. Desktop publishing (109)
6. Electronic mail (107)
7. Electronic spreadsheet software (109)
8. File management (119)
9. Fourth-generation language (124)
10. General-purpose application programs (104)
11. Graphical user interface (106)
12. Groupware (112)
13. High-level language (124)
14. HTML (125)
15. Instant messaging (108)
16. Integrated package (106)
17. Java (127)
18. Language translator program (130)
19. Machine language (123)
20. Middleware (122)
21. Multitasking (119)
22. Natural language (124)
23. Object-oriented language (124)
24. Operating system (117)
25. Personal information manager (111)
26. Presentation graphics software (110)
27. Programming tools (130)
28. Resource management (118)
29. Software suites (106)
30. System management programs (115)
31. System software (104)
32. Task management (119)
33. User interface (117)
34. Utility programs (121)
35. Virtual memory (118)
36. Web browser (107)
37. Web services (128)
38. Word processing software (109)
39. XML (126)

Review Quiz

Match one of the previous key terms and concepts with one of the brief examples or definitions that follow. Try to find the best fit for answers that seem to fit more than one term or concept. Defend your choices.

_____ 1. Programs that manage and support the operations of computers.

_____ 2. Programs that direct the performance of a specific use of computers.

_____ 3. A system of programs that manages the operations of a computer system.

_____ 4. Managing the processing of tasks in a computer system.

_____ 5. Managing the use of CPU time, primary and secondary storage, telecommunications processors, and input/output devices.

_____ 6. Managing the input/output, storage, and retrieval of files.

_____ 7. The function that provides a means of communication between end users and an operating system.

_____ 8. The use of icons, bars, buttons, and other image displays to help you get things done.

_____ 9. Provides a greater memory capability than a computer's actual memory capacity.

_____ 10. The ability to do several computing tasks concurrently.

_____ 11. System software that includes programs like operating systems, network management systems, and database management systems.

_____ 12. Converts numeric data into graphic displays.

_____ 13. Translates high-level instructions into machine language instructions.

_____ 14. Performs housekeeping chores for a computer system.

_____ 15. A category of application software that performs common information processing tasks for end users.

_____ 16. Software available for the specific applications of end users in business, science, and other fields.

_____ 17. Helps you surf the Web.

_____ 18. Use your networked computer to send and receive messages.

_____ 19. Creates and displays a worksheet for analysis.

_____ 20. Allows you to create and edit documents.

_____ 21. You can produce your own brochures and newsletters.

_____ 22. Helps you keep track of appointments and tasks.

_____ 23. A program that performs several general-purpose applications.

_____ 24. A combination of individual general-purpose application packages that work easily together.

_____ 25. Software to support the collaboration of teams and workgroups.

_____ 26. Uses instructions in the form of coded strings of ones and zeros.

_____ 27. Uses instructions consisting of symbols representing operation codes and storage locations.

_____ 28. Uses instructions in the form of brief statements or the standard notation of mathematics.

_____ 29. Might take the form of query languages and report generators.

_____ 30. Languages that tie together data and the actions that will be performed upon the data.

_____ 31. As easy to use as one's native tongue.

_____ 32. Includes programming editors, debuggers, and code generators.

_____ 33. Produces hyperlinked multimedia documents for the Web.

_____ 34. A Web document content description language.

_____ 35. A popular object-oriented language for Web-based applications.

_____ 36. Middleware that helps Web-based application programs run faster and more efficiently.

_____ 37. Software that helps diverse applications work together.

_____ 38. Enables you to communicate and collaborate in real time with the online associates in your workgroup.

_____ 39. Links business functions within applications for the exchange of data between companies via the Web.

Discussion Questions

1. What major trends are occurring in software? What capabilities do you expect to see in future software packages?

2. How do the different roles of system software and application software affect you as a business end user? How do you see this changing in the future?

3. Refer to the Real World Case on Intuit and Lone Star Doughnuts in the chapter. What does the experience of Lone Star Doughnuts reveal about the nature of the small business software market, and the challenges faced by Microsoft, SAP, and Oracle in competing in that market with Intuit? How should that shape their software product and marketing strategies?

4. Why is an operating system necessary? That is, why can't an end user just load an application program in a computer and start computing?

5. Should a Web browser be integrated into an operating system? Why or why not?

6. Refer to the Real World Case on Wells Fargo and Others in the chapter. Use Google and other search engines to research the topic of Web services, and then visit the Web services links of BEA, IBM, and Microsoft provided at the end of that case. What can be done to improve the business use of Web services today?

7. Are software suites, Web browsers, and groupware merging together? What are the implications for a business and its end users?

8. How are HTML, XML, and Java affecting business applications on the Web?

9. Do you think Linux will surpass other operating systems for network and Web servers? Why or why not?

10. Which application software packages are the most important for a business end user to know how to use? Explain the reasons for your choices.

Analysis Exercises

Complete the following exercises as individual or group projects that apply chapter concepts to real world business situations.

1. **ABC Department Stores: Software Selection**
ABC Department Stores would like to acquire software to do the following tasks. Identify what software packages they need.

   a. Surf the Web and their intranets and extranets.
   b. Send messages to each other's computer workstations.
   c. Help employees work together in teams.
   d. Use a group of productivity packages that work together easily.
   e. Help sales reps keep track of meetings and sales calls.
   f. Type correspondence and reports.
   g. Analyze rows and columns of sales figures.
   h. Develop a variety of graphical presentations.

2. **Evaluating Software Packages**
Which of the software packages mentioned in this chapter have you used?

   a. Briefly describe the advantages and disadvantages of one of these packages.
   b. How would such a package help you in a present or future job situation?
   c. How would you improve the package you used?
   d. Search the Internet for a comparison between the software package with which you are most familiar

and its competitors. What were the comparative strengths and weaknesses of your package?

3. **Tracking Project Work at AAA Systems**
You are responsible for managing information systems development projects at AAA Systems. To better track progress in completing projects you have decided to maintain a simple database table to track the time your employees spend on various tasks and the projects with which they are associated. It will also allow you to keep track of employees' billable hours each week. The table below provides a sample data set.

   a. Build a database table to store the data shown and enter the records as a set of sample data.
   b. Create a query that will list the hours worked for all workers who worked more than 40 hours during production week 20.
   c. Create a report grouped by project that will show the number of hours devoted to each task on the project and the total number of hours devoted to each project as well as a ground total of hours worked.
   d. Create a report grouped by employee that will show their hours worked on each task and total hours worked. The user should be able to select a production week and have data for just that week presented.

Project_Name	Task_Name	Employee_ID	Production_Week	Hours Worked
Fin-Goods-Inv	App. Devel.	456		
Fin-Goods-Inv	DB Design	345		20
Fin-Goods-Inv	UI Design	234		16
HR	Analysis	234		24
HR	Analysis	456		48
HR	UI Design	123		8
HR	UI Design	123		40
HR	UI Design	234		32
Shipmt-Tracking	DB Design	345		24
Shipmt-Tracking	DB Design	345		16
Shipmt-Tracking	DB Development	345		20
Shipmt-Tracking	UI Design	123		32
Shipmt-Tracking	UI Design	234		24

4. Matching Training to Software Use

You have responsibility for managing software training for Sales, Accounting, and Operations Department workers in your organization. You have surveyed the workers to get a feel for the amounts of time spent using various packages and the results are shown below. The values shown are the total number of workers in each department and the total weekly hours the department's workers spend using each software package. You have been asked to prepare a spreadsheet summarizing this data and comparing the use of the various packages across departments.

Department	Employees	Spreadsheet	Database	Presentations
Sales	225	410	1100	650
Operations	75	710	520	405
Accounting	30	310	405	50

a. Create a spreadsheet illustrating each application's average use per department. To do this, you will first enter the data shown below. Then compute the average weekly spreadsheet use by dividing spreadsheet hours by the number of Sales workers. Do this for each department. Repeat these three calculations for both database and presentation use. Round results to the nearest 1/100th.

b. Create a three-dimensional bar graph illustrating the averages by department and software package.

c. A committee has been formed to plan software training classes at your company. Prepare a slide presentation with four slides illustrating your findings. The first slide should serve as an introduction to the data. The second slide should contain a copy of the original data table (without the averages). The third slide should contain a copy of the three-dimensional bar graph from the previous answer. The fourth slide should contain your conclusions regarding key applications per department. Use professional labels, formatting, and backgrounds.

REAL WORLD CASE 3

Merrill Lynch and Others: The Growth of Linux in Business

Over the past two years Linux has spread like wild-fire through corporate data centers. Companies once dependent on expensive proprietary systems from Sun, IBM, or Hewlett-Packard have replaced them with dirt-cheap Dell or no-name servers that are Intel-powered and loaded with the Linux operating system. Linux now runs almost 15 percent of all servers and is growing at about 23 percent a year. And even mainframe systems have joined in, with IBM estimating that over 10 percent of its mainframe sales are for running Linux applications.

Though PC users haven't switched to Linux—less than 1 percent of all computers run Linux—a 2002 survey by *CIO* magazine found that almost 30 percent of chief technologists were considering moving their companies' PCs to a Linux PC operating system like Lindows. Wal-Mart, which began selling Lindows-ready PCs on its website in September 2002, had such success with that offering that by Christmas it was having trouble meeting demand. Almost every major PC electronics maker, from HP in printers to Epson in scanners, is making sure it has Linux-compatible offerings. And Sun has poured millions of dollars into its Star Office software suite, which gives Linux users programs that work like—and more important, are compatible with—Microsoft PowerPoint, Word, and Excel.

Backed by technology titans such as Intel, IBM, Hewlett-Packard, and Dell, Linux is just now going mainstream. From DaimlerChrysler to Tommy Hilfiger— not to mention just about every major brokerage on Wall Street—Linux is gaining ground. Coming from near zero three years ago, Linux grabbed 13.7 percent of the $50.9 billion market for server computers in 2002. That figure is expected to jump to 25.2 percent in 2006, putting Linux in the No. 2 position, according to market researcher IDC. And get this: Starting in 2003, No. 1 Microsoft's 59.9 percent share in the server market will reverse its long climb and slowly slide backwards. Even the surprise but shaky assault on Linux by SCO in its suit of IBM is not expected to slow the steady growth of Linux.

Meanwhile, Linux is finding its way into countless consumer-electronics gizmos, including Sony PlayStation video-game consoles and TiVo TV-program recorders. "Has Linux come of age? The answer is absolutely, positively, unequivocally yes," says Steven A. Mills, group executive for IBM Software.

How did Linux make the jump into the mainstream? A trio of powerful forces converged. First, credit the sagging economy. Corporations under intense pressure to reduce their computing bills began casting about for low-cost alternatives. Second, Intel Corp., the dominant maker of processors for PCs, loosened its tight links with Microsoft and started making chips for Linux; at the same time a resurgent IBM made a $1 billion investment in Linux compatibility across its entire product line. This made it possible for corporations to get all the computing power they wanted at a fraction of the price. The third ingredient was widespread resentment of Microsoft

and fear that the company was on the verge of gaining a stranglehold on corporate customers. "I always want to have the right competitive dynamics. That's why we focus on Linux. Riding that wave will give us choices going forward," says John A. McKinley Jr., executive vice-president for global technology and services at Merrill Lynch & Co., which runs some key securities trading applications on Linux.

Using open-source software like Linux is a no-brainer for many companies. It's stable and can be fixed easily if bugs appear, and you can't beat the price. But some companies and government organizations are taking their commitment to open source a step further by actively participating in the open-source community that develops Linux. When their developers write patches, modifications or new implementations of open-source software for in-house use, these organizations are releasing that new code back to the open-source community, thereby assisting in the software's ongoing development.

What's the payoff? It makes for better software. "If we find a bug or a problem, we're interested in fixing that problem. We're also interested in not fixing it again in the next version," explains Robert M. Lefkowitz, director of open-source strategy at Merrill Lynch & Co. in New York.

This is why Merrill Lynch sent the fixes it made to open-source software during one of its projects back to the open-source community. "The way a typical open-source project works is that there is a core team in the open-source community with direct access to modifying the code on its central website," Lefkowitz says. "People who want to contribute to that community submit their code, which is looked at by a core team and integrated if found appropriate."

For all contributions, Lefkowitz emphasizes the importance of creating a corporate policy with help from the departments that could be affected by open-source involvement. At Merrill Lynch, an eight-member Open-Source Review Board determines when contributing is appropriate.

Case Study Questions

1. Should businesses continue to switch to the Linux operating system on servers and mainframes? Why or why not?

2. Should business and consumer PC users switch to Linux PC operating systems like Lindows and software suites like Sun's StarOffice? Why or why not?

3. Should the IT departments of companies like Merrill Lynch contribute their software improvements to the open-source community for products like Linux? Explain your reasoning.

Source: Adapted from Fred Vogelstein, "Bringing Linux to the Masses," *Fortune*, February 3, 2003, pp. 98–100; Jay Greene, "The Linux Uprising," *Business Week*, March 3, 2003, pp. 78–86; and Minda Zetlin, "In the Linux Loop," *Computerworld*, April 7, 2003, pp. 37–38.

REAL WORLD CASE 4

Mark's Work Wearhouse and Others: Using Java in Business

Growing numbers of retailers and other companies are deploying Java-based point-of-sale (POS) systems and e-commerce portals. Many said they like the fact that the software can run on any hardware or operating system and also noted that they're finding the Java code easy to modify as their needs expand.

Mark's Work Wearhouse. Robin Lynas, CIO at Mark's Work Wearhouse Ltd., a Calgary, Alberta-based chain found himself peppered with questions from fellow retailers at the National Retail Federation Conference & Expo in New York recently. The Canadian retailer has rolled out its Java POS system from Retek Inc. to new Linux-based IBM terminals at 70 stores, with the rollout to the remaining 240 stores to be completed by the middle of 2003.

"My guys said, 'Do we really want to pay Microsoft licensing fees? Why don't you go to open systems?'" Lynas recalled. Once they proved that the POS system would run on Linux, he was sold. Mark's Work Wearhouse claims to have lowered store opening costs by 30 percent and maintenance costs by 50 percent, in part because it no longer needs in-store servers. The registers connect directly via frame relay to central servers at the home office, thanks in part to Java's networking capabilities, according to Retek Chief Technology Officer John Gray.

Another advantage that Mark's Work Wearhouse has found is the ease with which developers can bolt on new applications that connect to the POS system. Those include website, time sheet, business account, and Web reporting applications, Lynas said.

"Retek gives you the Java source code for their POS application," Lynas said. "You just take the objects they've got and extend them and write your new functionality."

Home Depot. Atlanta-based The Home Depot Inc., whose IT shop is heavily invested in Java, settled on a Java POS system so it would be able to migrate code between clients and servers running disparate operating systems, said Ray Alien, director of IT. The POS terminals run Windows 2000, and the servers run different flavors of Unix from Hewlett-Packard Co. and IBM, Alien noted. "POS applications typically live for 10 to 12 years, and they're very tightly integrated with whatever the retailer chooses to provide," he said. "So you're trying to make the best guesses for what might be going on five to six years down the road." Alien said changes can be made "much easier and faster with a component-based solution and object-oriented language like Java."

Jerry Rightmer, CTO at 360Commerce, Home Depot's Java POS system provider, said building a POS system in Java was "a fairly risky decision" in 1997 when his company began developing products. But, "The language is easier to work with than previous generations of languages, it's more productive than C or C++, and it has all the benefits of object-oriented languages without some of the traps and pitfalls of C++ in particular," he said. "Plus, it has an extremely rich set of application programming interfaces that has made it easy for us to integrate the POS software with middleware and database systems."

GE Power Systems. GE Power Systems used Java to develop an e-commerce Web portal called PartsEdge as an online resource that let GE Power's customers purchase parts from the company while giving them a single interface to its many business units and partners. One of the biggest challenges the Schenectady, New York-based company faced when building the portal was finding a way to share data across a variety of legacy systems, enterprise resource planning (ERP) software, and Web-based applications. The company, a subsidiary of General Electric Co., "had systems that had been built in silos that were not communicating" with one another, recalls Alan Boehme, former e-technology CIO at GE Power and now CIO at Best Software Inc. "The objective was to provide a seamless method for the selection of parts and service, with information being able to come into the system through multiple means, such as Web browsers, EDI [electronic data interchange], XML exchanges, or an ERP system," he says.

To address the issue, GE Power decided to build PartsEdge as a Web services application using Java 2 Enterprise Edition (J2EE). The J2EE framework lets GE developers use Java and XML to integrate the various applications that form the core of the PartsEdge Web portal. PartsEdge is the largest of sixty or so applications that are supported by GE's J2EE-based application development framework. The benefits of this Java platform include increased portability of applications across multiple operating systems, application servers and hardware; reusable application and legacy system business logic; a common presentation layer for business systems; and reduced costs and cycle times for application development and upgrades.

Case Study Questions

1. What are the benefits of Java as a programming language for retail POS applications compared to other programming languages?

2. What are the benefits of Java for the development of e-commerce portals for customers and suppliers like PartsEdge?

3. Why do companies like Mark's Work Wearhouse frequently team Java with the Linux operating system?

Source: Adapted from Carol Sliwa, "Retailers Explore Java POS Systems," *Computerworld*, January 27, 2003, p. 7; and Jaikumar Vijayan, "Application Framework Allows Easy Portal Access," *Computerworld*, February 24, 2003, p. 51.

CHAPTER 5

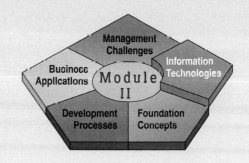

DATA RESOURCE MANAGEMENT

Chapter Highlights

Section I
Managing Data Resources

Data Resource Management

Real World Case: Argosy Gaming Co.: Challenges in Building a Data Warehouse

Foundation Data Concepts

Types of Databases

Data Warehouses and Data Mining

Traditional File Processing

The Database Management Approach

Section II
Technical Foundations of Database Management

Database Management

Real World Case: Owens & Minor and Vivendi Universal Games: Protecting Strategic Data Resources

Database Structures

Database Development

Real World Case: Henry Schein Inc.: The Business Value of a Data Warehouse

Real World Case: Anadarko Petroleum and Prudential Financial: Challenges of Data Resource Management

Learning Objectives

After reading and studying this chapter, you should be able to:

1. Explain the business value of implementing data resource management processes and technologies in an organization.

2. Outline the advantages of a database management approach to managing the data resources of a business, compared to a file processing approach.

3. Explain how database management software helps business professionals and supports the operations and management of a business.

4. Provide examples to illustrate each of the following concepts:

   a. Major types of databases.

   b. Data warehouses and data mining.

   c. Logical data elements.

   d. Fundamental database structures.

   e. Database development.

Managing Data Resources

Data Resource Management

Data are a vital organizational resource that need to be managed like other important business assets. Today's business enterprises cannot survive or succeed without quality data about their internal operations and external environment.

With each online mouse click, either a fresh bit of data is created or already-stored data are retrieved from all those business websites. All that's on top of the heavy demand for industrial-strength data storage already in use by scores of big corporations. What's driving the growth is a crushing imperative for corporations to analyze every bit of information they can extract from their huge data warehouses for competitive advantage. That has turned the data storage and management function into a key strategic role of the information age [9].

That's why organizations and their managers need to practice **data resource management,** a managerial activity that applies information systems technologies like *database management, data warehousing,* and other data management tools to the task of managing an organization's data resources to meet the information needs of their business stakeholders. This chapter will show you the managerial implications of using data resource management technologies and methods to manage an organization's data assets to meet business information requirements.

Analyzing Argosy Gaming Co.

Read the Real World Case on Argosy Gaming Co. on the next page. We can learn a lot from this case about the challenges of developing data warehouses to support business decision making. See Figure 5.1.

Argosy Gaming decided to build a data warehouse to consolidate all of their data about customers and thus give their management a unified view of their operations and customer relationships. As part of the data warehouse development process, an extract, transform, and load (ETL) software tool was acquired to access company

FIGURE 5.1

Data warehousing analyst Jason Fortenberry led the development process for building a data warehouse of customer data for Argosy Gaming Co.

Source: Marc Berlow

REAL WORLD CASE 1

Argosy Gaming Co.: Challenges in Building a Data Warehouse

When you've got half a dozen riverboat gambling operations, it's important that everyone plays by the same rules. Argosy Gaming Co. (www.argosycasinos.com), with headquarters in Alton, Illinois, and a fleet of six Mississippi riverboat casinos, had decided that bringing all customer data together would enhance management's view of operations and potentially help strengthen customer relationships. To accomplish those goals, though, the company needed to access a variety of databases and develop an extract, transform, and load (ETL) system to help construct and maintain a central data warehouse.

Jason Fortenberry, a data-warehousing analyst, came aboard at Argosy just as the company's data warehouse project started in 2001. His job was made easier, he says, by the adoption of Hummingbird Ltd.'s Genio ETL software tool, which helped bridge systems and automate processes. But like others going through such projects, he learned the hard way that preparing for the ETL process is just as important as having the right software.

The riverboats each had unique and incompatible ways of defining a host of operational activities and customer characteristics—in essence, the floating casinos were each playing the same game but with different rules. But those problems remained hidden until reports from the company's data warehouse began to turn up inconsistent or troubling data. That's when Fortenberry and his staff discovered conflicting definitions for a wide range of data types—problems he wishes he had identified much earlier. Fortenberry's troubles—and his successes—are typical of ETL, the complex and often expensive prelude to data warehouse success.

ETL is often problematic because of its inherent complexity and underlying business challenges, such as making sure you plan adequately and have quality data to process. Analysts, users, and even vendors say all bets are off if you don't have a clear understanding of your data resources and what you want to achieve with them. Then there are choices, like whether to go for a centralized architecture—the simplest and most common configuration—or a distributed system, with ETL processing spread across various software tools, system utilities, and target databases, which is sometimes a necessity in larger, more complicated data warehouses. Even if you navigate those waters successfully, you still need to ensure that the ETL foundation you build for your data warehouse can meet growing data streams and future information demands.

As the term implies, ETL involves extracting data from various sources, transforming it, (usually the trickiest part), and loading it into the data warehouse. A transformation could be as simple as reordering the fields of a record from a source system. But, as Philip Russom, a Giga Information Group analyst explains, a data warehouse often contains data values and data structures that never existed in a source system. Since many analytical questions a business user would ask of a data warehouse can be answered only with calculated values (like averages, rankings or metrics), the ETL tool must calculate these from various data sources and load them into the warehouse. Similarly, notes Russom, a data warehouse typically contains "time-series" data. The average operational application keeps track of the current state of a value such as a bank account balance. It's the job of the ETL tool to regularly add new states of a value to the series.

For his yearlong ETL project, Argosy's Fortenberry says Hummingbird's Genio Suite, a data integration and ETL tool, quickly became the project's "central nervous system," coordinating the process for extracting source data and loading the warehouse.

But for Argosy, getting all that data into the warehouse didn't produce immediate usable and dependable results. "The lesson was that people thought that they were talking about the same thing, but they actually were not," says Fortenberry. For example, he explains, riverboats calculated visits differently. One riverboat casino would credit a customer with a visit only if he actually played at a slot machine or table. Another had an expanded definition and credited customers with visits when they redeemed coupons, even if they didn't play. So identical customer activity might have one riverboat reporting 4 player visits and another reporting 10. "This type of discovery was repeated for everything from defining what a 'player' is to calculating a player's profitability," says Fortenberry.

IT played a lead role in identifying problems and helping to hammer out a consensus among the business units about how to define and use many categories of data, he says. Now, the data warehouse is running smoothly and producing dependable results for business analysis and management reporting, so the number of problem-resolution meetings has dropped dramatically. Still, Fortenberry reckons that three-quarters of the meetings he attends nowadays have a business focus. "For our part, we now know better what questions to ask business users as we continue with the data warehouse development process," he says.

Case Study Questions

1. What is the business value of a data warehouse? Use Argosy Gaming as an example.

2. Why did Argosy use an ETL software tool? What benefits and problems arose? How were they solved?

3. What are some of the major responsibilities that business professionals and managers have in data warehouse development? Use Argosy Gaming as an example.

databases, extract relevant customer data, transform it into common formats, and load it into the new data warehouse. One of the major problems Argosy discovered in the process was that the riverboat casinos were reporting and submitting data about common business transactions and customer activities using different views and definitions of such events, which were then processed by various business systems and stored in company databases. This resulted in poor quality results for management reports based on the data warehouse. So Argosy's IT department led a series of problem resolution meetings in which the various riverboat casinos and other business units worked out agreements on data definitions for all commonly reported business events and customer characteristics. As a result, the data warehouse is operational and producing dependable results for business analysis and management reporting.

Foundation Data Concepts

Before we go any further, let's discuss some fundamental concepts about how data are organized in information systems. A conceptual framework of several levels of data has been devised that differentiates between different groupings, or elements, of data. Thus, data may be logically organized into characters, fields, records, files, and databases, just as writing can be organized in letters, words, sentences, paragraphs, and documents. Examples of these logical data elements are shown in Figure 5.2.

Character

The most basic logical data element is the **character,** which consists of a single alphabetic, numeric, or other symbol. One might argue that the bit or byte is a more elementary data element, but remember that those terms refer to the physical storage elements provided by the computer hardware, discussed in Chapter 3. From a user's point of view (that is, from a *logical* as opposed to a physical or hardware view of data), a character is the most basic element of data that can be observed and manipulated.

Field

The next higher level of data is the **field,** or data item. A field consists of a grouping of related characters. For example, the grouping of alphabetic characters in a person's name may form a name field, (or typically, last name, first name, and middle initial fields) and the grouping of numbers in a sales amount forms a sales amount field. Specifically, a data field represents an **attribute** (a characteristic or quality) of some **entity** (object, person, place, or event). For example, an employee's salary is an attribute that is a typical data field used to describe an entity who is an employee of a business.

FIGURE 5.2

Examples of the logical data elements in information systems. Note especially the examples of how data fields, records, files, and databases are related.

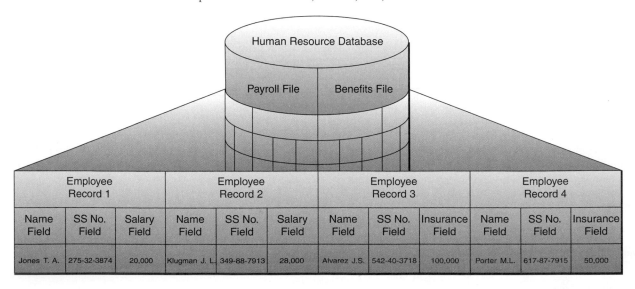

Employee Record 1			Employee Record 2			Employee Record 3			Employee Record 4		
Name Field	SS No. Field	Salary Field	Name Field	SS No. Field	Salary Field	Name Field	SS No. Field	Insurance Field	Name Field	SS No. Field	Insurance Field
Jones T. A.	275-32-3874	20,000	Klugman J. L.	349-88-7913	28,000	Alvarez J.S.	542-40-3718	100,000	Porter M.L.	617-87-7915	50,000

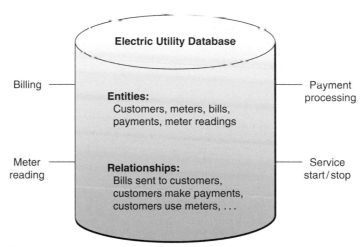

Source: Adapted from Michael V. Mannino, *Database Application Development and Design* (Burr Ridge, IL: McGraw-Hill/Irwin, 2001), p. 6.

Record

Related fields of data are grouped to form a **record**. Thus, a record represents a collection of *attributes* that describe an *entity*. An example is the payroll record for a person, which consists of data fields describing attributes such as the person's name, Social Security number, and rate of pay. *Fixed-length* records contain a fixed number of fixed-length data fields. *Variable-length* records contain a variable number of fields and field lengths.

File

A group of related records is a data **file,** or *table*. Thus, an employee file would contain the records of the employees of a firm. Files are frequently classified by the application for which they are primarily used, such as a *payroll file* or an *inventory file*, or the type of data they contain, such as a *document file* or a *graphical image* file. Files are also classified by their permanence, for example, a payroll *master file* versus a payroll *weekly transaction file*. A transaction file, therefore, would contain records of all transactions occurring during a period and might be used periodically to update the permanent records contained in a master file. A *history file* is an obsolete transaction or master file retained for backup purposes or for long-term historical storage called *archival storage*.

Database

A **database** is an integrated collection of logically related data elements. A database consolidates records previously stored in separate files into a common pool of data elements that provides data for many applications. The data stored in a database are independent of the application programs using them and of the type of storage devices on which they are stored.

Thus, databases contain data elements describing entities and relationships among entities. For example, Figure 5.3 outlines some of the entities and relationships in a database for an electric utility. Also shown are some of the business applications (billing, payment processing) that depend on access to the data elements in the database.

Types of Databases

Continuing developments in information technology and its business applications have resulted in the evolution of several major types of databases. Figure 5.4 illustrates several major conceptual categories of databases that may be found in many organizations. Let's take a brief look at some of them now.

Operational Databases

Operational databases store detailed data needed to support the business processes and operations of a company. They are also called *subject area databases* (SADB), *transaction databases*, and *production databases*. Examples are a customer database, human resource database, inventory database, and other databases containing data generated by business operations. For example, a human resource database like that shown in

FIGURE 5.4 Examples of some of the major types of databases used by organizations and end users.

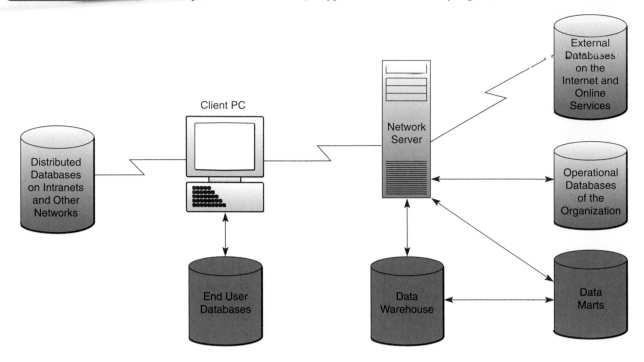

Figure 5.2 would include data identifying each employee and their time worked, compensation, benefits, performance appraisals, training and development status, and other related human resource data. Figure 5.5 illustrates some of the common operational databases that can be created and managed for a small business using Microsoft Access database management software.

Distributed Databases

Many organizations replicate and distribute copies or parts of databases to network servers at a variety of sites. These **distributed databases** can reside on network servers on the World Wide Web, on corporate intranets or extranets, or on other company

FIGURE 5.5

Examples of operational databases that can be created and managed for a small business by microcomputer database management software like Microsoft Access.

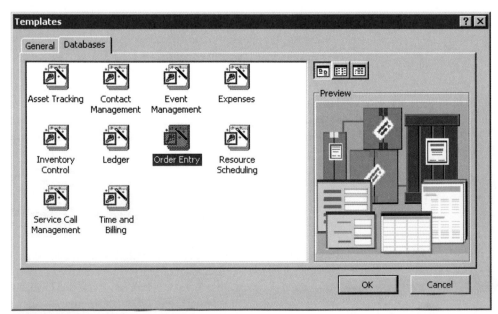

Source: Courtesy of Microsoft Corporation

FIGURE 5.6   The components of a Web-based information system include Web browsers, servers, and hypermedia databases.

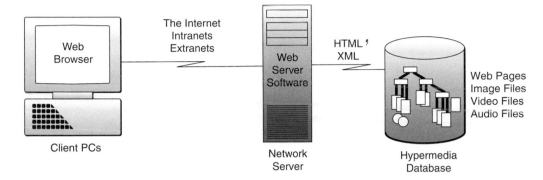

networks. Distributed databases may be copies of operational or analytical databases, hypermedia or discussion databases, or any other type of database. Replication and distribution of databases are done to improve database performance at end user worksites. Ensuring that the data in an organization's distributed databases are consistently and concurrently updated is a major challenge of distributed database management.

External Databases

Access to a wealth of information from **external databases** is available for a fee from commercial online services, and with or without charge from many sources on the World Wide Web. Websites provide an endless variety of hyperlinked pages of multimedia documents in *hypermedia databases* for you to access. Data are available in the form of statistics on economic and demographic activity from *statistical* data banks. Or you can view or download abstracts or complete copies of hundreds of newspapers, magazines, newsletters, research papers, and other published material and other periodicals from *bibliographic* and *full text* databases.

Hypermedia Databases

The rapid growth of websites on the Internet and corporate intranets and extranets has dramatically increased the use of databases of hypertext and hypermedia documents. A website stores such information in a **hypermedia database** consisting of hyperlinked pages of multimedia (text, graphic, and photographic images, video clips, audio segments, and so on). That is, from a database management point of view, the set of interconnected multimedia pages at a website is a database of interrelated hypermedia page elements, rather than interrelated data records [3].

Figure 5.6 shows how you might use a Web browser on your client PC to connect with a Web network server. This server runs Web server software to access and transfer the Web pages you request. The website illustrated in Figure 5.6 uses a hypermedia database consisting of Web page content described by HTML (Hypertext Markup Language) code or XML (Extended Markup Language) labels, image files, video files, and audio. The Web server software acts as a database management system to manage the transfer of hypermedia files for downloading by the multimedia plug-ins of your Web browser.

Data Warehouses and Data Mining

A **data warehouse** stores data that have been extracted from the various operational, external, and other databases of an organization. It is a central source of the data that have been cleaned, transformed, and cataloged so they can be used by managers and other business professionals for data mining, online analytical processing, and other forms of business analysis, market research, and decision support. Data warehouses may be subdivided into **data marts,** which hold subsets of data from the warehouse that focus on specific aspects of a company, such as a department or a business process.

FIGURE 5.7 The components of a complete data warehouse system.

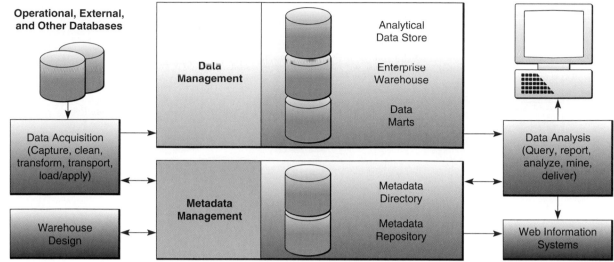

Source: Adapted courtesy of Hewlett-Packard.

Figure 5.7 illustrates the components of a complete data warehouse system. Notice how data from various operational and external databases are captured, cleaned, and transformed into data that can be better used for analysis. This acquisition process might include activities like consolidating data from several sources, filtering out unwanted data, correcting incorrect data, converting data to new data elements, and aggregating data into new data subsets.

This data is then stored in the enterprise data warehouse, from where it can be moved into data marts or to an *analytical data store* that holds data in a more useful form for certain types of analysis. *Metadata* (data that defines the data in the data warehouse) is stored in a metadata repository and cataloged by a metadata directory. Finally, a variety of analytical software tools can be provided to query, report, mine, and analyze the data for delivery via Internet and intranet Web systems to business end users. See Figure 5.8.

Shell Exploration: The Business Value of a Data Warehouse	Redundant data, wrong data, missing data, miscoded data. Every company has some of each, probably residing in IT nooks that don't communicate much. It's not a new problem, but these days the jumble becomes very apparent during high-profile projects, such as installing enterprise resource planning (ERP) or supply chain management (SCM) software. That's when companies often focus on the business processes and not on the form and congruity of the resulting data, says John Hagerty, an analyst at AMR Research Inc. in Boston. When a company does that, its IT department has to step back to cleanse, reconcile, and integrate data from various databases around the company into a data warehouse.

Shell Exploration and Production is in the throes of such a project. Early last year, the fuel company wanted to combine data from its ERP financial applications with data from its mishmash of volumetric systems, which process information on how much gas and oil the company finds and collects. "Every different system has its own internal sets of codes," explains Steve Mutch, data warehouse team leader at Shell Exploration in Aberdeen, Scotland. "Going back and cleansing and integrating the data in those host systems wasn't an option." It would have taken too much time and been too expensive, he says. Instead, Mutch found a tool from Kalido Ltd. in London that analyzes and maps the data from various systems and then combines it

A data warehouse and its data mart subsets hold data that has been extracted from various operational databases for business analysis, market research, decision support, and data mining applications.

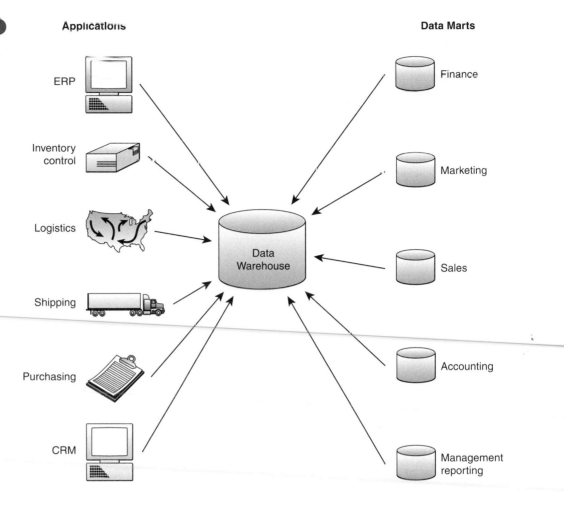

Applications

ERP

Inventory control

Logistics

Shipping

Purchasing

CRM

Data Warehouse

Data Marts

Finance

Marketing

Sales

Accounting

Management reporting

into one data warehouse. After nearly seven months of data analysis and mapping work, 27 data sources now come together in one 450GB warehouse, Mutch says.

Corporate politics weren't too bad because no single business unit lost control of its data, he says. And now they all contribute to a greater understanding of the information for the company as a whole. "Once the concept was proved, we had pressure from the top executives to integrate data from other applications as well," he says. "They could see for themselves what information they could now get from a data warehouse, and how powerful it is" [12].

Data Mining

Data mining is a major use of data warehouse databases. In data mining, the data in a data warehouse are analyzed to reveal hidden patterns and trends in historical business activity. This can be used to help managers make decisions about strategic changes in business operations to gain competitive advantages in the marketplace [2]. See Figure 5.9.

Data mining can discover new correlations, patterns, and trends in vast amounts of business data (frequently several terabytes of data), stored in data warehouses. Data mining software uses advanced pattern recognition algorithms, as well as a variety of mathematical and statistical techniques to sift through mountains of data to extract previously unknown strategic business information. For example, many companies use data mining to:

- Perform "market-basket analysis" to identify new product bundles.
- Find root causes to quality or manufacturing problems.

FIGURE 5.9 How data mining extracts business knowledge from a data warehouse.

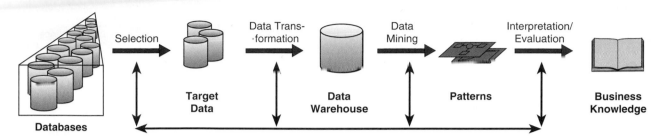

- Prevent customer attrition and acquire new customers.
- Cross-sell to existing customers.
- Profile customers with more accuracy [8].

We will discuss data mining, further, as well as online analytical processing (OLAP), and other technologies that analyze the data in databases and data warehouses to provide vital support for business decisions in Chapter 9. Let's look at a real world example.

Bank of America: Benefits of Data Mining	The Bank of America (BofA) is using a data warehouse and data mining software to develop more accuracy in marketing and pricing financial products, such as home equity loans. BofA's data warehouse is so large—for some customers, there are 300 data points—that traditional analytic approaches are overwhelmed. For each market, BofA can offer a variety of tailored product packages by adjusting fees, interest rates, and features. The result is a staggering number of potential strategies for reaching profitable customers. Sifting through the vast number of combinations requires the ability to identify very fine opportunity segments. Data extracted from the data warehouse were analyzed by data mining software to discover hidden patterns. For example, data mining discovered that a certain set of customers were 15 times more likely to purchase a high-margin lending product. The bank also wanted to determine the sequence of events leading to purchasing. They fed the parameters to the Discovery data mining software from HYPERparallel and built a model for finding other customers. This model proved to be so accurate that it discovered people already in the process of applying and being approved for the lending product. Using this profile, a final list of quality prospects for solicitation was prepared. The resulting direct marketing response rates have dramatically exceeded past results [11].

Traditional File Processing

How would you feel if you were an executive of a company and were told that some information you wanted about your employees was too difficult and too costly to obtain? Suppose the vice president of information services gave you the following reasons:

- The information you want is in several different files, each organized in a different way.
- Each file has been organized to be used by a different application program, none of which produces the information you want in the form you need.
- No application program is available to help get the information you want from these files.

That's how end users can be frustrated when an organization relies on **file processing** systems in which data are organized, stored, and processed in independent files of data records. In the traditional file processing approach that was used in business data processing for many years, each business application was designed to use one or more specialized data files containing only specific types of data records. For example, a bank's checking account processing application was designed to access and

Examples of file processing systems in banking. Note the use of separate computer programs and independent data files in a file processing approach to the savings, installment loan, and checking account applications.

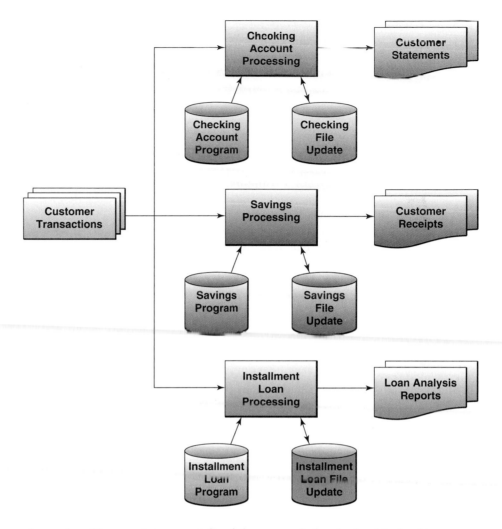

update a data file containing specialized data records for the bank's checking account customers. Similarly, the bank's installment loan processing application needed to access and update a specialized data file containing data records about the bank's installment loan customers. See Figure 5.10.

Problems of File Processing

The file processing approach finally became too cumbersome, costly, and inflexible to supply the information needed to manage modern business, and as we shall soon see, was replaced by the *database management approach*. File processing systems had the following major problems:

Data Redundancy. Independent data files included a lot of duplicated data; the same data (such as a customer's name and address) was recorded and stored in several files. This *data redundancy* caused problems when data had to be updated, since separate *file maintenance* programs had to be developed and coordinated to ensure that each file was properly updated. Of course, this proved difficult in practice, so a lot of inconsistency occurred among data stored in separate files.

Lack of Data Integration. Having data in independent files made it difficult to provide end users with information for ad hoc requests that required accessing data stored in several different files. Special computer programs had to be written to retrieve data from each independent file. This was so difficult, time-consuming, and costly for some organizations that it was impossible to provide end users or management with such information. If necessary, end users had to manually extract the required information from the various reports produced by each separate application and prepare customized reports for management.

Data Dependence. In file processing systems, major components of a system—the organization of files, their physical locations on storage hardware, and the application software used to access those files—depended on one another in significant ways. For example, application programs typically contained references to the specific *format* of the data stored in the files they used. Thus, changes in the format and structure of data and records in a file required that changes be made to all of the programs that used that file. This *program maintenance* effort was a major burden of file processing systems. It proved difficult to do properly, and it resulted in a lot of inconsistency in the data files.

Other Problems. In file processing systems, it was easy for data elements such as stock numbers and customer addresses to be defined differently by different end users and applications. This caused serious inconsistency problems in the development of programs to access such data. In addition, the *integrity* (i.e., the accuracy and completeness) of the data was suspect because there was no control over their use and maintenance by authorized end users. Thus, a lack of standards caused major problems in application program development and maintenance, and in the security and integrity of the data files needed by the organization.

The Database Management Approach

The file processing approach was replaced by the **database management approach** as the foundation of modern methods of managing organizational data. The database management approach consolidates data records formerly in separate files into databases that can be accessed by many different application programs. In addition, a *database management system* (DBMS) serves as a software interface between users and databases. This helps users easily access the data in a database. Thus, database management involves the use of database management software to control how databases are created, interrogated, and maintained to provide information needed by end users.

For example, customer records and other common types of data are needed for several different applications in banking, such as check processing, automated teller systems, bank credit cards, savings accounts, and installment loan accounting. These data can be consolidated into a common *customer database*, rather than being kept in separate files for each of those applications. See Figure 5.11.

Alberta Central: Converting to Database Management

Alberta Central is the administrative services organization for thirty-eight credit unions with more than half a million customers in Alberta, Canada. Alberta Central recently moved from a traditional file processing system to a database management approach to support their banking system's vision to provide credit union analysts and managers with more meaningful and timely information to analyze and manage their credit union's performance and risk. The primary business driver for the project was feedback from the credit unions, which wanted more detailed customer demographics, account and product analysis, and profitability forecasting than was possible when all credit union information was in specialized data files tied to specific applications.

Alberta Central's new DB2 Universal Database software from IBM manages a database that stores demographic information as well as account and product information such as the type and amount of loan or investment products and interest rate yields. Users at each credit union access the database via a corporate intranet using the Business Objects query and reporting software tool.

According to Bill Gnenz, Alberta Central's project manager of Retail Banking and Corporate Systems, the new database management approach has delivered dramatic reductions in response times for queries and generation of reports. The system's new user interface, ease of use, and flexibility have also boosted the business creativity and productivity of credit union staff. And Gnenz expects the cost of the project to achieve full payback soon [6].

FIGURE 5.11

An example of a database management approach in a banking information system. Note how the savings, checking, and installment loan programs use a database management system to share a customer database. Note also that the DBMS allows a user to make a direct, ad hoc interrogation of the database without using application programs.

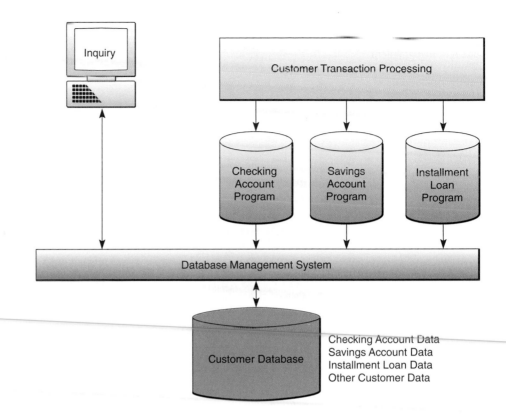

Database Management Software

A **database management system** (DBMS) is the main software tool of the database management approach, since it controls the creation, maintenance, and use of the databases of an organization and its end users. As we saw in Figure 5.5, microcomputer database management packages such as Microsoft Access, Lotus Approach, or Corel Paradox allow you to set up and manage databases on your PC, network server, or the World Wide Web. In mainframe and server computer systems, the database management system is an important system software package that controls the development, use, and maintenance of the databases of computer-using organizations. Examples of popular mainframe and server versions of DBMS software are IBM's DB2 Universal Database, Oracle 9i by Oracle Corporation, and MySQL, a popular open-source DBMS. See Figure 5.12. Common DBMS components and functions are summarized in Figure 5.13.

The three major functions of a database management system are (1) to **create** new databases and database applications, (2) to **maintain** the quality of the data in an organization's databases, and (3) to **use** the databases of an organization to provide the information needed by its end users. See Figure 5.14.

Database development involves defining and organizing the content, relationships, and structure of the data needed to build a database. *Database application development* involves using a DBMS to develop prototypes of queries, forms, reports, and Web pages for a proposed business application. *Database maintenance* involves using transaction processing systems and other tools to add, delete, update, and correct the data in a database. The primary use of database by end users involves employing the *database interrogation* capabilities of a DBMS to access the data in a database to selectively retrieve and display information and produce reports, forms, and other documents. We will discuss the use and maintenance of databases and database application development in this section, and cover the development of databases in Section II of this chapter.

Database Interrogation

A database interrogation capability is a major benefit of the database management approach. End users can use a DBMS by asking for information from a database using a *query* feature or a *report generator.* They can receive an immediate response in the form

Database management software like MySQL, a popular open-source DBMS, support the development, maintenance, and use of the databases of an organization.

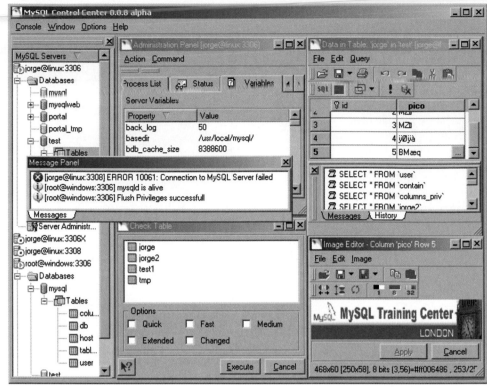

Source: Courtesy of MySQL.com.

of video displays or printed reports. No difficult programming is required. The **query language** feature lets you easily obtain immediate responses to ad hoc data requests: You merely key in a few short inquiries. The **report generator** feature allows you to quickly specify a report format for information you want presented as a report. Figure 5.15 illustrates the use of a DBMS report generator.

SQL Queries. SQL, or Structured Query Language, is an international standard query language found in many DBMS packages. The basic form of an SQL query is:

```
SELECT . . . FROM . . . WHERE . . .
```

After SELECT you list the data fields you want retrieved. After FROM you list the files or tables from which the data must be retrieved. After WHERE you specify conditions that limit the search to only those data records in which you are interested.

FIGURE 5.13

Common software components and functions of a database management system.

Common DBMS Software Components	
● **Database definition**	Language and graphical tools to define entities, relationships, integrity constraints, and authorization rights
● **Nonprocedural access**	Language and graphical tools to access data without complicated coding
● **Application development**	Graphical tools to develop menus, data entry forms, and reports
● **Procedural language interface**	Language that combines nonprocedural access with full capabilities of a programming language
● **Transaction processing**	Control mechanisms to prevent interference from simultaneous users and recover lost data after a failure
● **Database tuning**	Tools to monitor and improve database performance

Source: Adapted from Michael V. Mannino, *Database Application Development and Design* (Burr Ridge, IL: McGraw-Hill/Irwin, 2001), p. 7.

FIGURE 5.14

The three major uses of DBMS software are to create, maintain, and use the databases of an organization.

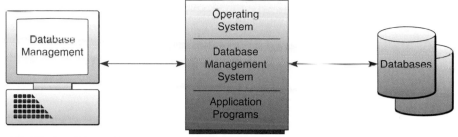

- Create: Database and Application Development
- Maintain: Database Maintenance
- Use: Database Interrogation

Figure 5.16 compares an SQL query to a natural language query for information on customer orders.

Graphical and Natural Queries. Many end users (and IS professionals) have difficulty correctly phrasing SQL and other database language queries. So most end user database management packages offer GUI (graphical user interface) point-and-click methods, which are easier to use and are translated by the software into SQL commands. See Figure 5.17. Other packages are available that use *natural language* query statements similar to conversational English (or other languages), as was illustrated in Figure 5.16.

Database Maintenance

The **database maintenance** process is accomplished by *transaction processing systems* and other end user applications, with the support of the DBMS. End users and information specialists can also employ various utilities provided by a DBMS for database maintenance. The databases of an organization need to be updated continually to reflect new business transactions (such as sales made, products produced, or inventory shipped) and other events. Other miscellaneous changes must also be made to update and correct data, (such as customer or employee name and address changes), to ensure accuracy of the data in the databases. We introduced transaction processing systems in Chapter 1 and will discuss them in more detail in Chapter 7.

Application Development

DBMS packages also play a major role in **application development.** End users, systems analysts, and other application developers can use the internal 4GL programming language and built-in software development tools provided by many DBMS packages to develop custom application programs. For example, you can use a DBMS to easily develop the data entry screens, forms, reports, or Web pages of a business application that accesses a company database to find and update the data it needs. A DBMS also makes the job of application software developers easier, since they do not have to develop detailed data-handling procedures using conventional programming

FIGURE 5.15

Using the report generator of Microsoft Access to create an employee report.

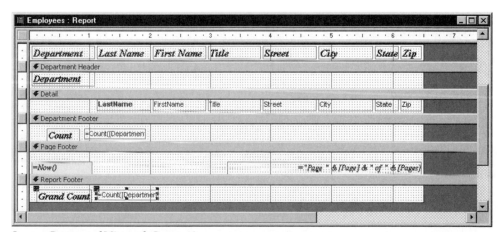

Source: Courtesy of Microsoft Corporation

Comparing a natural language query with an SQL query.

A Sample Natural Language-to-SQL Translation for Microsoft Access

Natural Language

WHAT CUSTOMERS HAD NO ORDERS LAST MONTH?

SQL

SELECT [Customers].[Company Name],[Customers].[Contact Name]

FROM [Customers]

WHERE not Exists {SELECT [Ship Name] FROM [Orders]

 WHERE Month {[Order Date]}=1 and Year {[Order Date]}=2004 and
 [Customers].[Customer ID]=[Orders].{[Customer ID]}

languages every time they write a program. Instead, they can include features such as *data manipulation language* (DML) statements in their software that call on the DBMS to perform necessary data-handling activities.

WH Smith PLC: Transaction Processing and Database Interrogation

WH Smith (www.whsmith.com) wanted to get a grasp on customers' buying patterns, anticipate trends, and more carefully align inventory to maximize profits in its 1,200 U.K.-based stores. At WH Smith, with sales of over $4 billion in 2002, there was no integration or insight about the most profitable items among the more than 60,000 CDs, books, games, stationery, and gifts the stores offer.

So Trevor Dukes, the company's head of information strategy, worked with a team that included store managers and central office executives to install a new business intelligence system from MicroStrategy Inc. The goal was to cut the amount of paper shuttling back and forth between stores and the corporate headquarters in Swindon, England, and give store managers greater insight into what was happening in their own stores and throughout the WH Smith network.

Now, the new Web-based system begins generating reports in template form from the time a customer makes a purchase in a store. Sales and inventory data are captured by point-of-sale terminals at retail locations and processed by a retail transaction processing system, which updates company databases and a retail data mart that store managers can access via an intranet. The software tools available for managers to use include report templates and wizards so managers can develop their own customized views of updated inventory statistics based on criteria such as highest-margin items ranked by sales.

Barrie Stewart, manager of the WH Smith store in Dunbartonshire, Scotland, says he can now see which specific products in the store are selling well, badly, or according to expected trends, allowing him to take appropriate action [4].

Using the Query Wizard of the Microsoft Access database management package to develop a query about employee health plan choices.

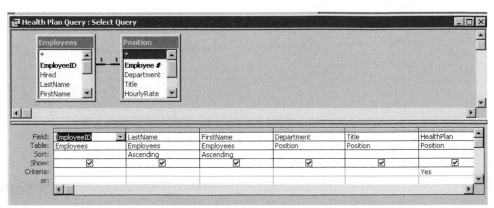

Source: Courtesy of Microsoft Corporation.

SECTION II	Technical Foundations of Database Management

Database Management

Just imagine how difficult it would be to get any information from an information system if data were stored in an unorganized way, or if there was no systematic way to retrieve it. Therefore, in all information systems, data resources must be organized and structured in some logical manner so that they can be accessed easily, processed efficiently, retrieved quickly, and managed effectively. Thus, data structures and access methods ranging from simple to complex have been devised to efficiently organize and access data stored by information systems. In this section, we will explore these concepts, as well as more technical concepts of database management.

Analyzing Owens & Minor and Vivendi Universal

Read the Real World Case on Owens & Minor and Vivendi Universal on the next page. We can learn a lot from this case about security issues in data resource management. See Figure 5.18.

Owens & Minor is a billion-dollar medical supplies distributor that began using data mining in 1996 to discover strategic information about their business operations and stored it in an Oracle-managed database. Access to the database is determined by the business roles of employees, such as sales managers being given access to data about sales in their region. In 1998, Owens & Minor developed an extranet Web portal that enabled their customers and suppliers, including high-profile companies like 3M and Johnson & Johnson, to access their own transaction data and use a Web-based business intelligence tool to generate sophisticated analysis and reports. This called for a new level of security for customers and suppliers based on secure database views using security tables managed by the Oracle database management system. Now Owens & Minor can even load a customer's own materials management data into their system, so customers can use the Web portal and its business intelligence software to analyze their data. This calls for another level of security to protect such data. And Vivendi Universal Games faces some of the same security issues for their financial databases, and thus will use a combination of Web portals and business roles to control access to the data.

FIGURE 5.18

Don Stoller is senior director of Information Systems at Owens & Minor, and has responsibility for the security of company, customer, and supplier data resources.

Source: Katherine Lambert.

Owens & Minor and Vivendi Universal Games: Protecting Strategic Data Resources

It's no secret that somewhere in a back room in the typical Fortune 500 company, there's a team of analytical wizards running sophisticated data mining queries that mine for gems such as data about the company's best customers—those top 20 percent of clients that produce 80 percent of the company's profits. These jewels can be a business's most valuable intellectual property, which makes them very valuable to competitors. What's to prevent that data set from walking out the door or falling into the wrong hands? Sometimes, not much. Many companies lack the internal controls to prevent that information from leaking. The problem is that such data is as hard to protect as it is to find.

Owens & Minor Inc. (www.owens-minor.com), a $4 billion medical supplies distributor, counts some of the nation's largest health care organizations among its customers. In late 1996, it started mining data internally using business intelligence software from Business Objects SA.

"From the beginning, we were aware of security issues around this strategic information about our operations," says Don Stoller, senior director of information systems at Owens & Minor. "For example, a sales executive in Dallas should only have access to analyses from his region." It is always possible that someone who has legitimate access will abuse that trust, but companies can minimize that potential by strictly limiting access to only those who need it. Thus, Owens & Minor uses role-level security functions that clearly define who has access to which data. "This meant we had to build a separate security table in our Oracle database," says Stoller.

A few years later, when the company wanted to open its systems to suppliers and customers, security became even more important. In 1998, Owens & Minor moved quickly to take advantage of Web-intelligence software from Business Objects that's designed to Web-enable business intelligence systems. The result was Wisdom, an extranet Web portal that lets Owens & Minor's suppliers and customers access their own transactional data and generate sophisticated analyses and reports from it.

"In business-to-business transactions, security is key," says Stoller. "We had to make absolutely sure that Johnson & Johnson, for example, could not see any of 3M's information. This meant we had to set up specific customer and supplier security tables, and we had to maintain new, secured database views using the Oracle DBMS and Business Objects."

Wisdom was such a success that Owens & Minor decided to go into the intelligence business with the launch of Wisdom2 in the spring of 2000. "We capture data out of a hospital's materials management system and load it into our data warehouse," Stoller explains. A hospital can then make full use of its business-intelligence software to mine and an-

alyze purchasing data. Owens & Minor receives a licensing and maintenance fee for the service.

Layers of security and encryption require a considerable amount of overhead data for systems administration. Both Stoller and Michael Rasmussen, an analyst at Giga Information Group, say that's the main reason security concerns about business intelligence are often swept under the carpet. The issues of authentication (identifying the user) and authorization (what things the user is allowed to do) must be addressed, usually across different applications, Rasmussen says, adding, "Systems administration can be a real nightmare."

"We are going through some of this," says David Merager, director of Web services and corporate applications at Vivendi Universal Games Inc. (www.vugames.com). "Our business intelligence needs more security attention." Business intelligence reports come from two systems: an Oracle-based general ledger database on Unix, and a data entry application for budgets on a Microsoft SQL Server database. The heart of the business intelligence system consists of Microsoft's OLAP application and software from Comshare Inc. that provides the Web-based front end for the analytics. "Our budget teams use these reports to do real-time analyses," says Merager.

Rodger Sayles, manager of data warehousing at Vivendi Universal, says one way to secure such a system is to assign roles to all users within the Microsoft application. Roles determine precisely what a user is allowed to see and do and are usually managed within a directory. If your computing architecture is amenable to a single, centralized directory that supports roles, this may be an attractive solution. "The problem is that once you have over 40 distinct roles, you run into performance issues, and we have identified about 70 user roles," Sayles explains. He says there's a way around this difficulty. "I think we are going to use a combination of Web portals and user roles. A user would sign on through a particular Web portal, which would effectively place the user in a role category. This reduces the overhead burden on the application," says Sayles.

Case Study Questions

1. Why have developments in IT helped to increase the value of the data resources of many companies?

2. How have these IT capabilities increased the security challenges for a company's data resources?

3. How can companies use IT to meet the challenges of data resource security?

Source: Adapted from Mark Leon, "Keys to the Kingdom," *Computerworld*, April 14, 2003. Copyright © 2003 by Computerworld, Inc. Framingham, MA 01701. All rights reserved.

Database Structures

The relationships among the many individual data elements stored in databases are based on one of several logical data structures, or models. Database management system packages are designed to use a specific data structure to provide end users with quick, easy access to information stored in databases. Five fundamental database structures are the hierarchical, network, relational, object-oriented, and multidimensional models. Simplified illustrations of the first three database structures are shown in Figure 5.19.

Hierarchical Structure

Early mainframe DBMS packages used the **hierarchical structure,** in which the relationships between records form a hierarchy or treelike structure. In the traditional hierarchical model, all records are dependent and arranged in multilevel structures, consisting of one *root* record and any number of subordinate levels. Thus, all of the relationships

FIGURE 5.19

Example of three fundamental database structures. They represent three basic ways to develop and express the relationships among the data elements in a database.

Hierarchical Structure

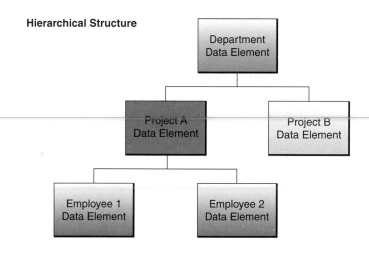

Network Structure

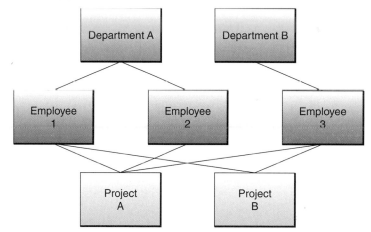

Relational Structure

Department Table

Deptno	Dname	Dloc	Dmgr
Dept A			
Dept B			
Dept C			

Employee Table

Empno	Ename	Etitle	Esalary	Deptno
Emp 1				Dept A
Emp 2				Dept A
Emp 3				Dept B
Emp 4				Dept B
Emp 5				Dept C
Emp 6				Dept B

among records are *one-to-many*, since each data element is related to only one element above it. The data element or record at the highest level of the hierarchy (the department data element in this illustration) is called the root element. Any data element can be accessed by moving progressively downward from a root and along the branches of the tree until the desired record (for example, the employee data element) is located.

Network Structure

The **network structure** can represent more complex logical relationships, and is still used by some mainframe DBMS packages. It allows *many-to-many* relationships among records; that is, the network model can access a data element by following one of several paths, because any data element or record can be related to any number of other data elements. For example, in Figure 5.19, departmental records can be related to more than one employee record, and employee records can be related to more than one project record. Thus, one could locate all employee records for a particular department, or all project records related to a particular employee.

Relational Structure

The **relational model** is the most widely used of the three database structures. It is used by most microcomputer DBMS packages, as well as by most midrange and mainframe systems. In the relational model, all data elements within the database are viewed as being stored in the form of simple **tables.** Figure 5.19 illustrates the relational database model with two tables representing some of the relationships among departmental and employee records. Other tables, or **relations,** for this organization's database might represent the data element relationships among projects, divisions, product lines, and so on. Database management system packages based on the relational model can link data elements from various tables to provide information to users. For example, a DBMS package could retrieve and display an employee's name and salary from the employee table in Figure 5.19, and the name of the employee's department from the department table, by using their common department number field (Deptno) to link or join the two tables. See Figure 5.20.

Multidimensional Structure

The multidimensional database structure is a variation of the relational model that uses multidimensional structures to organize data and express the relationships between data. You can visualize multidimensional structures as cubes of data and cubes within cubes of data. Each side of the cube is considered a dimension of the data. Figure 5.21 is an example that shows that each dimension can represent a different category, such as product type, region, sales channel, and time [7].

Each cell within a multidimensional structure contains aggregated data related to elements along each of its dimensions. For example, a single cell may contain the total sales for a product in a region for a specific sales channel in a single month. A major benefit of multidimensional databases is that they are a compact and easy-to-understand way to visualize and manipulate data elements that have many interrelationships. So multidimensional databases have become the most popular database structure for the analytical databases that support *online analytical processing* (OLAP) applications, in which fast answers to complex business queries are expected. We discuss OLAP applications in Chapter 9.

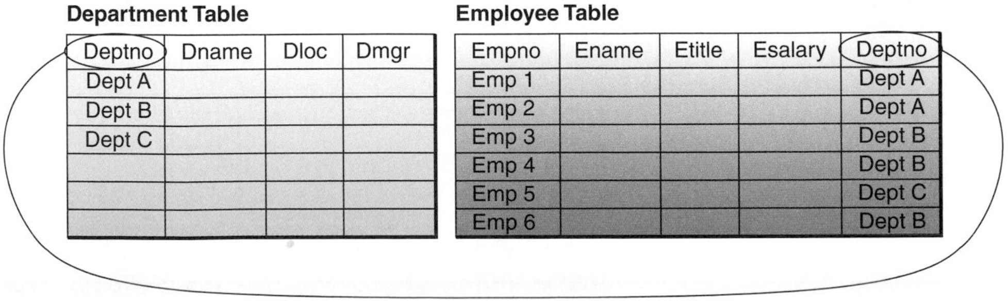

FIGURE 5.20

Joining the Employee and Department tables in a relational database enables you to selectively access data in both tables at the same time.

Department Table

Deptno	Dname	Dloc	Dmgr
Dept A			
Dept B			
Dept C			

Employee Table

Empno	Ename	Etitle	Esalary	Deptno
Emp 1				Dept A
Emp 2				Dept A
Emp 3				Dept B
Emp 4				Dept B
Emp 5				Dept C
Emp 6				Dept B

FIGURE 5.21   An example of the different dimensions of a multidimensional database.

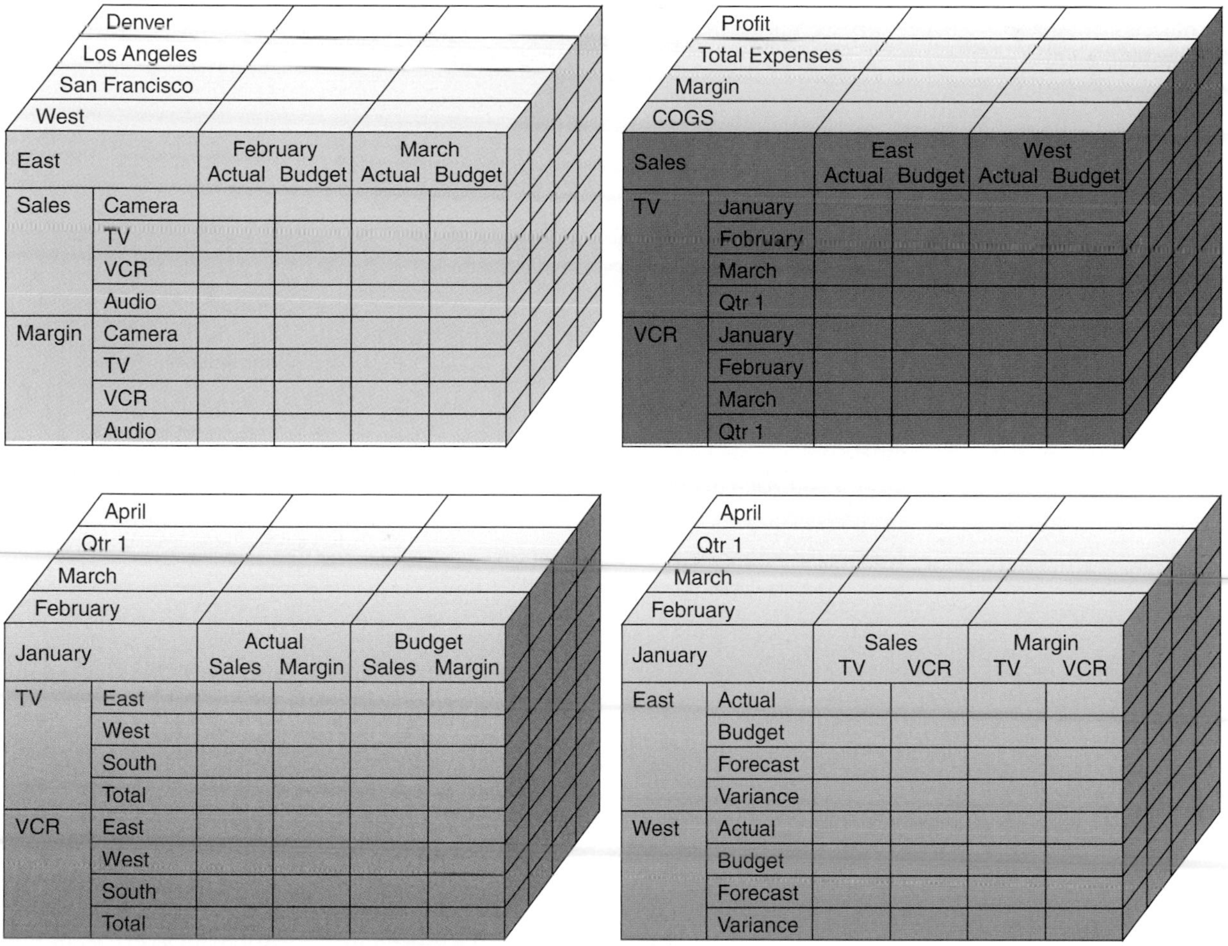

Object-Oriented Structure

The **object-oriented** database model is considered to be one of the key technologies of a new generation of multimedia web-based applications. As Figure 5.22 illustrates, an **object** consists of data values describing the attributes of an entity, plus the operations that can be performed upon the data. This *encapsulation* capability allows the object-oriented model to better handle more complex types of data (graphics, pictures, voice, text) than other database structures.

The object-oriented model also supports *inheritance*; that is, new objects can be automatically created by replicating some or all of the characteristics of one or more *parent* objects. Thus, in Figure 5.22, the checking and savings account objects can both inherit the common attributes and operations of the parent bank account object. Such capabilities have made *object-oriented database management systems* (OODBMS) popular in computer-aided design (CAD) and in a growing number of applications. For example, object technology allows designers to develop product designs, store them as objects in an object-oriented database, and replicate and modify them to create new product designs. In addition, multimedia web-based applications for the Internet and corporate intranets and extranets have become a major application area for object technology.

Object technology proponents argue that an object-oriented DBMS can work with *complex data types* such as document and graphic images, video clips, audio segments, and other subsets of Web pages much more efficiently than relational database management systems. However, major relational DBMS vendors have countered by adding object-oriented modules to their relational software. Examples

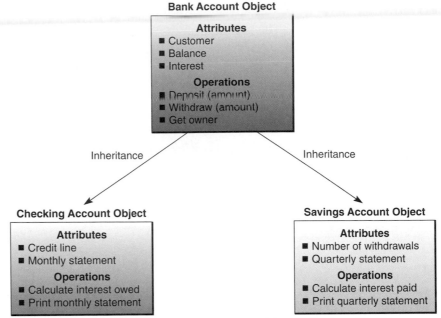

Source: Adapted from Ivar Jacobsen, Maria Ericsson, and Ageneta Jacobsen, *The Object Advantage: Business Process Reengineering with Object Technology* (New York: ACM Press, 1995), p. 65. Copyright © 1995, Association for Computing Machinery. By permission.

FIGURE 5.22

The checking and savings account objects can inherit common attributes and operations from the bank account object.

include multimedia object extensions to IBM's DB2, and Oracle's object-based "cartridges" for Oracle 9i. See Figure 5.23.

Evaluation of Database Structures

The hierarchical data structure was a natural model for the databases used for the structured, routine types of transaction processing that was a characteristic of many business operations. Data for these operations can easily be represented by groups of records in a hierarchical relationship. However, there are many cases where information is needed about records that do not have hierarchical relationships. For example, it is obvious that, in some organizations, employees from more than one department

FIGURE 5.23

This claims analysis graphics display provided by the CleverPath enterprise portal is powered by the Jasmine ii object-oriented database management system of Computer Associates.

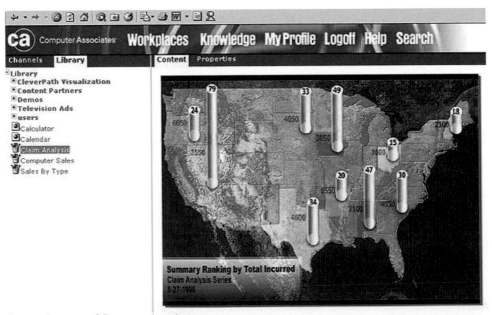

Source: Courtesy of Computer Associates.

limitation can't do M:M

can work on more than one project (refer back to Figure 5.19). A network data structure could easily handle this many-to-many relationship. It is thus more flexible than the hierarchical structure in support of databases for many types of business operations. However, like the hierarchical structure, because its relationships must be specified in advance, the network model cannot easily handle ad hoc requests for information.

Relational databases, on the other hand, allow an end user to easily receive information in response to ad hoc requests. That's because not all of the relationships between the data elements in a relationally-organized database need to be specified when the database is created. Database management software (such as Oracle 9i, DB2, Access, and Approach) creates new tables of data relationships using parts of the data from several tables. Thus, relational databases are easier for programmers to work with and easier to maintain than the hierarchical and network models.

The major limitation of the relational model is that relational database management systems cannot process large amounts of business transactions as quickly and efficiently as those based on the hierarchical and network models, or complex, high-volume applications as well as the object-oriented model. This performance gap has narrowed with the development of advanced relational DBMS software with object-oriented extensions. The use of database management software based on the object-oriented and multidimensional models is growing steadily, as these technologies are playing a greater role for OLAP and web-based applications.

Experian Automotive: The Business Value of Relational Database Management	Experian Inc. (www.experian.com), a unit of London-based GUS PLC, runs one of the largest credit reporting agencies in the United States. But Experian wanted to expand its business beyond credit checks for automobile loans. If it could collect vehicle data from the various motor-vehicle departments in the U.S. and blend that with other data, such as change-of-address records, then its Experian Automotive division could sell the enhanced data to a variety of customers. For example, car dealers could use the data to make sure their inventory matches local buying preferences. And toll collectors could match license plates to addresses to find motorists who sail past toll booths without paying.

But to offer new services, Experian first needed a way to extract, transfer, and load data from the 50 different U.S. state department of motor vehicles (DMV) systems (plus Puerto Rico) into a single database. That was a big challenge. "Unlike the credit industry that writes to a common format, the DMVs do not," says Ken Kauppila, vice president of IT at Experian Automotive in Costa Mesa, California.

Of course, Experian didn't want to replicate the hodgepodge of file formats it inherited when the project began in January 1999—175 formats among 18,000 files. So Kauppila decided to transform and map the data to a common relational database format.

Fortunately, off-the-shelf software tools for extracting, transforming, and loading data (called ETL tools) make it economical to combine very large data repositories. Using ETL Extract from Evolutionary Technologies, Experian created a database that can incorporate vehicle information within 48 hours of its entry into any of the nation's DMV computers. This is one of the areas in which data management software tools can excel, says Guy Creese, analyst at Aberdeen Group in Boston. "It can simplify the mechanics of multiple data feeds, and it can add to data quality, making fixes possible before errors are propagated to data warehouses," he says.

Using the ETL extraction and transformation tools along with IBM's DB2 database system, Experian Automotive created a database that processes 175 million transactions per month and has created a variety of profitable new revenue streams. Experian's automotive database is the 10th largest database in the world—now, with up to 16 billion rows of data. But the company says the relational database is managed by just three IT professionals. Experian says this demonstrates how efficiently database software like DB2 and the ETL tools can work with a large database to handle vast amounts of data quickly.

Database Development

Database management packages like Microsoft Access or Lotus Approach allow end users to easily develop the databases they need. See Figure 5.24. However, large organizations usually place control of enterprisewide database development in the hands of **database administrators** (DBAs) and other database specialists. This improves the integrity and security of organizational databases. Database developers use the *data definition language* (DDL) in database management systems like Oracle 9i or IBM's DB2 to develop and specify the data contents, relationships, and structure of each database, and to modify these database specifications when necessary. Such information is cataloged and stored in a database of data definitions and specifications called a *data dictionary*, or *metadata repository*, which is managed by the database management software and maintained by the DBA.

A **data dictionary** is a database management catalog or directory containing **metadata,** that is, data about data. A data dictionary relies on a DBMS software component to manage a database of data definitions, that is, metadata about the structure, data elements, and other characteristics of an organization's databases. For example, it contains the names and descriptions of all types of data records and their interrelationships, as well as information outlining requirements for end users' access and use of application programs, and database maintenance and security.

Data dictionaries can be queried by the database administrator to report the status of any aspect of a firm's metadata. The administrator can then make changes to the definitions of selected data elements. Some *active* (versus *passive*) data dictionaries automatically enforce standard data element definitions whenever end users and application programs use a DBMS to access an organization's databases. For example, an active data dictionary would not allow a data entry program to use a nonstandard

FIGURE 5.24

Creating a database table using the Table Wizard of Microsoft Access.

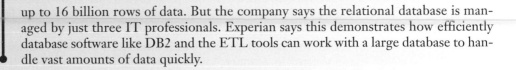

Source: Courtesy of Microsoft Corporation

FIGURE 5.25

Database development involves data planning and database design activities. Data models that support business processes are used to develop databases that meet the information needs of users.

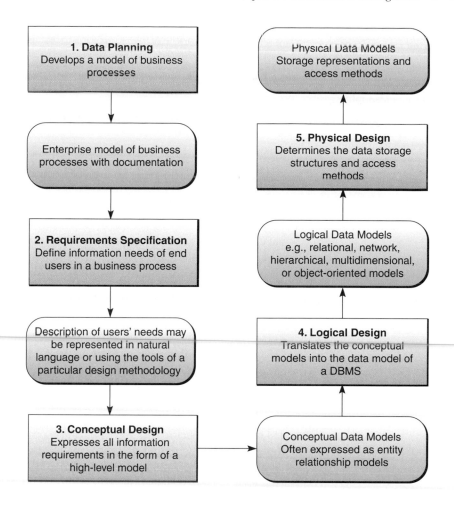

definition of a customer record, nor would it allow an employee to enter a name of a customer that exceeded the defined size of that data element.

Developing a large database of complex data types can be a complex task. Database administrators and database design analysts work with end users and systems analysts to model business processes and the data they require. Then they determine (1) what data definitions should be included in the database and (2) what structure or relationships should exist among the data elements.

Data Planning and Database Design

As Figure 5.25 illustrates, database development may start with a top-down **data planning process.** Database administrators and designers work with corporate and end user management to develop an *enterprise model* that defines the basic business process of the enterprise. Then they define the information needs of end users in a business process, such as the purchasing/receiving process that all businesses have.

Next, end users must identify the key data elements that are needed to perform their specific business activities. This frequently involves developing *entity relationship diagrams* (ERDs) that model the relationships among the many entities involved in business processes. For example, Figure 5.26 illustrates some of the relationships in a purchasing/receiving process. End users and database designers could use database management or business modeling software to help them develop ERD models for the purchasing/receiving process. This would help identify what supplier and product data are required to automate their purchasing/receiving and other business processes using enterprise resource management (ERP) or supply chain management (SCM) software.

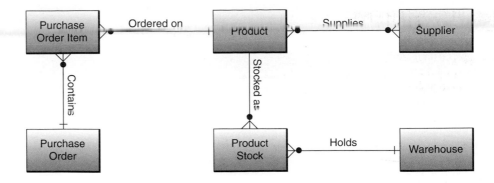

FIGURE 5.26

This entity relationship diagram illustrates some of the relationships among the entities (product, supplier, warehouse, etc.) in a purchasing/receiving business process.

Such user views are a major part of a **data modeling** process where the relationships between data elements are identified. Each data model defines the logical relationships among the data elements needed to support a basic business process. For example, can a supplier provide more than one type of product to us? Can a customer have more than one type of account with us? Can an employee have several pay rates or be assigned to several project workgroups?

Answering such questions will identify data relationships that have to be represented in a data model that supports a business process. These data models then serve as logical frameworks (called *schemas and subschemas*) on which to base the *physical design* of databases and the development of application programs to support the business processes of the organization. A schema is an overall logical view of the relationships among the data elements in a database, while the subschema is a logical view of the data relationships needed to support specific end user application programs that will access that database.

Remember that data models represent *logical views* of the data and relationships of the database. Physical database design takes a *physical view* of the data (also called the internal view) that describes how data are to be physically stored and accessed on the storage devices of a computer system. For example, Figure 5.27 illustrates these different database views and the software interface of a bank database processing system. In this example, checking, savings, and installment lending are the business processes whose data models are part of a banking services data model that serves as a logical data framework for all bank services.

| Aetna and Shop at Home Network: Development Solutions | Database administrators maintain the more than 15,000 database table definitions with the ERWin data modeling tool, according to Michael Mathias, an information systems data storage expert at Aetna Inc. Mathias sees the importance of viewing the maintenance of large amounts of data from a logical perspective. While the physical management of large data stores is certainly a nontrivial effort, Mathias says that failing to keep the data organized leads inexorably to user workflow problems, devaluation of the data as a corporate asset and, eventually, customer complaints.

Shop At Home Network has created a team of three senior developers for its Oracle database management system. One team member is responsible for creating the data models that define the entities and relationships that represent the end user's view into the data. Another is a business analyst and project lead who finds out what types of queries are needed by business end users and how users want to see information summarized to create the best system design. The third, a database administrator, is responsible for the physical structure of the warehouse itself and making sure it gets loaded correctly so users get the right information at the right time [11]. |
| --- | --- |

FIGURE 5.27   Example of the logical and physical database views and the software interface of a banking services information system.

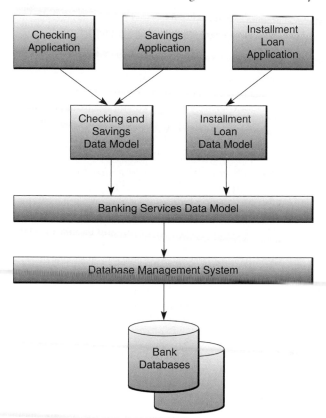

Logical User Views
Data elements and relationships (the subschemas) needed for checking, savings, or installment loan processing

Data elements and relationships (the schema) needed for the support of all bank services

Software Interface
The DBMS provides access to the bank's databases

Physical Data Views
Organization and location of data on the storage media

Summary

- **Data Resource Management.** Data resource management is a managerial activity that applies information technology and software tools to the task of managing an organization's data resources. Early attempts to manage data resources used a file processing approach in which data were organized and accessible only in specialized files of data records that were designed for processing by specific business application programs. This approach proved too cumbersome, costly, and inflexible to supply the information needed to manage modern business processes and organizations. Thus, the database management approach was developed to solve the problems of file processing systems.

- **Database Management.** The database management approach affects the storage and processing of data. The data needed by different applications are consolidated and integrated into several common databases, instead of being stored in many independent data files. Also, the database management approach emphasizes updating and maintaining common databases, having users' application programs share the data in the database, and providing a reporting and an inquiry/response capability so end users can easily receive reports and quick responses to requests for information.

- **Database Software.** Database management systems are software packages that simplify the creation, use, and maintenance of databases. They provide software tools so end users, programmers, and database administrators can create and modify databases, interrogate a database, generate reports, do application development, and perform database maintenance.

- **Types of Databases.** Several types of databases are used by business organizations, including operational, distrib-

uted, and external databases. Data warehouses are a central source of data from other databases that have been cleaned, transformed and cataloged for business analysis and decision support applications. That includes data mining, which attempts to find hidden patterns and trends in the warehouse data. Hypermedia databases on the World Wide Web and corporate intranets and extranets store hyperlinked multimedia pages at a website. Web server software can manage such databases for quick access and maintenance of the Web database.

- **Data Access.** Data must be organized in some logical manner on physical storage devices so that they can be efficiently processed. For this reason, data are commonly organized into logical data elements such as characters, fields, records, files, and databases. Database structures, such as the hierarchical, network, relational, and object-oriented models, are used to organize the relationships among the data records stored in databases. Databases and files can be organized in either a sequential or direct manner and can be accessed and maintained by either sequential access or direct access processing methods.

- **Database Development.** The development of databases can be easily accomplished using microcomputer database management packages for small end-user applications. However, the development of large corporate databases requires a top-down data planning effort. This may involve developing enterprise and entity relationship models, subject area databases, and data models that reflect the logical data elements and relationships needed to support the operation and management of the basic business processes of the organization.

Key Terms and Concepts

These are the key terms and concepts of this chapter. The page number of their first explanation is in parentheses.

1. Data dictionary (160)
2. Data mining (145)
3. Data modeling (162)
4. Data resource management (138)
5. Database administrator (160)
6. Database management approach (148)
7. Database management system (149)
8. Database structures (155)
   - *a.* Hierarchical (155)
   - *b.* Multidimensional (156)

   - *c.* Network (156)
   - *d.* Object-oriented (157)
   - *e.* Relational (156)
9. DBMS uses (149)
   - *a.* Application development (151)
   - *b.* Database development (149)
   - *c.* Database interrogation (149)
   - *d.* Database maintenance (151)
10. File processing (146)
11. Logical data elements (140)
    - *a.* Character (140)
    - *b.* Field (140)

   - *c.* Record (141)
   - *d.* File (141)
   - *e.* Database (141)
12. Metadata (160)
13. Query language (150)
14. Report generator (150)
15. Types of databases (141)
    - *a.* Data warehouse (143)
    - *b.* Distributed (142)
    - *c.* External (143)
    - *d.* Hypermedia (143)
    - *e.* Operational (141)

Review Quiz

Match one of the key terms and concepts listed previously with one of the brief examples or definitions that follow. Try to find the best fit for answers that seem to fit more than one term or concept. Defend your choices.

_____ 1. The use of integrated collections of data records and files for data storage and processing.

_____ 2. A DBMS allows you to create, interrogate, and maintain a database, create reports, and develop application programs.

_____ 3. A specialist in charge of the databases of an organization.

_____ 4. This DBMS feature allows users to easily interrogate a database.

_____ 5. Defines and catalogs the data elements and data relationships in an organization's database.

_____ 6. Helps you specify and produce reports from a database.

_____ 7. The main software package that supports a database management approach.

_____ 8. Databases are dispersed to the Internet and corporate intranets and extranets.

_____ 9. Databases that organize and store data as objects.

_____ 10. Databases of hyperlinked multimedia documents on the Web.

_____ 11. The management of all the data resources of an organization.

_____ 12. Processing data in a data warehouse to discover key business factors and trends.

_____ 13. Developing conceptual views of the relationships among data in a database.

_____ 14. A customer's name.

_____ 15. A customer's name, address, and account balance.

_____ 16. The names, addresses, and account balances of all of your customers.

_____ 17. An integrated collection of all of the data about your customers.

_____ 18. Business application programs use specialized data files.

_____ 19. A treelike structure of records in a database.

_____ 20. A tabular structure of records in a database.

_____ 21. Records are organized as cubes within cubes in a database.

_____ 22. Databases that support the major business processes of an organization.

_____ 23. A centralized and integrated database of current and historical data about an organization.

_____ 24. Databases available on the Internet or provided by commercial information services.

Discussion Questions

1. How should a business store, access, and distribute data and information about their internal operations and external environment?

2. What role does database management play in managing data as a business resource?

3. What are the advantages of a database management approach to the file processing approach? Give examples to illustrate your answer.

4. Refer to the Real World Case on Argosy Gaming Co. in the chapter. Why do analysts, users, and vendors say that the benefits of data warehouses depend on whether companies "know their data resources and what they want to achieve with them?" Use Argosy Gaming as an example.

5. What is the role of a database management system in a business information system?

6. Databases of information about a firm's internal operations were formerly the only databases that were

considered to be important to a business. What other kinds of databases are important for a business today?

7. Refer to the Real World Case on Owens & Minor and Vivendi Universal Games in the chapter. What are several major threats today to the security of the data resources of a company and its business partners? Explain several ways a company could protect such data resources from the threats you identify.

8. What are the benefits and limitations of the relational database model for business applications today?

9. Why is the object-oriented database model gaining acceptance for developing applications and managing the hypermedia databases at business websites?

10. How have the Internet, intranets, and extranets affected the types and uses of data resources available to business professionals? What other database trends are also affecting data resource management in business?

Analysis Exercises

Complete the following exercises as individual or group projects that apply chapter concepts to real world business.

1. **Training Cost Management Part 1**

   You have the responsibility for managing technical training classes within your organization. These classes fall under two general types: highly technical training, and end-user training. Software engineers sign up for the former, and administrative staff sign up for the latter. Your supervisor measures your effectiveness in part based upon the average cost per training hour and type of training. In short, your supervisor expects the best training for the least cost.

   To meet this need, you have negotiated an exclusive on-site training contract with Hands On Technology Transfer, Inc. (HOTT) (www.traininghott.com), a high quality technical training provider. Your negotiated rates are reproduced below in the pricing table. A separate table contains a sample list of courses you routinely make available for your organization.

   a. Using the data below, design and populate a table that includes basic training rate information. Designate the "Technical" field type as "Yes/No" (Boolean).

   b. Using the data below, design and populate a course table. Designate the CourseID field as a "Primary Key" and allow your database to automatically generate a value for this field. Designate the "Technical" field type as "Yes/No" (Boolean).

   c. Prepare a query that lists each course name and its cost per day of training.

   d. Prepare a query that lists the cost per student for each class. Assume maximum capacity and that you will schedule two half-day classes on the same day to take full advantage of HOTT's per day pricing schedule.

Pricing Table

Technical	Price Per Day	Capacity
Yes	2680	15
No	2144	30

Course Table

Course ID	Course Name	Duration	Technical
1	ASP Programming	5	Yes
2	XML Programming	5	Yes
3	PHP Programming	4	Yes
4	Microsoft Word–Advanced	.5	No
5	Microsoft Excel–Advanced	.5	No
. . .			

2. **Training Cost Management Part 2**

   Having determined the cost per student for each of the classes in the previous problem, you now must carefully manage class registration. Since you pay the same flat rates no matter how many students attend (up to capacity), you want to do all you can to ensure maximum attendance. Your training provider, Hands

On Technology Transfer, Inc., requires two week's notice in the event that you need to reschedule a class. You want to make sure your classes are at least two thirds full before this deadline. You also want to make sure you send timely reminders to all attendees so they do not needlessly forget to show up. Use the database you created in problem #1 above to perform the following activities.

   a. Using the information provided in the sample below, add a course schedule table to your training database. Designate the ScheduleID field as a "Primary Key" and allow your database program to automatically generate a value for this field. Make the CourseID field a number field and the StartDate field a date field.

   b. Using the information provided in the sample below, add a class roster table to your training database. Make ScheduleID field a number field. Make the Reminder and Confirmed fields both "yes/no" (Boolean) fields.

   c. Since the Class Schedule table relates back to the Course Table and the Course Table relates to the Pricing Table, why is it appropriate to record the Price Per Day information in the Class Schedule table, too?

   d. What are the advantages and disadvantages of using the participant's name and e-mail address in the Class Roster table? What other database design might you use to record this information?

   e. Write a query that shows how many people have registered for each scheduled class. Include the class name, capacity, date, and count of attendees.

Class Schedule

Schedule ID	Course ID	Location	StartDate	PricePer Day
1	1	101-A	7/12/2004	2680
2	1	101-A	7/19/2004	2680
3	1	101-B	7/19/2004	2680
4	4	101-A&B	7/26/2004	2144
5	5	101-A&B	8/2/2004	2144
. . .				

Class Roster

Schedule ID	Participant	e-mail	Reminder	Confirmed
1	Linda Adams	adams.l@ . . .	Yes	Yes
1	Fatima Ahmad	ahmad.f@ . . .	Yes	No
1	Adam Alba	alba.a@ . . .	Yes	Yes
4	Denys Alyea	alyea.d@ . . .	No	No
4	Kathy Bara	bara.k@ . . .	Yes	No
...				

4 took 24rs to do all of this

REAL WORLD CASE 3

Henry Schein Inc.: The Business Value of a Data Warehouse

Most companies store reams of data about their customers. The IT challenge has been how to integrate and massage that information so the business units can respond immediately to changes in sales and customer preferences.

Henry Schein Inc. (www.henryschein.com) has it figured out. The $2.8 billion distributor of health care products designed and built a data warehouse with an in-house team of six IS professionals. CIO Jim Harding says he knew that having the right skills was critical to the data warehouse project, yet at the time, Schein had zero warehousing experience in its IT shop. So he and Grace Monahan, vice president of business systems, hired people for what they call "Team Schein."

Because Harding had chosen two key tools for the data warehouse—data extraction software from Informatica Corp. and user query and reporting software from MicroStrategy Inc.—the focus was on finding people who had experience with those tools. So Monahan hired three people from outside: project director Daryll Kelly, data modeler Christine Bates, and front-end specialist Rena Levy, who's responsible for the user interface and data analysis, as well as user support and training. Dawen Sun, who handles extract, transform, and load issues, and database administrator Jamil Uddin hold two other key positions. Another team member is rotated in from Schein's application development group.

Besides having the right skills, the other top priority was ensuring data quality. "It seems kind of obvious," says Harding, "but sometimes these projects forget about quality, and then the data warehouse ends up being worthless because nobody trusts it." So at the outset of the project, the team interviewed about 175 potential business users to determine the information they needed to access and the reports they wanted to see. Plus, the team analyzed the old paper reports and the condition of the data housed in the company's core transaction system. Monahan says those steps brought to light the importance of cleansing data in a system that's designed for transactional purposes but not suitable for a data warehouse. That led to a long period of standardizing transactional codes in order to produce the sales reporting that business analysts needed.

"It's the in-house people who have this gold coin of knowledge of how their systems really work, which data is really good and not so good, and how the end users really want to use the data," Kimball says. "Data quality is the hardest part of the project, because it's very time-consuming and detailed, and not everyone appreciates it unless they've been through a couple of projects, like Daryll has," Harding says.

And there was yet another tedious obstacle. The data warehouse was designed to provide a very granular level of detail about customers, "so we can slice and dice at will," Harding says. But the result was sluggish system performance. So the team created summary tables to make the queries work faster, and those tables needed to be tested. It was a lengthy process, Harding says, but in the end, it worked very well. The journey has taken well over two years. The system went live 18 months ago but "really came into its own" in February, Harding says.

Of course, building a data warehouse is a never-ending job. New companies are acquired, products are added, customers come and go, and new features and enhancements are ongoing. But from an IT standpoint, the data warehouse is complete and has 85 percent of the data from the core transactional system. The next major goal is to provide the European operation with its own data warehouse system and tie it into the one in the U.S.

Harding says his project will surely justify the costs, but he lacks hard numbers. "We didn't have a formal ROI that you could track later. I don't even know how you would do it," he says. "The reason we're doing the project is because of the value it brings to the business."

Lou Ferraro, vice president and general manager of Schein's medical group, says the business benefits are outstanding. He can now figure out who his most profitable customers are, target customers for certain types of promotions, and look at the business by product categories or sales territories. Ferraro says the data warehouse also helps select customers for direct-mail marketing campaigns that range "upward of 25 million pieces annually."

One of the most valuable features of the data warehouse has been the ability it gives users to add more fields to reports as they are using the system. "Once you create a basic report, draw a conclusion, and drill further based on those assumptions, it allows you to use that data and go even further, as opposed to creating a new report, and another and another," Ferraro says. The IT department used to create, edit, revise, run, download, reprogram, and print piles of paper reports—daily, weekly, monthly and quarterly—for the analysis of sales and market trends. But today, business users search, sort, and drill down for that information themselves in a fraction of the time. The data warehouse has become "a part of our culture," says Harding. "It's got that kind of aura about it within the company".

Case Study Questions

1. What are some of the key requirements for building a good data warehouse? Use Henry Schein Inc. as an example.

2. What are the key software tools needed to construct and use a data warehouse?

3. What is the business value of a data warehouse to Henry Schein? To any company?

Anadarko Petroleum and Prudential Financial: Challenges of Data Resource Management

For Joan Dunn, being out on the front lines of IT is just part of the job. In her role as manager of enterprise computing at Anadarko Petroleum Corp. (www.anadarko.com), Dunn says she's encouraged to take risks and demonstrate leadership. Witness the energy firm's willingness to create a massive infrastructure to handle the storage and modeling of 2-D and 3-D seismic data related to oil and gas exploration.

Anadarko acquires huge amounts of data for its geologists, geophysicists, and engineers to interpret. The decision was made to put all that data in one central repository—a move in keeping with the company's desire to consolidate its IT infrastructure as much as possible to save money, says Dunn.

The project had its risks. It required rolling out new networked storage units that replaced machines from various vendors. The project took approximately 20 months, and the system went live two years ago. "At the time, that move was very risky," says Dunn. "But it paid off very well, providing improved performance and reduced administration and maintenance costs." The new storage units provide 110TB of data storage capacity for Anadarko.

Dunn says one of the most challenging aspects of the project involved IT specialists themselves, because they were accustomed to handling only their own types of systems—either dedicated data storage or transaction processing systems. To make the project succeed, the IT team had to work hard on communication, planning, and change management with affected IT staffers and business users. But the rewards have been great: The networked storage model has become standard for the petroleum and gas industry, and Anadarko is ahead of its competitors and is already getting payback from the implementation, says Dunn.

One of the keys to success, she says, is making sure the technology is closely wedded to business strategy. "There are always more technical options out there than make sense for any company," she says. "We take business opportunities and technical opportunities and match them to be successful." Morris Helbach, CIO at Anadarko, says Dunn's across-the-board leadership has been crucial to the firm. "An exploration and production company lives and dies by the way it acquires, manages, and provides access to data," he says.

Prudential Financial. Patricia Graham knows that the most effective way to sell a project is to form relationships with end users and explain what's in it for them. As director of information systems at Prudential Financial (www.prudential.com), Graham's latest challenge is pitching the strategic benefits of data modeling, XML support, and metadata management to the 80 or so business units that she and her department of 16 people support. "I'm always in a selling mode," she says. Over the past two years, Graham has been convincing business units of the time savings and quality improvements that can be gained from using industry and XML standards. "Her strength is making them aware of all the things they can gain holistically," says Curtis Mitchell, vice president of IS and Graham's boss.

For example, Graham's role in a metadata management project might be to make sure that all life insurance data is available to business units, and to foster communication between business and systems groups by providing a more precise and business-friendly language. The ultimate goal is to free the business units so they can spend more time running the business and serving customers and less time deciphering technical specifications or reports.

During her 19 years at Prudential, Graham has used her innate talent to win the cooperation of developers, project managers, and analysts. And that has been a difficult task at times, as business units must now pay for her department's IT services by the project.

"It's hard for people to see the business value of a data architecture project right away," Graham says. "They could be working on the next project before realizing the benefits from the first one." And Graham knows firsthand the expense of not building to standard. Without a blueprint to guide design and development, the project team could start to see incorrect information, increased maintenance costs, and the same data analysis repeated over and over, she says.

"The criticism that the creation of data models and metadata directories are bottlenecks or unnecessary overhead quickly dissipate when key people on project teams start to see the benefit in adhering to standards," she says. And Graham recently demonstrated the positive return on investment from a project when, after building an XML interface for a customer of the company, she was able to send the interface and data exchange to a second customer—without doing additional development work.

Case Study Questions

1. How did Anadarko Petroleum meet its data resource management challenges? What is the business value of their approach?

2. What are the business benefits of the data resource management processes that Patricia Graham is selling to business users at Prudential Financial?

3. How does effective data resource management contribute to the strategic business goals of companies? Use Anadarko and Prudential Financial as examples.

CHAPTER 6

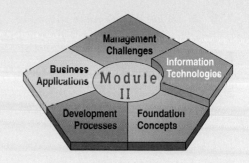

TELECOMMUNICATIONS AND NETWORKS

Chapter Highlights

Section I
The Networked Enterprise

Networking the Enterprise

Real World Case: Celanese Chemicals and Others: Wireless Business Applications

Trends in Telecommunications

The Business Value of Telecommunications Networks

The Internet Revolution

Business Use of the Internet

The Business Value of the Internet

The Role of Intranets

The Role of Extranets

Section II
Telecommunications Network Alternatives

Telecommunications Alternatives

Real World Case: Con-Way NOW and Trimble Navigation: The Business Value of GPS Satellite Networks

A Telecommunications Network Model

Types of Telecommunications Networks

Telecommunications Media

Wireless Technologies

Telecommunications Processors

Telecommunications Software

Network Topologies

Network Architectures and Protocols

Bandwidth Alternatives

Switching Alternatives

Real World Case: UPS, Wells Dairy, Novell, and GM: The Business Value and Challenge of Wi-Fi Networks

Real World Case: Grant Thornton and Others: Return on Investement Challenges of Internet Phone Systems

Learning Objectives

After reading and studying this chapter; you should be able to:

1. Identify several major developments and trends in the industries, technologies, and business applications of telecommunications and Internet technologies.

2. Provide examples of the business value of Internet, intranet, and extranet applications.

3. Identify the basic components, functions, and types of telecommunications networks used in business.

4. Explain the functions of major types of telecommunications network hardware, software, media, and services.

SECTION I The Networked Enterprise

Networking the Enterprise

When computers are networked, two industries—computing and communications converge, and the result is vastly more than the sum of the parts. Suddenly, computing applications become available for business-to-business coordination and commerce, and for small as well as large organizations. The global Internet creates a public place without geographic boundaries—cyberspace—where ordinary citizens can interact, publish their ideas, and engage in the purchase of goods and services. In short, the impact of both computing and communications on our society and organizational structures is greatly magnified [14].

Thus, telecommunications and network technologies are internetworking and revolutionizing business and society. Businesses have become **networked enterprises.** The Internet, the Web, and intranets and extranets are networking business processes and employees together, and connecting them to their customers, suppliers, and other business stakeholders. Companies and workgroups can thus collaborate more creatively, manage their business operations and resources more effectively, and compete successfully in today's fast-changing global economy. This chapter presents the telecommunications and network foundations for these developments.

Analyzing Celanese Chemicals and Others

Read the Real World Case on Celanese Chemicals and Others on the next page. We can learn a lot about how businesses are using wireless technologies from this case. See Figure 6.1.

This case examines the business applications of wireless technology in a variety of industries. At Celanese Chemicals, wireless PDA applications are moving from supporting salespeople in the field to empowering maintenance workers in their chemical plants. At Fidelity Investments, wireless applications for over 170,000 customers include stock

FIGURE 6.1

Companies like Celanese Chemicals use wireless PDAs and laptops for plant maintenance and inventory control.

Source: John Madera/Corbis

REAL WORLD CASE 1

Celanese Chemicals and Others: Wireless Business Applications

Chemicals. Like most executives in the chemicals industry, the upper echelons of Celanese Chemicals Ltd. (www.celanesechemicals.com), are fairly conservative, says Bill Schmitt, the director of e-business at Celanese. "Anything that looks or smells like bleeding-edge technology makes us pretty nervous," he says. But the $3 billion chemicals company was comfortable enough with handheld devices and wireless LANs by 2002 to adopt the technology primarily as a productivity tool for their salespeople in the field. Now the Dallas-based company is looking at wireless technology to speed maintenance at its chemical plants.

"When you run continuous production units, time is money," Schmitt says, When a pump goes down, for example, maintenance workers travel through football-field-size plants by foot or bicycle to inspect the problem and then travel back to the control room and storage room to arrange for repairs—which could take up to an hour, he says. Soon, however, employees will use Hewlett-Packard Pocket PCs to report problems and arrange for repair equipment to be brought to the site.

Finance and Investments. Soon after launching its first wireless offering in 1998, Fidelity Investments (www.fidelity.com) realized that wireless subscribers were very attractive customers. "They have more assets, they're more financially active and more tech-savvy," says Joe Ferra, chief wireless officer. That appealing and profitable combination keeps the Boston-based firm listening to its customers' demands for new wireless features and monitoring their use of every new function.

Today the company's wireless offering, Fidelity Anywhere, lets over 170,000 customers get real-time stock quotes, make after-hours trades, short-sell, and, with phone-integrated BlackBerry handhelds, call a Fidelity rep with the touch of a button. The firm also now lets customers manage their retirement accounts, charitable donations, and insurance needs wirelessly.

Ferra says security remains a paramount concern, and Fidelity continues to "look at what's out there" in terms of security standards. But right now it relies on encryption and authentication developed using the Handheld Device Markup Language. The firm even chooses which functions will be offered on each type of device based on security concerns, browser capabilities, and the latency of wireless transmissions. But Ferra says that once security challenges are met; "I'm convinced this will become a predominant way that people conduct their business with us. These devices are convenient, more reasonably priced, and easier to use than ever before."

Manufacturing. Automotive and aerospace plants lead the manufacturing pack in wireless device use, with about two-thirds of all companies actively using the technology. General Motors Corp.'s Cadillac and Buick assembly plants mounted wireless handheld-size computers from Symbol Technologies Inc., on forklifts so drivers can wirelessly collect and transmit data from the factory or warehouse floor.

The forklift operators can also receive work instructions and updates without leaving their vehicles.

The wireless network is expected to save $1 million at one GM assembly plant, according to a company statement. Forklift traffic has declined by 400 miles each day. After nine months of wireless use, forklift operators now average 60 to 70 deliveries a day, double the number of deliveries they were making before the system went live.

Retailing. Retailers are old-time users of wireless technology for communicating between the checkout counter and the backroom and mobile point-of-sale terminals. But today's wireless technology can improve inventory accuracy, fight fraud, and increase sales. Forward-thinking retailers are venturing into RFID (radio frequency identification) technology, which involves chip-embedded tags that hold more information than a bar code and don't require direct contact with a reading device. But most retailers are holding off on full-blown implementations because of the poor economy, the high cost of RFID equipment, or complicated supply chains.

RFID readers mounted on display shelves in stores can survey item tags and send inventory data to back-end systems rather than relying on point-of-sale data or manual counts. In the stockroom, a tagged box's contents can be identified without opening the box.

While retailers such as Wal-Mart Stores Inc., and Target Corp. have piloted RFID tags on boxes and pallets, retailers that manufacture their own clothing lines are experimenting with individual garment tags. But at 25 to 50 cents apiece, the cost of individual tags is keeping item-level RFID at bay for many retailers. "I foresee the use of RFID at the item level in five to seven years," Alien predicts. "I foresee more applications used for RFID for the carton and pallet level. We are not anywhere near being able to provide retailers with a 5-cent or penny tag. The technology is just not there yet."

Case Study Questions

1. What is the business value of wireless technologies in the chemicals and automotive manufacturing industries? What other manufacturing applications might benefit from wireless technologies? Why?

2. What are some of the business benefits of wireless technologies in finance and investments? What other applications would you recommend? Why? Check the website of Fidelity.com to help you answer.

3. What are some of the business benefits and challenges of using wireless technologies in retailing? What are some other applications that might be beneficial to consumers, as well as retailers? Why?

Source: Adapted from Stacy Collette, "Wireless Gets Down to Business," *Computerworld*, May 5, 2003. Copyright © 2003 by Computerworld, Inc. Framingham, MA 01701. All rights reserved.

quotes and securities trading, as well as accomplishing other investment and insurance transactions. Fidelity has found that these wireless customers have more assets and are more financially active, and thus are a more profitable customer segment, enabling Fidelity to serve them with even more wireless applications, especially as more security is built into the wireless systems. In manufacturing, General Motors has seen the productivity of forklift drivers double after the forklifts were outfitted with wireless handheld computers. Retailing has been using wireless handheld computers for several years to connect the selling floor with backroom inventory systems. Several large retailers are trying out RFID technology, where chip-embedded tags on boxes or pallets of merchandise can wirelessly communicate to company computers. However, adoption of RFID tags for individual items of merchandise must wait for the cost of the chips to drop significantly.

Trends in Telecommunications

Telecommunications is the exchange of information in any form (voice, data, text, images, audio, video) over computer-based networks. Major trends occurring in the field of telecommunications have a significant impact on management decisions in this area. You should thus be aware of major trends in telecommunications industries, technologies, and applications that significantly increase the decision alternatives confronting business managers and professionals. See Figure 6.2.

Industry Trends

The competitive arena for telecommunications service has changed dramatically in many countries in recent years. The telecommunications industry has changed from government-regulated monopolies to a deregulated market with fiercely competitive suppliers of telecommunications services. Numerous companies now offer businesses and consumers a choice of everything from local and global telephone services to communications satellite channels, mobile radio, cable TV, cellular phone services, and Internet access [6]. See Figure 6.3.

The explosive growth of the Internet and the World Wide Web has spawned a host of new telecommunications products, services, and providers. Driving and responding to this growth, business firms have dramatically increased their use of the Internet and the Web for electronic commerce and collaboration. Thus, the service and vendor options available to meet a company's telecommunications needs have increased significantly, as have a business manager's decision-making alternatives.

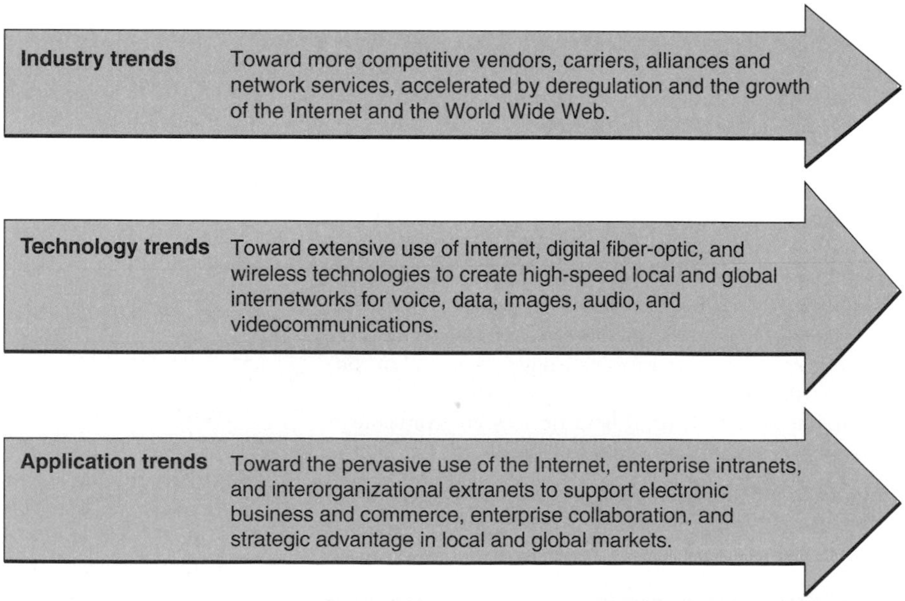

FIGURE 6.2

Major trends in business telecommunications.

Industry trends Toward more competitive vendors, carriers, alliances and network services, accelerated by deregulation and the growth of the Internet and the World Wide Web.

Technology trends Toward extensive use of Internet, digital fiber-optic, and wireless technologies to create high-speed local and global internetworks for voice, data, images, audio, and videocommunications.

Application trends Toward the pervasive use of the Internet, enterprise intranets, and interorganizational extranets to support electronic business and commerce, enterprise collaboration, and strategic advantage in local and global markets.

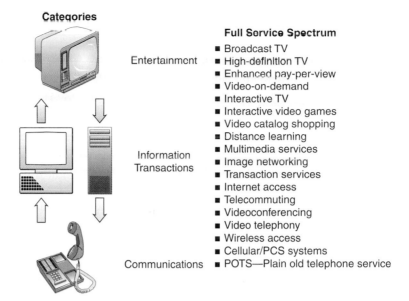

FIGURE 6.3

The spectrum of telecommunications-based services available today.

Categories

Entertainment

Information Transactions

Communications

Full Service Spectrum

- Broadcast TV
- High-definition TV
- Enhanced pay-per-view
- Video-on-demand
- Interactive TV
- Interactive video games
- Video catalog shopping
- Distance learning
- Multimedia services
- Image networking
- Transaction services
- Internet access
- Telecommuting
- Videoconferencing
- Video telephony
- Wireless access
- Cellular/PCS systems
- POTS—Plain old telephone service

Technology Trends

Open systems with unrestricted connectivity, using **Internet networking technologies** as their technology platform, are today's primary telecommunications technology drivers. Web browser suites, HTML Web page editors, Internet and intranet servers and network management software, TCP/IP Internet networking products, and network security firewalls are just a few examples. These technologies are being applied in Internet, intranet, and extranet applications, especially those for electronic commerce and collaboration. This trend has reinforced previous industry and technical moves toward building client/server networks based on an open systems architecture.

Open systems are information systems that use common standards for hardware, software, applications, and networking. Open systems, like the Internet and corporate intranets and extranets, create a computing environment that is open to easy access by end users and their networked computer systems. Open systems provide greater **connectivity**, that is, the ability of networked computers and other devices to easily access and communicate with each other and share information. Any open systems architecture also provides a high degree of network **interoperability.** That is, open systems enable the many different applications of end users to be accomplished using the different varieties of computer systems, software packages, and databases provided by a variety of interconnected networks. Frequently, software known as *middleware* may be used to help diverse systems work together.

Telecommunications is also being revolutionized by the rapid change from analog to **digital network technologies.** Telecommunication systems have always depended on voice-oriented analog transmission systems designed to transmit the variable electrical frequencies generated by the sound waves of the human voice. However, local and global telecommunications networks are rapidly converting to digital transmission technologies that transmit information in the form of discrete pulses, as computers do. This provides (1) significantly higher transmission speeds, (2) the movement of larger amounts of information, (3) greater economy, and (4) much lower error rates than analog systems. In addition, digital technologies allow telecommunications networks to carry multiple types of communications (data, voice, video) on the same circuits.

Another major trend in telecommunications technology is a change from reliance on copper wire-based media and land-based microwave relay systems to fiber-optic lines and cellular, PCS, communications satellite, and other **wireless technologies**. Fiber-optic transmission, which uses pulses of laser-generated light, offers significant advantages in terms of reduced size and installation effort, vastly greater communication capacity, much faster transmission speeds, and freedom from electrical interference. Satellite transmission offers significant advantages for organizations that need to transmit massive quantities of data, audio, and video over global networks, especially to isolated areas. Cellular, PCS, mobile radio, and other wireless systems are connecting cellular and PCS phones, PDAs, and other wireless appliances to the Internet and corporate networks.

Business Application Trends

The changes in telecommunications industries and technologies just mentioned are causing a significant change in the business use of telecommunications. The trend toward more vendors, services, Internet technologies, and open systems, and the rapid growth of the Internet, the World Wide Web, and corporate intranets and extranets dramatically increase the number of feasible telecommunications applications. Thus, telecommunications networks are now playing vital and pervasive roles in Web-enabled e-business processes, electronic commerce, enterprise collaboration, and other business applications that support the operations, management, and strategic objectives of both large and small business enterprises.

The Business Value of Telecommunications Networks

What *business value* is created when a company capitalizes on the trends in telecommunications we have just identified? Use of the Internet, intranets, extranets, and other telecommunications networks can dramatically cut costs, shorten business lead times and response times, support electronic commerce, improve the collaboration of workgroups, develop online operational processes, share resources, lock in customers and suppliers, and develop new products and services. This makes applications of telecommunications more strategic and vital for businesses that must increasingly find new ways to compete in both domestic and global markets.

Figure 6.4. illustrates how telecommunications-based business applications can help a company overcome geographic, time, cost, and structural barriers to business success. Note the examples of the business value of these four strategic capabilities

FIGURE 6.4   Examples of the business value of business applications of telecommunications networks.

Strategic Capabilities	e-Business Examples	Business Value
Overcome geographic barriers: Capture information about business transactions from remote locations	Use the Internet and extranets to transmit customer orders from traveling salespeople to a corporate data center for order processing and inventory control	Provides better customer service by reducing delay in filling orders and improves cash flow by speeding up the billing of customers
Overcome time barriers: Provide information to remote locations immediately after it is requested	Credit authorization at the point of sale using online POS networks	Credit inquiries can be made and answered in seconds
Overcome cost barriers: Reduce the cost of more traditional means of communication	Desktop videoconferencing between a company and its business partners using the Internet, intranets, and extranets	Reduces expensive business trips; allows customers, suppliers, and employees to collaborate, thus improving the quality of decisions reached
Overcome structural barriers: Support linkages for competitive advantage	Business-to-business electronic commerce websites for transactions with suppliers and customers using the Internet and extranets	Fast, convenient services lock in customers and suppliers

of telecommunications networks. This figure emphasizes how several e-business applications can help a firm capture and provide information quickly to end users at remote geographic locations at reduced costs, as well as supporting its strategic organizational objectives.

For example, traveling salespeople and those at regional sales offices can use the Internet, extranets, and other networks to transmit customer orders from their laptop or desktop PCs, thus breaking geographic barriers. Point-of-sale terminals and an online sales transaction processing network can break time barriers by supporting immediate credit authorization and sales processing. Teleconferencing can be used to cut costs by reducing the need for expensive business trips since it allows customers, suppliers, and employees to participate in meetings and collaborate on joint projects. Finally, business-to-business electronic commerce websites are used by the business to establish strategic relationships with their customers and suppliers by making business transactions fast, convenient, and tailored to the needs of the business partners involved.

The Internet Revolution

The explosive growth of the **Internet** is a revolutionary phenomenon in computing and telecommunications. The Internet has become the largest and most important network of networks today, and has evolved into a global *information superhighway*. The Internet is constantly expanding, as more and more businesses and other organizations and their users, computers, and networks join its global web. Thousands of business, educational, and research networks now connect millions of computer systems and users in more than 200 countries to each other. For example, the worldwide population of Internet users was estimated at between 580 million and 655 million in 2002, with estimates of 710 million to 945 million Internet users projected for 2004 [9].

The Net doesn't have a central computer system or telecommunications center. Instead, each message sent has a unique address code so any Internet server in the network can forward it to its destination. Also, the Internet does not have a headquarters or governing body. International advisory and standards groups of individual and corporate members (such as the Internet Society (www.isoc.org) and the World Wide Web Consortium (www.w3.org)), promote use of the Internet and the development of new communications standards. These common standards are the key to the free flow of messages among the widely different computers and networks of the many organizations and *Internet service providers* (ISPs) in the system.

Internet Applications

The most popular Internet applications are e-mail, instant messaging, browsing the sites on the World Wide Web, and participating in *newsgroups* and *chat rooms*. Internet e-mail messages usually arrive in seconds or a few minutes anywhere in the world, and can take the form of data, text, fax, and video files. Internet browser software like Netscape Navigator and Internet Explorer enables millions of users to surf the World Wide Web by clicking their way to the multimedia information resources stored on the hyperlinked pages of businesses, government, and other websites. Websites offer information and entertainment, and are the launch sites for electronic commerce transactions between businesses and their suppliers and customers. As we will discuss in Chapter 8, e-commerce websites offer all manner of products and services via online retailers, wholesalers, service providers, and online auctions. See Figure 6.5.

The Internet provides electronic discussion forums and bulletin board systems formed and managed by thousands of special-interest newsgroups. You can participate in discussions or post messages on thousands of topics for other users with the same interests to read and respond to. Other popular applications include downloading software and information files and accessing databases provided by thousands of business, government, and other organizations. You can make online searches for information at websites in a variety of ways, using search sites and search engines such as Yahoo!,

FIGURE 6.5

Popular uses of the Internet.

- **Surf.** Point and click your way to thousands of hyperlinked websites and resources for multimedia information, entertainment, or electronic commerce.
- **e-Mail.** Use e-mail and instant messaging to exchange electronic messages with colleagues, friends, and other Internet users.
- **Discuss.** Participate in discussion forums of special-interest newsgroups, or hold real-time text conversations in website chat rooms.
- **Publish.** Post your opinion, subject matter, or creative work to a website or weblog for others to read.
- **Buy and Sell.** You can buy and sell practically anything via e-commerce retailers, wholesalers, service providers, and online auctions.
- **Download.** Transfer data files, software, reports, articles, pictures, music, videos, and other types of files to your computer system.
- **Compute.** Log on to and use thousands of Internet computer systems around the world.
- **Other Uses:** Make long-distance phone calls, hold desktop videoconferences, listen to radio programs, watch television, play video games, explore virtual worlds, etc.

Google, and Fast Search. Logging on to other computers on the Internet and holding real-time conversations with other Internet users in *chat rooms* are also popular uses of the Internet.

Business Use of the Internet

As Figure 6.6. illustrates, business use of the Internet has expanded from an electronic information exchange to a broad platform for strategic business applications. Notice how applications like collaboration among business partners, providing customer and vendor support, and electronic commerce have become major business uses of the Internet. Companies are also using Internet technologies for marketing, sales, and customer relationship management applications, as well as cross-functional business applications, and applications in engineering, manufacturing, human resources, and accounting. Let's look at a real world example.

GE Power Systems: Using the Internet

General Electric Co. (GE) provides a fascinating glimpse of how the Net changes things. At GE Power Systems, customers and designers can use intranets, extranets, the Internet, and project collaboration technology to help construct a power plant from the ground up on the Web, says Jose A. Lopez, the subsidiary's general manager of e-business.

GE and customer engineers can now hold virtual meetings in which blueprints can be exchanged and manipulated in real time. Then customers can use the Web to watch from anywhere in the world as a turbine is built and moves down the production line, ordering last-minute changes as needed. Because the turbines cost an average of $35 million each and contain about 18,000 parts, catching changes—and errors—early is priceless. And after the turbine is delivered, a new Net-powered system called the Turbine Optimizer lets both customers and GE compare the performances of the turbines with other GE turbines around the world.

While GE's new systems should give the company a 20 percent to 30 percent reduction in the time it takes to build a turbine and could improve the annual output of each turbine by 1 percent to 2 percent, that's just the beginning. "Sure, there are productivity gains for us, but this is mainly a competetive advantage," says Lopez. "If customers find this helps them, they'll come back." So far, so good: Sales at GE Power Systems have increased significantly since customers have been able to use the Net to monitor GE's production systems [19].

FIGURE 6.6 — Examples of how a company can use the Internet for business.

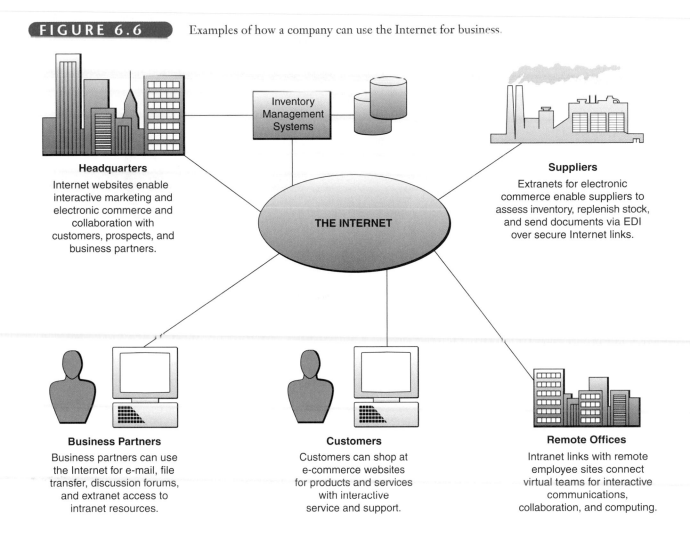

Headquarters
Internet websites enable interactive marketing and electronic commerce and collaboration with customers, prospects, and business partners.

Inventory Management Systems

THE INTERNET

Suppliers
Extranets for electronic commerce enable suppliers to assess inventory, replenish stock, and send documents via EDI over secure Internet links.

Business Partners
Business partners can use the Internet for e-mail, file transfer, discussion forums, and extranet access to intranet resources.

Customers
Customers can shop at e-commerce websites for products and services with interactive service and support.

Remote Offices
Intranet links with remote employee sites connect virtual teams for interactive communications, collaboration, and computing.

The Business Value of the Internet

The Internet provides a synthesis of computing and communication capabilities that adds value to every part of the business cycle [8].

What business value do companies derive from their business applications on the Internet? Figure 6.7 summarizes how many companies perceive the business value of the Internet for electronic commerce. Substantial cost savings can arise because applications that use the Internet and Internet-based technologies (like intranets and extranets) are typically less expensive to develop, operate, and maintain than traditional systems. For example, American Airlines saves money every time customers use their website instead of their customer support telephone system.

Other primary sources of business value include attracting new customers with innovative marketing and products, and retaining present customers with improved customer service and support. Of course, generating revenue through electronic commerce applications is a major source of business value, which we will discuss in Chapter 8. To summarize, most companies are building e-business and e-commerce websites to achieve six major business values:

- Generate new revenue from online sales.
- Reduce transaction costs through online sales and customer support.
- Attract new customers via Web marketing and advertising and online sales.
- Increase the loyalty of existing customers via improved Web customer service and support.

FIGURE 6.7

How companies are
deriving business value from
their e-business and
e-commerce applications.

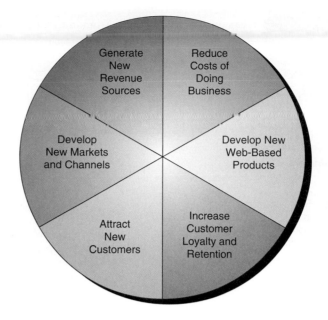

- Develop new Web-based markets and distribution channels for existing products.
- Develop new information-based products accessible on the Web [11].

The Role of Intranets

Many companies have sophisticated and widespread intranets, offering detailed data retrieval, collaboration tools, personalized customer profiles, and links to the Internet. Investing in the intranet, they feel, is as fundamental as supplying employees with a telephone [15].

Before we get any further, let's redefine the concept of an intranet, to specifically emphasize how intranets are related to the Internet and extranets. An **intranet** is a network inside an organization that uses Internet technologies (such as Web browsers and servers, TCP/IP network protocols, HTML hypermedia document publishing and databases, and so on) to provide an Internet-like environment within the enterprise for information sharing, communications, collaboration, and the support of business processes. An intranet is protected by security measures such as passwords, encryption, and firewalls, and thus can be accessed by authorized users through the Internet. A company's intranet can also be accessed through the intranets of customers, suppliers, and other business partners via *extranet* links.

The Business Value of Intranets

Organizations of all kinds are implementing a broad range of intranet uses. One way that companies organize intranet applications is to group them conceptually into a few user services categories that reflect the basic services that intranets offer to their users. These services are provided by the intranet's portal, browser, and server software, as well as by other system and application software and groupware that are part of a company's intranet software environment. Figure 6.8 illustrates how intranets provide an *enterprise information portal* that supports communication and collaboration, Web publishing, business operations and management, and intranet portal management. Notice also how these applications can be integrated with existing IS resources and applications, and extended to customers, suppliers, and business partners via the Internet and extranets.

Communications and Collaboration. Intranets can significantly improve communications and collaboration within an enterprise. For example, you can use your intranet browser and your PC or NC workstation to send and receive e-mail, voicemail,

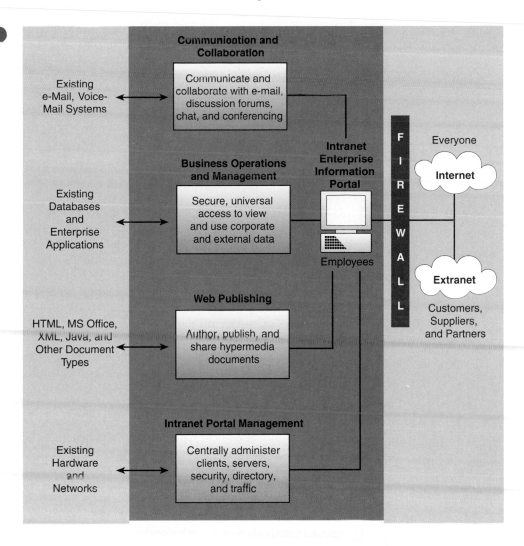

FIGURE 6.8

Intranets can provide an enterprise information portal for applications in communication and collaboration, business operations and management, Web publishing, and intranet portal management.

paging, and faxes to communicate with others within your organization, and externally through the Internet and extranets. You can also use intranet groupware features to improve team and project collaboration with services such as discussion groups, chat rooms, and audio- and videoconferencing.

Web Publishing. The advantages of developing and publishing hyperlinked multimedia documents to hypermedia databases accessible on World Wide Web servers has moved to corporate intranets. The comparative ease, attractiveness, and lower cost of publishing and accessing multimedia business information internally via intranet websites have been the primary reasons for the explosive growth in the use of intranets in business. For example, information products as varied as company newsletters, technical drawings, and product catalogs can be published in a variety of ways, including hypermedia Web pages, e-mail, and net broadcasting, and as part of in-house business applications. Intranet software browsers, servers, and search engines can help you easily navigate and locate the business information you need.

Business Operations and Management. Intranets have moved beyond merely making hypermedia information available on Web servers, or pushing it to users via net broadcasting. Intranets are also being used as the platform for developing and deploying critical business applications to support business operations and managerial decision making across the internetworked enterprise. For example, many companies are developing custom applications like order processing, inventory control, sales management, and enterprise information portals that can be implemented on intranets, extranets, and the Internet. Many of these applications are designed to interface with, and access, existing company databases and legacy systems. The software for such business uses is then installed on intranet Web servers. Employees within the company, or external business partners, can access and run such applications using Web browsers from anywhere on the network whenever needed.

Now let's look at one company's use of an intranet in more detail to get a better idea of how intranets are used in business.

Cadence OnTrack: Business Value of an Intranet

Cadence Design Systems is the leading supplier of electronic design automation (EDA) software tools and professional services for managing the design of semiconductors, computer systems, networking and telecommunications equipment, consumer electronics, and other electronics-based products. The company employs more than 3,000 people in offices worldwide to support the requirements of the world's leading electronics manufacturers. Cadence developed an intranet for 500 managers, sales reps, and customer support staff. Called OnTrack, the intranet project provides sales support for a Cadence product line of over 1,000 products and services.

The OnTrack system uses a home page with links to other pages, information sources, and other applications to support each phase of the sales process with supporting materials and reference information. For example, at any point in the sales process, such as one called "Identify Business Issues," a sales rep can find customer presentations, sample letters, and the internal forms needed to move effectively through this step.

With OnTrack, sales reps now use the intranet as a single enterprise information portal that provides all of the information and data needed to go through the sales process, from prospecting, to closing a deal, to account management. In addition, global account teams have their own home page where they can collaborate and share information. Information on customers or competitors is now available instantly through access to an outside provider of custom news. The sales rep simply searches using a company name to get everything from financial information to recent news articles and press releases about the customer or competitor [5].

The Role of Extranets

As businesses continue to use open Internet technologies [extranets] to improve communication with customers and partners, they can gain many competitive advantages along the way—in product development, cost savings, marketing, distribution, and leveraging their partnerships [2].

As we have explained earlier, **extranets** are network links that use Internet technologies to interconnect the intranet of a business with the intranets of its customers, suppliers, or other business partners. Companies can establish direct private network links between themselves, or create private secure Internet links between them called *virtual private networks*. Or a company can use the unsecured Internet as the extranet link between its intranet and consumers and others, but rely on encryption of sensitive data and its own firewall systems to provide adequate security. Thus, extranets enable customers, suppliers, consultants, subcontractors, business prospects, and others to access selected intranet websites and other company databases. See Figure 6.9.

Business Value of Extranets

The business value of extranets is derived from several factors. First, the Web browser technology of extranets makes customer and supplier access of intranet resources a lot easier and faster than previous business methods. Second, as you will see in two upcoming examples, extranets enable a company to offer new kinds of interactive Web-enabled services to their business partners. Thus, extranets are another way that a

FIGURE 6.9 Extranets connect the internetworked enterprise to consumers, business customers, suppliers, and other business partners.

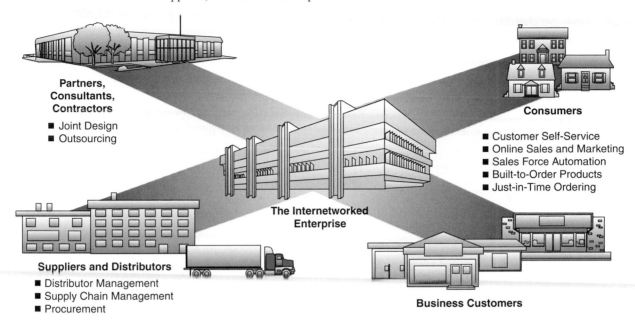

Partners, Consultants, Contractors

- Joint Design
- Outsourcing

The Internetworked Enterprise

Consumers

- Customer Self-Service
- Online Sales and Marketing
- Sales Force Automation
- Built-to-Order Products
- Just-in-Time Ordering

Suppliers and Distributors

- Distributor Management
- Supply Chain Management
- Procurement

Business Customers

business can build and strengthen strategic relationships with its customers and suppliers. Also, extranets can enable and improve collaboration by a business with its customers and other business partners. Extranets facilitate an online, interactive product development, marketing, and customer-focused process that can bring better-designed products to market faster.

Countrywide and Snap-on: Extranet Examples	Countrywide Home Loans has created an extranet called Platinum Lender Access for its lending partners and brokers. About 500 banks and mortgage brokers can access Countrywide's intranet and selected financial databases. The extranet gives them access to their account and transaction information, status of loans, and company announcements. Each lender or broker is automatically identified by the extranet and provided with customized information on premium rates, discounts, and any special business arrangements they have negotiated with Countrywide [2].

Snap-on Incorporated spent $300,000 to create an extranet link to their intranet called the Franchise Information Network. The extranet lets Snap-on's 4,000 independent franchises for automotive tools access a secured intranet website for customized information and interactive communications with Snap-on employees and other franchisees. Franchisers can get information on sales plus marketing updates. Tips and training programs about managing a franchise operation and discussion forums for employees and franchisees to share ideas and best practices are also provided by the extranet. Finally, the Franchise Information Network provides interactive news and information on car racing and other special events sponsored by Snap-on, as well as corporate stock prices, business strategies, and other financial information [17].

SECTION II Telecommunications Network Alternatives

Telecommunications Alternatives

Telecommunications is a highly technical, rapidly changing field of information systems technology. Most business professionals do not need a detailed knowledge of its technical characteristics. However, it is necessary that you understand some of the important characteristics of the basic components of telecommunications networks. This understanding will help you participate effectively in decision making regarding telecommunications alternatives.

Analyzing Con-Way NOW and Trimble Navigation

Read the Real World Case on Con-Way NOW and Trimble Navigation on the next page. We can learn a lot about the business value of GPS satellite networks from this case. See Figure 6.10.

This case looks at how GPS satellite tracking systems are used by trucking and cement companies and other businesses. Con-Way NOW uses GPS to track shipments by truck, and thus is able to offer its business customers guaranteed "time-definite delivery" of shipments in the United States and parts of Canada. The Omni TRACKS satellite tracking system is provided by Qualcomm. Inc., which monitors and provides data to all GPS antenna-equipped trucks and its business customers from its network management control center in San Diego. For example, Con-Way NOW'S business customers frequently include automotive industry suppliers and manufacturers, who are willing to pay a premium for guaranteed shipment of the auto parts that are needed to keep automobile factory assembly lines in operation. And Trimble Navigation is working with cement companies who have installed GPS devices on cement mixer trucks to better manage these time-sensitive mobile resources with GPS data accessed over the Internet.

FIGURE 6.10

The Qualcomm network management control center provides GPS satellite tracking services to trucking companies like Con-Way NOW.

Source: Amanda Friendman.

REAL WORLD CASE 2

Con-Way NOW and Trimble Navigation: The Business Value of GPS Satellite Networks

t's a little past noon in the utterly ordinary offices of a space-age trucking company called Con-Way NOW (www.con-waynow.com). When companies need something big moved quickly, they call an outfit like Con-Way NOW, a unit of transportation giant CNF, which operates 41,000 trucks, tractors, and trailers. Con-Way NOW, just seven years old, is based in Ann Arbor, Michigan. With only about 350 trucks, it is still a tiny part of CNF.

The whole operation is built around a simple guarantee: When you call Con-Way NOW and book a shipment, that shipment will arrive at the time promised, whether it's going across the state or across three time zones. In the trucking business, it's called "time-definite delivery." If the shipment is more than two hours late, it's half price. If it's more than four hours late, it's free.

A global positioning system (GPS) makes the whole thing possible. Con-Way NOW knows where every GPS antenna-equipped truck is, all the time. Not roughly where every truck is, but where every truck is to within less than one-tenth of a mile. When an order comes in, a dispatcher punches a computer function labeled FIND NEAREST, and a list of trucks comes up, displaying a full array of detailed information on the status of each of them. If a truck is running more than 15 minutes late, or if a truck strays off route by more than 200 feet, Qualcomm Inc.'s (www.qualcom.com) OmniTRACKS system based in San Diego, which supplies satellite tracking and mobile communications services to over 300,000 trucks in North America, notices and sends dispatchers an alert. Con-Way NOW says that it has only had to compensate customers for late shipments on less than 1 percent of orders.

In 10 years, GPS has quietly become an indispensable tool across the U.S. economy. Truckers use it, of course, as do fishermen, hikers, and surveyors. So do the terrestrial- and cellular-phone networks. Power companies and farmers use GPS, as do archaeologists, police departments, school districts, and concrete companies. Construction firms use it to navigate bulldozers, and several big seaports use it to guide robotic cranes that load and unload shipping containers. And the technology is just taking hold. It's predicted that, in 2003, just as many GPS devices of all kinds will be produced as in the previous 25 years that the constellation of 28 GPS satellites have been in orbit at 10,988 miles above the earth, financed by $9 billion from U.S. taxpayers, and managed and maintained by the U.S. Air Force. And predictions are that, in 2004, the number of consumer and commercial GPS devices will double again.

One of the oldest GPS companies is Trimble Navigation Ltd. (www.trimble.com), in Sunnyvale, California. Michael Lesyna, vice president of Trimble's mobile-solutions division, is focusing on bringing a highly refined version of the tracking system that Con-Way NOW uses to all kinds of commercial truck fleets. Trimble has begun with the ready-mix concrete business, equipping some of the over 80,000 cement mixer trucks on U.S. roads with GPS sensors and cell-phone data communicators.

What Trimble and others are quickly discovering is that GPS is what might be called a doorway technology. Once concrete companies know where their cement mixers are, "they want to know everything," says Lesyna. "When the truck left the cement plant, when it arrived at the job site, how fast it went, when it started to pour concrete, when it finished pouring, when it left the job site, when it arrived back at the plant."

This kind of GPS and communications equipment—it costs about $2,900 per truck, plus $50 per truck per month—makes a vast array of data about a company's truck fleet available. How long do trucks idle in the morning before being loaded? How long do they wait before being unloaded? Are the drivers driving safely? Are routes and job assignments efficient? All of the data is available instantly over the Internet.

"This business is not about the cost of moving something," says Chris Hance, a regional sales manager who just spent three years as a regional account executive for Con-Way NOW. "It's about the opportunity cost of not getting it there when you need it." The company routinely handles equipment for the military, medical supplies, newspaper inserts that are time sensitive, and, most often, auto parts, the kind of equipment that keeps an assembly line up and running. Ford books an average of 1,000 such shipments of auto parts each month. To a big manufacturer, spending a few thousand dollars to move equipment is nothing compared with letting an assembly line sit idle at a cost of $100,000 an hour. "We are Big Brother," says Hance. "That's what we are selling to our customers. They always know where the shipment is. We've got what it takes to let them sleep at night."

Case Study Questions

1. What is the business value of GPS satellite tracking and communications systems to Con-Way NOW? To their customers?

2. Visit the website of Qualcomm and check out the other satellite services besides OmniTRACKS. What is the business value of several of these services?

3. What is the business value of the GPS services offered by Trimble Navigation to cement companies? To other types of businesses? Visit their website to help you answer.

Source: Adapted from "The Sky's the Limit" by Charles Fishman. This article was originally published in the July 2003 issue of FAST COMPANY, © 2003 by FAST COMPANY. All rights reserved.

FIGURE 6.11

Key telecommunications network components and alternatives.

Network Alternative	Examples of Alternatives
Networks	Internet, intranet, extranet, wide area, local area, client/server, network computing, peer-to-peer
Media	Twisted-pair wire, coaxial cable, fiber optics, microwave radio, communications satellites, cellular and PCS systems, wireless mobile and LAN systems
Processors	Modems, multiplexers, switches, routers, hubs, gateways, front-end processors, private branch exchanges
Software	Network operating systems, telecommunications monitors, Web browsers, middleware
Channels	Analog/digital, switched/nonswitched, circuit/message/packet/cell switching, bandwidth alternatives
Topology/architecture	Star, ring, and bus topologies, OSI and TCP/IP architectures and protocols

Figure 6.11 outlines key telecommunications components and alternatives. Remember, a basic understanding and appreciation, not a detailed knowledge, are sufficient for most business professionals.

A Telecommunications Network Model

Before we begin our discussion of telecommunications network alternatives, we should understand the basic components of a **telecommunications network.** Generally, a *communications network* is any arrangement where a *sender* transmits a message to a *receiver* over a *channel* consisting of some type of *medium.* Figure 6.12 illustrates a simple conceptual model of a telecommunications network, which shows that it consists of five basic categories of components:

- **Terminals,** such as networked personal computers, network computers, or information appliances. Any input/output device that uses telecommunications networks to transmit or receive data is a terminal, including telephones and the various computer terminals that were discussed in Chapter 3.

- **Telecommunications processors,** which support data transmission and reception between terminals and computers. These devices, such as modems, switches, and routers, perform a variety of control and support functions in a telecommunications network. For example, they convert data from digital to analog and back,

FIGURE 6.12

The five basic components in a telecommunications network: (1) terminals, (2) telecommunications processors, (3) telecommunications channels, (4) computers, and (5) telecommunications software.

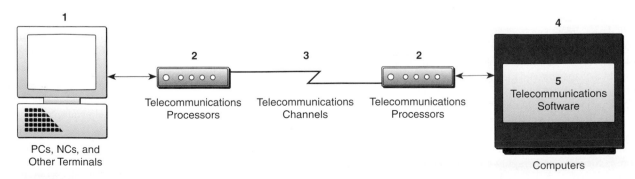

code and decode data, and control the speed, accuracy, and efficiency of the communications flow between computers and terminals in a network

- **Telecommunications channels** over which data are transmitted and received. Telecommunications channels may use combinations of **media,** such as copper wires, coaxial cables, or fiber-optic cables, or use wireless systems like microwave, communications satellite, radio, and cellular systems to interconnect the other components of a telecommunications network.

- **Computers** of all sizes and types are interconnected by telecommunications networks so that they can carry out their information processing assignments. For example, a mainframe computer may serve as a *host computer* for a large network, assisted by a midrange computer serving as a *front-end processor*, while a microcomputer may act as a *network server* in a small network.

- **Telecommunications control software** consists of programs that control telecommunications activities and manage the functions of telecommunications networks. Examples include network management programs of all kinds, such as *telecommunications monitors* for mainframe host computers, *network operating systems* for network servers, and *Web browsers* for microcomputers.

No matter how large and complex real world telecommunications networks may appear to be, these five basic categories of network components must be at work to support an organization's telecommunications activities. This is the conceptual framework you can use to help you understand the various types of telecommunications networks in use today.

Types of Telecommunications Networks

Many different types of networks serve as the telecommunications infrastructure for the Internet and the intranets and extranets of internetworked enterprises. However, from an end user's point of view, there are only a few basic types, such as wide area and local area networks and client/server, network computing, and peer-to-peer networks.

Wide Area Networks

Telecommunications networks covering a large geographic area are called **wide area networks** (WANs). Networks that cover a large city or metropolitan area (*metropolitan area networks*) can also be included in this category. Such large networks have become a necessity for carrying out the day-to-day activities of many business and government organizations and their end users. For example, WANs are used by many multinational companies to transmit and receive information among their employees, customers, suppliers, and other organizations across cities, regions, countries, and the world. Figure 6.13 illustrates an example of a global wide area network for a major multinational corporation.

Local Area Networks

Local area networks (LANs) connect computers and other information processing devices within a limited physical area, such as an office, classroom, building, manufacturing plant, or other work site. LANs have become commonplace in many organizations for providing telecommunications network capabilities that link end users in offices, departments, and other workgroups.

LANs use a variety of telecommunications media, such as ordinary telephone wiring, coaxial cable, or even wireless radio and infrared systems, to interconnect microcomputer workstations and computer peripherals. To communicate over the network, each PC usually has a circuit board called a *network interface card*. Most LANs use a more powerful microcomputer having a large hard disk capacity, called a *file server* or **network server,** that contains a **network operating system** program that controls telecommunications and the use and sharing of network resources. For example, it distributes copies of common data files and software packages to the other

FIGURE 6.13 A global wide area network (WAN): The Chevron MPI (Multi-Protocol Internetwork).

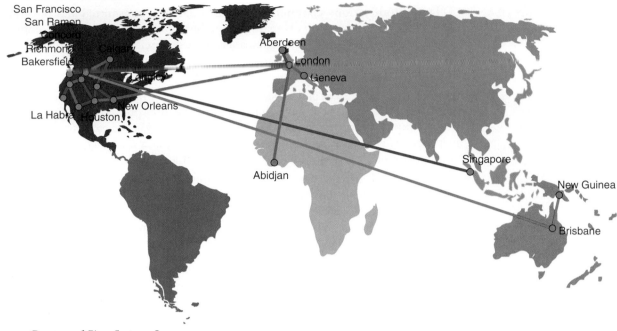

Source: Courtesy of Cisco Systems, Inc.

microcomputers in the network and controls access to shared laser printers and other network peripherals. See Figure 6.14.

Virtual Private Networks

Many organizations use *virtual private networks* (VPNs) to establish secure intranets and extranets. A **virtual private network** is a secure network that uses the Internet as its main *backbone network*, but relies on network firewalls, encryption, and other security features of its Internet and intranet connections and those of participating organizations. Thus, for example, VPNs would enable a company to use the Internet to

FIGURE 6.14

A local area network (LAN). Note how the LAN allows users to share hardware, software, and data resources.

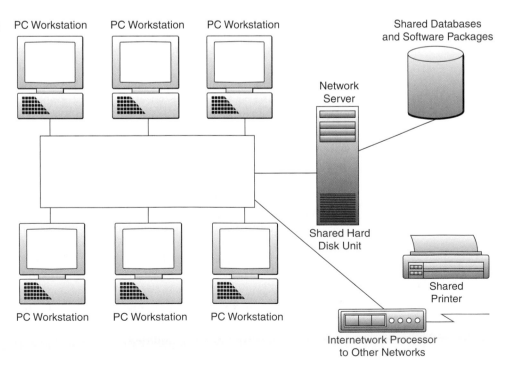

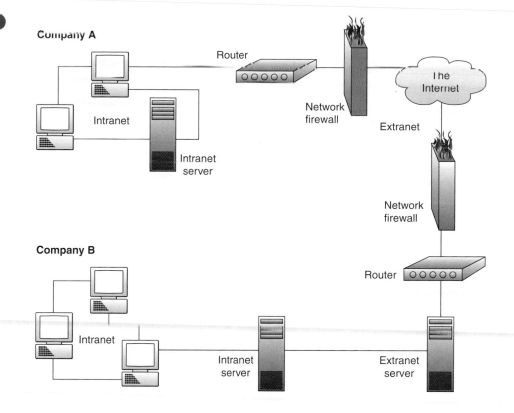

An example of a virtual private network protected by network firewalls.

establish secure intranets between its distant branch offices and manufacturing plants, and secure extranets between itself and its business customers and suppliers. Figure 6.15 illustrates a VPN where network routers serve as firewalls to screen Internet traffic between two companies. We will discuss firewalls, encryption, and other network security features in Chapter 11. Let's look at a real world example.

Link Staffing: Challenges of VPN Services

George Gaulda, CIO at Link Staffing Inc. (www.linkstaffing.com) wanted to securely connect 49 branch offices in 23 states to his company's Houston headquarters. Gaulda decided he needed to build a virtual private network (VPN) to tie the far-flung parts of Link Staffing together. Trouble was, he lacked the staff to design and manage the system. So Gaulda chose OpenReach Inc. to provide Link Staffing with a secure VPN over the Internet.

Link Staffing is one of many companies that are turning to outsourced VPN services. Some are pinched for security-savvy network personnel. And even some that have the staffs simply want to off-load the hassle of policing increased network infrastructure to a firm that provides VPNs for a living. The offerings of those providers, however, vary significantly and require users to evaluate their needs thoroughly and select their providers carefully. Prior to cutting a deal with OpenReach, Gaulda says, he had a "very bad experience with a major service provider." Gaulda won't name the company, but he says it was unwilling to provide the support his firm needed. His technicians ended up doing most of the VPN support work, which contradicted the idea of using a service provider in the first place, he says.

Although OpenReach manages the network, Gaulda says he never feels out of the control loop because he can view VPN performance from his own desktop PC through a special browser-based interface provided by the VPN's network management software. "I can drill down to the workstation level on a remote location to see how the VPN is performing," he says [7].

FIGURE 6.16

The functions of the computer systems in client/server networks.

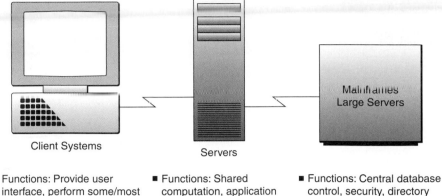

Client Systems

Servers

Mainframes Large Servers

■ Functions: Provide user interface, perform some/most processing on an application.

■ Functions: Shared computation, application control, distributed databases.

■ Functions: Central database control, security, directory management, heavy-duty processing.

Client/Server Networks

Client/server networks have become the predominant information architecture of enterprisewide computing. In a client/server network, end user PC or NC workstations are the **clients.** They are interconnected by local area networks and share application processing with network **servers,** which also manage the networks. (This arrangement of clients and servers is sometimes called a *two-tier* client/server architecture.) Local area networks are also interconnected to other LANs and wide area networks of client workstations and servers. Figure 6.16 illustrates the functions of the computer systems that may be in client/server networks, including optional host systems and superservers.

A continuing trend is the **downsizing** of larger computer systems by replacing them with client/server networks. For example, a client/server network of several interconnected local area networks may replace a large mainframe-based network with many end user terminals. This typically involves a complex and costly effort to install new application software that replaces the software of older, traditional mainframe-based business information systems, now called **legacy systems.** Client/server networks are seen as more economical and flexible than legacy systems in meeting end user, workgroup, and business unit needs, and more adaptable in adjusting to a diverse range of computing workloads.

Network Computing

The growing reliance on the computer hardware, software, and data resources of the Internet, intranets, extranets, and other networks has emphasized that for many users, "the network is the computer." This **network computing** or *network-centric* concept views networks as the central computing resource of any computing environment.

Figure 6.17 illustrates that in network computing, **network computers** and other *thin clients* provide a browser-based user interface for processing small application programs called *applets.* Thin clients include network computers, Net PCs, and other low-cost network devices or information appliances. Application and database servers provide the operating system, application software, applets, databases, and database management software needed by the end users in the network. Network computing is sometimes called a *three-tier* client/server model, since it consists of thin clients, application servers, and database servers.

Peer-to-Peer Networks

The emergence of peer-to-peer (P2P) networking technologies and applications for the Internet is being hailed as a development that will have a major impact on e-business and e-commerce and the Internet itself. Whatever the merits of such claims, it is clear that peer-to-peer networks are a powerful telecommunications networking tool for many business applications.

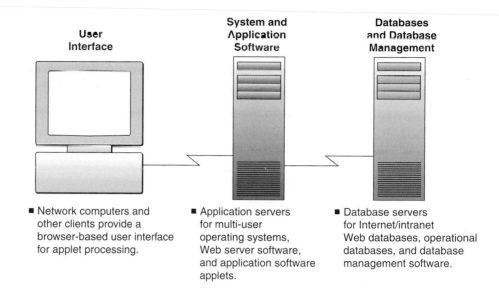

FIGURE 6.17

The functions of the computer systems in network computing.

User Interface

- Network computers and other clients provide a browser-based user interface for applet processing.

System and Application Software

- Application servers for multi-user operating systems, Web server software, and application software applets.

Databases and Database Management

- Database servers for Internet/intranet Web databases, operational databases, and database management software.

Figure 6.18 illustrates two major models of **peer-to-peer networking** technology. In the central server architecture, P2P file-sharing software connects your PC to a central server that contains a directory of all of the other users *(peers)* in the network. When you request a file, the software searches the directory for any other users who have that file and are online at that moment. It then sends you a list of user names that are active links to all such users. Clicking on one of these user names prompts the software to connect your PC to their PC (making a *peer-to-peer* connection) and automatically transfers the file you want from their hard drive to yours.

FIGURE 6.18

The two major forms of peer-to-peer networks.

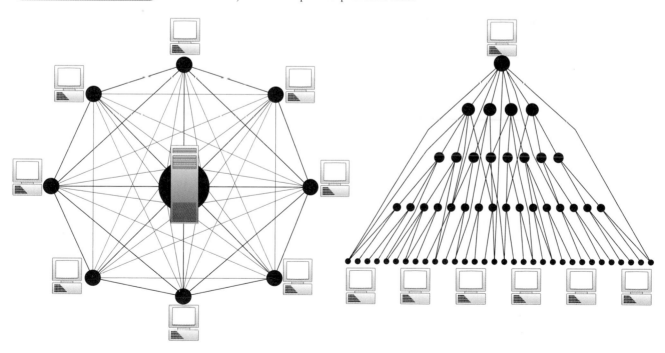

- A peer-to-peer network architecture with a directory of all peers on a central server

- A pure peer-to-peer network architecture with no central directory server

The *pure* peer-to-peer network architecture has no central directory or server. First, the file sharing software in the P2P network connects your PC with one of the online users in the network. Then an active link to your user name is transmitted from peer to peer to all the online users in the network that the first user (and the other online users) encountered in previous sessions. In this way, active links to more and more peers spread throughout the network the more it is used. When you request a file, the software searches every online user and sends you a list of active file names related to your request. Clicking on one of these automatically transfers the file from their hard drive to yours.

One of the major advantages and limitations of the central server architecture is its reliance on a central directory and server. The directory server can be slowed or overwhelmed by too many users or technical problems. However, it also provides the network with a platform that can better protect the integrity and security of the content and users of the network. Some applications of pure P2P networks, on the other hand, have been plagued by slow response times and bogus and corrupted files.

Telecommunications Media

Telecommunications channels make use of a variety of **telecommunications media.** These include twisted-pair wire, coaxial cables, and fiber-optic cables, all of which physically link the devices in a network. Also included are terrestrial microwave, communications satellites, cellular phone systems, and packet and LAN radio, all of which use microwave and other radio waves. In addition, there are infrared systems, which use infrared light to transmit and receive data.

Twisted-Pair Wire

Ordinary telephone wire, consisting of copper wire twisted into pairs (**twisted-pair wire**), is the most widely used medium for telecommunications. These lines are used in established communications networks throughout the world for both voice and data transmission. Twisted-pair wiring is wrapped or shielded in a variety of forms, and used extensively in home and office telephone systems and many local area networks and wide area networks. Transmission speeds can range from 2 million bits per second (unshielded) to 100 million bits per second (shielded).

Coaxial Cable

Coaxial cable consists of a sturdy copper or aluminum wire wrapped with spacers to insulate and protect it. The cable's cover and insulation minimize interference and distortion of the signals the cable carries. Groups of coaxial cables may be bundled together in a big cable for ease of installation. These high-quality lines can be placed underground and laid on the floors of lakes and oceans. They allow high-speed data transmission (from 200 million to over 500 million bits per second—200 Mbps to 500 Mbps), and are used instead of twisted-pair wire lines in high-service metropolitan areas, for cable TV systems, and for short-distance connection of computers and peripheral devices. Coaxial cables are also used in many office buildings and other work sites for local area networks.

Fiber Optics

Fiber optics uses cables consisting of one or more hair-thin filaments of glass fiber wrapped in a protective jacket. They can conduct pulses of visible light elements (*photons*) generated by lasers at transmission rates as high as trillions of bits per second (terabits per second or Tbps). This is about hundreds of times greater than coaxial cable and thousands of times better than twisted-pair wire lines. Fiber-optic cables provide substantial size and weight reductions as well as increased speed and greater carrying capacity. A half-inch-diameter fiber-optic cable can carry over 500,000 channels, compared to about 5,500 channels for a standard coaxial cable.

Fiber-optic cables are not affected by and do not generate electromagnetic radiation; therefore, multiple fibers can be placed in the same cable. Fiber-optic cables have less need for repeaters for signal retransmissions than copper wire media. Fiber optics also has a much lower data error rate than other media and is harder to tap than electrical wire and cable. Fiber-optic cables have already been installed in many parts of the world, and they are expected to replace other communications media in many applications.

New optical technologies such as *dense wave division multiplexing* (DWDM) can split a strand of glass fiber into 40 channels, which enables each strand to carry 5 million calls. In the future, DWDM technology is expected to split each fiber into 1,000 channels, enabling each strand to carry up to 122 million calls. In addition, newly developed *optical routers* will be able to send optical signals up to 2,500 miles without needing regeneration, thus eliminating the need for repeaters every 370 miles to regenerate signals [19].

Wireless Technologies

Wireless telecommunications technologies rely on radio wave, microwave, infrared, and visible light pulses to transport digital communications without wires between communications devices. Wireless technologies include terrestrial microwave, communications satellites, cellular and PCS telephone and pager systems, mobile data radio, wireless LANs, and various wireless Internet technologies. Each technology utilizes specific ranges within the electromagnetic spectrum (in megahertz) of electromagnetic frequencies that are specified by national regulatory agencies to minimize interference and encourage efficient telecommunications. Let's briefly review some of these major wireless communications technologies. See Figure 6.19.

Terrestrial Microwave

Terrestrial microwave involves earthbound microwave systems that transmit high-speed radio signals in a line-of-sight path between relay stations spaced approximately 30 miles apart. Microwave antennas are usually placed on top of buildings, towers, hills, and mountain peaks, and they are a familiar sight in many sections of the country. They are still a popular medium for both long-distance and metropolitan area networks.

Communications Satellites

Communications satellites also use microwave radio as their telecommunications medium. Typically, high-earth orbit (HEO) communications satellites are placed in stationary geosynchronous orbits approximately 22,000 miles above the equator.

FIGURE 6.19

The Ericsson Smartphone gives users wireless Internet access for e-mail and website services.

Source: Courtesy of Ericsson.

Satellites are powered by solar panels and can transmit microwave signals at a rate of several hundred million bits per second. They serve as relay stations for communications signals transmitted from earth stations. Earth stations use dish antennas to beam microwave signals to the satellites that amplify and retransmit the signals to other earth stations thousands of miles away.

While communications satellites were used initially for voice and video transmission, they are now also used for high-speed transmission of large volumes of data. Because of time delays caused by the great distances involved, they are not suitable for interactive, real-time processing. Communications satellite systems are operated by several firms, including Comsat, American Mobile Satellite, and Intellsat.

A variety of other satellite technologies are being implemented to improve global business communications. For example, many companies use networks of small satellite dish antennas known as VSAT (very-small-aperture terminal) to connect their stores and distant work sites via satellite. Other satellite networks use many low-earth orbit (LEO) satellites orbiting at an altitude of only 500 miles above the earth. Companies like Globalstar offer wireless phone, paging, and messaging services to users anywhere on the globe. Let's look at a real world example.

Bob Evans Farms: The Case for Satellite Networks

The network connecting the Bob Evans Farms, Inc., 459 restaurants and six food production plants to each other and the Internet runs via satellite, a technology choice that came as something of a surprise to company executives. "Truthfully, we didn't want to do satellite at first," says Bob Evans Farms CIO Larry Beckwith. The company looked at frame relay, ISDN lines, a virtual private network over the Internet, and DSL services. But a VSAT (very small aperture terminal) communications satellite network was the only technology that supported Bob Evans' goals, was available at all sites, and was cost-effective, Beckwith says.

But until last year, the computers at Bob Evans restaurants dialed in daily over ordinary phone lines to the Columbus, Ohio, headquarters to report sales, payroll, and other data. That worked well enough, Beckwith says. Credit card authorization, especially on busy weekend mornings, was another story. "With dial-up, every time you swipe a credit card, a modem dials the credit card authorization site, makes the connection, then verifies the card, which takes another 15 seconds," Beckwith says. If the connection fails, it restarts after timing out for 30 seconds, "a long time when you've got a line of people waiting to pay. We needed a persistent IP connection."

Satellite would give the restaurants the connection and sufficient bandwidth— 8M bit/second outbound from remote sites, and 153K bit/second inbound. After talks with satellite network vendors, Beckwith ran tests for two months, first in the lab, then in one restaurant, on a Skystar Advantage system from Spacenet Inc. Only after a further month-long pilot project with 10 stores was Beckwith sold on satellite. During the next five weeks, Spacenet rolled out earth stations to 440 stores, and the network went live in September 2000.

"Average time to do a credit card authorization is about three seconds now, including getting your printed receipt," Beckwith says. Also running over satellite are nightly automatic polling of financial data from the point-of-sale (POS) systems, Lotus Notes e-mail to managers, and online manuals of restaurant procedures, restaurant POS systems, facilities and physical plant maintenance, "things the restaurants never had live access to before," Beckwith says.

New applications planned include online inventory management, with XML-based electronic ordering to follow. In-store audio for music and promotional messages, and video broadcasting for employee training and corporate communications (Skystar supports IP multicasting) are also in the works for the near future [13].

Cellular and PCS Systems

Cellular and PCS telephone and pager systems use several radio communications technologies. However, all of them divide a geographic area into small areas, or *cells*, typically from one to several square miles in area. Each cell has its own low-power transmitter or radio relay antenna device to relay calls from one cell to another. Computers and other communications processors coordinate and control the transmissions to and from mobile users as they move from one area to another.

Cellular phone systems have long used analog communications technologies operating at frequencies in the 800 to 900 MHz cellular band. Newer cellular systems use digital technologies, which provide greater capacity and security, and additional services such as voice mail, paging, messaging, and caller ID. These capabilities are also available with PCS (Personal Communications Services) phone systems. PCS operates at 1,900 MHz frequencies using digital technologies that are related to digital cellular. However, PCS phone systems cost substantially less to operate and use than cellular systems and have lower power consumption requirements.

Wireless LANs

Wiring an office or a building for a local area network is often a difficult and costly task. Older buildings frequently do not have conduits for coaxial cables or additional twisted-pair wire, and the conduits in newer buildings may not have enough room to pull additional wiring through. Repairing mistakes and damages to wiring is often difficult and costly, as are major relocations of LAN workstations and other components. One solution to such problems is installing a **wireless LAN,** using one of several wireless technologies. Examples include a high-frequency radio technology similar to digital cellular, and a low-frequency radio technology called *spread spectrum*.

The use of wireless LANs is growing rapidly as new high-speed technologies are implemented. A prime example is a new open-standard wireless radio-wave technology technically known as IEEE 802.11b, or more popularly as Wi-Fi (for wireless fidelity). Wi-Fi is faster (11 Mbps) and less expensive than Standard Ethernet and other common wire-based LAN technologies. Thus, Wi-Fi wireless LANs enable laptop PCs, PDAs, and other devices with Wi-Fi modems to easily connect to the Internet and other networks in a rapidly increasing number of business, public, and home environments. An even faster version (802.11g) with speeds of 54 Mbps promises to make this technology even more widely used.

In addition, a short-range wireless technology called "Bluetooth" is rapidly being built in to computers and other devices. Bluetooth serves as a wire- and cable-free wireless connection to peripheral devices such as computer printers and scanners. Bluetooth operates at about one Mbps, and has an effective range between 10 to 100 meters [4].

The Wireless Web

Wireless access to the Internet, intranets, and extranets is growing as more Web-enabled information appliances proliferate. Smart telephones, pagers, PDAs, and other portable communications devices have become *very thin clients* in wireless networks. Agreement on a standard *wireless application protocol* (WAP) has encouraged the development of many wireless Web applications and services. The telecommunications industry continues to work on *third generation* (3G) wireless technologies whose goal is to raise wireless transmission speeds to enable streaming video and multimedia applications on mobile devices.

For example, the Smartphone, a PCS phone shown in Figure 6.19, can send and receive e-mail and provide Web access via a "Web clipping" technology that generates custom-designed Web pages from many popular financial, securities, travel, sport, entertainment, and e-commerce websites. Another example is the Sprint PCS Wireless Web phone, which delivers similar Web content and e-mail services via a Web-enabled PCS phone.

Figure 6.20 illustrates the wireless application protocol that is the foundation of wireless mobile Internet and Web applications. The WAP standard specifies how Web pages in HTML or XML are translated into a *wireless markup language* (WML) by *filter* software and preprocessed by *proxy* software to prepare the Web pages for wireless transmission from a Web server to a Web-enabled wireless device [14].

FIGURE 6.20 The wireless application protocol (WAP) architecture for wireless Internet services to mobile information appliances.

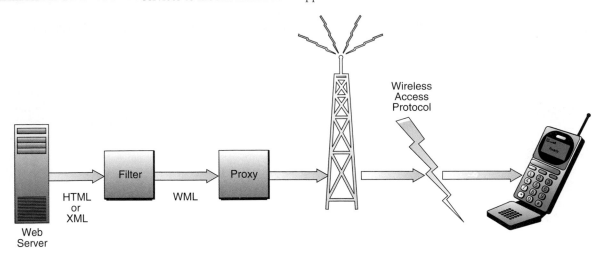

UPS: Wireless LANs and M-Commerce	Atlanta-based UPS uses wireless as part of UPScan, a companywide, global initiative to streamline and standardize all scanning hardware and software used in their package distribution centers. For package tracking, UPScan will consolidate multiple scanning applications into one wireless LAN application, while maintaining interfaces with critical control and repository systems. The project is part of a $100 million upgraded and expanded effort throughout the decade.

UPS will use Bluetooth, a short-range wireless networking protocol for communications with cordless peripherals (such as ring-mounted wireless manual scanners), linked to wireless LANs, which communicate with corporate systems. The project calls for fixed-mount, wearable, and portable devices, which are expected to serve most UPS applications, from package tracking to equipment monitoring to two-way communications. UPS will also install advanced wireless LANs using WiFi technology at all of its 2,000 facilities worldwide.

UPS has also developed application programming interfaces (APIs) in-house to link its legacy tracking systems to business customers, such as retailers that wanted to provide order-status information on their websites from UPS to their customers. When UPS decided to offer its customers wireless shipment tracking as part of a mobile commerce/information services package, it hired Air2Web, Inc., a wireless application service provider in Atlanta. The company used the existing APIs to link UPS business applications to multiple types of wireless networks from different providers and configure them for a range of wireless devices, from PDAs to cell phones [18].

Telecommunications Processors

Telecommunications processors such as modems, multiplexers, switches, and routers perform a variety of support functions between the computers and other devices in a telecommunications network. Let's take a look at some of these processors and their functions. See Figure 6.21.

Modems

Modems are the most common type of communications processor. They convert the digital signals from a computer or transmission terminal at one end of a communications link into analog frequencies that can be transmitted over ordinary telephone lines. A modem at the other end of the communications line converts the transmitted data back into digital form at a receiving terminal. This process is known as *modulation* and *demodulation*, and the word *modem* is a combined abbreviation of those two words. Modems come in several forms, including small stand-alone units, plug-in circuit boards, and removable

FIGURE 6.21

Examples of some of the communications processors involved in an Internet connection.

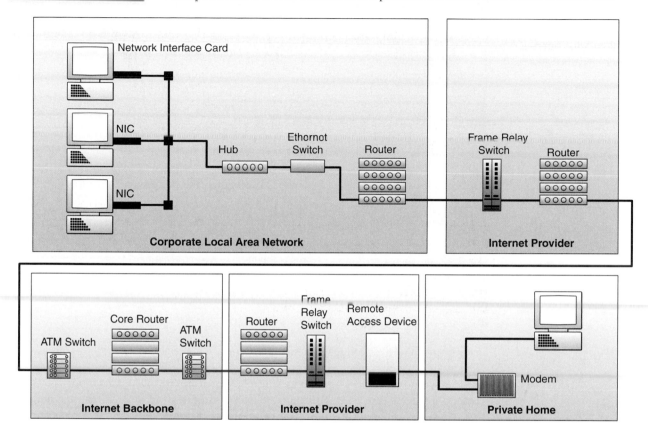

modem cards for laptop PCs. Most modems also support a variety of telecommunications functions, such as transmission error control, automatic dialing and answering, and a faxing capability.

Modems are used because ordinary telephone networks were first designed to handle continuous analog signals (electromagnetic frequencies), such as those generated by the human voice over the telephone. Since data from computers are in digital form (voltage pulses), devices are necessary to convert digital signals into appropriate analog transmission frequencies and vice versa. However, digital communications networks that use only digital signals and do not need analog/digital conversion are becoming commonplace. Since most modems also perform a variety of telecommunications support functions, devices called digital modems are still used in digital networks.

Figure 6.22 compares several modem and telecommunications technologies for access to the Internet and other networks by home and business users.

Multiplexers

A **multiplexer** is a communications processor that allows a single communications channel to carry simultaneous data transmissions from many terminals. This is accomplished in two basic ways. In *frequency division multiplexing* (FDM), a multiplexer effectively divides a high-speed channel into multiple slow-speed channels. In *time division multiplexing* (TDM), the multiplexer divides the time each terminal can use the high-speed line into very short time slots, or time frames.

Internetwork Processors

Telecommunications networks are interconnected by special-purpose communications processors called **internetwork processors** such as switches, routers, hubs, and gateways. A *switch* is a communications processor that makes connections between telecommunications circuits in a network. Switches are now available in managed

Comparing modem and telecommunications technologies for Internet and other network access.

Modem (56K bit/sec)	DSL (Digital Subscriber Line) Modem
• Receives at 56K bit/sec.	• Receives at 1.5M to 5.0M bit/sec.
• Sends at 33.6K bit/sec.	• Sends at 128K to 640K bit/sec.
• Slowest technology	• Users must be near switching centers
ISDN (Integrated Services Digital Network)	**Cable Modem**
• Sends and receives at 128K bit/sec.	• Receives at 1.5M to 5M bit/sec.
• Users need extra lines	• Sends at 128K to 2.5M bit/sec.
• Becoming obsolete	• Speed degrades with many local users
Home Satellite	**Local Microwave**
• Receives at 400K bit/sec.	• Sends and receives at 512K to 1.4M bit/sec.
• Sends via phone modem	• Higher cost alternative
• Slow sending, higher cost	• May require line of sight to base antenna

versions with network management capabilities. A *router* is an intelligent communications processor that interconnects networks based on different rules or *protocols*, so a telecommunications message can be routed to its destination. A *hub* is a port switching communications processor. Advanced versions of both hubs and switches provide automatic switching among connections called *ports* for shared access to a network's resources. Workstations, servers, printers, and other network resources are typically connected to ports. Networks that use different communications architectures are interconnected by using a communications processor called a *gateway*. All these devices are essential to providing connectivity and easy access between the multiple LANs and wide area networks that are part of the intranets and client/server networks in many organizations.

Telecommunications Software

Software is a vital component of all telecommunications networks. Telecommunications and network management software may reside in PCs, servers, mainframes, and communications processors like multiplexers and routers. These programs are used by network servers and other computers in a network to manage network performance. Network management programs perform such functions as automatically checking client PCs for input/output activity, assigning priorities to data communications requests from clients and terminals, and detecting and correcting transmission errors and other network problems.

For example, mainframe-based wide area networks frequently use *telecommunications monitors or teleprocessing* (TP) monitors. CICS (Customer Identification Control System) for IBM mainframes is a typical example. Servers in local area and other networks frequently rely on *network operating systems* like Novell NetWare, or operating systems like UNIX, Linux, or Microsoft Windows 2003 Servers for network management. Many software vendors also offer telecommunications software as *middleware*, which can help diverse networks communicate with each other.

Telecommunications functions built into Microsoft Windows and other operating systems provide a variety of communications support services. For example, they work with a communications processor (such as a modem) to connect and disconnect communications links and establish communications parameters such as transmission speed, mode, and direction.

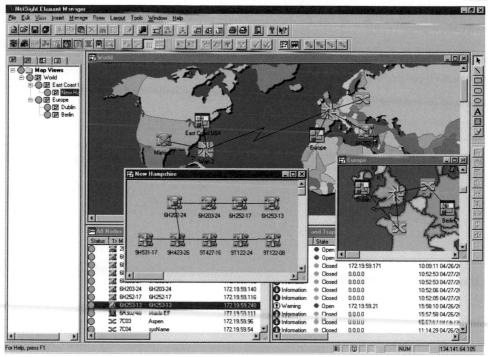

FIGURE 6.23

Network management software monitors and manages network performance.

Source: Courtesy of Avnet.

Network Management

Network management packages such as network operating systems and telecommunications monitors determine transmission priorities, route (switch) messages, poll terminals in the network, and form waiting lines (queues) of transmission requests. They also detect and correct transmission errors, log statistics of network activity, and protect network resources from unauthorized access. See Figure 6.23.

Examples of major **network management** functions include:

- **Traffic management.** Manage network resources and traffic to avoid congestion and optimize telecommunications service levels to users.

- **Security.** Security is one of the top concerns of network management today. Thus, telecommunications software must provide authentication, encryption, firewall, and auditing functions, and enforce security policies. Encryption, firewalls, and other network security defenses are covered in Chapter 11.

- **Network monitoring.** Troubleshoot and watch over the network, informing network administrators of potential problems before they occur.

- **Capacity planning.** Survey network resources and traffic patterns and users' needs to determine how best to accommodate the needs of the network as it grows and changes.

Nielsen Media Research and Others: Network Bandwidth Management Challenges

Kim Ross, CIO at Nielsen Media Research (www.nielsenmedia.com) in Dunedin, Florida, says "With Internet applications, more resources are shared. If you add more bandwidth capacity to a shared pool without a clear idea of why or where it's needed, you're unlikely to get the result you want. The way we deal with it is we watch bandwidth utilization day by day, week by week and watch for spikes in utilization," Ross says. "Usually it's someone trying something new, but 9 times out of 10, it's not something that's business-critical. We'll do the detective work to find out where it's coming from," Ross adds, "One aspect of our control policy is to be sure our IT governance system communicates guidelines to our users. Clear, well-understood policies can help you prevent some problems from even coming up."

Online gaming and peer-to-peer networking services that allow downloading of audio files, software, and movies, such as those offered at the Morpheus, Kazaa, and Grokster websites, can quickly gobble up bandwidth. Part of tuning the network at investment management services firm Ark Asset Management Co. (www.the-ark.com) in New York was "toughening up on users," says Danny Shpak, manager of Ark's IT group. "That means no gaming, for one thing."

Ark uses Eye of the Storm software from New York–based Entuity Ltd. to monitor its network and locate and ease the pain points. Streaming stock quotes constitute the single greatest use of bandwidth, says Shpak, but "no one thing really put us over the top." Monitoring helped him identify bottlenecks such as those resulting from misconfigured connections between clients and servers. Sometimes the fix was as simple as moving an application server closer to those workers who used it most. In other cases, he had to invest in larger routers or switches or more bandwidth. "Tuning was most important," Shpak says. "I'm interested in solving problems, not measuring bandwidth. For me, the more important issue is to have my network run cleanly." [12].

Network Topologies

There are several basic types of network *topologies*, or structures, in telecommunications networks. Figure 6.24 illustrates three basic topologies used in wide area and local area telecommunications networks. A star network ties end user computers to a central computer. A *ring* network ties local computer processors together in a ring on a more equal basis. A *bus* network is a network in which local processors share the same bus, or communications channel. A variation of the ring network is the *mesh* network. It uses direct communications lines to connect some or all of the computers in the ring to each other.

FIGURE 6.24 The ring, star, and bus network topologies.

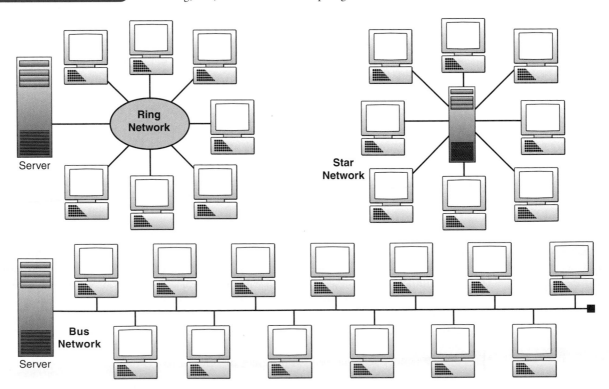

Client/server networks may use a combination of star, ring, and bus approaches. Obviously, the star network is more centralized, while ring and bus networks have a more decentralized approach. However, this is not always the case. For example, the central computer in a star configuration may be acting only as a *switch*, or message-switching computer, that handles the data communications between autonomous local computers. Star, ring, and bus networks differ in their performances, reliabilities, and costs. A pure star network is considered less reliable than a ring network, since the other computers in the star are heavily dependent on the central host computer. If it fails, there is no backup processing and communications capability, and the local computers are cut off from each other. Therefore, it is essential that the host computer be highly reliable. Having some type of multiprocessor architecture to provide a fault tolerant capability is a common solution.

Network Architectures and Protocols

Until quite recently, there was a lack of sufficient standards for the interfaces between the hardware, software, and communications channels of telecommunications networks. This situation hampered the use of telecommunications, increased its costs, and reduced its efficiency and effectiveness. In response, telecommunications manufacturers and national and international organizations have developed standards called *protocols* and master plans called *network architectures* to support the development of advanced data communications networks.

Protocols. A protocol is a standard set of rules and procedures for the control of communications in a network. However, these standards may be limited to just one manufacturer's equipment, or to just one type of data communications. Part of the goal of communications network architectures is to create more standardization and compatibility among communications protocols. One example of a protocol is a standard for the physical characteristics of the cables and connectors between terminals, computers, modems, and communications lines. Other examples are the protocols that establish the communications control information needed for *handshaking*, which is the process of exchanging predetermined signals and characters to establish a telecommunications session between terminals and computers. Other protocols deal with control of data transmission reception in a network, switching techniques, inter-network connections, and so on.

Network Architectures. The goal of network architectures is to promote an open, simple, flexible, and efficient telecommunications environment. This is accomplished by the use of standard protocols, standard communications hardware and software interfaces, and the design of a standard multilevel interface between end users and computer systems.

The OSI Model

The International Standards Organization (ISO) has developed a seven-layer Open Systems Interconnection (OSI) model to serve as a standard model for network architectures. Dividing data communications functions into seven distinct layers promotes the development of modular network architectures, which assists the development, operation, and maintenance of complex telecommunications networks. Figure 6.25 illustrates the functions of the seven layers of the OSI model architecture.

The Internet's TCP/IP

The Internet uses a system of telecommunications protocols that has become so widely used that it is now accepted as a network architecture. The Internet's protocol suite is called Transmission Control Protocol/Internet Protocol and is known as TCP/IP. As Figure 6.25 shows, TCP/IP consists of five layers of protocols that can be related to the seven layers of the OSI architecture. TCP/IP is used by the Internet and by all intranets and extranets. Many companies and other organizations are thus converting their client/server and wide-area networks to TCP/IP technology, which are now commonly called IP networks.

FIGURE 6.25 The seven layers of the OSI communications network architecture, and the five layers of the Internet's TCP/IP protocol suite.

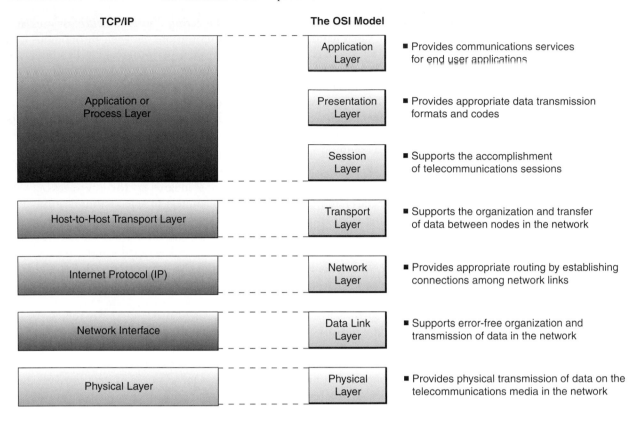

Bandwidth Alternatives

The communications speed and capacity of telecommunications networks can be classified by **bandwidth.** This is the frequency range of a telecommunications channel; it determines the channel's maximum transmission rate. The speed and capacity of data transmission rates are typically measured in bits per second (bps). This is sometimes referred to as the *baud* rate, though baud is more correctly a measure of signal changes in a transmission line.

Narrow-band channels typically provide low-speed transmission rates up to 64K bps, but can now handle up to 2 million bps. They are usually unshielded twisted-pair lines commonly used for telephone voice communications, and for data communications by the modems of PCs and other devices. Medium-speed channels *(medium-band)* use shielded twisted-pair lines for transmission speeds up to 100 Mbps.

Broadband channels provide high-speed transmission rates at intervals from 256,000 bps to several billion bps. Typically, they use microwave, fiber optics, or satellite transmission. Examples are 1.54 million bps for T1 and 45M bps for T3 communications channels, up to 100 Mbps for communications satellite channels, and between 52 Mbps and 10 Gbps for fiber-optic lines. See Figure 6.26.

Switching Alternatives

Regular telephone service relies on *circuit switching*, in which a switch opens a circuit to establish a link between a sender and receiver; it remains open until the communication session is completed. In message switching, a message is transmitted a block at a time from one switching device to another.

FIGURE 6.26

Examples of the telecommunications transmission speeds of various network technologies.

Network Technologies	Typical–Maximum bps
WiFi: wireless fidelity	11–54M
Standard Ethernet or token ring	10–16M
High-speed Ethernet	100M–1G
FDDI: fiber distributed data interface	100M
DDN: digital data network	2.4K–2M
PSN: packet switching network–X.25	64K–1.5M
Frame relay network	1.5M–45M
ISDN: integrated services digital network	64K/128K–2M
ATM: asynchronous transfer mode	25/155M–2.4G
SONET: synchronous optical network	45M–40G

Kbps = thousand bps or kilobits per second.   Gbps = billion bps or gigabits per second.
Mbps = million bps or megabits per second.

Packet switching involves subdividing communications messages into fixed or variable groups called packets. For example, in the X.25 protocol, packets are 128 characters long, while they are of variable length in the *frame relay* technology. Packet switching networks are frequently operated by *value-added carriers* who use computers and other communications processors to control the packet switching process and transmit the packets of various users over their networks.

Early packet switching networks were X.25 networks. The X.25 protocol is an international set of standards governing the operations of widely used, but relatively slow, packet switching networks. *Frame relay* is another popular packet switching protocol, and is used by many large companies for their wide area networks. Frame relay is considerably faster than X.25, and is better able to handle the heavy telecommunications traffic of interconnected local area networks within a company's wide area client/server network. ATM *(asynchronous transfer mode)* is an emerging high-capacity *cell switching* technology. An ATM switch breaks voice, video, and other data into fixed cells of 53 bytes (48 bytes of data and 5 bytes of control information) and routes them to their next destination in the network. ATM networks are being developed by many companies needing their fast, high-capacity multimedia capabilities for voice, video, and data communications [16]. See Figure 6.27.

FIGURE 6.27

Why four large retail chains chose different network technologies to connect their stores.

Company	Technology	Why
Sears	Frame relay	Reliable, inexpensive, and accommodates mainframe and Internet protocols
Rack Room	VSAT	Very inexpensive way to reach small markets and shared satellite dishes at malls
Hannaford	ATM	Very high bandwidth; combines voice, video, and data
7-Eleven	ISDN	Can use multiple channels to partition traffic among different uses

Summary

- **Telecommunications Trends.** Organizations are becoming networked enterprises that use the Internet, intranets, and other telecommunications networks to support business operations and collaboration within the enterprise, and with their customers, suppliers, and other business partners. Telecommunications has entered a deregulated and fiercely competitive environment with many vendors, carriers, and services. Telecommunications technology is moving toward open, internetworked digital networks for voice, data, video, and multimedia. A major trend is the pervasive use of the Internet and its technologies to build interconnected enterprise and global networks, like intranets and extranets, to support enterprise collaboration, electronic commerce, and other e-business applications.

- **The Internet Revolution.** The explosive growth of the Internet and the use of its enabling technologies have revolutionized computing and telecommunications. The Internet has become the key platform for a rapidly expanding list of information and entertainment services and business applications, including enterprise collaboration, electronic commerce, and other e-business systems. Open systems with unrestricted connectivity using Internet technologies are the primary telecommunications technology drivers in e-business systems. Their primary goal is to promote easy and secure access by business professionals and consumers to the resources of the Internet, enterprise intranets, and interorganizational extranets.

- **The Business Value of the Internet.** Companies are deriving strategic business value from the Internet, which enables them to disseminate information globally, communicate and trade interactively with customized information and services for individual customers, and foster collaboration of people and integration of business processes within the enterprise and with business partners. These capabilities allow them to generate cost savings from using Internet technologies, revenue increases from electronic commerce, and better customer service and relationships through better supply chain management and customer relationship management.

- **The Role of Intranets.** Businesses are installing and extending intranets throughout their organizations (1) to improve communications and collaboration among individuals and teams within the enterprise;

(2) to publish and share valuable business information easily, inexpensively, and effectively via enterprise information portals and intranet websites and other intranet services, and (3) to develop and deploy critical applications to support business operations and decision making.

- **The Role of Extranets.** The primary role of extranets is to link the intranet resources of a company to the intranets of its customers, suppliers, and other business partners. Extranets can also provide access to operational company databases and legacy systems to business partners. Thus, extranets provide significant business value by facilitating and strengthening the business relationships of a company with customers and suppliers, improving collaboration with its business partners, and enabling the development of new kinds of Web-based service for its customers, suppliers, and others.

- **Telecommunications Networks.** The major generic components of any telecommunications network are (1) terminals, (2) telecommunications processors, (3) communications channels, (4) computers, and (5) telecommunications software. There are several basic types of telecommunications networks, including wide area networks (WANs) and local area networks (LANs). Most WANs and LANs are interconnected using client/server, network computing, peer-to-peer, and Internet networking technologies.

- **Network Alternatives.** Key telecommunications network alternatives and components are summarized in Figure 6.11 for telecommunications media, processors, software, channels, and network architectures. A basic understanding of these major alternatives will help business end users participate effectively in decisions involving telecommunications issues. Telecommunications processors include modems, multiplexers, internetwork processors, and various devices to help interconnect and enhance the capacity and efficiency of telecommunications channels. Telecommunications networks use such media as twisted-pair wire, coaxial cables, fiber-optic cables, terrestrial microwave, communications satellites, cellular and PCS systems, wireless LANs, and other wireless technologies. Telecommunications software, such as network operating systems and telecommunications monitors, controls and manages the communications activity in a telecommunications network.

Key Terms and Concepts

These are the key terms and concepts of this chapter. The page number of their first explanation is in parentheses.

1. Bandwidth alternatives (200)
2. Business applications of the Internet (176)
3. Business value of the Internet (177)
4. Business value of telecommunications networks (174)
5. Cellular phone systems (193)
6. Client/server networks (188)
7. Coaxial cable (190)
8. Communications satellites (191)
9. Downsizing (188)
10. Extranets (180)
11. Fiber optics (190)
12. Internet revolution (175)
13. Internet technologies (173)
14. Internetwork processors (195)
15. Intranets (178)
16. Legacy systems (188)
17. Local area networks (185)
18. Modems (194)
19. Multiplexer (195)
20. Network architectures (199)
    a. OSI (199)
    b. TCP/IP (199)
21. Network computing (188)
22. Network management (197)
23. Network operating system (185)
24. Network server (185)
25. Network topologies (198)
26. Open systems (173)
27. Peer-to-peer networks (188)
28. Protocol (199)
29. Switching alternatives (200)
30. Telecommunications channels (185)
31. Telecommunications media (190)
32. Telecommunications network components (184)
33. Telecommunications processors (184)
34. Telecommunications software (185)
35. Trends in telecommunications (172)
36. Virtual private network (186)
37. Wide area networks (185)
38. Wireless LAN (193)
39. Wireless technologies (191)

Review Quiz

Match one of the key terms and concepts listed previously with one of the brief examples or definitions that follow. Try to find the best fit for answers that seem to fit more than one term or concept. Defend your choices.

_____ 1. Fundamental changes have occurred in the competitive environment, the technology, and the application of telecommunications.

_____ 2. Telecommunications networks help companies overcome geographic, time, cost, and structural barriers to business success.

_____ 3. Companies are using the Internet for electronic commerce and enterprise collaboration.

_____ 4. Companies are cutting costs, generating revenue, improving customer service, and forming strategic business alliances via the Internet.

_____ 5. The rapid growth in the business and consumer use of the Internet, and the use of its technologies in internetworking organizations.

_____ 6. Internet-like networks that improve communications and collaboration, publish and share information, and develop applications to support business operations and decision making within an organization.

_____ 7. Provide Internet-like access to a company's operational databases and legacy systems by its customers and suppliers.

_____ 8. Includes terminals, telecommunications processors, channels, computers, and control software.

_____ 9. A communications network covering a large geographic area.

_____ 10. A communications network in an office, a building, or other work site.

_____ 11. Communications data move in these paths using various media in a network.

_____ 12. Coaxial cable, microwave, and fiber optics are examples.

_____ 13. A communications medium that uses pulses of laser light in glass fibers.

_____ 14. A wireless mobile telephone technology.

_____ 15. Includes modems, multiplexers, and internetwork processors.

_____ 16. Includes programs such as network operating systems and Web browsers.

_____ 17. A common communications processor for microcomputers.

_____ 18. Helps a communications channel carry simultaneous data transmissions from many terminals.

_____ 19. Star, ring, and bus networks are examples.

_____ 20. Cellular and PCS systems can connect mobile information appliances to the Internet.

_____ 21. A computer that handles resource sharing and network management in a local area network.

_____ 22. Intranets and extranets can use their network firewalls and other security features to establish secure Internet links within an enterprise or with its trading partners.

_____ 23. The software that manages a local area network.

_____ 24. Standard rules or procedures for control of communications in a network.

_____ 25. An international standard, multilevel set of protocols to promote compatibility among telecommunications networks.

_____ 26. The standard suite of protocols used by the Internet, intranets, extranets, and some other networks.

_____ 27. Information systems with common hardware, software, and network standards that provide easy access for end users and their networked computer systems.

_____ 28. Interconnected networks need communications processors such as switches, routers, hubs, and gateways.

_____ 29. Websites, Web browsers, HTML documents, hypermedia databases, and TCP/IP networks are examples.

_____ 30. Networks where end user PCs are tied to network servers to share resources and application processing.

_____ 31. Network computers provide a browser-based interface for software and databases provided by servers.

_____ 32. End user computers connect directly with each other to exchange files.

_____ 33. Replacing mainframe-based systems with client/server networks.

_____ 34. Older, traditional mainframe-based business information systems.

_____ 35. Telecommunications networks come in a wide range of speed and capacity capabilities.

_____ 36. Examples are packet switching using frame relay and cell switching using ATM technologies.

_____ 37. Provides wireless network access for laptop PCs in business settings.

_____ 38. Monitoring and optimizing network traffic and service.

Discussion Questions

1. The Internet is the driving force behind developments in telecommunications, networks, and other information technologies. Do you agree or disagree? Why?

2. How is the trend toward open systems, connectivity, and interoperability related to business use of the Internet, intranets, and extranets?

3. Refer to the Real World Case on Celanese Chemicals and Others in the chapter. What are some of the major challenges limiting the widespread use of wireless technologies in many business applications? What can be done to meet such challenges?

4. How will wireless information appliances and services affect the business use of the Internet and the Web? Explain.

5. What are some of the business benefits and management challenges of client/server networks? Network computing? Peer-to-peer networks?

6. What is the business value driving so many companies to rapidly install and extend intranets throughout their organizations?

7. What strategic competitive benefits do you see in a company's use of extranets?

8. Refer to the Real World Case on Con-Way NOW and Trimble Navigation in the chapter. What is the business value of several other business uses for communications satellites not mentioned in this case? Check out the websites of satellite services providers like Hughes Network Systems (www.hns.com) or G-Com International (www.g-com.com) to help you answer.

9. Do you think that business use of the Internet, intranets, and extranets has changed what businesspeople expect from information technology in their jobs? Explain.

10. The insatiable demand for everything wireless, video, and Web-enabled everywhere will be the driving force behind developments in telecommunications, networking, and computing technologies for the foreseeable future. Do you agree or disagree? Why?

Analysis Exercises

1. Network Growth

The Internet is an international network of networks. Each new node added to the Internet increases the number of new possible connections by many millions. Telecommunications networks have come a long way since the invention of telegraph, telephone, and radio. When Alexander Graham Bell invented the telephone, he began with a two-node network. If he had wanted to order a pizza, his network had little to offer. However, each time he added a new node to the network, he created more than one new connection. With the third node, Bell created two additional connections. With the fourth node, Bell created three new connections to his existing network for a total of six unique pairs of connections between nodes.

If we had a network of 100 nodes, adding the 101st node would create 100 new possible connections, one for each of the first 100 nodes. To calculate the total possible connections, we add these 100 new connections to the 99 new connections made when we added the 100th node, the 98 new connections made when we added the 99th node, and so on.

As you can see, large networks have tremendous power to help people connect.

a. Prepare a spreadsheet formula that calculates the total number of unique pairs of connections for a network with n nodes. Use a cell reference for n so that users can enter a network of any size and see the correct answer calculated.

b. Each node on the Internet has a specific and unique IP address. IP addresses are expressed as four sets of numbers separated by dots. Each number ranges from 0 to 255. For example: 143.43.222.103 would be a valid IP address that refers to a specific node on the Internet. Given this addressing scheme, calculate the total number of possible IP addresses available.

c. Search the internet for IPv4, IPv6, and references to running out of IP addresses. Prepare a one page paper describing the issue, the global distribution of IP addresses, and why this issue has become a concern. Conclude your paper with the recommended solution.

d. How many IP addresses would a 128 bit address provide?

2. Evaluating Online Banking Websites

Some of the biggest banks want your business, and they are putting it on the line, on-line. The information about financial products and services goes to naught if users have difficulty finding or understanding the information they need.

American Express (www.americanexpress.com)
Why leave home? Amex offers very attractive interest rates on deposits, lots of personal finance information, and links to on-line trading.

Bank of America (www.bankofamerica.com)
Sleek, no-nonsense design is pitched to retail and business customers alike.

Citi (www.citi.com)
Citigroup wants to help you round up all your financial activity and park it here. The site updates your finances to include your latest credit card bill, for instance. Security is top notch.

Wells Fargo (www.wellsfargo.com)
This West Coast innovator has taken its act nationally. Good design aimed at both consumers and commercial

accounts. The color scheme looks odd unless you're a San Francisco 49'ers fan.

Bank One
(www.bankone.com)
This recently re-branded site has learned from experience. The home page provides space for brand, image, navigation, log-in, and promotions all without appearing overly cluttered or confusing.

a. Assume you need an auto loan to buy a new car. Evaluate three sites from the list provided. Use a table to illustrate your evaluation of the following features: ease of navigation, clarity of information, lowest rates, ability to obtain pre-approval, and interest rates. List the banks you examined in the first column and each of these criteria as column headings to the right. Explain which loan product appealed to you the most.

b. Enter the following into a search engine "[bank name] sucks" where [bank name] is the name of the bank you selected in the question above. Select and review several of the links that appear likely to provide a second opinion regarding your selected bank. Summarize what you learned about the bank. Did anything you read change your opinion about the bank? If you were the bank's director of marketing, how would you respond to what you read?

3. MNO Incorporated Communications Network
MNO Incorporated is considering acquiring its own leased lines to handle its voice and data communications between its 14 distribution sites in three regions around the country. The peak load of communications for each site is expected to be a function of the number of phone links and the number of computers at that site. You have been asked to gather this information, as shown in the first table below, and place it in a database file.

a. Create a database table with an appropriate structure to store the data below. Enter records shown below and get a printed listing of your table.

b. Survey results suggest that the peak traffic to and from a site will be approximately 2 kilobits per second for each phone line plus 10 kilobits per second for each computer. Create a report showing the estimated peak demand for the telecommunications system at each site in kilobits. Create a second report grouped by region and showing regional subtotals and a total for the system as a whole.

Site Location	Region	Phone Lines	Computers
Boston	East	228	95
New York	East	468	205
Richmond	East	189	84
Atlanta	East	192	88
Detroit	East	243	97
Cincinnati	East	156	62
New Orleans	Central	217	58
Chicago	Central	383	160
Saint Louis	Central	212	91
Houston	Central	238	88
Denver	West	202	77
Los Angeles	West	364	132
San Francisco	West	222	101
Seattle	West	144	54

4. Wireless Threat a Cause for Concern?
Radio waves, microwaves, and infrared all belong to the electromagnetic radiation spectrum. These terms reference ranges of radiation frequencies we use every day in our wireless networking environments. However, the very word "radiation" strikes fear in many people. With all this radiation zapping about, should we be concerned?

a. Use an Internet search engine and report back what the World Health Organization (WHO) has had to say about microwave radiation or non-ionizing radiation.

b. Use an Internet search engine to identify the various complaints posed by stakeholders regarding cell phone towers. Write a one page paper describing an alternative to cell phone towers that would enable cell phone use and yet mitigate all or most of these complaints?

UPS, Wells Dairy, Novell, and GM: The Business Value and Challenges of Wi-Fi Networks

Wi-Fi is beaming its way into the corporate world. Its superfast wireless connections to the Web cost only a quarter as much as the gaggle of wires companies use today. And they're proving irresistible to businesses willing to venture onto the wireless edge. From General Motors to United Parcel Service, companies are using Wi-Fi for mission-critical jobs in factories, trucks, stores, and even hospitals.

What is Wi-Fi? It's a radio signal that beams Internet connections out 300 feet. Attach it to a broadband modem and any nearby computers equipped with Wi-Fi access cards can log on to the Net, whether they're in the cubicle across the hall, the apartment next door, or the hammock out back. To date, Wi-Fi has grown on the scruffy fringes of the networked world. It shares an unregulated radio spectrum with a motley crew of contraptions, including cordless phones and baby monitors.

The challenge facing the tech industry is to transform this unruly phenomenon into a global business. That involves transforming a riot of hit-or-miss hot spots into coherent, dependable networks. It means coming up with billing systems, roaming agreements, and technical standards—jobs the phone companies are busy tackling. The goal, says Anand Chandrasekher, vice-president and general manager of the mobile-platforms group at Intel, is to "take Wi-Fi from a wireless rogue activity to an industrial-strength solution that corporations can bet on."

Corporations aren't waiting for fine-tuned industrial versions of Wi-Fi to hit the market. The potential productivity gains are so compelling that many are investing in custom-built systems. United Parcel Service Inc. (www.ups.com), is equipping its worldwide distribution centers with wireless networks at a cost of $120 million. The company says that as loaders and packers scan packages, the information zips instantly to the the UPS network, leading to a 35 percent productivity gain.

But let's go back to the Spring of 2000, when LeMars, Iowa, ice-cream maker Wells' Dairy (www.wellsdairy.com), rolled out Wi-Fi to 120 users in its new corporate annex. One thousand miles west, in Provo, Utah, network software supplier Novell launched a wireless local area network (WLAN) in its IT department.

"This was very cutting edge when we did it, but it's just standard now," says Jim Kirby, senior network architect at Wells', which churns out over 60 million gallons of Blue Bunny brand ice cream each year. Ditto for Novell, whose employees say they think about Wi-Fi only at those rare times when it is not accessible. About 90 percent of the company's 6,000 employees can access the wireless network at any of Novell's 96 offices worldwide.

Thus Wi-Fi is no stranger to the business world, but up until now deployments have been mostly limited to schools, stores, airports, hospitals, and warehouses. This year roughly 90 percent of the nation's public and private universities have WLANs, which accounts for over 80 percent of the $1.6-billion-a-year business wireless LAN market.

Of course, there are downsides to Wi-Fi. Having everyone online during a meeting can be toxic to productivity. When there are laptops everywhere, culturally it can create a whole lot of problems," says Novell CIO Debra Anderson. "We're finding the balance between Wi-Fi as an intrusion and as a powerful, productive tool." To minimize disruptions and keep people focused, Novell and other companies now institute "no laptop" policies for important meetings.

Wi-Fi is also not for everyone. Deskbound employees in finance or customer service really have no compelling need for wireless. IT managers need to learn where it makes sense, which can be difficult when everyone is wailing for Wi-Fi, "There is enormous pressure on IT managers from upper management to add wireless technology because it's sexy," says analyst Stan Schatt.

Take the Wells' Dairy plant floor, where quality-assurance technicians audit products every two hours. Supervisor Jan Wagner has asked for Wi-Fi, but Kirby doesn't think the cost justifies the benefit. Installing it in Wells' massive, two-story, 550,000-square-foot south plant would require many more access points than usual, as the production machines would generate a good deal of interference.

Also, it's clear that business adoption of Wi-Fi won't accelerate until security reaches industrial grade. Corporations are hankering for the power and flexibility of Wi-Fi networks, but many are postponing rollouts in strategic areas until they're convinced that hackers, spies, and competitors can't intercept wireless data. For example, General Motors has deployed Wi-Fi in 90 manufacturing plants but is holding off on Wi-Fi at its headquarters until next year. Why? Execs worry that until new encryption is in place, guests at a Marriott Hotel across the street could log on to GM's network and make off with vital memos and·budgets.

Case Study Questions

1. What are the business benefits of Wi-Fi networks?

2. What are some of the problems faced by companies who are using Wi-Fi networks? What are some solutions to those problems?

3. What are some other business uses for Wi-Fi networks not mentioned in this case? What are their business benefits and challenges?

Source: Adapted from Mathew Boyle, "Wi-Fi USA," *Fortune*, November 25, 2002, pp. 205–214; and Heather Green, "Wi-Fi Means Business," *Business Week*, April 28, 2003, pp. 86–92.

REAL WORLD CASE 4

Grant Thornton and Others: Return on Investment Challenges of Internet Phone Systems

The return on investment from voice-over-Internet protocol (VOIP) technology has proved difficult, in part because upfront costs can be high and traditional long-distance phone charges have dropped in recent years. Adding voice requires that all elements of the corporate network be tested—and in some cases replaced or upgraded—for VOIP applications.

Grant Thornton. Chicago-based Grant Thornton Inc., (www.grantthornton.com), a global accounting and auditing firm, has set up a VOIP network in the United States featuring centralized management, five-digit dialing for calls between offices and employees, hub-based voice mail, and unified messaging. With 51 offices and 2,800 employees nationwide, "We really wanted our geographically dispersed sales teams to be able to communicate more quickly and easily, enabling us to provide faster, more flexible service," says Kevin Lopez, national manager of telecommunications at Grant Thornton.

The new network has been in place since last spring. Grant Thornton has cut communication costs by routing voice traffic over its wide-area network and eliminating toll charges. It has also reduced network management requirements and consolidated 28 stand-alone systems into four hubs—all without replacing its existing private branch exchange (PBX) and digital phones. The payoff? Grant Thornton has saved $800,000 in its first year on intracompany long-distance toll charges and $160,000 on equipment lease payments, Lopez says.

Grant Thornton selected Avaya Inc. (www.avaya.com) to provide their VOIP functions because that supplier was best able to leverage its existing PBX and digital phone investments, and because its leasing plan lowered the company's monthly costs, Lopez says. For Grant Thornton, the savings in administration and monthly recurring costs were too great to ignore. Now, says Lopez, the company is looking to enhance the network so it's more robust and to improve visibility into the network by using specialized systems management tools. "And in the next year, we hope to boost bandwidth for audio- and videoconferencing, which will further reduce our costs," he says.

Lillian Vernon. Cutting the costs of leasing T1 lines from the phone company was the key at Rye, New York-based catalog retailer Lillian Vernon Corp. (www.lillianvernon.com). For example, in late 2001, Lillian Vernon replaced an aging automated call distribution (ACD) system with a VOIP-enabled multimedia contact center, reducing the number of T1 lines used from six to two. That move saved the company $100,000 during 2001's peak holiday sales season, says Ellis Admire, director of MIS operations. "By converting voice calls from analog to digital signals, we can carry up to 72 calls on a single T1 line, versus the previous high of 24 simultaneous analog voice calls," Admire says.

Lillian Vernon chose the eQueue multimedia contact center from eOn Communications Corp. (www.eoncommunications.com), because it lets customer service representatives handle e-mail and Web contacts with the same ease as a phone call. Admire says eOn's VOIP-enabled ACD system was chosen because it uses open, Linux-based technology that is up to date and reliable.

H.B. Fuller. H.B. Fuller Co. (www/hbfuller.com), St. Paul, Minnesota, expects a payback on its new VOIP deployment in about a year, says Kevin Wetzel, manager of global network services at the manufacturer of adhesives, sealants, coatings, and paints. VOIP technology finally proved reliable and sturdy enough for use this past summer, Wetzel says. The reliability comes from the addition of centralized processing, which reduces the overhead of having multiple local processing locations and provides remote-site recoverability. So if a WAN circuit fails, the calls can still be completed.

H.B. Fuller uses VOIP at 30 sites globally, incorporating about 3,500 digital phones. Most of the sites are in the United States, with the remainder scattered throughout Europe, South America, and the Asia-Pacific Rim, in places where the cost savings were almost immediate, Wetzel says. The network uses Cisco Systems' (www.cisco.com) CallManager and other related call center and unified-messaging products.

The savings vary dramatically—from 20 to 80 percent—depending on the application and the age of the analog phone systems replaced. But Wetzel says the average savings delivered by switching from traditional analog phone services to VOIP has been about 50 percent. By the end of this year, H.B. Fuller hopes to expand the VOIP network to 41 locations in 30 countries. That will mean more toll-bypass savings, and will reduce travel and long-distance bills when employees use the internal audioconferencing capability. Over the next four years, Wetzel estimates that H.B. Fuller will save about $2 million because of its VOIP investment.

Case Study Questions

1. What are the main business benefits that can be gained by companies that switch to VOIP telephone systems?

2. What are some of the major cost factors that may limit a positive rate of return from investments in VOIP projects?

3. Should more companies switch to VOIP systems? Visit the websites of Avaya, eOn Communications, and Cisco Systems to view their VOIP news, products, and services to help you answer.

MODULE III

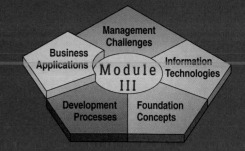

BUSINESS APPLICATIONS

How do Internet technologies and other forms of IT support business processes, electronic commerce, and business decision making? The three chapters of this module show you how such business applications of information systems are accomplished in today's networked enterprises.

- **Chapter 7: Electronic Business Systems** describes how information systems integrate and support enterprise-wide business processes, especially customer relationship management, enterprise resource planning, and supply chain management, as well as the business functions of marketing, manufacturing, human resource management, accounting, and finance.

- **Chapter 8: Electronic Commerce Systems** introduces the basic process components of e-commerce systems, and discusses important trends, applications, and issues in e-commerce.

- **Chapter 9: Decision Support Systems** shows how management information systems, decision support systems, executive information systems, expert systems, and artificial intelligence technologies can be applied to decision-making situations faced by business managers and professionals in today's dynamic business environment.

CHAPTER 7

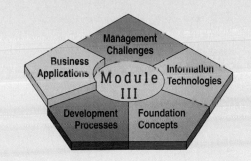

ELECTRONIC BUSINESS SYSTEMS

Chapter Highlights

Section I
Enterprise Business Systems

Introduction
Real World Case: Salesforce.com and Others: Challenges of Customer Relationship Management Systems
Cross-Functional Enterprise Applications
Enterprise Resource Planning
Customer Relationship Management
Supply Chain Management
Enterprise Application Integration
Transaction Processing Systems
Enterprise Collaboration Systems

Section II
Functional Business Systems

Introduction
Real World Case: GE Power Systems and Corporate Express: The Business Case for Enterprise Application Integration
IT in Business
Marketing Systems
Manufacturing Systems
Human Resource Systems
Accounting Systems
Financial Management Systems
Real World Case: Welch's, Straightline, Skyworks, and Pella: The Business Value of Supply Chain Management
Real World Case: Lowe and HP: The Business Case for Swarming Collaboration

Learning Objectives

After reading and studying this chapter, you should be able to:

1. Identify the following cross-functional enterprise systems, and give examples of how they can provide significant business value to a company:
   a. Enterprise resource planning
   b. Customer relationship management
   c. Supply chain management
   d. Enterprise application integration
   e. Transaction processing systems
   f. Enterprise collaboration systems

2. Give examples of how Internet and other information technologies support business processes within the business functions of accounting, finance, human resource management, marketing, and production and operations management.

SECTION I   Enterprise Business Systems

Introduction

Contrary to popular opinion, e-business is not synonymous with e-commerce. E-business is much broader in scope, going beyond transactions to signify use of the Net, in combination with other technologies and forms of electronic communication, to enable any type of business activity [26].

This chapter introduces the fast-changing world of business applications of information technology, which increasingly consists of what is popularly called *e-business* applications. Remember that **e-business** is the use of the Internet and other networks and information technologies to support electronic commerce, enterprise communications and collaboration, and Web-enabled business processes both within a networked enterprise, and with its customers and business partners. E-business includes *e-commerce* which involves the buying and selling, and marketing and servicing of products, services, and information over the Internet and other networks. We will cover e-commerce in Chapter 8.

In this chapter, we will explore some of the major concepts and applications of e-business. We will begin by focusing in Section I on examples of cross-functional enterprise systems, especially customer relationship management, enterprise resource planning, and supply chain management. In Section II, we will explore examples of information systems that support essential processes in the functional areas of business.

Analyzing Salesforce.com and Others

Read the Real World Case on Salesforce.com and Others in the chapter. We can learn a lot from this case about the challenges and benefits of customer relationship management systems. See Figure 7.1.

Salesforce.com founder and CEO Marc Benioff is capitalizing on the widespread dissatisfaction with the high costs, complexity, and difficult implementation requirements of traditional CRM software from vendors like Siebel Systems, Oracle, and SAP. Instead, Salesforce.com is an application service provider that offers CRM as a

FIGURE 7.1

Marc Benioff is founder and CEO of Salesforce.com and leads their drive to make CRM systems available to businesses as a Web-based service.

Source: Marc Asnin/Corbis Saba

REAL WORLD CASE 1

Salesforce.com and Others: Challenges of Customer Relationship Management Systems

Customer relationship management (CRM) systems were pioneered and are still dominated by Siebel Systems (www.siebel.com). But Siebel's software has come under increasing attack as too complex and hard to implement: In 2002, Siebel had $1.6 billion in sales, down from $2 billion in 2001. Application service provider Salesforce.com's (www.salesforce.com) sales, on the other hand, are soaring. Salesforce's Web-based CRM services for business are built on the shoulders of Siebel Systems. That company's founder, Tom Siebel, previously worked for Larry Ellison at Oracle Corporation. So did Marc Benioff, founder and CEO of Salesforce.com, who eventually became one of the most successful sales executives in Oracle's history. In 1994, he was one of seven seed investors in Siebel Systems. Five years later he left Oracle, sold the bulk of his initial $50,000 Siebel stake for more than $25 million, and founded Salesforce.com.

From the start, Benioff has gotten a lot of mileage from a fundamental characteristic of traditional CRM systems: For a lot of customers, it has been a nightmare. "CRM is the most oversold, under-implemented concept of the past five years," says management consultant Michael Treacy. Many clients have found CRM too expensive and too complicated. Research firm Gartner estimates that 42 percent of all CRM software sold is not even being used.

Benioff sells his Web-based services as the antidote to CRM's problems. Salesforce's CRM software helps salespeople manage their accounts, track leads, and evaluate marketing campaigns. It helps companies monitor the sales cycle "from campaign to cash," Benioff says, fingering invisible money with his right hand. Yet unlike traditional CRM software from Siebel and others that can cost hundreds of thousands of dollars to install and take months to get up and running, Salesforce costs as little as $65 a month per user.

Siebel, SAP, and other CRM stalwarts typically send in scores of consultants to get their systems up and running. Salesforce.com provides the same systems with hardly any consultants, since it hosts the applications on its own Web servers. There are no associated hardware or IT labor costs. Customers access the software over the Web and pay by the number of users. When a new version comes out, everyone gets upgraded at the same time, for the same price as before. The software is so cheap that sales managers often sign up for it themselves, bypassing their IT departments.

But as Salesforce goes after bigger and bigger customers, the sales challenges mount. The company was recently put through the wringer to get its first contract for 1,000 users at SunGard Data Systems, which provides data recovery and other IT products to financial services firms. "They sent an army of people and drilled deeper than any other customer," recalls Salesforce president Jim Steele. "It was an excruciating four-month process." Bettina Slusar, SunGard's head of global accounts, says she was prepared to walk away from the deal at any time if her simulations, demos, and security reviews turned up anything questionable. Yet she had "no appetite for the five-year implementation or the $18,000-a-head" cost of traditional CRM software. The ultimate test, Slusar says, is that "unless the sales reps like it, it is never going to work." The verdict? "The reps like it."

To keep winning those big accounts, Salesforce will have to overcome several perceived disadvantages to its software utility. "Customers are still the largest form of resistance against" the rent-an-app idea, says investor Roger McNamee of Silver Lake Partners. He ticks off a list of concerns: security, lack of control, problems with customizing, and the difficulty of integrating the software with other corporate applications. "Customers would rather buy than rent," he concludes flatly. Gartner analyst Beth Eisenfeld characterizes Salesforce as a "stripped-down system" that's a "good low-cost option," but says the gulf between it and a full-fledged CRM package is "the difference between a tract house and a custom-built home."

Benioff, of course, has an answer to every objection. To protect customers' data, Salesforce employs state-of-the-art encryption and security systems. And, at the insistence of large corporate customers, Benioff recently built a redundant data center in Dublin, Ireland, He is also addressing the one-size-fits-all criticism of Salesforce's software: The recently released version S3 gives users more flexibility to tailor the software to their needs. It also contains upgraded features meant to allay concerns that Salesforce software doesn't have the firepower of more expensive CRM packages from Siebel or SAP.

In addition, Salesforce has come up with Sforce, a new set of Web-based application development tools that enable programmers in IT departments to more easily integrate Salesforce CRM software with data from other vendors' enterprise applications. So both corporate customers and software partners can now use Sforce to build their own Web-based applications on top of Salesforce's CRM system.

Case Study Questions

1. Why have traditional CRM software implementations been so problematic for many businesses?

2. What are the benefits and drawbacks of the Salesforce Web-based CRM services approach?

3. Which approach do you prefer? Why? Visit the websites of Salesforce.com and Siebel Systems for more information and customer examples of their CRM systems.

Source: Adapted from Erick Schonfeld. "The Biggest Mouth in Silicon Valley." *Business 2.0*, September 2003, pp. 107–112.

Web-based service for a monthly fee per user. Though Salesforce is an easy to implement and use CRM service, it has been criticized as a stripped-down one-size-fits-all CRM solution without adequate security and integration links to other enterprise systems. Benioff has responded by using state-of-the-art encryption and security systems and building a redundant data center in Ireland. He has also released an S3 version of Salesforce with more CRM features, more customization flexibility, and Web-based application development tools so customers and software partners can build applications that integrate with Salesforce.

Cross-Functional Enterprise Applications

Many companies today are using information technology to develop integrated **cross-functional enterprise systems** that cross the boundaries of traditional business functions in order to reengineer and improve vital business processes all across the enterprise. These organizations view cross-functional enterprise systems as a strategic way to use IT to share information resources and improve the efficiency and effectiveness of business processes, and develop strategic relationships with customers, suppliers, and business partners. Figure 7.2 illustrates a cross-functional business process.

Many companies first moved from functional mainframe-based *legacy systems* to integrated cross-functional *client/server* applications. This typically involved installing *enterprise resource planning*, *supply chain management*, or *customer relationship management* software from SAP America, PeopleSoft, Oracle, and others. Instead of focusing on the information processing requirements of business functions, such enterprise software focuses on supporting integrated clusters of business processes involved in the operations of a business.

Now, as we see continually in the Real World Cases in this text, business firms are using Internet technologies to help them reengineer and integrate the flow of information among their internal business processes and their customers and suppliers. Companies all across the globe are using the World Wide Web and their intranets and extranets as a technology platform for their cross-functional and interenterprise information systems.

Enterprise Application Architecture

Figure 7.3 presents an **enterprise application architecture,** which illustrates the interrelationships of the major cross-functional enterprise applications that many companies have or are installing today. This architecture does not provide a detailed or exhaustive application blueprint, but provides a conceptual framework to help you visualize the basic components, processes, and interfaces of these major e-business applications, and their interrelationships to each other. This application architecture also spotlights the roles these business systems play in supporting the customers, suppliers, partners, and employees of a business.

Notice that instead of concentrating on traditional business functions, or only supporting the internal business processes of a company, enterprise applications are focused on accomplishing fundamental business processes in concert with a company's

---

FIGURE 7.2

The new product development process in a manufacturing company. This is an example of a business process that must be supported by cross-functional information systems that cross the boundaries of several business functions.

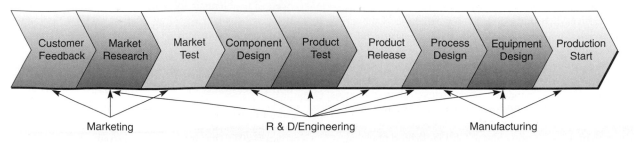

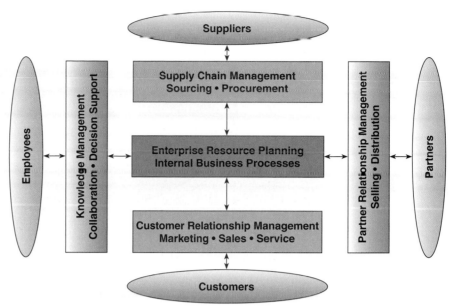

FIGURE 7.3

This enterprise application architecture presents an overview of the major cross-functional enterprise applications and their interrelationships.

Source: Adapted from Mohan Sawhney and Jeff Zabin, *Seven Steps to Nirvana: Strategic Insights into e-Business Transformation* (New York, McGraw-Hill, 2001), p. 175.

customer, supplier, partner, and employee stakeholders. Thus, enterprise resource planning (ERP) concentrates on the efficiency of a firm's internal production, distribution, and financial processes. Customer relationship management (CRM) focuses on acquiring and retaining profitable customers via marketing, sales, and service processes. Partner relationship management (PRM) aims at acquiring and retaining partners who can enhance the selling and distribution of a firm's products and services. Supply chain management (SCM) focuses on developing the most efficient and effective sourcing and procurement processes with suppliers for the products and services needed by a business. Knowledge management (KM) applications focus on providing a firm's employees with tools that support group collaboration and decision support [26]

We will discuss CRM, ERP, PRM, and SCM applications in this section, and cover knowledge management applications in Chapter 9. Now let's look at a real world example of a cross-functional enterprise system in action.

IBM Corporation: Global Cross-Functional Enterprise Systems

An enterprise e-business system requires end-to-end connectivity across all of the different processes, from the innards of a company's legacy systems to the outer reaches of its suppliers, customers, and partners. Consider the real-time, configure-to-order system that IBM has created for its personal systems division. A customer in Europe can configure a personal computer on IBM's website and get real-time availability and order confirmation. Seems simple, doesn't it? But behind the scenes, it takes a team of rocket scientists and a hundred man-years of effort to stitch together the myriad business processes and systems that need to work together to make this simple action possible.

Here's what happens when the customer places the order: The order travels to IBM's fulfillment engine located in the United Kingdom; its e-commerce engine located in Boulder, Colorado; its ERP and production management systems located in Raleigh, North Carolina; its sales reporting system located in Southbury, Connecticut; its product database located in Poughkeepsie, New York; and back to the customer's browser in Europe. Every system updates its status and communicates with every other system in real time. And every order placed in Europe zips across the Atlantic an average of four times. In its journey, it touches dozens of geographical units, legacy systems, and databases strewn across the globe [26].

FIGURE 7.4

The major application components of enterprise resource planning demonstrate the cross-functional approach of ERP systems.

ERP: The Business Backbone

ERP is the technological backbone of e-business, an enterprise-wide transaction framework with links into sales order processing, inventory management and control, production and distribution planning, and finance [15].

Businesses of all kinds have now implemented **enterprise resource planning** (ERP) systems. ERP serves as a cross-functional enterprise backbone that integrates and automates many internal business processes and information systems within the manufacturing, logistics, distribution, accounting, finance, and human resource functions of a company. Large companies throughout the world began installing ERP systems in the 1990s as a conceptual framework and catalyst for reengineering their business processes. ERP also served as the vital software engine needed to integrate and accomplish the cross-functional processes that resulted. Now, ERP is recognized as a necessary ingredient that many companies need in order to gain the efficiency, agility, and responsiveness required to succeed in today's dynamic business environment.

Enterprise resource planning is a cross-functional enterprise system driven by an integrated suite of software modules that supports the basic internal business processes of a company. For example, ERP software for a manufacturing company will typically process the data from and track the status of sales, inventory, shipping, and invoicing, as well as forecast raw material and human resource requirements. Figure 7.4 presents the major application components of an ERP system [15].

ERP gives a company an integrated real-time view of its core business processes, such as production, order processing, and inventory management, tied together by the ERP application software and a common database maintained by a database management system. ERP systems track business resources (such as cash, raw materials, and production capacity), and the status of commitments made by the business (such as customer orders, purchase orders, and employee payroll), no matter which department (manufacturing, purchasing sales, accounting, etc.) has entered the data into the system.

ERP software suites typically consist of integrated modules of manufacturing, distribution, sales, accounting, and human resource applications. Examples of manufacturing processes supported are material requirements planning, production planning, and capacity planning. Some of the sales and marketing processes supported by ERP are sales analysis, sales planning, and pricing analysis, while typical distribution applications include order management, purchasing, and logistics planning. ERP systems support many vital human resource processes, from personnel requirements planning to salary and benefits administration, and accomplish most required financial record-keeping and managerial accounting applications. Figure 7.5 illustrates the processes supported by the ERP system installed by the Colgate-Palmolive Company [15]. Let's take a closer look at their experience with ERP.

FIGURE 7.5 The business processes and functions supported by the ERP system implemented by the Colgate-Palmolive Company

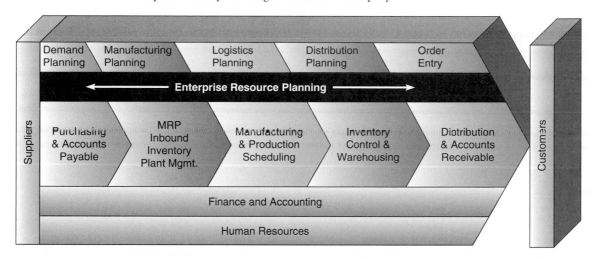

Colgate-Palmolive: The Business Value of ERP	Colgate-Palmolive is a global consumer products company that implemented the SAP R/3 enterprise resource planning system. Colgate embarked on an implementation of SAP R/3 to allow the company to access more timely and accurate data, get the most out of working capital, and reduce manufacturing costs. An important factor for Colgate was whether it could use the software across the entire spectrum of the business. Colgate needed the ability to coordinate globally and act locally. The implementation of SAP across the Colgate supply chain contributed to increased profitability. Now installed in operations that produce most of Colgate's worldwide sales, SAP was expanded to all Colgate divisions worldwide during 2001. Global efficiencies in purchasing—combined with product and packaging standardization—also produced large savings.

- Before ERP, it took Colgate U.S. anywhere from one to five days to acquire an order, and another one to two days to process the order. Now, order acquisition and processing combined takes four hours, not up to seven days. Distribution planning and picking used to take up to four days; today, it takes 14 hours. In total, the order-to-delivery time has been cut in half.

- Before ERP, on-time deliveries used to occur only 91.5 percent of the time, and cases ordered were delivered correctly 97.5 percent of the time. After R/3 the figures are 97.5 percent and 99.0 percent, respectively.

- After ERP, domestic inventories have dropped by one-third and receivables outstanding have dropped to 22.4 days from 31.4. Working capital as a percentage of sales has plummeted to 6.3 percent from 11.3 percent. Total delivered cost per case has been reduced by nearly 10 percent [15].

Benefits of ERP

As the example of Colgate-Palmolive has just shown, ERP systems can generate significant business benefits for a company. Many other companies have found major business value in their use of ERP in several basic ways [21].

- **Quality and Efficiency.** ERP creates a framework for integrating and improving a company's internal business processes that results in significant improvements in the quality and efficiency of customer service, production, and distribution.

- **Decreased Costs.** Many companies report significant reductions in transaction processing costs and hardware, software, and IT support staff compared to the nonintegrated legacy systems that were replaced by their new ERP systems.

- **Decision Support.** ERP provides vital cross-functional information on business performance quickly to managers to significantly improve their ability to make better decisions in a timely manner across the entire business enterprise.

- **Enterprise Agility.** Implementing ERP systems breaks down many former departmental and functional walls or "silos" of business processes, information systems, and information resources. This results in more flexible organizational structures, managerial responsibilities, and work roles, and therefore a more agile and adaptive organization and workforce that can more easily capitalize on new business opportunities.

Failures in ERP

An ERP implementation is like the corporate equivalent of a brain transplant. We pulled the plug on every company application and moved to PeopleSoft software. The risk was certainly disruption of business, because if you do not do ERP properly, you can kill your company, guaranteed [15].

So says Jim Prevo, CIO of Green Mountain Coffee of Vermont, commenting on their successful implementation of an ERP system. Though the benefits of ERP are many, the costs and risks are also considerable, as we will continue to see in some of the real world cases and examples in the text. Most companies have had successful ERP implementations, but a sizable minority of firms experienced spectacular and costly failures that heavily damaged their overall business. Big losses in revenue, profits, and market share resulted when core business processes and information systems failed or did not work properly. In many cases, orders and shipments were lost, inventory changes were not recorded correctly, and unreliable inventory levels caused major stock-outs to occur for weeks or months. Companies like Hershey Foods, Nike, A-DEC, and Connecticut General sustained losses running into hundreds of millions of dollars in some instances. In the case of FoxMeyer Drugs, a $5 billion pharmaceutical wholesaler, the company had to file for bankruptcy protection, and then was bought out by its arch competitor McKesson Drugs [15]. Let's take a look at an example of a more recent failed ERP project.

Sobeys Inc.: Failure in ERP Implementation

SAP AG's software applications for retailers continue to be stung by a series of high-profile installation problems that many say illustrate the complexity of trying to fit an integrated suite of enterprise resource planning (ERP) software into a retail operation. A major example came late in January 2001, when Canadian supermarket chain, Sobeys Inc., abandoned an $89.1 million SAP Retail implementation. "SAP Retail has insufficient core functionality . . . to effectively deal with the extremely high number of transactions in our retail operating environment," said Bill McEwan, president and CEO of the Stellarton, Nova Scotia–based retail chain.

Sobeys isn't alone. Jo-Ann Stores, Inc. in Hudson, Ohio, and pet supply retailer Petsmart Inc. in Phoenix both attributed low financial results to problems with their SAP Retail rollouts. Both, however, said they're pleased with the system overall. SAP officials continued to defend the capabilities of SAP Retail. Geraldine McBride, general manager of the consumer sector business unit at SAP America, Inc., said the German vendor has signed up 264 retailers as customers, 128 of which have gone live. But Greg Girard, an analyst at AMR Research in Boston, said most of the retailers are running SAP's financial and human resources applications, not the SAP Retail core ERP application itself. "I can't point to a single happy SAP Retail account in North America," said Girard.

Canada's second largest supermarket chain abandoned the $80 million implementation of SAP AG's business applications for retailers after a five-day database and systems shutdown affected the company's business operations for nearly a month. McEwan said during a conference that all "growing pains" expected by the 1,400-store retail chain in the two-year-old project became "in fact systemic problems of a much more serious nature." McEwan, who inherited the SAP implementation when he joined Sobeys in November 2000, added that it would have taken another two years to finish the software rollout.

The system shutdown in December 2000 resulted in "unprecedented" out-of-stock issues with products at many of Sobeys' corporate-owned stores, McEwan said. The disruption also forced Sobeys to implement work-arounds for its accounting department. Sobeys plans to replace the SAP applications with software that can be installed more quickly and that "will fully meet all the business requirements" at the company, McEwan said [20].

Causes of ERP Failures

What have been the major causes of failure in ERP projects? In almost every case, the business managers and IT professionals of these companies underestimated the complexity of the planning, development, and training that were needed to prepare for a new ERP system that would radically change their business processes and information systems. Failure to involve affected employees in the planning and development phases and change management programs, or trying to do too much too fast in the conversion process, were typical causes of failed ERP projects. Insufficient training in the new work tasks required by the ERP system, and failure to do enough data conversion and testing, were other causes of failure. In many cases, ERP failures were also due to overreliance by company or IT management on the claims of ERP software vendors or on the assistance of prestigious consulting firms hired to lead the implementation [19].

CRM: The Business Focus

Managing the full range of the customer relationship involves two related objectives: one, to provide the organization and all of its customer facing employees with a single, complete view of every customer at every touchpoint and across all channels; and, two, to provide the customer with a single, complete view of the company and its extended channels [28].

That's why companies are turning to **customer relationship management** to help them become customer-focused businesses. CRM uses information technology to create a cross-functional enterprise system that integrates and automates many of the *customer serving* processes in sales, marketing, and customer services that interact with a company's customers. CRM systems also create an IT framework of Web-enabled software and databases that integrates these processes with the rest of a company's business operations, and supports collaboration among a business and its customers and partners [15]. See Figure 7.6.

CRM systems include a family of software modules that provides the tools that help a business and its employees provide fast, convenient, dependable, and consistent service to its customers. Siebel Systems, Oracle, PeopleSoft, SAP AG, and Epiphany are some of the leading vendors of CRM software. Figure 7.7 illustrates some of the major application components of a CRM system [15]. Let's take a look at each of them.

Contact and Account Management

CRM software helps sales, marketing, and service professionals capture and track relevant data about every past and planned contact with prospects and customers, as well as other business and life cycle events of customers. Information is captured from all customer touchpoints, such as telephone, fax, e-mail, the company's website, retail stores, kiosks, and personal contact. CRM systems store the data in a common customer

CRM systems support an integrated and collaborative relationship between a business and its customers and partners with Web-enabled software and shared databases.

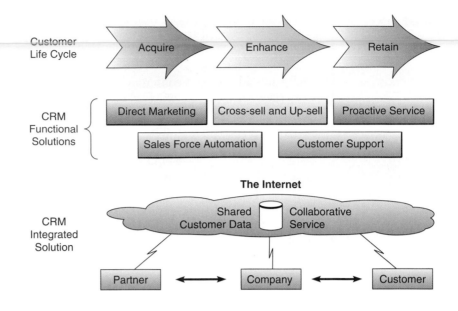

database that integrates all customer account information and makes it available throughout the company via Internet, intranet, or other network links for sales, marketing, service, and other CRM applications.

Sales

A CRM system provides sales reps with the software tools and company data sources they need to support and manage their sales activities, and optimize cross-selling and up-selling. Examples include sales prospect and product information, product configuration, and sales quote generation capabilities. CRM also gives them real-time access to a single common view of the customer, enabling them to check on all aspects of a customer's account status and history before scheduling their sales calls. For example, a CRM system would alert a bank sales rep to call customers who make large deposits to sell them premier credit or investment services. Or it would alert a salesperson of unresolved service, delivery, or payment problems that could be resolved through a personal contact with a customer.

The major application clusters in customer relationship management.

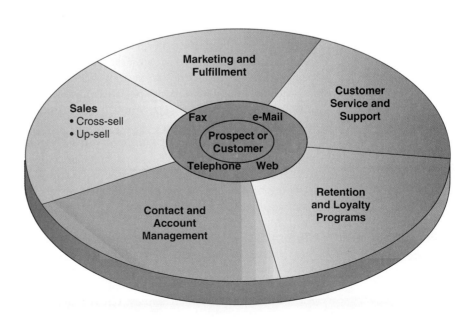

Marketing and Fulfillment

CRM systems help marketing professionals accomplish direct marketing campaigns by automating such tasks as qualifying leads for targeted marketing, and scheduling and tracking direct marketing mailings. Then the CRM software helps marketing professionals capture and manage prospect and customer response data in the CRM database, and analyze the customer and business value of a company's direct marketing campaigns. CRM also assists in the fulfillment of prospect and customer responses and requests by quickly scheduling sales contacts and providing appropriate information on products and services to them, while capturing relevant information for the CRM database.

Customer Service and Support

A CRM system provides service reps with software tools and real-time access to the common customer database shared by sales and marketing professionals. CRM helps customer service managers create, assign, and manage requests for service by customers. *Call center* software routes calls to customer support agents based on their skills and authority to handle specific kinds of service requests. *Help desk* software assists customer service reps in helping customers who are having problems with a product or service, by providing relevant service data and suggestions for resolving problems. Web-based self-service enables customers to easily access personalized support information at the company website, while giving them an option to receive further assistance online or by phone from customer service personnel.

Retention and Loyalty Programs

- It costs six times more to sell to a new customer than to sell to an existing one.
- A typical dissatisfied customer will tell eight to ten people about his or her experience.
- A company can boost its profits 85 percent by increasing its annual customer retention by only 5 percent.
- The odds of selling a product to a new customer are 15 percent, whereas the odds of selling a product to an existing customer are 50 percent.
- Seventy percent of complaining customers will do business with the company again if it quickly takes care of a service snafu [15].

That's why enhancing and optimizing customer retention and loyalty is a major business strategy and primary objective of customer relationship management. CRM systems try to help a company identify, reward, and market to their most loyal and profitable customers. CRM analytical software includes data mining tools and other analytical marketing software, while CRM databases may consist of a customer data warehouse and CRM data marts. These tools are used to identify profitable and loyal customers and direct and evaluate a company's targeted marketing and relationship marketing programs toward them.

Telstra Corporation: The Business Value of CRM

Australia's Telstra Corporation provides fixed, wireless, and e-commerce services to a customer base in nineteen countries. In addition, Telstra offers voice, data, Internet, multimedia, managed communications services, and customer-contact center solutions globally through its strategic alliances and partnerships. The Melbourne company is Australia's largest communications carrier and the clear market leader.

To succeed in transforming its relationship with its customers, Telstra determined that it needed a CRM solution that would provide both its customer-facing employees and channel partners a single view of each customer relationship. The solution would also require the integration of more than 20 core legacy billing and operations databases across all of its product lines. After exploring several options, Telstra chose a variety of Siebel Systems products to provide its e-business solution.

For its initial deployment, Telstra rolled out a Siebel Call Center to more than 250 telesales representatives and 150 telephone account managers in its outbound call centers, which are geographically dispersed throughout Australia. "This was where we could most quickly impact our business," explains Ross Riddoch, general manager of Retail Technology Products. "We rolled out account, contact, and opportunity management modules." This Siebel CRM product was deployed in approximately three months, on time and on budget.

User acceptance and business benefits quickly followed. "Users found Siebel Call Center's Web-based interface to be extremely intuitive and easy to use," says Riddoch. "This enabled us to reduce our training time and get our users up to speed in record time. Within four months of employing Siebel Call Center, our account management team doubled its weekly revenue, and we achieved a three-fold gain in employee productivity" [28].

The success of Telstra's initial implementation of a CRM system led the company to expand its CRM deployment to target four work streams: sales and account management, commissions, order fulfillment, and marketing. Based on this strategy, Telstra is now managing seven concurrent projects and rolling out e-business applications to the majority of its field sales, call center, telesales, and business partners.

Within its marketing organization, for example, Telstra has deployed Siebel Marketing and Siebel eAnalytics applications to more than 80 marketing professionals. These CRM applications enable Telstra's marketing managers to perform customer segmentation analysis using customer information from across all touchpoints and create targeted campaigns that effectively reach their customers through call centers, direct mail, and e-mail. They also help Telstra manage, analyze, and track channel and marketing effectiveness through real-time reporting, enabling the company to continually refine its marketing efforts across all channels.

To better integrate partners into its channel system, Telstra also is deploying Siebel eChannel—a Web-based partner relationship management portal for communication of customer and sales data between Telstra and its many business partners. By integrating its channel partners into its CRM system, Telstra wants to ensure that it maintains a seamless view of the customer across all points of interaction between customers, partners, and Telstra customer-facing professionals [28].

Benefits and Challenges of CRM

The potential business benefits of customer relationship management are many. For example, CRM allows a business to identify and target their best customers—those who are the most profitable to the business—so they can be retained as lifelong customers for greater and more profitable services. It makes possible real-time customization and personalization of products and services based on customer wants, needs, buying habits, and life cycles. CRM can also keep track of when a customer contacts the company, regardless of the contact point. And CRM systems can enable a company to provide a consistent customer experience and superior service and support across all the contact points a customer chooses. All of these benefits would provide strategic business value to a company and major customer value to its customers [11, 12, 14].

CRM Failures

The business benefits of customer relationship management are not guaranteed and, instead, have proven elusive at many companies. Surveys by industry research groups include a report that over 50 percent of CRM projects did not produce the results that were promised. In another research report, 20 percent of businesses surveyed reported that CRM implementations had actually damaged long-standing customer relationships. And in a survey of senior management satisfaction with 25 management tools, CRM ranked near the bottom in user satisfaction, even though 72 percent expected to have CRM systems implemented shortly [23].

What is the reason for such a high rate of failure or dissatisfaction with CRM initiatives? Research shows that the major reason is a familiar one: lack of understanding and preparation. That is, too often, business managers rely on a major new application of information technology (like CRM) to solve a business problem without first developing the business process changes and change management programs that are required. For example, in many cases, failed CRM projects were implemented without the participation of the business stakeholders involved. Therefore, employees and customers were not prepared for the new processes or challenges that were part of the new CRM implementation. We will discuss the topic of failures in information technology management, system implementation, and change management further in Chapters 10 and 12.

Gevity HR and Monster.com: Failures in CRM Implementation	No amount of high-level cooperation will protect a CRM project from rank-and-file employees who hate it. Lisa Harris, CIO at HR-services firm Gevity HR based in Bradenton, Florida, faced rebellion from the staff when she installed Oracle CRM software that helped solve some customers' problems online—without the help of a live operator. Call-center employees felt that the software threatened their jobs, so they quietly discouraged customers from using it. "Our operators would say, 'Wouldn't you rather call up? I'll take care of everything you need,'" Harris says. She stuck with the online CRM, but also belatedly began talking to employees about software. She changed their work routines to include more customer hand-holding and less data entry, which was increasingly done online.

CRM software is complex to install because it often touches many different legacy systems. Harris says she spent millions of dollars integrating a CRM application in 1997 for a previous employer. But when the project was finished, it took operators too long to get data on screen. The company had bogged down the performance of the new CRM implementation by trying to integrate too many complex business systems. The project ended up a total failure, she says [4].

And when Monster.com rolled out a CRM program in 1998, it was sure it had a new money-making strategy on its hands. The Massachusetts-based job-listings company had invested over $1 million in customized software and integrated all its computer systems in an attempt to boost the efficiency of its sales force. These CRM applications had been specially developed to allow Monster.com's sales representatives instant access to data for prospective customers.

However, the new system proved to be frighteningly slow—so slow, in fact, that salespeople in the field found themselves unable to download customer information from the company's databases onto their laptops. Every time they tried, their machines froze. Eventually, Monster.com was forced to rebuild the entire system. It lost millions of dollars along the way, not to mention the goodwill of both customers and employees [23].

SCM: The Business Network

Legacy supply chains are clogged with unnecessary steps and redundant stockpiles. For instance, a typical box of breakfast cereal spends an incredible 104 days getting from factory to supermarket, struggling its way through an unbelievable maze of wholesalers, distributors, brokers, and consolidators, each of which has a warehouse. The e-business opportunity lies in the fusing of each company's internal systems to those of its suppliers, partners, and customers. This fusion forces companies to better integrate interenterprise supply chain processes to improve manufacturing efficiency and distribution effectiveness [15].

Many companies today are making supply chain management (SCM) a top strategic objective and major e-business application development initiative. Fundamentally, supply chain management helps a company get the right products to the right place at the right time, in the proper quantity and at an acceptable cost. The goal of SCM is to efficiently manage this process by forecasting demand; controlling inventory; enhancing the network of business relationships a company has with customers, suppliers, distributors, and others, and receiving feedback on the status of every link in the supply chain. To achieve this goal, many companies today are turning to Internet technologies to Web-enable their supply chain processes, decision making, and information flows.

Supply chain management is a cross-functional interenterprise system that uses information technology to help support and manage the links between some of a company's key business processes and those of its suppliers, customers, and business partners. The goal of SCM is to create a fast, efficient, and low-cost network of business relationships, or **supply chain**, to get a company's products from concept to market.

What exactly is a company's supply chain? Let's suppose a company wants to build and sell a product to other businesses. Then it must buy raw materials and a variety of contracted services from other companies. The interrelationships with suppliers, customers, distributors, and other businesses that are needed to design, build, and sell a product make up the network of business entities, relationships, and processes that is called a supply chain. And since each supply chain process should add value to the products or services a company produces, a supply chain is frequently called a *value chain*, a different but related concept we discussed in Chapter 2. In any event, many companies today are using Internet technologies to create interenterprise information systems for supply chain management that help a company streamline its traditional supply chain processes.

Figure 7.8 illustrates the basic business processes in the supply chain life cycle and the functional SCM processes that support them [15]. It also emphasizes how many companies today are reengineering their supply chain processes, aided by Internet technologies and supply chain management software. For example, the demands of today's competitive business environment are pushing manufacturers to use their intranets, extranets, and e-commerce Web portals to help them reengineer their relationships with their suppliers, distributors, and retailers. The objective is to significantly reduce costs, increase efficiency, and improve their supply chain cycle times. SCM software can also help to improve interenterprise coordination among supply chain process players. The result is much more effective distribution and channel networks among business partners. The Web initiatives of Moen Inc. and TaylorMade Golf illustrate these developments.

Moen Inc. and TaylorMade Golf: Web-Enabling the Supply Chain	In late 1998, faucet maker Moen Inc. started sending electronic files of new product designs by e-mail. A few months later, it launched ProjectNet, an online extranet site where Moen can share digital designs simultaneously with suppliers worldwide. Every supplier can make changes immediately. Moen consolidates all the design changes on a master Web file. That way, design problems are discovered instantly and adjustments can be made just as fast, cutting the time it takes to lock in a final design to three days.

Next, the company attacked the cumbersome process of ordering parts from suppliers and updating them by fax or phone. In October 2000, the company launched its SupplyNet extranet site that allows parts suppliers to check the status of Moen's orders online. Every time Moen changes an order, the supplier receives an e-mail. If a supplier can't fill an order in time, it can alert Moen right away so the faucet maker can search elsewhere for the part. Today, the 40 key suppliers who make 80 percent of the parts that Moen buys use SupplyNet. The result: The company has shaved $3 million, or almost 6 percent, off its raw materials and work-in-progress inventories [17].

Although golf-equipment makers generally stage their competition in the public eye, with star-studded ads or with logos that are plastered on players as thickly as on racing cars, TaylorMade Golf Co. (www.taylormadegolf. com) took a less glamorous approach. It spent two years moving its key business information systems with its network of suppliers and distributors to the Web. Of course, to implement its Web

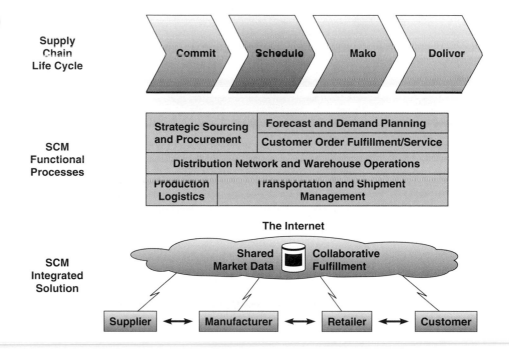

FIGURE 7.8

Supply chain management software and Internet technologies can help companies reengineer and integrate the functional SCM processes that support the supply chain life cycle.

strategy, TaylorMade did spend $10 million to develop a secure extranet website to efficiently handle the administrative details of dealing with the systems of its suppliers and distributors, and to more easily share forecasts and inventory information with them. Mark Leposky, the vice president of global operations, says that Taylor-Made may save $50 million in production costs in 2002—Tiger Woods–type money—based on just that $10 million investment in moving online.

The new Web-based system has compressed TaylorMade's production schedule for a set of off-the-shelf golf clubs by more than half. And the company can now make a set of custom clubs in less than seven days, instead of taking six weeks. As a result, TaylorMade's custom-club business has doubled in the past year. "In a supply chain, how you execute creates competitive advantage," Leposky says. "We definitely see ours as a competitive weapon [8].

Benefits and Challenges of SCM

Creating a real-time SCM infrastructure is a daunting and ongoing issue and quite often, a point of failure, for several reasons. The chief reason is that the planning, selection, and implementation of SCM solutions is becoming more complex as the pace of technological change accelerates and the number of a company's partners increases [15].

The real world experiences of companies like Moen, Inc. and TaylorMade Golf emphasize the major business benefits that are possible with effective supply chain management systems. Companies know that SCM systems can provide them with key business benefits such as faster, more accurate order processing, reductions in inventory levels, quicker time to market, lower transaction and materials costs, and strategic relationships with their suppliers. All of these benefits of SCM are aimed at helping a company achieve agility and responsiveness in meeting the demands of their customers and the needs of their business partners.

But developing effective SCM systems has proven to be a complex and difficult application of information technology to business operations. So achieving the business value and customer value goals and objectives of supply chain management, as illustrated in Figure 7.9, has been a major challenge for most companies [15].

FIGURE 7.9

Achieving the goals and objectives of supply chain management is a major challenge for many companies today.

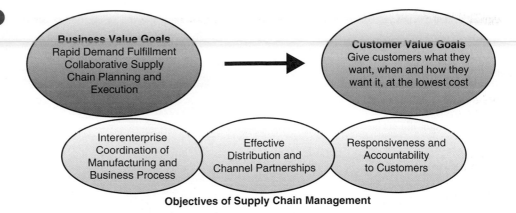

Objectives of Supply Chain Management

What are the causes of problems in supply chain management? Several reasons stand out. A lack of proper demand planning knowledge, tools, and guidelines is a major source of SCM failure. Inaccurate or overoptimistic demand forecasts will cause major production, inventory, and other business problems, no matter how efficient the rest of the supply chain management process is constructed. Inaccurate production, inventory, and other business data provided by a company's other information systems are a frequent cause of SCM problems. And lack of adequate collaboration among marketing, production, and inventory management departments within a company, and with suppliers, distributors, and others, will sabotage any SCM system. Even the SCM software tools themselves are considered to be immature, incomplete, and hard to implement by many companies who are installing SCM systems [1]. These problems are spotlighted in the real world example of Solectron Corporation.

Solectron Corp.: Failures in SCM

SCM theory contends that technologically driven improvements in inventory management—like "just-in-time" production, direct online sales, and supply-chain management software—will prompt increased efficiency and allow managers to tailor output to match demand exactly. That, in turn, would increase working capital, boost margins, and help companies smooth out the ups and downs in the business cycle.

SCM lesson one is that killer software applications can't compensate for old-fashioned business judgment. There's a flaw in the premise that technology can synchronize every party in the product chain by providing a transparent view of supply and demand: The forecasts driving the entire flow of work are still concocted by people, not by real-time blips of data from retail shelves. No matter how mechanized the system becomes, sales managers and CEOs still shoot for the moon in a boom and don't share internal market intelligence with outsiders.

The experience of Solectron Corp., the world's biggest electronics contract manufacturer, is a case in point. In the fall of 2000, company officials say they could tell a supply glut of telecom equipment was brewing. Each of their big customers, which include Cisco, Ericsson, and Lucent, was expecting explosive growth for wireless phones and networking gear. But since Solectron supplies every major player, it knew the numbers didn't add up, even under the rosiest scenario.

Nevertheless, the telecom giants told Solectron and other contractors to produce flat out, assuring them that they would pay for excess materials. But when the bottom finally fell out and its clients ordered production cutbacks, it was too late for Solectron to halt orders from all of its 4,000 suppliers. By the spring of 2001, Solectron was left holding the bag for $4.7 billion in inventory [9].

FIGURE 7.10

Enterprise application integration software interconnects front-office and back-office applications like customer relationship management and enterprise resource planning.

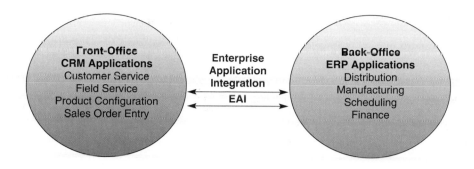

Enterprise Application Integration

How does a business interconnect some of the cross-functional enterprise systems we have discussed in this chapter? **Enterprise application integration** (EAI) software is being used by many companies to connect major e-business applications like CRM and ERP. See Figure 7.10. EAI software enables users to model the business processes involved in the interactions that should occur between business applications. EAI also provides *middleware* that performs data conversion and coordination, application communication and messaging services, and access to the application interfaces involved. Thus, EAI software can integrate a variety of enterprise application clusters by letting them exchange data according to rules derived from the business process models developed by users. For example, a typical rule might be:

> *When an order is complete, have the order application tell the accounting system to send a bill and alert shipping to send out the product.*

Thus, as Figure 7.10 illustrates, EAI software can integrate the front-office and back-office applications of a business so they work together in a seamless, integrated way [15]. This is a vital capability that provides real business value to a business enterprise that must respond quickly and effectively to business events and customer demands. For example, the integration of enterprise application clusters has been shown to dramatically improve customer call center responsiveness and effectiveness. That's because EAI integrates access to all of the customer and product data customer reps need to quickly serve customers. EAI also streamlines sales order processing so products and services can be delivered faster. Thus, EAI improves customer and supplier experience with the business because of its responsiveness [15, 22]. See Figure 7.11.

Dell Inc.: Enterprise Application Integration

In a survey of just 75 companies it deals with, Dell Inc. found they used 18 different software packages, says Terry Klein, vice president of e-business for Dell's "relationship group." This lack of integration means that companies aren't getting the seamless processing that reduces costs and speeds up customer responsiveness.

Dell knew that figuring out how to get its system to talk to each of those 18 different systems in its partners' back offices, one at a time, would be impractical, to say the least. So Dell installed software from WebMethods, a maker of industrial-strength business-to-business integration software, based in Fairfax, Virginia. WebMethods' enterprise application integration (EAI) technology acts as a software translator and creates a kind of hub that, using the Web, allows instantaneous communication among networked companies' internal business systems.

For Dell, the first fruit of installing the WebMethods software is what Dell calls e-procurement, and it goes like this. A business customer pulls product information directly from Dell's server into the customer's purchasing system, which creates an electronic requisition. After the requisition is approved online by the customer, a computer-generated purchase order shoots over the Internet back to Dell.

The entire process can take 60 seconds. Dell says the system, which went live in the spring of 2000, has automatically cut errors in its procurement processes from about

FIGURE 7.11 An example of a new customer order process showing how EAI middleware connects several business information systems within a company.

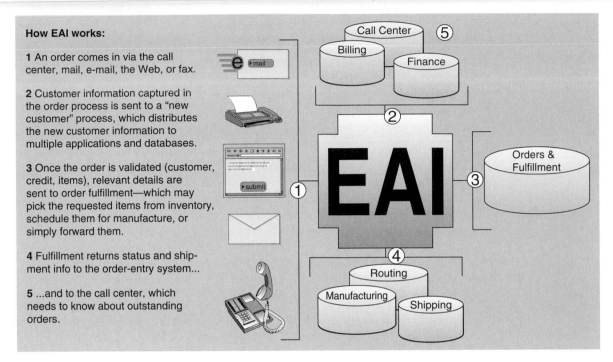

How EAI works:

1 An order comes in via the call center, mail, e-mail, the Web, or fax.

2 Customer information captured in the order process is sent to a "new customer" process, which distributes the new customer information to multiple applications and databases.

3 Once the order is validated (customer, credit, items), relevant details are sent to order fulfillment—which may pick the requested items from inventory, schedule them for manufacture, or simply forward them.

4 Fulfillment returns status and shipment info to the order-entry system...

5 ...and to the call center, which needs to know about outstanding orders.

200 per million transactions to 10 per million. And Dell has been able to shave $40 to $50 off the cost of processing each order. That adds up to $5 million a year in cost savings, since thousands of orders flow to Dell through its WebMethods system daily.

The EAI software also enabled Dell to build links to 40 or so of its biggest customers, allowing a customer to buy, say, a truckload of new laptops online while Dell simultaneously enters the order for those laptops into the customer's procurement system. Think of it as one-click shopping for corporate buyers. Just as Amazon.com automates the process of entering credit card information to speed purchases by consumers, Dell is able to update its customers' procurement tracking systems every time they make a purchase [3].

Transaction Processing Systems

Transaction processing systems (TPS) are cross-functional information systems that process data resulting from the occurrence of business transactions. We introduced transaction processing systems in Chapter 1 as one of the major application categories of information systems in business.

Transactions are events that occur as part of doing business, such as sales, purchases, deposits, withdrawals, refunds, and payments. Think, for example, of the data generated whenever a business sells something to a customer on credit, whether in a retail store or at an e-commerce site on the Web. Data about the customer, product, salesperson, store, and so on, must be captured and processed. This in turn causes additional transactions, such as credit checks, customer billing, inventory changes, and increases in accounts receivable balances, that generate even more data. Thus, transaction processing activities are needed to capture and process such data, or the operations of a business would grind to a halt. Therefore, transaction processing systems play a vital role in supporting the operations of an e-business enterprise.

Online transaction processing systems play a strategic role in electronic commerce. Many firms are using the Internet, extranets, and other networks that tie them

FIGURE 7.12 The Syntellect pay-per-view online transaction processing system.

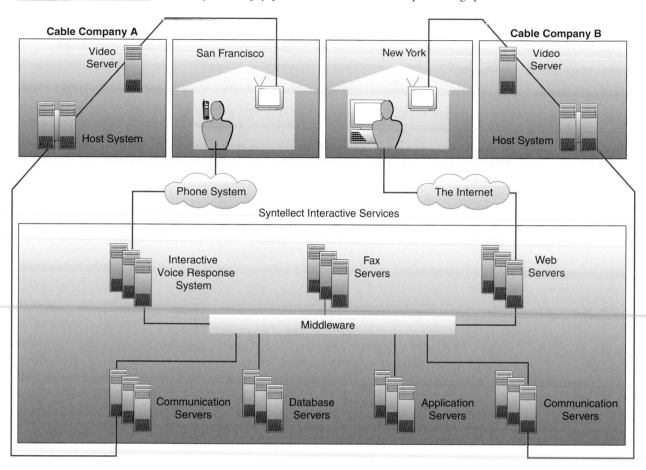

electronically to their customers or suppliers for online transaction processing (OLTP). Such *real-time* systems, which capture and process transactions immediately, can help firms provide superior service to customers and other trading partners. This capability adds value to their products and services, and thus gives them an important way to differentiate themselves from their competitors.

Syntellect's Online Transaction Processing

For example, Figure 7.12 illustrates an online transaction processing system for cable pay-per-view systems developed by Syntellect Interactive Services. Cable TV viewers can select pay-per-view events offered by their cable companies using the phone or the World Wide Web. The pay-per-view order is captured by Syntellect's interactive voice response system or Web server, then transported to Syntellect database application servers. There the order is processed, customer and sales databases are updated, and the approved order is relayed back to the cable company's video server, which transmits the video of the pay-per-view event to the customer. Thus, Syntellect teams with over 700 cable companies to offer a very popular and very profitable service [30].

The Transaction Processing Cycle

Transaction processing systems, such as Syntellect's, capture and process data describing business transactions, update organizational databases, and produce a variety of information products. You should understand this as a **transaction processing cycle** of several basic activities, as illustrated in Figure 7.13.

FIGURE 7.13

The transaction processing cycle. Note that transaction processing systems use a five-stage cycle of data entry, transaction processing, database maintenance, document and report generation, and inquiry processing activities.

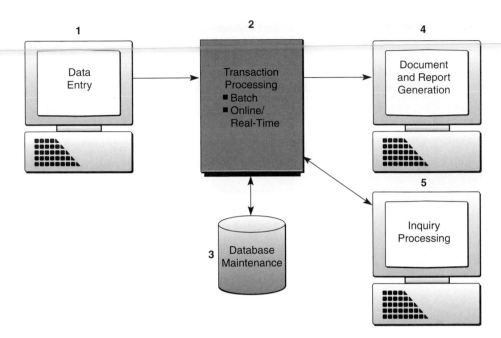

- **Data Entry.** The first step of the transaction processing cycle is the capture of business data. For example, transaction data may be collected by point-of-sale terminals using optical scanning of bar codes and credit card readers at a retail store or other business. Or transaction data can be captured at an electronic commerce website on the Internet. The proper recording and editing of data so they are quickly and correctly captured for processing is one of the major design challenges of information systems discussed in Chapter 10.

- **Transaction Processing.** Transaction processing systems process data in two basic ways: (1) **batch processing,** where transaction data are accumulated over a period of time and processed periodically, and (2) **real-time processing** (also called online processing), where data are processed immediately after a transaction occurs. All online transaction processing systems incorporate real-time processing capabilities. Many online systems also depend on the capabilities of *fault tolerant* computer systems that can continue to operate even if parts of the system fail. We will discuss this fault tolerant concept in Chapter 11.

- **Database Maintenance.** An organization's database must be maintained by its transaction processing systems so that they are always correct and up-to-date. Therefore, transaction processing systems update the corporate databases of an organization to reflect changes resulting from day-to-day business transactions. For example, credit sales made to customers will cause customer account balances to be increased and the amount of inventory on hand to be decreased. Database maintenance ensures that these and other changes are reflected in the data records stored in the company's databases.

- **Document and Report Generation.** Transaction processing systems produce a variety of documents and reports. Examples of transaction documents include purchase orders, paychecks, sales receipts, invoices, and customer statements. Transaction reports might take the form of a transaction listing such as a payroll register, or edit reports that describe errors detected during processing.

- **Inquiry Processing.** Many transaction processing systems allow you to use the Internet, intranets, extranets, and Web browsers or database management query languages to make inquiries and receive responses concerning the results of transaction processing activity. Typically, responses are displayed in a variety of prespecified formats or screens. For example, you might check on the status of a sales order, the balance in an account, or the amount of stock in inventory and receive immediate responses at your PC.

Enterprise Collaboration Systems

Really difficult business problems always have many aspects. Often a major decision depends on an impromptu search for one or two key pieces of auxiliary information and a quick ad hoc analysis of several possible scenarios. You need software tools that easily combine and recombine data from many sources. You need Internet access for all kinds of research. Widely scattered people need to be able to collaborate and work the data in different ways [10].

Enterprise collaboration systems (ECS) are cross-functional information systems that enhance communication, coordination, and collaboration among the members of business teams and workgroups. Information technology, especially Internet technologies, provides tools to help us collaborate—to communicate ideas, share resources, and coordinate our cooperative work efforts as members of the many formal and informal process and project teams and workgroups that make up many of today's organizations. Thus, the goal of **enterprise collaboration systems** is to enable us to work together more easily and effectively by helping us to:

- **Communicate:** Sharing information with each other.
- **Coordinate:** Coordinating our individual work efforts and use of resources with each other.
- **Collaborate:** Working together cooperatively on joint projects and assignments.

For example, engineers, business specialists, and external consultants may form a virtual team for a project. The team may rely on intranets and extranets to collaborate via e-mail, videoconferencing, discussion forums, and a multimedia database of work-in-progress information at a project website. The enterprise collaboration system may use PC workstations networked to a variety of servers on which project, corporate, and other databases are stored. In addition, network servers may provide a variety of software resources, such as Web browsers, groupware, and application packages, to assist the team's collaboration until the project is completed.

Tools for Enterprise Collaboration

The capabilities and potential of the Internet, as well as intranets and extranets, are driving the demand for better enterprise collaboration tools in business. On the other hand, it is Internet technologies like Web browsers and servers, hypermedia documents and databases, and intranets and extranets that provide the hardware, software, data, and network platforms for many of the groupware tools for enterprise collaboration that business users want. Figure 7.14 provides an overview of some of the software tools for electronic communication, electronic conferencing, and collaborative work management.

Electronic communication tools include electronic mail, voice mail, faxing, Web publishing, bulletin board systems, paging, and Internet phone systems. These tools enable you to electronically send messages, documents, and files in data, text, voice, or multimedia over computer networks. This helps you share everything from voice and text messages to copies of project documents and data files with your team members, wherever they may be. The ease and efficiency of such communications are major contributors to the collaboration process.

Electronic conferencing tools help people communicate and collaborate while working together. A variety of conferencing methods enables the members of teams and workgroups at different locations to exchange ideas interactively at the same time, or at different times at their convenience. These include data and voice conferencing, videoconferencing, chat systems, and discussion forums. Electronic

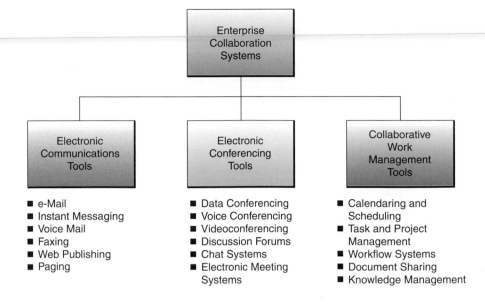

FIGURE 7.14

Electronic communications, conferencing, and collaborative work software tools enhance enterprise collaboration.

conferencing options also include *electronic meeting systems* and other *group support systems* where team members can meet at the same time and place in a *decision room* setting, or use the Internet to work collaboratively anywhere in the world. See Figure 7.15.

Collaborative work management tools help people accomplish or manage group work activities. This category of software includes calendaring and scheduling tools, task and project management, workflow systems, and knowledge management tools. Other tools for joint work, such as joint document creation, editing, and revision, are found in the software suites discussed in Chapter 4.

General Electric Co.: Committed to Enterprise Collaboration	GE has made a huge commitment to the Lotus Development tools QuickPlace (which lets employees set up Web-based work spaces) and Sametime (for real-time online meetings), which permit ad hoc collaboration without help from the IT department. These tools streamline the company's communication in myriad ways. Thus, GE's recruiting teams can set up QuickPlaces to trade information about prospective hires. And GE engineers share drawings, design requirements, and production schedules with supervisors on manufacturing floors. In all, GE has created almost 18,000 QuickPlaces for 250,000 users, says CTO Larry Biagini. "And if we have an engineering project with someone outside the company, we'll set up a QuickPlace or Sametime session and invite outside people."

There's also Support Central, a companywide knowledge management system developed using software from GE's Fanuc division. Employees sign on and complete a survey about their areas of expertise. The responses are added to a knowledge base so people with questions anywhere in GE can find people with answers. "Someone may have a question about, say, titanium metallurgy, and they'll be able to find documents about it, or send e-mail or initiate an online chat with someone who can help," says Stuart Scott, CIO of GE Industrial Systems. The result of all this collaboration? Faster workflow and quicker, smarter decisions, GE executives say [7].

FIGURE 7.15

QuickPlace by Lotus Development helps virtual workgroups set up Web-based work spaces for collaborative work assignments.

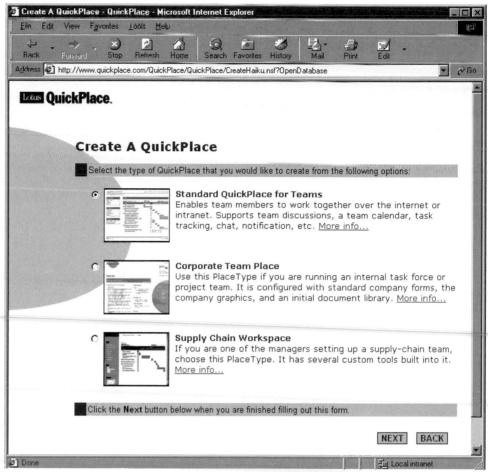

Source: Courtesy of Lotus Development Corp.

SECTION II Functional Business Systems

Introduction

Business managers are moving from a tradition where they could avoid, delegate, or ignore decisions about IT to one where they cannot create a marketing, product, international, organization, or financial plan that does not involve such decisions [16].

There are as many ways to use information technology in business as there are business activities to be performed, business problems to be solved, and business opportunities to be pursued. As a business professional, you should have a basic understanding and appreciation of the major ways information systems are used to support each of the functions of business that must be accomplished in any company that wants to succeed. Thus, in this section, we will discuss **functional business systems,** that is, a variety of types of information systems (transaction processing, management information, decision support, etc.) that support the business functions of accounting, finance, marketing, operations management, and human resource management.

Analyzing GE Power and Corporate Express

Read the Real World Case on GE Power and Corporate Express on the next page. We can learn a lot about the business value and challenges of implementing e-business systems from this case. See Figure 7.16.

GE Power began an enterprise application integration project three years ago to interconnect the information systems of their various divisions, including a variety of legacy business systems and enterprise resource planning and Web-based applications. The EAI projects of the business units were managed and coordinated by a project management office established by GE Power's IT department. Benefits from the EAI projects have included the ability to send data in real time between systems and the improved quality and accuracy of the data. The EAI projects of Corporate Express were primarily focused on developing Web-based interfaces between their business systems and the e-procurement systems of their customers. The company credits this integration with record increases in its online sales to customers.

FIGURE 7.16

GE Power Systems is a global leader in the manufacture of electric power plant control systems.

Source: Digital Vision/Getty Images.

REAL WORLD CASE 2	GE Power Systems and Corporate Express: The Business Case for Enterprise Application Integration

GE Power Systems. Enterprise application integration is not new at GE Power Systems in Atlanta (www.gepower.com), which began an EAI project three years ago and is now reaping the benefits. The subsidiary of General Electric Co. had "a collection of business units running as independent operations, with the majority of their systems not interconnected," says Alan Boehme, former e-technology CIO at GE Power who recently left to join Best Software Inc. as executive vice president and CIO. GE Power used the WebMethods EAI development system to build an EAI platform to share data among a variety of legacy systems, ERP software, and Web-based applications. The benefits have included the ability to send data in real time from one system to another, and improved quality and accuracy of the data.

EAI involves using software to connect a variety of applications into a cohesive unit and thereby helps enterprises align systems more closely with business processes. It's become a critical part of the IT strategy at many organizations looking to meld disparate systems and quickly deliver data to employees, customers, and partners.

EAI was the third most-cited project Premier 100 IT Leaders said they plan to undertake in 2003. And while IT managers who have completed or launched EAI projects say there can be significant benefits, they also point out that such efforts require specific IT skills and extensive coordination among multiple departments, which can be a major challenge in some organizations.

For example, the IT department at GE Power set up a project management office to manage the implementation of EAI by various business units and track its benefits to the company. Boehme says. Although it's centrally managed, EAI is funded by individual projects run by various functional units within the business divisions. "That's where the benefit accrues, so we pushed the cost and the actual physical work into the functional units." Boehme says. The decision on whether to invest in EAI was determined by each functional unit based on the estimated cost of implementing EAI interfaces among their systems, compared with the perceived benefits.

Corporate Express. Corporate Express Inc. (www.corporate express.com), a fastgrowing office supplies distributor in Broomfield, Colorado, used an EAI project to dramatically improve customer service by almost doubling the number of its Web-based interfaces to the systems of its business partners, from 120 to more than 200. The aim of Corporate Express was to cut costs both internally and for its customers, so it would remain attractive as a preferred supplier. The company has also completed a handful of other EAI projects recently, including integrating its warehouse management application with its PeopleSoft enterprise resource planning system.

"The integration effort is probably even more successful than we planned," says Andy Miller, vice president of technical architecture at Corporate Express. "We didn't think that we would replace as many legacy interfaces as we did. We actually went back to quite a few older interfaces between applications and retrofitted them."

One of the results was that the company set a new record for online sales this past January, selling more than $7 million in office products online in one day. Online sales now represent more than 50 percent of its total sales. In addition, Corporate Express's integrated business-to-business systems, which include EDI and XML interfaces with customers' e-procurement systems, achieved a new daily high of more than $2 million. Corporate Express has integrated with more than 250 customer e-procurement systems, including platforms such as SAP AG, Oracle Corp., Ariba Inc., and Commerce One Inc. The company expects its 2003 e-commerce sales to exceed $1.5 billion.

Corporate Express is using EAI development technology from WebMethods Inc. By the end of 2003, Miller says, he expects to complete five more strategic EAI projects that will, among other things, expand the company's products and enhance its delivery capabilities. "We haven't measured it officially, but we know of cases where we've won business because of our integration capability with customers," he says.

"A lot of IT departments held off on investing in EAI because they were waiting for a maturation in the technology and for the market to shake out and a few clear leaders to emerge," says Mark Ehr of Enterprise Management Associates. "EAI products have reached a maturation level in the past couple of years that make them considerably easier to implement, resulting in a more rapid ROI than was possible before."

Case Study Questions

1. Why has EAI recently "become a critical part of the IT strategy at many organizations," and a high-ranking project of top IT executives? Use GE Power and Corporate Express as examples.

2. What is the major difference in the business value of the EAI projects at GE Power and Corporate Express?

3. What are some of the challenges in developing and implementing EAI systems? How can companies meet these challenges?

Source: Adapted from Bob Violino, "How Will You Integrate Technology with Business?" *Computerworld*, January 6, 2003, pp. 20–21; and Maria Trombly, "Piecing it All Together," *Computerworld*, July 7, 2003, p. 40.

FIGURE 7.17 Examples of functional business information systems. Note how they support the major functional areas of business.

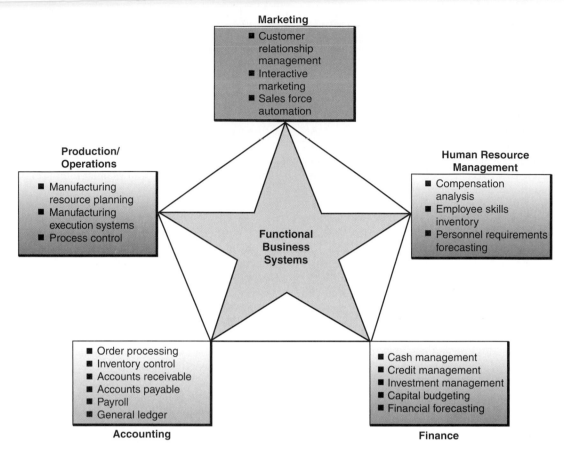

Marketing
- Customer relationship management
- Interactive marketing
- Sales force automation

Production/ Operations
- Manufacturing resource planning
- Manufacturing execution systems
- Process control

Human Resource Management
- Compensation analysis
- Employee skills inventory
- Personnel requirements forecasting

Functional Business Systems

- Order processing
- Inventory control
- Accounts receivable
- Accounts payable
- Payroll
- General ledger

Accounting

- Cash management
- Credit management
- Investment management
- Capital budgeting
- Financial forecasting

Finance

IT in Business

As a business professional, it is also important that you have a specific understanding of how information systems affect a particular business function—marketing, for example—or a particular industry (e.g., banking) that is directly related to your career objectives. For example, someone whose career objective is a marketing position in banking should have a basic understanding of how information systems are used in banking and how they support the marketing activities of banks and other firms.

Figure 7.17 illustrates how information systems can be grouped into business function categories. Thus, information systems in this section will be analyzed according to the business function they support by looking at a few key examples in each functional area. This should give you an appreciation of the variety of functional business systems that both small and large business firms may use.

Marketing Systems

The business function of marketing is concerned with the planning, promotion, and sale of existing products in existing markets, and the development of new products and new markets to better attract and serve present and potential customers. Thus, marketing performs a vital function in the operation of a business enterprise. Business firms have increasingly turned to information technology to help them perform vital marketing functions in the face of the rapid changes of today's environment.

Figure 7.18 illustrates how **marketing information systems** provide information technologies that support major components of the marketing function. For example, Internet/intranet websites and services make an *interactive marketing* process possible where customers can become partners in creating, marketing, purchasing, and im-

FIGURE 7.18

Marketing information systems provide information technologies to support major components of the marketing function.

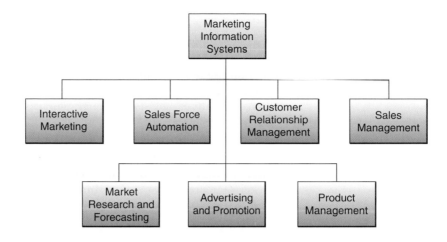

proving products and services. *Sales force automation* systems use mobile computing and Internet technologies to automate many information processing activities for sales support and management. Other marketing information systems assist marketing managers in customer relationship management, product planning, pricing, and other product management decisions, advertising, sales promotion, and targeted marketing strategies, and market research and forecasting. Let's take a closer look at three of these marketing applications.

Interactive Marketing

The term **interactive marketing** has been coined to describe a customer focused marketing process that is based on using the Internet, intranets, and extranets to establish two-way transactions between a business and its customers or potential customers. The goal of interactive marketing is to enable a company to profitably use those networks to attract and keep customers who will become partners with the business in creating, purchasing, and improving products and services.

In interactive marketing, customers are not just passive participants who receive media advertising prior to purchase, but are actively engaged in a network-enabled proactive and interactive processes. Interactive marketing encourages customers to become involved in product development, delivery, and service issues. This is enabled by various Internet technologies, including chat and discussion groups, Web forms and questionnaires, instant messaging, and e-mail correspondence. Finally, the expected outcomes of interactive marketing are a rich mixture of vital marketing data, new product ideas, volume sales, and strong customer relationships.

Targeted Marketing

Targeted marketing has become an important tool in developing advertising and promotion strategies to strengthen a company's e-commerce initiatives, as well as its traditional business venues. As illustrated in Figure 7.19, targeted marketing is

FIGURE 7.19

The five major components of targeted marketing for electronic commerce.

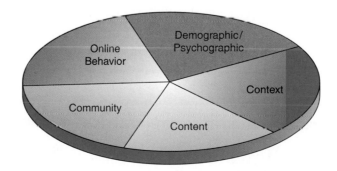

an advertising and promotion management concept that includes five targeting components [18].

- **Community.** Companies can customize their Web advertising messages and promotion methods to appeal to people in specific communities. They can be *communities of interest*, such as *virtual communities* of online sporting enthusiasts or arts and crafts hobbyists, or geographic communities formed by the websites of a city or other local organization.

- **Content.** Advertising such as electronic billboards or banners can be placed on a variety of selected websites, in addition to a company's website. They content of these messages is aimed at the targeted audience. An ad for a product campaign on the opening page of an Internet search engine is a typical example.

- **Context.** Advertising appears only in Web pages that are relevant to the content of a product or service. So advertising is targeted only at people who are already looking for information about a subject matter (vacation travel, for example) that is related to a company's products (car rental services, for example).

- **Demographic/Psychographic.** Web marketing efforts can be aimed only at specific types or classes of people: unmarried, twenty-something, middle income, male college graduates, for example.

- **Online Behavior.** Advertising and promotion efforts can be tailored to each visit to a site by an individual. This strategy is based on a variety of tracking techniques, such as Web "cookie" files recorded on the visitor's disk drive from previous visits. This enables a company to track a person's online behavior at a website so marketing efforts (such as coupons redeemable at retail stores or e-commerce websites) can be targeted to that individual at each visit to their website.

Sales Force Automation

Increasingly, computers and the Internet are providing the basis for **sales force automation.** In many companies, the sales force is being outfitted with notebook computers, Web browsers, and sales contact management software that connect them to marketing websites on the Internet, extranets, and their company intranets. This not only increases the personal productivity of salespeople, but dramatically speeds up the capture and analysis of sales data from the field to marketing managers at company headquarters. In return, it allows marketing and sales management to improve the delivery of information and the support they provide to their salespeople. Therefore, many companies are viewing sales force automation as a way to gain a strategic advantage in sales productivity and marketing responsiveness. See Figure 7.20.

For example, salespeople use their PCs to record sales data as they make their calls on customers and prospects during the day. Then each night, sales reps in the field can connect their computers by modem and telephone links to the Internet and extranets, which can access intranet or other network servers at their company. Then, they can upload information on sales orders, sales calls, and other sales statistics, as well as send electronic mail messages and access website sales support information. In return, the network servers may download product availability data, prospect lists of information on good sales prospects, and e-mail messages.

Baker Tanks: Web-Based Sales Force Automation

Baker Tanks, a nationwide leader in rentals of industrial containment and transfer equipment, serves customers throughout the country in industries ranging from construction to aerospace. Because of this varied client base, it's especially important—and challenging—for salespeople to be aware of the specifics of each account every time they speak to customers. The company's 50 sales professionals are on the road four days a week visiting customers on location. That creates additional

FIGURE 7.20

This Web-based sales force automation package supports sales lead management of qualified prospects, and management of current customer accounts.

Source: Courtesy of Salesforce.com.

challenges when it comes to keeping track of customer information and accessing it when it's needed.

In the past, salespeople filled out paper forms to track customer information, which was later entered into an electronic database. This left the reps with less time to do what they do best—selling. Even worse, the traveling representatives had no way of connecting to the electronic database from the customer's location. They were collecting plenty of information, but they couldn't access and use it effectively.

"They were recording everything on paper, and that's a very unproductive way of getting things done," says Scott Whitford, systems administrator and lead on the wireless Salesforce.com solution. "We were looking for a solution that would improve our communications, not only between corporate and field people, but between field people and our customers." "We were looking for a tool we could implement quickly, but that would still give us the flexibility we needed to become more efficient," adds Darrell Yoshinaga, marketing manager at Baker Tanks.

Baker Tanks was immediately drawn to the Web-based functionality, quick implementation time, and low capital investment of a sales force automation system. The ability to connect to sales information anywhere at anytime was also an attractive feature. So Baker Tanks moved from a paper-based system to a Web-based system, eliminating the extra step of transferring information from paper documents to the database. Next, sales reps were outfitted with personal digital assistants (PDAs) enabled with the Salesforce.com service. "Our salespeople are real road warriors, and we needed to extend the system to them rather than make them come to the system," Whitford reflects.

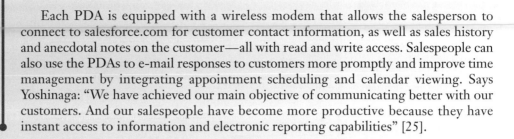

Each PDA is equipped with a wireless modem that allows the salesperson to connect to salesforce.com for customer contact information, as well as sales history and anecdotal notes on the customer—all with read and write access. Salespeople can also use the PDAs to e-mail responses to customers more promptly and improve time management by integrating appointment scheduling and calendar viewing. Says Yoshinaga: "We have achieved our main objective of communicating better with our customers. And our salespeople have become more productive because they have instant access to information and electronic reporting capabilities" [25].

Manufacturing Systems

Manufacturing information systems support the *production/operations* function that includes all activities concerned with the planning and control of the processes producing goods or services. Thus, the production/operations function is concerned with the management of the operational processes and systems of all business firms. Information systems used for operations management and transaction processing support all firms that must plan, monitor, and control inventories, purchases, and the flow of goods and services. Therefore, firms such as transportation companies, wholesalers, retailers, financial institutions, and service companies must use production/operations information systems to plan and control their operations. In this section, we will concentrate on computer-based manufacturing applications to illustrate information systems that support the production/operations function.

Computer-Integrated Manufacturing

Once upon a time, manufacturers operated on a simple build-to-stock model. They built 100 or 100,000 of an item and sold them via distribution networks. They kept track of the stock of inventory and made more of the item once inventory levels dipped below a threshold. Rush jobs were both rare and expensive, and configuration options limited. Things have changed. Concepts like just-in-time inventory, build-to-order (BTO) manufacturing, end-to-end supply chain visibility, the explosion in contract manufacturing, and the development of Web-based e-business tools for collaborative manufacturing have revolutionized plant management [24].

A variety of manufacturing information systems, many of them Web-enabled, are used to support **computer-integrated manufacturing** (CIM). See Figure 7.21. CIM is an overall concept that stresses that the objectives of computer-based systems in manufacturing must be to:

- **Simplify** (reengineer) production processes, product designs, and factory organization as a vital foundation to automation and integration.
- **Automate** production processes and the business functions that support them with computers, machines, and robots.
- **Integrate** all production and support processes using computer networks, cross-functional business software, and other information technologies.

The overall goal of CIM and such manufacturing information systems is to create flexible, agile, manufacturing processes that efficiently produce products of the highest quality. Thus, CIM supports the concepts of *flexible manufacturing systems*, *agile manufacturing*, and *total quality management*. Implementing such manufacturing concepts enables a company to quickly respond to and fulfill customer requirements with high-quality products and services.

Manufacturing information systems help companies simplify, automate, and integrate many of the activities needed to produce products of all kinds. For example, computers are used to help engineers design better products using both *computer-aided engineering* (CAE) and *computer-aided design* (CAD) systems, and better production

FIGURE 7.21

Manufacturing information systems support computer-integrated manufacturing. Note that manufacturing resources planning systems are one of the application clusters in an ERP system.

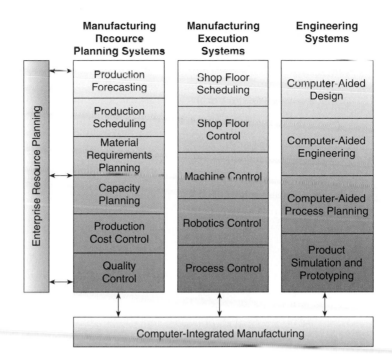

processes with *computer-aided process planning*. They are also used to help plan the types of material needed in the production process, which is called *material requirements planning* (MRP), and to integrate MRP with production scheduling and shop floor operations, which is known as *manufacturing resource planning*. Many of the processes within manufacturing resource planning systems are included in the manufacturing module of enterprise resource planning (ERP) software discussed earlier.

Computer-aided manufacturing (CAM) systems are those that automate the production process. For example, this could be accomplished by monitoring and controlling the production process in a factory (manufacturing execution systems) or by directly controlling a physical process (process control), a machine tool (machine control), or machines with some humanlike work capabilities (robots).

Manufacturing execution systems (MES) are performance monitoring information systems for factory floor operations. They monitor, track, and control the five essential components involved in a production process: materials, equipment, personnel, instructions and specifications, and production facilities. MES includes shop floor scheduling and control, machine control, robotics control, and process control systems. These manufacturing systems monitor, report, and adjust the status and performance of production components to help a company achieve a flexible, high-quality manufacturing process.

Process control is the use of computers to control an ongoing physical process. Process control computers control physical processes in petroleum refineries, cement plants, steel mills, chemical plants, food product manufacturing plants, pulp and paper mills, electric power plants, and so on. A process control computer system requires the use of special sensing devices that measure physical phenomena such as temperature or pressure changes. These continuous physical measurements are converted to digital form by analog-to-digital converters and relayed to computers for processing.

Machine control is the use of computers to control the actions of machines. This is also popularly called *numerical control*. The computer-based control of machine tools to manufacture products of all kinds is a typical numerical control application used by many factories throughout the world.

The Timken Company: Web-Based Manufacturing Systems	To outsiders, says president James W. Griffith, Timken may seem old-economy, but to people inside, it is a high-tech operation. Just walk through its huge R&D center and see the sophisticated instruments that some 450 scientists and engineers are applying to product design. The Timken Company, based in Canton, Ohio, is a global manufacturer of precision bearings and specialty alloys with operations in 24 countries. Timken has embarked on major e-business initiatives in electronic commerce, engineering design collaboration, and global e-manufacturing.

So Timken hired a GE executive, Curt J. Andersson, and named him to a new post, senior vice president for e-business. Andersson and his team have concentrated on establishing "electronic visibility" through Timken's global supply chain. Within eight weeks the team created a system that lets a Timken dealer see exactly where a part is available in any of a dozen warehouses spread around the world. Such searches previously took lots of faxing, telephoning, and paperwork. The improvement will save Timken millions of dollars annually.

Connecting design to the factory floor came next in the Andersson team's plans. Engineers in the company's main R&D center initiate, modify, and complete product designs jointly with customers in real time via the Internet. Now, newly developed e-manufacturing software allows the designs to flow immediately to Timken's sophisticated production plants all over the world.

Such instant access to information anywhere, anytime, and its meaningful manipulation, are what all e-manufacturers strive for. "We're combining the Internet benefits of speed and worldwide access with the real world capabilities of automated manufacturing plants, warehouses, freight, and global logistics management," says Timken's Andersson. "This bricks-and-clicks e-business combination is what the real Internet is all about" [2].

Human Resource Systems

The human resource management (HRM) function involves the recruitment, placement, evaluation, compensation, and development of the employees of an organization. The goal of human resource management is the effective and efficient use of the human resources of a company. Thus, **human resource information systems** are designed to support (1) planning to meet the personnel needs of the business, (2) development of employees to their full potential, and (3) control of all personnel policies and programs. Originally, businesses used computer-based information systems to (1) produce paychecks and payroll reports, (2) maintain personnel records, and (3) analyze the use of personnel in business operations. Many firms have gone beyond these traditional *personnel management* functions and have developed human resource information systems (HRIS) that also support (1) recruitment, selection, and hiring; (2) job placement; (3) performance appraisals; (4) employee benefits analysis; (5) training and development; and (6) health, safety, and security. See Figure 7.22.

HRM and the Internet

The Internet has become a major force for change in human resource management. For example, **online HRM systems** may involve recruiting for employees through recruitment sections of corporate websites. Companies are also using commercial recruiting services and databases on the World Wide Web, posting messages in selected Internet newsgroups, and communicating with job applicants via e-mail.

The Internet has a wealth of information and contacts for both employers and job hunters. Top websites for job hunters and employers on the World Wide Web include Monster.com, HotJobs.com, and Jobweb.org. These websites are full of reports, statistics, and other useful HRM information, such as job reports by industry, or listings of the top recruiting markets by industry and profession.

HRM and Corporate Intranets

Intranet technologies allow companies to process most common HRM applications over their corporate intranets. Intranets allow the HRM department to provide around-the-clock services to their customers: the employees. They can also disseminate

FIGURE 7.22 Human resource information systems support the strategic, tactical, and operational use of the human resources of an organization.

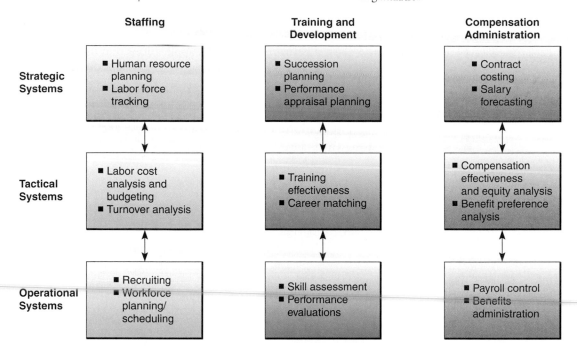

valuable information faster than through previous company channels. Intranets can collect information online from employees for input to their HRM files, and they can enable managers and other employees to perform HRM tasks with little intervention by the HRM department. See Figure 7.23.

For example, *employee self-service (ESS)* intranet applications allow employees to view benefits, enter travel and expense reports, verify employment and salary information, access and update their personal information, and enter data that has a time constraint to it. Through this completely electronic process, employees can use their Web browsers to look up individual payroll and benefits information online, right from their desktop PCs, mobile computers, or intranet kiosks located around a work site.

Another benefit of the intranet is that it can serve as a superior training tool. Employees can easily download instructions and processes to get the information or education they need. In addition, employees using new technology can view training videos over the intranet on demand. Thus, the intranet eliminates the need to loan out and track training videos. Employees can also use their corporate intranets to produce automated paysheets, the online alternative to time cards. These electronic forms have made viewing, entering, and adjusting payroll information easy for both employees and HRM professionals [13].

Charles Schwab & Co.: Web-Based Human Resource Systems

It receives 1.3 million page views per day, but it's not Yahoo or America Online or even CNN.com. It's an intranet created by Charles Schwab & Co. that enables Schwab's 23,000 employees to access detailed HR information about benefits, training, computer support, and scads of company information.

"As a company, we're very committed to using technology to benefit our customers and to provide good services to our employees," says Anne Barr, vice president of the intranet initiative known throughout the company as the "Schweb." The Schweb provides managers with online access to accurate information about employees. Because the directory is online, it's a lot easier to update and maintain than a set of desktop applications, notes Barr.

The intranet provides employees with more personalized information about themselves, their roles, and the organization than they'd otherwise be able to obtain from the company's human resources department. "The other benefit is that it helps employees find the information they need faster and serve customers faster, more effectively," says Barr. There are now 30 HR applications that link into the Schweb, including the Learning Intranet, an application that helps manage training for Schwab's customer-facing employees, and eTimesheets, which employees use to manage their own vacation time.

The productivity benefits alone from the use of the Schweb are huge. Schwab is saving hundreds of thousands of dollars annually by having employees fill out benefit forms online using an application called eForms, says Barr [13].

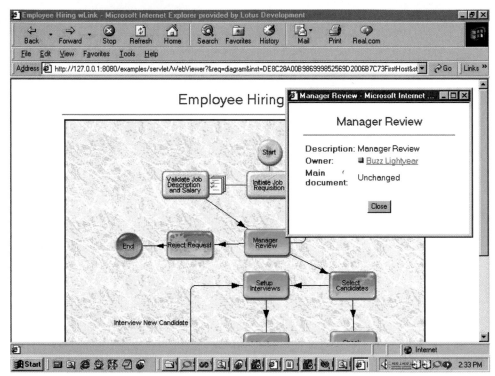

FIGURE 7.23

An example of an employee hiring review system.

Source: Courtesy of Lotus Development Corp.

Accounting Systems

Accounting information systems are the oldest and most widely used information systems in business. They record and report business transactions and other economic events. Computer-based accounting systems record and report the flow of funds through an organization on a historical basis and produce important financial statements such as balance sheets and income statements. Such systems also produce forecasts of future conditions such as projected financial statements and financial budgets. A firm's financial performance is measured against such forecasts by other analytical accounting reports.

Operational accounting systems emphasize legal and historical record-keeping and the production of accurate financial statements. Typically, these systems include transaction processing systems such as order processing, inventory control, accounts receivable, accounts payable, payroll, and general ledger systems. Management accounting systems focus on the planning and control of business operations. They emphasize cost accounting reports, the development of financial budgets and projected financial statements, and analytical reports comparing actual to forecasted performance.

Figure 7.24 illustrates the interrelationships of several important accounting information systems commonly computerized by both large and small businesses. Many

FIGURE 7.24   Important accounting information systems for transaction processing and financial reporting. Note how they are related to each other in terms of input and output flows.

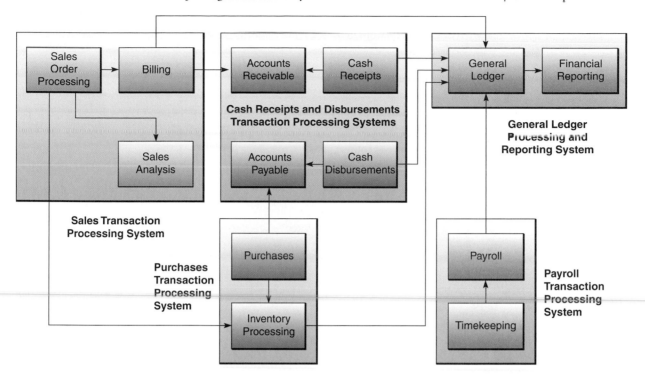

accounting software packages are available for these applications. Figure 7.25 provides a good summary of the essential purpose of six common, but important, accounting information systems used by both large and small business firms.

Online Accounting Systems

It should come as no surprise that the accounting information systems illustrated in Figures 7.24 and 7.25 are being transformed by Internet technologies. Using the Internet and other networks changes how accounting information systems monitor and track business activity. The online, interactive nature of such networks calls for new

FIGURE 7.25   A summary of six essential accounting information systems used in business.

Common Business Accounting Systems
● **Order Processing** Captures and processes customer orders and produces data for inventory control and accounts receivable.
● **Inventory Control** Processes data reflecting changes in inventory and provides shipping and reorder information.
● **Accounts Receivable** Records amounts owed by customers and produces customer invoices, monthly customer statements, and credit management reports.
● **Accounts Payable** Records purchases from, amounts owed to, and payments to suppliers, and produces cash management reports.
● **Payroll** Records employee work and compensation data and produces paychecks and other payroll documents and reports.
● **General Ledger** Consolidates data from other accounting systems and produces the periodic financial statements and reports of the business.

FIGURE 7.26

An example of an online
accounting report.

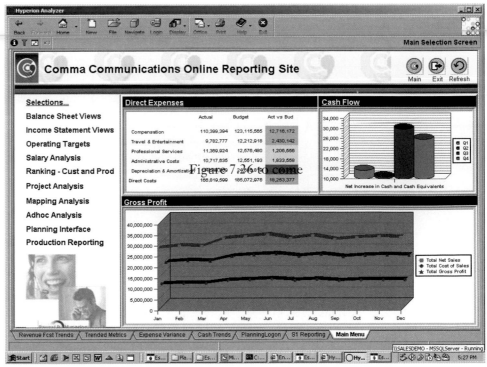

Source: Courtesy of Hyperion Solutions Corp.

forms of transaction documents, procedures, and controls. This particularly applies to systems like order processing, inventory control, accounts receivable, and accounts payable. As outlined in Figure 7.25, these systems are directly involved in the processing of transactions between a business and its customers and suppliers. So naturally, many companies are using Internet and other network links to these trading partners for such online transaction processing systems, as discussed in Section I. Figure 7.26 is an example of an online accounting report.

Financial Management Systems

Computer-based **financial management systems** support business managers and professionals in decisions concerning (1) the financing of a business and (2) the allocation and control of financial resources within a business. Major financial management system categories include cash and investment management, capital budgeting, financial forecasting, and financial planning. See Figure 7.27.

FIGURE 7.27

Examples of important
financial management
systems.

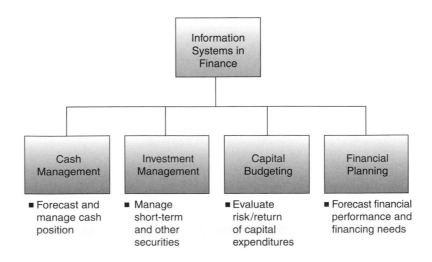

FIGURE 7.28

An example of strategic financial planning using a multiple scenario approach. Note the effect on earnings per share.

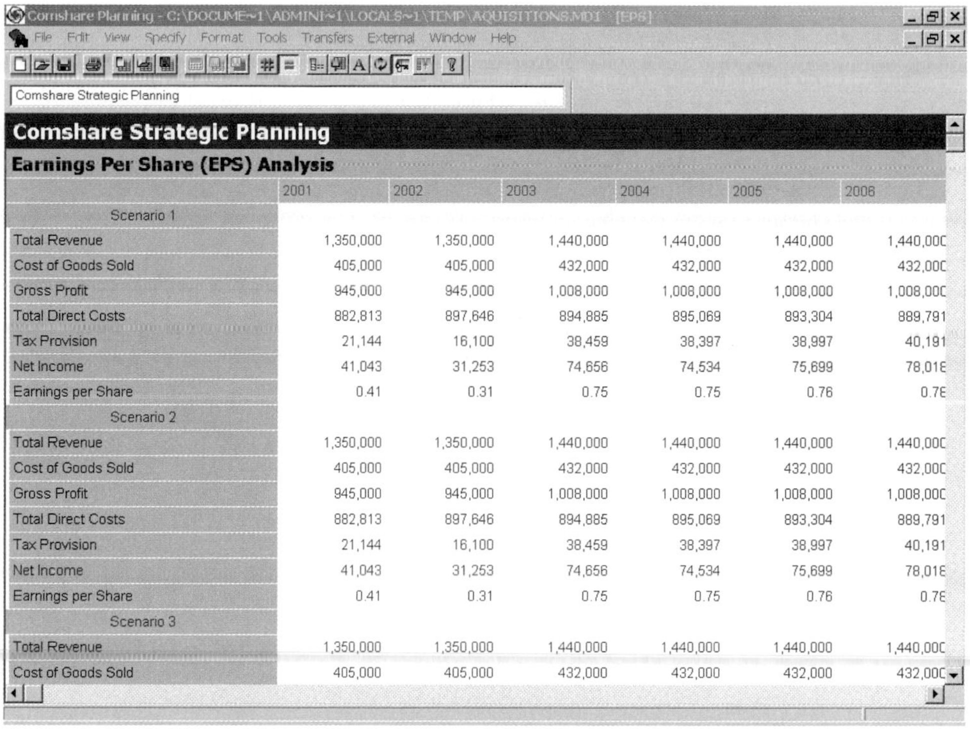

	2001	2002	2003	2004	2005	2006
Scenario 1						
Total Revenue	1,350,000	1,350,000	1,440,000	1,440,000	1,440,000	1,440,00C
Cost of Goods Sold	405,000	405,000	432,000	432,000	432,000	432,00C
Gross Profit	945,000	945,000	1,008,000	1,008,000	1,008,000	1,008,00C
Total Direct Costs	882,813	897,646	894,885	895,069	893,304	889,791
Tax Provision	21,144	16,100	38,459	38,397	38,997	40,191
Net Income	41,043	31,253	74,656	74,534	75,699	78,01E
Earnings per Share	0.41	0.31	0.75	0.75	0.76	0.7E
Scenario 2						
Total Revenue	1,350,000	1,350,000	1,440,000	1,440,000	1,440,000	1,440,00C
Cost of Goods Sold	405,000	405,000	432,000	432,000	432,000	432,00C
Gross Profit	945,000	945,000	1,008,000	1,008,000	1,008,000	1,008,00C
Total Direct Costs	882,813	897,646	894,885	895,069	893,304	889,791
Tax Provision	21,144	16,100	38,459	38,397	38,997	40,191
Net Income	41,043	31,253	74,656	74,534	75,699	78,01E
Earnings per Share	0.41	0.31	0.75	0.75	0.76	0.7E
Scenario 3						
Total Revenue	1,350,000	1,350,000	1,440,000	1,440,000	1,440,000	1,440,00C
Cost of Goods Sold	405,000	405,000	432,000	432,000	432,000	432,00C

Source: Courtesy of Comshare.

For example, the **capital budgeting** process involves evaluating the profitability and financial impact of proposed capital expenditures. Long-term expenditure proposals for facilities and equipment can be analyzed using a variety of return on investment (ROI) evaluation techniques. This application makes heavy use of spreadsheet models that incorporate present value analysis of expected cash flows and probability analysis of risk to determine the optimum mix of capital projects for a business.

Financial analysts also typically use electronic spreadsheets and other **financial planning** software to evaluate the present and projected financial performance of a business. They also help determine the financing needs of a business and analyze alternative methods of financing. Financial analysts use financial forecasts concerning the economic situation, business operations, types of financing available, interest rates, and stock and bond prices to develop an optimal financing plan for the business. Electronic spreadsheet packages, DSS software, and Web-based groupware can be used to build and manipulate financial models. Answers to what-if and goal-seeking questions can be explored as financial analysts and managers evaluate their financing and investment alternatives. We will discuss such applications further in Chapter 9. See Figure 7.28.

Summary

- **Cross-Functional Enterprise Systems.** Major e-business applications and their interrelationships are summarized in the enterprise application architecture of Figure 7.3. These applications are integrated cross-functional enterprise systems such as enterprise resource planning (ERP), customer relationship manage- ment (CRM), and supply chain management (SCM).

  These applications may be interconnected by enterprise application integration (EAI) systems so that business professionals can more easily access the information resources they need to support the needs of customers, suppliers, and business partners. Enterprise collaboration systems (ECS) are cross-functional systems that support and enhance communication and collaboration among the teams and workgroups in an organization. Refer to Figures 7.10 and 7.14 for summary views of the e-business applications in EAI systems and enterprise collaboration systems.

- **Enterprise Resource Planning: The Business Backbone.** Enterprise resource planning is a cross-functional enterprise system that integrates and automates many of the internal business processes of a company, particularly those within the manufacturing, logistics, distribution, accounting, finance, and human resource functions of the business. Thus, ERP serves as the vital backbone information system of the enterprise, helping a company achieve the efficiency, agility, and responsiveness required to succeed in a dynamic business environment. ERP software typically consists of integrated modules that give a company a real-time cross-functional view of its core business processes, such as production, order processing, and sales, and its resources, such as cash, raw materials, production capacity, and people. However, properly implementing ERP systems is a difficult and costly process that has caused serious business losses for some companies, who underestimated the planning, development, and training that were necessary to reengineer their business processes to accommodate their new ERP systems.

- **Customer Relationship Management: The Business Focus.** Customer relationship management is a cross-functional enterprise system that integrates and automates many of the customer serving processes in sales, marketing, and customer services that interact with a company's customers. The major application components of CRM include contact and account management, sales, marketing and fulfillment, customer service and support, and retention and loyalty programs, all aimed at helping a company acquire, enhance, and retain profitable relationships with its customers as a primary business goal. However, many companies have found CRM systems difficult to properly implement due to lack of adequate understanding and preparation by management and affected employees.

- **Supply Chain Management: The Business Network.** Supply chain management is a cross-functional inter-enterprise system that integrates and automates the network of business processes and relationships between a company and its suppliers, customers, distributors, and other business partners. The goal of SCM is to help a company achieve agility and responsiveness in meeting the demands of their customers and needs of their suppliers, by enabling it to design, build, and sell its products using a fast, efficient, and low-cost network of business partners, processes, and relationships, or supply chain. SCM is frequently subdivided into supply chain planning applications, such as demand and supply forecasting, and supply chain execution applications, such as inventory management, logistics management, and warehouse management. Developing effective supply chain systems and achieving the business goals of SCM have proven to be complex and difficult challenges for many firms.

- **Transaction Processing Systems.** Online transaction processing systems play a vital role in business. Transaction processing involves the basic activities of (1) data entry, (2) transaction processing, (3) database maintenance, (4) document and report generation, and (5) inquiry processing. Many firms are using the Internet, intranets, extranets, and other networks for online transaction processing to provide superior service to their customers and suppliers. Figure 7.13 illustrates the basic activities of transaction processing systems.

- **Functional Business Systems.** Functional business information systems support the business functions of marketing, production/operations, accounting, finance, and human resource management through a variety of e-business operational and management information systems summarized in Figure 7.17.

- **Marketing.** Marketing information systems support traditional and e-commerce processes and management of the marketing function. Major types of marketing information systems include interactive marketing at e-commerce websites, sales force automation, customer relationship management, sales management, product management, targeted marketing, advertising and promotion, and market research. Thus, marketing information systems assist marketing managers in electronic commerce product development and customer relationship decisions, as well as in planning advertising and sales promotion strategies and developing the e-commerce potential of new and present products, and new channels of distribution.

- **Manufacturing.** Computer-based manufacturing information systems help a company achieve computer-integrated manufacturing (CIM), and thus simplify, automate, and integrate many of the activities needed to quickly produce high-quality products to meet changing customer demands. For example, computer-aided design using collaborative manufacturing networks helps engineers collaborate on the design of new products and processes. Then manufacturing resource planning systems help plan the types of resources needed in the production process. Finally, manufacturing execution systems monitor and control the manufacture of products on the factory floor through shop floor scheduling and control systems, controlling a physical process (process control), a machine tool (numerical control), or machines with some human-like work capabilities (robotics).

- **Human Resource Management.** Human resource information systems support human resource management in organizations. They include information systems for staffing the organization, training and development, and compensation administration. HRM websites on the Internet or corporate intranets have become important tools for providing HR services to present and prospective employees.

- **Accounting and Finance.** Accounting information systems record, report, and analyze business transactions and events for the management of the business enterprise. Figure 7.25 summarizes six essential accounting systems including order processing, inventory control, accounts receivable, accounts payable, payroll, and general ledger. Information systems in finance support managers in decisions regarding the financing of a business and the allocation of financial resources within a business. Financial information systems include cash management, online investment management, capital budgeting, and financial forecasting and planning.

Key Terms and Concepts

These are the key terms and concepts of this chapter. The page number of their first explanation is in parentheses.

1. Accounting systems (244)
2. Accounts payable (245)
3. Accounts receivable (245)
4. Batch processing (230)
5. Computer-aided manufacturing (241)
6. Computer-integrated manufacturing (240)
7. Cross-functional enterprise systems (214)
8. Customer relationship management (219)
   a. Application components (220)
   b. Business benefits (222)
9. E-business (212)
10. Enterprise application architecture (214)
11. Enterprise application integration (227)
12. Enterprise collaboration systems (231)
13. Enterprise resource planning (216)
   a. Application components (216)
   b. Business benefits (217)
14. Financial management systems (246)
15. Functional business systems (234)
16. General ledger (245)
17. Human resource systems (242)
18. Interactive marketing (237)
19. Inventory control (245)
20. Machine control (241)
21. Manufacturing execution systems (241)
22. Manufacturing systems (240)
23. Marketing systems (236)
24. Online accounting systems (245)
25. Online HRM systems (242)
26. Online transaction processing systems (228)
27. Order processing (245)
28. Payroll (245)
29. Process control (241)
30. Real-time processing (230)
31. Sales force automation (238)
32. Supply chain (224)
33. Supply chain management (224)
   a. Application components (224)
   b. Business benefits (225)
34. Targeted marketing (237)
35. Transaction processing cycle (229)

Review Quiz

Match one of the key terms and concepts listed previously with one of the brief examples or definitions that follow. Try to find the best fit for the answers that seem to fit more than one term or concept. Defend your choices.

_____ 1. Using the Internet and other networks for e-commerce, enterprise collaboration, and Web-enabled business processes.

_____ 2. Information systems that cross the boundaries of the functional areas of a business in order to integrate and automate business processes.

_____ 3. Information systems that support marketing, production, accounting, finance, and human resource management.

_____ 4. E-business applications fit into a framework of interrelated cross-functional enterprise applications.

_____ 5. Software that interconnects enterprise application systems.

_____ 6. Information systems for customer relationship management, sales management, and promotion management.

_____ 7. Collaborating interactively with customers in creating, purchasing, servicing, and improving products and services.

_____ 8. Using mobile computing networks to support salespeople in the field.

_____ 9. Information systems that support manufacturing operations and management.

_____ 10. A conceptual framework for simplifying and integrating all aspects of manufacturing automation.

_____ 11. Using computers in a variety of ways to help manufacture products.

_____ 12. Use electronic communications, conferencing, and collaborative work tools to support and enhance collaboration among teams and workgroups.

_____ 13. Using computers to operate a petroleum refinery.

_____ 14. Using computers to help operate machine tools.

_____ 15. Information systems to support staffing, training and development, and compensation administration.

_____ 16. Using the Internet for recruitment and job hunting is an example.

_____ 17. Accomplishes legal and historical record-keeping and gathers information for the planning and control of business operations.

_____ 18. An example is using the Internet and extranets to do accounts receivable and accounts payable activities.

_____ 19. Handles sales orders from customers.

_____ 20. Keeps track of items in stock.

_____ 21. Keeps track of amounts owed by customers.

_____ 22. Keeps track of purchases from suppliers.

_____ 23. Produces employee paychecks.

_____ 24. Produces the financial statements of a firm.

_____ 25. Information systems for cash management, investment management, capital budgeting, and financial forecasting.

_____ 26. Performance monitoring and control systems for factory floor operations.

_____ 27. Customizing advertising and promotion methods to fit their intended audience.

_____ 28. Data entry, transaction processing, database maintenance, document and report generation, and inquiry processing.

_____ 29. Collecting and periodically processing transaction data.

_____ 30. Processing transaction data immediately after they are captured.

_____ 31. Systems that immediately capture and process transaction data and update corporate databases.

_____ 32. A cross-functional enterprise system that helps a business develop and manage its customer-facing business processes.

_____ 33. A cross-functional enterprise system that helps a business integrate and automate many of its internal business processes and information systems.

_____ 34. A cross-functional interenterprise system that helps a business manage its network of relationships and processes with its business partners.

_____ 35. A network of business partners, processes, and relationships that supports the design, manufacture, distribution, and sale of a company's products.

_____ 36. Includes contact and account management, sales, marketing and fulfillment, and customer service and support systems.

_____ 37. Includes order management, production planning, accounting, finance, and human resource systems.

_____ 38. Includes demand forecasting, inventory management, logistics management, and warehouse management systems.

_____ 39. Acquiring, enhancing, and retaining profitable relationships with customers.

_____ 40. Improvements in the quality, efficiency, cost, and management of internal business processes.

_____ 41. Development of a fast, efficient, and low cost network of business partners to get products from concept to market.

Discussion Questions

1. Refer to the Real World Case on Salesforce.com and Others in the chapter. What are several reasons why a business application of IT like CRM can be so costly and take so long to implement for many companies and be criticized as a "most oversold, under-implemented concept"?

2. Why would systems like CRM that enhance a company's relationships with its customers have such a high rate of failure?

3. How could some of the spectacular failures of ERP systems in business been avoided?

4. Refer to the example on Dell Computer in the chapter. What other solutions could there be for the problem of information systems incompatibility in business besides EAI systems?

5. Refer to the example on Charles Schwab & Co. in the chapter. What are the most important HR applications a company should offer to its employees via a Web-based system? Why?

6. How could sales force automation affect salesperson productivity, marketing management, and competitive advantage?

7. How can Internet technologies be involved in improving a process in one of the functions of business? Choose one example and evaluate its business value.

8. Refer to the Real World Case on GE Power and Corporate Express in the chapter. Why is there a need for enterprise application integration systems in business? Will this continue to be the case in the future? Why or why not?

9. What are several e-business applications that you might recommend to a small company to help it survive and succeed in challenging economic times? Why?

10. Refer to the example on General Electric in the chapter. How do enterprise collaboration systems contribute to bottom-line profits for a business?

Analysis Exercises

1. Application Service Provider Marketplace

The traditional ASP definition includes web interface (or thin client) and external, Internet based, server-side processing and data storage. However, the business world hasn't always felt constrained by these definitions. Microsoft, McAfee, QuickBooks, and others are providing Internet based application services without meeting these exact criteria.

Microsoft provides automatic Internet based application maintenance as part of its one-time licensing fee. Through "automatic updates," Microsoft provides updates, fixes, and security patches to its software without IT staff involvement and minimal end user inconvenience.

McAfee, on the other hand, charges an annual maintenance fee that includes daily application and virus definition updates. McAfee provides it for one year as part of its license. After the first year, license holders may continue to use the software, but they must pay a subscription fee if they want updates. Customers tend to pay for this subscription service in order to protect themselves from new virus threats.

a. Would you use or recommend any of Intuit's online application services (www.intuit.com) to a small business? Why or why not?

b. America Online provides a free instant messaging service (AIM). This service enables instant messaging, file sharing, and voice and video conferencing through a free application anyone can download and install. Is AOL operating as an ASP? How so?

c. Visit AOL's "Enterprise AIM services" website (enterprise.aim.com). What additional features does AOL provide to enterprises? Why do you suppose AOL moved away from the ASP model for their enterprise solution?

2. eWork Exchange and eLance.com: Online Job Matching and Auctions

Many opportunities await those who troll the big job boards, the free-agent sites, the auction services where applicants bid for projects, and the niche sites for specialized jobs and skills. Examples of top job matching and auction sites are eWorkExchange and eLance.com.

eWorkExchange (www.eworkexchange.com). No more sifting through irrelevant search results; fill out a list of your skills and let eWork Exchange's proprietary technology find the most suitable projects for you—no bidding required.

eLance.com (www.elance.com). This global auction marketplace covers more than just IT jobs; it runs the gamut from astrology and medicine to corporate work and cooking projects. Register a description of your services or go straight to browsing the listings of open projects—and then start bidding. A feedback section lets both employers and freelancers rate one another.

FIGURE 7.29

The QuickBooks Solutions Marketplace provides online application software services from Intuit and their many business partners.

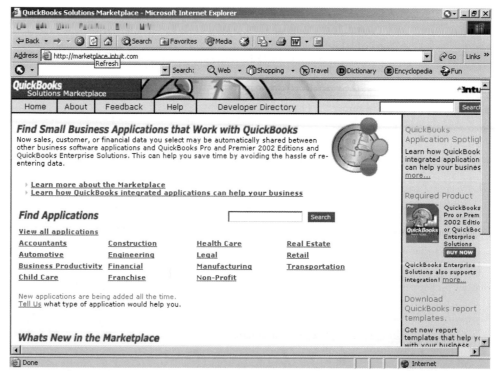

Source: Courtesy of Intuit

a. Check out eWork Exchange and eLance, and other online job sites on the Web.

b. Evaluate several sites based on their ease of use and their value to job seekers and employers.

c. Which website was your favorite? Why?

3. **Job Search Database**

Visit websites like Monster.com and others mentioned in this chapter to gather information about available jobs. Look up and record the relevant data for at least 10 current job openings that are of interest to you or that meet criteria provided by your instructor.

a. Create a database table to store key characteristics of these job opportunities. Include all of the job characteristics shown in the list that follows as fields in your table, but feel free to add fields of interest to you. If data are not available for some fields (such as salary range) for a particular job, leave that field blank.

b. Write a query that sorts jobs by region and then business function.

c. Create a report that groups jobs by region and sorts jobs within each region by business function.

Table: Jobs

Field	Sample Data (find your own for this exercise)
Employer	Techtron Inc.
Job Title	Systems Analyst
Region	North East
Location	Springfield, MA
Business Function	Information Technology
Description	Work with team to analyze design, and develop e-commerce systems. Skills in systems analysis, relational database design, and programming in Java are required
Qualifications	Bachelors degree in Information Systems or Computer Sciences, two years Java programming experience
Salary Range	48,000–60,000 depending on experience

4. **Performing an Industry Financial Analysis**

Employees apply their skills for the benefit of their organization. In addition to skills specific to their business function, employees need a keen understanding of their business environment. This environment includes their organization's business and financial structure as well its relationships with competitors, customers, and relevant regulatory agencies.

Interviewers expect job candidates to have basic knowledge in of each of these areas. Developing such an understanding demonstrates the candidate's interest in the position and helps assure the interviewer that the candidate indeed knows what he or she is getting in to. Indeed, after a modest amount of research, job hunters may rule out certain opportunities based upon what they discover. The Internet combined with good database skills can help simplify these tasks.

a. Go to the websites of at least three firms you identified in the problem above. Obtain information about their financial operations including net sales (or net revenue), after tax income, and any current information affecting the organization or industry.

b. Using the same database you created in the problem above create a new table that includes the fields described below. Add fields that may interest you as well.

c. Add a field called OrganizationID to the Jobs table you created in the previous problem. Make its field type Number (long integer). Write an update query that populates this new field with the appropriate values from the Organizations table's OrganizationID field. To do this, join the Jobs table and the Organizations table using the Employer/ Organization Name fields. This join will only work if the names used are identical, so be sure you've typed them in that way. Execute the query to complete the update. Since the tables already join using the Employer/Organization Name fields, why would you want to also join them on the OrganizationID field? Is the Employer field in the Jobs table still necessary?

d. Create a report that shows job opportunities by Industry. Within each industry, sort the records by the organization's name. Include Job Title, Globalization, Net Income, Competitors in each record. Be sure to join the Jobs table and the Organizations able using the OrganizationID field.

Table: Organizations

Field	Sample Data (find your own for this exercise)
OrganizationID	Set this as your primary key and let the database automatically generate the value
Organization Name	Be sure to spell the name exactly as you did in the job opportunity table (copy and paste works best for this)
Industry	Legal, medical, consulting, education, etc.
Globalization	Local, regional, national, international
Revenue	Net sales or revenue from the most current financial reports
Net Income (after tax)	From the most current financial reports
Competitors	Names of key competitors
Employees	Number of employees

REAL WORLD CASE 3

Welch's, Straightline, Skyworks, and Pella: The Business Value of Supply Chain Management

Welch's. Concord, Massachusetts-based fruit juice manufacturer Welch Foods Inc. (www.welchs.com) wanted to collaborate more closely with its customers to ensure its products were always stocked on retailer shelves. Welch's turned to Prescient Systems, a supply-chain planning vendor that focuses on the consumer packaged goods industry. "We like to do business with software companies who have a pretty ingrained understanding of the consumer products industry," says Dee Biggs, Welch's director of customer logistics. "This software didn't require a lot of customization. It was made specifically for us."

Welch's is leveraging the software to create orders and manage the inventories of one-third of its retail customers, allowing some retailers to double the number of times they turn Welch's products, Biggs adds. "The retailers share information with us, and we then take that information and create orders, and then send them back some information so they know the size of the orders we are placing for them." Biggs explains. "It's easy for the users to manipulate the software to get in and out of the screens . . . to create forecasts and be able to use those forecasts to increase their orders for our customers."

Because Prescient specializes in the consumer products market, its supply-chain application has built-in functionalities, including new packaging design support and the creation of forecasts from point-of-sale data—features that are key to the consumer packaged goods market—while leaving out engineering and product design options that are more attractive to other industries, says Kelly Vizzini, Prescient's vice president of marketing. This tight focus also allows implementations to move forward in an average of 100 days, she adds. "There is not a lot of functionality that needs to get turned off . . . . That is a significant contributing factor of why the implementations will go this fast. From a product development and product strategy perspective, you are able to better involve your clients . . . in build-to market requirements," Vizzini says.

Straightline. Straightline (www.straightline.com), the online distribution arm of U.S. Steel, is leveraging a supply-chain optimization solution from Strategic Systems Inc. (SSI) to help processors manage their inventories and thereby more effectively compete with overseas rivals. Straightline's processors help fulfill customized orders for configured steel materials from finished goods manufacturers such as automakers and appliance manufacturers.

"We are coordinating not only the inventory but taking the orders and allocating a variety of orders to specific processes," says Dan Pavlick, managing director of strategy and information at Pittsburgh-based Straightline. "That supply chain module is going through . . . and taking into account everything from freight costs, configuration of orders, similarity to other orders, inventory availability, and processors' capacity to handle orders. It helps select the inventory to process a customer order given the grade of the material."

Skyworks. Semiconductor company Skyworks Solutions (www.skyworksinc.com), in Woburn, Massachusetts, also tapped a supply-chain solution from Adexa to master its complex global supply chain and to access real-time data to give customers accurate product availability information. "We're trying to coordinate the capacity requirements and to coordinate the demand requirements to be able to deliver to our customer on time," explains David Halphide, Skyworks' manager of supply planning. "Most planning systems or ERP systems don't meet all of those requirements. We now have the ability to modify a customer's delivery date and have that change what the factory is building tomorrow. The system can replan the entire supply chain overnight. When our customers ask us what we can deliver to them and when, we can give them an answer in hours instead of days."

Pella. ERP vendors like Oracle, PeopleSoft, and SAP are now actively marketing their supply-chain applications as an "add-on" capability to their e-business suites, touting easy integration to back-end ERP systems. "We're pretty close to being truly complete with supply chain automation supporting all the data in one model," says Ron Wohl, executive vice president of applications at Redwood Shores, California-based Oracle. "You don't have to buy a separate software product and figure out how to integrate that product, instead, you can literally turn on different parts of the suite."

And some of Oracle's customers, such as window and door manufacturer Pella (www.pella.com), are buying into that philosophy to manage their supply chains. At Pella, any supply chain software that has to be bolted onto their present system is "suspect," says Bruce Baier, director of new business systems at the Pella, Iowa-based company. Instead, Pella leverages multiple Oracle E-Business Suite modules to help streamline its supply chain operations.

Case Study Questions

1. What is the business value of supply chain management systems for Welch's and other companies in the consumer packaged goods industry?

2. What is the business value of supply chain management systems for Straightline, Skyworks, and other manufacturing companies?

3. How does Pella's approach to supply chain management systems differ from that of the other companies in this case? Which is approach is better? Why?

Source: TAILOR-MADE SUPPLY CHAINS by HEATHER HAVENSTEIN. Copyright 2003 by INFOWORLD MEDIA GROUP, INC. Reproduced with permission of INFOWORLD MEDIA GROUP, INC in the format Textbook via Copyright Clearance Center.

Lowe and HP: The Business Case for Swarming Collaboration

At global advertising agency Lowe & Partners Worldwide (www.loweworldwide.com), when an account executive in Hong Kong gets a request for a proposal from a prospective client, he opens up a collaboration space on his PC and invites in subject-area experts, planners, and other creative types from India to England. Each can invite others from his personal network, whether inside or outside the company. In minutes, a swarm of creative talent is exploiting the opportunity. Artists post relevant images; content experts surf the Web in unison to find useful sites; researchers drop in pertinent files; copywriters type or edit documents together in real time. "This has shifted the landscape of expertise," says Ethan Schoonover, e-business director for the Asia-Pacific region at Lowe, "We're discovering resources we didn't know existed."

On the other side of the world, HP Services (www.hp.com/hps), which provides business services, systems integration, and consulting at Hewlett-Packard Co., is also swarming. When an HP field consultant has an opportunity to bid on a big ERP project, he opens up a collaboration space and solicits advice from people he knows who have recently worked on similar projects. They each tap their own contacts, and so on, to bring the right people into the team space quickly to plan and then execute what needs to be done.

Swarming is a type of collaboration in which large numbers of geographically dispersed people quickly self-organize in a peer-to-peer network to deal with a problem or opportunity. It's a fluid, shifting network with no central control or hub.

At Lowe, Schoonover was confronting an issue many global companies face: the need to match the agility of smaller competitors. "Clients want turnaround in a couple days with great ideas," he explains. "How do we—a large, multinational organization—respond against small, creative hot shops waiting to eat our lunch?"

For Lowe, software called Groove from Groove Networks (www.groove.net), is facilitating a swarming approach that enables quick collaboration among internal and external talent. Groove gets around connectivity problems in Asia by chopping files into small pieces and sending them one at a time as the connection allows. That means high-bandwidth messages and even video files, which previously often crashed in midtransmission, can be safely shared, Schoonover says.

Prospective clients have asked to see how the team space works, and they've been invited to come in by downloading free trial software from the Web. "They became something more than prospects—they became collaborators," Schoonover says, adding that swarm technology made the difference for at least two multinational client prospects who were concerned about Lowe's ability to communicate with talent around the world. After they saw swarming in action, they signed up as customers.

Clients' suppliers and other partners have also been brought into the collaboration space. "It makes it so much simpler to bring together a diverse group of minds," he says. Swarming has also saved on expenses such as international couriers, faxing, and travel. "It has paid for itself many times over in a half year," Schoonover says.

At HP Services, swarming helps ad hoc teams around the world collaborate in pursuing deals and delivering on consulting engagements. "We're connecting the right people faster, bringing them into the work stream, whoever they might be—company people or partners," says HP Services Chief Knowledge Officer Craig Samuel, who works from his home on the Isle of Bute off the coast of Scotland. "You have a sudden deadline, and people self-organize. We're getting proposals done faster and better." At HP Services, thousands of workers who deal with partners and customers are hooked into the swarm. "We're bridging organizations, suppliers, distributors—even corporations," says Samuel. "We compete on some things and partner on others, and we can all mobilize in a common team space."

Samuel says the return on investment from swarming mostly comes from opportunities that would have been lost without it. "What if you didn't get the $1 billion contract because you couldn't find the people or mobilize fast enough?" he says. "That is a huge impact to the organization." The ROI is as good as anything we do in IT today."

As swarming catches on in business, it will bring management challenges along with opportunities, Samuel cautions. "If I'm a high-level manager and I've got a lot of people self-allocating to projects arising on the fly, keeping other things those people are doing on track starts to be a problem," he says. "Some conventional-style managers will be getting new gray hairs."

The solution will be increased communication, and a clear understanding throughout the ranks, of the organization's top priorities, Samuel says. "You've got to give up a little control and trust your people." Swarming enables collaboration beyond the organization in a way that hasn't been possible before, Samuel says, adding, "If you're going to be effective going forward, you're going to need this kind collaboration."

Case Study Questions

1. What are the business benefits of swarming collaboration? Use Lowe Worldwide and HP as examples.

2. What are some possible limitations of swarming?

3. Visit the website of Groove Networks and experience their demo of working in a shared workspace. Would this support workgroup collaboration? Swarming collaboration? Why or why not?

CHAPTER 8

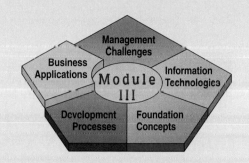

ELECTRONIC COMMERCE SYSTEMS

Chapter Highlights

Section I
Electronic Commerce Fundamentals

Introduction to e-Commerce

Real World Case: eBay Inc.: Managing Success in a Dynamic Online Marketplace

The Scope of e-Commerce

Essential e-Commerce Processes

Electronic Payment Processes

Section II
e-Commerce Applications and Issues

e-Commerce Application Trends

Real World Case: Corporate Express: The Business Value of Integrating Customer and Supplier Procurement Systems

Business-to-Consumer e-Commerce

Web Store Requirements

Business-to-Business e-Commerce

e-Commerce Marketplaces

Clicks and Bricks in e-Commerce

Real World Case: E-Trade and Wells Fargo: The Business Case for Clicks and Bricks e-Commerce

Real World Case: Providence Washington Insurance and Tharco: The Business Value of an Online Customer Interface

Learning Objectives

After reading and studying this chapter, you should be able to:

1. Identify the major categories and trends of e-commerce applications.

2. Identify the essential processes of an e-commerce system, and give examples of how they are implemented in e-commerce applications.

3. Identify and give examples of several key factors and Web store requirements needed to succeed in e-commerce.

4. Identify and explain the business value of several types of e-commerce marketplaces.

5. Discuss the benefits and trade-offs of several e-commerce clicks and bricks alternatives.

SECTION I

SECTION I   Electronic Commerce Fundamentals

Introduction to e-Commerce

E-commerce is changing the shape of competition, the speed of action, and the stream-lining of interactions, products, and payments from customers to companies and from companies to suppliers [12].

For most companies today, electronic commerce is more than just buying and selling products online. Instead, it encompasses the entire online process of developing, marketing, selling, delivering, servicing, and paying for products and services transacted on internetworked, global marketplaces of customers, with the support of a worldwide network of business partners. As we will see in this chapter, electronic commerce systems rely on the resources of the Internet and many other information technologies to support every step of this process. We will also see that many companies, large and small, are engaged in some form of e-commerce activities. Therefore, developing an e-commerce capability has become an important option that should be considered by most businesses today.

Analyzing eBay Inc.

Read the Real World case on eBay Inc. on the next page. We can learn a lot about the challenges and opportunities in the field of electronic commerce from this example. See Figure 8.1.

When eBay began, it was just another consumer-to-consumer online auction site specializing in collectibles and used goods. Now eBay is the dominant online marketplace for all kinds of products, sold at fixed prices as well as through auctions, with a fast

FIGURE 8.1

Founder Pierre Omidyar (left) and CEO Meg Whitman have successfully steered eBay into a profitable and dynamic user-driven online marketplace.

Source: Marc Asnin/Corbis Saba

REAL WORLD CASE 1

eBay Inc.: Managing Success in a Dynamic Online Marketplace

It began as a trading site for nerds, the newly jobless, home-bound housewives, and bored retirees to sell subprime goods: collectibles and attic trash. But eBay (www.ebay.com) quickly grew into a teeming marketplace of 30 million, with its own laws and norms, such as a feedback system in which buyers and sellers rate each other on each transaction. When that wasn't quite enough, eBay formed its own police force to patrol the listings for fraud and kick out offenders. The company even has something akin to a bank: Its PayPal payment-processing unit allows buyers to make electronic payments to eBay sellers who can't afford a merchant credit card account. "eBay is creating a second, virtual economy," says W. Brian Arthur, an economist at think tank Santa Fe Institute. "It's opening up a whole new medium of exchange."

eBay's powerful vortex is drawing diverse products and players into its profitable economy, driving its sellers into the heart of traditional retailing, a $2 trillion market. Among eBay's 12 million daily listings are products from giants such as Sears Roebuck, Home Depot, Walt Disney, and even IBM. More than a quarter of the offerings are listed at fixed prices. The result, says Bernard H. Tenenbaum, president of a retail buyout firm, is "They're coming right for the mainstream of the retail business."

So what started out as a pure consumer auction marketplace, is now also becoming a big time business-to-consumer and even business-to-business bazaar that is earning record profits for eBay's stockholders. And as the eBay economy expands, CEO Meg Whitman and her team may find that managing it could get a lot tougher, especially because eBay's millions of passionate and clamorous users demand a voice in all major decisions. This process is clear in one of eBay's most cherished institutions: the Voice of the Customer program. Every couple of months, the executives of eBay bring in as many as a dozen sellers and buyers, especially its high-selling "Power Sellers," to ask them questions about how they work and what else eBay needs to do. And at least twice a week, it holds hour-long teleconferences to poll users on almost every new feature or policy, no matter how small.

The result is that users feel like owners, and they take the initiative to expand the eBay economy—often beyond management's wildest dreams. Stung by an aerospace downturn, for instance, machine-tool shop Reliable Tools Inc., tried listing a few items on eBay in late 1998. Some were huge, hulking chunks of metal, such as a $7,000 2,300-pound milling machine. Yet they sold like ice cream in August. Since then, says Reliable's auction manager, Richard Smith, the company's eBay business has "turned into a monster." Now the Irwindale (California) shop's $1 million in monthly eBay sales constitutes 75% of its overall business. Pioneers such as Reliable prompted eBay to set up an industrial products marketplace in January that's on track to top $500 million in gross sales this year.

Then there is eBay Motors. When eBay manager Simon Rothman first recognized a market for cars on eBay in early 1999, he quickly realized that such high-ticket items would require a different strategy than simply opening a new category. To jump-start its supply of cars and customers, eBay immediately bought a collector-car auction company, Kruse International, for $150 million in stock, and later did a deal to include listings from online classifieds site, AutoTrader.com. Rothman also arranged insurance and warranty plans, an escrow service, and shipping and inspection services.

This approach worked wonders. Sales of cars and car parts, at a $5 billion-plus annual clip, are eBay's single largest market. That has catapulted eBay in front of No. 1 U.S. auto dealer AutoNation in number of used cars sold. About half of the sellers are brick-and-mortar dealers who now have a much larger audience than their local area. "eBay is by far one of my better sources for buyers," says Bradley Bonifacius, Internet sales director at Dean Stallings Ford in Oak Ridge, Tennessee.

And for now, the big corporations, which still account for under 5 percent of eBay's gross sales, seem to be bringing in more customers than they steal. Motorola Inc., for example, helped kick off a new wholesale business for eBay last year, selling excess and returned cell phones in large lots. Thanks to the initiative of established companies such as Motorola, eBay's wholesale business jumped ninefold, to $23 million, in the first quarter.

As businesses on eBay grow larger, they spur the creation of even more businesses. A new army of merchants, for example, is making a business out of selling on eBay for other people. From almost none a couple of years ago, these so-called Trading Assistants now number nearly 23,000. This kind of organic growth makes it exceedingly tough to predict how far the eBay economy can go. Whitman professes not to know. "We don't actually control this," she admits. "We are not building this company by ourselves. We have a unique partner—millions of people."

Case Study Questions

1. Why has eBay become such a successful and diverse online marketplace? Visit the eBay website to help you answer, and check out their many trading categories, specialty sites, international sites, and other features.

2. Why do you think eBay has become the largest online/offline seller of used cars, and the largest online seller of certain other products, like computers and photographic equipment?

3. Is eBay's move from a pure consumer-to-consumer auction marketplace to inviting large and small businesses to sell to consumers and other businesses, sometimes at fixed prices, a good long-term strategy? Why or why not?

Source: Adapted from Robert D. Hof, "The eBay Economy," *BusinessWeek*, August 25, 2003. Reprinted from 8/25/03 issue of *BusinessWeek* by special permission, copyright © 2003 by the McGraw-Hill Companies, Inc. And Adam Lashinsky, "Meg and the Machine," *Fortune*, September 1, 2003, pp. 70–78.

FIGURE 8.2 E-commerce involves accomplishing a range of business processes to support the electronic buying and selling of goods and services.

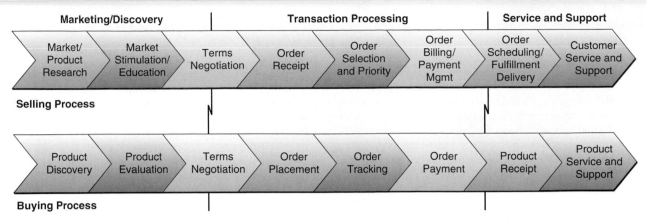

growing segment of business-to-consumer and business-to-business online sales driven by large corporations as well as small businesses. CEO Meg Whitman and her team of executives must manage this dynamic growth with the heavy involvement of eBay's sellers and buyers, since their cooperation in this largely self-regulating economy is essential for continued success. But eBay management has so far successfully steered this user-driven e-commerce marketplace into many new markets and services, and a strategic and profitable position in both online and offline markets for many products.

The Scope of e-Commerce

Figure 8.2 illustrates the range of business processes involved in the marketing, buying, selling, and servicing of products and services in companies that engage in e-commerce [6]. Companies involved in e-commerce as either buyers or sellers rely on Internet-based technologies, and e-commerce applications and services to accomplish marketing, discovery, transaction processing, and product and customer service processes. For example, electronic commerce can include interactive marketing, ordering, payment, and customer support processes at e-commerce catalog and auction sites on the World Wide Web. But e-commerce also includes e-business processes such as extranet access of inventory databases by customers and suppliers (transaction processing), intranet access of customer relationship management systems by sales and customer service reps (service and support), and customer collaboration in product development via e-mail exchanges and Internet newsgroups (marketing/discovery).

e-Commerce Technologies

What technologies are necessary for electronic commerce? The short answer is that most information technologies and Internet technologies that we discuss in this text are involved in electronic commerce systems. A more specific answer is illustrated in Figure 8.3, which is an example of the technology resources required by many e-commerce systems. The figure illustrates some of the hardware, software, data, and network components used by Free Markets Inc. to provide B2B online auction e-commerce services [5].

Categories of e-Commerce

Many companies today are participating in or sponsoring three basic categories of electronic commerce applications: business-to-consumer, business-to-business, and consumer-to-consumer e-commerce. Note: We will not explicitly cover business-to-government (B2G) and *e-government* applications in this text. However, many e-commerce concepts apply to such applications.

Business-to-Consumer (B2C) e-Commerce. In this form of electronic commerce, businesses must develop attractive electronic marketplaces to sell products and services to consumers. For example, many companies offer e-commerce websites

FIGURE 8.3

The hardware, software, network, and database components and IT architecture of B2B online auctions provider FreeMarkets Inc. are illustrated in this example of their Internet-based QuickSource auction service.

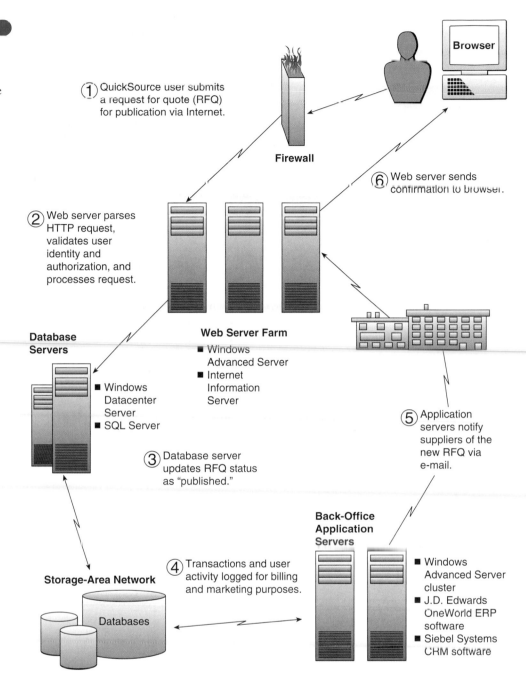

① QuickSource user submits a request for quote (RFQ) for publication via Internet.

Firewall

Browser

⑥ Web server sends confirmation to browser.

② Web server parses HTTP request, validates user identity and authorization, and processes request.

Web Server Farm
- Windows Advanced Server
- Internet Information Server

Database Servers
- Windows Datacenter Server
- SQL Server

③ Database server updates RFQ status as "published."

⑤ Application servers notify suppliers of the new RFQ via e-mail.

Back-Office Application Servers
- Windows Advanced Server cluster
- J.D. Edwards OneWorld ERP software
- Siebel Systems CRM software

Storage-Area Network

④ Transactions and user activity logged for billing and marketing purposes.

Databases

that provide virtual storefronts and multimedia catalogs, interactive order processing, secure electronic payment systems, and online customer support.

Business-to-Business (B2B) e-Commerce. This category of electronic commerce involves both electronic business marketplaces and direct market links between businesses. For example, many companies offer secure Internet or extranet e-commerce catalog websites for their business customers and suppliers. Also very important are B2B e-commerce portals that provide auction and exchange marketplaces for businesses. Others may rely on electronic data interchange (EDI) via the Internet or extranets for computer-to-computer exchange of e-commerce documents with their larger business customers and suppliers.

Consumer-to-Consumer (C2C) e-Commerce. The huge success of online auctions like eBay, where consumers (as well as businesses) can buy and sell with each other in an auction process at an auction website, makes this e-commerce model an important e-commerce business strategy. Thus, participating in or sponsoring consumer or business auctions is an important e-commerce alternative for B2C, C2B (consumer-to-business), or B2B e-commerce. Electronic personal advertising of products or services to buy or sell by consumers at electronic newspaper sites, consumer e-commerce portals, or personal websites is also an important form of C2C e-commerce.

Essential e-Commerce Processes

The essential **e-commerce processes** required for the successful operation and management of e-commerce activities are illustrated in Figure 8.4. This figure outlines the nine key components of an *e-commerce process architecture* that is the foundation of the e-commerce initiatives of many companies today [10]. We will concentrate on the role these processes play in e-commerce systems, but you should recognize that many of these components may also be used in internal, noncommerce e-business applications. An example would be an intranet-based human resource system used by a company's employees, which might use all but the catalog management and product payment processes shown in Figure 8.4. Let's take a brief look at each essential process category.

Access Control and Security

E-commerce processes must establish mutual trust and secure access between the parties in an e-commerce transaction by authenticating users, authorizing access, and enforcing security features. For example, these processes establish that a customer and e-commerce site are who they say they are through user names and passwords, encryption keys, or digital certificates and signatures. The e-commerce site must then authorize access to only those parts of the site that an individual user needs to accom-

FIGURE 8.4

This e-commerce process architecture highlights nine essential categories of e-commerce processes.

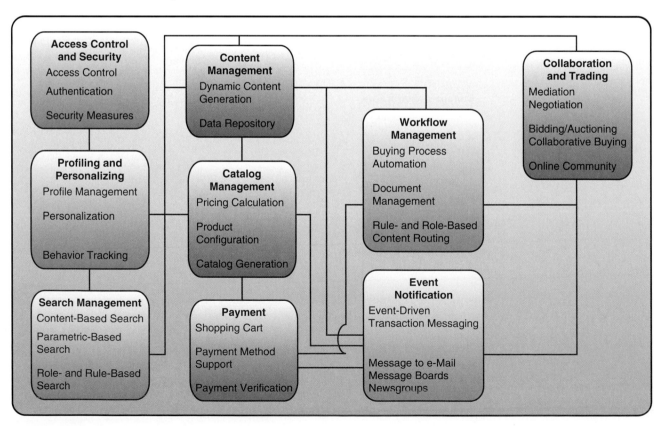

FIGURE 8.5

Bselect software gathers and analyzes the behavior of visitors to the Supergo Bike Shops website to help them personalize a customer's Web shopping experience.

Source: Courtesy of www.supergo.com.

plish his or her particular transactions. Thus, you usually will be given access to all resources of an e-commerce site except for other people's accounts, restricted company data, and webmaster administration areas. Companies engaged in B2B e-commerce may rely on secure industry exchanges for procuring goods and services, or Web trading portals that allow only registered customers access to trading information and applications. Other security processes protect the resources of e-commerce sites from threats such as hacker attacks, theft of passwords or credit card numbers, and system failures. We discuss many of these security threats and features in Chapter 11.

Profiling and Personalizing

Once you have gained access to an e-commerce site, profiling processes can occur that gather data on you and your website behavior and choices, and build electronic profiles of your characteristics and preferences. User profiles are developed using profiling tools such as user registration, cookie files, website behavior tracking software, and user feedback. These profiles are then used to recognize you as an individual user and provide you with a personalized view of the contents of the site, as well as product recommendations and personalized Web advertising as part of a *one-to-one marketing* strategy. Profiling processes are also used to help authenticate your identity for account management and payment purposes, and to gather data for customer relationship management, marketing planning, and website management. Some of the ethical issues in user profiling are discussed in Chapter 11. See Figure 8.5.

Be Free and Supergo Bike Shops: Personalizing e-Commerce

If you're looking to give your customers a unique experience at your e-store, Bselect by Be Free offers a personalization service at affordable prices. Setup costs around $5,000; after that you pay $5,000 per month, plus 15 cents every time someone buys a suggested sale item. Bselect works by tagging and tracking each page of your site. Frequent guests to your online store see products based on where they've been in the past and what they've bought. Bselect saves profile information by key, not a name or address. The system tracks customers anonymously, and they can delete profile details or opt out of future profiles through an online control panel (although Bselect saves customer purchase information indefinitely).

Steven Laff, Web developer for Santa Monica, California–based Supergo Bike Shops, started using Bselect about a year ago for the company's e-commerce site, Supergo.com. Before that Laff had developed his own recommendation tool, which didn't allow him to keep track of sale items. "If you have 600 items, manually recommending something becomes a nightmare," he says. "Bselect is ingenious. It doesn't recommend the same thing twice, and if it's a consumable product, you can set it up to be recommended again. Best of all, Bselect pays for itself 5, 10, 15 times over per month." Before Bselect, e-commerce orders made up only 33 percent of Supergo's overall mail-order sales; now they make up 60 percent [8].

Search Management

Efficient and effective search processes provide a top e-commerce website capability that helps customers find the specific product or service they want to evaluate or buy. E-commerce software packages can include a website search engine component, or a company may acquire a customized e-commerce search engine from search technology companies like Google and Requisite Technology. Search engines may use a combination of search techniques, including searches based on content (a product description, for example), or by parameters (above, below, or between a range of values for multiple properties of a product, for example).

Content and Catalog Management

Content management software helps e-commerce companies develop, generate, deliver, update, and archive text data and multimedia information at e-commerce websites. For example, German media giant Bertelsmann, part owner of BarnesandNoble.com, uses StoryServer content manager software to generate Web page templates that enable online editors from six international offices to easily publish and update book reviews and other product information, which are sold (syndicated) to other e-commerce sites.

E-commerce content frequently takes the form of multimedia catalogs of product information. So generating and managing catalog content is a major subset of content management. For example, W.W. Grainger & Co., a multibillion-dollar industrial parts distributor, uses the CenterStage catalog management software suite to retrieve data from more than 2,000 supplier databases, standardize the data and translate it into HTML or XML for Web use, and organize and enhance the data for speedy delivery as multimedia Web pages at their www.grainger.com website.

Content and catalog management software work with the profiling tools we mentioned earlier to personalize the content of Web pages seen by individual users. For example, Travelocity.com uses OnDisplay content manager software to push personalized promotional information about other travel opportunities to users while they are involved in an online travel-related transaction.

Finally, content and catalog management may be expanded to include *product configuration* processes that support Web-based customer self-service and the *mass customization* of a company's products. Configuration software helps online customers select the optimum feasible set of product features that can be included in a finished product. For example, both Dell Computer and Cisco Systems use configuration software to sell build-to-order computers and network processors to their online customers [3].

Cabletron Systems: e-Commerce Configuration

When $3 billion network equipment maker Cabletron Systems began selling its wares online, its sales reps knew full well that peddling made-to-order routers was not as simple as the mouse-click marvel of online book selling. Cabletron's big business customers—whether ISP EarthLink or motorcycle maker Harley-Davidson—

did not have the technical expertise to build their own router (which can be as small as a breadbox or as large as a television, depending upon the customer, and can include hundreds of components). Worse, Cabletron's website listed thousands of parts that presented users with nearly infinite combinations, most of which would work only when assembled in a certain way.

That's why part of Cabletron's new online sales team consists of a set of complex Web-based product configuration tools made by PeopleSoft Inc. Called eSales Configuration Workbench, it prompts customers the same way a salesperson might: It walks them through product features; analyzes their needs, budgets, and time constraints; and considers only components and options compatible with existing systems. The configurator also suggests various options—different kinds of backup power, the number of parts, types of connecting wires—and generates price quotes for up to 500 concurrent online users. When a customer clicks the Buy button, the configurator generates an order that is passed on to Cabletron's back-end order fulfillment systems, which update inventory, accounting, and shipping databases.

Within a year of completing a six-month implementation of PeopleSoft's software, Cabletron saw staggering results. Some 60 percent of the businesses using its website now use the configurator. Kirk Estes, Cabletron's director of e-commerce, estimates PeopleSoft's software saved $12 million in one year by whittling down the percentage of misconfigured orders—and subsequent returns—to nearly nothing. "We think it's 99.8 percent accurate," Estes says. Order processing costs also dropped 96 percent, and customers can now place online orders in 10 to 20 minutes—a fraction of the two to three days it takes through a sales rep [2].

Workflow Management

Many of the business processes in e-commerce applications can be managed and partially automated with the help of workflow management software. E-business workflow systems for enterprise collaboration help employees electronically collaborate to accomplish structured work tasks within knowledge-based business processes. Workflow management in both e-business and e-commerce depends on a *workflow software engine* containing software models of the business processes to be accomplished. The workflow models express the predefined sets of business rules, roles of stakeholders, authorization requirements, routing alternatives, databases used, and sequence of tasks required for each e-commerce process. Thus, workflow systems ensure that the proper transactions, decisions, and work activities are performed, and the correct data and documents are routed to the right employees, customers, suppliers, and other business stakeholders.

For example, Figure 8.6 illustrates the e-commerce procurement processes of the MS Market system of Microsoft Corporation. Microsoft employees use their global intranet and the catalog/content management and workflow management software engines built into MS Market to electronically purchase more than $3 billion annually of business supplies and materials from approved suppliers connected to the MS Market system by their corporate extranets [12].

Microsoft Corporation: e-Commerce Purchasing Processes

MS Market is an internal e-commerce purchasing system that works on Microsoft's intranet. MS Market drastically reduced the personnel required to manage low-cost requisitions and gives employees a quick, easy way to order materials without being burdened with paperwork and bureaucratic processes. These high-volume, low-dollar transactions represent about 70 percent of total volume, but only 3 percent of Microsoft's accounts payable. Employees were wasting time turning requisitions into purchase orders (POs) and trying to follow business rules and processes. Managers wanted to streamline this process, so the decision was made to create a requisitioning tool that would take all the controls and validations used by requisition personnel and push them onto the Web. Employees wanted an easy-to-use online form for ordering supplies that included extranet interfaces to procurement partners, such as Boise Cascade and Marriott.

How does this system work? Let's say a Microsoft employee wants a technical book. He goes to the MS Market site on Microsoft's intranet, and MS Market immediately identifies his preferences and approval code through his log-on ID. The employee selects the Barnes & Noble link, which brings up a catalog, order form, and a list of hundreds of books with titles and prices that have been negotiated between Microsoft buyers and Barnes & Noble. He selects a book, puts it in the order form, and completes the order by verifying his group's cost center number and manager's name.

The order is transmitted immediately to the supplier, cutting down on delivery time as well as accounting for the payment of the supplies. Upon submission of the order, MS Market generates an order tracking number for reference, sends notification via e-mail to the employee's manager, and transmits the order over the Internet to Barnes & Noble for fulfillment. In this case, since the purchase total is only $40, the manager's specific approval is not required. Two days later, the book arrives at the employee's office. Thus, MS Market lets employees easily order low-cost items in a controlled fashion at a low cost, without going through a complicated PO approval process [12].

Event Notification

Most e-commerce applications are *event-driven* systems that respond to a multitude of events—from a new customer's first website access, to payment and delivery processes, and to innumerable customer relationship and supply chain management activities. That is why **event notification** processes play an important role in e-commerce systems, since customers, suppliers, employees, and other stakeholders must be notified of all events that might affect their status in a transaction. Event notification software works with the workflow management software to monitor all e-commerce processes and record all relevant events, including unexpected changes or problem situations. Then it works with user-profiling software to automatically notify all involved stakeholders of important transaction events using appropriate user-preferred methods of electronic messaging, such as e-mail, newsgroup, pager, and

FIGURE 8.6

The role of catalog/content management and workflow management in a Web-based procurement process: the MS Market system used by Microsoft Corporation.

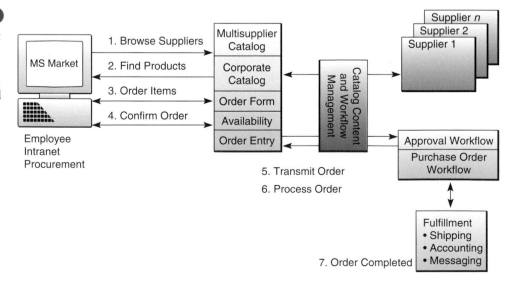

fax communications. This includes notifying a company's management so they can monitor their employees' responsiveness to e-commerce events and customer and supplier feedback.

For example, when you purchase a product at a retail e-commerce website like Amazon.com, you automatically receive an e-mail record of your order. Then you may receive e-mail notifications of any change in product availability or shipment status, and finally, an e-mail message notifying you that your order has been shipped and is complete.

Collaboration and Trading

This major category of e-commerce processes are those that support the vital collaboration arrangements and trading services needed by customers, suppliers, and other stakeholders to accomplish e-commerce transactions. Thus, in Chapter 2, we discussed how a customer-focused e-business uses tools such as e-mail, chat systems, and discussion groups to nurture online *communities of interest* among employees and customers to enhance customer service and build customer loyalty in e-commerce. The essential collaboration among business trading partners in e-commerce may also be provided by Internet-based trading services. For example, B2B e-commerce Web portals provided by companies like Ariba and Commerce One support matchmaking, negotiation, and mediation processes among business buyers and sellers. In addition, B2B e-commerce is heavily dependent on Internet-based trading platforms and portals that provide online exchange and auctions for e-business enterprises. Therefore, the online auctions and exchanges developed by companies like FreeMarkets are revolutionizing the procurement processes of many major corporations. We will discuss these and other e-commerce applications in Section II.

Electronic Payment Processes

Payment for the products and services purchased is an obvious and vital set of processes in electronic commerce transactions. But payment processes are not simple, because of the near-anonymous electronic nature of transactions taking place between the networked computer systems of buyers and sellers, and the many security issues involved. Electronic commerce payment processes are also complex because of the wide variety of debit and credit alternatives and financial institutions and intermediaries that may be part of the process. Therefore, a variety of **electronic payment systems** have evolved over time. In addition, new payment systems are being developed and tested to meet the security and technical challenges of electronic commerce over the Internet.

Web Payment Processes

Most e-commerce systems on the Web involving businesses and consumers (B2C) depend on credit card payment processes. But many B2B e-commerce systems rely on more complex payment processes based on the use of purchase orders, as was illustrated in Figure 8.6. However, both types of e-commerce typically use an electronic *shopping cart* process, which enables customers to select products from website catalog displays and put them temporarily in a virtual shopping basket for later checkout and processing. Figure 8.7 illustrates and summarizes a B2C electronic payment system with several payment alternatives.

Electronic Funds Transfer

Electronic funds transfer (EFT) systems are a major form of electronic payment systems in banking and retailing industries. EFT systems use a variety of information technologies to capture and process money and credit transfers between banks and businesses and their customers. For example, banking networks support teller terminals at all bank offices and automated teller machines (ATMs) at locations throughout the world. Banks, credit card companies, and other businesses may support pay-by-phone services. Very popular also are Web-based payment services, such as PayPal and

FIGURE 8.7

An example of a secure
electronic payment system
with many payment
alternatives.

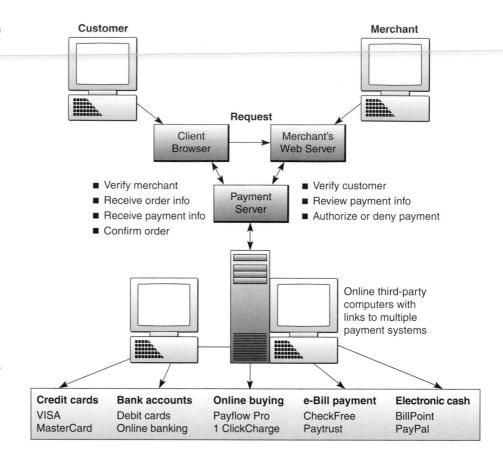

BillPoint for cash transfers, and CheckFree and PayTrust for automatic bill payment that enable the customers of banks and other bill payment services to use the Internet to electronically pay bills. In addition, most point-of-sale terminals in retail stores are networked to bank EFT systems. This makes it possible for you to use a credit card or debit card to instantly pay for gas, groceries, or other purchases at participating retail outlets.

Secure Electronic Payments

When you make an online purchase on the Internet, your credit card information is vulnerable to interception by *network sniffers*, software that easily recognizes credit card number formats. Several basic security measures are being used to solve this security problem: (1) encrypt (code and scramble) the data passing between the customer and merchant, (2) encrypt the data passing between the customer and the company authorizing the credit card transaction, or (3) take sensitive information offline. (Note: Because encryption and other security issues are discussed in Chapter 11, we will not explain how they work in this section.)

For example, many companies use the Secure Socket Layer (SSL) security method developed by Netscape Communications that automatically encrypts data passing between your Web browser and a merchant's server. However, sensitive information is still vulnerable to misuse once it's decrypted (decoded and unscrambled) and stored on a merchant's server. So a digital wallet payment system was developed. In this method, you add security software add-on modules to your Web browser. That enables your browser to encrypt your credit card data in such a way that only the bank that authorizes credit card transactions for the merchant gets to see it. All the merchant is told is whether your credit card transaction is approved or not.

The Secure Electronic Transaction, or SET, standard for electronic payment security extends this digital wallet approach. In this method, software encrypts a digital envelope of digital certificates specifying the payment details for each transaction.

FIGURE 8.8

VeriSign provides electronic payment, security, and many other e-commerce services.

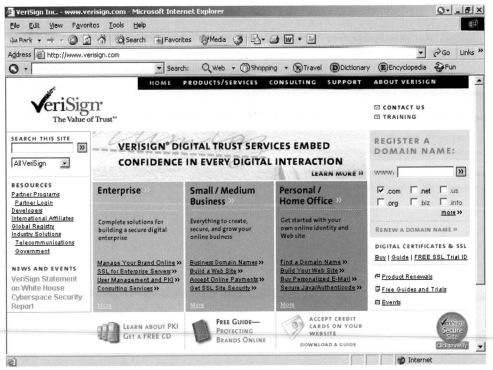

Source: Courtesy of VeriSign Inc.

SET has been agreed to by VISA, MasterCard, IBM, Microsoft, Netscape, and most other industry players. Therefore, a system like SET may become the standard for secure electronic payments on the Internet. However, SET has been stalled by the reluctance of companies to incur its increased hardware, software, and cost requirements [16]. See Figure 8.8.

SECTION II   e-Commerce Applications and Issues

e-Commerce Application Trends

E-commerce is here to stay. The Web and e-commerce are key industry drivers. It's changed how many companies do business. It's created new channels for our customers. Companies are at the e-commerce crossroads and there are many ways to go [12].

Thus, e-commerce is changing how companies do business both internally and externally with their customers, suppliers, and other business partners. How companies apply e-commerce to their business is also subject to change as their managers confront a variety of e-commerce alternatives. The applications of e-commerce by many companies have gone through several major stages as e-commerce matures in the world of business. For example, e-commerce between businesses and consumers (B2C) moved from merely offering multimedia company information at corporate websites *(brochureware)*, to offering products and services at Web storefront sites via electronic catalogs and online sales transactions. B2B e-commerce, on the other hand, started with website support to help business customers serve themselves, and then moved toward automating intranet and extranet procurement systems. But before we go any further, let's look at a real world example.

Analyzing Corporate Express

Read the Real World Case on the next page. We can learn a lot about the challenges and opportunities faced by companies as they integrate their e-commerce systems with those of their customers and suppliers. See Figure 8.9.

Corporate Express has been a very successful pioneer in integrating its online order processing and other systems with the procurement systems of its customers and suppliers. As a result, its customers find Corporate Express very easy to do business with, and trust it to handle most of their procurement needs for office supplies. Even small customers can take advantage of the customized procurement features of the Corporate Express E-Way Web portal, while larger customers' procurement systems

FIGURE 8.9

Vice-presidents Bret McIniss of e-business technologies (left) and Wayne Aiello of e-business services led the drive to integrate Corporate Express with the procurement systems of their customers.

Source: Patricia Barry Levy.

REAL WORLD CASE 2

Corporate Express: The Business Value of Integrating Customer and Supplier Procurement Systems

When you have consolidated computer systems from 500 corporate acquisitions, as Corporate Express Inc. has, you get pretty good at integrating information systems. Indeed, nothing so distinguishes IT at Corporate Express (www.corporateexpress.com) as the degree to which it seamlessly links major procurement systems—its own and those of customers and suppliers. The $5.5 billion, Broomfield, Colorado-based vendor of office supplies for the business market has, in essence, become an extension of the procurement systems of its largest customers.

"Integration is one of our core competencies," says CIO Lisa Peters, who has seen her IT shop grow from 12 people to more than 300 in the past nine years. Corporate Express has for years taken orders for furniture, paper, computer supplies and other office products by telephone, fax, and electronic data interchange. In 1997, it began offering customers Internet-based procurement via a simple CD-ROM catalog. Now, more than half of its 75,000 daily orders arrive electronically, most as XML transactions through a richly featured Web portal called E-Way. The smallest of Corporate Express's 30,000 customers, which typically lack their own automated procurement systems, log on to E-Way and conduct purchasing transactions much as a consumer might at Amazon.com. These buyers have also placed many of their unique procurement rules into E-Way, so that, for example, E-Way checks budgets, buyer authorizations, and other controls for customers.

But 750 of the company's largest customers—which account for some 80 percent of its sales volume—have a more direct connection to E-Way. Corporate Express has integrated E-Way into the processing fabric of their internal procurement systems. That has involved integrating with some 40 different commercial packages from companies ranging from Ariba to Commerce One Operations, and e-Scout. These customers start to build orders locally, but then bridge to E-Way by leveraging the integration features offered by their own e-commerce software.

Although customers can maintain their own versions of the Corporate Express catalog, more often the catalogs are maintained by and at Corporate Express. Every catalog is tailored to its user's format, terminology, and buying practices. "E-Way knows all the customer rules—for example, that they don't buy desks from us, so desks will be blocked out," says Wayne Aiello, vice president of e-business services. "E-Way actually becomes the customer's system, so every customer has to be examined and treated differently."

Corporate Express is doing about 10 new customer integrations per month. They take 10 to 20 days—with requirements definition, coding and testing taking equal amounts of time—but the first few projects took 10 times that long. "The hardest thing three to four years ago was that nobody in the industry had done it," Aiello says.

The company buys off-the-shelf software when it can, but much of E-Way and its other supply systems were developed in-house. Commercial packages often aren't scalable or flexible enough to accommodate the unique needs of customers, the company says. For example, Corporate Express developed its own search engine tailored to the characteristics of an office supply catalog.

Unocal Corp. in El Segundo, California, used to buy from Corporate Express by telephone and fax, but now has integrated its Oracle procurement system with E-Way. Michael Comeau, e-procurement tools manager at Unocal, says he likes E-Way's ability to send all invoices to a central point for payment, its buying controls, and its order-tracking ability. "Maverick spending is reduced tremendously," he says.

Meanwhile, Trisha Smallwood, manager of mail center operations at The Kroger Co. in Cincinnati, says she likes E-Way because it saves her five minutes on every order. No more filling out an order form, faxing it, and waiting for confirmation. The process is made even simpler, she says, by E-Way's ability to maintain a list of items that Kroger orders frequently, as well as the special prices and terms that the grocery chain has negotiated.

Corporate Express uses software from webMethods Inc. to integrate its major logistics and financial applications. The webMethods tool provides flexibility in deciding where data and logic are best placed, says Bret McInnis, vice president for e-business technologies, which is critical when dealing with a high volume of low-margin transactions. "Performance and scalability are always huge issues for us," McInnis says. "Our average order size is small so it takes a lot of transactions for $5 million a day on our website."

While grabbing data using webMethods is "theoretically easy," Aiello says, optimizing performance is not. "At any point, we have thousands of people on the site placing orders. Making something available to 3,000 users simultaneously is a real challenge."

Case Study Questions

1. What is the value to Corporate Express of integrating its systems with the procurement systems of customers?

2. What are the business benefits of the E-Way Web portal to smaller customers? Larger customers?

3. Should every business that has an e-commerce website integrate its systems with the procurement systems of its business customers? Why or why not?

Source: Adapted from Gary Anthes, "Corporate Express Goes Direct," *Computerworld*, September 1, 2003, pp. 17–18. Copyright © 2003 by Computerworld, Inc. Framingham, MA 01701. All rights reserved.

FIGURE 8.10 Trends in B2C and B2B e-commerce, and the business strategies and value driving these trends.

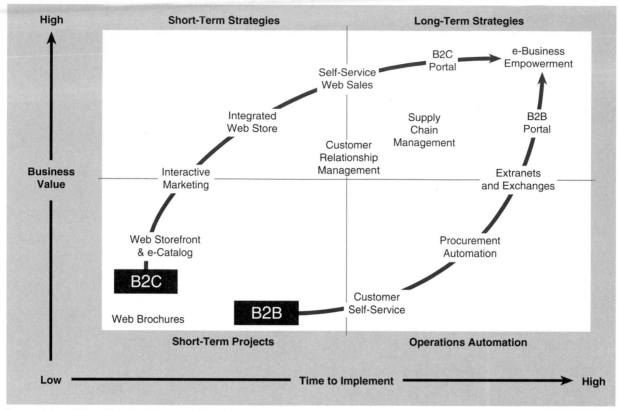

Source: Adapted from Jonathan Rosenoer, Douglas Armstrong, and J. Russell Gates, *The Clickable Corporation: Successful Strategies for Capturing the Internet Advantage* (New York: The Free Press, 1999), p. 24.

use E-Way to connect directly into the Corporate Express order processing and inventory systems. Such integration posed major technical challenges when Corporate Express first pioneered the development of such systems, and still continues to be a challenge in ensuring prompt response times when thousands of customers are online at the same time.

e-Commerce Trends

Figure 8.10 illustrates some of the trends taking place in the e-commerce applications that we introduced at the beginning of this section. Notice how B2C e-commerce moves from simple Web storefronts to interactive marketing capabilities that provide a personalized shopping experience for customers, and then toward a totally integrated Web store that supports a variety of customer shopping experiences. B2C e-commerce is also moving toward a self-service model where customers configure and customize the products and services they wish to buy, aided by configuration software and online customer support as needed.

B2B e-commerce participants moved quickly from self-service on the Web to configuration and customization capabilities and extranets connecting trading partners. As B2C e-commerce moves toward full-service and wide-selection retail Web portals, B2B is also trending toward the use of e-commerce portals that provide catalog, exchange, and auction markets for business customers within or across industries. Of course, both of these trends are enabled by e-business capabilities like customer relationship management and supply chain management, which are the hallmarks of the customer-focused and internetworked supply chains of a fully e-business-enabled company [18].

Business-to-Consumer e-Commerce

E-commerce applications that focus on the consumer share an important goal: to attract potential buyers, transact goods and services, and build customer loyalty through individual courteous treatment and engaging community features [10].

What does it take to create a successful B2C e-commerce business venture? That's the question that many are asking in the wake of the failures of many pure B2C *dot-com* companies. One obvious answer would be to create a Web business initiative that offers attractive products or services of great customer value, and whose business plan is based on realistic forecasts of profitability within the first year or two of operation—a condition that was lacking in many failed dot-coms. But such failures have not stemmed the tide of millions of businesses, both large and small, that are moving at least part of their business to the Web. So let's take a look at some essential success factors and website capabilities for companies engaged in either B2C or B2B e-commerce. Figure 8.11 provides examples of a few top-rated retail Web companies.

e-Commerce Success Factors

On the Internet, the barriers of time, distance, and form are broken down, and businesses are able to transact the sale of goods and services 24 hours a day, 7 days a week, 365 days a year with consumers all over the world. In certain cases, it is even possible to convert a physical good (CDs, packaged software, a newspaper) to a virtual good (MP3 audio, downloadable software, information in HTML format) [10].

A basic fact of Internet retailing is that all retail websites are created equal as far as the "location, location, location" imperative of success in retailing is concerned. No site is any closer to its Web customers, and competitors offering similar goods and services may be only a mouse click away. This makes it vital that businesses find ways to build customer satisfaction, loyalty, and relationships, so customers keep coming back to their Web stores. Thus the key to e-tail success is to optimize several key factors such as selection and value, performance and service efficiency, the look and feel of the site, advertising and incentives to purchase, personal attention, community relationships, and security and reliability. Let's briefly examine each of these factors that are essential to the success of a B2C Web business. See Figure 8.12.

FIGURE 8.11

Examples of a few top-rated retail websites.

Top Retail Websites
● **Amazon.com   www.amazon.com** Amazon.com is the exception to the rule that consumers prefer to shop "real world" retailers online. The mother of all shopping sites, Amazon features a vast selection of books, videos, DVDs, CDs, toys, kitchen items, electronics, and even home and garden goods sold to millions of loyal customers.
● **eBay   www.ebay.com** The fabled auction site operates the world's biggest electronic flea market, with everything from antiques, computers, and coins to Pez dispensers and baseball cards. This site boasts billions of page views per month, and millions of items for sale in thousands of categories supported by thousands of special-interest groups.
● **Eddie Bauer   www.eddiebauer.com** Sportswear titan Eddie Bauer has integrated its retail channels-store, website, and catalog. Shoppers can return an item to any Eddie Bauer store, no matter where it was purchased—a policy other merchants should follow.
● **Lands' End   www.landsend.com** With several seasons as an online retailer, Lands' End is a pro at meeting shoppers' expectations. One of the best features: Specialty Shoppers. A customer service rep will help you make your selections and answer questions by phone or via a live chat.

Source: Adapted from "Tech Lifestyles: Shopping," Technology Buyers Guide, *Fortune*, Winter 2001, pp. 288–90. © 2001 Time Inc. All rights reserved.

FIGURE 8.12

Some of the key factors for success in e-commerce.

e-Commerce Success Factors
● **Selection and Value.** Attractive product selections, competitive prices, satisfaction guarantees, and customer support after the sale.
● **Performance and Service.** Fast, easy navigation, shopping, and purchasing, and prompt shipping and delivery.
● **Look and Feel.** Attractive Web storefront, website shopping areas, multimedia product catalog pages, and shopping features.
● **Advertising and Incentives.** Targeted Web page advertising and e-mail promotions, discounts and special offers, including advertising at affiliate sites.
● **Personal Attention.** Personal Web pages, personalized product recommendations, Web advertising and e-mail notices, and interactive support for all customers.
● **Community Relationships.** Virtual communities of customers, suppliers, company representatives, and others via newsgroups, chat rooms, and links to related sites.
● **Security and Reliability.** Security of customer information and website transactions, trustworthy product information, and reliable order fulfillment.

Selection and Value. Obviously, a business must offer Web shoppers a good selection of attractive products and services at competitive prices or they will quickly click away from a Web store. But a company's prices don't have to be the lowest on the Web if they build a reputation for high quality, guaranteed satisfaction, and top customer support while shopping and after the sale. For example, top-rated e-tailer REI.com helps you select quality outdoor gear for hiking and other activities with a "How to Choose" section, and gives a money-back guarantee on your purchases.

Performance and Service. People don't want to be kept waiting when browsing, selecting, or paying in a Web store. A site must be efficiently designed for ease of access, shopping, and buying, with sufficient server power and network capacity to support website traffic. Web shopping and customer service must also be friendly and helpful, as well as quick and easy. In addition, products offered should be available in inventory for prompt shipment to the customer.

Look and Feel. B2C sites can offer customers an attractive Web storefront, shopping areas, and multimedia product catalogs. These could range from an exciting shopping experience with audio, video, and moving graphics, to a more simple and comfortable look and feel. Thus, most retail e-commerce sites let customers browse product sections, select products, drop them into a virtual shopping cart, and go to a virtual checkout station when they are ready to pay for their order.

Advertising and Incentives. Some Web stores may advertise in traditional media, but most advertise on the Web with targeted and personalized banner ads and other Web page and e-mail promotions. Most B2C sites also offer shoppers incentives to buy and return. Typically, this means coupons, discounts, special offers, and vouchers for other Web services, sometimes with other e-tailers at cross-linked websites. Many Web stores also increase their market reach by being part of Web banner advertising exchange programs with thousand of other Web retailers. Figure 8.13 compares major marketing communications choices in traditional and e-commerce marketing to support each step of the buying process [17].

Personal Attention. Personalizing your shopping experience encourages you to buy and make return visits. Thus, e-commerce software can automatically record details of your visits and build user profiles of you and other Web shoppers. Many sites also encourage you to register with them and fill out a personal interest pro-

FIGURE 8.13 How traditional and Web marketing communications differ in supporting each step of the buying process

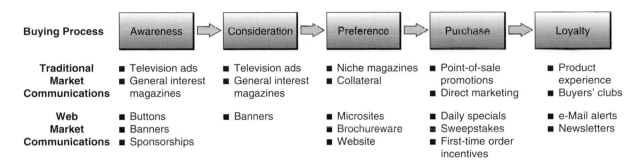

Buying Process	Awareness	Consideration	Preference	Purchase	Loyalty
Traditional Market Communications	■ Television ads ■ General interest magazines	■ Television ads ■ General interest magazines	■ Niche magazines ■ Collateral	■ Point-of-sale promotions ■ Direct marketing	■ Product experience ■ Buyers' clubs
Web Market Communications	■ Buttons ■ Banners ■ Sponsorships	■ Banners	■ Microsites ■ Brochureware ■ Website	■ Daily specials ■ Sweepstakes ■ First-time order incentives	■ e-Mail alerts ■ Newsletters

file. Then, whenever you return, you are welcomed by name or with a personal Web page, greeted with special offers, and guided to those parts of the site that you are most interested in. This *one-to-one marketing* and relationship building power is one of the major advantages of personalized Web retailing.

Community Relationships. Giving online customers with special interests a feeling of belonging to a unique group of like-minded individuals helps build customer loyalty and value. Thus, website relationship and affinity marketing programs build and promote virtual communities of customers, suppliers, company representatives, and others via a variety of Web-based collaboration tools. Examples include discussion forums or newsgroups, chat rooms, message board systems, and cross-links to related website communities.

Security and Reliability. As a customer of a successful Web store, you must feel confident that your credit card, personal information, and details of your transactions are secure from unauthorized use. You must also feel that you are dealing with a trustworthy business, whose products and other website information you can trust to be as advertised. Having your orders filled and shipped as you requested, in the time frame promised, and with good customer support are other measures of an e-tailer's reliability.

Amazon.com: Tops in B2C Retailing

Amazon (www.amazon.com) is rated as one of the biggest and best virtual retailers on the Web, and has regained some of its luster with investors because it is finally making operating profits after many years of losses. The site is designed to speed you through the process of browsing and ordering merchandise while giving you reassuring, personal service at discount prices. For example, the search engine for finding the products you want is quick and accurate, and the ordering process easy and fast. Confirmation is quick, notifications are accurate and friendly, and delivery is prompt. Buyers are e-mailed both when their order is confirmed, as well as the day their order is shipped. The company also offers customers a complete money-back guarantee.

In creating this potential powerhouse of shopping services and offerings, Amazon.com wants to be not simply a Wal-Mart of the Web but rather a next-generation retail commerce portal. Imagine a customized site where—through a personalized shopping service and alliances with thousands of other dealers—you can shop easily with a trusted brand as you research the features, prices, and availability of millions of products from a single storefront that has Amazon's—and your—name on it.

That's what has gotten Amazon this far in its first years of business: exhaustive focus on convenience, selection, and personalization. It lived up to its billing as "Earth's Biggest Selection" by building an inventory of millions of products. It was also among the first Net stores to facilitate credit card purchases; greet customers by name and offer customized home pages; send purchase recommendations via e-mail; and number and explain each step in the purchasing process. This combination of vast selection, efficiency, discount prices, and personal service is why Amazon is frequently mentioned as the top retailer on the Web [4, 20].

Web Store Requirements

Most business-to-consumer e-commerce ventures take the form of retail business sites on the World Wide Web. Whether a huge retail Web portal like Amazon.com, or a small specialty Web retailer, the primary focus of such e-tailers is to develop, operate, and manage their websites so they become high-priority destinations for consumers who will repeatedly choose to go there to buy products and services. Thus, these websites must be able to demonstrate the key factors for e-commerce success that we have just covered. In this section, let's discuss the essential Web store requirements that you would have to implement to support a successful retail business on the Web, as summarized and illustrated in Figure 8.14.

Developing a Web Store

Before you can launch your own retail store on the Internet, you must build an e-commerce website. Many companies use simple website design software tools and predesigned templates provided by their website hosting service to construct their Web retail store. That includes building your Web storefront and product catalog Web pages, as well as tools to provide shopping cart features, process orders, handle credit card payments, and so forth. Of course, larger companies can use their own software developers or hire an outside website development contractor to build a custom-designed e-commerce site. Also, like most companies, you can contract with your ISP (Internet service provider) or a specialized Web hosting company to operate and maintain your B2C website.

FIGURE 8.14 These Web store requirements must be implemented by a company or its website hosting service, in order to develop a successful e-commerce business.

Developing a Web Store		
● **Build**	● **Market**	
Website design tools	Web page advertising	
Site design templates	E-mail promotions	
Custom design services	Web advertising exchanges with affiliate sites	
Website hosting	Search engine registrations	
Serving Your Customers		
● **Serve**	● **Transact**	● **Support**
Personalized Web pages	Flexible order process	Website online help
Dynamic multimedia catalog	Credit card processing	Customer service e-mail
Catalog search engine	Shipping and tax calculations	Discussion groups and chat rooms
Integrated shopping cart	E-mail order notifications	Links to related sites
Managing a Web Store		
● **Manage**	● **Operate**	● **Protect**
Website usage statistics	24x7 website hosting	User password protection
Sales and inventory reports	Online tech support	Encrypted order processing
Customer account management	Scalable network capacity	Encrypted website administration
Links to accounting system	Redundant servers and power	Network firewalls and security monitors

Once you build your website, it must be developed as a retail Web business by marketing it in a variety of ways that attract visitors to your site and transform them into loyal Web customers. So your website should include Web page and e-mail advertising and promotions for Web visitors and customers, and Web advertising exchange programs with other Web stores. Also, you can register your Web business with its own domain name (for example, yourstore.com), as well as registering your website with the major Web search engines and directories to help Web surfers find your site more easily. In addition, you might consider affiliating as a small business partner with large Web portals like Yahoo! and Netscape, large e-tailers and auction sites like Amazon and eBay, and small business Web centers like Microsoft bCentral and Prodigy Biz.

Freemerchant and Prodigy Biz: Getting Started

Freemerchant and Prodigy Biz are examples of the many companies that help small businesses get on the Web. Freemerchant.com enables you to set up a Web store for free by choosing from nearly 60 design templates. That includes Web hosting on secure networks, shopping cart and order processing, and providing common database software for importing your product catalog data. Fee-based services include banner ad exchanges, domain and search engine registrations, and enabling product data to be listed on eBay and sales data to be exported to the QuickBooks accounting system.

Prodigybiz.com is designed to serve small e-tail businesses with a full range of Web store development services. Prodigy Biz features both free and fee-based site design and Web publishing tools, website hosting and site maintenance, full e-commerce order and credit card processing, Internet access and e-mail services, and a variety of management reports and affiliate marketing programs [19]. See Figure 8.15.

FIGURE 8.15

Prodigy Biz is one of many companies offering retail website development and hosting services.

Source: Courtesy of www.prodigybiz.com.

Serving Your Customers

Once your retail store is on the Web and receiving visitors, the website must help you welcome and serve them personally and efficiently so that they become loyal customers. So most e-tailers use several website tools to create user profiles, customer files, and personal Web pages and promotions that help them develop a one-to-one relationship with their customers. This includes creating incentives to encourage visitors to register, developing *Web cookie files* to automatically identify returning visitors, or contracting with website tracking companies like DoubleClick and others for software to automatically record and analyze the details of the website behavior and preferences of Web shoppers.

Of course, your website should have the look and feel of an attractive, friendly, and efficient Web store. That means having e-commerce features like a dynamically changing and updated multimedia catalog, a fast catalog search engine, and a convenient shopping cart system that is integrated with Web shopping, promotions, payment, shipping, and customer account information. Your e-commerce order processing software should be fast and able to adjust to personalized promotions and customer options like gift handling, special discounts, credit card or other payments, and shipping and tax alternatives. Also, automatically sending your customers e-mail notices to document when orders are processed and shipped is a top customer service feature of e-tail transaction processing.

Providing customer support for your Web store is an essential website capability. So many e-tail sites offer help menus, tutorials, and lists of FAQs (frequently asked questions) to provide self-help features for Web shoppers. Of course, e-mail correspondence with customer service representatives of your Web store offers more personal assistance to customers. Establishing website discussion groups and chat rooms for your customers and store personnel to interact helps create a more personal community that can provide invaluable support to customers, as well as building customer loyalty. Providing links to related websites from your Web store can help customers find additional information and resources, as well as earning commission income from the affiliate marketing programs of other Web retailers. For example, the Amazon.com Affiliate program pays commissions of up to 15 percent for purchases made by Web shoppers clicking to their Web store from your site.

Managing a Web Store

A Web retail store must be managed as both a business and a website, and most e-commerce hosting companies offer software and services to help you do just that. For example, companies like Freemerchant, Prodigy Biz, and Verio provide their hosting clients with a variety of management reports that record and analyze Web store traffic, inventory, and sales results. Other services build customer lists for e-mail and Web page promotions, or provide customer relationship management features to help retain Web customers. Also, some e-commerce software includes links to download inventory and sales data into accounting packages like QuickBooks for bookkeeping and preparation of financial statements and reports.

Of course, Web hosting companies must enable their Web store clients to be available online twenty-four hours a day and seven days a week all year. This requires them to build or contract for sufficient network capacity to handle peak Web traffic loads, and redundant network servers and power sources to respond to system or power failures. Most hosting companies provide e-commerce software that uses passwords and encryption to protect Web store transactions and customer records, and employ network firewalls and security monitors to repel hacker attacks and other security threats. Many hosting services also offer their clients 24-hour tech support to help them with any technical problems that arise. We will discuss these and other e-commerce security management issues in Chapter 11.

NTT/Verio Inc.: Website Management

NTT/Verio Inc. (www.verio.com) is an example of one of the world's leading Web hosting companies. Verio provides complete software, computing, and network resources to Web hosting companies, as well as offering e-commerce development and hosting services to Web retailers. Verio also offers a Web start-up and development service for small businesses called SiteMerlin (www.sitemerlin.com). Verio guarantees 99.9 percent website uptime to its e-commerce customers, with 24×7 server monitoring and customer support. Verio hosts more than 10,000 small and medium-sized Web businesses; has a network hosting alliance with Sun Microsystems and an Oracle Web database application service; and provides hosting services to Terra Lycos and other Web hosting companies [19].

Business-to-Business e-Commerce

Business-to-business electronic commerce is the wholesale and supply side of the commercial process, where businesses buy, sell, or trade with other businesses. B2B electronic commerce relies on many different information technologies, most of which are implemented at e-commerce websites on the World Wide Web and corporate intranets and extranets. B2B applications include electronic catalog systems, electronic trading systems such as exchange and auction portals, electronic data interchange, electronic funds transfers, and so on. All of the factors for building a successful retail website we discussed earlier also apply to wholesale websites for business-to-business electronic commerce.

In addition, many businesses are integrating their Web-based e-commerce systems with their e-business systems for supply chain management, customer relationship management, and online transaction processing, as well as to their traditional, or legacy, computer-based accounting and business information systems. This ensures that all electronic commerce activities are integrated with e-business processes and supported by up-to-date corporate inventory and other databases, which in turn are automatically updated by Web sales activities. Let's look at a successful example.

Cisco Systems: B2B Marketplace Success

The e-commerce website Cisco Connection Online enables corporate users to purchase routers, switches, and other hardware that enables customers to build high-speed information networks. Over 70 percent of Cisco's sales take place at this site.

So what has made Cisco so successful? Some would argue that its market—networking hardware—is a prime product to sell online because the customer base is composed almost entirely of IT department staffers and consultants. To some degree, this is certainly true. On the other hand, competitors initially scoffed at Cisco's efforts due to the inherent complexity of its product. However, it's difficult to dispute that Cisco has built an online store with functionality and usefulness that is a model of success in the B2B commerce world.

Cisco was able to achieve success largely due to the variety of service offerings made available throughout its purchasing process. In addition to simply providing a catalog and transaction processing facilities, Cisco includes a personalized interface for buyers, an extensive customer support section with contact information, technical documents, software updates, product configuration tools, and even online training and certification courses for Cisco hardware. Also, Cisco provides direct integration with its internal back-end systems for frequent customers, and makes software available that customers can use to design custom links to their own line-of-business software from such players as SAP America, PeopleSoft, and Oracle.

Cisco has also made a concerted effort to ensure that post-sale customer support is available to buyers of every kind. For most large corporations, this means diligent account management and dedicated support representatives to troubleshoot problems and aid in complex network design. For smaller businesses that may be installing their first routers or switches, Cisco includes recommended configurations and simple FAQs to get users up and running.

Like any mature virtual marketplace, Cisco Connection Online integrates directly with Cisco's internal applications and databases to automatically manage inventory and production. Cisco even allows vendors such as HP, PeopleSoft, and IBM to exchange design data to enable easy network configuration troubleshooting online [10].

e-Commerce Marketplaces

The latest e-commerce transaction systems are scaled and customized to allow buyers and sellers to meet in a variety of high speed trading platforms: auctions, catalogs, and exchanges [14].

Businesses of any size can now buy everything from chemicals to electronic components, excess electrical energy, construction materials, or paper products at business-to-business **e-commerce marketplaces.** Figure 8.16 outlines five major types of e-commerce marketplaces used by businesses today. However, many B2B **e-commerce portals** provide several types of marketplaces. Thus they may offer an electronic **catalog** shopping and ordering site for products from many suppliers in an industry. Or they may serve as an **exchange** for buying and selling via a bid-ask process, or at negotiated prices. Very popular are electronic **auction** websites for business-to-business auctions of products and services. Figure 8.17 illustrates a B2B trading system that offers exchange, auction, and reverse auction (where sellers bid for the business of a buyer) electronic markets [14].

Many of these B2B **e-commerce portals** are developed and hosted by third-party *market-maker* companies who serve as **infomediaries** that bring buyers and sellers together in catalog, exchange, and auction markets. Infomediaries are companies that serve as intermediaries in e-business and e-commerce transactions. Examples are Ariba, Commerce One, VerticalNet, and FreeMarkets, to name a few successful companies. All provide e-commerce marketplace software products and services to power business Web portals for e-commerce transactions.

These B2B e-commerce sites make business purchasing decisions faster, simpler, and more cost-effective, since companies can use Web systems to research and transact with many vendors. Business buyers get one-stop shopping and accurate purchasing information. They also get impartial advice from infomediaries that they can't get from the sites hosted by suppliers and distributors. Thus, companies can negotiate or bid for better prices from a larger pool of vendors. And of course, suppliers benefit from easy access to customers from all over the globe [14]. Now, let's look at a real world example.

ChemConnect and Heritage Services: Public and Private B2B Exchanges

Public B2B Exchanges. The pricing was becoming cutthroat in the closing minutes of the online auction. A North American chemical producer offered to sell a plastics stabilizer to a *Fortune* 20 firm for $4.35 per kilogram. But with two minutes left, a lower price from a Chinese company flashed across the computer screens at ChemConnect (www.chemconnect.com), the San Francisco operator of a public online marketplace for the chemical industry. The North American producer lowered

FIGURE 8.16

Types of e-commerce marketplaces.

e-Commerce Marketplaces
● **One to many:** Sell-side marketplaces. Host one major supplier, who dictates product catalog offerings and prices. Examples: Cisco.com and Dell.com.
● **Many to one:** Buy-side marketplaces. Attract many suppliers that flock to these exchanges to bid on the business of a major buyer like GE or AT&T.
● **Some to many:** Distribution marketplaces. Unite major suppliers who combine their product catalogs to attract a larger audience of buyers. Examples: VerticalNet and Works.com
● **Many to some:** Procurement marketplaces. Unite major buyers who combine their purchasing catalogs to attract more suppliers and thus more competition and lower prices. Examples: the auto industry's Covisint and energy industry's Pantellos.
● **Many to many:** Auction marketplaces used by many buyers and sellers that can create a variety of buyers' or sellers' auctions to dynamically optimize prices. Examples are eBay and FreeMarkets.

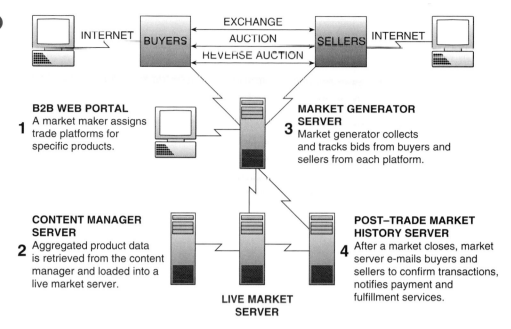

FIGURE 8.17

This is an example of a B2B e-commerce Web portal that offers exchange, auction, and reverse auction electronic markets.

B2B WEB PORTAL
1 A market maker assigns trade platforms for specific products.

MARKET GENERATOR SERVER
3 Market generator collects and tracks bids from buyers and sellers from each platform.

CONTENT MANAGER SERVER
2 Aggregated product data is retrieved from the content manager and loaded into a live market server.

POST–TRADE MARKET HISTORY SERVER
4 After a market closes, market server e-mails buyers and sellers to confirm transactions, notifies payment and fulfillment services.

LIVE MARKET SERVER

its price. Back and forth the two firms went as ChemConnect officials saw the price drop penny by penny. The Chinese offered $4.23. Finally, the North American company won the $500,000 contract with an offer of $4.20. The auction was just one of 20 taking place on ChemConnect's website one August morning, as companies from North America, Europe, and Asia bid on the lucrative six-month contracts.

ChemConnect hosted the event during several hours on a recent Monday morning. The same bidding process without the online auction would have taken at least three months, according to the company that held the event—even using e-mail. In the past, this company sent e-mail to all the suppliers it wanted to bid on its business. Then in a few days those companies would respond with their opening bids. The buyer would counter. Up to a week elapsed between every round.

Not only does ChemConnect help save companies time when they're buying, but it offers a central hub in a fragmented industry. More than 89,000 companies around the world produce chemicals, according to the American Chemical Council. ChemConnect, housed on one floor of a San Francisco high-rise, allows many of them to find suppliers or buyers they did not know existed.

Private B2B Exchanges. Heritage Environmental Services President Ken Price agreed to enter two B2B Web public auctions, hosted by FreeMarkets, to bid on contracts in 2001. But Heritage didn't end up winning. Not only that, the online auction process emphasized price, meaning Heritage had to lower its fee to compete.

Heritage managers quickly concluded that this flavor of Net commerce wasn't for them. Instead, they decided on a different strategy: building their own online portal to link Heritage with existing customers. Heritage's B2B Web-based exchange lets customers order hazardous-waste management services and keep tabs on their accounts. It also speeds up the billing process because it accepts payment for services online. "What we've got is a nice central focal point where everyone in the process can see what's going on," says Price, who expects his company to book up to 15 percent of its business this year through the private portal.

Heritage is at the forefront of business-to-business e-commerce: private exchanges. This form of online link appeals to a growing number of large and small companies disappointed by public Internet markets intended to facilitate auctions and group purchasing. Like Heritage, many suppliers have been unhappy with the downward price pressures they encounter in public Internet markets.

Businesses concerned that participating in public B2B exchanges would put sales information and other critical data in the hands of customers and competitors are also turning to private exchanges. Smaller companies such as Heritage as well as giants like Dell Computer, Intel, and Wal-Mart have set up private online exchanges to link to suppliers and customers, help streamline the business, and boost sales. Private exchanges offer more control, say executives at these companies, and permit easier customization—allowing automation of processes such as sending purchase orders or checking delivery schedules [24].

Electronic Data Interchange

Electronic data interchange (EDI) was one of the earliest uses of information technology for electronic commerce. EDI involves the electronic exchange of business transaction documents over the Internet and other networks between supply chain trading partners (organizations and their customers and suppliers). Data representing a variety of business transaction documents (such as purchase orders, invoices, requests for quotations, and shipping notices) are automatically exchanged between computers using standard document message formats. Typically, EDI software is used to convert a company's own document formats into standardized EDI formats as specified by various industry and international protocols. Thus, EDI is an example of the almost complete automation of an e-commerce supply chain process. And EDI over the Internet, using secure *virtual private networks*, is a growing B2B e-commerce application.

Formatted transaction data are transmitted over network links directly between computers without paper documents or human intervention. Besides direct network links between the computers of trading partners, third-party services are widely used. Value-added network companies like GE Global Exchange Services and Computer Associates offer a variety of EDI services for relatively high fees. But many EDI service providers now offer secure, lower cost EDI services over the Internet. Figure 8.18 illustrates a typical EDI system.

FIGURE 8.18 A typical example of electronic data interchange activities, an important form of business-to-business electronic commerce. EDI over the Internet is a major B2B e-commerce application.

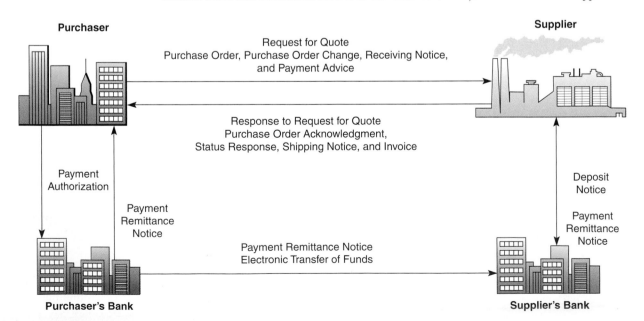

FIGURE 8.19 Companies have a spectrum of alternatives and benefits trade-offs when deciding upon an integrated or separate e-commerce business.

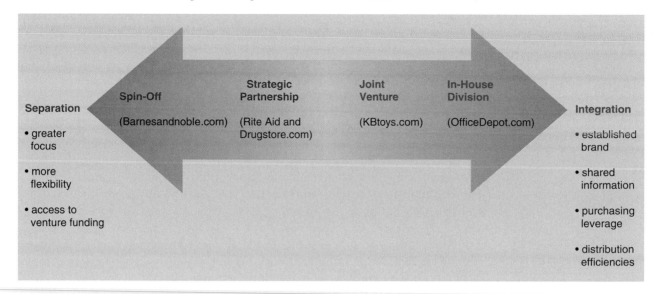

EDI is still a popular data-transmission format among major trading partners, primarily to automate repetitive transactions, though it is slowly being replaced by XML-based Web services. EDI automatically tracks inventory changes; triggers orders, invoices, and other documents related to transactions; and schedules and confirms delivery and payment. By digitally integrating the supply chain, EDI streamlines processes, saves time, and increases accuracy. And by using Internet technologies, lower cost Internet-based EDI services are now available to smaller businesses [21, 23].

Clicks and Bricks in e-Commerce

Companies are recognizing that success will go to those who can execute clicks-and-mortar strategies that bridge the physical and virtual worlds. Different companies will need to follow very different paths in deciding how closely — or loosely — to integrate their Internet initiatives with their traditional operations [9].

Figure 8.19 illustrates the spectrum of alternatives and benefit trade-offs that e-business enterprises face when choosing an e-commerce "clicks and bricks" strategy. E-business managers must answer this question: Should we integrate our e-commerce virtual business operations with our traditional physical business operations, or keep them separate? As Figure 8.19 shows, companies have been implementing a range of integration/separation strategies and made key benefits trade-offs in answering that question. Let's take a look at several alternatives [9].

e-Commerce Integration

The Internet is just another channel that gets plugged into the business architecture [9].

So says CIO Bill Seltzer of office supply retailer Office Depot, which fully integrates their OfficeDepot.com e-commerce sales channel into their traditional business operations. Thus, Office Depot is a prime example of why many companies have chosen integrated clicks and bricks strategies, where their e-commerce business is integrated in some major ways into the traditional business operations of a company. The business case for such strategies rests on:

- Capitalizing on any unique strategic capabilities that may exist in a company's traditional business operations that could be used to support an e-commerce business.

- Gaining several strategic benefits of integrating e-commerce into a company's traditional business; such as the sharing of established brands and key business information, and joint buying power and distribution efficiencies.

For example, Office Depot already had a successful catalog sales business with a professional call center and a fleet of over 2,000 delivery trucks. Its 1,825 stores and 30 warehouses were networked by a sophisticated information system that provided complete customer, vendor, order, and product inventory data in real time. These business resources made an invaluable foundation for coordinating Office Depot's e-commerce activities and customer services with its catalog business and physical stores. Thus, customers can shop at OfficeDepot.com at their home or business, or at in-store kiosks. Then they can choose to pick up their purchases at the stores or have them delivered. In addition, the integration of Web-enabled e-commerce applications within Office Depot's traditional store and catalog operations has helped to increase the traffic at their physical stores and improved the catalog operation's productivity and average order size.

Other Clicks and Bricks Strategies

As Figure 8.19 illustrates, other clicks and bricks strategies range from partial e-commerce integration using joint ventures and strategic partnerships, to complete separation via the spin-off of an independent e-commerce company.

For example, KBtoys.com is an e-commerce joint venture of KB Online Holdings LLC, created by toy retailer KB Toys and BrainPlay.com, formerly an e-tailer of children's products. The company is 80 percent owned by KB Toys, but has independent management teams and separate distribution systems. However, KBtoys.com has successfully capitalized on the shared brand name and buying power of KB Toys, and the ability of its customers to return purchases to over 1,300 KB Toys stores which also heavily promote their e-commerce site.

The strategic partnership of the Rite-Aid retail drugstore chain and Drugstore.com is a good example of a less integrated e-commerce venture. Rite-Aid only owns about 25 percent of Drugstore.com, which has an independent management team and a separate business brand. However, both companies share the decreased costs and increased revenue benefits of joint buying power, an integrated distribution center, co-branded pharmacy products, and joint prescription fulfillment at Rite-Aid stores.

Finally, let's look at an example of the benefits and challenges of a completely separate clicks and bricks strategy. Barnesandnoble.com was created as an independent e-commerce company that was spun off by the Barnes & Noble book retail chain. This enabled it to gain several hundred million dollars in venture capital funding, create an entrepreneurial culture, attract quality management, maintain a high degree of business flexibility, and accelerate decision making. But the book e-retailer has done poorly since its founding, and has failed to gain market share from Amazon.com, its leading competitor. Many business analysts say that the failure of Barnes & Noble to integrate some of the marketing and operations of Barnesandnoble.com within their thousands of bookstores forfeited a key strategic business opportunity.

e-Commerce Channel Choices

Some of the key questions that the management of companies must answer in making a clicks and bricks decision and developing the resulting e-commerce channel are outlined in Figure 8.20. An **e-commerce channel** is the marketing or sales channel created by a company to conduct and manage its chosen e-commerce activities. How this e-commerce channel is integrated with a company's traditional sales channels (retail/wholesale outlets, catalog sales, direct sales, etc.) is a major consideration in developing its e-commerce strategy [15].

Thus, the examples in this section emphasize that there is no universal clicks and bricks e-commerce strategy or e-commerce channel choice for every company, industry, or type of business. Both e-commerce integration and separation have major

FIGURE 8.20

Key questions for developing an e-commerce channel strategy.

A Checklist for Channel Development
1. What audiences are we attempting to reach?
2. What action do we want those audiences to take?—to learn about us, to give us information about themselves, to make an inquiry, to buy something from our site, to buy something through another channel?
3. Who owns the e-commerce channel within the organization?
4. Is the e-commerce channel planned alongside other channels?
5. Do we have a process for generating, approving, releasing, and withdrawing content?
6. Will our brands translate to the new channel or will they require modification?
7. How will we market the channel itself?

business benefits and shortcomings. Thus, deciding on a clicks and bricks strategy and e-commerce channel depends heavily on whether or not a company's unique business operations provide strategic capabilities and resources to successfully support a profitable business model for their e-commerce channel. As these examples show, most companies are implementing some measure of clicks and bricks integration, because "the benefits of integration are almost always too great to abandon entirely" [9].

Citigroup: From Failure to Success in e-Commerce Integration Strategies

Few companies blew more money trying to build independent e-commerce divisions than Citigroup, parent company of Citibank, Salomon Smith Barney, and Travelers Insurance. In 1997, it launched e-Citi with high hopes and a big task. e-Citi's job was to keep all of Citigroup on its toes—partly by competing with the very bank, credit card company, and other businesses that made Citigroup a $230 billion giant. There was to be an e-Citibank called Citi.f/i and a financial portal called Finance.com. The e-Citi unit soon had 1,600 employees and more than 100 U.S. websites. The idea: to cannibalize your business before someone else did.

The only thing e-Citi gobbled was money. Citigroup's e-commerce effort lost over $1 billion between 1998 and 2000. In online banking, for example, Citigroup was so determined to make Citi.f/i an independent operation that customers of the online bank couldn't use Citibank branches. That turned off depositors. The online bank drew 30,000 accounts versus 146 million for the rest of Citigroup's banking operation. By March 2000, word came down from Citigroup Chairman Sandy Weill: E-commerce initiatives must be part of the existing business, not self-appointed upstarts trying to overturn them. "At the beginning of 2000, people were dreaming that you could take e-Citi public," says Deryck C. Maughan, Citigroup's vice-chairman. "I looked very carefully and asked, could it make a profit? Not in our lifetime."

Still, Citigroup wanted to keep e-commerce innovation humming. So in 2000, the company formed an Internet Operating Group of top execs to help Citigroup units share e-business technology and to ensure that they all have a common look and feel.

By 2001, the results were easy to see. The number of online customers were up 80 percent because Citibank and Citi's credit card operations were pushing Web services themselves, instead of leaving that mostly to e-Citi. Citigroup now serves 10 million customers online. e-Citi has scaled back to only 100 people, who implement projects the operating groups propose. The 100 websites have been trimmed to 38. The reported loss for online efforts in the first half of 2001 was down 41 percent, to $67 million, from $114 million a year before. And counting savings from moving procurement, human resources, and other back-office functions online, Citigroup says e-business systems had cut $1 billion off annual costs. "I promise you, we are going to be saving a lot more than we are spending," Maughan pledges [13].

Summary

- **Electronic Commerce.** Electronic commerce encompasses the entire online process of developing, marketing, selling, delivering, servicing, and paying for products and services. The Internet and related technologies and e-commerce websites on the World Wide Web and corporate intranets and extranets serve as the business and technology platform for e-commerce marketplaces for consumers and businesses in the basic categories of business-to-consumer (B2C), business-to-business (B2B), and consumer-to-consumer (C2C) e-commerce. The essential processes that should be implemented in all e-commerce applications—access control and security, personalizing and profiling, search management, content management, catalog management, payment systems, workflow management, event notification, and collaboration and trading—are summarized in Figure 8.4.

- **e-Commerce Issues.** Many e-business enterprises are moving toward offering full-service B2C and B2B e-commerce portals supported by integrated customer-focused processes and internetworked supply chains as illustrated in Figure 8.10. In addition, companies must evaluate a variety of e-commerce integration or separation alternatives and benefit trade-offs when choosing a clicks and bricks strategy and e-commerce channel, as summarized in Figures 8.19 and 8.20.

- **B2C e-Commerce.** Businesses typically sell products and services to consumers at e-commerce websites that provide attractive Web pages, multimedia catalogs, interactive order processing, secure electronic payment systems, and online customer support. However, successful e-tailers build customer satisfaction and loyalty by optimizing factors outlined in Figure 8.12, such as selection and value, performance and service efficiency, the look and feel of the site, advertising and incentives to purchase, personal attention, community relationships, and security and reliability. In addition, a Web store has several key business requirements, including building and marketing a Web business, serving and supporting customers, and managing a Web store, as summarized in Figure 8.14.

- **B2B e-Commerce.** Business-to-business applications of e-commerce involve electronic catalog, exchange, and auction marketplaces that use Internet, intranet, and extranet websites and portals to unite buyers and sellers, as summarized in Figure 8.16 and illustrated in Figure 8.17. Many B2B e-commerce portals are developed and operated for a variety of industries by third-party market-maker companies called infomediaries, which may represent consortiums of major corporations.

Key Terms and Concepts

These are the key terms and concepts of this chapter. The page number of their first explanation is in parentheses.

1. Clicks and bricks alternatives (281)
2. E-commerce channel (282)
3. E-commerce marketplaces (278)
   a. Auction (278)
   b. Catalog (278)
   c. Exchange (278)
   d. Portal (278)
4. E-commerce success factors (271)
5. E-commerce technologies (258)

6. Electronic commerce (256)
   a. Business-to-business (259)
   b. Business-to-consumer (258)
   c. Consumer-to-consumer (260)
7. Electronic data interchange (280)
8. Electronic funds transfer (265)
9. Essential e-commerce processes (260)
   a. Access control and security (260)
   b. Catalog management (262)

c. Collaboration and trading (265)
d. Content management (262)
e. Electronic payment systems (265)
f. Event notification (264)
g. Profiling and personalizing (261)
h. Search management (262)
i. Workflow management (263)

10. Infomediaries (278)
11. Trends in e-commerce (270)
12. Web store requirements (274)

Review Quiz

Match one of the key terms and concepts listed previously with one of the brief examples or definitions that follow. Try to find the best fit for the answers that seem to fit more than one term or concept. Defend your choices.

_____ 1. The online process of developing, marketing, selling, delivering, servicing, and paying for products and services.

_____ 2. Business selling to consumers at retail Web stores is an example.

____ 3. Using an e-commerce portal for auctions by business customers and their suppliers is an example.

____ 4. Using an e-commerce website for auctions among consumers is an example.

____ 5. E-commerce depends on the Internet and the World Wide Web, and on other networks of browser-equipped client/server systems and hypermedia databases.

____ 6. E-commerce applications must implement several major categories of interrelated processes such as search management and catalog management.

____ 7. Helps to establish mutual trust between you and an e-tailer at an e-commerce site.

____ 8. Tracks your website behavior to provide you with an individualized Web store experience.

____ 9. Develops, generates, delivers, and updates information to you at a website.

____ 10. Ensures that proper e-commerce transactions, decisions, and activities are performed to better serve you.

____ 11. Sends you an e-mail when what you ordered at an e-commerce site has been shipped.

____ 12. Includes matchmaking, negotiation, and mediation processes among buyers and sellers.

____ 13. Companies that serve as intermediaries in e-commerce transactions.

____ 14. A website for e-commerce transactions.

____ 15. An e-commerce marketplace that may provide catalog, exchange, or auction service for businesses or consumers.

____ 16. Buyers bidding for the business of a seller.

____ 17. Marketplace for bid (buy) and ask (sell) transactions.

____ 18. The most widely used type of marketplace in B2C e-commerce.

____ 19. The marketing or sales channel created by a company to conduct and manage its e-commerce activities.

____ 20. The processing of money and credit transfers between businesses and financial institutions.

____ 21. Ways to provide efficient, convenient, and secure payments in e-commerce.

____ 22. Companies are increasingly developing full-service B2C and B2B e-commerce portals.

____ 23. Companies can evaluate and choose from several e-commerce integration alternatives.

____ 24. Successful e-commerce retailers build customer satisfaction and loyalty in several key ways.

____ 25. Successful e-commerce ventures must build, market, and manage their Web businesses while serving their customers.

____ 26. The automatic exchange of electronic business documents between the networked computers of business partners.

Discussion Questions

1. Most businesses should engage in electronic commerce on the Internet. Do you agree or disagree with this statement? Explain your position.

2. Are you interested in investing in, owning, managing, or working for a business that is primarily engaged in electronic commerce on the Internet? Explain your position.

3. Refer to the Real World Case on eBay in the chapter. What are the benefits and limitations of being an eBay Power Seller or Trading Assistant?

4. Why do you think there have been so many business failures among "dot-com" companies that were devoted only to retail e-commerce?

5. Do the e-commerce success factors listed in Figure 8.12 guarantee success for an e-commerce business venture? Give a few examples of what else could go wrong and how you would confront such challenges.

6. If personalizing a customer's website experience is a key success factor, then electronic profiling processes to track visitor website behavior are necessary. Do you

agree or disagree with this statement? Explain your position.

7. All corporate procurement should be accomplished in e-commerce auction marketplaces, instead of using B2B websites that feature fixed-price catalogs or negotiated prices. Explain your position on this proposal.

8. Refer to the Real World Case on Corporate Express in the chapter. What are some of the business and IT challenges that companies face in integrating their procurement systems with their customers and suppliers? What are several solutions to such problems?

9. If you were starting an e-commerce Web store, which of the business requirements summarized in Figure 8.14 would you primarily do yourself, and which would you outsource to a Web development or hosting company? Why?

10. Which of the e-commerce clicks and bricks alternatives illustrated in Figure 8.19 would you recommend to Barnes & Noble? Amazon.com? Wal-Mart? Any business? Explain your position.

Analysis Exercises

Complete the following exercises as individual or group projects that apply chapter concepts to real world business situations.

1. bCentral.com: Small Business e-Commerce Portals

On the net, small businesses have become big business. And a really big business, Microsoft, wants a piece of the action. The company's bCentral Web portal (www.bcental.com) is one of many sites offering advice and services for small businesses moving online. Most features, whether free or paid, are what you'd expect: lots of links and information along the lines established by Prodigy Biz (www.prodigybiz.com) or Entrabase.com. bCentral, however, stands out for its affordable advertising and marketing services. See Figure 8.21.

FIGURE 8.21

Microsoft's bCentral is a small business e-commerce portal.

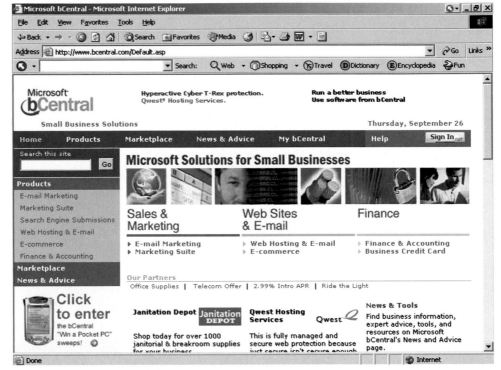

Source: Courtesy of Microsoft Corp.

One bCentral program helps businesses create banner ads and places them on a collection of websites that it claims are visited by 60% of the web surfing community. With its "Banner Network Ads" program, buyers don't pay a huge fee up front, and they don't run the risk that a huge number of visitors will unexpectedly drive up click-through commissions. Instead, this program allows small business to pay a small, fixed fee for a guaranteed number of click-throughs (people who click on your banner ad in order to visit your website). bCentral rotates these banner ads around a network of participating websites and removes the ad as soon as it has received the guaranteed number of click-through visitors. This eliminates the guesswork regarding both traffic and fees. The three packages, 100, 250, and 1,000 visitors, break down to 50 cents per visitor.

a. Check out bCentral and the other e-commerce portals mentioned. Identify several benefits and limitations for a business using these websites.

b. Which website is your favorite? Why?

c. Which site would you recommend or use to help a small business wanting to get into e-commerce? Why?

2. e-Commerce Websites for Car Buying

Nowadays new car buyers can configure the car of their dreams on Microsoft's MSN Autos website as well as those of Ford, GM, and other auto giants. Many independent online car purchase and research companies offer similar services. See Figure 8.22. Car buying information provided by manufacturers, brokerage sites, car dealers, financial institutions, and consumer advocate websites has exploded in the past few years.

Yet in the age of the Internet, the auto industry remains a steadfast holdout to innovations that might threaten the well established and well connected supply chain, the car dealership. U.S. new car buyers simply cannot skip the middleman and purchase an automobile directly from the manufacturer. That's not simply a business decision by the manufacturers either; that's the law.

Even so, many car buyers use the Internet as a place to research their purchases. Instead of selling new cars directly, websites such as Autobytel.com of Irvine, California, simply put consumers in touch with a local dealer where they test drive a vehicle and negotiate a price. Autobytel.com has been referring buyers to new and used car dealers since 1995. They also offer online financing and insurance.

Online car buying sites on the Web make consumers less dependent on what cars a dealer has on the lot. At online sites, buyers can customize a car—or van, truck, or sport utility vehicle—by selecting trim, paint, color, and other options before purchase. They can also use

websites such as CarBuyingTips.com to help prepare for the final negotiating process.

a. Check out several of the websites shown in Figure 8.22. Evaluate them based on ease of use, relevance of information provided, and other criteria you feel are important. Don't forget the classic: "Did they make you want to buy?"

b. Which sites would you use or recommend if you or a friend actually wanted to buy a car? Why?

c. Check out the Consumer Federation of America's study on anti-competitive new car buying state laws or similar studies online. How much do they estimate consumers would save if they could purchase cars directly from manufacturers online?

FIGURE 8.22

Top Car Buying Websites

- **Autobytel.com   www.autobytel.com**
  Enter make and model, and a local dealer will contact you with a price offer. Home delivery is an option.

- **AutoNation   www.autonation.com**
  Every make and model available, as well as financing and insurance information, home delivery, and test drives.

- **Microsoft MSN Autos   www.autos.msn.com**
  Auto reviews, detailed vehicle specifications, safety ratings, and buying services for new and used cars, including customizing your very own Ford.

- **cars.com   www.cars.com**
  Research tools include automotive reviews, model reports, dealer locators, and financing information.

- **CarsDirect.com   www.carsdirect.com**
  Research price and design, then order your car. CarsDirect will deliver it to your home. A top-rated site.

- **Edmunds.com   www.edmunds.com**
  For an objective opinion, Edmunds.com provides reviews, safety updates, and rebate news for car buyers.

- **FordVehicles.com   www.fordvehicles.com**
  Research, configure, price, and order your new Ford car, minivan, truck, or SUV at this website.

- **GM BuyPower   www.gmbuypower.com**
  With access to nearly 6,000 GM dealerships, car shoppers can get a price quote, schedule a test drive, and buy.

3. Comparing e-Commerce Sites
In this exercise you will experiment with electronic shopping and compare alternative electronic commerce sites. First you will need to select a category of product widely available on the Web such as books, CDs, toys, etcetera. Next select five specific products to price on the Internet, e.g., five specific CDs you might be interested in buying. Search three prominent e-commerce sites selling this type of product and record the price charged for each product by each site.

a. Using a spreadsheet, record a set of information similar to that shown for each product. (Categories describing the product will vary depending upon the type of product you select—Ds might require the title of the CD and the performer[s], while toys or similar products would require the name of the product and its description.)

b. For each product, rank each company based on the price charged. Give a rating of 1 for the lowest price and 3 for the highest and split the ratings for ties— two sites tying for 1st and 2nd lowest price would each receive a 1.5. If a site does not have one of the products available for sale, give that site a rating of 4 for that product. Add the ratings across your products to produce an overall price/availability rating for each site.

c. Based on your experience with these sites, rate them on their ease of use, completeness of information, and

order-filling and shipping options. As in part b, give a rating of 1 to the site you feel is best in each category, a 2 to the second best, and a 3 to the poorest site.

d. Prepare a set of PowerPoint slides or similar presentation materials summarizing the key results and including an overall assessment of the sites you compared.

TABLE 8.1

Title of Book	Author	Price Site A	Site B	Site C	Rating A	B	C
The Return of Little Big Man	Berger, T.	15.00	16.95	14.50	2	3	1
Learning Perl/Tk	Walsh, N. & Mui, L.	26.36	25.95	25.95	3	11.5	1.5
Business at the Speed of Thought	Gates, W.	21.00	22.95	21.00	1.5	3	1.5
Murders for the Holidays	Smith, G.		8.25	7.95	4	2	1
Designs for Dullards	Jones	17.95	18.50	18.50	1	2.5	3
Sum of ratings (low score represents most favorable rating)					11.5	12	8

4. e-Commerce: The Dark Side

Anonymous transactions on the Internet can have a dark side. Research each of the terms below on the web. Prepare a one page report for each term researched. Your paper should describe the problem and provide examples and illustrations where possible. Conclude each paper with recommendations on how to guard against each type of fraud.

a. Search using the terms "Ponzi Scheme" or "Pyramid Scheme." To find current examples in action, try searching for "plasma TV $50," "cash matrix," or "e-books" and "matrix," or "gifting" through a search engine or action site.

b. Search using the terms "phishing" and "identity." If possible include a printout of a real-world example

that you or an acquaintance may have received via e-mail.

c. Search using the term "third party escrow." What legitimate function does this serve? Provide an example of a legitimate third party escrow service for Internet transactions. How has the third party escrow system been used to commit fraud on the Internet?

d. Prepare a one page paper describing a type of online fraud not covered above. Prepare presentation materials and present your findings to the class. Be sure to include a description of the fraud, how to detect it, and how to avoid it. Use real-world illustrations if possible.

REAL WORLD CASE 3

E-Trade and Wells Fargo: The Business Case for Clicks and Bricks e-Commerce

E-Trade Inc. (www.etrade.com), should be gone—just like eToys, eAuto, and every other company founded on the belief that the prefix "e" exempted it from all the rules of business. So why is E-Trade not only still alive, but posted its largest profit ever—$36 million in the last quarter of 2002—when so many other online brokerages are either losing money or gone? Because E-Trade's survival is a victory not just for the new economy, but also for a key tenet of the old one: diversification.

During the past three years, E-Trade has moved beyond being a mere online brokerage to become the nation's 62nd-largest bank (bigger, for example, than Capital One), with $17 billion in assets and more than 500,000 accounts. Banking revenues—which last year topped $457 million, 35 percent of the company's total—have provided a lifesaving cushion.

E-Trade started its diversification campaign back in 1999, at the apex of the stock mania, when it gobbled up Telebanc Financial, a branchless bank, for $1.8 billion in stock. At the time, the move was widely criticized as a costly distraction from its core trading business. But the move allowed E-Trade to begin offering its customers and investors risk-free alternatives such as savings accounts, money-market checking accounts, and certificates of deposit.

Subsequent acquisitions brought E-Trade the nation's second-largest ATM network and, in February 2001, an entry into the mortgage origination business. The latter was especially timely, as it gave E-Trade a way to capitalize on the cooling economy's hottest sector. Since online banking's overhead is low, E-Trade can also offer savings yields more than twice the national average and loan rates that match or beat those of its brick-and-mortar competitors.

Still, diversification offers only so much protection in a weak or recovering economy. To further bolster its staying power, E-Trade has deliberately shed its free-spending dot-com ways and implemented a rigorous cost reduction program. All told, the company has squeezed $250 million out of its operating costs. So the new E-trade is in much better shape to expand on its present diversified business success.

Wells Fargo. At a 1999 meeting of Wells Fargo (www.wellsfargo.com) commercial banking executives, Steve Ellis asked the largest bank west of the Mississippi to radically reinvent itself online. As if that weren't stressful enough, just as he walked in to make his presentation, he learned that CEO Richard M. Kovacevich would be sitting in.

Ellis argued that it was time to allow Wells Fargo's wholesale customers—companies with revenues of $10 million and up—to do all their banking on the Web. It would make life far easier for the clients and allow wholesale banking reps to spend less time on routine services and more time selling new ones. Ellis cautioned that the system would not be cheap, requiring a total of 140 people and a budget in the tens of millions. At the end of Ellis's presentation, Kovace-

vich gave him the green light—with one condition: The online project had to be profitable.

Launched in July 2000, the Commercial Electronic Office (C.E.O.) is a one-stop shop on the Web for corporate banking needs, ranging from foreign exchange loan servicing to quarter-billion-dollar wire transfers. The C.E.O. turned profitable in April 2002, but the real payoff came during the next 12 months: As other big banks suffered along with their recession-wracked corporate customers, Wells Fargo's Internet-based revenues grew 25 percent. More than half of the bank's 30,000 wholesale customers are now signed up.

Where do the profits come from? Essentially from the Net's ability to deepen client relationships. "We found that the longer a customer has been online," says Danny Peltz, who now runs the wholesale Internet group that Ellis established, "the more of our products he is likely to have."

The Web's success at cross selling makes perfect sense: Regular Web users are exposed to all of Wells Fargo's banking products when they log on, and the bank's sales force emphasizes that if customers sign up for new services, they can access them through the same familiar interface. In 2000, more than half of Wells Fargo's commercial customers banked primarily with another institution. Today most consider Wells Fargo their main bank, and the average customer buys five Wells products.

Like many forays onto the Web, there were some mistakes. For example, Ellis and his team originally assumed that the C.E.O. needed to be a destination site, or portal. But Wells quickly learned that clients didn't care about financial news feeds or e-procurement of business supplies. So Ellis and Peltz focused on what customers *did* want: convenience, instantaneous account information, and, most of all, industrial-strength security and access controls.

Ellis, now executive VP for wholesale services, downplays C.E.O.'s role in Wells Fargo's corporate banking success. The Web is just one of the doors the bank opens to customers, he says, modestly. But Kovacevich brushes that aside. "I don't think our customers could live without the Internet," he says.

Case Study Questions

1. What lessons in business strategy can be applied to development of the e-commerce channels of other companies from the experience of E-Trade?

2. What is the business value of the C.E.O. online wholesale banking portal to Wells Fargo?

3. What can other companies learn from the successes and mistakes of the Wells Fargo e-commerce system?

Source: Adapted from Mark Athitakis and Thomas Mucha, "How to Make Money on the Net," *Business 2.0*, May 2003, pp. 83–90.

Providence Washington Insurance and Tharco: The Business Value of an Online Customer Interface

Buried under an avalanche of paper requests for insurance bids, Providence Washington Insurance Co. (www.providencewashington.com) sometimes took weeks to reply—a delay that proved costly. "We felt that we lost business in the past because we were too slow to get price quotations out," says Edward N. Leveille, vice president of systems and CIO at the East Providence, Rhode Island, insurance firm. The solution was a Web-based price quotation system—an extranet portal for independent insurance agents—that has sped up the accurate delivery of bids for custom business insurance contracts. The new Web-based system automates the sales process and saves money on internal paper shuffling.

In a tight budget year, e-commerce projects haven't lost their appeal. *Computerworld's* Premier 100 IT Leaders ranked e-commerce projects fourth on their list of top priorities for 2003. But the rules have changed. Required payback times are shorter, often no more than a year. And e-commerce initiatives tend to focus on improving order taking or sales-lead management, tuning the sales channel, or creating business partner self-service portals.

"The goal of e-commerce these days is to increase your sales volume with the same number of employees in order to bring down the cost per transaction," says Gene Alvarez, vice president of electronic-business strategies at Meta Group Inc. in Stamford, Connecticut. If you can take phone or fax transactions and do them via the Web, you can save money."

With Providence Washington's extranet portal, independent insurance agents no longer need to submit paper bid requests to the company via fax or conventional mail. The portal also replaces the time-consuming process of keying information into the computer system. With the new portal, Providence Washington will be able to make bids in minutes, versus taking up to three weeks with the paper-based system.

The e-commerce initiative started with a pilot project by agents in 2 states using the extranet portal to submit requests for bids, but will soon be expanded to agents in 14 additional states. The 18-month project cost about $3 million and is expected to reap a return on investment within three years, Leveille says. Payback should come from a combination of improved internal productivity and additional insurance revenue through the agents, he says.

Tharco. At Tharco Inc. (www.tharco.com) in San Lorenzo, California, a new Web-based e-commerce project allows customers to check on the availability of different types of packaging materials, create and track orders, and verify order delivery on the Web.

Tharco—which makes corrugated and foam packaging materials for customers such as electronics firms, grocery stores, and wineries—was looking for an interactive e-business approach that would both engage customers and cut Tharco's internal costs. It chose a Web front-end order processing system from Haht Commerce Inc. to interface with its own SAP enterprise resource planning system. Obtaining orders over the Web reduced the company's reliance on the customer service representatives, who typically receive orders by phone or fax and then key the orders into the computer system, says Bill Picton, Tharco's MIS director. "It saves money for us and for the customers, and it means one less chance for error in the order. And because it's linked to our SAP system, customers get specific, real-time pricing on every order." Picton says.

The Web-based ordering succeeded where earlier e-commerce attempts had failed. One unsuccessful approach involved a noninteractive catalog that didn't include prices. Another failure was a third-party Web-based hosting arrangement that didn't eliminate enough paperwork, Picton says.

Tharco's Web ordering method has proved popular with customers since it went live in March 2001, and it now accounts for about 10 percent of the firm's off-the-shelf packaging materials business, or about 6.5 percent of total revenue, Picton says. That success came partly because Tharco aggressively marketed the project to its customers. "We had to reach out to them and show the people who do the daily ordering how it works," Picton says. "We sent our people to the customers' facilities to train them in using it. Then we had to let customers try it out for free for a week. That was the only way that customers got into it."

Tharco's three-month Web project cost less than $1 million and has already paid for itself, Picton says. "We're waiting to show a real profit," he says. "But as the economy picks up, we will be able to support several times our current revenue with the combination of our existing customer service staff and this Web type of business approach."

Case Study Questions

1. What are the business reasons why even "in a tight budget year, e-commerce projects have not lost their appeal" and are still highly ranked by IT leaders from many companies?

2. What is the business value of Providence Washington's extranet portal? Of Tharco's Web-based order processing system?

3. What lessons on developing successful e-commerce projects for small businesses can be gained from the information in this case?

CHAPTER 9

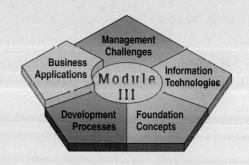

DECISION SUPPORT SYSTEMS

Chapter Highlights

Section I

Decision Support in Business

Introduction

Real World Case: Ben & Jerry's and GE Plastics: The Business Value of Business Intelligence

Decision Support Trends

Management Information Systems

Online Analytical Processing

Decision Support Systems

Using Decision Support Systems

Executive Information Systems

Enterprise Portals and Decision Support

Knowledge Management Systems

Section II

Artificial Intelligence Technologies in Business

Business and AI

Real World Case: Wal-Mart, BankFinancial, and HP: The Business Value of AI

An Overview of Artificial Intelligence

Neural Networks

Fuzzy Logic Systems

Genetic Algorithms

Virtual Reality

Intelligent Agents

Expert Systems

Developing Expert Systems

Real World Case: Procter & Gamble and Others: Using Agent-Based Modeling for Supply Chain Management

Real World Case: Boehringer Ingelheim: Using Web-Based Tools for Financial Analysis and Reporting

Learning Objectives

After reading and studying this chapter, you should be able to:

1. Identify the changes taking place in the form and use of decision support in business.

2. Identify the role and reporting alternatives of management information systems.

3. Describe how online analytical processing can meet key information needs of managers.

4. Explain the decision support system concept and how it differs from traditional management information systems.

5. Explain how the following information systems can support the information needs of executives, managers, and business professionals:

   a. Executive information systems

   b. Enterprise information portals

   c. Knowledge management systems

6. Identify how neural networks, fuzzy logic, genetic algorithms, virtual reality, and intelligent agents can be used in business.

7. Give examples of several ways expert systems can be used in business decision-making situations.

SECTION I   Decision Support in Business

Introduction

As companies migrate toward responsive e-business models, they are investing in new data-driven decision support application frameworks that help them respond rapidly to changing market conditions and customer needs [26].

So to succeed in business today, companies need information systems that can support the diverse information and decision-making needs of their managers and business professionals. In this section, we will explore in more detail how this is accomplished by several types of management information, decision support, and other information systems. We will concentrate our attention on how the Internet, intranets, and other Web-enabled information technologies have significantly strengthened the role that information systems play in supporting the decision-making activities of every manager and knowledge worker in business.

Analyzing Ben & Jerry's and GE Plastics

Read the Real World Case on Ben & Jerry's and GE Plastics on the next page. We can learn a lot from this case about the business value of business intelligence. See Figure 9.1.

Ben & Jerry's is a good example of the many companies that are using or implementing the software tools for analysis and reporting that are included under the umbrella-term of "business intelligence." Many of these tools are new Web-based variations of the management information systems and decision support systems that have been used in business for many years. Only now they are more easily available and usable by many business professionals and managers on company intranets and the Web. And one popular form the user interface of these BI systems is taking is the digital dashboard. At GE Plastics, over 300 managers can get business intelligence

FIGURE 9.1

GE Plastics CIO John Seral led the development of Web-based "digital cockpits" for reporting vital business statistics to over 300 managers that replaces dozens of analysts and management reports.

Source: Ann States.

**REAL WORLD
CASE 1**

Ben & Jerry's and GE Plastics: The Business Value of Business Intelligence

In the company's headquarters in Burlington, Vermont, just miles from where the founders opened their first shop 25 years ago, the life of each pint of Ben & Jerry's ice cream—from ingredients to sale—is tracked. Once the pint is stamped and sent out the door to over 50,000 stores in the United States and 12 other countries, Ben & Jerry's (www.benjerry.com), places its tracking number in an Oracle database; then it puts it under the microscope.

Using software from a company called Business Objects, the sales team can check to see if Chocolate Chip Cookie Dough is gaining ground on Cherry Garcia for the coveted No. 1 sales position. Down the hall in the marketing department, the company checks to see whether orders online require Ben & Jerry's to make a donation to one of its philanthropies. The finance people pop the number into their journals to show results. Since they started using the software, they've sharply cut the time it takes to close their monthly books. And the consumer affairs staff matches up the pint with the 225 calls and e-mails received each week, checking to see if there were any complaints, and if so, which supplier didn't meet the company's near-obsession with quality.

Ben & Jerry's may cultivate a down home image, but as a unit of $47-billion-a-year UK-conglomerate Unilever, it depends heavily on statistics for its success. To get those figures, it relies on business intelligence (BI) software: a plain-vanilla name for programs that crunch huge quantities of data in search of trends, problems, or new business opportunities.

While the concept of BI is hardly new, many of the companies and people using it are. Industrial giants like GE and Procter & Gamble have been slicing and dicing their data with a variety of analytical and reporting software tools for decades; now, pharmaceutical manufacturers, retailers, and other industries are demanding those tools and more.

Part of the interest comes from increasing pressure on CIOs to deliver on the investments they've made in information systems in the past few years. BI software is seen as an attractive way to do that. The software is relatively inexpensive—it typically costs between $35,000 and $75,000, though large enterprise installations can cost millions—and is easy to set up. Ben & Jerry's needed only a few weeks to install its system, whereas a large-scale data mining project can take years.

Until now diving through data was reserved for experts who would generate massive reports that would be handed out during meetings, flipped through, then shelved. BI companies now promise that anyone can use the technology. Typical BI applications first pull information out of giant data warehouses into so-called data marts—smaller clusters of information that can keep financial data in one area, inventory data in another. Then BI software is ready for the hunt.

When a Ben & Jerry's marketing manager wants to know, say, what the hottest-selling flavor has been in the last month, the BI software has to gather the relevant data from the right data mart, organize it, analyze it, translate it back, and offer an answer. The employee sees only the last part. And now just about every BI company offers stand-alone or browser-based software that the industry calls "dashboards," which presents graphical displays of inventory levels, sales info, and other urgent business intelligence of day-to-day business operations.

GE Plastics. "When the CEO asked how the quarter was looking," GE Plastics (www.geplastics.com) chief information officer John Seral explains, "he got a different answer depending on whom he asked. You had to ask an analyst, who'd use a query tool to dig the information out, then release a report. It could take hours or days." It just took too long for managers to get updates on sales and operations.

GE vice chairman Gary Rogers first hatched the idea for a digital dashboard—the continuously updated online display of business intelligence in the form of a company's vital stats. But it fell to Seral to build the system. GE Plastic's new "digital cockpits" now give over 300 managers access to the company's essential data—on desktop PCs and Blackberry PDAs. The old system required dozens of analysts to compile information and send it up the line; Seral's dashboards have slimmed down those ranks to six.

To get the project launched, Seral first asked several senior managers—from quality assurance, manufacturing, and IT—to decide what data each division would contribute. Then he hired an IT crew to enforce data input. The BI numbers he could generate would be a day old, but that was a fair compromise. "Live data would've cost 10 times more," Seral says, "and the payback wasn't there." Costs came in at just under $1 million—cheap for something that would link up senior management at a company with 11,000 workers, "This wasn't just an IT feat," Seral says. "It was about changing the culture so everyone has a common way to look at the business."

Case Study Questions

1. What is business intelligence? Why are BI systems becoming such a popular business application of IT?

2. What is the business value of Ben & Jerry's business intelligence system? Is their BI system an MIS or DSS? Explain.

3. What are the benefits and limitations of the "digital cockpits" of GE Plastics? Are these an example of an MIS or DSS? Explain.

Sources: Adapted from Julie Schlosser, "Looking for Intelligence in Ice Cream," *Fortune*, March 17, 2003, pp. 114–120; Bob Tedeschi, "End of the Paper Chase," *Business 2.0*, March 2003, p. 64; and Alice Dragoon, "Business Intelligence Gets Smarter," *CIO Magazine*, September 15, 2003, pp. 63–65.

FIGURE 9.2

Information requirements of decision makers. The type of information required by directors, executives, managers, and members of self-directed teams is directly related to the level of management decision making involved and the structure of decision situations they face.

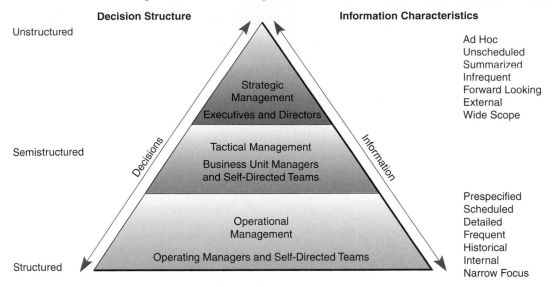

delivered to them in the form of a Web-based digital cockpit display of their company's vital sales and operating statistics.

Information, Decisions, and Management

Figure 9.2 emphasizes that the type of information required by decision makers in a company is directly related to the **level of management decision making** and the amount of structure in the decision situations they face. You should realize that the framework of the classic *managerial pyramid* shown in Figure 9.2 applies even in today's *downsized organizations* and *flattened* or nonhierarchical organizational structures. Levels of management decision making still exist, but their size, shape, and participants continue to change as today's fluid organizational structures evolve. Thus, the levels of managerial decision making that must be supported by information technology in a successful organization are:

- **Strategic Management.** Typically, a board of directors and an executive committee of the CEO and top executives develop overall organizational goals, strategies, policies, and objectives as part of a strategic planning process. They also monitor the strategic performance of the organization and its overall direction in the political, economic, and competitive business environment.

- **Tactical Management.** Increasingly, business professionals in self-directed teams as well as business unit managers develop short- and medium-range plans, schedules, and budgets and specify the policies, procedures, and business objectives for their subunits of the company. They also allocate resources and monitor the performance of their organizational subunits, including departments, divisions, process teams, project teams, and other workgroups.

- **Operational Management.** The members of self-directed teams or operating managers develop short-range plans such as weekly production schedules. They direct the use of resources and the performance of tasks according to procedures and within budgets and schedules they establish for the teams and other workgroups of the organization.

Information Quality

What characteristics would make information products valuable and useful to you? One way to answer this important question is to examine the characteristics or attributes of **information quality.** Information that is outdated, inaccurate, or hard to understand would not be very meaningful, useful, or valuable to you or other business professionals. People want information of high quality, that is, information products

FIGURE 9.3

A summary of the attributes of information quality. This outlines the attributes that should be present in high-quality information products.

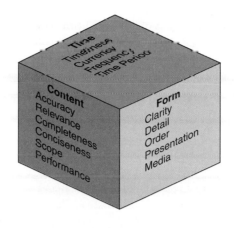

Time Dimension

Timeliness	Information should be provided when it is needed.
Currency	Information should be up-to-date when it is provided.
Frequency	Information should be provided as often as needed.
Time Period	Information can be provided about past, present, and future time periods.

Content Dimension

Accuracy	Information should be free from errors.
Relevance	Information should be related to the information needs of a specific recipient for a specific situation.
Completeness	All the information that is needed should be provided.
Conciseness	Only the information that is needed should be provided.
Scope	Information can have a broad or narrow scope, or an internal or external focus.
Performance	Information can reveal performance by measuring activities accomplished, progress made, or resources accumulated.

Form Dimension

Clarity	Information should be provided in a form that is easy to understand.
Detail	Information can be provided in detail or summary form.
Order	Information can be arranged in a predetermined sequence.
Presentation	Information can be presented in narrative, numeric, graphic, or other forms.
Media	Information can be provided in the form of printed paper documents, video displays, or other media.

whose characteristics, attributes, or qualities make the information more valuable to them. It is useful to think of information as having the three dimensions of time, content, and form. Figure 9.3 summarizes the important attributes of information quality and groups them into these three dimensions.

Decision Structure

Decisions made at the operational management level tend to be more *structured*, those at the tactical level more *semistructured*, and those at the strategic management level more *unstructured*. Structured decisions involve situations where the procedures to follow when a decision is needed can be specified in advance. The inventory reorder decisions faced by most businesses are a typical example. Unstructured decisions involve decision situations where it is not possible to specify in advance most of the decision procedures to follow. At best, many decision situations are semistructured. That is, some decision procedures can be prespecified, but not enough to lead to a definite recommended decision. For example, decisions involved in starting a new line of e-commerce services or making major changes to employee benefits would probably range from unstructured to semistructured. Figure 9.4 provides a variety of examples of business decisions by type of decision structure and level of management [21].

Therefore, information systems must be designed to produce a variety of information products to meet the changing needs of decision makers throughout an organization. For example, decision makers at the strategic management level may look to

FIGURE 9.4   Examples of decisions by the type of decision structure and by level of management.

Decision Structure	Operational Management	Tactical Management	Strategic Management
Unstructured	Cash management	Business process reengineering	New e-business initiatives
		Workgroup performance analysis	Company reorganization
Semistructured	Credit management	Employee performance appraisal	Product planning
	Production scheduling	Capital budgeting	Mergers and acquisitions
	Daily work assignment	Program budgeting	Site location
Structured	Inventory control	Program control	

decision support systems to provide them with more summarized, ad hoc, unscheduled reports, forecasts, and external intelligence to support their more unstructured planning and policy-making responsibilities. Decision makers at the operational management level, on the other hand, may depend on *management information systems* to supply more prespecified internal reports emphasizing detailed current and historical data comparisons that support their more structured responsibilities in day-to-day operations. Figure 9.5 compares the information and decision support capabilities of management information systems and decision support systems which we will explore in this chapter.

Decision Support Trends

The emerging class of applications focuses on personalized decision support, modeling, information retrieval, data warehousing, what-if scenarios, and reporting [26].

As we discussed in Chapter 1, using information systems to support business decision making has been one of the primary thrusts of the business use of information technology. However, during the 1990s, both academic researchers and business practitioners began reporting that the traditional managerial focus originating in classic management information systems (1960s), decision support systems (1970s), and executive information systems (1980s) was expanding. The fast pace of new information technologies like PC hardware and software suites, client/server networks, and networked PC versions of DSS/EIS software made decision support available to lower levels of management, as well as to nonmanagerial individuals and self-directed teams of business professionals [18, 37, 42].

This trend has accelerated with the dramatic growth of the Internet and intranets and extranets that internetwork companies and their stakeholders. The e-business and

FIGURE 9.5

Comparing the major differences in the information and decision support capabilities of management information systems and decision support systems.

	Management Information Systems	Decision Support Systems
● Decision support provided	Provide information about the performance of the organization	Provide information and decision support techniques to analyze specific problems or opportunities
● Information form and frequency	Periodic, exception, demand, and push reports and responses	Interactive inquiries and responses
● Information format	Prespecified, fixed format	Ad hoc, flexible, and adaptable format
● Information processing methodology	Information produced by extraction and manipulation of business data	Information produced by analytical modeling of business data

FIGURE 9.6

A business must meet the information and data analysis requirements of their stakeholders with more personalized and proactive Web-based decision support.

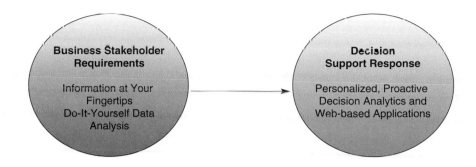

e-commerce initiatives that are being implemented by many companies are also expanding the information and decision support uses and expectations of a company's employees, managers, customers, suppliers, and other business partners. Figure 9.6 illustrates that all business stakeholders expect easy and instant access to information and Web-enabled self-service data analysis [26]. Today's businesses are responding with a variety of personalized and proactive Web-based analytical techniques to support the decision-making requirements of all of their constituents.

Thus, the growth of corporate intranets, extranets, as well as the Web, has accelerated the development and use of "executive class" information delivery and decision support software tools by lower levels of management and by individuals and teams of business professionals. In addition, this dramatic expansion has opened the door to the use of such **business intelligence** (BI) tools by the suppliers, customers, and other business stakeholders of a company for customer relationship management, supply chain management, and other e-business applications.

Figure 9.7 highlights several major information technologies which are being customized, personalized, and Web-enabled to provide key business information and analytical tools for managers, business professionals, and business stakeholders [24, 25, 32, 46]. We will highlight the trend toward such business intelligence applications in the various types of information and decision support systems that are discussed in this chapter.

Cisco Systems: MIS Dashboard	At Cisco (www.cisco.com), company executives say that ideally, everyone in the business should have access to real-time information. "The whole corporation is moving to real time," says Mike Zill, director of sales and finance IT at Cisco. "It's difficult to have applications stay in batch mode when the business architecture is message-based."

Channel account managers in the sales department use a Web-based "dashboard," or graphical user interface–based view, from OneChannel Inc. that gives them real-time

FIGURE 9.7

Business intelligence applications are based on personalized and Web-enabled information analysis, knowledge management, and decision support technologies.

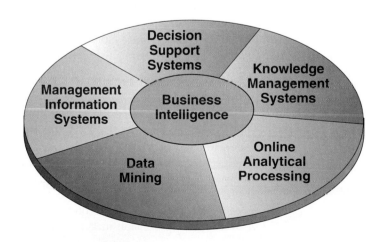

views of their accounts' activities. When a business condition hits a predetermined threshold, the software triggers an alert, sending a message or warning to the user's dashboard. For example, if Cisco's sales department has a top-10 list of new products it wants sold through, say, Ingram Micro, the application will let the Cisco channel manager know the instant the distributor's sales fall outside target levels.

To achieve this, Cisco had to build deep hooks into its supply chain, which wasn't easy to develop. The firm has established agreements with its partners to receive point-of-sale data via the Internet or, in some cases, through electronic data interchange. However, most of the data are batched. Few partners will feed real-time point-of-sale data to the company, Zill says.

Once it receives the data, Cisco couples it with real-time Web-based inventory information and processes it using analytics software from Hyperion Solutions Corp. Channel managers can then query the Hyperion software in detail through the OneChannel dashboard to find the underlying causes of any distribution problem. "The response time is fast enough so you're not waiting," Zill says. And that's the essence of real time for any user [22].

Management Information Systems

Management information systems were the original type of information system developed to support managerial decision making. An MIS produces information products that support many of the day-to-day decision-making needs of managers and business professionals. Reports, displays, and responses produced by management information systems provide information that these decision makers have specified in advance as adequately meeting their information needs. Such predefined information products satisfy the information needs of decision makers at the operational and tactical levels of the organization who are faced with more structured types of decision situations. For example, sales managers rely heavily on sales analysis reports to evaluate differences in performance among salespeople who sell the same types of products to the same types of customers. They have a pretty good idea of the kinds of information about sales results (by product line, sales territory, customer, salesperson, and so on) that they need to manage sales performance effectively.

Managers and other decision makers use an MIS to request information at their networked workstations that supports their decision-making activities. This information takes the form of periodic, exception, and demand reports and immediate responses to inquiries. Web browsers, application programs, and database management software provide access to information in the intranet and other operational databases of the organization. Remember, operational databases are maintained by transaction processing systems. Data about the business environment are obtained from Internet or extranet databases when necessary.

Management Reporting Alternatives

Management information systems provide a variety of information products to managers. Four major reporting alternatives are provided by such systems.

- **Periodic Scheduled Reports.** This traditional form of providing information to managers uses a prespecified format designed to provide managers with information on a regular basis. Typical examples of such periodic scheduled reports are daily or weekly sales analysis reports and monthly financial statements.

- **Exception Reports.** In some cases, reports are produced only when exceptional conditions occur. In other cases, reports are produced periodically but contain information only about these exceptional conditions. For example, a credit manager can be provided with a report that contains only information on customers who exceed their credit limits. Exception reporting reduces *information overload*, instead of overwhelming decision makers with periodic detailed reports of business activity.

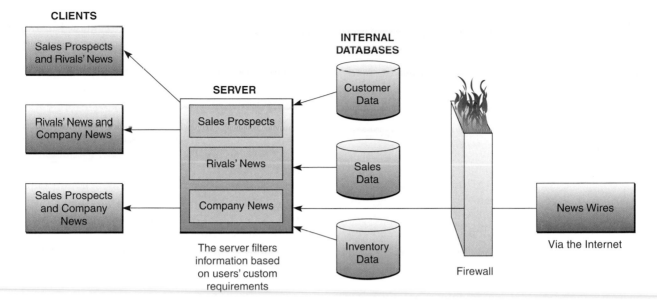

FIGURE 9.8 An example of the components in a marketing intelligence system that uses the Internet and a corporate intranet system to "push" information to employees.

- **Demand Reports and Responses.** Information is available whenever a manager demands it. For example, Web browsers and DBMS query languages and report generators enable managers at PC workstations to get immediate responses or find and obtain customized reports as a result of their requests for the information they need. Thus, managers do not have to wait for periodic reports to arrive as scheduled.

- **Push Reporting.** Information is *pushed* to a manager's networked workstation. Thus, many companies are using webcasting software to selectively broadcast reports and other information to the networked PCs of managers and specialists over their corporate intranets. See Figure 9.8.

| Microsoft: The Impact of MIS on District Sales Managers | At Microsoft, our information systems have changed the role of our district sales managers. When MS Sales (our intranet-based revenue measurement system) first came online, our Minneapolis general manager ran a variety of numbers for her district at a level of detail never possible before. She discovered that excellent sales among other customer segments were obscuring a poor showing among large customers in her district. In fact, the district was dead last among U.S. districts in that category. Finding that out was a shock but also a big motivator for the large-customer teams in the district. By the end of the year Minneapolis was the top-growing district for sales to large customers.

If you're a district manager at Microsoft today, you must be more than a good sales leader helping your team close the big deals, which has been the traditional district sales manager role. Now you can be a business thinker. You have numbers to help you run your business. Before, even if you were concerned about the retail store revenue in your area, you had no view whatsoever of those results. Now you can look at sales figures and evaluate where your business is strong, where your business is weak, and where your business has its greatest potential, product by product, relative to other districts. You can try out new promotions and see their impact. You can talk to other managers about what they're doing to get strong results. Being a district sales manager in our organization is a much broader role than what it was five years ago because of the digital tools we've developed and their ease of use [19]. |

Online Analytical Processing

At a recent stockholder meeting, the CEO of PepsiCo, D. Wayne Calloway, said: "Ten years ago I could have told you how Doritos were selling west of the Mississippi. Today, not only can I tell you how well Doritos sell west of the Mississippi, I can also tell you how well they are selling in California, in Orange County, in the town of Irvine, in the local Vons supermarket, in the special promotion, at the end of Aisle 4, on Thursdays" [47].

The competitive and dynamic nature of today's global business environment is driving demands by business managers and analysts for information systems that can provide fast answers to complex business queries. The IS industry has responded to these demands with developments like analytical databases, data marts, data warehouses, data mining techniques, and multidimensional database structures (discussed in Chapter 5), and with specialized servers and Web-enabled software products that support **online analytical processing** (OLAP).

Online analytical processing enables managers and analysts to interactively examine and manipulate large amounts of detailed and consolidated data from many perspectives. OLAP involves analyzing complex relationships among thousands or even millions of data items stored in data marts, data warehouses, and other multidimensional databases to discover patterns, trends, and exception conditions. An OLAP session takes place online in real time, with rapid responses to a manager's or analyst's queries, so that their analytical or decision-making process is undisturbed. See Figure 9.9.

Online analytical processing involves several basic analytical operations, including consolidation, "drill-down," and "slicing and dicing." See Figure 9.10.

- **Consolidation.** Consolidation involves the aggregation of data. This can involve simple roll-ups or complex groupings involving interrelated data. For example, sales offices can be rolled up to districts and districts rolled up to regions.

- **Drill-Down.** OLAP can go in the reverse direction and automatically display detail data that comprise consolidated data. This is called drill-down. For example, the sales by individual products or sales reps that make up a region's sales totals could be easily accessed.

- **Slicing and Dicing.** Slicing and dicing refers to the ability to look at the database from different viewpoints. One slice of the sales database might show all sales of product type within regions. Another slice might show all sales by sales channel within each product type. Slicing and dicing is often performed along a time axis in order to analyze trends and find time-based patterns in the data.

FIGURE 9.9

Online analytical processing may involve the use of specialized servers and multidimensional databases. OLAP provides fast answers to complex queries posed by managers and analysts using traditional and Web-enabled OLAP software.

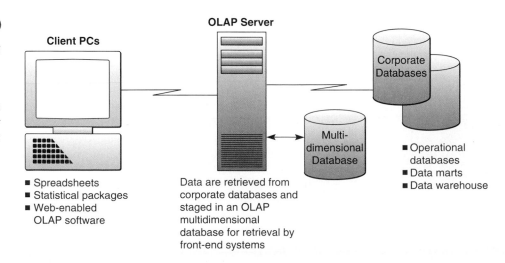

Client PCs
- Spreadsheets
- Statistical packages
- Web-enabled OLAP software

OLAP Server
Data are retrieved from corporate databases and staged in an OLAP multidimensional database for retrieval by front-end systems

Multi-dimensional Database

Corporate Databases
- Operational databases
- Data marts
- Data warehouse

FIGURE 9.10

Comshare's Management Planning and Control software enables business professionals to use Microsoft Excel as their user interface for Web-enabled online analytical processing.

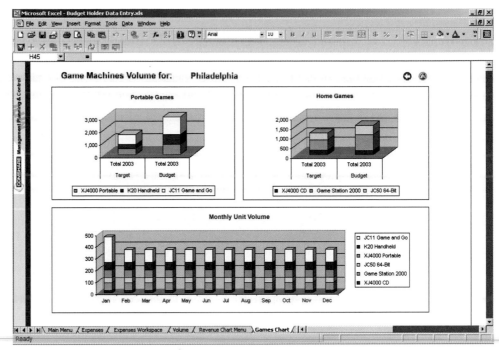

Source: Courtesy of Comshare.

International Rectifier: OLAP for Decision Support

At International Rectifier Corp., an El Segundo, California–based producer of power management semiconductors, manager of financial analytics Doug Burke says Hyperion Solutions' Essbase software has enabled the company to get a lot more out of their IBM midrange system by allowing the company to extract and analyze sales data very inexpensively. Rather than being forced to manipulate and e-mail each other huge spreadsheets, which ties up network bandwidth, users at networked PC workstations can now dynamically retrieve calculated views of just the data they need from the company's sales databases using the online analytical processing (OLAP) features of Essbase.

Burke says he expects more cost savings in a few weeks when he deploys a new version of Essbase, which includes attributes that will allow users to dynamically analyze data across additional dimensions (such as sales areas) without having to store those calculations and thus increase the size of the database. "That's a big payoff," he says, "especially when you want to scale this thing up to hundreds of thousands or even millions of products" to analyze.

International Rectifier is using Essbase not only to cut the costs and time it takes to collect data but also to standardize how the data is created to improve decision making, says Burke. Using Essbase, the company has built a multidimensional data cube for inventory analysis and will soon roll out another to analyze sales by market sector.

Now that everyone at International Rectifier is using these common databases, "you don't have costs defined three different ways or revenue defined four different ways by different divisions," Burke says. "Whether people like the numbers or not, everyone agrees on the numbers," and can focus more on analyzing the data than gathering it, he explains [41].

Decision Support Systems

Decision support systems are computer-based information systems that provide interactive information support to managers and business professionals during the decision-making process. Decision support systems use (1) analytical models, (2) specialized databases, (3) a decision maker's own insights and judgments, and (4) an interactive, computer-based modeling process to support the making of semistructured and unstructured business decisions.

Example. An example might help at this point. Sales managers typically rely on management information systems to produce sales analysis reports. These reports contain sales performance figures by product line, salesperson, sales region, and so on. A decision support system, on the other hand, would also interactively show a sales manager the effects on sales performance of changes in a variety of factors (such as promotion expense and salesperson compensation). The DSS could then use several criteria (such as expected gross margin and market share) to evaluate and rank several alternative combinations of sales performance factors.

Therefore, DSS systems are designed to be ad hoc, quick-response systems that are initiated and controlled by business decision makers. Decision support systems are thus able to directly support the specific types of decisions and the personal decision-making styles and needs of individual executives, managers, and business professionals.

DSS Components

Unlike management information systems, decision support systems rely on **model bases** as well as databases as vital system resources. A DSS model base is a software component that consists of models used in computational and analytical routines that mathematically express relationships among variables. For example, a spreadsheet program might contain models that express simple accounting relationships among variables, such as Revenue − Expenses = Profit. Or a DSS model base could include models and analytical techniques used to express much more complex relationships. For example, it might contain linear programming models, multiple regression forecasting models, and capital budgeting present value models. Such models may be stored in the form of spreadsheet models or templates, or statistical and mathematical programs and program modules [27]. See Figure 9.11.

DSS software packages can combine model components to create integrated models that support specific types of decisions [11]. DSS software typically contains built-in analytical modeling routines and also enables you to build your own models. Many DSS packages are now available in microcomputer and Web-enabled versions. Of course, electronic spreadsheet packages also provide some of the model building (spreadsheet models) and analytical modeling (what-if and goal-seeking analysis) offered by more powerful DSS software. See Figure 9.12.

FIGURE 9.11

Components of a Web-enabled marketing decision support system. Note the hardware, software, model, data, and network resources involved.

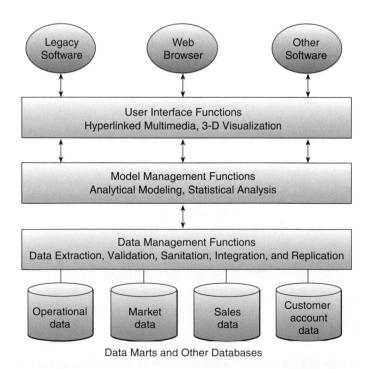

FIGURE 9.12

Examples of special-purpose DSS packages.

DSS Packages
• **Retail:** Information Advantage and Unisys offer the Category Management Solution Suite, an OLAP decision support system and industry-specific data model.
• **Insurance:** Computer Associates offers RiskAdvisor, an insurance risk decision support system whose data model stores information in insurance industry specific tables designed for optimal query performance.
• **Telecom:** NCR and SABRE Decision Technologies have joined forces to create the NCR Customer Retention program for the communications industry including data marts for telephone companies to use for decision support in managing customer loyalty, quality of service, network management, fraud, and marketing.

Web-Enabled DSS at PepsiCo

PepsiCo and Sedgwick James Inc., the world's second largest insurance broker, developed a risk management DSS to help minimize PepsiCo's losses from accidents, theft, and other causes. Every week, Sedgwick loads the latest casualty claims data from the nation's leading insurance carriers into a DSS database resident on IBM RS/6000 servers in the PepsiCo intranet. The database is then accessed by managers and analysts using desktop PCs and remote laptops equipped with the INFORM risk management system. Both the RS/6000 servers and local PCs use Information Builders' middleware to provide PepsiCo managers and business analysts with transparent data access from a variety of hardware/ software configurations.

The INFORM risk management system combines the analytical power of FOCUS decision support modeling with the graphical analysis capabilities of FOCUS/EIS for Windows. As a result, PepsiCo managers and business analysts at all levels can pinpoint critical trends, drill down for detailed backup information, identify potential problems, and plan ways to minimize risks and maximize profits [32].

Geographic Information and Data Visualization Systems

Geographic information systems (GIS) and *data visualization systems* (DVS) are special categories of DSS that integrate computer graphics with other DSS features. A geographic information system is a DSS that uses *geographic databases* to construct and display maps and other graphics displays that support decisions affecting the geographic distribution of people and other resources. Many companies are using GIS technology along with *global positioning system* (GPS) devices to help them choose new retail store locations, optimize distribution routes, or analyze the demographics of their target audiences. For example, companies like Levi Strauss, Arby's, Consolidated Rail, and Federal Express use GIS packages to integrate maps, graphics, and other geographic data with business data from spreadsheets and statistical packages. GIS software such as MapInfo and Atlas GIS is used for most business GIS applications.

Data visualization systems represent complex data using interactive three-dimensional graphical forms such as charts, graphs, and maps. DVS tools help users to interactively sort, subdivide, combine, and organize data while it is in its graphical form. This helps users discover patterns, links, and anomalies in business or scientific data in an interactive knowledge discovery and decision support process. Business applications like data mining typically use interactive graphs that let users drill down in real time and manipulate the underlying data of a business model to help clarify its meaning for business decision making [12, 23]. Figure 9.13 is an example of website activity data displayed by a data visualization system.

Eli Lilly: Data Visualization for Decision Support

A new idea in software is beginning to help companies reduce the time and money they spend searching for patterns and meaning in their data oceans. It's an approach that started as a doctoral thesis by Christopher Ahlberg, the 32-year-old Swedish-born founder of software company Spotfire, in Somerville, Massachusetts.

FIGURE 9.13

Using a data visualization system to analyze user activity on an e-commerce website.

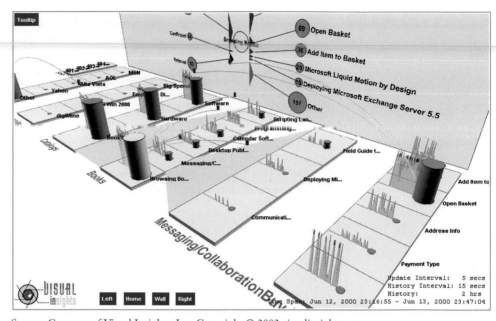

Source: Courtesy of Visual Insights, Inc. Copyright © 2002 visualinsights.com.

Spotfire's software is the first to combine both "data visualization" and a powerful database querying flexibility. Known as DecisionSite, the data visualization system (DVS) software isn't cheap—installations start at $100,000. That hasn't stopped customers in a wide range of industries from buying more than 16,000 licenses.

The magic in Spotfire's software is that it lets users easily do what-if queries and comparisons of data from different sources by moving sliders on a computer screen with a mouse. The results appear as brightly colored bar graphs, pie charts, scatter plots, and even maps.

When Spotfire rolled out its software in 1997, it aimed first at the drug industry, where the data explosion has been immense. An early adopter was Sheldon Ort, Eli Lilly's information officer for manufacturing and supply services. Ort now has some 1,500 company scientists around the world hooked up to Spotfire's software. "We primarily use it to facilitate decision making," Ort says. "With its ability to represent multiple sources of information and interactively change your view, it's helpful for homing in on specific molecules and deciding whether we should be doing further testing on them."

Using Spotfire, researchers avoid having to construct multiple queries in perfect syntax. Dragging the sliders to and fro, the user is actually launching a sequence of queries in rapid succession and seeing the outcomes expressed graphically onscreen. Lilly uses the software to conduct meetings among researchers at multiple sites who are linked on a computer network. As the person making a presentation moves the sliders on his or her screen, everyone can see the families, clusters, outliers, gaps, anomalies, and other statistical nuggets that database users fish for. Ideas can be tried out collaboratively in real time [8].

Using Decision Support Systems

Using a decision support system involves an interactive **analytical modeling** process. For example, using a DSS software package for decision support may result in a series of displays in response to alternative what-if changes entered by a manager. This differs from the demand responses of management information systems, since decision makers are not demanding prespecified information. Rather, they are exploring possible alternatives. Thus, they do not have to specify their information needs in advance. Instead, they use the DSS to find the information they need to help them make a decision. That is the essence of the decision support system concept.

FIGURE 9.14

Activities and examples of the major types of analytical modeling.

Type of Analytical Modeling	Activities and Examples
What if analysis	Observing how changes to selected variables affect other variables. *Example:* What if we cut advertising by 10 percent? What would happen to sales?
Sensitivity analysis	Observing how repeated changes to a single variable affect other variables. *Example:* Let's cut advertising by $100 repeatedly so we can see its relationship to sales.
Goal-seeking analysis	Making repeated changes to selected variables until a chosen variable reaches a target value. *Example:* Let's try increases in advertising until sales reach $1million.
Optimization analysis	Finding an optimum value for selected variables, given certain constraints. *Example:* What's the best amount of advertising to have, given our budget and choice of media?

Using a decision support system involves four basic types of analytical modeling activities: (1) what-if analysis, (2) sensitivity analysis, (3) goal-seeking analysis, and (4) optimization analysis. Let's briefly look at each type of analytical modeling that can be used for decision support. See Figure 9.14.

What-If Analysis

In **what-if analysis,** an end user makes changes to variables, or relationships among variables, and observes the resulting changes in the values of other variables. For example, if you were using a spreadsheet, you might change a revenue amount (a variable) or a tax rate formula (a relationship among variables) in a simple financial spreadsheet model. Then you could command the spreadsheet program to instantly recalculate all affected variables in the spreadsheet. A managerial user would be very interested in observing and evaluating any changes that occurred to the values in the spreadsheet, especially to a variable such as net profit after taxes. To many managers, net profit after taxes is an example of *the bottom line*, that is, a key factor in making many types of decisions. This type of analysis would be repeated until the manager was satisfied with what the results revealed about the effects of various possible decisions. Figure 9.15 is an example of what-if analysis.

Sensitivity Analysis

Sensitivity analysis is a special case of what-if analysis. Typically, the value of only one variable is changed repeatedly, and the resulting changes on other variables are observed. So sensitivity analysis is really a case of what-if analysis involving repeated changes to only one variable at a time. Some DSS packages automatically make repeated small changes to a variable when asked to perform sensitivity analysis. Typically, sensitivity analysis is used when decision makers are uncertain about the assumptions made in estimating the value of certain key variables. In our previous spreadsheet example, the value of revenue could be changed repeatedly in small increments, and the effects on other spreadsheet variables observed and evaluated. This would help a manager understand the impact of various revenue levels on other factors involved in decisions being considered.

Goal-Seeking Analysis

Goal-seeking analysis reverses the direction of the analysis done in what-if and sensitivity analysis. Instead of observing how changes in a variable affect other variables, goal-seeking analysis (also called *how can* analysis) sets a target value (a goal) for a variable and then repeatedly changes other variables until the target value is achieved. For example, you could specify a target value (goal) of $2 million for net profit after taxes for a business venture. Then you could repeatedly change the value of revenue or expenses in a

FIGURE 9.15

This what-if analysis involves the evaluation of probability distributions of net income and net present value (NPV) generated by changes to values for sales, competitors, product development, and capital expenses.

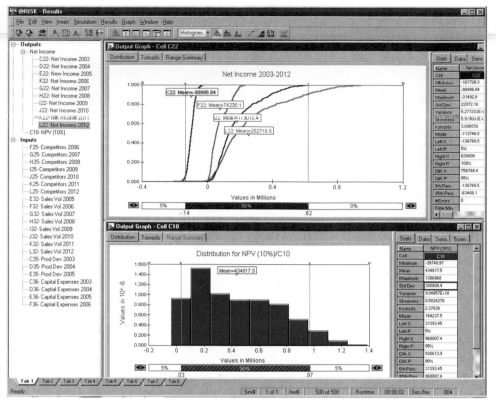

Source: Courtesy of Palisade Software.

spreadsheet model until a result of $2 million is achieved. Thus, you would discover what amount of revenue or level of expenses the business venture needs to achieve in order to reach the goal of $2 million in after-tax profits. Therefore, this form of analytical modeling would help answer the question, "How can we achieve $2 million in net profit after taxes?" instead of the question, "What happens if we change revenue or expenses?" Thus, goal-seeking analysis is another important method of decision support.

Optimization Analysis

Optimization analysis is a more complex extension of goal-seeking analysis. Instead of setting a specific target value for a variable, the goal is to find the optimum value for one or more target variables, given certain constraints. Then one or more other variables are changed repeatedly, subject to the specified constraints, until the best values for the target variables are discovered. For example, you could try to determine the highest possible level of profits that could be achieved by varying the values for selected revenue sources and expense categories. Changes to such variables could be subject to constraints such as the limited capacity of a production process or limits to available financing. Optimization typically is accomplished using software like the Solver tool in Microsoft Excel and other software packages for optimization techniques such as linear programming.

Lexis-Nexis: Web Tools for Decision Support

"Our new subscribers will grow geometrically with Web-based access to our information services," explains Keith Hawk, vice president of sales for the Nexis division of Lexis-Nexis. "And therefore our business model is changing from selling primarily to organizations to selling to individual users." To track their 1.7 million subscribers of legal and news documents, Lexis-Nexis replaced its old decision support system with new DSS tools and an NCR Teradata data warehouse system. The new customer data warehouse lets 475 salespeople and in-house analysts use the corporate intranet and Web browsers to look up daily detailed customer usage data.

The type of data that the company's salespeople sort through and analyze includes subscriber usage patterns—what they look up, what sources they use most often, when they're connecting—along with customer contract details. To get to that data, Lexis-Nexis uses decision support software from MicroStrategy Inc. Field sales representatives who need ad hoc reporting capabilities use MicroStrategy DSS WebPE, a Web-based reporting tool. Power users, such as market research analysts, use DSS Agent, an analytical modeling tool with Web access, to closely analyze and model business processes [13, 18].

Data Mining for Decision Support

We discussed data mining and data warehouses in Chapter 5 as vital tools for organizing and exploiting the data resources of a company. Thus, data mining's main purpose is to provide decision support to managers and business professionals through a process sometimes called *knowledge discovery*. Data mining software analyzes the vast stores of historical business data that have been prepared for analysis in corporate data warehouses, and tries to discover patterns, trends, and correlations hidden in the data that can help a company improve its business performance.

Data mining software may perform regression, decision tree, neural network, cluster detection, or market basket analysis for a business. See Figure 9.16. The data mining process can highlight buying patterns, reveal customer tendencies, cut redundant costs, or uncover unseen profitable relationships and opportunities. For example, many companies use data mining to find more profitable ways to perform successful direct mailings, including e-mailings, or to discover better ways to display products in a store, design a better e-commerce website, reach untapped profitable customers, or recognize customers or products that are unprofitable or marginal [15].

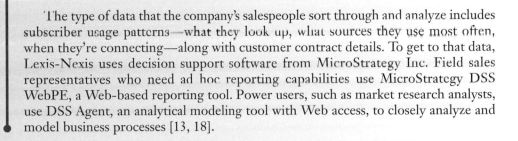

FIGURE 9.16

Data mining software helps discover patterns in business data like this analysis of customer demographic information.

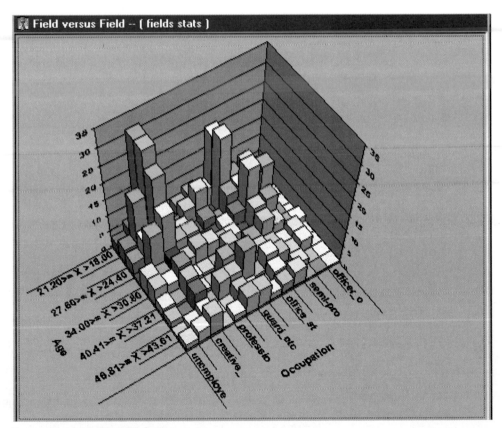

Source: Courtesy of Attar Software.

KeyCorp and Peoples Bank: Data Mining DSS	Quick payback and support for some surprising, counterintuitive decisions have been among the benefits users have found with IBM's DecisionEdge for Relationship Marketing decision support software. "We had a full return on our investment 14 months after installing the data mining component," said Jo Ann Boylan, an executive vice president in the Key Technology Service division at KeyCorp, one of the largest retail banks in the United States. She added that the data mining and analysis system helped raise the bank's direct-mail response rate from 1 to as high as 10 percent. It also helped identify unprofitable product lines.

The DecisionEdge decision support package includes application suites, analytical tools, a mining data tool, industry-specific data models, and consulting services. Pricing begins at around $150,000.

Peoples Bank & Trust Co. in Indianapolis used the DecisionEdge for Relationship Marketing to delve into some highly profitable bank offerings that turned out to be prohibitively expensive, said Bob Connors, a senior vice president of information services. The DSS pointed out how much it actually costs to bring in each highly profitable home equity loan customer. "Because those loans can be so profitable, it seems like a no-brainer that you'd want to market them," Connors explained. "But we found that the costs to bring them in were far too high, so we've cut way back on that spending. We still offer the loans, but we don't spend so much on advertising or direct mail any more" [14].

Executive Information Systems

Executive information systems (EIS) are information systems that combine many of the features of management information systems and decision support systems. When they were first developed, their focus was on meeting the strategic information needs of top management. Thus, the first goal of executive information systems was to provide top executives with immediate and easy access to information about a firm's *critical success factors* (CSFs), that is, key factors that are critical to accomplishing an organization's strategic objectives. For example, the executives of a retail store chain would probably consider factors such as its e-commerce versus traditional sales results, or its product line mix to be critical to its survival and success.

However, executive information systems are becoming so widely used by managers, analysts, and other knowledge workers that they are sometimes humorously called "everyone's information systems." More popular alternative names are enterprise information systems (EIS) and executive support systems (ESS). These names also reflect the fact that more features, such as Web browsing, electronic mail, groupware tools, and DSS and expert system capabilities, are being added to many systems to make them more useful to managers and business professionals [18, 19, 42].

Features of an EIS

In an EIS, information is presented in forms tailored to the preferences of the executives using the system. For example, most executive information systems stress the use of a graphical user interface and graphics displays that can be customized to the information preferences of executives using the EIS. Other information presentation methods used by an EIS include exception reporting and trend analysis. The ability to *drill down*, which allows executives to quickly retrieve displays of related information at lower levels of detail, is another important capability.

Figure 9.17 shows one of the displays provided by the Web-enabled Hyperion executive information system. Notice how simple and brief this display is. Also note how it provides users of the system with the ability to drill down quickly to lower levels of detail in areas of particular interest to them. Beside the drill-down capability, the Hyperion EIS also stresses trend analysis and exception reporting. Thus, a business user can quickly discover the direction key factors are heading and the extent to which critical factors are deviating from expected results.

EIS have spread into the ranks of middle management and business professionals as they recognized their feasibility and benefits, and as less-expensive systems for

FIGURE 9.17

This Web-based executive information system provides managers and business professionals with a variety of personalized information and analytical tools for decision support.

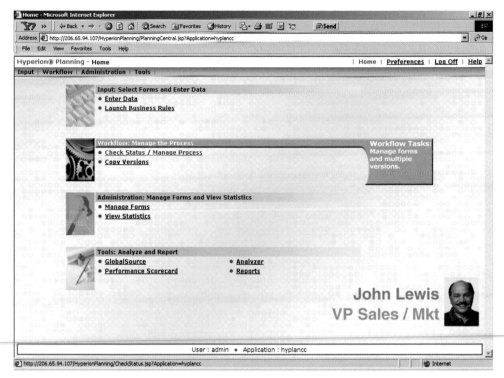

Source: Courtesy of Hyperion Solutions Corp.

client/server networks and corporate intranets became available. For example, one popular EIS software package reports that only 3 percent of its users are top executives. Another example is the EIS of Conoco, one of the world's largest oil companies. Conoco's EIS is used by most senior managers, and by over 4,000 employees located at corporate headquarters in Houston and throughout the world [4, 43, 46].

EIS at Conoco and KeyCorp

As we just mentioned, Conoco, Inc., has a widely used EIS. Conoco's EIS is a large system with 75 different applications and hundreds of screen displays. Senior executives and over 4,000 managers and analysts worldwide use EIS applications ranging from analyzing internal operations and financial results to viewing external events that affect the petroleum industry. Conoco's EIS is popular with its users and has resulted in improved employee productivity and decision making, and significant cost savings compared to alternative methods of generating information for managers and analysts [4].

KeyCorp is a large banking and financial services holding company. It developed Keynet, a corporate intranet that transformed their mainframe-based EIS into a new EIS—a Web-enabled system they call "everyone's information system." Now more than 1,000 managers and analysts have Web access to 40 major business information areas within Keynet, ranging from sales and financial statistics to human resource management [37].

Enterprise Portals and Decision Support

Don't confuse portals with the executive information systems that have been used in some industries for many years. Portals are for everyone in the company, and not just for executives. You want people on the front lines making decisions using browsers and portals rather than just executives using specialized executive information system software [37].

We mentioned earlier in this chapter that major changes and expansion are taking place in traditional MIS, DSS, and EIS tools for providing the information and modeling managers need to support their decision making. Decision support in business is changing, driven by rapid developments in end user computing and networking; Internet and Web technologies, and Web-enabled business applications. One of the key changes taking place in management information and decision support systems in business is the rapid growth of enterprise information portals.

Enterprise Information Portals

A user checks his e-mail, looks up the current company stock price, checks his available vacation days, and receives an order from a customer—all from the browser on his desktop. That is the next-generation intranet, also known as a corporate or enterprise information portal. With it, the browser becomes the dashboard to daily business tasks [36].

An **enterprise information portal** (EIP) is a Web-based interface and integration of MIS, DSS, EIS, and other technologies that gives all intranet users and selected extranet users access to a variety of internal and external business applications and services. For example, internal applications might include access to e-mail, project websites, and discussion groups; human resources Web self-services; customer, inventory, and other corporate databases; decision support systems, and knowledge management systems. External applications might include industry, financial, and other Internet news services; links to industry discussion groups; and links to customer and supplier Internet and extranet websites. Enterprise information portals are typically tailored or personalized to the needs of individual business users or groups of users, giving them a personalized *digital dashboard* of information sources and applications. See Figure 9.18.

The business benefits of enterprise information portals include providing more specific and selective information to business users, providing easy access to key corporate intranet website resources, delivering industry and business news, and providing better access to company data for selected customers, suppliers, or business partners. Enterprise information portals can also help avoid excessive surfing by

An enterprise information portal can provide a business professional with a personalized workplace of information sources, administrative and analytical tools, and relevant business applications.

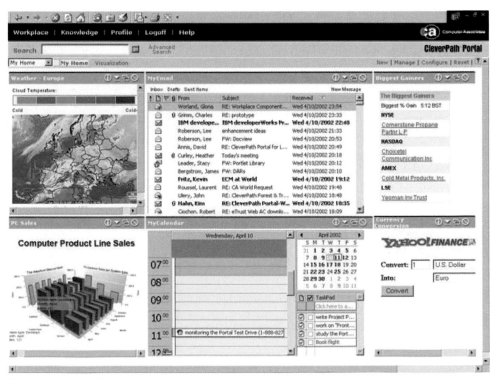

Source: Courtesy of Computer Associates.

FIGURE 9.19

The components of this enterprise information portal identify it as a Web-enabled decision support system that can be personalized for executives, managers, employees, suppliers, customers, and other business partners.

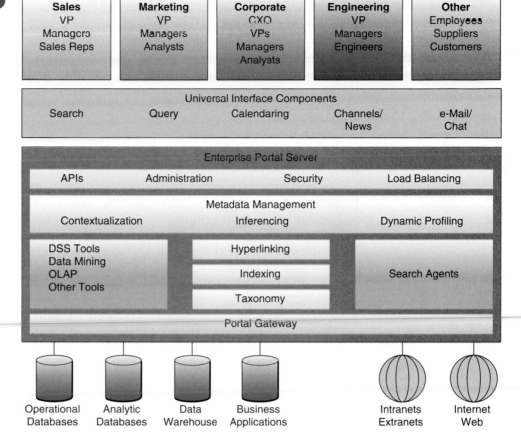

employees across company and Internet websites by making it easier for them to receive or find the information and services they need, thus improving the productivity of a company's workforce [37].

Figure 9.19 illustrates how companies are developing enterprise information portals as a way to provide Web-enabled information, knowledge, and decision support to their executives, managers, employees, suppliers, customers, and other business partners. The enterprise information portal is a customized and personalized Web based interface for corporate intranets, which gives users easy access to a variety of internal and external business applications, databases, and services. For example, the EIP in Figure 9.19 might give a qualified user secure access to DSS, data mining, and OLAP tools, the Internet and the Web, the corporate intranet, supplier or customer extranets, operational and analytical databases, a data warehouse, and a variety of business applications [35, 36, 37].

AmeriKing Inc.: The Business Value of an EIP	When Chief Information Officer Hernando Manrique arrived at AmeriKing in 2000, technology wasn't exactly on the front burner for the Westchester, Illinois–based Burger King franchisee. Though AmeriKing (www.ameriking.com) claims to be the largest Burger King franchisee in the country with some 376 stores and 13,000 employees scattered across the United States, its technology and applications infrastructures definitely weren't whoppers. Information ranging from financial reports to human resource policies was manually photocopied and distributed via monthly or bimonthly mailings and fax. "The technology side of the business was definitely underdeveloped," says Manrique.

So Manrique teamed with Carol Swanson, manager of Business Data & Intelligence, and Patti Cahanin, manager of Business Applications and Solutions, to help AmeriKing put its technology efforts into overdrive. At the beginning of 2001, the company began testing of its intranet portal, which is powered by Plumtree's Portal Server. And in June 2001, Manrique and his team officially launched AKInet, as the portal is called, to some 180 district managers, marketing directors, and marketing managers. And a rollout of the portal to the managers of all 376 stores began during 2002. Field personnel can now use Web browsers to access daily and monthly financial reports and over 71,000 corporate documents, use e-mail accounts, and order supplies from Boise Cascade online via the portal. Just the ability to access these reports and human resource information online is saving AmeriKing about $500,000 per year in reduced printing and distribution costs. "Those savings alone enabled us to justify the entire project, and we see it as just the beginning," Manrique says.

The AKInet portal provides several "communities" of applications accessible by all or selected employees, including an HR community of employee profiles and employee contact information; a MyInet community of personalized employee information; a Finance and Accounting community with access to sales and inventory data, P&L, payroll, and a decision support system; and a Marketing community with regional calendars and timely promotional information. Other portal components include an AKNews community with corporate content such as Burger King press releases, partner company news, and executive news; and a Training community with access to course scheduling and materials and the AmeriKing University for online training [39].

Knowledge Management Systems

We introduced **knowledge management systems** in Chapter 2 as the use of information technology to help gather, organize, and share business knowledge within an organization. In many organizations, hypermedia databases at corporate intranet websites have become the *knowledge bases* for storage and dissemination of business knowledge. This knowledge frequently takes the form of best practices, policies, and business solutions at the project, team, business unit, and enterprise levels of the company.

For many companies, enterprise information portals are the entry to corporate intranets that serve as their knowledge management systems. That's why such portals are called **enterprise knowledge portals** by their vendors. Thus, enterprise knowledge portals play an essential role in helping companies use their intranets as knowledge management systems to share and disseminate knowledge in support of business decision making by managers and business professionals [34, 35]. See Figure 9.20. Now let's look at an example of a Web-enabled knowledge management system in business.

Qwest Communications: Web Knowledge Management System

At Qwest Communications, knowledge management (KM) was the only way to be sure that call center representatives had the information they needed, when they needed it. Relying on print documentation or a supervisor's directive did not ensure cross-company accuracy or even that the information was delivered to all who needed it. Knowledge management was the only way to ensure that support would be available for every conceivable situation, and that the information was accurate and complete. Qwest has had an online procedures database for quite some time, but it was just online documentation. Each document looked different. Design was in the hands of the individual author, and there were lots of authors. Compounding the problem, authors had their own view about the content and the appropriate level of detail. Generally speaking, they wrote what *they* thought the representative needed to know, not necessarily what the representative *actually* needed to know.

In 1999 the old system was replaced by *InfoBuddy*, Qwest's Web-based knowledge management system. It supports a wide variety of job functions in addition to customer service representatives, including technical repair, installation and maintenance, etc. InfoBuddy uses a methods and procedures database with intelligent KM capabilities, such as searching, tagging, and customizable interface. It can reorder the information presentation based on who the user is.

When users identify themselves and their job function or role, the InfoBuddy intranet portal knows how to configure its user interface to provide information of most value to each person. In addition, users have the ability to personalize their portal through the "MyBuddy" feature, enabling representatives to place bookmarks on their home pages to the information they feel is most important. Over time, as users "learn" from the system, they can replace learned material with new, usually more advanced information.

In addition, the InfoBuddy system "pushes" information to specific users based on their needs. For example, if a new promotion were initiated, specific information—products, pricing, etc.—would appear on the "desktop" of those representatives who are involved in the marketing initiative [40].

FIGURE 9.20   This example of the capabilities and components of an enterprise knowledge portal emphasizes its use as a Web-based knowledge management system.

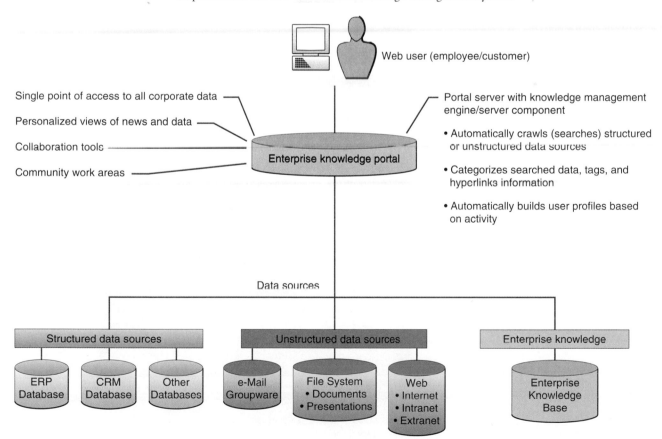

SECTION II	Artificial Intelligence Technologies in Business

Business and AI

Artificial intelligence (AI) technologies are being used in a variety of ways to improve the decision support provided to managers and business professionals in many companies. For example:

> *AI-enabled applications are at work in information distribution and retrieval, database mining, product design, manufacturing, inspection, training, user support, surgical planning, resource scheduling, and complex resource management.*
>
> *Indeed, for anyone who schedules, plans, allocates resources, designs new products, uses the Internet, develops software, is responsible for product quality, is an investment professional, heads up IT, uses IT, or operates in any of a score of other capacities and arenas, AI technologies already may be in place and providing competitive advantage* [48].

Analyzing Wal-Mart, BankFinancial, and HP

Read the Real World Case on Wal-Mart, BankFinancial, and HP on the next page. We can learn a lot about the business value of artificial intelligence technologies from this example. See Figure 9.21.

This case emphasizes that leading companies in many different industries are using artificial intelligence technologies as a vital ingredient of many strategic business applications such as manufacturing, process control, biomedical research, fraud detection,

FIGURE 9.21

William Connerty, assistant vice-president for market research at BankFinancial, is responsible for improving the bank's use of data mining for market research.

Source: David Joel.

REAL WORLD CASE 2

Wal-Mart, BankFinancial, and HP: The Business Value of AI

Some managers still think that artificial intelligence—the decades-long effort to create computer systems with humanlike smarts—has been a big flop. But executives at many companies know better. Artificial intelligence (AI) is often a crucial ingredient in their stellar performance. In fact, AI is now a part of the technology of many industries. AI software helps engineers create better jet engines. In factories, it boosts productivity by monitoring equipment and signaling when preventive maintenance is needed. And in the pharmaceutical sector, it is used to gain new insights into the tremendous amount of data on the human genome.

The finance industry is a real veteran in such technology. Banks, brokerages, and insurance companies have been relying on various AI tools for two decades. One variety, called a neural network, has become the standard for detecting credit-card fraud. Since 1992, neural nets have slashed such incidents by 70 percent or more for the likes of U.S. Bancorp and Wachovia Bank. Now, even small credit unions are required to use the software in order to qualify for debit-card insurance from Credit Union National Association.

Wal-Mart. Like banks, retailers collect huge amounts of data. Wal-Mart Stores Inc. (www.walmart.com), for instance, harnesses AI to transform that raw data into useful information. Wal-Mart consolidates point-of-sale details from its 3,000 stores. Data-mining systems sift instantly through the deluge to uncover patterns and relationships that would elude an army of human searchers. Data-mining software typically includes neural nets, statistical analysis, and so-called expert systems with if-then rules that mimic the logic of human experts. The results enable Wal-Mart to predict sales of every product at each store with uncanny accuracy, translating into huge savings in inventories and maximum payoff from promotional spending.

BankFinancial. The potential for mining cost-saving and revenue-boosting ideas from data is increasing as companies build bigger data warehouses, computers grow more powerful, and vendors of analytic software introduce products that are easier to use. But while many of the products that can answer those questions use esoteric techniques such as neural networks, logistic regression, and support-vector machines, they don't require a PhD in math, users say. Indeed, the biggest stumbling block to using "predictive analytics" is getting the data, not analyzing it, they say.

That has been the case so far at BankFinancial Corp. (www.bankfinancial.com) in Chicago. It uses the Clementine data-mining "workbench" from SPSS Inc., to develop models that predict customer behavior so the bank can, for example, more accurately target promotions to customers and prospects. The bank uses Clementine's neural network and regression routines for these models.

It's also beginning to use PredictiveMarketing, SPSS's new package of "best-practice templates" for helping users set up predictive models. PredictiveMarketing will reduce the time it takes the bank to develop a model by 50 percent to 75 percent, says William Connerty, assistant vice president of market research. The first major application is a model to predict customer "churn," the rate at which customers come and go. It will be used to identify the customers most likely to leave the bank during the coming month. The problem is, the model has access only to account information prepared from weekly and monthly summaries, not to the daily customer activity that would make it more timely.

"The biggest obstacle is getting transaction data and dealing with disparate data sources." Connerty says. The data that BankFinancial needs in order to assess customer loyalty comes from several bank systems and unintegrated customer survey databases. A lot of systems integration and interface work needs to be done before the bank will see the full fruits of its modeling tools, Connerty says.

HP Enterprise Systems. Hewlett-Packard (www.hp.com) has an Enterprise Systems Group that pulls together people with diverse backgrounds and strong analytical skills for its group that does predictive modeling of customer behavior. The group is part of "CRM operations" under a vice president for sales, says Randy Collica, a senior business/data mining analyst.

HP uses software from SAS Institute Inc. in Cary, North Carolina, to mine its database of customers and prospects, using AI techniques to predict customer churn, loyalty, and where to target promotions. HP also mines its huge stores of unformatted text data from its call centers, including e-mails from customers and prospects and text typed in during voice calls with SAS predictive analytics for text. The techniques use "lead ratings" of call center personnel's assessments of a caller's readiness to buy — coded as "hot," "warm," or "suspect," to predict the customer-led rating of non-coded text sources with 85 percent accuracy, Collica says.

Case Study Questions

1. What is the business value of AI technologies in business today? Use several examples from the case to illustrate your answer.

2. What are some of the benefits and limitations of data mining for business intelligence? Use BankFinancial's experience to illustrate your answer.

3. Why have banks and other financial institutions been leading users of AI technologies like neural networks? What are the benefits and limitations of this technology?

Sources: Adapted from Otis Port, Michael Arndt, and John Carey, "Smart Tools," *Business Week*, The Business Week 50, Spring 2003; and Gary Anthes, "The Forecast is Clear," *Computerworld*, April 14, 2003, pp. 31–32.

FIGURE 9.22

Some of the attributes of intelligent behavior. AI is attempting to duplicate these capabilities in computer-based systems.

Attributes of Intelligent Behavior
● Think and reason.
● Use reason to solve problems.
● Learn or understand from experience.
● Acquire and apply knowledge.
● Exhibit creativity and imagination.
● Deal with complex or perplexing situations.
● Respond quickly and successfully to new situations.
● Recognize the relative importance of elements in a situation.
● Handle ambiguous, incomplete, or erroneous information.

data mining, and market research. Examples include the use of neural net systems by most banks for credit card fraud detection, neural nets and expert systems in data mining applications by Wal-Mart and BankFinancial for sales and market forecasting, and predictive modeling of consumer behavior by HP Enterprise Systems. The major limitation mentioned in the case centers on the difficulties in obtaining and transforming data into the good quality business data needed to produce high-quality results.

An Overview of Artificial Intelligence

What is artificial intelligence? **Artificial intelligence** (AI) is a field of science and technology based on disciplines such as computer science, biology, psychology, linguistics, mathematics, and engineering. The goal of AI is to develop computers that can think, as well as see, hear, walk, talk, and feel. A major thrust of artificial intelligence is the development of computer functions normally associated with human intelligence, such as reasoning, learning, and problem solving, as summarized in Figure 9.22.

Debate has raged around artificial intelligence since serious work in the field began in the 1950s. Not only technological, but moral and philosophical questions abound about the possibility of intelligent, thinking machines. For example, British AI pioneer Alan Turing in 1950 proposed a test for determining if machines could think. According to the Turing test, a computer could demonstrate intelligence if a human interviewer, conversing with an unseen human and an unseen computer, could not tell which was which [29, 42].

Though much work has been done in many of the subgroups that fall under the AI umbrella, critics believe that no computer can truly pass the Turing test. They claim that developing intelligence to impart true humanlike capabilities to computers is simply not possible. But progress continues, and only time will tell if the ambitious goals of artificial intelligence will be achieved and equal the popular images found in science fiction.

The Domains of Artificial Intelligence

Figure 9.23 illustrates the major domains of AI research and development. Note that AI applications can be grouped under three major areas: cognitive science, robotics, and natural interfaces, though these classifications do overlap each other, and other classifications can be used. Also note that expert systems are just one of many important AI applications. Let's briefly review each of these major areas of AI and some of their current technologies. Figure 9.24 outlines some of the latest developments in commercial applications of artificial intelligence.

Cognitive Science. This area of artificial intelligence is based on research in biology, neurology, psychology, mathematics, and many allied disciplines. It focuses on

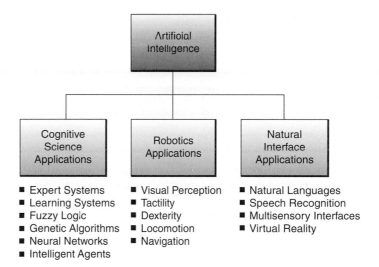

FIGURE 9.23

The major application areas of artificial intelligence. Note that the many applications of AI can be grouped into the three major areas of cognitive science, robotics, and natural interfaces.

researching how the human brain works and how humans think and learn. The results of such research in *human information processing* are the basis for the development of a variety of computer-based applications in artificial intelligence.

Applications in the cognitive science area of AI include the development of *expert systems* and other *knowledge-based systems* that add a knowledge base and some reasoning capability to information systems. Also included are *adaptive learning systems* that can modify their behaviors based on information they acquire as they operate. Chess-playing systems are primitive examples of such applications, though many more applications are being implemented. *Fuzzy logic* systems can process data that are incomplete or ambiguous, that is, *fuzzy data*. Thus, they can solve unstructured problems with incomplete knowledge by developing approximate inferences and answers, as humans do. *Neural network* software can learn by processing sample problems and their solutions. As neural nets start to recognize patterns, they can begin to program themselves to solve such problems on their own. *Genetic algorithm* software uses Darwinian (survival of the fittest), randomizing, and other mathematics functions to simulate evolutionary processes that can generate increasingly better solutions to problems. And *intelligent agents* use expert system and other AI technologies to serve as software surrogates for a variety of end user applications.

Robotics. AI, engineering, and physiology are the basic disciplines of robotics. This technology produces robot machines with computer intelligence and computer-controlled, humanlike physical capabilities. This area thus includes applications designed to give robots the powers of sight, or visual perception; touch, or tactile capabilities; dexterity, or skill in handling and manipulation; locomotion, or the physical ability to move over any terrain; and navigation, or the intelligence to properly find one's way to a destination [29].

Natural Interfaces. The development of natural interfaces is considered a major area of AI applications and is essential to the natural use of computers by humans. For example, the development of *natural languages* and speech recognition are major thrusts of this area of AI. Being able to talk to computers and robots in conversational human languages and have them "understand" us as easily as we understand each other is a goal of AI research. This involves research and development in linguistics, psychology, computer science, and other disciplines. Other natural interface research applications include the development of multisensory devices that use a variety of body movements to operate computers. This is related to the emerging application area of *virtual reality*.

FIGURE 9.24

Examples of some of the latest commercial applications of AI.

Commercial Applications of AI
Decision Support
● Intelligent work environment that will help you capture the *why* as well as the *what* of engineered design and decision making
● Intelligent human-computer interface (HCI) systems that can understand spoken language and gestures, and facilitate problem solving by supporting organizationwide collaborations to solve particular problems
● Situation assessment and resource allocation software for uses that range from airlines and airports to logistics centers
Information Retrieval
● AI-based intra- and Internet systems that distill tidal waves of information into simple presentations
● Natural language technology to retrieve any sort of online information, from text to pictures, videos, maps, and audio clips, in response to English questions
● Database mining for marketing trend analysis, financial forecasting, maintenance cost reduction, and more
Virtual Reality
● X-raylike vision enabled by enhanced-reality visualization that allows brain surgeons to "see through" intervening tissue to operate, monitor, and evaluate disease progression
● Automated animation and haptic interfaces that allow users to interact with virtual objects via touch (i.e., medical students can "feel" what it's like to suture severed aortas)
Robotics
● Machine vision inspections systems for gauging, guiding, identifying, and inspecting products and providing competitive advantage in manufacturing
● Cutting-edge robotics systems from micro robots and hands and legs to cognitive robotic and trainable modular vision systems

Virtual reality involves using multisensory human-computer interfaces that enable human users to experience computer-simulated objects, spaces, activities, and "worlds" as if they actually exist.

BAE Systems: Using AI for Knowledge Management

It's one of those blue-sky goals to which many big companies only aspire: capturing the seemingly infinite amount of intellectual capital that's carried by tens of thousands of employees around the world and using it to achieve competitive advantage. But it's a flight that's well under way at London-based BAE Systems PLC (www.baesystems.com), formerly British Aerospace, which is getting solid returns on a knowledge management intranet-based system. Thousands of BAE engineers scattered across five continents in 100 offices are using the system to search for information that may be vital to big initiatives and to identify and eliminate redundant project work.

Like other far-flung multinationals, the $20 billion-plus aerospace and engineering giant suspected that its engineers and other workers might be wasting a lot of time searching for information scattered across the enterprise. So BAE Systems invested roughly $150,000 to study its global operations to see whether "we had the right information to support decision-making processes and if people had the right learning systems to help them support their day-to-day jobs," says Richard West, BAE's organizational and e-learning manager in Farnborough, England.

The results, says West, "were certainly eye-opening." BAE Systems discovered that nearly two-thirds of its top 120 decision makers didn't have the right information at key stages. The company also found that 80 percent of employees were "wasting" an average of 30 minutes each day trying to find the information they needed to do their jobs. Another 60 percent were spending an hour or more duplicating the work of others.

One of the problems BAE Systems officials discovered through the study was information overload on its intranets. The information itself was often unstructured, and the search engines were inadequate for conducting keyword searches to find information, says West. The company decided to test two or three of the top intranet search engines over three months and compare their ability to find information, says West.

One of the search engines BAE Systems tested was from San Francisco–based Autonomy Corp. The Autonomy search engine uses advanced pattern matching, intelligent agents, and other artificial intelligence (AI) technologies whose "ability to retrieve information was second to none," says West. What sold BAE Systems on Autonomy's AI-based technology was its ability to flag whether other people in the organization are searching against similar information and, perhaps, working on common problems.

That kind of matching identification helped the Autonomy system pay for itself just seven months after it was installed. One of the system's first big payoffs came when two disparate groups of engineers in the U.K. were working on wing construction issues for the company's Harrier 2 military aircraft. After using the Autonomy system to search for wing specification information across the company's intranet, one of the engineering groups discovered that the other group was working on the same problem. Catching the redundancy early in the cycle helped save the company millions, says West. And a year into using the Autonomy search engine, BAE Systems evaluated its performance and determined that it was able to reduce the time needed to retrieve information from its intranet by 90 percent [24].

Neural Networks

Neural networks are computing systems modeled after the brain's meshlike network of interconnected processing elements, called *neurons*. Of course, neural networks are a lot simpler in architecture (the human brain is estimated to have over 100 billion neuron brain cells!). However, like the brain, the interconnected processors in a neural network operate in parallel and interact dynamically with each other. This enables the network to "learn" from data it processes. That is, it learns to recognize patterns and relationships in the data it processes. The more data examples it receives as input, the better it can learn to duplicate the results of the examples it processes. Thus, the neural network will change the strengths of the interconnections between the processing elements in response to changing patterns in the data it receives and the results that occur [6, 42]. See Figure 9.25.

For example, a neural network can be trained to learn which credit characteristics result in good or bad loans. Developers of a credit evaluation neural network could provide it with data from many examples of credit applications and loan results to process, and opportunities to adjust the signal strengths between its neurons. The neural network would continue to be trained until it demonstrated a high degree of accuracy in correctly duplicating the results of recent cases. At that point it would be trained enough to begin making credit evaluations of its own.

FIGURE 9.25

Evaluating the training status of a neural network application.

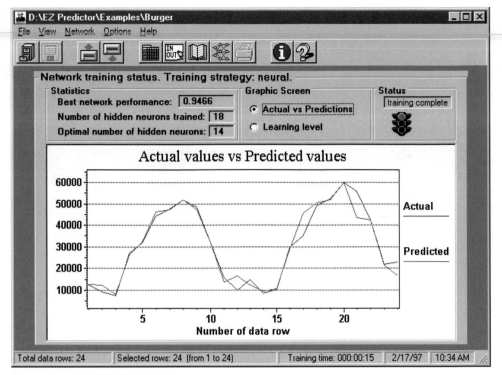

Source: Courtesy of Trading Solutions.

Neural Nets at Go.com

Go.com has a targeted marketing service that more closely targets advertising on its Internet search engine to users' interests by keeping track of every search that a user makes. The service uses neural network technology from Aptex Software to observe all the searches users run every time they use the Go.com search engine. The neural net software then calculates a numeric value, or "vector," that describes users' interests. Go.com uses that information to match users to the online ads it sells to advertisers on its Web search pages.

Other commercial World Wide Web sites use this technology to build up the usefulness of their websites or encourage repeat business. Many electronic commerce websites use customizing software to track user behavior and predict what a user will be interested in seeing in the future. For example, Aptex has a version of its neural net software designed for sites that sell products and services online. Select-Cast for Commerce Servers analyzes customer buying patterns, and predicts products and services the customer will be likely to buy, based on past behavior [44].

Fuzzy Logic Systems

In spite of the funny name, **fuzzy logic** systems represent a small, but serious application of AI in business. Fuzzy logic is a method of reasoning that resembles human reasoning since it allows for approximate values and inferences (fuzzy logic) and incomplete or ambiguous data (fuzzy data) instead of relying only on *crisp data*, such as binary (yes/no) choices. For example, Figure 9.26 illustrates a partial set of rules (fuzzy rules) and a fuzzy SQL query for analyzing and extracting credit risk information on businesses that are being evaluated for selection as investments.

Notice how fuzzy logic uses terminology that is deliberately imprecise, such as *very high, increasing, somewhat decreased, reasonable,* and *very low*. This enables fuzzy systems to process incomplete data and quickly provide approximate, but acceptable, solutions to problems that are difficult for other methods to solve. Thus, fuzzy logic queries of a database, such as the SQL query shown in Figure 9.26, promise to improve the extraction of data from business databases [10, 25].

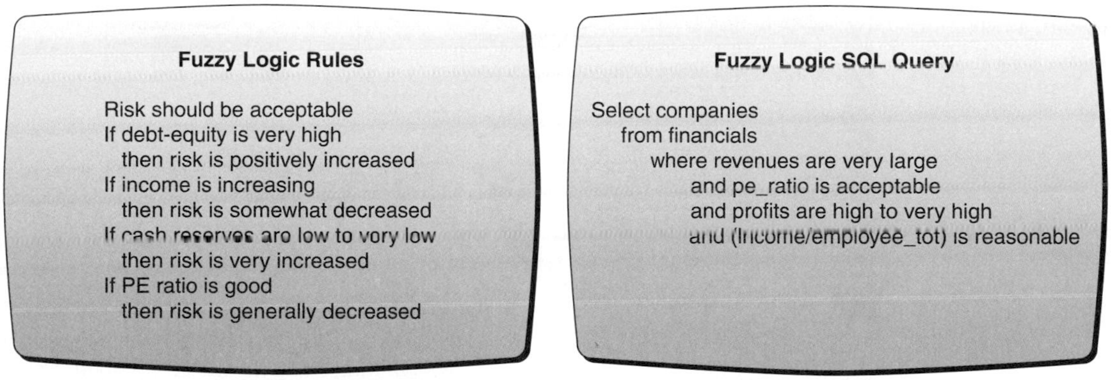

FIGURE 9.26   An example of fuzzy logic rules and a fuzzy logic SQL query in a credit risk analysis application.

Fuzzy Logic Rules

Risk should be acceptable
If debt-equity is very high
   then risk is positively increased
If income is increasing
   then risk is somewhat decreased
If cash reserves are low to very low
   then risk is very increased
If PE ratio is good
   then risk is generally decreased

Fuzzy Logic SQL Query

Select companies
  from financials
    where revenues are very large
    and pe_ratio is acceptable
    and profits are high to very high
    and (Income/employee_tot) is reasonable

Fuzzy Logic in Business

Examples of applications of fuzzy logic are numerous in Japan, but rare in the United States. The United States has tended to prefer using AI solutions like expert systems or neural networks. But Japan has implemented many fuzzy logic applications, especially the use of special-purpose fuzzy logic microprocessor chips, called fuzzy process controllers. Thus, the Japanese ride on subway trains, use elevators, and drive cars that are guided or supported by fuzzy process controllers made by Hitachi and Toshiba. Many models of Japanese-made products also feature fuzzy logic microprocessors. The list is growing, but includes autofocus cameras, autostabilizing camcorders, energy-efficient air conditioners, self-adjusting washing machines, and automatic transmissions [33].

Genetic Algorithms

The use of **genetic algorithms** is a growing application of artificial intelligence. Genetic algorithm software uses Darwinian (survival of the fittest), randomizing, and other mathematical functions to simulate an evolutionary process that can yield increasingly better solutions to a problem. Genetic algorithms were first used to simulate millions of years in biological, geological, and ecosystem evolution in just a few minutes on a computer. Now genetic algorithm software is being used to model a variety of scientific, technical, and business processes [3, 20].

Genetic algorithms are especially useful for situations in which thousands of solutions are possible and must be evaluated to produce an optimal solution. Genetic algorithm software uses sets of mathematical process rules *(algorithms)* that specify how combinations of process components or steps are to be formed. This may involve trying random process combinations *(mutation)*, combining parts of several good processes *(crossover)*, and selecting good sets of processes and discarding poor ones *(selection)* in order to generate increasingly better solutions. Figure 9.27 illustrates a business use of genetic algorithm software.

GE's Engeneous

General Electric's design of a more efficient jet engine for the Boeing 777 is a classic example of a genetic algorithm application in business. A major engineering challenge was to develop more efficient fan blades for the engine. GE's engineers estimated that it would take billions of years, even with a supercomputer, to mathematically evaluate the astronomical number of performance and cost factors and combinations involved. Instead, GE used a hybrid genetic algorithm/expert system, called Engeneous, that produced an optimal solution in less than a week [3].

Virtual Reality

Virtual reality (VR) is a computer-simulated reality. Virtual reality is a fast-growing area of artificial intelligence that had its origins in efforts to build more natural, realistic, multisensory human-computer interfaces. So virtual reality relies on multisensory input/output devices such as a tracking headset with video goggles and stereo

FIGURE 9.27

Risk Optimizer software combines genetic algorithms with a risk simulation function in this airline yield optimization application.

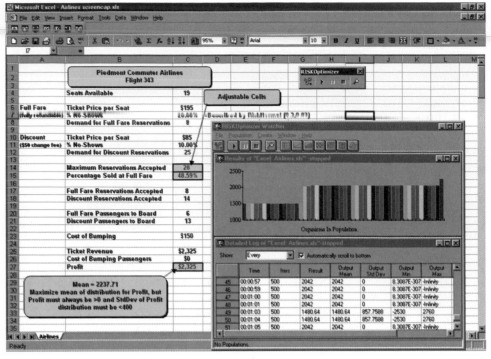

Source: Courtesy of Palisade Software.

earphones, a *data glove* or jumpsuit with fiber-optic sensors that track your body movements, and a *walker* that monitors the movement of your feet. Then you can experience computer-simulated "virtual worlds" three-dimensionally through sight, sound, and touch. Thus, virtual reality is also called *telepresence*. For example, you can enter a computer-generated virtual world, look around and observe its contents, pick up and move objects, and move around in it at will. Thus, virtual reality allows you to interact with computer-simulated objects, entities, and environments as if they actually exist [2, 38]. See Figure 9.28.

FIGURE 9.28

Using a virtual reality system to design the interiors of an office building.

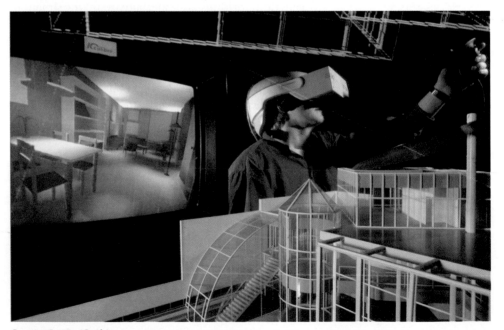

Source: Sygma/Corbis.

VR Applications

Current applications of virtual reality are wide ranging and include computer-aided design (CAD), medical diagnostics and treatment, scientific experimentation in many physical and biological sciences, flight simulation for training pilots and astronauts, product demonstrations, employee training, and entertainment, especially 3-D video arcade games. CAD is the most widely used industrial VR application. It enables architects and other designers to design and test electronic 3-D models of products and structures by entering the models themselves and examining, touching, and manipulating sections and parts from all angles. This scientific-visualization capability is also used by pharmaceutical and biotechnology firms to develop and observe the behavior of computerized models of new drugs and materials, and by medical researchers to develop ways for physicians to enter and examine a virtual reality of a patient's body.

VR becomes *telepresence* when users who can be anywhere in the world use VR systems to work alone or together at a remote site. Typically, this involves using a VR system to enhance the sight and touch of a human who is remotely manipulating equipment to accomplish a task. Examples range from virtual surgery, where surgeon and patient may be on either side of the globe, to the remote use of equipment in hazardous environments such as chemical plants or nuclear reactors.

VR at Morgan Stanley

The Market Risks Department of Morgan Stanley & Co. uses Discovery virtual reality software by Visible Decisions to model risks of financial investments in varying market conditions. Discovery displays three-dimensional results using powerful Silicon Graphics workstations.

Morgan Stanley also uses VRML (virtual reality modeling language) as a way to display the results of risk analyses in three dimensions on PCs in their corporate intranet. (VRML allows developers to create hyperlinks between 3-D objects in files and databases on the World Wide Web and corporate intranets.) 3-D results are displayed on ordinary PCs in a virtual reality experience over an intranet connection to a Sun Microsystems SPARCstation server running a Sun VRML browser. Seeing data in three dimensions and experiencing relationships among data in a virtual reality process make it easier for analysts to make intuitive connections than it would be with a 2-D chart or table of numbers [45].

Intelligent Agents

Intelligent agents are growing in popularity as a way to use artificial intelligence routines in software to help users accomplish many kinds of tasks in e-business and e-commerce. An intelligent agent is a *software surrogate* for an end user or a process that fulfills a stated need or activity. An intelligent agent uses its built-in and learned knowledge base about a person or process to make decisions and accomplish tasks in a way that fulfills the intentions of a user. Sometimes an intelligent agent is given a graphic representation or persona, such as Einstein for a science advisor, Sherlock Holmes for an information search agent, and so on. Thus, intelligent agents (also called *software robots* or "bots") are special-purpose knowledge-based information systems that accomplish specific tasks for users. Figure 9.29 summarizes major types of intelligent agents [31].

One of the most well-known uses of intelligent agents is the wizards found in Microsoft Office and other software suites. These wizards are built-in capabilities that can analyze how an end user is using a software package and offer suggestions on how to complete various tasks. Thus, wizards might help you change document margins, format spreadsheet cells, query a database, or construct a graph. Wizards and other software agents are also designed to adjust to your way of using a software package so that they can anticipate when you will need their assistance. See Figure 9.30.

The use of intelligent agents is growing rapidly as a way to simplify software use, search websites on the Internet and corporate intranets, and help customers do

FIGURE 9.29

Examples of different types of intelligent agents

Types of Intelligent Agents
User Interface Agents
● **Interface Tutors.** Observe user computer operations, correct user mistakes, and provide hints and advice on efficient software use.
● **Presentation Agents.** Show information in a variety of reporting and presentation forms and media based on user preferences.
● **Network Navigation Agents.** Discover paths to information and provide ways to view information that are preferred by a user.
● **Role-Playing Agents.** Play what-if games and other roles to help users understand information and make better decisions.
Information Management Agents
● **Search Agents.** Help users find files and databases, search for desired information, and suggest and find new types of information products, media, and resources.
● **Information Brokers.** Provide commercial services to discover and develop information resources that fit the business or personal needs of a user.
● **Information Filters.** Receive, find, filter, discard, save, forward, and notify users about products received or desired, including e-mail, voice mail, and all other information media.

comparison shopping among the many e-commerce sites on the Web. Intelligent agents are becoming necessary as software packages become more sophisticated and powerful, as the Internet and the World Wide Web become more vast and complex, and as information sources and e-commerce alternatives proliferate exponentially. In fact, some commentators forecast that much of the future of computing will consist of intelligent agents performing their work for users.

FIGURE 9.30

Intelligent agents like those in Ask Jeeves help you find information in a variety of categories from many online sources.

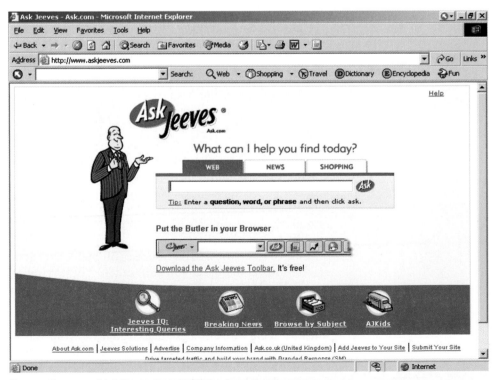

Source: Courtesy of Ask Jeeves, Inc., © 2000.

Dow Jones & Co.: Intelligent Web Agents	Websites such as Amazon.com's Shop the Web, Excite's Jango.com, and MySimon's MySimon.com use intelligent agent technology to help users compare prices for fragrances, book titles, or other items on multiple sites. Other types of agents can answer e-mail, conduct intelligent searches, or help users find news reports and useful sites based on stated preferences.

For example, dozens of sites can show you the news, but Dow Jones & Co.'s Dow Jones Interactive (www.djinteractive.com) is different. Nearly 600,000 customers pay to search through stories from its 6,000 licensed and internal publications. That's a huge amount of data to filter and the company has applied intelligent agent and other artificial intelligence (AI) technologies to manage the task.

One of the site's most important features is Custom Clips, which allows users to create folders based on predefined topics—such as agribusiness or IBM—or to build their own using custom key words. When the site IS agent retrieves relevant articles, it can post them to a database-generated Web page or send the stories to the user's e-mail address [30, 31].

Expert Systems

One of the most practical and widely implemented applications of artificial intelligence in business is the development of expert systems and other knowledge-based information systems. A *knowledge-based information system* (KBIS) adds a knowledge base to the major components found in other types of computer-based information systems. An **expert system** (ES) is a knowledge-based information system that uses its knowledge about a specific, complex application area to act as an expert consultant to end users. Expert systems provide answers to questions in a very specific problem area by making humanlike inferences about knowledge contained in a specialized knowledge base. They must also be able to explain their reasoning process and conclusions to a user. So expert systems can provide decision support to end users in the form of advice from an expert consultant in a specific problem area [16, 29].

Components of an Expert System

The components of an expert system include a knowledge base and software modules that perform inferences on the knowledge in the knowledge base and communicate answers to a user's questions. Figure 9.31 illustrates the interrelated components of an expert system. Note the following components:

- **Knowledge Base.** The knowledge base of an expert system contains (1) facts about a specific subject area (for example, *John is an analyst*) and (2) heuristics (rules of thumb) that express the reasoning procedures of an expert on the subject (for example: IF John is an analyst, THEN he needs a workstation). There are many ways that such knowledge is represented in expert systems. Examples are *rule-based*, *frame-based*, *object-based*, and *case-based* methods of knowledge representation. See Figure 9.32.

- **Software Resources.** An expert system software package contains an inference engine and other programs for refining knowledge and communicating with users. The **inference engine** program processes the knowledge (such as rules and facts) related to a specific problem. It then makes associations and inferences resulting in recommended courses of action for a user. User interface programs for communicating with end users are also needed, including an explanation program to explain the reasoning process to a user if requested. Knowledge acquisition programs are not part of an expert system but are software tools for knowledge base development, as are *expert system shells*, which are used for developing expert systems.

Expert System Applications

Using an expert system involves an interactive computer-based session in which the solution to a problem is explored, with the expert system acting as a consultant to an end user. The expert system asks questions of the user, searches its knowledge base for

FIGURE 9.31

Components of an expert system. The software modules perform inferences on a knowledge base built by an expert and/or knowledge engineer. This provides expert answers to an end user's questions in an interactive process.

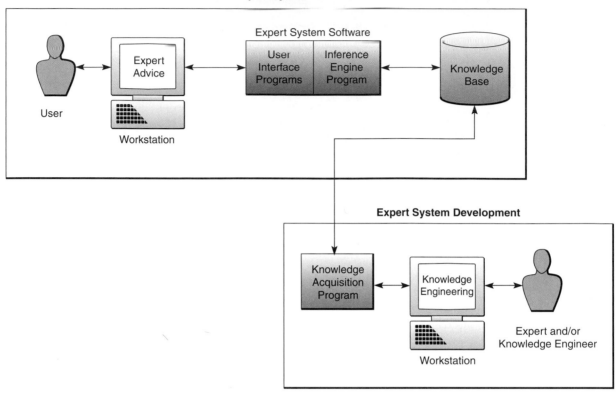

facts and rules or other knowledge, explains its reasoning process when asked, and gives expert advice to the user in the subject area being explored. For example, Figure 9.33 illustrates an expert system application.

Expert systems are being used for many different types of applications, and the variety of applications is expected to continue to increase. However, you should realize that expert systems typically accomplish one or more generic uses. Figure 9.34 outlines six generic categories of expert system activities, with specific examples of actual expert system applications. As you can see, expert systems are being used in many different fields, including medicine, engineering, the physical sciences, and business. Expert systems now help diagnose illnesses, search for minerals, analyze compounds, recommend repairs, and do financial planning. So from a strategic business standpoint,

FIGURE 9.32

A summary of four ways that knowledge can be represented in an expert system's knowledge base.

Methods of Knowledge Representation
● **Case-Based Reasoning.** Representing knowledge in an expert system's knowledge base in the form of cases, that is, examples of past performance, occurrences, and experiences.
● **Frame-Based Knowledge.** Knowledge represented in the form of a hierarchy or network of *frames*. A frame is a collection of knowledge about an entity consisting of a complex package of data values describing its attributes.
● **Object-Based Knowledge.** Knowledge represented as a network of objects. An object is a data element that includes both data and the methods or processes that act on those data.
● **Rule-Based Knowledge.** Knowledge represented in the form of rules and statements of fact. Rules are statements that typically take the form of a premise and a conclusion such as: If (condition), Then (conclusion).

FIGURE 9.33

Tivoli Systems Manager by IBM automatically monitors and manages the computers in a network with proactive expert system software components based on IBM's extensive mainframe systems management expertise.

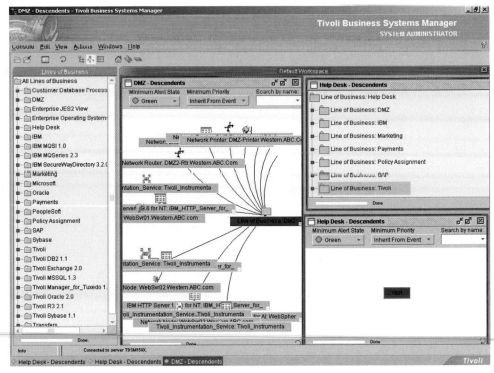

Source: Courtesy of IBM Corporation.

expert systems can and are being used to improve every step of the product cycle of a business, from finding customers to shipping products to providing customer service.

Benefits of Expert Systems

An expert system captures the expertise of an expert or group of experts in a computer-based information system. Thus, it can outperform a single human expert in many problem situations. That's because an expert system is faster and more consistent, can have the knowledge of several experts, and does not get tired or distracted by overwork or stress. Expert systems also help preserve and reproduce the knowledge of experts. They allow a company to preserve the expertise of an expert before she leaves the organization. This expertise can then be shared by reproducing the software and knowledge base of the expert system.

Limitations of Expert Systems

The major limitations of expert systems arise from their limited focus, inability to learn, maintenance problems, and developmental cost. Expert systems excel only in solving specific types of problems in a limited domain of knowledge. They fail miserably in solving problems requiring a broad knowledge base and subjective problem solving. They do well with specific types of operational or analytical tasks, but falter at subjective managerial decision making.

Expert systems may also be difficult and costly to develop and maintain properly. The costs of knowledge engineers, lost expert time, and hardware and software resources may be too high to offset the benefits expected from some applications. Also, expert systems can't maintain themselves. That is, they can't learn from experience but must be taught new knowledge and modified as new expertise is needed to match developments in their subject areas.

Cutler-Hammer: Strategic Expert System

Cutler-Hammer's IT people were pioneers when they began work in 1995 on an expert system software program called Bid Manager. Its original purpose was to let customers' engineers deal more directly with the factory. Today Bid Manager has grown into a giant software package with six million lines of code, a far-reaching

FIGURE 9.34

Major application categories and examples of typical expert systems. Note the variety of applications that can be supported by such systems.

Application Categories of Expert Systems

- **Decision management**—Systems that appraise situations or consider alternatives and make recommendations based on criteria supplied during the discovery process:
  - Loan portfolio analysis
  - Employee performance evaluation
  - Insurance underwriting
  - Demographic forecasts

- **Diagnostic/troubleshooting**—Systems that infer underlying causes from reported symptoms and history:
  - Equipment calibration
  - Help desk operations
  - Software debugging
  - Medical diagnosis

- **Design/configuration**—Systems that help configure equipment components, given existing constraints:
  - Computer option installation
  - Manufacturability studies
  - Communications networks
  - Optimum assembly plan

- **Selection/classification**—Systems that help users choose products or processes, often from among large or complex sets of alternatives:
  - Material selection
  - Delinquent account identification
  - Information classification
  - Suspect identification

- **Process monitoring/control**—Systems that monitor and control procedures or processes:
  - Machine control (including robotics)
  - Inventory control
  - Production monitoring
  - Chemical testing

all-embracing e-manufacturing weapon with a sharp competitive edge. Not surprisingly, Cutler-Hammer has kept it largely under wraps.

To start with, the program allows a customer, a distributor, or one of the company's sales engineers in the field to easily configure the sometimes devilishly complex innards of Cutler-Hammer equipment with its convoluted wiring patterns and precise placement of dozens of electronic and electrical components. The software automatically checks that the engineer does everything right. If he places a switch or a wire in the wrong spot, he gets a gentle electronic slap on the wrist—an onscreen message pointing out the mistake. Bid Manager contains literally thousands of rules to ensure that designs are done correctly; at the same time, it allows for idiosyncrasies—a user may want the equipment to turn on electric motors in a certain way, for instance.

"No outsider could possibly know an industry such as ours well enough to cover it the way Bid Manager does," says Barbara J. Riesmeyer, manager of IT at Cutler-Hammer's power and control systems division and a developer of Bid Manager. To create the software, the company enlisted not only 15 software writers but also experts at the plants, sales engineers, and many others. Director of e-business Ray L. Huber led the team and, with Riesmeyer, created what they call the design-to-delivery (D2D) vision.

With more than 61,000 orders processed electronically in one year at Cutler-Hammer, the expert system unquestionably has proved itself. Plant managers Frank C. Campbell at Sumter and Steven R. Kavanaugh at Fayetteville overflow with praise for the software. It's easy to see why. Where in the past paperwork stifled production flow, now Bid Manager takes care of even small but significant details. What's more, says Huber, "Bid Manager has helped us think differently about products." For example, Cutler-Hammer has standardized its products and models, slimming down the number of steel enclosure sizes from more than 400 to only 100.

There's no question that the expert system has decisively helped Cutler-Hammer's business. CEO Randy Carson reports that Bid Manager has increased Cutler-Hammer's market share for configured products—motor control centers, control panels, and the like—by 15 percent. He adds that Bid Manager has boosted sales of the larger assemblies by 20 percent, doubling profits, increasing productivity by 35 percent, and reducing quality costs by 26 percent. He concludes, "Bid Manager has transformed Cutler-Hammer into a customer-driven company [9]."

Developing Expert Systems

What types of problems are most suitable to expert system solutions? One way to answer this is to look at examples of the applications of current expert systems, including the generic tasks they can accomplish, as were summarized in Figure 9.34. Another way is to identify criteria that make a problem situation suitable for an expert system. Figure 9.35 outlines some important criteria.

Figure 9.35 should emphasize that many real world situations do not fit the suitability criteria for expert system solutions. Hundreds of rules may be required to capture the assumptions, facts, and reasoning that are involved in even simple problem situations. For example, a task that might take an expert a few minutes to accomplish might require an expert system with hundreds of rules and take several months to develop [42].

The easiest way to develop an expert system is to use an **expert system shell** as a developmental tool. An expert system shell is a software package consisting of an expert system without its kernel, that is, its knowledge base. This leaves a *shell* of software (the inference engine and user interface programs) with generic inferencing and user interface capabilities. Other development tools (such as rule editors and user interface generators) are added in making the shell a powerful expert system development tool.

Expert system shells are now available as relatively low-cost software packages that help users develop their own expert systems on microcomputers. They allow trained users to develop the knowledge base for a specific expert system application. For example, one shell uses a spreadsheet format to help end users develop IF-THEN rules, automatically generating rules based on examples furnished by a user. Once a knowledge base is constructed, it is used with the shell's inference engine and user interface modules as a complete expert system on a specific subject area. Other software tools may require an IT specialist to develop expert systems. See Figure 9.36.

FIGURE 9.35

Criteria for applications that are suitable for expert systems development.

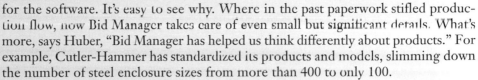

Suitability Criteria for Expert Systems
● **Domain:** The domain, or subject area, of the problem is relatively small and limited to a well-defined problem area.
● **Expertise:** Solutions to the problem require the efforts of an expert. That is, a body of knowledge, techniques, and intuition is needed that only a few people possess.
● **Complexity:** Solution of the problem is a complex task that requires logical inference processing, which would not be handled as well by conventional information processing.
● **Structure:** The solution process must be able to cope with ill-structured, uncertain, missing, and conflicting data, and a problem situation that changes with the passage of time.
● **Availability:** An expert exists who is articulate and cooperative, and who has the support of the management and end users involved in the development of the proposed system.

FIGURE 9.36

Using the Visual Rule Studio and Visual Basic to develop rules for a credit management expert system.

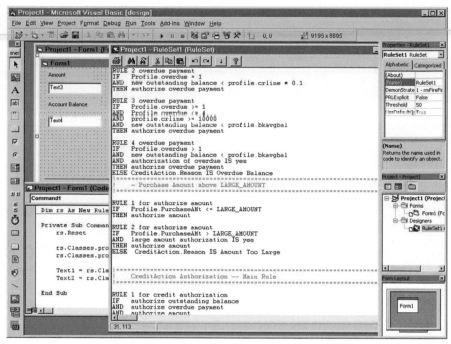

Source: Courtesy of MultiLogic Inc.

Knowledge Engineering

A **knowledge engineer** is a professional who works with experts to capture the knowledge (facts and rules of thumb) they possess. The knowledge engineer then builds the knowledge base (and the rest of the expert system if necessary), using an iterative, prototyping process until the expert system is acceptable. Thus, knowledge engineers perform a role similar to that of systems analysts in conventional information systems development.

Once the decision is made to develop an expert system, a team of one or more domain experts and a knowledge engineer may be formed. Or experts skilled in the use of expert system shells could develop their own expert systems. If a shell is used, facts and rules of thumb about a specific domain can be defined and entered into a knowledge base with the help of a rule editor or other knowledge acquisition tool. A limited working prototype of the knowledge base is then constructed, tested, and evaluated using the inference engine and user interface programs of the shell. The knowledge engineer and domain experts can modify the knowledge base, then retest the system and evaluate the results. This process is repeated until the knowledge base and the shell result in an acceptable expert system.

ES Development at MacMillan Bloedel

MacMillan Bloedel Corp. is a forest products conglomerate in British Columbia, Canada, that produces particleboard used in building items such as bookshelves, furniture, and kitchen cupboards. Due to high staff turnover and a reorganization of divisional personnel at the particleboard plant, only two senior employees had the comprehensive, operational know-how and training needed to operate the facility. After they retired, MacMillan had to call back a former manager, named Herb, as a very expensive consultant to keep the mill running. So MacMillan decided to develop an expert system to capture his knowledge of plant operations. The expert system that resulted documents the procedures needed to efficiently run the facility, and is also used for training and upgrading employees.

Knowledge engineers used the ACQUIRE expert system shell from Acquired Intellup for the particleboard coating line. The line consisted of machines whose operations parameters changed according to the coating to be applied. Herb was able to provide expert information, in the form of facts and rules, that was captured in the expert system's knowledge base. The resulting expert system consistently provides quality maintenance and operations advice to the mill operators [16].

Summary

- **Information, Decisions, and Management.** Information systems can support a variety of management decision-making levels and decisions. These include the three levels of management activity (strategic, tactical, and operational decision making) and three types of decision structures (structured, semistructured, and unstructured). Information systems provide a wide range of information products to support these types of decisions at all levels of the organization.

- **Decision Support Trends.** Major changes are taking place in traditional MIS, DSS, and EIS tools for providing the information and modeling managers need to support their decision making. Decision support in business is changing, driven by rapid developments in end user computing and networking; Internet and Web technologies; and Web-enabled business applications. The growth of corporate intranets, extranets, as well as the Web, has accelerated the development of "executive class" interfaces like enterprise information portals and Web-enabled business intelligence software tools, and their use by lower levels of management and by individuals and teams of business professionals. In addition, the growth of e-commerce and e-business applications has expanded the use of enterprise portals and DSS tools by the suppliers, customers, and other business stakeholders of a company.

- **Management Information Systems.** Management information systems provide prespecified reports and responses to managers on a periodic, exception, demand, or push reporting basis, to meet their need for information to support decision making.

- **OLAP and Data Mining.** Online analytical processing interactively analyzes complex relationships among large amounts of data stored in multidimensional databases. Data mining analyzes the vast amounts of historical data that have been prepared for analysis in data warehouses. Both technologies discover patterns, trends, and exception conditions in a company's data that support their business analysis and decision making.

- **Decision Support Systems.** Decision support systems are interactive, computer-based information systems that use DSS software and a model base and database to provide information tailored to support semistructured and unstructured decisions faced by individual managers. They are designed to use a decision maker's own insights and judgments in an ad hoc, interactive, analytical modeling process leading to a specific decision.

- **Executive Information Systems.** Executive information systems are information systems originally designed to support the strategic information needs of top management. However, their use is spreading to lower levels of management and business professionals. EIS are easy to use and enable executives to retrieve information tailored to their needs and preferences. Thus, EIS can provide information about a company's critical success factors to executives to support their planning and control responsibilities.

- **Enterprise Information and Knowledge Portals.** Enterprise information portals provide a customized and personalized Web-based interface for corporate intranets to give their users easy access to a variety of internal and external business applications, databases, and information services that are tailored to their individual preferences and information needs. Thus, an EIP can supply personalized Web-enabled information, knowledge, and decision support to executives, managers, and business professionals, as well as customers, suppliers, and other business partners. An enterprise knowledge portal is a corporate intranet portal that extends the use of an EIP to include knowledge management functions and knowledge base resources so that it becomes a major form of knowledge management system for a company.

- **Artificial Intelligence.** The major application domains of artificial intelligence (AI) include a variety of applications in cognitive science, robotics, and natural interfaces. The goal of AI is the development of computer functions normally associated with human physical and mental capabilities, such as robots that see, hear, talk, feel, and move, and software capable of reasoning, learning, and problem solving. Thus, AI is being applied to many applications in business operations and managerial decision making, as well as in many other fields.

- **AI Technologies.** The many application areas of AI are summarized in Figure 9.23, including neural networks, fuzzy logic, genetic algorithms, virtual reality, and intelligent agents. Neural nets are hardware or software systems based on simple models of the brain's neuron structure that can learn to recognize patterns in data. Fuzzy logic systems use rules of approximate reasoning to solve problems where data are incomplete or ambiguous. Genetic algorithms use selection, randomizing, and other mathematics functions to simulate an evolutionary process that can yield increasingly better solutions to problems. Virtual reality systems are multisensory systems that enable human users to experience computer-simulated environments as if they actually existed. Intelligent agents are knowledge-based software surrogates for a user or process in the accomplishment of selected tasks.

- **Expert Systems.** Expert systems are knowledge-based information systems that use software and a knowledge base about a specific, complex application area to act as expert consultants to users in many business and technical applications. Software includes an inference engine program that makes inferences based on the facts and rules stored in the knowledge base. A knowledge base consists of facts about a specific subject area and heuristics (rules of thumb) that express the reasoning procedures of an expert. The benefits of expert systems (such as preservation and replication of expertise) must be balanced with their limited applicability in many problem situations.

Key Terms and Concepts

These are the key terms and concepts of this chapter. The page number of their first explanation is in parentheses.

1. Analytical modeling (304)
   a. Goal-seeking analysis (305)
   b. Optimization analysis (306)
   c. Sensitivity analysis (305)
   d. What-if analysis (305)
2. Artificial intelligence (316)
   a. Application areas (316)
   b. Domains (316)
3. Business intelligence (297)
4. Data mining (307)
5. Data visualization system (303)
6. Decision structure (295)
7. Decision support system (301)
8. Decision support trends (296)
9. DSS components (302)
10. Enterprise information portal (310)
11. Enterprise knowledge portal (312)
12. Executive information system (308)
13. Expert system (325)
    a. Applications (325)
    b. Benefits and limitations (327)
    c. Components (325)
    d. System development (329)
14. Expert system shell (329)
15. Fuzzy logic (320)
16. Genetic algorithms (321)
17. Geographic information system (303)
18. Inference engine (325)
19. Intelligent agent (323)
20. Knowledge base (325)
21. Knowledge engineer (330)
22. Knowledge management system (312)
23. Level of management decision making (294)
24. Management information system (298)
25. Model base (302)
26. Neural network (319)
27. Online analytical processing (300)
28. Reporting alternatives (298)
29. Robotics (317)
30. Virtual reality (321)

Review Quiz

Match one of the key terms and concepts listed previously with one of the brief examples or definitions that follow. Try to find the best fit for answers that seem to fit more than one term or concept. Defend your choices.

_____ 1. Internet technologies and e-business developments have expanded the form and use of decision support in business.

_____ 2. Decision support systems rely on DSS software, model bases, and databases as system resources.

_____ 3. A CEO and a production team may have different needs for decision making.

_____ 4. Decision-making procedures cannot be specified in advance for some complex decision situations.

_____ 5. Information systems for the strategic information needs of top and middle managers.

_____ 6. Systems that produce predefined reports for management.

_____ 7. Managers can receive reports periodically, on an exception basis, or on demand.

_____ 8. Provide an interactive modeling capability tailored to the specific information needs of managers.

_____ 9. Provides business information and analytical tools for managers, business professionals, and business stakeholders.

_____ 10. A collection of mathematical models and analytical techniques.

_____ 11. Analyzing the effect of changing variables and relationships and manipulating a mathematical model.

_____ 12. Changing revenues and tax rates to see the effect on net profit after taxes.

_____ 13. Changing revenues in many small increments to see revenue's effect on net profit after taxes.

_____ 14. Changing revenues and expenses to find how you could achieve a specific amount of net profit after taxes.

_____ 15. Changing revenues and expenses subject to certain constraints in order to achieve the highest profit after taxes.

_____ 16. Realtime analysis of complex business data.

_____ 17. Attempts to find patterns hidden in business data in a data warehouse.

_____ 18. Represents complex data using three-dimensional graphical forms.

_____ 19. A customized and personalized Web interface to internal and external information resources available through a corporate intranet.

_____ 20. Using intranets to gather, store, and share a company's best practices among employees.

_____ 21. An enterprise information portal that can access knowledge management functions and company knowledge bases.

_____ 22. Information technology that focuses on the development of computer functions normally associated with human physical and mental capabilities.

_____ 23. Applications in cognitive science, robotics, and natural interfaces.

_____ 24. Development of computer-based machines that possess capabilities such as sight, hearing, dexterity, and movement.

_____ 25. Computers that can provide you with computer-simulated experiences.

_____ 26. An information system that integrates computer graphics, geographic databases, and DSS capabilities.

_____ 27. A knowledge-based information system that acts as an expert consultant to users in a specific application area.

_____ 28. Applications such as diagnosis, design, prediction, interpretation, and repair.

_____ 29. These systems can preserve and reproduce the knowledge of experts but have a limited application focus.

_____ 30. A collection of facts and reasoning procedures in a specific subject area.

_____ 31. A software package that manipulates a knowledge base and makes associations and inferences leading to a recommended course of action.

_____ 32. A software package consisting of an inference engine and user interface programs used as an expert system development tool.

_____ 33. One can either buy a completely developed expert system package, develop one with an expert system shell, or develop one from scratch by custom programming.

_____ 34. An analyst who interviews experts to develop a knowledge base about a specific application area.

_____ 35. AI systems that use neuron structures to recognize patterns in data.

_____ 36. AI systems that use approximate reasoning to process ambiguous data.

_____ 37. Knowledge-based software surrogates that do things for you.

_____ 38. Software that uses mathematical functions to simulate an evolutionary process.

Discussion Questions

1. Is the form and use of information and decision support systems for managers and business professionals changing and expanding? Why or why not?

2. Has the growth of self-directed teams to manage work in organizations changed the need for strategic, tactical, and operational decision making in business?

3. What is the difference between the ability of a manager to retrieve information instantly on demand using an MIS and the capabilities provided by a DSS?

4. Refer to the Real World Case on Ben & Jerry's and GE Plastics in the chapter. How might a digital dashboard help you as a business professional or manager in your work activities? Give several examples to illustrate your answer.

5. In what ways does using an electronic spreadsheet package provide you with the capabilities of a decision support system?

6. Are enterprise information portals making executive information systems unneccessary? Explain your reasoning.

7. Refer to the Real World Case on Wal-Mart, BankFinancial, and HP in the chapter. Why are neural network and expert system technologies used in many data-mining applications?

8. Can computers think? Will they ever be able to? Explain why or why not.

9. What are some of the most important applications of AI in business? Defend your choices.

10. What are some of the limitations or dangers you see in the use of AI technologies such as expert systems, virtual reality, and intelligent agents? What could be done to minimize such effects?

Analysis Exercises

1. BizRate.com: eCommerce Website Reviews

Visit *www.bizrate.com* and you instantly have information about hundreds of online stores. Stores include books, music, electronics, clothes, hardware, gifts, and more. Thousands of previous shoppers also provide their opinion about each retailer. See Figure 9.37.

Over the course of four clicks from BizRate's home page, you will find increasing detailed information about a product and prospective online retailers. By the fourth click, you find yourself at my chosen retailer's website and ready to add the CD to your virtual shopping cart.

a. Use BizRate.com to check out retailers for a product you want to buy. How thorough, valid, and valuable were the reviews to you? Explain.

b. How could other businesses use a similar web-enabled review system? Give an example.

c. How is BizRate.com similar to a web enabled decision support system (DSS)?

2. Enterprise Application Integration

Information coming from a variety of business systems can appear on the executive desktop as a consolidated whole. The information contained in such a view might include the executive's schedule, current e-mail, a brief list of production delays, major accounts past due, current sales summaries, and a financial market summary. While it isn't possible to fit all an organization's information on a single screen, it is possible to summarize data in ways specified by the executive and then act as a launching point or portal for further point and click enquiries.

How might such a system look? Portals such as my.Excite.com, my.MSN.com, my.Lycos.com, and my.Yahoo.com make good general-purpose information portals. These websites contain characteristics in common with their business-oriented brethren. They provide information from many different sources and they allow users to determine what information sources they see. They also allow a user to drill down into the information they find important to receive more detail.

Once a user has set up an account and identified his or her preferences, these public portals remember the user's preferences and deliver only what the user has requested. Users may change their preferences as often as they wish, and the controls to make these changes require only point and click programming skills.

a. Visit one of the portal sites listed above. Configure the site to meet your own information needs. Provide a printout of the result.

b. Look up product reviews for one enterprise application integration (or EAI) solution using a search engine. Outline the strengths and weaknesses identified for that product.

FIGURE 9.37

The BizRate website offers customer reviews of online stores.

Source: Courtesy of www.bizrate.com.

3. Case-Based System Sells Books on Amazon.com

A case-based reasoning system is a type of "expert system." It attempts to match the facts on hand to a database of prior "cases." When a case-based reasoning system finds one or more cases in its database that match the facts at hand, it then evaluates and reports the most common outcomes. Given enough cases, such a system can prove very useful. Even better, if a case-based system can automatically capture cases as they occur, then it will become a powerful tool that continually fine-tunes its results as it gains "experience."

One can see just such a system in operation at the Amazon.com website. Amazon.com offers a search engine that helps visitors find books by subject, author, or title. Amazon.com offers a tool that allows users to both rate and review books they have read. So how does Amazon.com use case-based reasoning systems to boost sales? Amazon.com takes its database interactivity a step farther than simple searches and customer ratings. Given a particular book title, Amazon.com's case-based reasoning engine examines all past sales of that book to see if the customers who bought that book shared other book purchases in common. It then produces a short list and presents that list to the user. The overall effect approaches that of a sales clerk who says "oh! If you like this book, then you'll really like reading these as well." However, Amazon's system has the experience of hundreds of millions more transactions than the most wizened and well-read sales clerk.

Equipped with this information, customers can then learn more about similar books before making a purchase decision. This information may encourage customers to buy several books, or it may increase the customers' confidence that they have selected the right book. In either case, this information translates to more book sales.

a. Using Figure 9.22, indicate whether or not each of the attributes of artificially intelligent behavior applies to Amazon.com's case-based reasoning system.

b. For those attributes that apply as indicated by your answers above, explain how Amazon.com's system creates that behavior. For example, Amazon.com handles ambiguous, incomplete, or erroneous information by linking its recommendations to a specific book rather than to the user's search terms. In short, Amazon.com's system works to reduce ambiguity by forcing a user to select a specific book first.

4. Palm City Police Department

The Palm City Police Department has eight defined precincts. The police station in each precinct has primary responsibility for all activities in its precinct area. The table below lists the current population of each precinct, the number of violent crimes committed in each precinct, and the number of officers assigned to each precinct. The department has established a goal of equalizing access to police services. Ratios of population per police officer and violent crimes per police officer should be calculated for each precinct. These ratios for the city as a whole are shown below.

a. Build a spreadsheet to perform the analysis described above and print it out.

b. Currently, no funds are available to hire additional officers. Based on the citywide ratios, the department has decided to develop a plan to shift resources as needed in order to ensure that no precinct has more than 1,100 residents per police officer and no precinct has more than seven violent crimes per police officer. The department will transfer officers from precincts that easily meet these goals to precincts that violate one or both of these ratios. Use "goal seeking" on your spreadsheet to move police officers between precincts until the goals are met. You can use the goal seek function to see how many officers would be required to bring each precinct into compliance and then judgmentally reduce officers in precincts that are substantially within the criteria. Print out a set of results that allow the departments to comply with these ratios and a memorandum to your instructor summarizing your results and the process you used to develop them.

Precinct	Population	Violent Crimes	Police Officers
Shea Blvd.	96,552	318	85
Lakeland Heights	99,223	582	108
Sunnydale	68,432	206	77
Old Town	47,732	496	55
Mountainview	101,233	359	82
Financial District	58,102	511	70
Riverdale	78,903	537	70
Cole Memorial	75,801	306	82
Total	**625,978**	**3,315**	**629**
Per officer	**995.196**	**5.270**	

Procter & Gamble and Others: Using Agent-Based Modeling for Supply Chain Management

When it comes to IT projects, it doesn't get much better than this: Procter & Gamble Co. (www.pg.com), saves $300 million annually on an investment of less than 1 percent of that amount. Indeed, P&G's use of agent-based modeling helped it transform its supply chain system so fundamentally that the company no longer even calls it a supply chain. The Cincinnati-based maker of over 300 consumer products now calls its connections to 5 billion consumers in 140 countries a "supply network." "*Chain* connotes something that is sequential, that requires handing off information in sequence," says Larry Kellam, P&G's director of supply network innovation. "We believe it has to operate like a network, like an internet, so everybody has visibility to the information."

Many of the insights that have enabled P&G to transform a chain into a network come from agent-based computer models it developed with the BiosGroup, recently aquired by NuTech Solutions Inc. (www.nutechsolutions. com). Their work is a real-world example of what mathematicians call "agent-based modeling of complex, adaptive systems." The idea is that many systems that are enormously complex overall are in fact made up of semiautonomous local "agents" acting on a few simple rules. By modeling and changing the agents' behavior, one can understand and optimize the entire system.

In P&G's computer simulations, software agents represent the individual components of the supply system, such as trucks, drivers, stores, and so on. The behavior of each agent is programmed via rules that mimic actual behavior, such as, "Dispatch this truck only when it is full," or "Make more shampoo when inventory falls to x days' demand." The simulations let P&G perform what-if analyses to test the impact of new logistics rules on three key metrics: inventory levels, transportation costs, and in-store stock-outs. The models considered alternate rules on ordering and shipping frequencies, distribution center product allocation policies, demand forecasting, and so on.

"Some of the conclusions were surprising, and some confirmed what we believed but didn't have the data to support," Kellam says. For example, he says, the models showed that it would often be advantageous to send out trucks with less than full loads, something P&G almost never did before. Although transportation costs would be higher as a result, P&G could more than make that up by reducing the frequency of in-store stock-outs, which often result in lost sales. "Agent-based modeling convinced us of some changes we fundamentally had to make if we were to be flexible and adaptable," Kellam says, explaining that changes fell into the following three broad areas:

- Relaxation of rigid rules, often counterintuitively, in order to improve the overall performance of the supply network. That required some cultural changes, such as convincing freight managers that it's sometimes OK to let a truck go half-full.

- More flexibility in manufacturing. As a result of insights gained by the models, P&G is "fundamentally retooling" its manufacturing processes so that it no longer produces long runs of a single product but instead is able to produce every product every day. The benefits include fewer stock-outs and happier customers.

- More flexibility in distribution. For example, it's possible to restock a retailer in 24 hours rather than the customary 48 to 72 hours.

P&G uses supply chain management software from SAP AG, but it turned to BiosGroup's agent modeling technology when its long efforts to decrease inventory levels produced only marginal improvements. Agent-based modeling, while not yet commonplace, is catching on, especially at companies with large, complex supply or transportation networks. In addition to P&G, the following companies have tried it and cite benefits that include cost savings, reduced inventories, and better customer service:

- Southwest Airlines Co. used software agents to optimize cargo routing.
- Air Liquide America LP, a Houston-based producer of liquefied industrial gases, reduced both production and distribution costs with agent-based modeling.
- Ford Motor Co. used agents to simulate buyer preferences, suggesting packages of car options that optimized the trade-offs between production costs and customer demands.

Computer modeling of supply chain operations, like that done by BiosGroup and P&G, today requires a combination of custom software development and consulting. But that could change as a result of a development agreement that P&G had fostered between SAP and BiosGroup. SAP has already demonstrated a prototype agent capability in its replenishment software. SAP may introduce the prototype technology in its products, Knoll says, but for now it's helping a few key customers try it out on a project basis.

Case Study Questions

1. Do you agree with Proctor & Gamble that a supply chain should be called a supply network? Why or why not?

2. What is the business value of agent-based modeling? Use P&G and other companies in this case as examples.

3. Visit the website of NuTech Solutions. How does NuTech use AI techniques to help companies gain "adaptive" business intelligence? Give several examples from the website case studies.

Source: Adapted from Gary Anthes, "Agents of Change," *Computerworld*, January 27, 2003, pp. 26–27. Copyright © 2003 by Computerworld, Inc. Framingham, MA 01701. All rights reserved.

REAL WORLD CASE 4

REAL WORLD CASE 4

Boehringer Ingelheim: Using Web-Based Tools for Financial Analysis and Reporting

Boehringer Ingelheim (www.boehringer-ingelheim. com), is a huge company, with $7.6 billion in revenue and 32,000 employees in 60 nations. But the Ingelheim, Germany-based pharmaceutical maker says Web-enabled reporting and financial applications are making the company as nimble as some of its smaller competitors when it comes to running financials.

Like many large corporations, Boehringer is turning to Web-based financial and analytical tools to rapidly consolidate and present key financial data on a daily, weekly, or monthly basis. The company uses a Web-enabled version of SAP AG's financial software, which allows it to drill down and draw conclusions based on the latest available financial and operational data. "I want to be told where I stand and where we are heading" says Boehringer's chief financial officer, Holger Huels. "I like to be able to see negative trends and counter them as fast as possible." More important, Boehringer is now able to close its books for most of its divisions just two hours after the close of business at the end of each month, says Huels.

That's a big change for Boehringer's accounting department, which previously had to wait for printed reports and then pick through them manually. The staff used a variety of software tools for financial analysis, says Tony Ciancio, Boehringer's director of accounting. The closing process spanned three days each month, including the time required to reconcile data from the disparate systems.

The pharmaceutical company switched to the SAP Financials SAP R/3 system a little more than a year ago, after a 14-month rollout. Delivering the necessary information required some integration work with several procurement systems that tied into SAP. Boehringer also had to write custom interfaces to link its SAP system to its Manugistics production planning application.

The new system uses the Cognos Inc. (www.cognos.com) Impromptu reporting tool to report financial results from an Oracle-managed data warehouse, which takes feeds from the SAP system each night, says Ciancio. Impromptu then creates standard income statements, cost center reporting, and account-level analysis. Impromptu also lets the accounting staff drill down to individual transactions. Ciancio says that with three and a half years worth of SAP data, his department can spot product sales trends and track expenses such as personnel costs, which are frequently reviewed and compared with net sales and other metrics.

The biggest difficulty in implementing the new system was training staff to deal with the unique way the SAP application deals with pharmaceutical-specific accounting procedures as it reports revenue, says Ciancio. Despite the amount of time required for training, the system has made the accounting department much more productive, in part because the staff can now run up-to-date reports whenever needed, according to Ciancio.

Boehringer also uses the Cognos PowerPlay business intelligence tool, which permits multidimensional views of profit-and-loss data. "We can quickly analyze revenue and expense information by switching the columnar and row data, and also bring in different dimensions or measures such as budget or prior year, then drill down and get subsets of the data," Ciancio says. Executives can access this data through Cognos Upfront, which securely delivers the reports via a browser over the Boehringer intranet. The system also allows for ad hoc analyses. The most common of these are transaction reviews that let users get fast summaries by customer account or product.

Ciancio says the new system is running as efficiently as possible, but it has limitations. For instance, there is still a one-day lag in reporting because some parts of the global organization are still using different systems. Boehringer usually closes the books for four of its divisions in 12 hours, typically on the first business day of the month, Ciancio explains. However, three units don't use the SAP Financials system and its general ledger. So those units have to close independently, and then the financial data is consolidated through Excel spreadsheets into the Cognos Finance tool for reporting, which requires manual intervention and takes another day. "For many reports, this is acceptable. For others, we are evaluating options for getting real-time updates and reporting up to the minute to the Web," Ciancio says.

But Boehringer plans to roll out the Web-based SAP Financials system to most of its subsidiaries worldwide over the next few years says Ciancio. Despite some problems, the company is convinced that the savings from the new system have already exceeded expectations, he says.

Case Study Questions

1. What are the business benefits and limitations of Boehringer's Web-based financial analysis and reporting systems?

2. Which of Boehringer's financial analysis and reporting systems are MIS tools? DSS tools? Why?

3. How could the Cognos tools used by Boehringer be used for marketing and other business analysis and reporting applications? Visit the Cognos website to help you answer.

MODULE IV

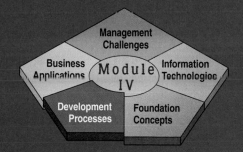

Management
Challenges

Business
Applications

Module
IV

Information
Technologies

Development
Processes

Foundation
Concepts

DEVELOPMENT PROCESSES

How can business professionals develop and implement information system solutions to meet the challenges and opportunities faced in today's business environment? Answering that question is the goal of the chapter of this module, which concentrates on the processes for developing and implementing IT-based business applications.

- Chapter 10, **Developing Business/IT Solutions,** introduces the traditional, prototyping, and end user approaches to the development of information systems, and discusses the processes and managerial issues in the implementation of new business applications of information technology.

CHAPTER 10

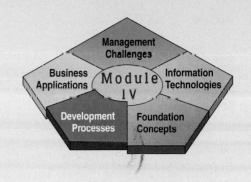

DEVELOPING BUSINESS/IT SOLUTIONS

Chapter Highlights

Section I
Developing Business Systems

IS Development

Real World Case: Blue Cross, AT&T Wireless, and CitiStreet: Development Challenges of Self-Service Web Systems

The Systems Approach

The Systems Development Cycle

Prototyping

Starting the Systems Development Process

Systems Analysis

Systems Design

End User Development

Section II
Implementing Business Systems

Implementation

Real World Case: InterContinental Hotels, Del Taco, and Cardinal Health: Implementation Strategies

Implementing New Systems

Evaluating Hardware, Software, and Services

Other Implementation Activities

Managing Organizational Change

Real World Case: Du Pont and Southwire: Implementing Successful Enterprise Information Portals

Real World Case: Wyndham International and Amazon.com: Cost-Effective IT

Learning Objectives

After reading and studying this chapter, you should be able to:

1. Use the systems development process outlined in this chapter, and the model of IS components from Chapter 1 as problem-solving frameworks to help you propose information systems solutions to simple business problems.

2. Describe and give examples to illustrate how you might use each of the steps of the information systems development cycle to develop and implement a business information system.

3. Explain how prototyping improves the process of systems development for end users and IS specialists.

4. Identify the activities involved in the implementation of new information systems.

5. Describe several evaluation factors that should be considered in evaluating the acquisition of hardware, software, and IS services.

6. Identify several change management solutions for end user resistance to the implementation of new information systems.

SECTION I	Developing Business Systems

IS Development

Suppose the chief executive of the company where you work asks you to find a Web-enabled way to get information to and from the salespeople in your company. How would you start? What would you do? Would you just plunge ahead and hope you could come up with a reasonable solution? How would you know whether your solution was a good one for your company? Do you think there might be a systematic way to help you develop a good solution to the CEO's request? There is. It's a problem-solving process called *the systems approach.*

When the systems approach to problem solving is applied to the development of information systems solutions to business problems, it is called *information systems development or application development.* This section will show you how the systems approach can be used to develop e-business systems and applications that meet the business needs of a company and its employees and stakeholders.

Analyzing Blue Cross, AT&T Wireless, and CitiStreet

Refer to the Real World Case on Blue Cross, AT&T Wireless, and CitiStreet in the chapter. We can learn a lot about the design challenges in designing and developing websites from this example. See Figure 10.1.

This case highlights some of the reasons why over a third of the users of self-service websites leave without finishing and call a help center instead. Such sites are now a business necessity for many companies. For example, Blue Cross–Blue Shield of Minnesota had to offer Web self-service systems for client employees of several major corporations or lose their health plan business. One of the challenges in the development process for the new systems involved redesigning drop-down dialog boxes that a focus group of users found confusing. AT&T Wireless had to redesign a process in

FIGURE 10.1

Andy Marsh, CIO of CitiStreet, acquired a software tool that enables business analysts to change the business rules encoded in the software of their benefit plan systems.

Source: Kelly Laduke.

REAL WORLD CASE 1

Blue Cross, AT&T Wireless, and CitiStreet: Development Challenges of Self-Service Web Systems

When Web-based self-service is good, it's really good. Customer satisfaction soars and call center costs plummet as customers answer their own questions, enter their own credit card numbers, and change their own passwords without expensive live help.

But when Web-based self-service is bad, it's really bad. Frustrated customers click to a competitor's site or dial up your call center—meaning you've paid for both a self-service website and for a call center, and the customer is still unhappy. A poorly designed Web interface that greets self-service users with a confusing sequence of options or asks them questions they can't answer is a sure way to force them to call a help center.

Blue Cross-Blue Shield. For Blue Cross–Blue Shield of Minnesota (www.bluecrossmn.com), developing Web self-service capabilities for employee health insurance plans meant the difference between winning and losing several major clients, including retailer Target, Northwest Airlines, and General Mills. "Without it, they would not do business with us," explains John Ounjian, CIO and senior vice president of information systems and corporate adjudication services at the $5 billion insurance provider. So when Ounjian explained to executives that the customer relationship management (CRM) project that would enable Web-based self-service by client employees would cost $15 million for the first two phases, they didn't blink.

Blue Cross–Blue Shield also learned the importance of communicating with business units during the design phase of its Web self-service system. Ounjian and his technical team designed screen displays that featured drop-down boxes that they thought were logical, but a focus group of end users that examined a prototype system found the feature cumbersome and the wording hard to understand. "We had to adjust our logic," he says, of the subsequent redesign.

AT&T Wireless. When AT&T Wireless Services (www.attws.com) began rolling out its new high-bandwidth wireless networks, its self-service website required customers to say whether their phones used the older Time Division Multiple Access (TDMA) network or the newer, third-generation network. Most people didn't know which network they used, only which calling plan they had signed up for, says Scott Cantrell, e-business IT program manager at AT&T Wireless. So AT&T had to redesign the site so the customer just enters his user ID and password, "And the application follows built-in rules to automatically send you to the right website," Cantrell says.

According to Gartner Inc., more than a third of all customers or users who initiate queries over the Web eventually get frustrated and end up calling a help center to get their questions answered.

Whether a self-service application is aimed at external customers or internal users such as employees, two keys to success remain the same: setting aside money and time for maintaining the site, and designing flexibility into application interfaces and business rules so the site can be changed as needed.

CitiStreet. CitiStreet (www.citistreetonline.com), is a global benefits services provider managing over $170 billion in savings and pension funds and is owned by Citigroup and State Street Corp. CitiStreet is using the JRules software development tool to make rules changes in its benefits plan administration systems, many of them featuring Web-based employee self-service. JRules manages thousands of business rules related to client policies, government regulations, and customer preferences. Previously, business analysts developed the required business rules for each business process, and IT developers did the coding. But now analysts use JRules to create and change rules, without help from developers, says Andy Marsh, CitiStreet's CIO. "We've effectively eliminated the detail design function and 80 percent of the development function," says Marsh. IT is involved in managing the systems and platforms, but it's less involved in rules management, he says.

The software helps speed the development process for new business systems or features, says Marsh. For example, it used to take CitiStreet six months to set up benefit plans for clients; it now takes three months. CitiStreet can also react more quickly to market changes and new government regulations. It has used the rules development software to quickly revise business rules to accommodate the changes in pension programs required by new legislation. And Marsh says that when a client company recently added a savings plan to its benefits program, CitiStreet was able to easily develop and implement changes with JRules.

Case Study Questions

1. Why do more than a third of all Web self-service customers get frustrated and end up calling a help center? Use the experiences of Blue Cross–Blue Shield and AT&T Wireless to help you answer.

2. What are some solutions to the problems users may have with Web self-service? Use the experiences of the companies in this case to propose several solutions.

3. Visit the websites of Blue Cross–Blue Shield and AT&T Wireless. Investigate the details of obtaining an individual health plan or a new cell phone plan. What is your appraisal of the self-service features of these websites? Explain your evaluations.

Sources: Adapted from Stacy Collete, "How Will You Connect with Customers?" *Computerworld*, January 6, 2003, p. 19; Robert Scheier, "Know Thy Customer," *Computerworld*, March 24, 2003, pp. 27–28; and Bob Violino, "Who's Changing the Rules?" *Computerworld*, July 28, 2003, p. 38.

their self-service website which required information that many customers didn't know. And CitiStreet is relying on rules development software that can be used by business analysts to expedite changes to the business rules in the software for Web self-service and other benefit plan systems that are frequently required by changes in new client policies, government regulations, or customer preferences.

The Systems Approach

The **systems approach** to problem solving uses a systems orientation to define problems and opportunities and develop solutions. Analyzing a problem and formulating a solution involves the following interrelated activities:

1. Recognize and define a problem or opportunity using *systems thinking*.
2. Develop and evaluate alternative system solutions.
3. Select the system solution that best meets your requirements.
4. Design the selected system solution.
5. Implement and evaluate the success of the designed system.

Systems Thinking

Using **systems thinking** to understand a problem or opportunity is one of the most important aspects of the systems approach. Management consultant and author Peter Senge calls systems thinking *the fifth discipline*. Senge argues that mastering systems thinking (along with the disciplines of personal mastery, mental models, shared vision, and team learning) is vital to personal fulfillment and business success in a world of constant change. The essence of the discipline of systems thinking is "seeing the forest *and* the trees" in any situation by:

- Seeing *interrelationships* among *systems* rather than linear cause-and-effect chains whenever events occur.
- Seeing *processes* of change among *systems* rather than discrete "snapshots" of change, whenever changes occur [24].

One way of practicing systems thinking is to try to find systems, subsystems, and components of systems in any situation you are studying. This is also known as using a *systems context*, or having a *systemic view* of a situation. For example, the business organization or business process in which a problem or opportunity arises could be viewed as a system of input, processing, output, feedback, and control components. Then to understand a problem and solve it, you would determine if these basic systems functions are being properly performed. See Figure 10.2.

Example The sales process of a business can be viewed as a system. You could then ask: Is poor sales performance (output) caused by inadequate selling effort (input), out-of-date sales procedures (processing), incorrect sales information (feedback), or inadequate sales management (control)? Figure 10.2 illustrates this concept.

FIGURE 10.2

An example of systems thinking. You can better understand a sales problem or opportunity by identifying and evaluating the components of a sales system.

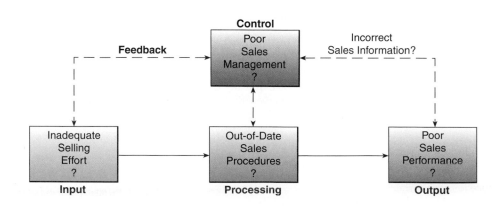

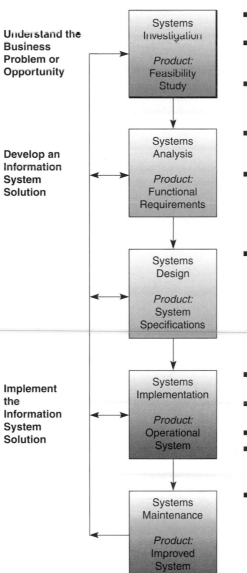

The traditional information systems development cycle. Note how the five steps of the cycle are based on the stages of the systems approach. Also note the products that result from each step in the cycle, and that you can recycle back to any previous step if more work is needed.

Understand the Business Problem or Opportunity

Systems Investigation

Product: Feasibility Study

- Determine how to address business opportunities and priorities.
- Conduct a feasibility study to determine whether a new or improved business system is a feasible solution.
- Develop a project management plan and obtain management approval.

Develop an Information System Solution

Systems Analysis

Product: Functional Requirements

- Analyze the information needs of employees, customers, and other business stakeholders.
- Develop the functional requirements of a system that can meet business priorities and the needs of all stakeholders.

Systems Design

Product: System Specifications

- Develop specifications for the hardware, software, people, network, and data resources, and the information products that will satisfy the functional requirements of the proposed business information system.

Implement the Information System Solution

Systems Implementation

Product: Operational System

- Acquire (or develop) hardware and software.
- Test the system, and train people to operate and use it.
- Convert to the new business system.
- Manage the effects of system changes on end users.

Systems Maintenance

Product: Improved System

- Use a postimplementation review process to monitor, evaluate, and modify the business system as needed.

The Systems Development Cycle

Using the systems approach to develop information system solutions can be viewed as a multistep process called the **information systems development cycle,** also known as the *systems development life cycle* (SDLC). Figure 10.3 illustrates what goes on in each stage of this process, which includes the steps of (1) investigation, (2) analysis, (3) design, (4) implementation, and (5) maintenance.

You should realize, however, that all of the activities involved are highly related and interdependent. Therefore, in actual practice, several developmental activities can occur at the same time, so different parts of a development project can be at different stages of the development cycle. In addition, you and IS specialists may recycle back at any time to repeat previous activities in order to modify and improve a system you are developing. We will discuss the activities and products of each step of the systems development cycle in this chapter.

Prototyping

The systems development process frequently takes the form of, or includes, a *prototyping* approach. **Prototyping** is the rapid development and testing of working models, or **prototypes,** of new applications in an interactive, iterative process that can

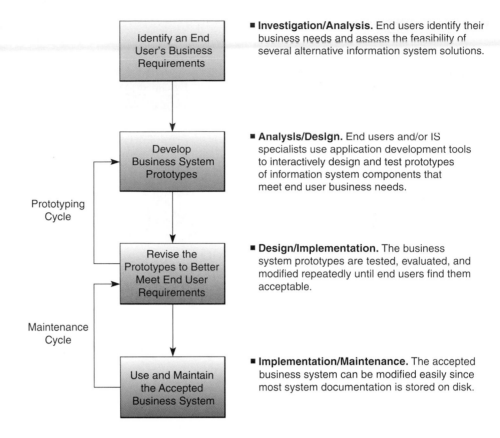

FIGURE 10.4

Application development using prototyping. Note how prototyping combines the steps of the systems development cycle and changes the traditional roles of IS specialists and end users.

Identify an End User's Business Requirements

■ **Investigation/Analysis.** End users identify their business needs and assess the feasibility of several alternative information system solutions.

Develop Business System Prototypes

■ **Analysis/Design.** End users and/or IS specialists use application development tools to interactively design and test prototypes of information system components that meet end user business needs.

Prototyping Cycle

Revise the Prototypes to Better Meet End User Requirements

■ **Design/Implementation.** The business system prototypes are tested, evaluated, and modified repeatedly until end users find them acceptable.

Maintenance Cycle

Use and Maintain the Accepted Business System

■ **Implementation/Maintenance.** The accepted business system can be modified easily since most system documentation is stored on disk.

be used by both IS specialists and business professionals. Prototyping makes the development process faster and easier, especially for projects where end user requirements are hard to define. Thus, prototyping is sometimes called *rapid application design* (RAD). Prototyping has also opened up the application development process to end users because it simplifies and accelerates systems design. Thus prototyping has enlarged the role of the business stakeholders affected by a proposed system, and helps make possible a quicker and more responsive development process called *agile systems development* (ASD). See Figure 10.4.

The Prototyping Process

Prototyping can be used for both large and small applications. Typically, large business systems still require using a traditional systems development approach, but parts of such systems can frequently be prototyped. A prototype of a business application needed by an end user is developed quickly using a variety of application development software tools. The prototype system is then repeatedly refined until it is acceptable.

As Figure 10.4 illustrates, prototyping is an iterative, interactive process that combines steps of the traditional systems development cycle. End users with sufficient experience with application development tools can do prototyping themselves. Alternatively, you could work with an IS specialist to develop a prototype system in a series of interactive sessions. For example, you could develop, test, and refine prototypes of management reports, data entry screens, or output displays.

Usually, a prototype is modified several times before end users find it acceptable. Any program modules that are not generated by application development software can then be coded by programmers using conventional programming languages. The final version of the application system is then turned over to its end users for operational use. Figure 10.5 outlines a typical prototyping-based systems development process for a business application.

FIGURE 10.5

An example of a typical prototyping-based systems development process for a business application.

Example of Prototyping Development
● **Team.** A few end users and IS developers form a team to develop a business application.
● **Schematic.** The initial prototype schematic design is developed.
● **Prototype.** The schematic is converted into a simple point-and-click prototype using prototyping tools.
● **Presentation.** A few screens and routine linkages are presented to users.
● **Feedback.** After the team gets feedback from users, the prototype is reiterated.
● **Reiteration.** Further presentations and reiterations are made.
● **Consultation.** Consultations are held with IT consultants to identify potential improvements and conformance to existing standards.
● **Completion.** The prototype is converted into a finished application.
● **Acceptance.** Users review and sign off on their acceptance of the new business system.
● **Installation.** The new business software is installed on network servers.

Frito-Lay Inc.: Failure and Success in Systems Development

Frito-Lay created national sales teams to focus on top customers such as supermarket chains. But the teams, used to working regionally, found nationwide collaboration difficult. Although Frito-Lay had rich stores of market research and other pertinent customer information housed in databases at its headquarters, there was no easy way for team members to find what they needed. Frustration rose, performance suffered, and sales team turnover reached 25 percent.

So Mike Marino, Frito-Lay's vice president for category and customer development engaged Dallas-based Navigator Systems to help. Navigator consultants envisioned a Web-based enterprise knowledge portal that would combine tools for knowledge management and collaboration, enabling the team to better serve the customer while helping reduce frustration and turnover.

A portal development project team was formed to work with the national supermarket sales team because it had the most centralized and demanding customers. "We knew if we could deliver there, we could satisfy any customer," Marino says. The supermarket sales team told the project team what kind of knowledge they needed. The request ranged from simple information, such as why Frito-Lay merchandises Lays and Ruffles products in one part of a store and Doritos in another, to more complex research on what motivates shoppers as they move through a store.

A few months later, the project team presented a working prototype they had developed to a group of beta users from the supermarket sales team only to find that in the quest for speed, a classic and crippling error had been made. Because the project team had not involved the Frito-Lay team in the design of the prototype, the portal they had built wasn't specific enough for the supermarket sales team.

"Conceptually, it was a great idea," says Frito-Lay sales team leader Joe Ackerman. "But when folks are not on the front line, their view of what is valuable is different from those running 100 miles an hour in the field." The project team needed to backtrack and plug in the missing features, but it also had to win back the sales force, who now suspected that even a revised tool would be a waste of time.

The project team then spent the next four months working with salespeople to evolve the prototype into a system they would embrace. For example, a call-reporting feature was added. "So many people want to know what happened on a sales call, the account manager involved can be on the phone for days," Ackerman explains. "Now, we're able to post that to a website. It frees up the account manager to document the call once and move on."

Other changes included enabling users to analyze and manipulate data rather than just viewing it, and developing reports tailored to customers' needs. "The original reports were very general," Ackerman says, so users would have had to spend lots of time reformatting them for customer presentations. Ackerman was also enlisted for the official rollout of the portal.

Now Ackerman says that better collaboration with the portal has helped to significantly reduce turnover, while improved access to knowledge-base data has enabled account managers to present themselves to customers as consultants with important data to share [16].

Starting the Systems Development Process

Do we have business opportunities? What are our business priorities? How can information technologies provide information system solutions that address our business priorities? These are the questions that have to be answered in the **systems investigation stage**—the first step in the systems development process. This stage may involve consideration of proposals generated by a business/IT planning process, which we will discuss in Chapter 12. The investigation stage also includes the preliminary study of proposed information system solutions to meet a company's business priorities and opportunities as identified in a planning process [10]. See Figure 10.6.

Feasibility Studies

Because the process of development can be costly, the systems investigation stage typically requires a preliminary study called a **feasibility study.** A feasibility study is a preliminary study where the information needs of prospective users and the resource requirements, costs, benefits, and feasibility of a proposed project are determined. Then a team of business professionals and IS specialists might formalize the findings of this study in a written report that includes preliminary specifications and a developmental plan for a proposed business application. If the management of the company approves the recommendations of the feasibility study, the development process can continue.

Thus, the goal of feasibility studies is to evaluate alternative system solutions and to propose the most feasible and desirable business application for development. The feasibility of a proposed business system can be evaluated in terms of four major categories, as illustrated in Figure 10.7.

The focus of **organizational feasibility** is on how well a proposed system supports the strategic business priorities of the organization. **Economic feasibility** is concerned with whether expected cost savings, increased revenue, increased profits, reductions in required investment, and other types of benefits will exceed the costs of

---

The systems investigation stage involves consideration of IT proposals for addressing the strategic business priorities of a company developed in a business/IT planning process.

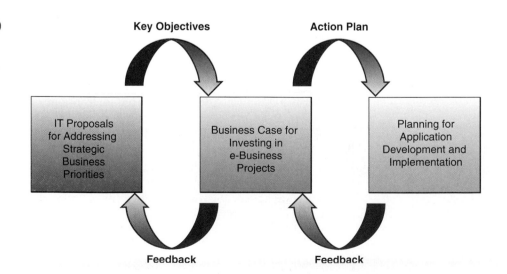

FIGURE 10.7

Organizational, economic, technical, and operational feasibility factors. Note that there is more to feasibility than cost savings or the availability of hardware and software.

Organizational Feasibility	Economic Feasibility
• How well the proposed system supports the business priorities of the organization	• Cost savings • Increased revenue • Decreased investment requirements • Increased profits
Technical Feasibility	**Operational Feasibility**
• Hardware, software, and network capability, reliability, and availability	• Employee, customer, supplier acceptance • Management support • Government or other requirements

developing and operating a proposed system. For example, if a proposed human resource system can't cover its development costs, it won't be approved, unless mandated by government regulations or strategic business considerations.

Technical feasibility can be demonstrated if reliable hardware and software capable of meeting the needs of a proposed system can be acquired or developed by the business in the required time. Finally, **operational feasibility** is the willingness and ability of the management, employees, customers, suppliers, and others to operate, use, and support a proposed system. For example, if the software for a new business system is too difficult to use, customers or employees may make too many errors and avoid using it. Thus, it would fail to show operational feasibility. See Figure 10.8.

Cost/Benefit Analysis. Feasibility studies typically involve **cost/benefit analysis.** If costs and benefits can be quantified, they are called tangible; if not, they are called intangible. Examples of tangible costs are the costs of hardware and software, employee salaries, and other quantifiable costs needed to develop and implement an IS solution. **Intangible costs** are difficult to quantify; they include the loss of customer goodwill or employee morale caused by errors and disruptions arising from the installation of a new system.

Tangible benefits are favorable results, such as the decrease in payroll costs caused by a reduction in personnel or a decrease in inventory carrying costs caused by reduction in inventory. **Intangible benefits** are harder to estimate. Such benefits as better customer service or faster and more accurate information for management fall into this category. Figure 10.9 lists typical tangible and intangible benefits with examples. Possible tangible and intangible costs would be the opposite of each benefit shown.

FIGURE 10.8

Examples of how a feasibility study might measure the feasibility of a proposed e-commerce system for a business.

Organizational Feasibility	Economic Feasibility
• How well a proposed e-commerce system fits the company's plans for developing Web-based sales, marketing, and financial systems	• Savings in labor costs • Increased sales revenue • Decreased investment in inventory • Increased profits
Technical Feasibility	**Operational Feasibility**
• Capability, reliability and availability of Web store hardware, software, and management services	• Acceptance of employees • Management support • Customer and supplier acceptance

FIGURE 10.9

Possible benefits of new information systems, with examples. Note that an opposite result for each of these benefits would be a cost or disadvantage of new systems.

Tangible Benefits	Example
● Increase in sales or profits	● Development of IT-based products
● Decrease in information processing costs	● Elimination of unnecessary documents
● Decrease in operating costs	● Reduction in inventory carrying costs
● Decrease in required investment	● Decrease in inventory investment required
● Increased operational efficiency	● Less spoilage, waste, and idle time

Intangible Benefits	Example
● Improved information availability	● More timely and accurate information
● Improved abilities in analysis	● OLAP and data mining
● Improved customer service	● More timely service response
● Improved employee morale	● Elimination of burdensome job tasks
● Improved management decision making	● Better information and decision analysis
● Improved competitive position	● Systems that lock in customers
● Improved business image	● Progressive image as perceived by customers, suppliers, and investors

Systems Analysis

What is **systems analysis?** Whether you want to develop a new application quickly or are involved in a long-term project, you will need to perform several basic activities of systems analysis. Many of these activities are an extension of those used in conducting a feasibility study. However, systems analysis is not a preliminary study. It is an in-depth study of end user information needs that produces *functional requirements* that are used as the basis for the design of a new information system. Systems analysis traditionally involves a detailed study of:

- The information needs of a company and end users like yourself.
- The activities, resources, and products of one or more of the present information systems being used.
- The information system capabilities required to meet your information needs, and those of other business stakeholders that may use the system.

Organizational Analysis

An **organizational analysis** is an important first step in systems analysis. How can anyone improve an information system if they know very little about the organizational environment in which that system is located? They can't. That's why the members of a development team have to know something about the organization, its management structure, its people, its business activities, the environmental systems it must deal with, and its current information systems. Someone on the team must know this information in more detail for the specific business units or end user workgroups that will be affected by the new or improved information system being proposed. For example, a new inventory control system for a chain of department stores cannot be designed unless someone on a development team knows a lot about the company and the types of business activities that affect its inventory. That's why business end users are frequently added to systems development teams.

Analysis of the Present System

Before you design a new system, it is important to study the system that will be improved or replaced (if there is one). You need to analyze how this system uses hardware, software, network, and people resources to convert data resources, such as transactions data, into information products, such as reports and displays. Then, you should document how the information system activities of input, processing, output, storage, and control are accomplished.

FIGURE 10.10

A Web page from BuyerZone's e-commerce site at www.buyerzone.com.

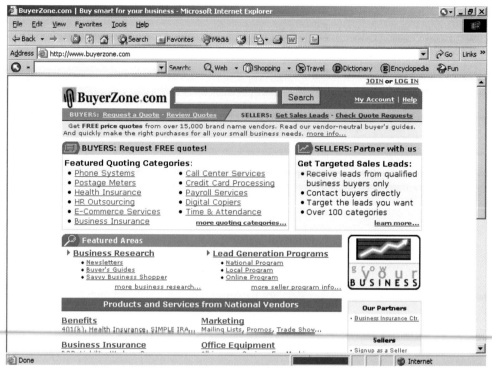

Source: Courtesy of BuyerZone.com.

For example, you might evaluate the format, timing, volume, and quality of input and output activities. Such *user interface* activities are vital to effective interaction between end users and a computer-based system. Then, in the systems design stage, you can specify what the resources, products, and activities should be to support the user interface in the system you are designing. Figure 10.10 presents a Web page from the analysis of an e-commerce website.

BuyerZone and OfficeMax: Evaluating Customer Website Experiences

Customers of business-to-business sites are faced with much more difficult decisions than the customers of business-to-consumer sites. Jakob Nielsen of Nielsen Norman Group recently studied the reactions of users who were trying to decide whether to lease or buy office equipment.

BuyerZone.com and OfficeMax both failed in the study because they didn't support users going through a process. In order to support a customer's process, businesses need to understand it from the user's perspective. If users feel pushed through a process or can't figure out what to do next, you're skipping steps that matter to them. Don't just design Web pages. Design support for users' tasks. Here's how:

Support Processes before Pushing Transactions. Customers need compelling reasons to complete complex tasks on the Web. It's usually easier to pick up the phone and deal with a salesperson than to go it alone on the Web. Users often say that the Web is OK for preliminary research, but useless for closing deals. Most B2B sites overlook their users' perspectives in their eagerness to move them to the checkout line. For example, users don't want to click Buy Now until they select their payment options on BuyerZone.com. Unfortunately, clicking Buy Now is the only way to see both leasing and purchase prices.

Examples of Functional Requirements
● **User Interface Requirements** Automatic entry of product data and easy-to-use data entry screens for Web customers.
● **Processing Requirements** Fast, automatic calculation of sales totals and shipping costs.
● **Storage Requirements** Fast retrieval and update of data from product, pricing, and customer databases.
● **Control Requirements** Signals for data entry errors and quick e-mail confirmation for customers.

Provide the Right Tools at the Right Time. Complex processes require different tools for different stages of the process. Early in a process, customers need ways to quickly look at their purchasing options in many ways, without commitment. Let users easily manipulate data they care about, and carry that forward to their transaction when they're ready. For example, while it's good that BuyerZone.com offers a calculator to explore leasing prices, users struggle to understand the leasing terminology and want more guidance and recommendations from the tool.

Integrate Related Tasks. From a customer's prospective, leasing is just a payment option and is a part of a larger acquisition process, not a separate task. Yet OfficeMax separates leasing from purchasing, as if a user would get leases in an independent project. A user who has selected office equipment on OfficeMax's website can't explore how to lease that equipment. Instead, she must abandon her selection, find leasing services from the site's Business Services section, and then suffer through an awkward registration process [18, 19].

Functional Requirements Analysis

This step of systems analysis is one of the most difficult. You may need to work as a team with IS analysts and other end users to determine your specific business information needs. For example, first you need to determine what type of information each business activity requires; what its format, volume, and frequency should be; and what response times are necessary. Second, you must try to determine the information processing capabilities required for each system activity (input, processing, output, storage, control) to meet these information needs. *Your main goal is to identify what should be done, not how to do it.*

Finally, you should try to develop **functional requirements.** Functional requirements are end user information requirements that are not tied to the hardware, software, network, data, and people resources that end users presently use or might use in the new system. That is left to the design stage to determine. For example, Figure 10.11 shows examples of functional requirements for a proposed e-commerce application for a business.

Systems Design

Systems analysis describes *what* a system should do to meet the information needs of users. **Systems design** specifies *how* the system will accomplish this objective. Systems design consists of design activities that produce system specifications satisfying the functional requirements that were developed in the systems analysis process.

FIGURE 10.12 Systems design can be viewed as the design of user interfaces, data, and processes.

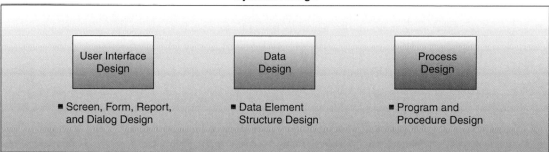

A useful way to look at systems design is illustrated in Figure 10.12. This concept focuses on three major products, or *deliverables* that should result from the design stage. In this framework, systems design consists of three activities: user interface, data, and process design. This results in specifications for user interface methods and products, database structures, and processing and control procedures.

User Interface Design

Let's take a closer look at user interface design, since it is the system component closest to business end users, and the one they will most likely help design. The user interface design activity focuses on supporting the interactions between end users and their computer-based applications. Designers concentrate on the design of attractive and efficient forms of user input and output, such as easy-to-use Internet or intranet Web pages.

As we mentioned earlier, user interface design is frequently a *prototyping* process, where working models or prototypes of user interface methods are designed and modified several times with feedback from end users. The user interface design process produces detailed design specifications for information products such as display screens, interactive user/computer dialogues (including the sequence or flow of dialogue), audio responses, forms, documents, and reports. Figure 10.13 gives examples of user interface design elements and other guidelines suggested for the multimedia Web pages of e-commerce websites [7]. Figure 10.14 presents actual before and after screen displays of the user interface design process for a work scheduling application of State Farm Insurance Company [20].

FIGURE 10.13 Useful guidelines for the design of business websites.

Checklist for Corporate Websites

- **Remember the Customer:** Successful websites are built solely for the customer, not to make company vice presidents happy.
- **Aesthetics:** Successful designs combine fast-loading graphics and simple color palettes for pages that are easy to read.
- **Broadband Content:** The Web's coolest stuff can't be accessed by most Web surfers. Including a little streaming video isn't bad, but don't make it the focus of your site.
- **Easy to Navigate:** Make sure it's easy to get from one part of your site to another. Providing a site map, accessible from every page, helps.

- **Searchability:** Many sites have their own search engines; very few are actually useful. Make sure yours is.
- **Incompatibilities:** A site that looks great on a PC using Internet Explorer can often look miserable on an iBook running Netscape.
- **Registration Forms:** Registration forms are a useful way to gather customer data. But make your customers fill out a three-page form, and watch them flee.
- **Dead Links:** Dead links are the bane of all Web surfers—be sure to keep your links updated. Many Web-design software tools can now do this for you.

FIGURE 10.14 An example of the user interface design process. State Farm developers changed this work scheduling and assignment application's interface after usability testing showed that end users working with the old interface (at left) didn't realize that they had to follow a six-step process. If users jumped to a new page out of order, they would lose their work. The new interface (at right) made it clearer that a process had to be followed.

(a)
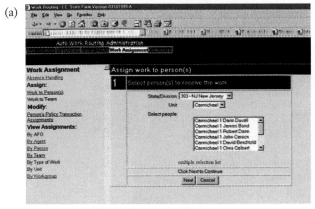

(b)
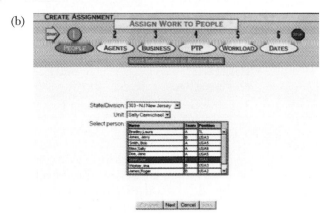

Source: Courtesy of the Usability Lab of State Farm.

Priceline.com: Designing a User Interface

The natural tendency when designing a website is to give users more—more features, more options—but by simplifying an interface and making it more visually compelling Priceline.com (www.priceline.com) saw a 50 percent increase in the number of visitors to its ticket site. On the old Priceline.com home page, customers had to click a specific button to order a plane ticket, rent a car, or make hotel reservation. A new feature, packaged prominently in a gold box on the home page, asks customers where they are going and when. This change paid off. Now 50 percent more people start down the path to buying a ticket, and 5 to 10 percent of them actually finish the process. The old format is still available, but only 1 percent of people who use it buy a ticket. In this case, simplicity rules. "Anytime you can take a thought out of the process for the user, it's always a good thing," says Brian Harniman, vice president of marketing at Priceline.com [23].

FIGURE 10.15

Examples of system specifications for a new e-commerce system for a business.

Examples of System Specifications
● **User Interface Specifications** Use personalized screens that welcome repeat Web customers and make product recommendations.
● **Database Specifications** Develop databases that use object/relational database management software to organize access to all customer and inventory data, and multimedia product information.
● **Software Specifications** Acquire an e-commerce software engine to process all e-commerce transactions with fast responses, i.e., retrieve necessary product data, and compute all sales amounts in less than one second.
● **Hardware and Network Specifications** Install redundant networked Web servers and sufficient high-bandwidth telecommunications lines to host the company e-commerce website.
● **Personnel Specifications** Hire an e-commerce manager and specialists and a webmaster and Web designer to plan, develop, and manage e-commerce operations.

FIGURE 10.16 End user development should focus on the basic information processing activity components of an information system.

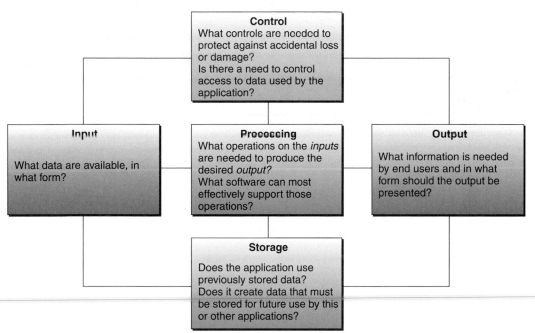

Source: Adapted from James N. Morgan, *Application Cases in MIS*, 4th ed. (New York: Irwin/McGraw-Hill, 2002), p. 31.

System Specifications

System specifications formalize the design of an application's user interface methods and products, database structures, and processing and control procedures. Therefore, systems designers will frequently develop hardware, software, network, data, and personnel specifications for a proposed system. Figure 10.15 shows examples of system specifications that could be developed for an e-commerce system of a company.

End User Development

In a traditional systems development cycle, your role as a business end user is similar to that of a customer or a client. Typically, you make a request for a new or improved system, answer questions about your specific information needs and information processing problems, and provide background information on your existing business systems. IS professionals work with you to analyze your problem and suggest alternative solutions. When you approve the best alternative, it is designed and implemented. Here again, you may be involved in a prototyping design process or be on an implementation team with IS specialists.

However, in **end user development,** IS professionals play a consulting role, while you do your own application development. Sometimes a staff of user consultants may be available to help you and other end users with your application development efforts. This may include training in the use of application packages; selection of hardware and software; assistance in gaining access to organization databases; and, of course, assistance in analysis, design, and implementing the business application of IT that you need.

Focus on IS Activities

It is important to remember that end user development should focus on the fundamental activities of any information system: input, processing, output, storage, and control, as we described in Chapter 1. Figure 10.16 illustrates these system components and the questions they address.

In analyzing a potential application, you should focus first on the **output** to be produced by the application. What information is needed and in what form should it be presented? Next, look at the **input** data to be supplied to the application.

FIGURE 10.17

Microsoft FrontPage is an example of an easy-to-use end user website development tool.

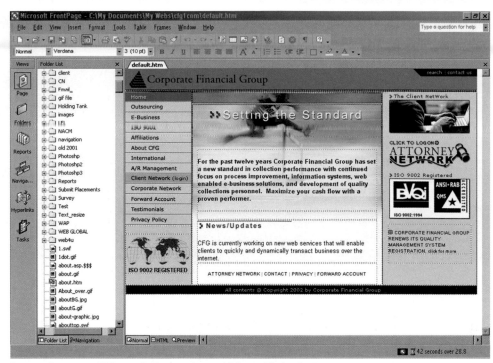

Source: Courtesy of Microsoft Corporation and Murnet Technologies.

What data are available? From what sources? In what form? Then you should examine the **processing** requirements. What operations or transformation processes will be required to convert the available inputs into the desired output? Among software packages the developer is able to use, which package can best perform the operations required?

You may find that the desired output cannot be produced from the inputs that are available. If this is the case, you must either make adjustments to the output expected, or find additional sources of input data, including data stored in files and databases from external sources. The **storage** component will vary in importance in end user applications. For example, some applications require extensive use of stored data or the creation of data that must be stored for future use. These are better suited for database management development projects than for spreadsheet applications.

Necessary **control** measures for end user applications vary greatly depending upon the scope and duration of the application, the number and nature of the users of the application, and the nature of the data involved. For example, control measures are needed to protect against accidental loss or damage to end user files. The most basic protection against this type of loss is simply to make backup copies of application files on a frequent and systematic basis. Another example is the cell protection feature of spreadsheets that protects key cells from accidental erasure by users.

Doing End User Development

In end user development, you and other business professionals can develop new or improved ways to perform your jobs without the direct involvement of IS specialists. The application development capabilities built into a variety of end user software packages have made it easier for many users to develop their own computer-based solutions. For example, Figure 10.17 illustrates a website development tool you could use to help you develop, update, and manage an intranet website for your business unit. Or you might use an electronic spreadsheet package as a tool to develop a way to easily analyze weekly sales results for the sales managers in a company. Or you could use a website development package to design Web pages for a small business Web

FIGURE 10.18

How companies are encouraging and managing intranet website development by business end users.

Encouraging End User Web Development
● **Look for Tools That Make Sense.** Some Web development tools may be too powerful and more costly than what your business end users really need.
● **Spur Creativity.** Consider a competition among business departments for the best website, to help spur users to more creative uses of their intranet sites.
● **Set Some Limits.** Yes, you have to keep some control. Consider putting limits on exactly what parts of a Web page users can change and who can change what pages. You still want some consistency across the organization.
● **Give Managers Responsibility.** Make business unit managers sign off on who will be Web publishing from their groups, and make the managers personally responsible for the content that goes on their websites. That will help prevent the publishing of inappropriate content by some users.
● **Make Users Comfortable.** Training users well on the tools will help users become confident in their ability to properly manage and update their sites—and save IT the trouble of fixing problems later on or providing continuous support for minor problems.

store or a departmental intranet website. Let's take a look at a real world example of how many companies are encouraging business end users to do their own website development [21]. See Figure 10.18.

Providence Health System: End User Web Development

Business groups at Providence Health System in Portland, Oregon, complained to information technology staff about the sometimes outdated and incorrect content of the company's intranet websites. That was especially frustrating to IT workers, because the content originated from and belonged to the business groups, says Erik Sargent, lead Internet developer at the health care provider. So Providence Health's IT and Web development group did what many companies are considering. They gave up some of their central power to let business personnel in different departments contribute directly to corporate Internet and intranet sites with the help of Web content development tools.

More IT groups can do this because the tools have made it easier for users to create, manage, and update websites without knowing the intricacies of the Internet programming language HTML. Sargent and his team at Providence Health used Microsoft FrontPage on their development efforts. And because the company standardized on Microsoft Office productivity tools, it made sense to stay with FrontPage when allowing employees to do the intranet publishing duties.

One reason was that FrontPage maintained the same look and feel as Office, so there was a gentler learning curve. The other reason: FrontPage was cheaper to roll out to the 108 non-IT people now contributing to the intranet, rather than buying high-end tools with big price tags [21].

Implementing Business Systems

Implementation

Once a new information system has been designed, it must be implemented as a working system, and maintained to keep it operating properly. The implementation process we will cover in this section follows the investigation, analysis, and design stages of the systems development cycle we discussed in Section I. Implementation is a vital step in the deployment of information technology to support the employees, customers, and other business stakeholders of a company.

Analyzing InterContinental, Del Taco, and Cardinal Health

Read the Real World Case on InterContinental Hotels, Del Taco, and Cardinal Health on the next page. We can learn a lot from this case about the challenges of implementing business systems. See Figure 10.19.

This case reveals some of the challenges and strategies involved in managing the upgrading of core business systems. For InterContinental Hotels, that involved installing a new central reservation system and the local operations management systems for 3,200 hotels. InterContinental's strategies included heavy user involvement, hiring subcontractors to deploy the new systems in the hotels and conduct training, and the work of talented project managers. Del Taco is upgrading the point-of-sale systems in its stores by outsourcing the installation of the new hardware to a subcontractor, working with Microsoft consultants to design the inventory database, and hiring top project managers. Cardinal Health is improving its core business systems with the planning and participation of the company's executive committees, and the use of CRM software development tools, and the cooperation of the management of its business units.

Implementing New Systems

Figure 10.20 illustrates that the **systems implementation** stage involves hardware and software acquisition, software development, testing of programs and procedures, conversion of data resources, and a variety of conversion alternatives. It also involves the education and training of end users and specialists who will operate a new system.

FIGURE 10.19

InterContinental Hotels used subcontractors to install new hardware and software and train its employees in the use of new reservation and operations management systems.

Source: Corbis

REAL WORLD CASE 2

InterContinental Hotels, Del Taco, and Cardinal Health: Implementation Strategies

There are few IT projects more fraught with danger than upgrading a core business system. If you do things wrong, you've crippled the workhorse that carries the business. On the other hand, the benefits of such a project can be enormous, says W. Douglas Lewis, executive vice president and CIO at InterContinental Hotels Group (www.ichotelsgroup.com), an international hotel management company, in Atlanta. Lewis is in the midst of installing a new central reservation system and local operations management systems for 3,200 hotels.

To make the project succeed, InterContinental partnered with end users from the start, says Lewis. "Involving the people who leave fingerprints on the keyboards is critical, because it's the employees and managers who know what the hotels need," says Lewis. "If we had approached this from an IT point of view, it's likely we would have built the wrong solution."

InterContinental hired subcontractors to deploy the new systems in the hotels and conduct training, "It doesn't make sense to build that capability internally for a one-time activity," says Lewis. But he relies on his staff to do the application programming because they know the business better than an outsider would. Lewis also lays the credit for keeping his project on track at the feet of talented project managers. "I can't brag about anything unique we did," he says. "We just managed the heck out of it." Lewis adds, "I have a premise that big-bang projects blow up CIOs." So he stops every few steps to evaluate the results of the latest "little bang." For example, he says, putting the new system in a few hotels for beta testing revealed a problem with the communication systems. It was easier to change course at that point than after several hundred hotels were involved, he says.

Del Taco. Cutting costs, improving efficiency, and increasing functionality for business end users is the typical business case when improving a company's core information systems, says Allison Bacon, an analyst at AMR Research Inc. in Boston. But it's harder to pin down a return on investment for a core system upgrade because you're spending money on something that already works. Selling the project to upper management often requires making a compelling argument in favor of hard-to-measure benefits and new features. And once the executive committee approves the funds for such projects, the IT group is on the spot to make the project happen on time and within its budget.

Henry Volkman, director of IT and CIO at Del Taco Inc. (www.deltaco.com) in Lake Forest, California, says, "My CFO can make a vendor cry and a nickel scream." Volkman, who meets with his company's top financial executive weekly, says he's the reason the upgrade project is on budget. If the project runs into a snag, IT has to find a way to fix it with what money is on hand. "You'll never get him to agree it was right to spend more money than budgeted," he says.

Volkman says his company is making use of outside help to upgrade its 254 point-of-sale systems. The fast-food chain is outsourcing the job of installing the hardware in its restaurants. It's also working with Microsoft Corp. consultants to design a SQL Server inventory database. The vendor of an application always knows its ins and outs better than you do, says Volkman, so it only makes sense to marry its expertise with your business knowledge.

Bacon says that having a mix of internal and external development teams gets you the most skills at the lowest cost. Using your own people means spending less and moving faster. But you need to lean judiciously on experienced vendors and outsourcers in order to gain the greatest benefits out of something that is new to your team, she says. Volkman adds that it pays to hire only the best project managers. "You can take a good manager with a mediocre crew and run rings around a poor manager with a high-quality crew."

Cardinal Health. At Cardinal Health Inc. (www.cardinal.com), a $7 billion maker of medical, surgical, and laboratory products, Richard Gius, senior vice president of IT, is on the company's capital review and operating committees, where IT projects are approved and funded. "That way, there are no surprises," he says. Too often, business units approve projects, and then confusion sets in when the IT staff is asked to deliver on something that's unclear. At Cardinal Health, "all of that is resolved before approval," Gius explains. His IT team is using CRM software development tools to improve product returns, pricing and availability, and order fulfillment for the company.

Customer relationship management projects can redefine a company's entire operational infrastructure, so cooperation among executives and the management of business units is critical to CRM project success. "Even the CEO must say customer service is Job 1," says Gius. Overall, CIOs agree that disruption to the organization is inevitable with CRM projects and that the entire company should be prepared. "These transformations are disruptive and need an initiative right at the heel to add quality improvements, which will bring stability," says Gius.

Case Study Questions

1. What are the benefits and limitations of the key implementation strategies that are being used by InterContinental Hotels?

2. Do you agree with how Del Taco is managing the implementation of its IT project? Why or why not?

3. What are several change management techniques to ensure the successful implementation of CRM projects? Use Cardinal Health to illustrate your answer.

Sources: Adapted from Amy Johnson, "How Will You Improve Your Core Systems?" *Computerworld*, January 6, 2003, p. 22; and Stacy Collette, "How Will You Connect with Customers?" *Computerworld*, January 6, 2003, p. 19.

FIGURE 10.20 An overview of the implementation process. Implementation activities are needed to transform a newly developed information system into an operational system for end users.

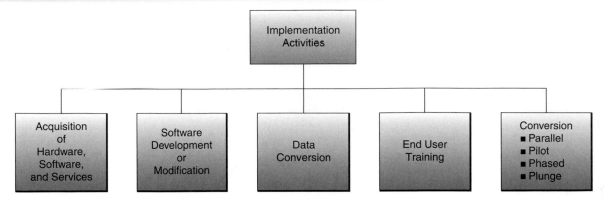

Implementation can be a difficult and time-consuming process. However, it is vital in ensuring the success of any newly developed system, for even a well-designed system will fail if it is not properly implemented. That is why the implementation process typically requires a **project management** effort on the part of IT and business unit managers. They must enforce a project plan which includes job responsibilities, time lines for major stages of development, and financial budgets. This is necessary if a project is to be completed on time and within its established budget, while still meeting its design objectives. Figure 10.21 illustrates the activities and time lines that might be required to implement an intranet for a new employee benefits system in the human resources department of a company [9].

Zurich North America: IT Project Management	Dave Patterson is a big believer in what he describes as full project transparency. "Every project we're working on and its status is reported through the intranet," says Patterson, vice president of IT at Zurich North America, the Baltimore-based insurance arm of Zurich Financial Services (www.zurich.com). "The status of projects is all very fact-based. You're either making your dates or you're not; you're on budget or you're not; you either have an issue or you don't."

Patterson says Zurich applies the same black-and-white, fact-based thinking when it comes to paying salaries and bonuses to members of an IT project team. The bulk of each project team member's salary is based on market pay rates and the worker's competency. "But about 10 to 20 percent of compensation is based on whether the company makes money and whether we deliver a project as promised," Patterson says.

His other financial rule of thumb is to always get the budget and funding arrangements of a project in writing. "At the start of every project, there is a project agreement," Patterson says. "It needs to contain the full scope of the project plans, risk analysis, costs and benefits, and it has to be signed by the business partners willing to pay for the project. I will not allow a project to initiate if I don't have a customer who is willing to pay for it [11]."

Evaluating Hardware, Software, and Services

How do companies evaluate and select hardware, software, and IT services, such as those shown in Figure 10.22? Large companies may require suppliers to present bids and proposals based on system specifications developed during the design stage of systems development. Minimum acceptable physical and performance characteristics for all hardware and software requirements are established. Most large business firms and all government agencies formalize these requirements by listing them in a document

FIGURE 10.21

An example of the implementation process activities and time lines for a company installing an intranet-based employee benefits system in its human resource management department.

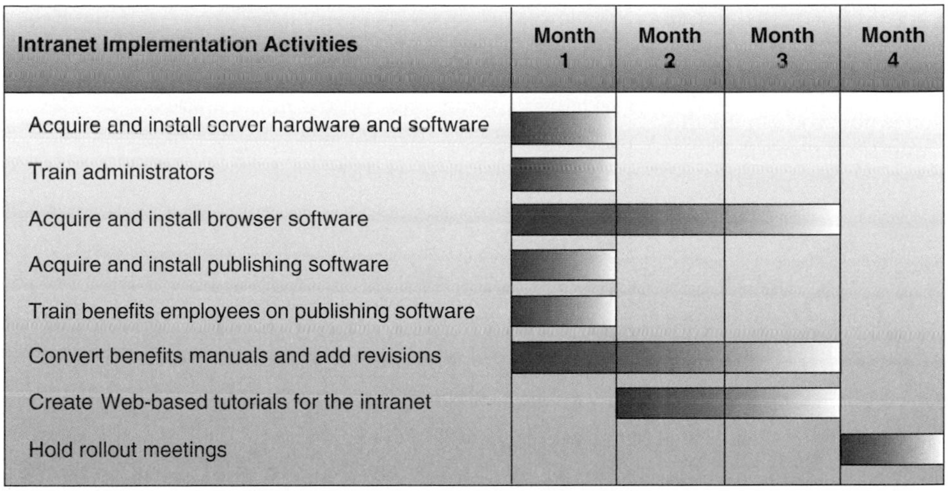

Intranet Implementation Activities	Month 1	Month 2	Month 3	Month 4
Acquire and install server hardware and software	▓			
Train administrators	▓			
Acquire and install browser software	▓	▓		
Acquire and install publishing software	▓			
Train benefits employees on publishing software	▓			
Convert benefits manuals and add revisions	▓	▓		
Create Web-based tutorials for the intranet		▓		
Hold rollout meetings				▓

called an RFP (request for proposal) or RFQ (request for quotation). Then they send the RFP or RFQ to appropriate vendors, who use it as the basis for preparing a proposed purchase agreement.

Companies may use a *scoring* system of evaluation when there are several competing proposals for a hardware or software acquisition. They give each **evaluation factor** a certain number of maximum possible points. Then they assign each competing proposal points for each factor, depending on how well it meets the user's specifications. Scoring evaluation factors for several proposals helps organize and document the evaluation process. It also spotlights the strengths and weaknesses of each proposal.

Whatever the claims of hardware manufacturers and software suppliers, the performance of hardware and software must be demonstrated and evaluated. Independent

FIGURE 10.22

Examples from the IBM Corporation of the kinds of hardware, software, and IS services that many companies are evaluating and acquiring to support their e-commerce initiatives.

Hardware
Full range of offerings, including xSeries servers, iSeries midrange servers for small and midsize businesses, RS6000 servers for UNIX customers and z900 mainframes for large enterprises. Also has full range of storage options.

Software
Web server: Lotus DominoGo Web server.
Storefront: WebSphere Commerce Suite (formerly known as Net.Commerce) for storefront and catalog creation, relationship marketing, and order management. Can add Commerce Integrator to integrate with back-end systems and Catalog Architect for content management.
Middleware/transaction services: WebSphere application server manages transactions. MQ Series queues messages and manages connections. CICS processes transactions.
Database: DB2 Universal Database.
Tools: WebSphere Studio includes set of predefined templates and common business logic.
Other applications include: IBM Payment Suite for handling credit cards and managing digital certificates.

Services
IBM Global Services, which includes groups organized by each major industry, including retail and financial. Can design, build, and host e-commerce applications.

FIGURE 10.23

A summary of ten major hardware evaluation factors. Notice how you can use this to evaluate a computer system or a peripheral device.

Hardware Evaluation Factors	Rating
Performance What is its speed, capacity, and throughput?	
Cost What is its lease or purchase price? What will be its cost of operations and maintenance?	
Reliability What are the risk of malfunction and its maintenance requirements? What are its error control and diagnostic features?	
Compatibility Is it compatible with existing hardware and software? Is it compatible with hardware and software provided by competing suppliers?	
Technology In what year of its product life cycle is it? Does it use a new untested technology or does it run the risk of obsolescence?	
Ergonomics Has it been "human factors engineered" with the user in mind? Is it user-friendly, designed to be safe, comfortable, and easy to use?	
Connectivity Can it be easily connected to wide area and local area networks that use different types of network technologies and bandwidth alternatives?	
Scalability Can it handle the processing demands of a wide range of end users, transactions, queries, and other information processing requirements?	
Software Is system and application software available that can best use this hardware?	
Support Are the services required to support and maintain it available?	
Overall Rating	

hardware and software information services (such as Datapro and Auerbach) may be used to gain detailed specification information and evaluations. Other users are frequently the best source of information needed to evaluate the claims of manufacturers and suppliers. That's why Internet newsgroups established to exchange information about specific software or hardware vendors and their products have become one of the best sources for obtaining up-to-date information about the experiences of users of the products.

Large companies frequently evaluate proposed hardware and software by requiring the processing of special *benchmark* test programs and test data. Benchmarking simulates the processing of typical jobs on several computers and evaluates their performances. Users can then evaluate test results to determine which hardware device or software package displayed the best performance characteristics.

Hardware Evaluation Factors

When you evaluate the hardware needed by a new business application, you should investigate specific physical and performance characteristics for each computer system or peripheral component to be acquired. Specific questions must be answered concerning many important factors. Ten of these **hardware evaluation factors** and questions are summarized in Figure 10.23.

Notice that there is much more to evaluating hardware than determining the fastest and cheapest computing device. For example, the question of obsolescence must be addressed by making a technology evaluation. The factor of ergonomics is also very important. Ergonomic factors ensure that computer hardware and software

FIGURE 10.24

A summary of selected software evaluation factors. Note that most of the hardware evaluation factors in Figure 10.23 can also be used to evaluate software packages.

Software Evaluation Factors	Rating
Quality Is it bug free, or does it have many errors in its program code?	
Efficiency Is the software a well-developed system of program code that does not use much CPU time, memory capacity, or disk space?	
Flexibility Can it handle our business processes easily, without major modification?	
Security Does it provide control procedures for errors, malfunctions, and improper use?	
Connectivity Is it *Web-enabled* so it can easily access the Internet, intranets, and extranets, on its own, or by working with Web browsers or other network software?	
Maintenance Will new features and bug fixes be easily implemented by our own software developers?	
Documentation Is the software well documented? Does it include help screens and helpful software agents?	
Hardware Does existing hardware have the features required to best use this software?	
Other Factors What are its performance, cost, reliability, availability, compatibility, modularity, technology, ergonomics, scalability, and support characteristics? (Use the hardware evaluation factor questions in Figure 10.23)	
Overall Rating	

are user-friendly, that is, safe, comfortable, and easy to use. Connectivity is another important evaluation factor, since so many network technologies and bandwidth alternatives are available to connect computer systems to the Internet, intranet, and extranet networks.

Software Evaluation Factors

You should evaluate software according to many factors that are similar to those used for hardware evaluation. Thus, the factors of performance, cost, reliability, availability, compatibility, modularity, technology, ergonomics, and support should be used to evaluate proposed software acquisitions. In addition, however, **the software evaluation factors** summarized in Figure 10.24 must also be considered. You should answer the questions they generate in order to properly evaluate software purchases. For example, some software packages are notoriously slow, hard to use, bug-filled, or poorly documented. They are not a good choice, even if offered at attractive prices.

Evaluating IS Services

Most suppliers of hardware and software products and many other firms offer a variety of **IS services** to end users and organizations. Examples include assistance in developing a company website, installation or conversion of new hardware and software, employee training, and hardware maintenance. Some of these services are provided without cost by hardware manufacturers and software suppliers.

Other types of IS services needed by a business can be outsourced to an outside company for a negotiated price. For example, *systems integrators* take over complete responsibility for an organization's computer facilities when an organization outsources its computer operations. They may also assume responsibility for developing and implementing large systems development projects that involve many vendors and subcontractors. Value-added resellers (VARs) specialize in providing industry-specific hardware, software, and services from selected manufacturers. Many other services are available to end users, including systems design, contract programming, and consulting services. Evaluation factors and questions for IS services are summarized in Figure 10.25.

OshKosh B'Gosh, Inc.: Evaluating IT Vendors and Products	Jon Dell'Antonia, vice president of MIS at OshKosh B'Gosh, Inc. (www.oshkoshbgosh.com), in Oshkosh, Wisconsin, starts the buying process by working with end users to determine exactly what they want the system to do. Then Dell'Antonia and the end users come up with a list of potential vendors, rank their top two or three priorities, and meet with the vendors. "If you've got your requirements defined, then it's 'Here's what we need, tell us what your product can do to help us,'" he says. If vendors "waltz around" the topic, Dell' Antonia says he just asks flat out if they're able to meet a specific requirement. If they can't, he'll end the meeting right there. He also recommends that you ask vendors for customer references and then check with those customers to find out how their products were installed, how the support was, whether the product still works and so on. "If they can't give you good, solid, positive references, then you've got to wonder," Dell'Antonia says. Finally, before making a decision, Dell'Antonia sits down with his entire team—IT staffers and end users—to review the offerings and take a vote. "It is not just an IT-driven process," he says. "It's not, 'We pick it, you get it.' If you don't involve your end user in the selection of your system, it ain't going to work. You're just setting yourself up for failure [26]."

FIGURE 10.25

Evaluation factors for IS services. These factors focus on the quality of support services business users may need.

Evaluation Factors for IS Services	Rating
Performance What has been their past performance in view of their past promises?	
Systems Development Are website and other e-business developers available? What are their quality and cost?	
Maintenance Is equipment maintenance provided? What are its quality and cost?	
Conversion What systems development and installation services will they provide during the conversion period?	
Training Is the necessary training of personnel provided? What are its quality and cost?	
Backup Are similar computer facilities available nearby for emergency backup purposes?	
Accessibility Does the vendor provide local or regional sites that offer sales, systems development, and hardware maintenance services? Is a customer support center at the vendor's website available? Is a customer hot line provided?	
Business Position Is the vendor financially strong, with good industry market prospects?	
Hardware Do they provide a wide selection of compatible hardware devices and accessories?	
Software Do they offer a variety of useful e-business software and application packages?	
Overall Rating	

Other Implementation Activities

Testing, data conversion, documentation, and training are keys to successful implementation of a new business system.

Testing

System testing may involve testing and debugging software, testing website performance, and testing new hardware. An important part of testing is the review of prototypes of displays, reports, and other output. Prototypes should be reviewed by end users of the proposed systems for possible errors. Of course, testing should not occur only during the system's implementation stage, but throughout the system's development process. For example, you might examine and critique prototypes of input documents, screen displays, and processing procedures during the systems design stage. Immediate end user testing is one of the benefits of a prototyping process.

Data Conversion

Implementing new information systems for many organizations today frequently involves replacing a previous system and its software and databases. One of the most important implementation activities required when installing new software in such cases is called **data conversion.** For example, installing new software packages may require converting the data elements in databases that are affected by a new application into new data formats. Other data conversion activities that are typically required include correcting incorrect data, filtering out unwanted data, consolidating data from several databases, and organizing data into new data subsets, such as databases, data marts, and data warehouses. A good data conversion process is essential, because improperly organized and formatted data is frequently reported to be one of the major causes of failures in implementing new systems.

Documentation

Developing good user **documentation** is an important part of the implementation process. Sample data entry display screens, forms, and reports are good examples of documentation. When *computer-aided systems engineering* methods are used, documentation can be created and changed easily since it is stored and accessible on disk in a *system repository.* Documentation serves as a method of communication among the people responsible for developing, implementing, and maintaining a computer-based system. Installing and operating a newly designed system or modifying an established application requires a detailed record of that system's design. Documentation is extremely important in diagnosing errors and making changes, especially if the end users or systems analysts who developed a system are no longer with the organization.

Training

Training is a vital implementation activity. IS personnel, such as user consultants, must be sure that end users are trained to operate a new business system or its implementation will fail. Training may involve only activities like data entry, or it may also involve all aspects of the proper use of a new system. In addition, managers and end users must be educated in how the new technology impacts the company's business operations and management. This knowledge should be supplemented by training programs for any new hardware devices, software packages, and their use for specific work activities. Figure 10.26 illustrates how one business coordinated its end user training program with each stage of its implementation process for developing intranet and Internet access within the company [5].

Clarke American Checks: Web-Based ERP Training

If it's 10 a.m., workers at Clarke American Checks, Inc. are firing up their Web browsers for a collaborative training lesson on how to perform purchasing with their new SAP AG enterprise resource planning (ERP) software. During the daily sessions, end users in more than 20 locations either watch their colleagues perform simulated transactions with the software, or do it themselves.

Self-paced ERP training delivered via the Web is becoming a popular concept. Users say training eats up 10 to 20 percent of an ERP project's budget and is one of the more vexing parts of an ERP development project. Many ERP systems have tricky user interfaces and are highly customized, making generic, computer-based training courses ineffective. Clarke American, a San Antonio–based check printer, is in a growing group of companies using Web-based training to get workers up to speed on enterprise resource planning applications. Doing so can trim up to 75 percent off the cost of traditional training methods, such as instructor-led sessions, users said [3].

Conversion Methods

The initial operation of a new business system can be a difficult task. This typically requires a **conversion** process from the use of a present system to the operation of a new or improved application. Conversion methods can soften the impact of introducing new information technologies into an organization. Four major forms of system conversion are illustrated in Figure 10.27. They include:

- Parallel conversion.
- Phased conversion.
- Pilot conversion.
- Plunge or direct cutover.

Conversions can be done on a *parallel basis*, whereby both the old and the new systems are operating until the project development team and end user management agree to

FIGURE 10.26 How one company developed training programs for the implementation of an e-commerce website and intranet access for its employees.

FIGURE 10.27

The four major forms of conversion to a new system.

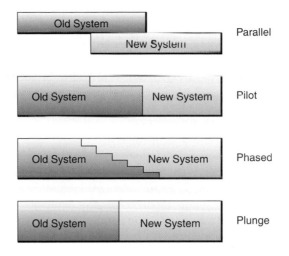

switch completely over to the new system. It is during this time that the operations and re-sults of both systems are compared and evaluated. Errors can be identified and corrected, and the operating problems can be solved before the old system is abandoned. Installation can also be accomplished by a direct cutover or *plunge* to a newly developed system.

Conversion can also be done on a *phased basis*, where only parts of a new application or only a few departments, branch offices, or plant locations at a time are converted. A phased conversion allows a gradual implementation process to take place within an or-ganization. Similar benefits accrue from using a *pilot conversion*, where one department or other work site serves as a test site. A new system can be tried out at this site until developers feel it can be implemented throughout the organization.

IS Maintenance

Once a system is fully implemented and is being used in business operations, the mainte-nance function begins. **Systems maintenance** is the monitoring, evaluating, and modify-ing of operational business systems to make desirable or necessary improvements. For example, the implementation of a new system usually results in the phenomenon known as the *learning curve*. Personnel who operate and use the system will make mistakes simply because they are not familiar with it. Though such errors usually diminish as experience is gained with a new system, they do point out areas where a system may be improved.

Maintenance is also necessary for other failures and problems that arise during the operation of a system. End users and information systems personnel then perform a *troubleshooting* function to determine the causes of and solutions to such problems.

The maintenance activity includes a **postimplementation review** process to en-sure that newly implemented systems meet the business objectives established for them. Errors in the development or use of a system must be corrected by the mainte-nance process. This includes a periodic review or audit of a system to ensure that it is operating properly and meeting its objectives. This audit is in addition to continually monitoring a new system for potential problems or necessary changes.

Maintenance also includes making modifications to an established system due to changes in the business organization or the business environment. For example, new tax legislation, company reorganizations, and new e-business and e-commerce initia-tives may require major changes to current business systems.

| GM Locomotive Group: Failure in System Implementation | The Locomotive Group of GM's Electromotive Division (www.gmemd.com), is the world's largest builder of diesel-electric locomotives. The General Motors locomotive unit encountered such severe problems during a rollout of SAP AG's R/3 enterprise resource planning applications in 2001 that its spare parts business virtually ground to a halt, forcing GM to launch an emergency turnaround effort six months after the |

software went live. Officials at GM's Locomotive Group said order backlogs and fulfillment cycle times still needed improvement over a year later, although business operations started to improve shortly after the rescue effort began in July 2001.

The SAP software had to be reconfigured, flushed, and repopulated with clean data, said Mike Duncan, director of worldwide aftermarket sales and development at the LaGrange, Illinois-based Electromotive Division. The $2 billion GM subsidiary hired a second consulting firm to help fix the enterprise resource planning and supply chain management systems after its first systems integrator completed the initial rollout. The GM unit, which makes locomotives, diesel engines and armored vehicles such as tanks, also had to retrain end users and remap all the business processes that were being built into the new system.

The locomotive unit launched a SAP-based ERP and supply chain system during 2001 in order to improve its financial reporting and its ability to forecast spare parts needs. The problems started when the Locomotive Group went live with R/3. The plan was to make aftermarket operations more efficient by replacing legacy mainframe systems with ERP system modules powered by R/3 that could handle parts distribution, order entry procurement, and financial reporting, said David Scott, the locomotive unit's executive director. He said the software wasn't configured well enough to match internal business processes, and legacy mainframe data weren't properly formatted for the new system.

Scott said there were no problems with the R/3 software itself, but the applications weren't properly configured to meet GM's needs. As a result, the aftermarket department couldn't accurately forecast demand or ensure that it had the right mix of parts inventories on hand. "Our business processes were largely arrested by what happened," Scott said. "We spent a lot of money and expected to get something for it, and got something else instead. It was very disappointing."

The Locomotive Group brought in Chicago-based Technology Solutions Co. to help reconfigure the ERP systems. Scott said that although most aftermarket operations have returned to normal, GM is still looking for continued improvements from both IT and business process standpoints. The Locomotive Group is also outsourcing SAP-related application support, end-user training, and follow-on software implementation for the new ERP system to Technology Solutions [27].

Managing Organizational Change

Implementing new business/IT strategies requires managing the effects of major changes in key organizational dimensions such as business processes, organizational structures, managerial roles, employee work assignments, and stakeholder relationships that arise from the deployment of new business information systems. For example, Figure 10.28 emphasizes the variety and extent of the challenges reported by 100 companies that developed and implemented new enterprise information portals and ERP systems [14, 22].

End User Resistance and Involvement

Any new way of doing things generates some resistance by the people affected. For example, the implementation of new work support technologies can generate fear and resistance to change by employees. Let's look at a real world example that demonstrates the challenges of implementing major business/IT strategies and applications, and the change management challenges that confront management. Customer relationship management (CRM) is a prime example of a key e-business application for many companies today. It is designed to implement a business strategy of using IT to support a total customer care focus for all areas of a company. Yet CRM projects have a history of a high rate of failure in meeting their objectives. For example, according to a report from Meta Group, a staggering 55 percent to 75 percent of CRM projects fail to meet their objectives, often as a result of sales force automation problems and "unaddressed cultural issues"—sales staffs are often resistant to, or even fearful of, using CRM systems [13].

FIGURE 10.28

The ten greatest challenges of developing and implementing intranet enterprise portals and enterprise resource planning systems reported by 100 companies.

Intranet Enterprise Portal Challenges	Enterprise Resource Planning Challenges
• Security, security, security	• Getting end-user buy-in
• Defining the scope and purpose of the portal	• Scheduling/planning
• Finding the time and the money	• Integrating legacy systems/data
• Ensuring consistent data quality	• Getting management buy-in
• Getting employees to use it	• Dealing with multiple/international sites and partners
• Organizing the data	• Changing culture/mind-sets
• Finding technical expertise	• IT training
• Integrating the pieces	• Getting, keeping IT staff
• Making it easy to use	• Moving to a new platform
• Providing all users with access	• Performance/system upgrades

One of the keys to solving problems of **end user resistance** to new information technologies is proper education and training. Even more important is **end user involvement** in organizational changes, and in the development of new information systems. Organizations have a variety of strategies to help manage business change, and one basic requirement is the involvement and commitment of top management and all business stakeholders affected by a new business application.

Direct end user participation in business planning and application development projects before a new system is implemented is especially important in reducing the potential for end user resistance. That is why end users frequently are members of systems development teams or do their own development work. Such involvement helps ensure that end users assume ownership of a system, and that its design meets their needs. Systems that tend to inconvenience or frustrate users cannot be effective systems, no matter how technically elegant they are and how efficiently they process data. For example, Figure 10.29 illustrates some of the major obstacles to knowledge management systems in business [4]. Notice that end user resistance to sharing knowledge is the biggest obstacle to the implementation of knowledge management applications. Let's look at a real world example that spotlights end user resistance and some of its solutions.

FIGURE 10.29

Obstacles to knowledge management systems. Note that end user resistance to knowledge sharing is the biggest obstacle.

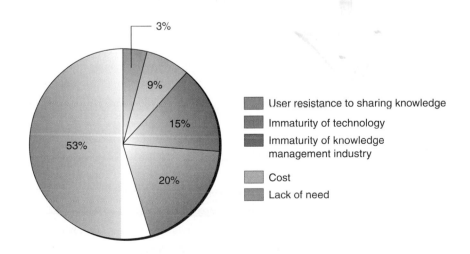

Crane Engineering: Overcoming User Resistance to CRM

"Our biggest challenge was our sales guys—changing their habits, getting them to use it for planning. They'd make comments like, 'I don't have time to enter the information.' Some are afraid of using Windows, not to mention CRM," says Jeff Koeper, vice president of operations at Crane Engineering, a Kimberly, Wisconsin-based industrial equipment distributor.

Crane initially had formed a cross-functional team with IT sales and customer service staffers to hear sales automation software vendors' presentations and mutually decide on the desired goals. After a vendor was chosen in 1999, a cross-functional pilot project was formed to iron out any kinks before the system was rolled out companywide. Two full-day training classes have been held since the initial implementation. But now, Crane is requiring sales managers to ride herd on foot-draggers, and using peer pressure from salespeople selling different products to the same accounts. A cross-functional CRM steering committee meets monthly to discuss problem areas.

"Salespeople want to know what's in it for them; it's not enough to tell them they have to do it. But give them a panoramic view of what their customer is doing in call centers and on the company website, such as buying other products or complaints. That's a very powerful motivator—they respond to revenue potential and growing their customer base," says Liz Shahnam, a Meta Group analyst.

But companies face a bigger challenge: CRM is a mind-set—a business philosophy that reshapes a company's sales, marketing, customer service, and analytics and presents a radical cultural shift for many organizations. "It's a change from a product-centered or internal focus to a customer-centered or external focus. It's a change from a monologue to a dialogue with the customer; with the advent of the Internet, customers want to converse with a company. Also, it's a change from targeting customers to becoming the target. Customers are now the hunters," says Ray McKenzie, Seattle-based director of management consulting at DMR Consulting.

This switch means getting IT professionals to "think customer" and breaking down the barriers between IT and the employees who interact with customers. It also means structural changes in how the company operates, like sharing information and resources across departments and job functions, which translates into giving up control over who "owns" it; retraining employees in new roles, responsibilities and skills; and measuring their job performance, and even how they're paid [13].

Change Management

People are a major focus of organizational **change management.** This includes activities such as developing innovative ways to measure, motivate, and reward performance. So is designing programs to recruit and train employees in the core competencies required in a changing workplace. Change management also involves analyzing and defining all changes facing the organization, and developing programs to reduce the risks and costs and to maximize the benefits of change. For example, implementing a new business application such as customer relationship management might involve developing a *change action plan*, assigning selected managers as *change sponsors*, developing employee *change teams*, and encouraging open communications and feedback about organizational changes [6]. Some key tactics change experts recommend include:

- Involve as many people as possible in business/IT planning and application development.
- Make constant change an expected part of the culture.
- Tell everyone as much as possible about everything as often as possible, preferably in person.
- Make liberal use of financial incentives and recognition.
- Work within the company culture, not around it.

Duke Energy: A Guerrilla Approach to Business Change	Duke Energy initiated a guerrilla approach to encouraging the development of e-business applications. A small band of advocates began to roam the utility, living in the business units, seeding pilot projects, assisting with implantations, coordinating resources, and spreading success stories. Eighteen months later, having launched more than a dozen successful Internet initiatives that saved the company $52 million in one year alone, the "e-team" handed off the projects to the business units.

Duke's corporate policy committee, at the urging of CIO Cecil Smith, authorized senior vice president and chief e-business officer A. R. Mullinax to begin to harness the Internet. The goal was to weave e-business applications into the Duke fabric. "We didn't want to turn Duke into a dot-com," Mullinax recalls. "We wanted to find uses of the Internet that would advance our existing business."

Mullinax, then senior vice president for procurement, was given free reign to recruit a team and carry out the mission. He chose Ted Schultz from strategic planning; Steve Bush, finance and administration; Dave Davies, IT project management; Amy Baxter and Dennis Wood, procurement; Elizabeth Henry, customer focus; and Anne Narang, Web design. "Everybody brought strengths to the table," Mullinax says, "and the other ingredient was chemistry. We worked well as a team."

Team members literally moved into the businesses. If a unit had already launched an Internet initiative, a team member would advise on strategy and implementation. If a unit was new to the Web, a team member would spearhead an initiative.

The e-team had a budget, but its mantra was "Invest little, save big." It looked for business units that could use Internet tools in the most effective way, particularly those units where customers were dependent on information, and easy access to that information would add value to the relationship. "We could have taken on hundreds of initiatives, but we looked for the ones that would give us the most return compared with the level of effort it was going to take," Mullinax explains [15].

FIGURE 10.30

An overview of the implementation process. Implementation activities are needed to transform a newly developed information system into an operational system for end users.

Implementing New Systems
● **Acquisition**   Evaluate and acquire necessary hardware and software resources and information system services. Screen vendor proposals.
● **Software Development**   Develop any software that will not be acquired externally as software packages. Make any necessary modifications to software packages that are acquired.
● **Data Conversion**   Convert data in company databases to new data formats and subsets required by newly installed software.
● **Training**   Educate and train management, end users, customers and other business stakeholders. Use consultants or training programs to develop user competencies.
● **Testing**   Test and make necessary corrections to the programs, procedures, and hardware used by a new system.
● **Documentation**   Record and communicate detailed system specifications, including procedures for end users and IS personnel and examples of input screens and output displays and reports.
● **Conversion**   Convert from the use of a present system to the operation of a new or improved system. This may involve operating both new and old systems in *parallel* for a trial period, operation of a *pilot* system on a trial basis at one location, *phasing* in the new system one location at a time, or an immediate *plunge* or *cut over* to the new system.

Summary

- **The Systems Development Cycle.** Business end users and IS specialists may use a systems approach to help them develop information system solutions to meet business opportunities. This frequently involves a systems development cycle where IS specialists and end users conceive, design, and implement business systems. The stages, activities, and products of the information systems development cycle are summarized in Figure 10.3.

- **Prototyping.** Prototyping is a major alternative methodology to the traditional information systems development cycle. It includes the use of prototyping tools and methodologies, which promote an iterative, interactive process that develops prototypes of user interfaces and other information system components. See Figure 10.4.

- **End User Development.** The application development capabilities built into many end user software packages have made it easier for end users to develop their own business applications. End users should focus their development efforts on the system components of business processes that can benefit from the use of information technology, as summarized in Figure 10.16.

- **Implementing IS.** The implementation process for information system projects is summarized in Figure 10.30. Implementation involves acquisition, testing, documentation, training, installation, and conversion activities that transform a newly designed business system into an operational system for end users.

- **Evaluating Hardware, Software, and Services.** Business professionals should know how to evaluate the acquisition of information system resources. IT vendors' proposals should be based on specifications developed during the design stage of systems development. A formal evaluation process reduces the possibility of incorrect or unnecessary purchases of hardware or software. Several major evaluation factors, summarized in Figures 10.23, 10.24, and 10.25, can be used to evaluate hardware, software, and IS services.

- **Implementing Business Change.** Implementation activities include managing the introduction and implementation of changes in business processes, organizational structures, job assignments, and work relationships resulting from business/IT strategies and applications such as e-business initiatives, reengineering projects, supply chain alliances, and the introduction of new technologies. Companies use change management tactics such as user involvement in business/IT planning and systems development to reduce and user resistance and maximize acceptance of business changes by all stakeholders.

Key Terms and Concepts

These are the key terms and concepts of this chapter. The page number of their first explanation is in parentheses.

1. Change management (368)
2. Conversion methods (364)
3. Cost/benefit analysis (347)
4. Data conversion (363)
5. Documentation (363)
6. Economic feasibility (346)
7. End user involvement (367)
8. End user resistance (366)
9. End user development (353)
10. Evaluation factors (360)
    a. Hardware (360)
    b. IS services (361)
    c. Software (361)
11. Feasibility study (346)
12. Functional requirements (350)
13. Implementation process (358)
14. Intangible (347)
    a. Benefits (347)
    b. Costs (347)
15. Operational feasibility (347)
16. Organizational analysis (348)
17. Organizational feasibility (346)
18. Postimplementation review (365)
19. Project management (358)
20. Prototype (343)
21. Prototyping (343)
22. Systems analysis (350)
23. Systems approach (342)
24. Systems design (350)
25. Systems development life cycle (343)
26. Systems implementation (356)
27. Systems investigation (346)
28. Systems maintenance (365)
29. Systems specifications (353)
30. System testing (363)
31. Systems thinking (342)
32. Tangible (347)
    a. Benefits (347)
    b. Costs (347)
33. Technical feasibility (347)
34. User interface design (351)

Match one of the key terms and concepts listed previously with one of the brief examples or definitions that follow. Try to find the best fit for answers that seem to fit more than one term or concept. Defend your choices.

_____ 1. Using an organized sequence of activities to study a problem or opportunity using systems thinking.

_____ 2. Trying to recognize systems and the new interrelationships and components of systems in any situation.

_____ 3. Evaluating the success of a solution after it has been implemented.

_____ 4. Your evaluation shows that benefits outweigh costs for a proposed system.

_____ 5. The costs of acquiring computer hardware, software, and specialists.

_____ 6. Loss of customer goodwill caused by errors in a new system.

_____ 7. Increases in profits caused by a new system.

_____ 8. Improved employee morale caused by efficiency and effectiveness of a new system.

_____ 9. A multistep process to conceive, design, and implement an information system.

_____ 10. The first stage of the systems development cycle.

_____ 11. Determines the organizational, economic, technical, and operational feasibility of a proposed information system.

_____ 12. Cost savings and additional profits will exceed the investment required.

_____ 13. Reliable hardware and software are available to implement a proposed system.

_____ 14. Customers will not have trouble using a proposed system.

_____ 15. The proposed system supports the strategic plan of the business.

_____ 16. Studying in detail the information needs of users and any information systems presently used.

_____ 17. A detailed description of user information needs and the input, processing, output, storage, and control capabilities required to meet those needs.

_____ 18. The process that results in specifications for the hardware, software, people, network, and data resources and information products needed by a proposed system.

_____ 19. Systems design should focus on developing user-friendly input and output methods for a system.

_____ 20. A detailed description of the hardware, software, people, network, and data resources and information products required by a proposed system.

_____ 21. Acquiring hardware and software, testing and documenting a proposed system, and training people to use it.

_____ 22. Making improvements to an operational system.

_____ 23. A working model of an information system.

_____ 24. An interactive and iterative process of developing and refining information system prototypes.

_____ 25. Managers and business specialists can develop their own e-business applications.

_____ 26. Includes acquisition, testing, training, and conversion to a new system.

_____ 27. Performance, cost, reliability, technology, and ergonomics are examples.

_____ 28. Performance, cost, efficiency, language, and documentation are examples.

_____ 29. Maintenance, conversion, training, and business position are examples.

_____ 30. Operate in parallel with the old system, use a test site, switch in stages, or cut over immediately to a new system.

_____ 31. Checking whether hardware and software work properly for end users.

_____ 32. A user manual communicates the design and operating procedures of a system.

_____ 33. Modifying an operational system by adding e-commerce website access would be an example.

_____ 34. Keeping an IS project on time and within its budget would be a major goal.

_____ 35. Installing new software may require new data formats.

_____ 36. End users frequently resist the introduction of new technology.

_____ 37. End users should be part of planning for organizational change and business/IT project teams.

_____ 38. Companies should try to minimize the resistance and maximize the acceptance of major changes in business and information technology.

Discussion Questions

1. Why has prototyping become a popular way to develop business applications? What are prototyping's advantages and disadvantages?

2. Refer to the Real World Case on Blue Cross, AT&T Wireless, and CitiStreet in the chapter. What are your top three complaints about the self-service features of the websites you visit regularly? Defend the value of several solutions you propose to address your complaints.

3. Review the BuyerZone and OfficeMax and Priceline real world examples in the chapter. What design changes should BuyerZone and OfficeMax make to correct the design flaws at their site and bring their website design up to Priceline's standard? Explain your reasoning.

4. What are the three most important factors you would use in evaluating computer hardware? Computer software? Explain why.

5. Assume that in your first week on a new job you are asked to use a type of business software that you have never used before. What kind of user training should your company provide to you before you start?

6. Refer to the Real World Case on InterContinental Hotels, Del Taco, and Cardinal Health in the chapter. Should companies outsource the tasks required for the implementation of new systems? Why or why not?

7. What is the difference between the parallel, plunge, phased, and pilot forms of IS conversion? Which conversion strategy is best? Explain why.

8. Review the Frito-Lay and GM Locomotive real world examples in the chapter. How could these failures have been avoided?

9. Review the Crane Engineering and Duke Energy real world examples in the chapter. What else could these companies do to increase user acceptance of their business/IT projects?

10. Pick a business task you would like to computerize. How could you use the steps of the information systems development cycle as illustrated in Figure 10.3 to help you? Use examples to illustrate your answer.

Analysis Exercises

1. **Alternative Web Page Targets and Styles**
   The appropriate look and feel of a Web page are very much affected by its purpose and target audience.

   Identify three successful websites—one from each category listed below. Identify and describe the principle purpose of each site. Find examples from each site that make the site unique to its category. Assess how well these differences fit the varying purposes and target audiences of the three websites.

   Categories:

   - Government – regulatory agency
   - Manufacturing – product support
   - Non-Governmental Organization (NGO) – eg., a hunger/medical aid agency

   a. Prepare a set of presentation materials summarizing your results and highlighting key findings. Include sample screen captures from the sites or links that can be used to call up the appropriate pages in an oral presentation. Be prepared to present your results.
   b. Prepare a short report summarizing your results. Include website addresses to key Web pages illustrating your main points.

   Source: Adapted from James N. Morgan, *Application Cases in MIS*, 4th ed. (New York, McGraw-Hill/Irwin, 2002), p. 20.

2. **e-Business System Report**
   Study an e-business application described in a case study in this text or one used by an organization to which you have access.

   a. Write up the results in an e-business system report.
   b. Make a presentation to the class based on the results of your study of an e-business system
   c. Use the outline in Figure 10.31 as a table of contents for your report and the outline of your presentation.
   d. Use presentation software and/or overhead transparencies to display key points of your analysis.

3. **SDLC in Practice**
   The Systems Development Life Cycle (SDLC) provides a structured problem solving approach frequently used to develop software systems. However, what works for information system related problems also works for business problems in general. The SDLC provides a framework for problem solving that requires adherents to follow a logical sequence that promotes credibility and helps ensure organizations you are *doing the right thing* as well as *doing the thing* right.

   Form student teams of three or four students. Use the Systems Development Life Cycle as illustrated in Figure 10.3 and outlined starting on page 343 to tackle a problem or opportunity within your immediate

FIGURE 10.31   Outline of an e-business system report.

- **Introduction to the organization and e-business application.** Briefly describe the organization you selected and the type of e-business application you have studied.

- **Analysis of an e-business system.** Identify the following system components of a current business use of the Internet, intranets, or extranets for an e-business or e-commerce application.

  - Input, processing, output, storage, and control methods currently used.

  - Hardware, software, networks, and people involved.

  - Data captured and information products produced.

  - Files and databases accessed and maintained.

- **Evaluation of the system.**

  - **Efficiency:** Does it do the job right? Is the system well organized? Inexpensive? Fast? Does it require minimum resources? Process large volumes of data, produce a variety of information products?

  - **Effectiveness:** Does it do the right job? The way the employees, customers, suppliers, or other end users want it done? Does it give them the information they need, the way they want it? Does it support the business objectives of the organization? Provide significant customer and business value?

- **Design and implementation of a system proposal.**

  - Do end users need a new system or just improvements? Why?

  - What exactly are you recommending they do?

  - Is it feasible? What are its benefits and costs?

  - What will it take to implement your recommendations?

---

community. Your community may include your campus, your work, or your neighborhood. Your instructor will provide additional guidelines and constraints.

Identify an existing problem or opportunity within your community and obtain approval from your instructor to pursue this topic. Investigate the problem or opportunity. Include the cause of the problem or nature of the opportunity. Include facts (not anecdotes) quantifying the problem or opportunity. These facts should focus on measures that your team plans to target for improvement. Interview the appropriate experts as needed. Identify by name the authorities directly responsible for your team's topic area. Identify all stakeholder groups associated with the problem or opportunity.

Research the current processes associated with the current problem or opportunity. Develop specific targets and measures for improvement. During this phase, do *not* focus on possible solutions or solution steps.

Determine how much time, money, and other resources your solution will require. Compare your recommended solution to other solutions considered but rejected. Explain the rationale behind your team's choice. Include a detailed description of your implementation plan. The plan should address the needs of each stakeholder group affected. Include a plan for measuring your proposed project's success.

a. Present to your class what you learned about your team's problem or opportunity. Following this initial presentation, solicit from your classmates suggestions about information sources useful in preparing a solid case for advancing to the *analysis stage* of the 3DLC.

b. Identify new performance levels your team would like to achieve and obtain agreement from the responsible authority (or your instructor) that your team has properly defined and measured the problem or opportunity and has established meaningful objectives.

c. Test the plan for feasibility. This may simply entail sharing your plan with the various stakeholder groups and obtaining their recommendations and approval.

d. Prepare a report covering the problem or opportunity, your team's analysis, solution, and implementation plan. Make your presentation to your class (for practice). Be sure to explain to the class at the presentation's outset what person or group constitutes the actual responsible authorities. Modify your report based on class and instructor feedback and make a final, formal presentation to the actual authorities responsible for your team's topic area (if feasible).

Du Pont and Southwire: Implementing Successful Enterprise Information Portals

Companies typically plan and deploy enterprise information portals to provide employees, customers, and suppliers with a single Web-based access point for data, content, and both new and legacy applications across the enterprise. But things don't always go as planned. Too often, companies build portals, but users just don't come. In a recent Delphi survey of 500 companies spanning 20 industries, 37 percent of the companies that had installed portals said they were disappointed by the lack of "adequate interest among target users."

According to Delphi's findings, the reason people aren't using portals is because there isn't a strategy for keeping people involved—what Delphi calls change management, explains analyst Nathaniel Palmer. "There's a lack of strategy beyond the technical architecture," he says. Indeed, too many companies got caught up in the hoopla surrounding portal technology. Meanwhile, critical usability issues get shortchanged, such as educating users about the portal's capabilities, training them to use it efficiently, and marketing the value of using the portal, especially its value in addressing very specific business problems a company may have.

Du Pont. At Du Pont Co.'s (www.dupont.com) $3.8 billion Performance Coatings group, the critical issue was content management. "We have a very large number of documents for marketing: brochures, press releases, warranty information on products, and general support content for our distributors and car repair body shops," explains Catherine Marchand, the group's e-business strategy manager. "Our salesmen were driving around with 50 pounds of obsolete literature in their trunk."

Du Pont opted to deliver the information through a Web-based intranet/extranet portal, using technology from Bowstreet, a portal software and Web development tools company. Du Pont wanted the ability to customize information about its half-dozen coating brands. It also wanted each of its 2,500 distributors and repair shops worldwide to see the information displayed in almost 4,000 different site views, which the technology would allow it to do.

Since the content capability was initiated, Du Pont's site has grown rapidly. The body shops can now get training, benchmarking tools, and car paint color formulas via the portal. There's also a job-posting and resume service, Marchand says. And for the distributors, Du Pont is researching adding order-tracking and order-accuracy capabilities soon.

Southwire. At Southwire Co. (www.mysouthwire.com), a $1.7 billion, Carrollton, Georgia-based manufacturer of cable and wire, the critical business issue was streamlining business processes. Southwire didn't set out in 1999 to build an ideal portal. The privately held firm just wanted a spot on the Web where customers could place orders. It also wanted to clean up multiple internal and corporate websites, which had been set up by IT on behalf of various departments, each using different Web development software. But four years later, Southwire's portal is yielding impressive business results.

Customer orders are up 33 percent, and 25 percent of all orders are electronic, with online customers ordering twice as many items as those who place orders via fax, telephone, or electronic data interchange. And thanks to content management and workflow capabilities added in the past year, Southwire's managers can approve and post announcements to the portal without involving IT.

"We had several independent websites and a fairly robust e-commerce site. The portal provides an umbrella to bring all those separate websites under, along with providing a single sign-on, multilevel security access, customization, and personalization," says Sheda Simpson, development manager in Southwire's IT Services group. The underlying portal technology is from Sybase Inc. "Southwire was trying to be ahead of the game—at the urging of our CEO," recalls Simpson.

Southwire's initial portal offered only 1,200 commonly ordered products out of the company's 65,000 stock numbers. The emphasis wasn't on creating a "pretty front-end storefront" for the ordering site, according to Simpson. The true business need was cutting costs associated with processing lots of paper and increasing productivity. "We didn't want the behind-the-scenes manual processing," says Simpson. "Southwire was trying to become more efficient. We did not need to create more work; we needed to eliminate work, to streamline," she says.

Thus came the emphasis on integrating the order site to the back-end systems. The company eliminated a significant chunk of manual work which means fewer telephone calls to answer and less faxed information to rekey into the computer system. This streamlining of operations is a big part of the portal's popularity at Southwire.

Case Study Questions

1. Why do so many enterprise information portals fail to attract "adequate interest among targeted users?" What can be done to improve the usage of portals in business?

2. What is the business value of their enterprise portal to Du Pont's Performance Coatings group? How could it be improved?

3. What are the business benefits of Southwire's enterprise portal? Describe several ways it might be improved.

Source: Adapted from Connie Winkler, "Drawing a Crowd," *Computerworld*, March 3, 2003, pp. 38–39. Copyright © 2003 by Computerworld, Inc. Framingham, MA 01701. All rights reserved.

REAL WORLD CASE 4
Wyndham International and Amazon.com: Cost-Effective IT

Having spent the past two years paring back staff, consolidating servers and storage equipment, renegotiating vendor contracts, and conducting selective outsourcing, CIOs are struggling to find new ways to reduce costs while still developing and implementing the new or improved business systems their companies need. "We've done all those things, and yet management still wants us to cut costs further," says a CIO at a Midwestern bank who requested anonymity. "I just don't know where else to cut." In their quest to come up with even more ways to keep a lid on costs, dauntless IT leaders are exploring everything from barter agreements with vendors to reselling services and joining purchasing consortiums for volume price discounts on equipment.

Wyndham International. A good example is Wyndham International Inc.'s (www.wyndham.com) chief technology officer, Mark Hedley. Like many IT executives, Hedley has taken advantage of the cutthroat competition that the economy has stirred up in the telecommunications sector and has reworked the hospitality firm's private branch exchange, data, and voice networking agreements, thus paring $850,000 from the Dallas-based company's annual telecom budget. Now Hedley is evaluating a shift from Wyndham's private frame relay network to a virtual private network on the Internet as a way to further reduce data communications costs by as much as 50 percent annually. But he is still weighing the major money-saving benefits of doing so against the security, stability, and reliability issues involved with moving to the less secure public network infrastructure of the Internet.

Amazon.com. Like a lot of people who buy software for their businesses, CIO Rick Dalzell saw his budget frozen last year. Unlike most of those people, though, that still leaves Dalzell with about $200 million to spend—but then, as chief information officer at Amazon.com (www.amazon.com), he has a lot to do. Most important, Dalzell has to maintain Amazon's edge in technology—an edge that is more critical than ever as Amazon increasingly squares off against sophisticated e-commerce survivors like eBay.

But that's why Jeff Bezos hired Dalzell away from Wal-Mart five years ago. In Bentonville, Arkansas, Dalzell made a name for himself by slashing $ 1.4 billion out of inventory costs; he has continued in the same vein in Seattle. Just two and a half years ago, Amazon spent 11 cents on information technology for every $1 in sales. Now, under Dalzell's new austerity regimen, the company spends only about 6 cents per sales dollar. All told, Dalzell has cut Amazon's tech spending 25 percent from its September 2000 peak, even as the company added nine new categories to its retail lineup, and signed on dozens of new corporate partners. Here are the strategies Dalzell has followed to success at Amazon.

Embrace open source. Dalzell says the single most effective move he made was to replace Sun servers with Linux boxes from Hewlett-Packard. For every $1 spent on the new hardware, he saved $10 in license fees, maintenance, and expected hardware upgrades. Some companies, Microsoft chief among them, have long warned that Linux savings are deceptive, certain to be offset by the costs of maintaining an operating system unsupported by a corporate proprietor. Dalzell doesn't buy it. "I haven't found any of the hidden, secret costs that others would make you believe exist for Linux," he says.

Recognize when you have to spend to save. Amazon maintains its own warehouse-management software, even though ready-made alternatives like Logility might cost as little as $375,000. But with its own software, Amazon can tweak inventory algorithms whenever it wants—so that, for example, a book isn't shipped to New York from a Nevada warehouse when it could be sent faster and cheaper from Delaware.

Help your partners help you. Dalzell recently began to invest in Web services—tools that make it easy for partners to hook into applications Amazon had developed for its own use. Now retailers like Nordstrom and Gap can feed their inventories into Amazon's new apparel store without a lot of custom coding. It also means that freelance programmers and retailers can build their own online stores using Amazon's payment, fulfillment, and customer services. (These associated stores get a 5 to 15 percent cut of the orders they bring to Amazon.) For example, a Romanian coder created www.simplest-shop.com, which uses Amazon's Web services tools to extract product data from Amazon and other websites and then fashions side-by-side comparison tables.

Use a tight budget as an excuse to get creative. Austerity forces you to focus on what really works. And in a perverse way, that frees up creativity. "First you think about the problem in a million different ways," Dalzell advises. "You'll come up with something really innovative. Then you apply the real world constraints, and figure out how to solve the problem." Dalzell looks at his stagnant budget as an engineering challenge. And as every engineer knows, it's the constraints that make a problem interesting.

Case Study Questions

1. Are the resource acquisition challenges faced by CIOs any different than those faced by other business managers in times of tight budgets? Why or why not?

2. What are the business benefits and limitations of Rick Dalzell's IT resource acquisition strategies for Amazon?

3. Are Dalzell's strategies applicable to small as well as large businesses? Explain your answer.

Sources: Adapted from Thomas Hoffman, "Squeeze Play," *Computerworld*, February 10, 2003, pp. 41–42; and Owen Thomas, "Amazon's Tightwad of Tech," *Business 2.0*, February 2003.

MODULE V

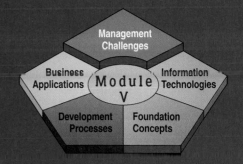

MANAGEMENT CHALLENGES

W hat managerial challenges do information systems pose for today's business enterprises? The two chapters of this module emphasize how managers and business professionals can manage the successful use of information technologies in a global economy.

- Chapter 11, **Security and Ethical Challenges,** discusses the threats against and defenses needed for the performance and security of business information systems, as well as the ethical implications and societal impacts of information technology.

- Chapter 12, **Enterprise and Global Management of Information Technology,** emphasizes the impact of business applications of information technology on management and organizations, the components of information systems management, and the managerial implications of the use of information technology in global business.

CHAPTER 11

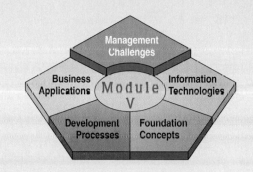

SECURITY AND ETHICAL CHALLENGES

Chapter Highlights

Section I
Security, Ethical, and Societal Challenges of IT
Introduction
Real World Case: F-Secure, Microsoft, GM, and Verizon: The Business Challenge of Computer Viruses
Ethical Responsibility of Business Professionals
Computer Crime
Privacy Issues
Other Challenges
Health Issues
Societal Solutions

Section II
Security Management of Information Technology
Introduction
Real World Case: Geisinger Health Systems and Du Pont: Security Management
Tools of Security Management
Internetworked Security Defenses
Other Security Measures
System Controls and Audits
Real World Case: Banner Health, Arlington County, and Others: Security Management of Windows Software
Real World Case: Online Resources, Lehman Brothers, and Others: Managing Network Security Systems

Learning Objectives

After reading and studying this chapter, you should be able to:

1. Identify several ethical issues in how the use of information technologies in business affects employment, individuality, working conditions, privacy, crime, health, and solutions to societal problems.

2. Identify several types of security management strategies and defenses, and explain how they can be used to ensure the security of business applications of information technology.

3. Propose several ways that business managers and professionals can help to lessen the harmful effects and increase the beneficial effects of the use of information technology.

SECTION I	Security, Ethical, and Societal Challenges of IT

Introduction

There is no question that the use of information technology in business presents major security challenges, poses serious ethical questions, and affects society in significant ways. Therefore, in this section we will explore the threats to businesses and individuals posed by many types of computer crime and unethical behavior. In Section II, we will examine a variety of methods that companies use to manage the security and integrity of their business systems. Now let's look at a real world example.

Analyzing F-Secure, Microsoft, GM, and Verizon

Read the Real World Case on F-Secure, Microsoft, GM, and Verizon on the next page. We can learn a lot from this case about the security and ethical issues in business that arise from the challenges caused by computer viruses. See Figure 11.1.

Computer virus attacks are increasingly causing major disruptions in business worldwide as the frequency of attacks and their potential for damage to networked business resources continue to escalate. On the spot is Microsoft Corporation and their Windows operating system, whose many vulnerabilities are being exploited by the virus creators. Microsoft has started a major Trustworthy Computing initiative to improve the security of Windows, but their many critics say that the problem lies in Microsoft's software development process itself, which emphasizes speed to market and software features over security, thus producing software with many system vulnerabilities. So far the burden has fallen on companies, business professionals, and consumers to use and update antivirus software and apply security patches to fix Windows vulnerabilities that are continually being discovered by Microsoft and others, before virus creators can take advantage of them.

Business/IT Security, Ethics, and Society

The use of information technologies in business has had major impacts on society, and thus raises ethical issues in the areas of crime, privacy, individuality, employment, health, and working conditions. See Figure 11.2.

FIGURE 11.1

Mikko Hypponen is the research director of F-Secure Corporation of Finland, which cracked the SoBig virus before it completed its attack process.

Source: Mark Richards.

REAL WORLD CASE 1

F-Secure, Microsoft, GM, and Verizon: The Business Challenge of Computer Viruses

Mikko Hypponen and his band of Finnish computer virus hunters know the odds are stacked against them in the Web's wild frontier. "Tracking down a virus is rare," says Vincent Gullotto of the antivirus research lab at software maker Network Associates. So you'll have to pardon Hypponen, the antivirus research manager at Helsinki-based software company F-Secure Corp. (www.fsecure.com), if he got a little excited when he and his team were able to crack the SoBig virus before it finished doing whatever it was meant to do. Thanks to research from F-Secure, a 300-employee company known for cracking tough computer problems, virus experts and government investigators in several countries were able to shut down a network of computers hijacked by the virus just minutes before SoBig was to launch what was expected to be the next phase of its attack. "It was a very close call," says Hypponen. "The virus writers will make sure it's not as easy next time."

Indeed, to those most affected, it seemed as if the onslaught of viruses had reached epidemic proportions in August 2003, as the world's computer systems were blitzed by hundreds of viruses. On August 11, the Blaster virus and related bugs struck, hammering dozens of corporations, including Air Canada's reservation and airport check-in systems. Ten days later, the SoBig virus took over, causing delays in freight traffic at rail giant CSX Corp. and shutting down more than 3,000 computers belonging to the city of Fort Worth. Worldwide, 15 percent of large companies and 30 percent of small companies were affected by SoBig, according to virus software tracker TruSecure Corp. Market researcher Computer Economics Inc. estimates damage will total $2 billion—one of the costliest viruses ever. All told, damage from viruses may amount to more than $13 billion in one year.

Even as the damage reports pour in, the summer of SoBig provides a jangling wake-up call to businesses, consumers, and the software industry: Get serious about cybersecurity. At the same time, technology experts are warning of the dangers of relying so heavily on just one outfit—Microsoft Corp. (www.microsoft.com)—to provide the backbone of the computing and Internet world. With a 95 percent market share, Microsoft's Windows desktop operating system is a fat, juicy target for the bad guys.

Some critics even say that Microsoft, as a virtually essential service, has an obligation to ensure that its software is sufficiently hostile to hackers. Tech experts are calling on the company to make fundamental changes in the way it designs programs. "Microsoft has to write better software," says Paul Saffo, director of think tank Institute for the Future in Menlo Park, California. "It's outrageous that a company this profitable does such a lousy job."

Security experts and corporate tech purchasers say the glitches exist because Microsoft and other software companies have placed a high priority on getting products out quickly and loading them with features, rather than attending to security. They're calling on the industry—and Microsoft in particular—to make software more secure. Ralph Szygenda, chief information officer at General Motors Corp. (www.gm.com), got fed up when his computers were hit by the Nimda virus in late 2001. He called Microsoft executives. "I told them I'm going to move GM away from Windows," Szygenda recalls. "They started talking about security all of a sudden."

Amid much fanfare, Microsoft launched its Trustworthy Computing initiative in 2002, a campaign it claimed would put security at the core of its software design. As part of the campaign, more than 8,500 Microsoft engineers stopped developing Windows Server 2003 and conducted a security analysis of millions of lines of freshly written code. Microsoft ultimately spent $200 million on beefing up security in Windows Server 2003 alone. "It's a fundamental change in the way we write software," says Mike Nash, vice-president for security business. "If there was some way we could spend more money or throw more people on it, believe me, we'd do it." Yet, embarrassingly, Windows Server 2003, released in April 2003, was one of the systems easily exploited by Blaster.

But the burden for combating viruses lies with computer users themselves. Most large corporations already have basic antivirus software. But security experts maintain that they need to come up with better procedures for frequently updating their computers with the latest security patches to programs and inoculations against new viruses. Verizon Communications (www.verizon.com) has gotten serious about security in the past couple of years and already has a system for automatically updating its 200,000 computers as soon as patches are available. As a result, it escaped unscathed from the summer attacks. "As far as business impact, it was a nonevent for us," says Chief Information Officer Shaygan Kheradpir.

Case Study Questions

1. What security measures should companies, business professionals, and consumers take to protect their systems from being damaged by computer worms and viruses?

2. What is the ethical responsibility of Microsoft in helping to prevent the spread of computer viruses? Have they met this responsibility? Why or why not?

3. What are several possible reasons why some companies (like GM) were seriously affected by computer viruses, while others (like Verizon) were not?

Source: Adapted from Steve Hamm, Jay Greene, Cliff Edwards and Jim Kerstetter, "Epidemic," *BusinessWeek*, September 2, 2003. Reprinted from 9/02/03 issue of Business Week by special permission, copyright © 2003 by the McGraw-Hill Companies, Inc.

FIGURE 11.2

Important aspects of the security, ethical, and societal dimensions of the use of information technology in business. Remember that information technologies can support both beneficial and detrimental effects on society in each of the areas shown.

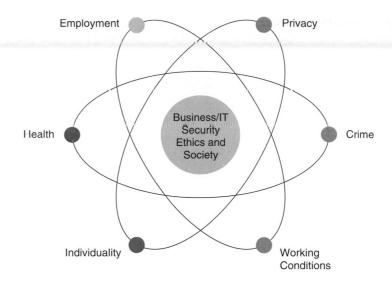

However, you should also realize that information technology has had beneficial results as well as detrimental effects on society and people in each of these areas. For example, computerizing a manufacturing process may have the adverse effect of eliminating people's jobs, but also have the beneficial result of improving working conditions and producing products of higher quality at less cost. So your job as a manager or business professional should involve managing your work activities and those of others to minimize the detrimental effects of business applications of information technology and optimize their beneficial effects. That would represent an ethically responsible use of information technology.

Ethical Responsibility of Business Professionals

As a business professional, you have a responsibility to promote ethical uses of information technology in the workplace. Whether you have managerial responsibilities or not, you should accept the ethical responsibilities that come with your work activities. That includes properly performing your role as a vital human resource in the business systems you help develop and use in your organization. As a manager or business professional, it will be your responsibility to make decisions about business activities and the use of information technologies, which may have an ethical dimension that must be considered.

For example, should you electronically monitor your employees' work activities and electronic mail? Should you let employees use their work computers for private business or take home copies of software for their personal use? Should you electronically access your employees' personnel records or workstation files? Should you sell customer information extracted from transaction processing systems to other companies? These are a few examples of the types of decisions you will have to make that have a controversial ethical dimension. So let's take a closer look at several ethical foundations in business and information technology.

Business Ethics

Business ethics is concerned with the numerous ethical questions that managers must confront as part of their daily business decision making. For example, Figure 11.3 outlines some of the basic categories of ethical issues and specific business practices that have serious ethical consequences. Notice that the issues of intellectual property rights, customer and employee privacy, security of company records, and workplace safety are highlighted because they have been major areas of ethical controversy in information technology [16].

How can managers make ethical decisions when confronted with business issues such as those listed in Figure 11.3? Several important alternatives based on theories of

FIGURE 11.3

Basic categories of ethical business issues. Information technology has caused ethical controversy in the areas of intellectual property rights, customer and employee privacy, security of company information, and workplace safety.

Equity	Rights	Honesty	Exercise of Corporate Power
Executive Salaries	Corporate Due Process	Employee Conflicts	Product Safety
Comparable Worth	Employee Health	of Interest	Environmental Issues
Product Pricing	Screening	**Security of Company**	Disinvestment
Intellectual	**Customer Privacy**	**Information**	Corporate Contributions
Property Rights	**Employee Privacy**	Inappropriate Gifts	Social Issues Raised by
Noncompetitive	Sexual Harassment	Advertising Content	Religious Organizations
Agreements	Affirmative Action	Government Contract	Plant/Facility Closures and
	Equal Employment	Issues	Downsizing
	Opportunity	Financial and Cash	Political Action Committees
	Shareholder Interests	Management Procedures	**Workplace Safety**
	Employment at Will	Questionable Business	
	Whistle-Blowing	Practices in Foreign	
		Countries	

corporate social responsibility can be used [21, 28]. For example, in business ethics, the **stockholder theory** holds that managers are agents of the stockholders, and their only ethical responsibility is to increase the profits of the business without violating the law or engaging in fraudulent practices.

However, the **social contract theory** states that companies have ethical responsibilities to all members of society, which allow corporations to exist based on a social contract. The first condition of the contract requires companies to enhance the economic satisfaction of consumers and employees. They must do that without polluting the environment or depleting natural resources, misusing political power, or subjecting their employees to dehumanizing working conditions. The second condition requires companies to avoid fraudulent practices, show respect for their employees as human beings, and avoid practices that systematically worsen the position of any group in society.

The **stakeholder theory** of business ethics maintains that managers have an ethical responsibility to manage a firm for the benefit of all its stakeholders, which are all individuals and groups that have a stake in or claim on a company. This usually includes the corporation's stockholders, employees, customers, suppliers, and the local community. Sometimes the term is broadened to include all groups who can affect or be affected by the corporation, such as competitors, government agencies and special interest groups. Balancing the claims of conflicting stakeholders is obviously not an easy task for managers.

Technology Ethics

Another important ethical dimension deals specifically with the ethics of the use of any form of technology. For example, Figure 11.4 outlines four principles of technology ethics. These principles can serve as basic ethical requirements that companies should meet to help ensure the ethical implementation of information technologies and information systems in business.

One common example of technology ethics involves some of the health risks of using computer workstations for extended periods in high-volume data entry job positions. Many organizations display ethical behavior by scheduling work breaks and limiting the CRT exposure of data entry workers to minimize their risk of developing a variety of work-related health disorders, such as hand injuries and over-exposure to CRT radiation. The health impact of information technology is discussed later in this chapter.

FIGURE 11.4

Ethical principles to help evaluate the potential harms or risks of the use of new technologies.

Principles of Technology Ethics
● **Proportionality.** The good achieved by the technology must outweigh the harm or risk. Moreover, there must be no alternative that achieves the same or comparable benefits with less harm or risk.
● **Informed Consent.** Those affected by the technology should understand and accept the risks.
● **Justice.** The benefits and burdens of the technology should be distributed fairly. Those who benefit should bear their fair share of the risks, and those who do not benefit should not suffer a significant increase in risk.
● **Minimized Risk.** Even if judged acceptable by the other three guidelines, the technology must be implemented so as to avoid all unnecessary risk.

Ethical Guidelines

We have outlined a few ethical principles that can serve as the basis for ethical conduct by managers, end users, and IS professionals. But what more specific guidelines might help your ethical use of information technology? Many companies and organizations answer that question today with detailed policies for ethical computer and Internet usage by their employees. For example, most policies specify that company computer workstations and networks are company resources that must be used only for work-related uses, whether using internal networks or the Internet.

Another way to answer this question is to examine statements of responsibilities contained in codes of professional conduct for IS professionals. A good example is the code of professional conduct of the Association of Information Technology Professionals (AITP), an organization of professionals in the computing field. Its code of conduct outlines the ethical considerations inherent in the major responsibilities of an IS professional. Figure 11.5 is a portion of the AITP code of conduct.

Business and IS professionals would live up to their ethical responsibilities by voluntarily following such guidelines. For example, you can be a **responsible profes-**

FIGURE 11.5

Part of the AITP standards of professional conduct. This code can serve as a model for ethical conduct by business end users as well as IS professionals.

AITP Standards of Professional Conduct
In recognition of my obligation to my employer I shall:
● Avoid conflicts of interest and ensure that my employer is aware of any potential conflicts.
● Protect the privacy and confidentiality of all information entrusted to me.
● Not misrepresent or withhold information that is germane to the situation.
● Not attempt to use the resources of my employer for personal gain or for any purpose without proper approval.
● Not exploit the weakness of a computer system for personal gain or personal satisfaction.
In recognition of my obligation to society I shall:
● Use my skill and knowledge to inform the public in all areas of my expertise.
● To the best of my ability, ensure that the products of my work are used in a socially responsible way.
● Support, respect, and abide by the appropriate local, state, provincial, and federal laws.
● Never misrepresent or withhold information that is germane to a problem or a situation of public concern, nor will I allow any such known information to remain unchallenged.
● Not use knowledge of a confidential or personal nature in any unauthorized manner to achieve personal gain.

sional by (1) acting with integrity, (2) increasing your professional competence, (3) setting high standards of personal performance, (4) accepting responsibility for your work, and (5) advancing the health, privacy, and general welfare of the public. Then you would be demonstrating ethical conduct, avoiding computer crime, and increasing the security of any information system you develop or use.

Enron Corporation: Failure In Business Ethics	Much has been said about the driven, cultlike ethos of the organization that styled itself "the world's leading company." Truth to tell, for all its razzle-dazzle use of Internet technology, a lot of the things Enron did weren't so very exceptional: paying insanely large bonuses to executives, for example, often in the form of stock options (that practice not only hid true compensation costs but also encouraged managers to keep the stock price up by any means necessary); promising outlandish growth, year after year, and making absurdly confident predictions about every new market it entered, however untested; scarcely ever admitting a weakness to the outside world, and showing scant interest in the questions or doubts of some in its own ranks about its questionable, unethical, and even illegal business and accounting practices.

But credibility comes hard in business. You earn it slowly, by conducting yourself with integrity year in and year out, or by showing exceptional leadership in exceptional circumstances, such as September 11. The surest way to lose it, short of being caught in an outright lie, is to promise much and deliver little. Those, at least, are two conclusions suggested by an exclusive survey of executives conducted by Clark Martire & Bartolomeo for *Business 2.0*.

Executives rated Enron Chairman and CEO Ken Lay least credible of the business figures in the survey. Perhaps it had something to do with statements like:

- "Our performance has never been stronger; our business model has never been more robust; our growth has never been more certain . . . I have never felt better about the prospects for the company." —E-mail to employees, Aug. 14, 2001

- "The company is probably in the strongest and best shape that it has ever been in." —Interview in *Business Week*, Aug. 24, 2001

- "Our 26 percent increase in [profits] shows the very strong results of our core wholesale and retail energy businesses and our natural gas pipelines." —Press release, Oct. 16, 2001

But three weeks later, Enron admitted that it had overstated earnings by $586 million since 1997. Within a few more weeks, Enron also disclosed a stunning $638 million third-quarter loss, then filed for Chapter 11 bankruptcy [14].

Dick Hudson, former CIO of Houston-based oil drilling company Global Marine Inc. and now president of Hudson & Associates, an executive IT consulting firm in Katy, Texas, thinks Enron started with a good business strategy, and that if it hadn't pushed the envelope, it could well have been a successful *Fortune* 1,000 firm. But its sights were set on the *Fortune* 10, so it got into markets such as broadband, which is a tough nut to crack even for the industry's leaders. "Those good old boys in Houston, they had to walk with the big dogs," said Hudson. "They are a textbook case of greed and mismanagement [29]."

Computer Crime

Cybercrime is becoming one of the Net's growth businesses. Today, criminals are doing everything from stealing intellectual property and committing fraud to unleashing viruses and committing acts of cyber terrorism [26].

Computer crime is a growing threat to society caused by the criminal or irresponsible actions of individuals who are taking advantage of the widespread use and

FIGURE 11.6

How large companies are protecting themselves from cybercrime.

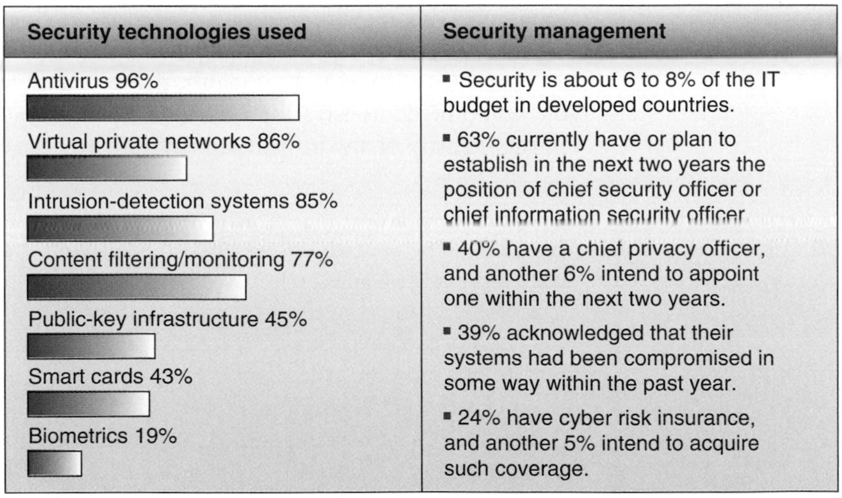

Security technologies used	Security management
Antivirus 96%	▪ Security is about 6 to 8% of the IT budget in developed countries.
Virtual private networks 86%	▪ 63% currently have or plan to establish in the next two years the position of chief security officer or chief information security officer.
Intrusion-detection systems 85%	
Content filtering/monitoring 77%	▪ 40% have a chief privacy officer, and another 6% intend to appoint one within the next two years.
Public-key infrastructure 45%	▪ 39% acknowledged that their systems had been compromised in some way within the past year.
Smart cards 43%	
Biometrics 19%	▪ 24% have cyber risk insurance, and another 5% intend to acquire such coverage.

Source: 2003 Global Security Survey by Deloitte Touche Tohmatsu, New York, June 2003, in Mitch Betts, "The Almanac." *Computerworld*, July 14, 2003, p. 42.

vulnerability of computers and the Internet and other networks. It thus presents a major challenge to the ethical use of information technologies. Computer crime poses serious threats to the integrity, safety, and survival of most business systems, and thus makes the development of effective security methods a top priority [11]. See Figure 11.6.

Computer crime is defined by the Association of Information Technology Professionals (AITP) as including (1) the unauthorized use, access, modification, and destruction of hardware, software, data, or network resources; (2) the unauthorized release of information; (3) the unauthorized copying of software; (4) denying an end user access to his or her own hardware, software, data, or network resources; and (5) using or conspiring to use computer or network resources to illegally obtain information or tangible property. This definition was promoted by the AITP in a Model Computer Crime Act, and is reflected in many computer crime laws.

PayPal, Inc.: Cybercrime on the Internet

At PayPal, Inc. (www.paypal.com), an online payment processing company now a subsidiary of eBay, security specialists noticed one day that there were too many Hudsens and Stivensons opening accounts with the company. John Kothanek, PayPal's lead fraud investigator (and a former military intelligence officer), discovered 10 names opening batches of 40 or more accounts that were being used to buy high-value computer goods in auctions on eBay.com. So PayPal froze the funds used to pay for the eBay goods (all to be shipped to an address in Russia) and started an investigation. Then one of PayPal's merchants reported that it had been redirected to a mock site called PayPal.

Kothanek's team set up sniffer software, which catches packet traffic, at the mock site. The software showed that operators of the mock site were using it to capture PayPal user log-ins and passwords. Investigators also used the sniffer to log the perpetrators' own IP address, which they then used to search against PayPal's database. It turned out that all of the accounts under scrutiny were opened by the same Internet address.

Using two freeware network-discovery tools, TraceRoute and Sam Spade, PayPal found a connection between the fake PayPal server address and the shipping address in Russia to which the accounts were trying to send goods. Meanwhile, calls were pouring in from credit card companies disputing the charges made from the suspect PayPal accounts. The perpetrators had racked up more than $100,000 in fraudulent charges using stolen credit cards—and PayPal was fully liable to repay them.

"Carders typically buy high-value goods like computers and jewelry so they can resell them," says Ken Miller, PayPal's fraud control director. PayPal froze the funds in those accounts and began to receive e-mail and phone calls from the perpetrators, who demanded that the funds be released. "They were blatant," says Kothanek. "They thought we couldn't touch them because they were in Russia."

Then PayPal got a call from the FBI. The FBI had lured the suspects into custody by pretending to be a technology company offering them security jobs. Using a forensics tool kit called EnCase, Kothanek's team helped the FBI tie its case to PayPal's by using keyword and pattern searches familiar to the PayPal investigators to analyze the slack and ambient space—where deleted files remain until overwritten—on a mirror-image backup of the suspects' hard drives.

"We were able to establish a link between their machine's IP address, the credit cards they were using in our system, and the Perl scripts they were using to open accounts on our system," Kothanek says. The alleged perpetrators, Alexey Ivanov and Vasili Gorchkov, were charged with multiple counts of wire fraud and convicted in the fall of 2001 [22].

Hacking

Cyber thieves have at their fingertips a dozen dangerous tools, from "scans" that ferret out weaknesses in website software programs to "sniffers" that snatch passwords [36].

Hacking, in computerese, is the obsessive use of computers, or the unauthorized access and use of networked computer systems. Hackers can be outsiders or company employees who use the Internet and other networks to steal or damage data and programs. One of the issues in hacking is what to do about a hacker who commits only *electronic breaking and entering;* that is, gets access to a computer system, reads some files, but neither steals nor damages anything. This situation is common in computer crime cases that are prosecuted. In most cases, courts have found that the typical computer crime statute language prohibiting malicious access to a computer system did apply to anyone gaining unauthorized access to another's computer networks [26]. See Figure 11.7.

Hackers can monitor e-mail, Web server access, or file transfers to extract passwords or steal network files, or to plant data that will cause a system to welcome intruders. A hacker may also use remote services that allow one computer on a network to execute programs on another computer to gain privileged access within a network. Telnet, an Internet tool for interactive use of remote computers, can help hackers discover information to plan other attacks. Hackers have used Telnet to access a computer's e-mail port, for example, to monitor e-mail messages for passwords and other information about privileged user accounts and network resources. These are just some of the typical types of computer crimes that hackers commit on the Internet on a regular basis. That's why Internet security measures like encryption and firewalls, as discussed in the next section, are so vital to the success of electronic commerce and other e-business applications.

Cyber Theft

Many computer crimes involve the theft of money. In the majority of cases, they are "inside jobs" that involve unauthorized network entry and fraudulent alteration of computer databases to cover the tracks of the employees involved. Of course, many computer crimes involve the use of the Internet. One early example was the theft of $11 million from Citibank in late 1994. Russian hacker Vladimir Levin and his accomplices in St. Petersburg used the Internet to electronically break into Citibank's mainframe

FIGURE 11.7

Examples of common hacking tactics to assault companies through the Internet and other networks.

Common Hacking Tactics

Denial of Service This is becoming a common networking prank. By hammering a website's equipment with too many requests for information, an attacker can effectively clog the system, slowing performance or even crashing the site. This method of overloading computers is sometimes used to cover up an attack.

Scans Widespread probes of the Internet to determine types of computers, services, and connections. That way the bad guys can take advantage of weaknesses in a particular make of computer or software program.

Sniffer Programs that covertly search individual packets of data as they pass through the Internet, capturing passwords or the entire contents.

Spoofing Faking an e-mail address or Web page to trick users into passing along critical information like passwords or credit card numbers.

Trojan Horse A program that, unknown to the user, contains instructions that exploit a known vulnerability in some software.

Back Doors In case the original entry point has been detected, having a few hidden ways back makes reentry easy—and difficult to detect.

Malicious Applets Tiny programs, sometimes written in the popular Java computer language, that misuse your computer's resources, modify files on the hard disk, send fake e-mail, or steal passwords.

War Dialing Programs that automatically dial thousands of telephone numbers in search of a way in through a modem connection.

Logic Bombs An instruction in a computer program that triggers a malicious act.

Buffer Overflow A technique for crashing or gaining control of a computer by sending too much data to the buffer in a computer's memory.

Password Crackers Software that can guess passwords.

Social Engineering A tactic used to gain access to computer systems by talking unsuspecting company employees out of valuable information such as passwords.

Dumpster Diving Sifting through a company's garbage to find information to help break into their computers. Sometimes the information is used to make a stab at social engineering more credible.

systems in New York. They then succeeded in transferring the funds from several Citibank accounts to their own accounts at banks in Finland, Israel, and California.

In most cases, the scope of such financial losses is much larger than the incidents reported. Most companies don't reveal that they have been targets or victims of computer crime. They fear scaring off customers and provoking complaints by shareholders. In fact, several British banks, including the Bank of London, paid hackers more than a half million dollars not to reveal information about electronic break-ins [24].

Recourse Technologies: Insider Computer Crime

"Often, there are feelings of betrayal and grudges," particularly during times of financial hardship at companies, said Eugene Schultz, an engineer at Lawrence Berkeley National Laboratory and an adjunct professor at the University of California, Berkeley. "There's no question that there is a link between insider [computer crime] activity and bad times at organizations."

Schultz, who has written a study on the corporate use of "honey pots"—phony servers populated with false data designed to attract hackers—for Recourse Technologies Inc., a security software firm in Palo Alto, California, also said there's a clear link between job roles and insider activity. Surprisingly, systems administrators, network security personnel, and senior executives are often the culprits.

Recourse Technologies CEO Frank Huera recently conducted a live demonstration of his company's Mantrap honey pot software during a sales call at a major computer manufacturer. Within 30 seconds, the software detected that a member of the company's network security team was attempting to hack into the honey pot server.

In another case, a very large financial firm discovered it was losing money from its payroll systems. So it set up two dozen honey pots and gave each server an interesting name, such as "payroll server." The next day, the company's chief operating officer was caught trying to jury-rig another executive's payroll account [31].

Unauthorized Use at Work

The unauthorized use of computer systems and networks can be called *time and resource theft*. A common example is unauthorized use of company-owned computer networks by employees. This may range from doing private consulting or personal finances, or playing video games, to unauthorized use of the Internet on company networks. Network monitoring software, called *sniffers*, are frequently used to monitor network traffic to evaluate network capacity, as well as reveal evidence of improper use. See Figures 11.8 and 11.9.

According to one survey, 90 percent of U.S. workers admit to surfing recreational sites during office hours, and 84 percent say they send personal e-mail from work. So this kind of activity alone may not get you fired from your job. However, other Internet activities at work can bring instant dismissal. For example, *The New York Times* fired 23 workers because they were distributing racist and sexually offensive jokes on the company's e-mail system [36].

FIGURE 11.8

Internet abuses in the workplace.

Internet Abuses	Activity
General e-Mail Abuses	Include spamming, harassments, chain letters, solicitations, spoofing, propagations of viruses/worms, and defamatory statements.
Unauthorized Usage and Access	Sharing of passwords and access into networks without permission.
Copyright Infringement/ Plagiarism	Using illegal or pirated software that cost organizations millions of dollars because of copyright infringements. Copying of websites and copyrighted logos.
Newsgroup Postings	Posting of messages on various non-work-related topics from sex to lawn care advice.
Transmission of Confidential Data	Using the Internet to display or transmit trade secrets.
Pornography	Accessing sexually explicit sites from workplace as well as the display, distribution, and surfing of these offensive sites.
Hacking	Hacking of websites, ranging from denial-of-service attacks to accessing organizational databases.
Non-Work-Related Download/Upload	Propagation of software that ties up office bandwidth. Use of programs that allow the transmission of movies, music, and graphical materials.
Leisure Use of the Internet	Loafing around the Internet, which includes shopping, sending e-cards and personal e-mail, gambling online, chatting, game playing, auctioning, stock trading, and doing other personal activities.
Usage of External ISPs	Using an external ISP to connect to the Internet to avoid detection.
Moonlighting	Using office resources such as networks and computers to organize and conduct personal business (side jobs).

Source: Adapted from Keng Fiona Fui-Hoon Nah, and Limei Teng, "Acceptable Internet Use Policy," *Communications of the ACM*, January 2002, p. 76.

Network monitoring software (sniffers) like SurfWatch is used to monitor the use of the Internet by employees at work. SurfWatch can also block access to unauthorized websites.

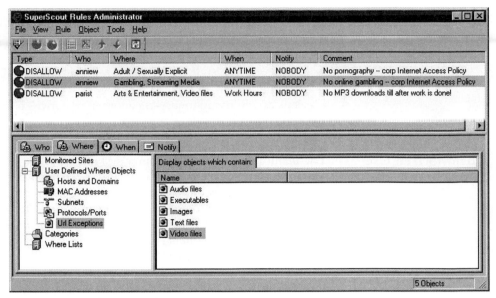

Source: Courtesy of SurfControl.

Xerox Corporation fired more than 40 workers for spending up to eight hours a day on pornography sites on the Web. Several employees even downloaded pornographic videos which took so much network bandwidth that it choked the company network and prevented co-workers from sending or receiving e-mail. Xerox instituted an eight-member SWAT team on computer abuse that uses software to review every website its 40,000 computer users view each day. Other companies clamp down even harder, by installing software like SurfWatch, which enables them to block, as well as monitor access to off-limit websites [19].

| AGM Container Controls: Stealing Time and Resources | It's not hard to see why the Net provides all kinds of productivity-frittering distractions—from instant messaging socializing, to eBay, pornography, and sports scores. Worse, company secrets may be floating across your firewall. And what you dismiss as simple time wasting could be setting you up for harassment, discrimination, copyright infringement, and other lawsuits. Lawsuits are not the only risk employers face. Intellectual property can make its way out of the office more easily than ever with the help of electronic communications. |

There are two ways to remedy cyber-slacking: monitoring Internet use (and making sure employees know you're doing it) and simply blocking sites deemed unrelated to work. Neither is an easy—or bulletproof—fix. If nothing else, a monitoring system with the right amount of follow-up can help employees realize how much company time they waste on the Internet—and help get them back on track.

Howard Stewart, president of AGM Container Controls in Tucson, Arizona, had a feeling that one of his employees was using her PC for personal use a little too much. "When I talked to the employee, she denied she was using e-mail or the Internet for personal use," he says, explaining that the company has a written policy against using the Internet for anything other than work. "However, I knew that this policy was ineffective because a few of my employees had come to the realization that I couldn't monitor their usage."

Stewart chose a simple program from Strategic Business Solutions called Resource Monitor. "Was that employee ever surprised when I was able to negate point-by-point each of her denials that she was using the computer for personal business," Stewart says. "She was shocked to discover that I could give her the exact dates and times she was on and how long she had been at inappropriate sites. Up to that point, she had claimed that she didn't have enough time to take on additional projects at work" [32].

Software Piracy

Computer programs are valuable property and thus are the subject of theft from computer systems. However, unauthorized copying of software, or **software piracy,** is also a major form of software theft. Widespread unauthorized copying of software by company employees is a major form of software piracy. This has resulted in lawsuits by the Software Publishers Association, an industry association of software developers, against major corporations that allowed unauthorized copying of their programs.

Unauthorized copying is illegal because software is intellectual property that is protected by copyright law and user licensing agreements. For example, in the United States, commercial software packages are protected by the Computer Software Piracy and Counterfeiting Amendment to the Federal Copyright Act. In most cases, the purchase of a commercial software package is really a payment to license its fair use by an individual end user. Therefore, many companies sign *site licenses* that allow them to legally make a certain number of copies for use by their employees at a particular location. Other alternatives are *shareware*, which allows you to make copies of software for others, and *public domain software*, which is not copyrighted.

Piracy of Intellectual Property

Software is not the only intellectual property subject to computer-based piracy. Other forms of copyrighted material, such as music, videos, images, articles, books and other written works are especially vulnerable to copyright infringement, which most courts have deemed illegal. Digitized versions can easily be captured by computer systems and made available for people to access or download at Internet websites, or can be readily disseminated by e-mail as file attachments. The development of peer-to-peer (P2P) networking technologies (discussed in Chapter 6) have made digital versions of copyrighted material even more vulnerable to unauthorized use. For example, P2P file-sharing software enables direct MP3 audio file transfers of specified tracks of music between your PC and those of other users on the Internet. Thus, such software creates a *peer-to-peer network* of millions of Internet users who electronically trade digital versions of copyrighted or public domain music stored on their PC's hard drives. Let's look at the ongoing debate in this controversial area more closely with a real world example that emphasizes the threat of developments in IT to intellectual property rights.

Copying Music CDs: Intellectual Property Controversy

Only a few short years after Napster's launch, online song-swapping floats dead in the water. A dogged legal campaign by the Recording Industry Association of America shut down the top services, Napster and Audiogalaxy. The other ones—KaZaA and Morpheus—are on the run as are their users, who are being sued by the RIAA.

There are others, like Gnutella, that have been built to withstand legal assault. By avoiding centralized servers and spreading the goods around the globe, the free-music hackers hope their networks will be impossible to shut down. Too bad they're also impossible to use. Shawn Fanning had a hit because Napster provided quick and easy access to a huge trove of music. His deservedly nameless imitators require us to do far more work to find far fewer tunes, all in the name of playing keep-away from the Man.

Why bother? The P2P music Maoists are wasting their time fighting a battle that no longer matters. The real action in music sharing isn't online. It's on foot.

Look at the numbers: Industry estimates say over 6 billion blank CDs will be sold worldwide in 2003—that's one for every person alive today—along with 44 million drives on which to burn them. And 140 million people now own writable drives—far more than the most optimistic membership claims made by Napster or any of its heirs. "You'll find one on nearly every consumer PC," says Gartner analyst Mary Craig, one of the more bearish forecasters in the business. "They're not using them for backups."

A previous generation of computer junkies called it sneakernet. Rather than relying on the slow, buggy network connections of the day, we hand-carried tapes and floppies to one another's mainframes. Now, sneakernet is in the schoolyard, bringing reluctant musicians to fans royalty-free, without the Net's assistance [4].

FIGURE 11.10

Facts about recent computer viruses and worms.

Worm and Virus Facts

Nimda Worm

- It spreads via both network-based e-mail and Web browsers.
- It modifies critical system files and registry keys.
- It creates a guest account with administrator privileges for hackers to use.

Code Red Worm

- It propagated through TCP/IP Web port 80.
- It identified itself by defacing English language websites with "Welcome to www.worm. com!—Hacked by Chinese!"
- Self-propagation was controlled by means of a "random" IP address generator—that had a bug in it.
- After the initial infection and incubation periods, Code Red was programmed to unleash a denial-of-service attack on the Whitehouse.gov website.

Economic Impact

The research firm Computer Economics estimates the Code Red worm cost society about $2.6 billion in July and August 2001 alone. Add to that $8.7 billion for the Love Bug, $1.2 billion for Melissa, $1 billion for Explorer, and another $1 billion for Sir Cam. These estimates include approximately equal losses resulting from returning the computer systems to preinfection operating status and lost productivity.

Computer Viruses and Worms

One of the most destructive examples of computer crime involves the creation of **computer viruses** or *worms*. *Virus* is the more popular term but, technically, a virus is a program code that cannot work without being inserted into another program. A worm is a distinct program that can run unaided. In either case, these programs copy annoying or destructive routines into the networked computer systems of anyone who accesses computers infected with the virus or who uses copies of magnetic disks taken from infected computers. Thus, a computer virus or worm can spread destruction among many users. Though they sometimes display only humorous messages, they more often destroy the contents of memory, hard disks, and other storage devices. Copy routines in the virus or worm spread the virus and destroy the data and software of many computer users [33]. See Figure 11.10.

Computer viruses typically enter a computer system through e-mail and file attachments via the Internet and online services, or through illegal or borrowed copies of software. Copies of *shareware* software downloaded from the Internet can be another source of viruses. A virus usually copies itself into the files of a computer's operating system. Then the virus spreads to the main memory and copies itself onto the computer's hard disk and any inserted floppy disks. The virus spreads to other computers through e-mail, file transfers, other telecommunications activities, or floppy disks from infected computers. Thus, as a good practice, you should avoid using software from questionable sources without checking for viruses. You should also regularly *use antivirus programs* that can help diagnose and remove computer viruses from infected files on your hard disk. We will discuss virus defenses further in Section II.

University of Chicago: The Nimda Worm

The Nimda worm—reports of which first began flooding into mailing lists and security firms on Sept. 18, 2001, is a mass-mailed piece of malicious code that infects systems running Microsoft Corp.'s Windows 95, 98, ME, NT, and 2000. Unlike other worms and viruses, Nimda is capable of spreading via both network-based e-mail and Web browsers. It was also written to scan for and exploit back doors left behind by previous viruses such as Code Red and Sadmind.

"The newness of this is that it leverages a number of different vulnerabilities in order to propagate itself," said Allen Householder, an analyst at the CERT Coordination Center at Carnegie Mellon University in Pittsburgh. Nimda propagates via various means, including modifying Web content on vulnerable systems running Microsoft's Internet Information Server software, Householder said. In the process, Nimda clogged part of the Internet, slowing down or even stopping Web traffic for some users. Many sites also experienced high volumes of e-mail and network traffic as a result of the worm.

In a four-hour period, the University of Chicago's Web servers were scanned by almost 7,000 unique IP addresses looking for vulnerabilities to exploit, said Larry Lidz, a senior network security officer at the school. As a result of the attacks, about 20 university servers were infected with the Nimda worm and had to be disconnected from the network, Lidz said. He recommended to school officials that those systems be reformatted and all software reinstalled. "If somebody has used a back door left by worms such as Code Red to infect your systems, you never really know what they have done to the system," Lidz said [33].

Privacy Issues

Information technology makes it technically and economically feasible to collect, store, integrate, interchange, and retrieve data and information quickly and easily. This characteristic has an important beneficial effect on the efficiency and effectiveness of computer-based information systems. However, the power of information technology to store and retrieve information can have a negative effect on the **right to privacy** of every individual. For example, confidential e-mail messages by employees are monitored by many companies. Personal information is being collected about individuals every time they visit a site on the World Wide Web. Confidential information on individuals contained in centralized computer databases by credit bureaus, government agencies, and private business firms has been stolen or misused, resulting in the invasion of privacy, fraud, and other injustices. The unauthorized use of such information has seriously damaged the privacy of individuals. Errors in such databases could seriously hurt the credit standing or reputation of an individual.

Important privacy issues are being debated in business and government, as Internet technologies accelerate the ubiquity of global telecommunications connections in business and society. For example:

- Accessing individuals' private e-mail conversations and computer records, and collecting and sharing information about individuals gained from their visits to Internet websites and newsgroups (violation of privacy).
- Always knowing where a person is, especially as mobile and paging services become more closely associated with people rather than places (computer monitoring).
- Using customer information gained from many sources to market additional business services (computer matching).
- Collecting telephone numbers, e-mail addresses, credit card numbers, and other personal information to build individual customer profiles (unauthorized personal files).

Privacy on the Internet

If you don't take the proper precautions, any time you send an e-mail, access a website, post a message to a newsgroup, or use the Internet for banking and shopping . . . whether you're online for business or pleasure, you're vulnerable to anyone bent on collecting data about you without your knowledge. Fortunately, by using tools like encryption and anonymous remailers—and by being selective about the sites you visit and the information you provide—you can minimize, if not completely eliminate, the risk of your privacy being violated [25].

The Internet is notorious for giving its users a feeling of anonymity, when in actuality, they are highly visible and open to violations of their privacy. Most of the Internet and its World Wide Web, e-mail, chat, and newsgroups are still a wide open, unsecured electronic frontier, with no tough rules on what information is personal and private. Information about Internet users is captured legitimately and automatically each time you visit a website or newsgroup and recorded as a "cookie file" on your hard disk. Then the website owners, or online auditing services like DoubleClick may sell the information from cookie files and other records of your Internet use to third parties. To make matters worse, much of the net and Web are easy targets for the interception or theft by hackers of private information furnished to websites by Internet users.

Of course, you can protect your privacy in several ways. For example, sensitive e-mail can be protected by encryption, if both e-mail parties use compatible encryption software built into their e-mail programs. Newsgroup postings can be made privately by sending them through *anonymous remailers* that protect your identity when you add your comments to a discussion. You can ask your Internet service provider not to sell your name and personal information to mailing list providers and other marketers. Finally, you can decline to reveal personal data and interests on online service and website user profiles to limit your exposure to electronic snooping [25].

Acxiom Inc.: Challenges to Consumer Privacy

What detail of your private life would you least like to see splashed across the Internet? Or added to a database, linked to your name and sold in a mailing list?

The privacy problem is simple. Companies need to glean information that will help target sales. Consumers want the convenience of secure e-commerce without worrying about having their identities stolen, being spammed, or having the aggregators of personal data knowing—and profiting from—every detail of their lives. As retailers and consumers force this issue, e-commerce could get squeezed in the process—particularly among companies that minimize the privacy concerns of their customers. Take Acxiom.

You may not know Acxiom. But the Conway, Arkansas, company probably knows you, having spent 30 years amassing a monster database of consumer information. It has dossiers on 160 million Americans—90 percent of U.S. households.

Acxiom has 20 million unlisted telephone numbers—gleaned mostly from those warranty cards you filled out when you bought that new coffeemaker—that it sells to law enforcement agencies, lawyers, private investigators, debt collectors, and just about anybody else willing to pay its fee. Acxiom is often better at tracking down deadbeat dads than the police. That's because Acxiom combines the most extensive public records database ever gathered by a nongovernmental entity with consumer information it purchases from the private sector.

The company's biggest clients are data-hungry telemarketers, retailers, e-commerce companies, and direct mail marketers. For example, Acxiom advises Wal-Mart on how to stock its shelves, while helping Citicorp decide the creditworthiness of potential customers [9].

Computer Matching

Computer profiling and mistakes in the **computer matching** of personal data are other controversial threats to privacy. Individuals have been mistakenly arrested and jailed, and people have been denied credit because their physical profiles or personal data have been used by profiling software to match them incorrectly or improperly with the wrong individuals. Another threat is the unauthorized matching of computerized information about you extracted from the databases of sales transaction processing systems, and sold to information brokers or other companies. A more recent threat is the unauthorized matching and sale of information about you collected from Internet websites and newsgroups you visit, as we discussed earlier. You are then subjected to a barrage of unsolicited promotional material and sales contacts as well as having your privacy violated [25].

Privacy Laws

Many countries strictly regulate the collection and use of personal data by business corporations and government agencies. Many government **privacy laws** attempt to enforce the privacy of computer-based files and communications. For example, in the United States, the Electronic Communications Privacy Act and the Computer Fraud and Abuse Act prohibit intercepting data communications messages, stealing or destroying data, or trespassing in federal-related computer systems. Since the Internet includes federal-related computer systems, privacy attorneys argue that the laws also require notifying employees if a company intends to monitor Internet usage. Another example is the U.S. Computer Matching and Privacy Act, which regulates the matching of data held in federal agency files to verify eligibility for federal programs.

Computer Libel and Censorship

The opposite side of the privacy debate is the right of people to know about matters others may want to keep private (freedom of information), the right of people to express their opinions about such matters (freedom of speech), and the right of people to publish those opinions (freedom of the press). Some of the biggest battlegrounds in the debate are the bulletin boards, e-mail boxes, and online files of the Internet and public information networks such as America Online and the Microsoft Network. The weapons being used in this battle include *spamming*, *flame mail*, libel laws, and censorship.

Spamming is the indiscriminate sending of unsolicited e-mail messages *(spam)* to many Internet users. Spamming is the favorite tactic of mass-mailers of unsolicited advertisements, or *junk e-mail*. Spamming has also been used by cyber criminals to spread computer viruses or infiltrate many computer systems.

Flaming is the practice of sending extremely critical, derogatory, and often vulgar e-mail messages *(flame mail)*, or newsgroup postings to other users on the Internet or online services. Flaming is especially prevalent on some of the Internet's special-interest newsgroups.

There have been many incidents of racist or defamatory messages on the Web that have led to calls for censorship and lawsuits for libel. In addition, the presence of sexually explicit material at many World Wide Web locations has triggered lawsuits and censorship actions by various groups and governments.

Other Challenges

Let's now explore some other important challenges that arise from the use of information technologies in business that were illustrated in Figure 11.2. These challenges include the potential ethical and societal impacts of business applications of IT in the areas of employment, individuality, working conditions, and health.

Employment Challenges

The impact of information technologies on **employment** is a major ethical concern and is directly related to the use of computers to achieve automation of work activities. There can be no doubt that the use of information technologies has created new jobs and increased productivity, while also causing a significant reduction in some types of job opportunities. For example, when computers are used for accounting systems or for the automated control of machine tools, they are accomplishing tasks formerly performed by many clerks and machinists. Also, jobs created by information technology may require different types of skills and education than do the jobs that are eliminated. Therefore, individuals may become unemployed unless they can be retrained for new positions or new responsibilities.

FIGURE 11.11

Computer monitoring can be used to record the productivity and behavior of people while they work.

Source: Charles Gupton Photography/Corbis.

However, there can be no doubt that Internet technologies have created a host of new job opportunities. Many new jobs, including Internet webmasters, e-commerce directors, systems analysts, and user consultants, have been created to support e-business and e-commerce applications. Additional jobs have been created because information technologies make possible the production of complex industrial and technical goods and services that would otherwise be impossible to produce. Thus, jobs have been created by activities that are heavily dependent on information technology, in such areas as space exploration, microelectronic technology, and telecommunications.

Computer Monitoring

One of the most explosive ethical issues concerning workplace privacy and the quality of working conditions in business is **computer monitoring.** That is, computers are being used to monitor the productivity and behavior of millions of employees while they work. Supposedly, computer monitoring is done so employers can collect productivity data about their employees to increase the efficiency and quality of service. However, computer monitoring has been criticized as unethical because it monitors individuals, not just work, and is done continually, thus violating workers' privacy and personal freedom. For example, when you call to make a reservation, an airline reservation agent may be timed on the exact number of seconds he or she took per caller, the time between calls, and the number and length of breaks taken. In addition, your conversation may also be monitored. See Figure 11.11.

Computer monitoring has been criticized as an invasion of the privacy of employees because, in many cases, they do not know that they are being monitored or don't know how the information is being used. Critics also say that an employee's right of due process may be harmed by the improper use of collected data to make personnel decisions. Since computer monitoring increases the stress on employees who must work under constant electronic surveillance, it has also been blamed for causing health problems among monitored workers. Finally, computer monitoring has been blamed for robbing workers of the dignity of their work. In effect, computer monitoring creates an "electronic sweatshop," where workers are forced to work at a hectic pace under poor working conditions.

Political pressure is building to outlaw or regulate computer monitoring in the workplace. For example, public advocacy groups, labor unions, and many legislators are pushing for action at the state and federal level in the United States. The proposed laws would regulate computer monitoring and protect the worker's right to know and right to privacy. In the meantime, lawsuits by monitored workers against employers are increasing. So computer monitoring of workers is one ethical issue in business that won't go away.

Challenges in Working Conditions

Information technology has eliminated monotonous or obnoxious tasks in the office and the factory that formerly had to be performed by people. For example, word processing and desktop publishing make producing office documents a lot easier to do, while robots have taken over repetitive welding and spray painting jobs in the automotive industry. In many instances, this allows people to concentrate on more challenging and interesting assignments, upgrades the skill level of the work to be performed, and creates challenging jobs requiring highly developed skills in the computer industry and within computer-using organizations. Thus, information technology can be said to upgrade the quality of work because it can upgrade the *quality of working conditions* and the content of work activities.

Of course, it must be remembered that some jobs in information technology—data entry, for example—are quite repetitive and routine. Also, to the extent that computers are utilized in some types of automation, IT must take some responsibility for the criticism of assembly-line operations that require the continual repetition of elementary tasks, thus forcing a worker to work like a machine instead of like a skilled craftsperson. Many automated operations are also criticized for relegating people to a "do-nothing" standby role, where workers spend most of their time waiting for infrequent opportunities to push some buttons. Such effects do have a detrimental effect on the quality of work, but they must be compared to the less burdensome and more creative jobs created by information technology.

Challenges to Individuality

A frequent criticism of information systems concerns their negative effect on the **individuality** of people. Computer-based systems are criticized as impersonal systems that dehumanize and depersonalize activities that have been computerized, since they eliminate the human relationships present in noncomputer systems.

Another aspect of the loss of individuality is the regimentation of the individual that seems to be required by some computer-based systems. These systems do not seem to possess any flexibility. They demand strict adherence to detailed procedures if the system is to work. The negative impact of IT on individuality is reinforced by horror stories that describe how inflexible and uncaring some organizations with computer-based processes are when it comes to rectifying their own mistakes. Many of us are familiar with stories of how computerized customer billing and accounting systems continued to demand payment and send warning notices to a customer whose account has already been paid, despite repeated attempts by the customer to have the error corrected.

However, many business applications of IT are designed to minimize depersonalization and regimentation. For example, many e-commerce systems are designed to stress personalization and community features to encourage repeated visits to e-commerce websites. Thus, the widespread use of personal computers and the Internet has dramatically improved the development of people-oriented and personalized information systems.

Health Issues

The use of information technology in the workplace raises a variety of **health issues.** Heavy use of computers is reportedly causing health problems like job stress, damaged arm and neck muscles, eye strain, radiation exposure, and even death by computer-caused accidents. For example, computer monitoring is blamed as a major cause of

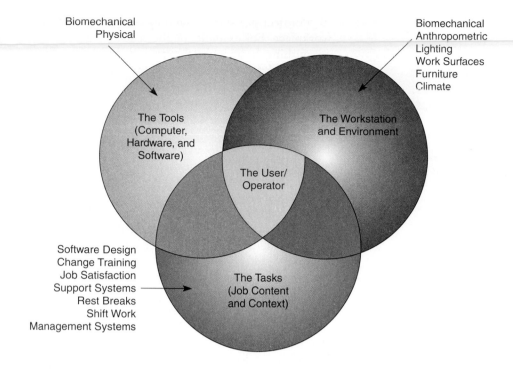

FIGURE 11.12

Ergonomic factors in the workplace. Note that good ergonomic design considers tools, tasks, the workstation, and environment.

computer-related job stress. Workers, unions, and government officials criticize computer monitoring as putting so much stress on employees that it leads to health problems.

People who sit at PC workstations or visual display terminals (VDTs) in fast-paced, repetitive keystroke jobs can suffer a variety of health problems known collectively as *cumulative trauma disorders* (CTDs). Their fingers, wrists, arms, necks, and backs may become so weak and painful that they cannot work. Many times strained muscles, back pain, and nerve damage may result. In particular, some computer workers may suffer from *carpal tunnel syndrome*, a painful, crippling ailment of the hand and wrist that typically requires surgery to cure.

Prolonged viewing of video displays causes eyestrain and other health problems in employees who must do this all day. Radiation caused by the cathode ray tubes (CRTs) that produce most video displays is another health concern. CRTs produce an electromagnetic field that may cause harmful radiation of employees who work too close for too long in front of video monitors. Some pregnant workers have reported miscarriages and fetal deformities due to prolonged exposure to CRTs at work. However, several studies have failed to find conclusive evidence concerning this problem. Still, several organizations recommend that female workers minimize their use of CRTs during pregnancy [6, 8].

Ergonomics

Solutions to some of these health problems are based on the science of **ergonomics,** sometimes called *human factors engineering.* See Figure 11.12. The goal of ergonomics is to design healthy work environments that are safe, comfortable, and pleasant for people to work in, thus increasing employee morale and productivity. Ergonomics stresses the healthy design of the workplace, workstations, computers and other machines, and even software packages. Other health issues may require ergonomic solutions emphasizing job design, rather than workplace design. For example, this may require policies providing for work breaks from heavy VDT use every few hours, while limiting the CRT exposure of pregnant workers. Ergonomic job design can also provide more variety in job tasks for those workers who spend most of their workday at computer workstations.

Societal Solutions

As we said at the beginning of the chapter, the Internet and other information technologies can have many beneficial effects on society. We can use information technologies to solve human and social problems through **societal solutions** such as medical diagnosis, computer-assisted instruction, governmental program planning, environmental quality control, and law enforcement. For example, computers can help diagnose an illness, prescribe necessary treatment, and monitor the progress of hospital patients. Computer-assisted instruction (CAI) and computer-based training (CBT) enable interactive instruction tailored to the needs of students. Distance learning is supported by telecommunications networks, video conferencing, e-mail, and other technologies.

Information technologies can be used for crime control through various law enforcement applications. For example, computerized alarm systems allow police to identify and respond quickly to evidences of criminal activity. Computers have been used to monitor the level of pollution in the air and in bodies of water, to detect the sources of pollution, and to issue early warnings when dangerous levels are reached. Computers are also used for the program planning of many government agencies in such areas as urban planning, population density and land use studies, highway planning, and urban transit studies. Computers are being used in job placement systems to help match unemployed persons with available jobs. These and other applications illustrate that information technology can be used to help solve the problems of society.

It should be obvious to you that many of the detrimental effects of information technology are caused by individuals or organizations that are not accepting the ethical responsibility for their actions. Like other powerful technologies, information technology possesses the potential for great harm or great good for all humankind. If managers, business professionals, and IS specialists accept their ethical responsibilities, then information technology can help make this world a better place for all of us.

Security Management of Information Technology

Introduction

With Internet access proliferating rapidly, one might think that the biggest obstacle to electronic commerce would be bandwidth. But it's not; the number one problem is security. And part of the problem is that the Internet was developed for interoperability, not impenetrability [32].

As we saw in Section I, there are many significant threats to the security of information systems in business. That's why this section is dedicated to exploring the methods that companies can use to manage their security. Business managers and professionals alike are responsible for the security, quality, and performance of the business information systems in their business units. Like any other vital business assets, hardware, software, networks, and data resources need to be protected by a variety of security measures to ensure their quality and beneficial use. That's the business value of security management.

Analyzing Geisinger Health Systems and Du Pont

Read the Real World Case on Geisinger Health Systems and Du Pont on the next page. We can learn a lot about the security management issues and challenges in securing company data resources and process control networks from this case. See Figure 11.13.

Geisinger Health Systems is responding to government legislation mandating the security of patient medical data by developing security measures to protect such data resources. For example, one wireless application that lets physicians use mobile devices to access patient data is being secured by requiring the use of electronic

FIGURE 11.13

Tom Good is a project engineer at Du Pont and leads their campaign to reduce the security vulnerabilities of their process control networks.

Source: Michael Branscom.

REAL WORLD CASE 2

Geisinger Health Systems and Du Pont: Security Management

Whether balancing the needs of security with the push for greater access to data, coping with government mandates, or planning for possible budget cuts, IT security managers have their hands full. Frank M. Richards has been scrambling to deal with those challenges. As CIO at Geisinger Health System (www.geisinger.org), a health care network in Danville, Pennsylvania, that serves more than 2 million people, he faced an April 2003 deadline for compliance with the U.S. Health Insurance Portability and Accountability Act (HIPAA). The law required health care organizations to safeguard patient data from unauthorized access and disclosure. But HIPAA set goals without giving specifics on how to get there, so Richards had to balance the legal requirements with a demand from health professionals for ease of access—a daunting challenge.

"This can be particularly problematic in the medical field, where care providers are under tremendous time pressures," he says. Understanding workflow, assessing risk, and educating users are all key components of a security system that achieves the correct balance between access and control, he says. Geisinger's Electronic Medical Record (EMR) program focuses on easing access to data. It lets physicians at 50 clinics use mobile devices to order medications, receive alerts, enter patient progress notes, and communicate with patients. Another program, MyChart, lets patients access their medical information via the Internet.

Both programs raised security issues. For example, security needs dictated that the database that powers MyChart be installed on hardware separate from the EMK system. Richards's staff is also evaluating biometric and proximity devices as ways to streamline secure network access. And caregivers accessing patient information via the Internet will be required to use electronic token identification in addition to a virtual private network or other encryption method, he says.

Richards expects security technologies such as intrusion detection systems to finally begin delivering on their promises. "Inadequate analysis tools, incompatibility with existing network management software, and inability to handle large volumes of data have combined to keep us from deploying these security tools until very recently," he says.

Du Pont Co. Process control networks are one of the essential applications of IT in manufacturing environments. For example, more than 2,400 oil, natural gas, and chemical companies in the United States employ process-control networks in their manufacturing systems. Other heavy users of process networks include the power, water, food, drug, automobile, metal, mining, and manufacturing industries. For example, process networks in the chemical industry control chemical-making equipment and monitor sensors. If anything goes wrong, such networks react by adjusting the environment in predefined ways, such as shutting off gas flow to prevent leaks or explosions.

One company that's taking process network security seriously and involving IT is Du Pont Co. (www.dupont.com) in Wilmington, Delaware. Tom Good, a project engineer at the chemical manufacturer, has been leading its 20-month-old effort to categorize and reduce its process-control system vulnerabilities. Du Pont's philosophy for dealing with this problem, he says, is that "On all of our critical manufacturing processes, we are either going to totally isolate our process systems from our business systems by not connecting our networks, or we're going to put in firewalls to control access."

To tackle process-control network security, Good says Du Pont formed a team made up of IT staffers, who understand networks and cybersecurity; process-control engineers, who understand the process-control equipment; and manufacturing employees, who understand manufacturing risks and vulnerabilities. To give the three groups visibility, each reports to a separate member of a committee that's leading the effort. The team first discerned which control devices are critical to manufacturing, safety and continuity of production. Next the team identified the assets of each—hardware, data, and software applications—then researched relevant vulnerabilities. Only then did it begin the arduous task of testing fixes and workarounds to see which ones might work for which machines.

Even in a manufacturing environment that uses similar process-control hardware and software, precise vulnerabilities differ by environment. "Dealing with a water treatment process on effluents out of a plant is considerably different than dealing with a production operation, where you might be dealing with vessels under high-temperature and high-pressure conditions," says Good. On the basis of its research, the team is also deciding how to separate networks and where process-control firewall appliances should go. "The greater cost is in the network equipment and reengineering activities to separate networks and place critical process-control devices together on the clean side of the firewall," says Good. "The challenge for us is to accomplish these tasks while keeping the processes running."

Case Study Questions

1. What is Geisinger Health Systems doing to protecting the security of their data resources? Are these measures adequate? Explain your evaluation.

2. What security measures is Du Pont taking to protect their process-control networks? Are these measures adequate? Explain your evaluation.

3. What are several other steps Geisinger and Du Pont could take to increase the security of their data and network resources? Explain the value of your proposals.

Sources: Adapted from Dan Verton, "How Will You Secure Your Company Data?" *Computerworld*, January 6, 2003, p. 24; and Mathew Schwartz, "Wanted: Security Tag Team," *Computerworld*, June 30, 2003, pp. 38–40.

FIGURE 11.14

Examples of important security measures that are part of the security management of information systems.

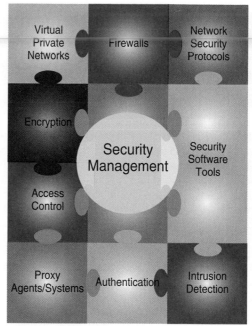

Source: Courtesy of Wang Global.

tokens, virtual private networks, and encryption. Du Pont is in the midst of a major campaign to reduce the security vulnerabilities of its many process control networks, using a team of IT security specialists, process control engineers, and manufacturing employees to evaluate all of their process control systems. Major security measures being implemented are the separation of process control networks from business networks, and the installation of process control firewall appliances on the networks.

Tools of Security Management

The goal of **security management** is the accuracy, integrity, and safety of all information system processes and resources. Thus, effective security management can minimize errors, fraud, and losses in the information systems that interconnect today's companies and their customers, suppliers, and other stakeholders. As Figure 11.14 illustrates, security management is a complex task. As you can see, security managers must acquire and integrate a variety of security tools and methods to protect a company's information system resources. We will discuss many of these security measures in this section.

Providence Health and Cervalis: Security Management Issues	The need for security management is being driven by both the increasing threat of cybercrimes and the growing use of the Internet to link companies with partners and customers, says David Rymal, director of technology at Providence Health System (www.providence.org) in Everett, Washington. "There is an increasing pressure to enable wide and unfettered access from our business units. We are getting so many requests to open up ports in our firewall that pretty soon it is going to look like Swiss cheese," Rymal says. "The more of them you have open, the more vulnerabilities you create."

The whole notion of "Web services," under which companies will use common Web protocols to link their business systems with those of external partners and |

suppliers, is only going to increase the need for better security, users say. Adding to the pressures is the growing number of remote workers and the trend toward wireless applications. This has meant finding better ways of identifying and authenticating users and controlling the access they have on the network. "You have to keep in mind that the minute you open your servers or services to the Internet, you are going to have bad people trying to get in," says Edward Rabbinovitch, vice president of global networks and infrastructure operations at Cervalis Inc. (www.cervalis.com), a Stamford, Connecticut–based Internet hosting service.

While it's impossible to guarantee 100 percent security, companies should make things as difficult as possible for outsiders or insiders to steal or damage IT assets, IT managers say. Cervalis's security, for instance, begins at its ingress points—where the Internet meets its networks. The company uses strict port control and management on all of its Internet-facing routers to ensure that open ports don't provide easy access for malicious attackers. Redundant, load-balanced firewalls that are sandwiched between two layers of content switches filter all traffic coming in from the Internet. Network-based intrusion-detection systems are sprinkled throughout the Cervalis network [34].

Internetworked Security Defenses

Few professionals today face greater challenges than those IT managers who are developing Internet security policies for rapidly changing network infrastructures. How can they balance the need for Internet security and Internet access? Are the budgets for Internet security adequate? What impact will intranet, extranet, and Web application development have on security architectures? How can they come up with best practices for developing Internet security policy? [32]

Thus, the security of today's networked business enterprises is a major management challenge. Many companies are still in the process of getting fully connected to the Web and the Internet for e-commerce, and reengineering their internal business processes with intranets, e-business software, and extranet links to customers, suppliers, and other business partners. Vital network links and business flows need to be protected from external attack by cyber criminals or subversion by the criminal or irresponsible acts of insiders. This requires a variety of security tools and defensive measures, and a coordinated security management program. Let's take a look at some of these important security defenses.

Encryption

Encryption of data has become an important way to protect data and other computer network resources especially on the Internet, intranets, and extranets. Passwords, messages, files, and other data can be transmitted in scrambled form and unscrambled by computer systems for authorized users only. Encryption involves using special mathematical algorithms, or keys, to transform digital data into a scrambled code before they are transmitted, and to decode the data when they are received. The most widely used encryption method uses a pair of public and private keys unique to each individual. For example, e-mail could be scrambled and encoded using a unique *public key* for the recipient that is known to the sender. After the e-mail is transmitted, only the recipient's secret *private key* could unscramble the message [25]. See Figure 11.15.

Encryption programs are sold as separate products or built into other software used for the encryption process. There are several competing software encryption standards, but the top two are RSA (by RSA Data Security) and PGP (pretty good privacy), a popular encryption program available on the Internet. Software products including Microsoft Windows XP, Novell Netware, and Lotus Notes offer encryption features using RSA software.

FIGURE 11.15   How public key/private key encryption works.

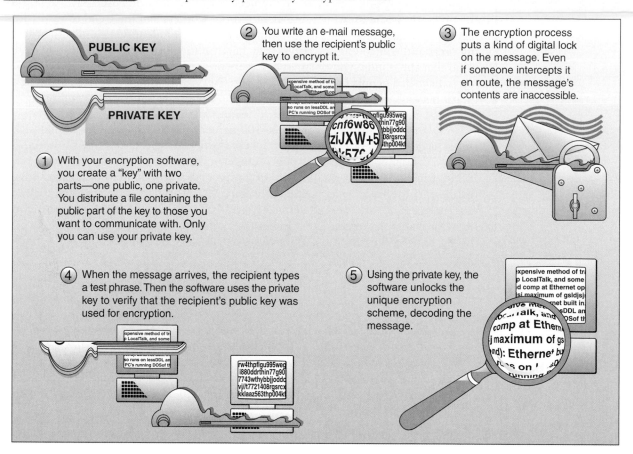

Firewalls

Another important method for control and security on the Internet and other networks is the use of **firewall** computers and software. A network firewall can be a communications processor, typically a *router*, or a dedicated server, along with firewall software. A firewall serves as a "gatekeeper" system that protects a company's intranets and other computer networks from intrusion by providing a filter and safe transfer point for access to and from the Internet and other networks. It screens all network traffic for proper passwords or other security codes, and only allows authorized transmissions in and out of the network. Firewall software has also become an essential computer system component for individuals connecting to the Internet with DSL or cable modems, because of their vulnerable, "always-on" connection status. Figure 11.16 illustrates an Internet/intranet firewall system for a company [14].

Firewalls can deter, but not completely prevent, unauthorized access (hacking) into computer networks. In some cases, a firewall may allow access only from trusted locations on the Internet to particular computers inside the firewall. Or it may allow only "safe" information to pass. For example, a firewall may permit users to read e-mail from remote locations but not to run certain programs. In other cases, it is impossible to distinguish safe use of a particular network service from unsafe use and so all requests must be blocked. The firewall may then provide substitutes for some network services (such as e-mail or file transfer) that perform most of the same functions but are not as vulnerable to penetration.

FIGURE 11.16 An example of the Internet and intranet firewalls in a company's networks.

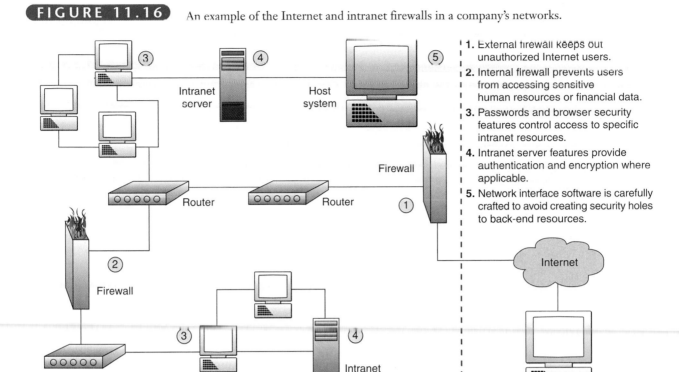

1. External firewall keeps out unauthorized Internet users.
2. Internal firewall prevents users from accessing sensitive human resources or financial data.
3. Passwords and browser security features control access to specific intranet resources.
4. Intranet server features provide authentication and encryption where applicable.
5. Network interface software is carefully crafted to avoid creating security holes to back-end resources.

Barry Nance: Testing PC Firewall Security	From all over the world, and even from your hometown, the bad guys' software is constantly probing the Internet, examining consecutive IP addresses for information. Ah! The software finds an active IP address. What sort of device is it? Does it have a network management agent? Whose protocol stack is the device running? Is the IP address permanently assigned? Might the device be a good target for a virus, Trojan, or worm? Is port 23, which is used by Telnet, open? Might it be worth flooding the device with denial-of-service packets? Does the IP address correspond to a registered domain name? Is the network node running Web server, FTP server, database server, or file sharing software?

A sophisticated probe can discover a staggering amount of data and store it for future use. If an employee's home PC has a persistent Internet connection via Digital Subscriber Line (DSL) or cable, the probe's database almost certainly contains his IP address and network node data. Even dial-up users with dynamically assigned IP addresses can be at risk if connections last more than a half-day. An employee who routinely handles company business and confidential data from his home computer is also at risk.

A number of companies offer personal firewall products to help block Internet-based intruders. Software developer Barry Nance tested some of the best-known, including Norton Personal Firewall and Black Ice Defender, to find out which offers the best deterrent to Internet probes.

A software firewall to protect your home PC intercepts and examines each inbound or outbound Internet message. It distinguishes, for example, between legitimate messages that are responses to your Web browsing and illegitimate messages that you never asked for. The software also uses network address translation to substitute a bogus IP address inside your computer's outgoing Internet messages. When the bad guys don't know who you are, they can't penetrate your PC.

Nance used many tools to test security, to try to penetrate each firewall and scan for ports. He also launched a 10-minute barrage of network request messages on all common ports and measured the time it took each firewall to resolve the requests.

The results were gratifying for anyone concerned about Internet security. All of the firewalls successfully blocked unsolicited Internet messages, port scans, and denial-of-service attacks. They slowed Internet access only slightly as they protected the computer from Nance's hacking efforts [18].

Denial of Service Defenses

Major attacks against e-commerce and corporate websites in the past few years have demonstrated that the Internet is extremely vulnerable to a variety of assaults by criminal hackers, especially **distributed denial of service** (DDOS) attacks. Figure 11.17 outlines the steps organizations can take to protect themselves from DDOS attacks.

Denial of service assaults via the Internet depend on three layers of networked computer systems: (1) the victim's website, (2) the victim's Internet service provider (ISP), and (3) the sites of "zombie" or slave computers that were commandeered by the cyber criminals. For example, in early 2000, hackers broke into hundreds of servers, mostly poorly protected servers at universities, and planted Trojan Horse .exe programs, which were then used to launch a barrage of service requests in a concerted attack at e-commerce websites like Yahoo! and eBay [15].

As Figure 11.17 shows, defensive measures and security precautions need to be taken at all three levels of the computer networks involved. These are the basic steps companies and other organizations can take to protect their websites from denial of service and other hacking attacks. Now let's take a look at a real world example of a more sophisticated defense technology.

MTV Networks: Denial of Service Defenses

MTV.com, the website for the cable TV music channel, is the target of distributed denial of service (DDOS) attacks each fall when the MTV Video Music Awards are televised. But the attacks, in which MTV.com's network servers are deliberately overloaded by massive automated requests for service by hackers, are now blunted because New York–based Viacom International's (www.viacom.com) MTV Networks division is protecting its 15 entertainment websites (including the MTV, VH-1, and Nickelodeon sites) with Enforcer, a network security software tool from Mazu Networks Inc. in Cambridge, Massachusetts.

"During the MTV Awards and other highly publicized TV events, some folks try to knock us out of the water," says Brian Amirian, director of Web hosting and development at MTV Networks Online Technology. So last year, MTV attached Mazu's Enforcer to telecom uplinks between the MTV websites and the company's Internet service provider.

Amirian says one reason he selected Mazu's product is the efficient way it uses proprietary hardware to filter out DDOS attacks. Some other products that he evaluated, but rejected, used software that relied on the more limited filtering capabilities of existing network routers. Mazu's Enforcer builds a statistical model of website traffic when no attack is occurring, says Carty Castaldi, vice president of engineering at Mazu Networks. During a DDOS attack, Enforcer identifies data packets associated

FIGURE 11.17

How to defend against
denial of service attacks.

Defending against Denial of Service
● **At the zombie machines:** Set and enforce security policies. Scan regularly for Trojan Horse programs and vulnerabilities. Close unused ports. Remind users not to open .exe mail attachments.
● **At the ISP:** Monitor and block traffic spikes. Filter spoofed IP addresses. Coordinate security with network providers.
● **At the victim's website:** Create backup servers and network connections. Limit connections to each server. Install multiple intrusion-detection systems and multiple routers for incoming traffic to reduce choke points.

with the attack based on their statistical differences from the norm and recommends a filter that typically blocks 80 percent of the attack packets and about 5 percent of nonattack packets, he says.

In any event, MTV Networks' Amirian is happy. According to his calculations, he recouped the $32,000 investment in Enforcer within about two months because the Mazu device kept MTV's website from being disrupted during the heavy advertising period surrounding the Video Music Awards [1].

e-Mail Monitoring

Spot checks just aren't good enough anymore. The tide is turning toward systematic monitoring of corporate e-mail traffic using content-monitoring software that scans for troublesome words that might compromise corporate security. The reason: Users of monitoring software said they're concerned about protecting their intellectual property and guarding themselves against litigation [5].

As we mentioned in Section I, Internet and other online e-mail systems are one of the favorite avenues of attack by hackers for spreading computer viruses or breaking into networked computers. E-mail is also the battleground for attempts by companies to enforce policies against illegal, personal, or damaging messages by employees, and the demands of some employees and others, who see such policies as violations of privacy rights.

Sonalysts, Inc.: Corporate e-Mail Monitoring

John Conlin is browsing around some company's network again. This time he's searching employees' e-mail by key words. But he can also sniff out which websites workers have visited and can see how long they were there and at what time. All this snooping leaves no tracks. What Conlin does is not illegal. In fact, it's probably already happening at your company. If not, just wait. Conlin's company, eSniff, sells an electronic monitoring device that allows businesses to spy on their workers. It may sound like a scene from a movie, but as either an employee or a manager, you'd better get used to it. Some 82 percent of businesses monitor their employees in some way, according to the American Management Association.

eSniff logs all Internet traffic, recording and reporting anything that's been labeled as suspicious. For example, an administrator can view e-mail log summaries and quickly drill down to the actual content of any questionable e-mail to make sure it hasn't fallen into the wrong in-box. "It's rare for eSniff to be installed on a network and not find a lot of inappropriate activity," Conlin says, adding that close to 100 percent of workers register some kind of improper use.

But Randy Dickson, a systems analyst for the Connecticut-based multimedia production firm Sonalysts, Inc., had different results. His firm uses eSniff to monitor all Internet activity. Dickson was pleased to find there was less abuse going on than he thought. For instance, Dickson had been concerned about time wasted using instant messaging, but found that most employee IM activity was for legitimate business use and was actually saving the company money on phone bills [32].

Virus Defenses

Is your PC protected from the latest viruses, worms, Trojan horses, and other malicious programs that can wreak havoc on your PC? Chances are it is, if it's periodically linked to the corporate network. These days, corporate antivirus protection is a centralized function of information technology. Someone installs it for you on your PC and notebook or, increasingly, distributes it over the network. The antivirus software runs in the background, popping up every so often to reassure you. The trend right now is to automate the process entirely [9].

Thus many companies are building defenses against the spread of viruses by centralizing the distribution and updating of antivirus software as a responsibility of their IS departments. Other companies are outsourcing the virus protection responsibility to their Internet service providers or to telecommunications or security management companies.

One reason for this trend is that the major antivirus software companies like Trend Micro (eDoctor and PC-cillin), McAfee (VirusScan), and Symantec (Norton Antivirus) have developed network versions of their programs which they are marketing to ISPs and others as a service they should offer to all their customers. The antivirus companies are also marketing *security suites* of software that integrate virus protection with firewalls, Web security, and content blocking features [10]. See Figure 11.18.

TrueSecure and 724 Inc.: Limitations of Antivirus Software

Much of the standard antivirus software that was available at the time the Nimda worm struck failed to keep the worm from spreading, users and analysts said. The worm does a number of insidious things, such as modifying critical system files and registry keys, making every directory available as a file share, and creating a guest account with administrator privileges, said Russ Cooper, an analyst at TruSecure Corp., a Reston, Virginia–based security firm. "These characteristics make it incredibly difficult to clean the worm from an infected system," he said.

"Running antivirus software alone will not fix the problem," said Edward York, chief technical officer at 724 Inc., an application hosting service in Lompoc, California. "The server must be secured all over again, all open shares closed, the hot fixes reapplied, the guest account disabled again and all traces of any file called root.exe or admin.dll deleted from the system," York said. Administrators also need to ensure that any registry items added by Nimda have been removed, he indicated. And, says York, until more sophisticated fixes become available, the only sure course is to disconnect infected systems from the network, reformat their hard drives, reinstall software from a clean source, and apply the appropriate security patches [33].

FIGURE 11.18

An example of security suite PC software that includes antivirus and firewall protection.

Source: Courtesy of McAfee

Other Security Measures

Let's now briefly examine a variety of security measures that are commonly used to protect business systems and networks. These include both hardware and software tools like fault tolerant computers and security monitors, and security policies and procedures like passwords and backup files. All of them are part of an integrated security management effort at many companies today.

Security Codes

Typically, a multilevel **password** system is used for security management. First, an end user logs on to the computer system by entering his or her unique identification code, or user ID. The end user is then asked to enter a password in order to gain access into the system. (Passwords should be changed frequently and consist of unusual combinations of upper- and lowercase letters and numbers.) Next, to access an individual file, a unique file name must be entered. In some systems, the password to read the contents of a file is different from that required to write to a file (change its contents). This feature adds another level of protection to stored data resources. However, for even stricter security, passwords can be scrambled, or *encrypted*, to avoid their theft or improper use, as we will discuss shortly. In addition, *smart cards*, which contain microprocessors that generate random numbers to add to an end user's password, are used in some secure systems.

Backup Files

Backup files, which are duplicate files of data or programs, are another important security measure. Files can also be protected by *file retention* measures that involve storing copies of files from previous periods. If current files are destroyed, the files from previous periods can be used to reconstruct new current files. Sometimes, several generations of files are kept for control purposes. Thus, master files from several recent periods of processing (known as *child, parent, grandparent* files, etc.) may be kept for backup purposes. Such files may be stored off-premises, that is, in a location away from a company's data center, sometimes in special storage vaults in remote locations.

FIGURE 11.19

The eTrust security monitor manages a variety of security functions for major corporate networks, including monitoring the status of Web-based applications throughout a network.

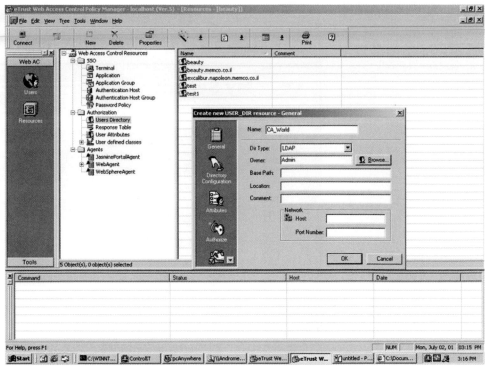

Source: Courtesy of Computer Associates.

Security Monitors

Security of a network may be provided by specialized system software packages known as **system security monitors.** See Figure 11.19. System security monitors are programs that monitor the use of computer systems and networks and protect them from unauthorized use, fraud, and destruction. Such programs provide the security measures needed to allow only authorized users to access the networks. For example, identification codes and passwords are frequently used for this purpose. Security monitors also control the use of the hardware, software, and data resources of a computer system. For example, even authorized users may be restricted to the use of certain devices, programs, and data files. Additionally, security programs monitor the use of computer networks and collect statistics on any attempts at improper use. They then produce reports to assist in maintaining the security of the network.

Biometric Security

Biometric security is a fast-growing area of computer security. These are security measures provided by computer devices that measure physical traits that make each individual unique. This includes voice verification, fingerprints, hand geometry, signature dynamics, keystroke analysis, retina scanning, face recognition, and genetic pattern analysis. Biometric control devices use special-purpose sensors to measure and digitize a biometric profile of an individual's fingerprints, voice, or other physical trait. The digitized signal is processed and compared to a previously processed profile of the individual stored on magnetic disk. If the profiles match, the individual is allowed entry into a computer network and given access to secure system resources [2]. See Figure 11.20.

Computer Failure Controls

Sorry, our computer systems are down is a well-known phrase to many end users. A variety of controls can prevent such computer failure or minimize its effects. Computer systems fail for several reasons—power failure, electronic circuitry malfunctions, telecommunications network problems, hidden programming errors, computer

FIGURE 11.20

An evaluation of common biometric security techniques based on user requirements, accuracy, and cost.

Evaluation of Biometric Techniques	User Criteria		System Criteria	
	Intrusiveness	Effort	Accuracy	Cost
Dynamic signature verification	Excellent	Fair	Fair	Excellent
Face geometry	Good	Good	Fair	Good
Finger scan	Fair	Good	Good	Good
Hand geometry	Fair	Good	Fair	Fair
Passive iris scan	Poor	Excellent	Excellent	Poor
Retina scan	Poor	Poor	Very good	Fair
Voice print	Very good	Poor	Fair	Very good

viruses, computer operator errors, and electronic vandalism. For example, computers are available with automatic and remote maintenance capabilities. Programs of preventive maintenance of hardware and management of software updates are commonplace. A backup computer system capability can be arranged with *disaster recovery organizations.* Major hardware or software changes are usually carefully scheduled and implemented to avoid problems. Finally, highly trained data center personnel and the use of performance and security management software help keep a company's computer system and networks working properly.

Fault Tolerant Systems

Many firms also use **fault tolerant** computer systems that have redundant processors, peripherals, and software that provide a *fail-over* capability to back up components in the event of system failure. This may provide a *fail-safe* capability where the computer system continues to operate at the same level even if there is a major hardware or software failure. However, many fault tolerant computer systems offer a *fail-soft* capability where the computer system can continue to operate at a reduced but acceptable level in the event of a major system failure. Figure 11.21 outlines some of the fault tolerant capabilities used in many computer systems and networks [20].

FIGURE 11.21

Methods of fault tolerance in computer-based information systems.

Layer	Threats	Fault Tolerant Methods
Applications	Environment, hardware, and software faults	Application-specific redundancy and rollback to previous checkpoint
Systems	Outages	System isolation, data security, system integrity
Databases	Data errors	Separation of transactions and safe updates, complete transaction histories, backup files
Networks	Transmission errors	Reliable controllers; safe asynchrony and handshaking; alternative routing; error-detecting and error-correcting codes
Processes	Hardware and software faults	Alternative computations, rollback to checkpoints
Files	Media errors	Replication of critical data on different media and sites; archiving, backup, retrieval
Processors	Hardware faults	Instruction retry; error-correcting codes in memory and processing; replication; multiple processors and memories

Visa International: Fault Tolerant Systems	"There is no such thing as 99.9 percent reliability; it has to be 100 percent," says Richard L. Knight, senior vice president for operations at Inovant, Inc., the Visa International subsidiary that runs its data centers. "Anything less than 100 percent, and I'm looking for a job." The company has had 98 minutes of downtime in 12 years. Visa fights the battle against outages and defects on two broad fronts: Its physical processing plant is protected by multiple layers of redundancy and backups, and the company's IT shop has raised software testing to a fine art.

There are more than 1 billion Visa payment cards outstanding around the world, spawning $2 trillion in transactions per year for 23 million merchants and automated teller machines and Visa's 21,000 member financial institutions. "We run the biggest payments engine in the world," says Sara Garrison, senior vice president for systems development at Visa U.S.A. Inc. in Foster City, California. "If you took all the traffic on all the stock markets in the world in 24 hours, we do that on a coffee break. And our capacity grows at 20 to 30 percent year to year, so every three years, our capacity doubles."

Visa has four global processing centers to handle that load, but the Washington, D.C., facility is the largest, with half of all global payment transactions flowing through the building. It shares U.S. traffic with a center in San Mateo, California, but it can instantly pick up the full United States if San Mateo goes down.

Indeed, everything in Visa's processing infrastructure—from entire data centers to computers, individual processors, and communications switches—has a backup. Even the backups have backups [3].

Disaster Recovery

Natural and man-made disasters do happen. Hurricanes, earthquakes, fires, floods, criminal and terrorist acts, and human error can all severely damage an organization's computing resources, and thus the health of the organization itself. Many companies, especially online e-commerce retailers and wholesalers, airlines, banks, and Internet service providers, for example, are crippled by losing even a few hours of computing power. Many firms could survive only a few days without computing facilities. That's why organizations develop **disaster recovery** procedures and formalize them in a *disaster recovery plan*. It specifies which employees will participate in disaster recovery and what their duties will be; what hardware, software, and facilities will be used; and the priority of applications that will be processed. Arrangements with other companies for use of alternative facilities as a disaster recovery site and offsite storage of an organization's databases are also part of an effective disaster recovery effort.

System Controls and Audits

Two final security management requirements that need to be mentioned are the development of information system controls and the accomplishment of business system audits. Let's take a brief look at these two security measures.

Information System Controls

Information system controls are methods and devices that attempt to ensure the accuracy, validity, and propriety of information system activities. Information system (IS) controls must be developed to ensure proper data entry, processing techniques, storage methods, and information output. Thus, IS controls are designed to monitor and maintain the quality and security of the input, processing, output, and storage activities of any information system. See Figure 11.22.

For example, IS controls are needed to ensure the proper entry of data into a business system and thus avoid the *garbage in, garbage out* (GIGO) syndrome.

FIGURE 11.22

Examples of information system controls. Note that they are designed to monitor and maintain the quality and security of the input, processing, output, and storage activities of an information system.

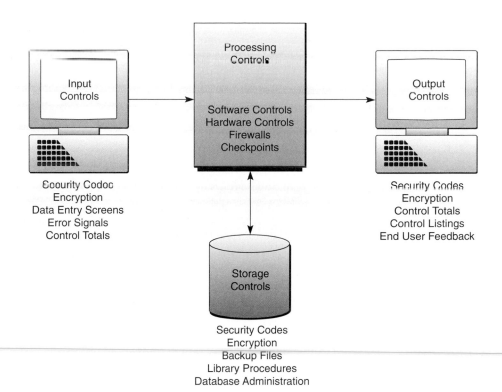

Examples include passwords and other security codes, formatted data entry screens, and audible error signals. Computer software can include instructions to identify incorrect, invalid, or improper input data as it enters the computer system. For example, a data entry program can check for invalid codes, data fields, and transactions, and conduct "reasonableness checks" to determine if input data exceed specified limits or are out of sequence.

Auditing IT Security

IT security management should be periodically examined, or audited, by a company's internal auditing staff or external auditors from professional accounting firms. Such audits review and evaluate whether proper and adequate security measures and management policies have been developed and implemented. This typically involves verifying the accuracy and integrity of the software used, as well as the input of data and output produced by business applications. Some firms employ special computer security auditors for this assignment. They may use special test data to test processing accuracy and the control procedures built into the software. The auditors may develop special test programs or use audit software packages.

Another important objective of business system audits is testing the integrity of an application's *audit trail*. An **audit trail** can be defined as the presence of documentation that allows a transaction to be traced through all stages of its information processing. This journey may begin with a transaction's appearance on a source document and may end with its transformation into information on a final output document or report. The audit trail of manual information systems is quite visible and easy to trace. However, computer-based information systems have changed the form of the audit trail. Now auditors must know how to search electronically through disk and tape files of past activity to follow the audit trail of today's networked computer systems.

Many times, this *electronic audit trail* takes the form of *control logs* that automatically record all computer network activity on magnetic disk or tape devices. This audit feature

How to protect yourself from cybercrime and other computer security threats.

Security Management for Internet Users	
1. Use antivirus and Firewall software and update if often to keep destructive programs off your computer.	6. Use the most up-to-date version of your Web browser, e-mail software, and other programs.
2. Don't allow online merchants to store your credit card information for future purchases.	7. Send credit card numbers only to secure sites; look for a padlock or key icons at the bottom of the browser.
3. Use a hard-to-guess password that contains a mix of numbers and letters, and change it frequently.	8. Use a security program that gives you control over "cookies" that send information back to websites.
4. Use different passwords for different websites and applications to keep hackers guessing.	9. Install firewall software to screen traffic if you use DSL or a cable modem to connect to the Net.
5. Install all operating system patches and upgrades.	10. Don't open e-mail attachments unless you know the source of the incoming message.

can be found on many online transaction processing systems, performance and security monitors, operating systems, and network control programs. Software that records all network activity is also widely used on the Internet, especially the World Wide Web, as well as corporate intranets and extranets. Such an audit trail helps auditors check for errors or fraud, but also helps IS security specialists trace and evaluate the trail of hacker attacks on computer networks.

Figure 11.23 summarizes ten security management steps you can take to protect your computer system resources from hacking and other forms of cybercrime [12].

Summary

- **Ethical and Societal Dimensions.** The vital role of information technologies and systems in society raises serious ethical and societal issues in terms of their impact on employment, individuality, working conditions, privacy, health, and computer crime as illustrated in Figure 11.2.

  Employment issues include the loss of jobs due to computerization and automation of work versus the jobs created to supply and support new information technologies and the business applications they make possible. The impact on working conditions involves the issues of computer monitoring of employees and the quality of the working conditions of jobs that make heavy use of information technologies. The effect of IT on individuality addresses the issues of the depersonalization, regimentation, and inflexibility of some computerized business systems.

  Health issues are raised by heavy use of computer workstations for long periods of time by employees which may cause work-related health disorders. Serious privacy issues are raised by the use of IT to access or collect private information without authorization, as well as for computer profiling, computer matching, computer monitoring, and computer libel and censorship. Computer crime issues surround activities such as hacking, computer viruses and worms, cyber theft, unauthorized use at work, software piracy, and piracy of intellectual property.

  Managers, business professionals, and IS specialists can help solve the problems of improper use of IT by as-

  suming their ethical responsibilities for the ergonomic design, beneficial use, and enlightened management of information technologies in our society.

- **Ethical Responsibility in Business.** Business and IT activities involve many ethical considerations. Basic principles of technology and business ethics can serve as guidelines for business professionals when dealing with ethical business issues that may arise in the widespread use of information technology in business and society. Examples include theories of corporate social responsibility, which outline the ethical responsibility of management and employees to a company's stockholders, stakeholders, and society, and the four principles of technology ethics summarized in Figure 11.4.

- **Security Management.** One of the most important responsibilities of the management of a company is to assure the security and quality of its IT-enabled business activities. Security management tools and policies can ensure the accuracy, integrity, and safety of the information systems and resources of a company, and thus minimize errors, fraud, and security losses in their business activities. Examples mentioned in the chapter include the use of encryption of confidential business data, firewalls, e-mail monitoring, antivirus software, security codes, backup files, security monitors, biometric security measures, computer failure controls, fault-tolerant systems, disaster recovery measures, information system controls, and security audits of business systems.

Key Terms and Concepts

These are the key terms and concepts of this chapter. The page number of their first explanation is in parentheses.

1. Antivirus software (406)
2. Audit trail (411)
3. Auditing business systems (411)
4. Backup files (407)
5. Biometric security (408)
6. Business ethics (380)
7. Computer crime (384)
8. Computer matching (392)
9. Computer monitoring (394)
10. Computer virus (390)
11. Denial of service (386)
12. Disaster recovery (410)

13. Encryption (401)
14. Ergonomics (396)
15. Ethical and societal impacts of business/IT (380)
    a. Employment (393)
    b. Health (395)
    c. Individuality (395)
    d. Societal solutions (397)
    e. Working conditions (395)
16. Ethical foundations (380)
17. Fault tolerant (409)
18. Firewall (402)
19. Flaming (393)

20. Hacking (385)
21. Information system controls (410)
22. Intellectual property piracy (389)
23. Passwords (407)
24. Privacy issues (391)
25. Responsible professional (383)
26. Security management (400)
27. Software piracy (389)
28. Spamming (393)
29. System security monitor (408)
30. Unauthorized use (387)

Review Quiz

Match one of the key terms and concepts listed previously with one of the brief examples or definitions that follow. Try to find the best fit for the answers that seem to fit more than one term or concept. Defend your choices.

_____ 1. Ensuring the accuracy, integrity, and safety of business/IT activities and resources.

_____ 2. Control totals, error signals, backup files, and security codes are examples.

_____ 3. Software that can control access and use of a computer system.

_____ 4. A computer system can continue to operate even after a major system failure if it has this capability.

_____ 5. A computer system that serves as a filter for access to and from other networks by a company's networked computers.

_____ 6. Periodically examine the accuracy and integrity of computer processing.

_____ 7. The presence of documentation that allows a transaction to be traced through all stages of information processing.

_____ 8. Using your voice or fingerprints to identify you electronically.

_____ 9. A plan to continue IS operations during an emergency.

_____ 10. Scrambling data during its transmission.

_____ 11. Ethical choices may result from decision-making processes, cultural values, or behavioral stages.

_____ 12. Managers must confront numerous ethical questions in their businesses.

_____ 13. Sending unsolicited e-mail indiscriminately.

_____ 14. Employees may have to retrain or transfer.

_____ 15. Computer-based systems may depersonalize human activities.

_____ 16. Constant long-term use of computers at work may cause health problems.

_____ 17. Computer-based monitoring of environmental quality is an example.

_____ 18. Tedious jobs are decreased and jobs are made more challenging.

_____ 19. Using computers to identify individuals that fit a certain profile.

_____ 20. Collecting information about you without your consent.

_____ 21. Using computers to monitor the activities of workers.

_____ 22. Overwhelming a website with requests for service from captive computers.

_____ 23. Using computers and networks to steal money, services, software, or data.

_____ 24. Using company computers to access the Internet during work hours for personal business.

_____ 25. Unauthorized copying of software.

_____ 26. Unauthorized copying of copyrighted material.

_____ 27. Electronic breaking and entering into a computer system.

_____ 28. A program makes copies of itself and destroys data and programs.

_____ 29. Finds and eliminates computer viruses.

_____ 30. Sending extremely critical, derogatory, and vulgar e-mail messages.

_____ 31. Designing computer hardware, software, and workstations that are safe, comfortable, and easy to use.

_____ 32. End users should act with integrity and competence in their use of information technology.

Discussion Questions

1. What can be done to improve the security of business uses of the Internet? Give several examples of security measures and technologies you would use.

2. What potential security problems do you see in the increasing use of intranets and extranets in business? What might be done to solve such problems? Give several examples.

3. Refer to the Real World Example about copying CDs in the chapter. Is copying music CDs an ethical practice? Explain.

4. What are your major concerns about computer crime and privacy on the Internet? What can you do about it? Explain.

5. What is disaster recovery? How could it be implemented at your school or work?

6. Refer to the Real World Case on F-Secure, Microsoft, GM, and Verizon in the chapter. What are the ethical responsibilities of companies and business professionals in helping to curb the spread of computer viruses?

7. Is there an ethical crisis in business today? What role does information technology play in unethical business practices?

8. What are several business decisions that you will have to make as a manager that have both an ethical and IT dimension? Give examples to illustrate your answer.

9. Refer to the Real World Case on Geisinger Health Systems and Du Pont in the chapter. What unique security challenges do mobile wireless applications like Geisinger's Electronic Medical Record system pose for companies? What are several ways these challenges can be met?

10. What would be examples of one positive and one negative effect of the use of information technologies in each of the ethical and societal dimensions illustrated in Figure 11.2? Explain several of your choices.

Analysis Exercises

1. Internet Privacy and Anonymity: An Ethical Dilemma

Some software allows you to cloak your identity on the Internet. Consider the implications this has on identity or anonymity on the Net. Suppose a political activist in a country with limited civil rights sends an e-mail to an American human-rights group describing dreadful working conditions in a U.S. owned factory. The plant's owners have to make changes—but not before local authorities, who monitor Internet traffic, throw the activist in jail. There, anonymity would have helped illuminate a problem.

Now suppose a child pornographer delivers his wares by e-mail. Authorities intercept the transmissions, but because the pornographer has successfully hidden his identity on the Net, they are unable to identify or find him. In that case, anonymity has protected a felon.

a. Should there be unrestricted use of software that provides anonymity on the Internet? Why or why not?

b. If you were able to decide this issue now, how would you decide for yourself? Your company? For society? Explain the reasons for your decision.

Source: Adapted from Stephen Wildtstrom, "A Big Boost for Net Privacy," *Business Week*, April 5, 1999, p. 23. Reprinted with special permission, copyright © 1999 by The McGraw-Hill Companies, Inc.

2. Your Internet Job Rights: Three Ethical Scenarios

Whether you're an employer or an employee, you should know what your rights are when it comes to Internet use in the workplace. Mark Grossman, a Florida attorney who specializes in computer and Internet law, gives answers to some basic questions.

Nobody told you that your Internet use in the office was being monitored. Now you've been warned you'll be fired if you use the Internet for recreational surfing again. What are your rights? Grossman advises that when you're using your office computer, you have virtually no rights. You'd have a tough time convincing a court that the boss invaded your privacy by monitoring your use of the company PC on company time. You should probably be grateful you got a warning.

What if your employees are abusing their Internet privileges, but you don't have an Internet usage policy?

What do you do? Grossman advises that although the law isn't fully developed in this area, courts are taking a straightforward approach: if it's a company computer, the company can control the way it's used. You don't need an Internet usage policy to prevent inappropriate use of your company computers. To protect yourself in the future, distribute an Internet policy to your employees as soon as possible.

Now assume that employee John Doe downloads adult material to his PC at work, and employee Jane Smith sees it. Smith then proceeds to sue the company for sexual harassment. As the employer, are you liable? Grossman advises that whether it comes from the Internet or from a magazine, adult material simply has no place in the office. So Smith could certainly sue the compay for making her work in a sexually hostile environment. The best defense is for the company to have an Internet usage policy that prohibits visits to adult sites. (Of course, you have to follow through. If someone is looking at adult material in the office, you must at least send the offending employee a written reprimand.) If the company lacks a strict Internet policy, though, Smith could prevail in court.

a. Do you agree with the advice of attorney Mark Grossman in each of the scenarios? Why or why not?

b. What would your advice be? Explain your positions.

c. Identify any ethical principles you may be using in explaining your position in each of the scenarios.

3. Social Engineering: Exploiting Security Weaknesses

An employee who needs permission to access an electronic workspace, database, or other information systems resource typically fills in a request form and obtains approval from the responsible manager. The manager then routes the request to one of the system's administrators.

Highly trusted and well-trained systems administrators spend a significant amount of time doing nothing more technical than adding or removing names from access control lists. In large organizations, it's not unusual for systems administrators to have never met any of the people involved in a specific request. The administrators may not even work in the same office.

Hackers have learned to take advantage of this approach to access authorization. They begin by "probing" an organization. The hacker doesn't expect to compromise the system during this initial probe. He or she simply starts by making a few phone calls to learn who is responsible for granting access and how to apply. A little more probing helps the hacker learn who's who within the organization's structure. Some organizations even post this information online in the form of employee directories. With this information in hand, the hacker knows who to talk to, what to ask for, and what names to use in order to sound convincing. The hacker is now ready to try to impersonate an employee and trick a systems administrator into revealing a password and unwittingly granting unauthorized access.

Organizations determine who needs access to what applications. They also need a system through which they can authenticate the identity of an individual making a request. Finally, they need to manage this process both effectively and inexpensively.

a. Describe the business problems presented by this exercise.

b. Suggest several ways to reduce an organization's exposure to social engineering.

c. Easy to memorize passwords are often easy to guess. Hackers' toolkits include programs that run "dictionary" attacks that attempt to guess a system's passwords using thousands of commonly used passwords (e.g. "smart1," "smart-one," "smart_one," "smartone," "smartypants," etc) or simply testing every word in the dictionary. On the other hand, difficult to guess passwords may be hard to memorize. Describe how you manage your own passwords. What are the strengths and weaknesses of your own approach?

d. Prepare an orientation memo to new-hires in your IT department describing "social engineering."

Suggest several ways employees can avoid being tricked by hackers.

4. **Privacy Statements and Spyware**

Web surfers may feel anonymous as they use the Internet, but that feeling isn't always justified. IP addresses, cookies, site login procedures, and credit card purchases all help track how often users visit and what pages they view. Some companies go further.

Some developers that provide free screensaver software or peer-to-peer file sharing also bundle "spyware" with their applications. Once loaded, these applications run in the background. What they actually track depends on the specific software. To stay on the "right side" of U.S. law, these companies outline their software's functions in general terms and include this information in the small print within their end user licensing agreement (EULA) and or privacy policy. In fact, these agreements may even include a stipulation that users *not* disable any part of their software as a condition for free use.

Since, most users don't read this information, they have no idea what privacy rights they may have given up. They may indeed get their free file sharing program or screen saver, but they may be getting a lot more. Indeed, users have reported that some spyware programs remain on their hard drives and stay active even after they have uninstalled the "free" software part of the software package.

a. Use a search engine to search on "spyware," "spyware removal," "adware," or other related terms. Prepare a one-page summary of your results. Include URLs for online sources.

b. Select three of your favorite websites and print out their privacy policies. What do they share in common? How do they differ?

c. Write your own website privacy policy striking a balance between both customer and business needs.

REAL WORLD CASE 3

Banner Health, Arlington County, and Others: Security Management of Windows Software

Computer viruses infect thousands of computers that run various Windows operating systems daily, worldwide. That presents an enormous challenge to companies to keep their systems up to date with patches for Windows software vulnerabilities, business users say. Companies that had installed Microsoft Corp.'s patch for a flaw identified last month before the Blaster virus hit, for example, said they felt no effects from the worm. But the seemingly constant work involved in guarding against such worms is becoming a burden that could prove unsustainable over time, complaining users said.

"The thing about patching is that it is so darn reactive. And that can kill you," said Dave Jahne, a senior security analyst at Phoenix-based Banner Health System (www.bannerhealth.com), which runs 22 hospitals. "You need to literally drop everything else to go take care of patching. And the reality is, we only have a finite amount of resources to do that," Jahne said. Banner had to patch more than 500 servers and 8,000 workstations to protect itself against the vulnerability that Blaster exploited. "I can tell you, it's been one heck of an effort on a lot of people's part to do that," Jahne added. For the longer term, Banner is studying the feasibility of partitioning its networks in order to minimize the effect of vulnerabilities, he said.

Adding to the patching problem is the fact that companies, especially larger and more distributed ones, need time to properly test each patch before they can deploy them. That's because patches haven't always worked or have broken the applications they were meant to protect, said Marc Willebeek-LeMair, chief technology officer at Tipping-Point Technologies (www.tippingpoint.com), an Austin-based vendor of intrusion-prevention products. Companies also need to schedule downtime in advance to deploy such patches, said Kevin Ott, vice president of technology at Terra Nova Trading LLC, (www.terranovatrading.com) a Chicago-based financial services firm. "We work in a 24-by-7 environment, so there is a limited scope for downtime in which to deploy patches," he said.

But the stunning quickness at which Blaster exploited Windows' remote procedure call vulnerability is a sign that companies are going to have to respond to new threats even faster than they do today, said Chuck Adams, chief security officer at NetSolve Inc., an IT services company in Austin. Although worms such as SQL Slammer didn't appear until eight months after the Windows vulnerability it exploited was announced, Blaster was released just one month after Microsoft announced the Windows vulnerability it attacked, Adams said.

That means companies will need to somehow find ways to lessen the time it takes to test and deploy patches, said

Vivek Kundra, director of infrastructure technologies for Arlington County, Virginia. Currently, Arlington County (www.co.arlington.va.us) needs about three or four days to push out patches across its networks. "Three or four days is not going to work any longer," Kundra said. "I need something that can cut the process down to a few hours, if not minutes." The county is looking at outsourcing its patch management process to a third party. Also under consideration is a plan to adopt a more automated process for testing and deploying software patches, Kundra said.

But Microsoft's Windows Update patch management program has a critical shortcoming that, in some cases, could fool users into thinking they have been properly patched against some vulnerabilities when in fact they have not, says Russ Cooper, an analyst at TruSecure Corp. The claim was strongly refuted by Microsoft as being unfounded since it made improvements to its Windows patching utility a few months earlier. But another security expert who requested anonymity said that there are many other serious security vulnerabilities concerning Microsoft patches that can easily be spoofed, including three critical vulnerabilities that were announced earlier in 2003.

And at least one user has finally given up on Windows Update altogether. Vivek Kundra of Arlington County said his department has had problems using the Windows Update server software to deploy the patches. Although the county government began the process using Microsoft's Windows Update process, it had to abandon the approach because the patches didn't always deploy properly on the county's 3,500 workstations. As a result, Arlington County has switched to Novell's ZEN-works to distribute the Windows patches, Kundra said.

Case Study Questions

1. What security problems are typically remedied by Microsoft's security patches for Windows? Why do such problems arise in the first place?

2. What challenges does the process of applying Windows patches pose for many businesses? What are some limitations of the patching process?

3. Does the business value of applying Windows patches outweigh its costs, limitations, and the demands it places on the IT function? Why or why not?

Sources: Adapted from Jaikumar Vijayan, "Patching Becoming a Major Resource Drain for Companies," *Computerworld*, August 18, 2003, 1, 15; and "Windows Update Patch Process Faulty, Expert Says," *Computerworld*, August 18, 2003, p. 15.

REAL WORLD CASE 4

Online Resources, Lehman Brothers, and Others: Managing Network Security Systems

Like many companies, Online Resources Corp. (www.onlineresources.com) has deployed network intrusion-detection systems, firewalls, and antivirus tools on its networks. But until it installed a security event management suite, the company had a hard time dealing with the deluge of data pouring in from its various security systems. Not only was the incoming data voluminous and highly unreliable, but the IT staff also had to collect it from each system and then manually correlate it. The Security Information Management suite from NetForensics, has changed that by automating the process of gathering, consolidating, correlating, and prioritizing that data, says Hugh McArthur, information security officer at the online bill processor. "It has given us a single place where we can go to get the information we need," he says.

The ever-increasing number of security tools and appliances around the network perimeter has created a stream of data that needs to be analyzed and correlated, says Michael Engle, vice president of information security at Lehman Brothers Holdings Inc. (www.lehman.com) in New York. Intrusion detection systems (IDS), intrusion prevention systems (IPS), firewalls and antivirus software, as well as operating systems and applications software, can detect and report an enormous number of security events daily.

For instance, the security incident management system at Lehman gathers and analyzes information about more than 1 million events from 15 different systems daily, according to Engle. This includes data from IDSs and authentication systems, a telephone password reset system, and an anomaly-detection system, as well as logs from Lehman's main e-commerce, Windows, and Unix systems. By year's end, the firm hopes to have an improved system in place that will help it gather and analyze more than 80 million daily events, including consolidated firewall log data.

Security information management tools typically "normalize" the security events data they collect by converting them into a common format and automatically filtering out duplicate data, such as multiple entries for the same virus attack. The normalized data is then dumped into a central database or repository, where correlation software can match data from different systems and look for patterns that might indicate an attack or threat. Finally, threats are prioritized based on their severity and the importance of the systems that are vulnerable. Data that suggests an attack against a critical e-commerce server, for instance, would be given a higher priority than an attack against a file server.

IT security administrators can view the information using a Web- or Java-based console, or dashboard, or the system can be configured to send alerts to pagers or other devices. Dashboards can give companies a real-time snapshot of what's going on inside the corporate network. "We are able to

see events happen more quickly. It allows us to react faster if we see some activity bubble up in our systems," says White.

The benefits of deploying such software can be enormous, Engle says. When Lehman first installed an IDS in 1999, it generated more than 600 alerts daily—most of them false alarms. Today, thanks to the event-correlation features of its management system, administrators receive fewer than 10 per day. The system today is "turning more than 1 million events down to less than 10 alerts," Engle says. Such technology allows companies like Lehman to pinpoint threats far more efficiently, identify trends that might indicate an emerging threat, and fine-tune incident response.

The data that centralized event management systems capture and store is also useful for forensic analysis of network intrusions, says Nitin Ved, chief operating officer at NetForensics (www.netforensics.com). Such systems let companies drill down into the details of an attack, piece together relevant information from different systems, and quickly build a composite of events leading up to a security incident.

But as with any other technology, there are several major precautions, especially concerning the quality of the data that is fed into such systems. The old adage "garbage in, garbage out" holds true with such software, says Sweta Duseja, a product manager at security vendor Check Point Software Technologies (www.checkpoint.com). That's why it's important to ensure that the right filters and rules are set for capturing the information that's fed into the system, Engle says. For example, every time an end user on Lehman's network clicked on CNN's website, it generated 144 separate log events on Lehman's security systems, most of which were useless data. "Initially, we were sending too much data into the system because we thought that would put us in a better security position," Engle says.

Case Study Questions

1. What is the function of each of the network security tools identified in this case? Visit the websites of security firms Check Point and NetForensics to help you answer.

2. What is the value of security information management software to a company? Use the companies in this case as examples.

3. What can smaller firms who cannot afford the cost of such software do to properly manage and use the information about security from their network security systems? Give several examples.

CHAPTER 12

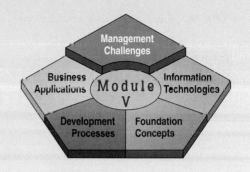

ENTERPRISE AND GLOBAL MANAGEMENT OF INFORMATION TECHNOLOGY

Chapter Highlights

Section I
Managing Information Technology

Business and IT

Real World Case: Chicago Board of Trade: From Failure to Success in Managing Information Technology

Managing Information Technology

Business/IT Planning

Managing the IS Function

Failures in IT Management

Section II
Managing Global IT

The International Dimension

Real World Case: Global Exchange Services and Allstate: Challenges and Solutions in Offshore Systems Development

Global IT Management

Cultural, Political, and Geoeconomic Challenges

Global Business/IT Strategies

Global Business/IT Applications

Global IT Platforms

Global Data Access Issues

Global Systems Development

Real World Case: Bio-ERA and Burlington Northern Santa Fe: The Business Case for Global Collaborative Development

Real World Case: Avon Products and Guardian Life Insurance: Successful Mangement of IT Projects

Learning Objectives

After reading and studying this chapter, you should be able to:

1. Identify each of the three components of information technology management and use examples to illustrate how they might be implemented in a business.

2. Explain how failures in IT management can be reduced by the involvement of business managers in IT planning and management.

3. Identify several cultural, political, and geoeconomic challenges that confront managers in the management of global information technologies.

4. Explain the effect on global business/IT strategy of the trend toward a transnational business strategy by international business organizations.

5. Identify several considerations that affect the choice of IT applications, IT platforms, data access policies, and systems development methods by a global business enterprise.

SECTION I	# Managing Information Technology

Business and IT

The strategic and operational importance of information technology in business is no longer questioned. As the 21st century unfolds, many companies throughout the world are intent on transforming themselves into global business powerhouses via major investments in global e-business, e-commerce, and other IT initiatives. Thus, there is a real need for business managers and professionals to understand how to manage this vital organizational function. In this section, we will explore how the IS function can be organized and managed, and stress the importance of a customer and business value focus for the management of information technologies. So whether you plan to be an entrepreneur and run your own business, a manager in a corporation, or a business professional, managing information systems and technologies will be one of your major responsibilities.

Analyzing the Chicago Board of Trade

Read the Real World Case on the Chicago Board of Trade on the next page. We can learn a lot from this case about the challenges of successfully managing information technology in business. See Figure 12.1.

This case portrays the dramatic failure and rebound to success of the IT function at the Chicago Board of Trade. The IT group was so ineffective and poorly managed that it seemed powerless to stop the weekly trading-floor system crashes that were costing CBOT millions of dollars in lost income. The IT infrastructure was ancient, unreliable, and undocumented. Project and budget controls were lacking, return on investment of IT projects had never been done, and quality control was substandard. Morale was low, and IT lacked credibility with the business units.

CIO Bill Farrow was hired in July 2001 to turn the IT function around, which he began to do quickly. For example, new computer systems and database software were installed, a project management office established, ROI evaluations of IT projects

FIGURE 12.1

Bill Farrow is Executive Vice President and CIO of the Chicago Board of Trade and led the dramatic turnaround of their IT function.

Source: Marc Berlow.

REAL WORLD CASE 1

Chicago Board of Trade: From Failure to Success in Managing Information Technology

Picture 3,000 traders in "the pit" waving their hands and screaming orders for stocks, bonds, and commodities. Millions of dollars in investments are changing hands every minute. Suddenly, screens freeze; orders won't execute. Mayhem reigns, as millions of dollars are lost with every tick of the clock. "That's the worst thing that can happen," says Carol Burke, executive vice president and chief of staff at the Chicago Board of Trade (CBOT) (www.cbot. com). But two years ago, trading-floor systems were crashing almost weekly because of a deteriorating IT infrastructure, costing the exchange and its members millions of dollars.

In July 2001, after two years of operating in the red, the board of directors brought in a new management team for CBOT, including Executive Vice President and CIO Bill Farrow. A total IT revamp got the exchange back to in-house profitability. By 2002, its profit had risen to $25 million, trading-system crashes were virtually unheard of, and CBOT was once again bullish on technology.

Farrow walked into an IT situation that was grim. "The chairman said, 'Bill, you have very small shoes to fill,'" he recalls. "That tells you a lot." "IT was in disarray," agrees Burke, a 20-year CBOT veteran. "There were a lot of good people in IT, but there was a real lack of leadership," says Chip Bennett, senior vice president of technology solutions and Farrow's first hire at CBOT. The infrastructure was ancient, unreliable, and undocumented." For example, desktop PCs ran a version of Windows no longer supported by Microsoft. Nearly every key process was routed through a group of old, midrange Tandem computers in an environment so complex that developing a new process took more than 90 steps. Project and budget controls were lacking, and quality control was substandard. IT was full of silos and fiefdoms, so there were no economies of scale.

Morale was low. There was a place called "the wall," where nearly 100 yellow sticky notes commemorated people who had gotten fed up and left. Yet many were complacent. "Tech jobs were called 'the golden hammock,'" Farrow says. "Once you got in, you could have a very easy, very, very long career in technology here." That attitude made no friends on the business side. "We would go to IT and say, 'Help us,'" recalls Kevin Lennon, vice president of real estate operations. "The feeling we got was that we were taking them away from something more important."

Other than Y2K, IT hadn't completed a single project in four years. As a result, people had no experience in project management disciplines, and return on investment was a foreign concept. "No ROIs were done—ever," Farrow says. "Technology did not have to provide a return for investing the money in it." There was such a lack of credibility between the business and IT sides that the business people had totally given up, Farrow says.

Farrow began by taking inventory of what he had. He documented systems and technical architecture, nailed down vendor relationships and service-level agreements, and evaluated

security systems. Simultaneously, he faced the bigger challenge of building new relationships with skeptical business managers. He assigned IT managers to counterparts on the business side to brainstorm regularly about how technology could support business goals. Denise Schaller, director of technology and data products for floor support applications, who has 21 years experience at CBOT, says her weekly meeting with the two vice presidents of exchange operations has changed everything. "If I have any business questions, issues, priorities—they help sort it out," she says.

Replacing the ancient Tandems with Sun Unix servers and Oracle databases, a process that Schaller thought would take two years, got done in half the time because her new partners in business helped with the analysis, legwork, and scope. Farrow boosted quality assurance with additional software testing and backed it up by putting IT troubleshooters on the trading floor every day when the market opened. "I'm on the spot, so I can see any problems and react immediately," says Schaller.

Farrow established a project management office to centralize the project portfolio and the IT skills pool. He also brought ROI to project agendas. Farrow used news of the turnaround to attract technology professionals with new skills, particularly in the areas of security and business analysis. But there were painful decisions as well, including letting 15 IT managers go. The permanent IT workforce shrank from 250 to fewer than 200, supplemented by temporary contract help as required by the project load.

In 2002, IT completed 66 projects. In February 2003, CBOT handled 33 million contracts—33 percent more than in the previous February, without a single system stutter. "We have a much more stable and robust environment with fail-over abilities," says Burke. "If there were a problem in a primary system, it would fail over to a backup and be seamless to the marketplace." Throughout the turnaround, IT has maintained a flat budget. "If you are wasting 35 percent of your money, that's a lot of money to put back into information technology to make it robust," Farrow says.

Case Study Questions

1. What were several major reasons the IT organization had failed at the Chicago Board of Trade? Explain the impact of each on CBOT.

2. What were several key management changes and initiatives that Bill Farrow implemented to make IT successful at CBOT? Explain the impact of each on CBOT.

3. Does the experience of CBOT prove that "IT is a business function that needs to be managed like any other business function?" Why or why not?

Source: Adapted from Kathleen Melymuka, "Market Rally," *Computerworld*, April 7, 2003, pp. 40–41.

FIGURE 12.2

The major components of information technology management. Note the executives with primary responsibilities in each area.

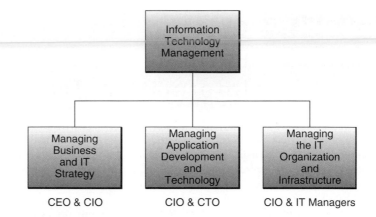

were required, and IT managers were assigned to work with business unit managers to assure that IT was supporting their business goals. Now IT is completing many new projects, and the trading floor systems are processing a third more transactions without any system failures.

Managing Information Technology

As we have seen throughout this text, information technology is an essential component of business success for companies today. But information technology is also a vital business resource that must be properly managed. Thus we have also seen many real world examples where the management of information technologies played a pivotal role in assuring the success or contributing to the failure of a company's strategic business initiatives. Therefore, managing the information systems and technologies that support the modern business processes of companies today is a major challenge for both business and IT managers and professionals.

How should information technology be managed? Figure 12.2 illustrates one popular approach to managing information technology in a large company [4]. This managerial approach has three major components:

- **Managing the joint development and implementation of business/IT strategies.** Led by the CEO and CIO (chief information officer), proposals are developed by business and IT managers and professionals for using IT to support the strategic business priorities of the company. This business/IT planning process *aligns* IT with strategic business goals. The process also includes evaluating the business case for investing in the development and implementation of each proposed business/IT project.

- **Managing the development and implementation of new business/IT applications and technologies.** This is the primary responsibility of the CIO and CTO (chief technology officer). This area of IT management involves managing the processes for information systems development and implementation we discussed in Chapter 10, as well as the responsibility for research into the strategic business uses of new information technologies.

- **Managing the IT organization and the IT infrastructure.** The CIO and IT managers share responsibility for managing the work of IT professionals who are typically organized into a variety of project teams and other organizational subunits. In addition, they are responsible for managing the IT infrastructure of hardware, software, databases, telecommunications networks, and other IT resources, which must be acquired, operated, monitored, and maintained.

Let's look at a real world example.

FIGURE 12.3

Comparing conventional and e-business-driven IT management approaches.

IT Management	Conventional Practices	Avnet Marshall's Business/IT Practices
Technology Management	• Approach to IT infrastructure may sacrifice match with business needs for vendor homogeneity and technology platform choices	• Best-of-breed approach to IT infrastructure in which effective match with business needs takes precedence over commitment to technology platform choices and vendor homogeneity
Managing the IT Organization	• Hire "best by position" who can bring specific IT expertise • Departments organized around IT expertise with business liaisons and explicit delegation of tasks • IT projects have separable cost/value considerations. Funding typically allocated within constraints of yearly budget for IT function	• Hire "best athletes" IS professionals who can flexibly integrate new IT and business competencies • Evolving workgroups organized around emerging IT-intensive business initiatives with little explicit delegation of tasks • IT funding typically based on value proposition around business opportunity related to building services for customers. IT project inseparable part of business initiative

Avnet Marshall: Managing IT

Figure 12.3 contrasts how Avnet Marshall's information technology management differs from conventional IT management [4]. Notice that they use the model of IT management illustrated in Figure 12.2. For example, in technology management, Avnet Marshall uses a best-of-breed approach that supports business needs, instead of enforcing a standardized and homogeneous choice of hardware, software, database, and networking technologies. In managing its IT organization, Avnet Marshall hires IS professionals who can integrate IT with business. These IS professionals are organized in workgroups around business/IT initiatives that focus on building IT-enabled business services for customers.

Business/IT Planning

Figure 12.4 illustrates the **business/IT planning** process, which focuses on discovering innovative approaches to satisfying a company's customer value and business value goals [10]. This planning process leads to development of strategies and business models for new business applications, processes, products, and services. Then a company can develop IT strategies and an IT architecture that supports building and implementing their newly planned business applications.

Both the CEO and the chief information officer (CIO) of a company must manage the development of complementary business and IT strategies to meet its customer value and business value vision. This *co-adaptation* process is necessary because as we have seen so often in this text, information technologies are a fast changing, but vital component in many strategic business initiatives. The business/IT planning process has three major components:

- **Strategy development.** Developing business strategies that support a company's business vision. For example, use information technology to create innovative e-business systems that focus on customer and business value. We will discuss this process in more detail shortly.

- **Resource management.** Developing strategic plans for managing or outsourcing a company's IT resources, including IS personnel, hardware, software, data, and network resources.

FIGURE 12.4 The business/IT planning process emphasizes a customer and business value focus for devoloping business strategies and models, and an IT architecture for business applications.

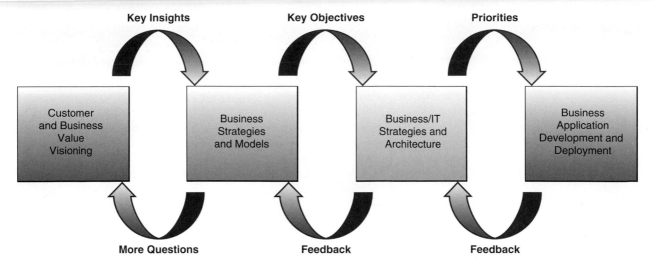

- **Technology architecture.** Making strategic IT choices that reflect an information technology architecture designed to support a company's business/IT initiatives.

Information Technology Architecture

The **IT architecture** that is created by the strategic business/IT planning process is a conceptual design, or blueprint, that includes the following major components:

- **Technology platform.** The Internet, intranets, extranets, and other networks, computer systems, system software, and integrated enterprise application software provide a computing and communications infrastructure, or platform, that supports the strategic use of information technology for e-business, e-commerce, and other business/IT applications.

- **Data resources.** Many types of operational and specialized databases, including data warehouses and Internet/intranet databases (as reviewed in Chapter 5) store and provide data and information for business processes and decision support.

- **Applications architecture.** Business applications of information technology are designed as an integrated architecture *or portfolio* of enterprise systems that support strategic business initiatives, as well as cross-functional business processes. For example, an applications architecture should include support for developing and maintaining the interenterprise supply chain applications, and integrated enterprise resource planning and customer relationship management applications we discussed in Chapter 7.

- **IT organization.** The organizational structure of the IS function within a company and the distribution of IS specialists are designed to meet the changing strategies of a business. The form of the IT organization depends on the managerial philosophy and business/IT strategies formulated during the strategic planning process.

Avnet Marshall: e-Business Planning

Figure 12.5 outlines Avnet Marshall's planning process for business/IT initiatives, and compares it to conventional IT planning approaches [4]. Avnet Marshall weaves both business and IT strategic planning together *co-adaptively* under the guidance of the CEO and the CIO, instead of developing IT strategy by just tracking and supporting

FIGURE 12.5

Comparing business/IT strategic and application planning approaches.

Conventional IT Planning	Avnet Marshall's Business/IT Planning
• Strategic alignment: IT strategy tracks specified enterprise strategy	• Strategic improvisation. IT strategy and enterprise business strategy co-adaptively unfold based on the clear guidance of a focus on customer value
• CEO endorses IT vision shaped through CIO	• CEO proactively shapes IT vision jointly with CIO as part of e-business strategy
• IT application development projects functionally organized as technological solutions to business issues	• IT application development projects co-located with e-business initiatives to form centers of IT-intensive business expertise
• Phased application development based on learning from pilot projects	• Perpetual application development based on continuous learning from rapid deployment and prototyping with end user involvement

business strategies. Avnet Marshall also locates IT application development projects within the business units that are involved in an e-business initiative to form centers of business/IT expertise throughout the company. Finally, Avnet Marshall uses a prototyping application development process with rapid deployment of new business applications, instead of a traditional systems development approach. This application development strategy trades the risk of implementing incomplete applications with the benefits of gaining competitive advantages from early deployment of new e-business services to employees, customers, and other stakeholders, and of involving them in the "fine-tuning" phase of application development.

Managing the IS Function

A radical shift is occurring in corporate computing—think of it as the recentralization of management. It's a step back toward the 1970s, when a data-processing manager could sit at a console and track all the technology assets of the corporation. Then came the 1980s and early 1990s. Departments got their own PCs and software; client/server networks sprang up all across companies.

Three things have happened in the past few years: The Internet boom inspired businesses to connect all those networks, companies put on their intranets essential applications without which their businesses could not function; and it became apparent that maintaining PCs on a network is very, very expensive. Such changes create an urgent need for centralization [12].

Organizing IT

In the early years of computing, the development of large mainframe computers and telecommunications networks and terminals caused a **centralization** of computer hardware and software, databases, and information specialists at the corporate level of organizations. Next, the development of minicomputers and microcomputers accelerated a **downsizing** trend, which prompted a move back toward **decentralization** by many business firms. Distributed client/server networks at the corporate, department, workgroup, and team levels came into being. This promoted a shift of databases and information specialists to some departments, and the creation of *information centers* to support end user and workgroup computing.

Lately, the trend is to establish more centralized control over the management of the IT resources of a company, while still serving the strategic needs of its business units, especially their e-business and e-commerce initiatives. This has resulted in the development of hybrid structures with both centralized and decentralized components. See Figure 12.6. For example, the IT function at Avnet Marshall is organized

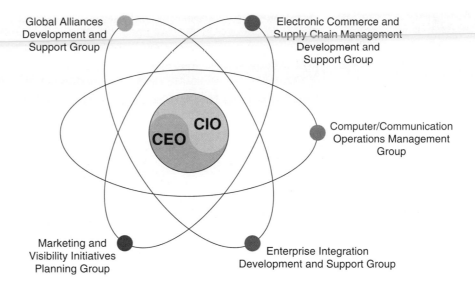

The organizational components of the IT function at Avnet Marshall.

into several business-focused development groups as well as operations management and planning groups [4].

Some companies spin off their information systems function into IS *subsidiaries* that offer IS services to external organizations as well as to their parent company. Other companies create or spin off their e-commerce and Internet-related business units or IT groups into separate companies or business units. Other corporations **outsource**, that is, turn over all or parts of their IS operations to outside contractors known as *systems integrators*. In addition, some companies are outsourcing software procurement and support to *application service providers* (ASPs), who provide and support business application and other software via the Internet and intranets to all of a company's employee workstations. Let's look at two companies as real world examples.

Fireman's Fund and FMC Corp: Outsourcing IT	Fireman's Fund Insurance Co. (www.firemansfund. com) in Novato, California, last fall signed a 10-year $380 million outsourcing deal with CGI Group Inc. (www.cgi.com) in Montreal, Canada. As part of the agreement, CGI will provide Fireman's Fund with IT support services to some 80 locations across the United States. CGI has taken over the insurance company's Phoenix data center, and about 300 Fireman's Fund employees have become CGI employees.

The growing challenge of maintaining and staffing Fireman's vital-but-aging legacy systems was a primary driver of the deal, says CIO Bill McCarter. The decision to hand over legacy operations to CGI has left Fireman's with a leaner IT organization focused on developing new applications that it hopes will give it a competitive market edge. But the contract with CGI has also resulted in a substantial 21 percent savings in infrastructure costs—a benefit that has assumed even bigger significance in today's economy, McCarter says.

Technology complexity is another consideration, says Ed Flynn, CIO at Philadelphia-based FMC Corp. (www.fmc.com), a $2 billion chemicals manufacturer. Handing over complex technologies to companies with the right know-how is both economical and efficient, Flynn says. It eliminates the risk and time involved in developing the knowledge in-house. FMC uses a variety of outsourcing vendors including IBM, Digex Inc., Genuity Inc. and Aventail Corp. "Cost has been an important priority in all these relationships. But our view on costs doesn't change based on the economy," says Flynn. "We are in some very competitive industries, and we look at costs all the time."[23]

Managing Application Development

Application development management involves managing activities such as systems analysis and design, prototyping, applications programming, project management, quality assurance, and system maintenance for all major business/IT development projects. Managing application development requires managing the activities of teams of systems analysts, software developers, and other IS professionals working on a variety of information systems development projects. Thus, project management is a key IT management responsibility if business/IT projects are to be completed on time, within their budgets, as well as meeting their design objectives. In addition, some systems development groups have established *development centers* staffed with IS professionals. Their role is to evaluate new application development tools and to help information systems specialists use them to improve their application development efforts.

Managing IS Operations

IS operations management is concerned with the use of hardware, software, network, and personnel resources in the corporate or business unit **data centers** (computer centers) of an organization. Operational activities that must be managed include computer system operations, network management, production control, and production support.

Most operations management activities are being automated by the use of software packages for computer system performance management. These **system performance monitors** monitor the processing of computer jobs, help develop a planned schedule of computer operations that can optimize computer system performance, and produce detailed statistics that are invaluable for effective planning and control of computing capacity. Such information evaluates computer system utilization, costs, and performance. This evaluation provides information for capacity planning, production planning and control, and hardware/software acquisition planning. It is also used in quality assurance programs, which stress quality of services to business end users. See Figure 12.7.

System performance monitors also supply information needed by **chargeback systems** that allocate costs to users based on the information services rendered. All costs

FIGURE 12.7

The CA-Unicenter TNG system performance monitor includes an Enterprise Management Portal module that helps IT specialists monitor and manage a variety of networked computer systems and operating systems.

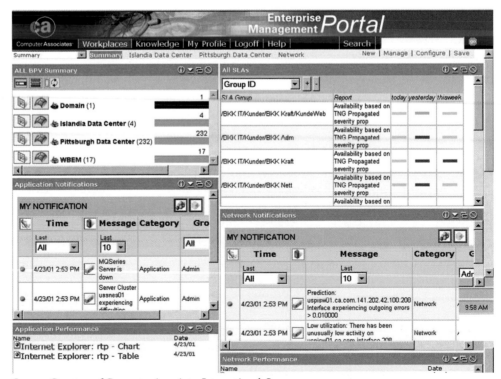

Source: Courtesy of Computer Associates International, Inc.

incurred are recorded, reported, allocated, and charged back to specific end user business units, depending on their use of system resources. When companies use this arrangement, the information services department becomes a service center whose costs are charged directly to business units, rather than being lumped with other administrative service costs and treated as an overhead cost.

Many performance monitors also feature **process control** capabilities. Such packages not only monitor but automatically control computer operations at large data centers. Some use built-in expert system modules based on knowledge gleaned from experts in the operations of specific computer systems and operating systems. These performance monitors provide more efficient computer operations than human-operated systems. They also enable "lights out" data centers at some companies, where computer systems are operated unattended, especially after normal business hours.

Human Resource Management of IT

The success or failure of an information services organization rests primarily on the quality of its people. Many computer-using firms consider recruiting, training, and retaining qualified IS personnel as one of their greatest challenges. Managing information services functions involves the management of managerial, technical, and clerical personnel. One of the most important jobs of information services managers is to recruit qualified personnel and to develop, organize, and direct the capabilities of existing personnel. Employees must be continually trained to keep up with the latest developments in a fast-moving and highly technical field. Employee job performances must be continually evaluated and outstanding performances rewarded with salary increases or promotions. Salary and wage levels must be set, and career paths must be designed so individuals can move to new jobs through promotion and transfer as they gain in seniority and expertise.

The CIO and Other IT Executives

The **chief information officer** (CIO) oversees all use of information technology in many companies, and brings them into alignment with strategic business goals. Thus, all traditional computer services, Internet technology, telecommunications network services, and other IS technology support services are the responsibility of this executive. Also, the CIO does not direct day-to-day information services activities. Instead, CIOs concentrate on business/IT planning and strategy. They also work with the CEO and other top executives to develop strategic uses of information technology in electronic business and commerce that help make the firm more competitive in the marketplace. Many companies have also filled the CIO position with executives from the business functions or units outside the IS field. Such CIOs emphasize that the chief role of information technology is to help a company meet its strategic business objectives.

Top IT Jobs: Requirements and Compensation

- **Chief technology officer**

Base salary range: $100,000 to $200,000-plus; varies by location
Bonus range: Up to 30% of salary

If you're second-in-command to the CIO or chief technology officer and you have years of applications development experience, your next move should be into the chief technology officer's spot. To land this job, you'll need to be a passionate problem-solver with a demonstrated record of reducing development time.

- **e-Commerce architect**

Base salary range: $100,000 to $150,000-plus; varies by location
Bonus range: Up to 20% of salary

If you know Java, Perl, C++, and Web services, have experience in systems architecture, and can design an Internet solution from concept through implementation, many companies want you to plan and develop their e-commerce sites.

- **Technical team leader**

  Base salary range: $75,000 to $100,000-plus; varies by location

  Bonus range: Up to 20% of salary

    Senior technical team leaders with good communication, project management, and leadership skills, as well as knowledge of Web languages and databases, are still highly sought after.

- **Practice manager**

  Base salary range: $70,000 to $100,000-plus; varies by location

  Bonus range: Up to 20% of salary

    If you've got a background in IT assessment and a pedigree in business development (MBA preferred), you can land a job as a point person for big projects. You'll need skills in IT operations and software assessment, as well as in marketing, staffing, budgeting, and building customer relationships [5, 22].

Technology Management

The management of rapidly changing technology is important to any organization. Changes in information technology, like the rise of the PC, client/server networks, and the Internet and intranets, have come swiftly and dramatically and are expected to continue into the future. Developments in information systems technology have had, and will continue to have, a major impact on the operations, costs, management work environment, and competitive position of many organizations.

Thus, all information technologies must be managed as a technology platform for integrating internally focused or externally facing business applications. Such technologies include the Internet, intranets, and a variety of electronic commerce and collaboration technologies, as well as integrated enterprise software for customer relationship management, enterprise resource planning, and supply chain management. In many companies, technology management is the primary responsibility of a *chief technology officer* (CTO) who is in charge of all information technology planning and deployment.

Managing User Services

Teams and workgroups of business professionals commonly use PC workstations, software packages, and the Internet, intranets, and other networks to develop and apply information technology to their work activities. Thus many companies have responded by creating **user services,** or *client services,* functions to support and manage end user and workgroup computing.

End user services provide both opportunities and problems for business unit managers. For example, some firms create an *information center* group staffed with user liaison specialists, or Web-enabled intranet help desks. IS specialists with titles such as user consultant, account executive, or business analyst may also be assigned to end user work groups. These specialists perform a vital role by troubleshooting problems, gathering and communicating information, coordinating educational efforts, and helping business professionals with application development.

In addition to these measures, most organizations still establish and enforce policies for the acquisition of hardware and software by end users and business units. This ensures their compatibility with company standards for hardware, software, and network connectivity. Also important is the development of applications with proper security and quality controls to promote correct performance and safeguard the integrity of corporate and departmental networks and databases.

Failures in IT Management

Managing information technology is not an easy task. The information systems function has performance problems in many organizations. The promised benefits of information technology have not occurred in many documented cases. Studies by management consulting firms and university researchers have shown that many businesses have not been successful in managing their use of information technology. Thus, it is evident that in many organizations, information technology is not being used effectively and efficiently. For example:

- Information technology is not being used *effectively* by companies that use IT primarily to computerize traditional business processes, instead of developing innovative e-business processes involving customers, suppliers, and other business partners, electronic commerce, and Web-enabled decision support.

- Information technology is not being used *efficiently* by information systems that provide poor response times and frequent downtimes, or IS professionals and consultants who do not properly manage application development projects.

Let's look closer at a real world example.

PeopleFirst Finance: Failure of a CRM Project

You've been warned: Putting in a decent customer relationship management (CRM) system is as perilous as installing enterprise resource planning (ERP) systems used to be. CRM projects fail more often than not, analysts say. The software is hard to install. It forces a lot of change, quickly, on business units. And even when companies manage to install and link applications that hold client information, they often don't serve customers any better, reports Gartner Inc. Mercer Management Consulting calls CRM a "money pit."

But some companies have gotten CRM to work well—on the second or third try. Some of the disappointment can be chalked up to classic bad habits in IT, such as not listening—sometimes not even talking—to end users about what they want. Or the CRM team may try to do too much at once, which almost guarantees delays and cost overruns.

PeopleFirst Finance LLC (www.peoplefirst.com), an online car loan company in San Diego, dived into CRM in June 2000, when it tried to install a complete CRM suite. It was clear about three months into the installation that things weren't going well, says Sharon Spooler, vice president of business intelligence at PeopleFirst. For example, there was no easy, automated way to manage bouncebacks from e-mail sales pitches that didn't reach intended recipients, she says. Also the software couldn't properly track multiple versions of e-mail sales letters. The result: PeopleFirst couldn't get an accurate view of which campaigns worked.

"We tried problem solving with the vendor. We tried a lot of different things to make it work. Every time you'd think you had a problem solved, another one would pop up," Spooler says. "It was like a game of whack-a-mole." Spooler declined to name the vendor, citing a deal struck when PeopleFirst killed the project in March 2001 [20].

Management Involvement and Governance

What is the solution to failures in the information systems function? There are no quick and easy answers. However, the experiences of successful organizations reveal that extensive and meaningful **managerial and end user involvement** is the key ingredient of high-quality information systems performance. Involving business managers in the governance of the IS function and business professionals in the development of IS applications should thus shape the response of management to the challenge of improving the business value of information technology [4, 10]. See Figure 12.8.

Involving managers in the management of IT (from the CEO to the managers of business units) requires the development of *governance structures* (such as executive councils and steering committees) that encourage their active participation in planning and controlling the business uses of IT. Thus, many organizations have policies that

FIGURE 12.8 Senior management needs to be involved in critical business/IT decisions to optimize the business value and performance of the IT function.

IT Decision	Senior Management's Role	Consequences of Abdicating the Decision
● **How much should we spend on IT?**	Define the strategic role that IT will play in the company and then determine the level of funding needed to achieve that objective.	The company fails to develop an IT platform that furthers its strategy, despite high IT spending.
● **Which business processes should receive our IT dollars?**	Make clear decisions about which IT initiatives will and will not be funded.	A lack of focus overwhelms the IT unit, which tries to deliver many projects that may have little companywide value or can't be implemented well simultaneously.
● **Which IT capabilities need to be companywide?**	Decide which IT capabilities should be provided centrally and which should be developed by individual businesses.	Excessive technical and process standardization limit the flexibility of business units, or frequent exceptions to the standards increase costs and limit business synergies.
● **How good do our IT services really need to be?**	Decide which features—for example, enhanced reliability or response time—are needed on the basis of their costs and benefits.	The company may pay for service options that, given its priorities, aren't worth their costs.
● **What security and privacy risks will we accept?**	Lead the decision making on the trade-offs between security and privacy on one hand and convenience on the other.	An overemphasis on security and privacy may inconvenience customers, employees, and suppliers; an underemphasis may make data vulnerable.
● **Whom do we blame if an IT initiative fails?**	Assign a business executive to be accountable for every IT project; monitor business metrics.	The business value of systems is never realized.

Source: Jeanne W. Ross and Peter Weill, "Six IT Decisions Your IT People Shouldn't Make," *Harvard Business Review*, November 2002, p. 87.

require managers to be involved in IT decisions that affect their business units. This helps managers avoid IS performance problems in their business units and development projects. With this high degree of involvement, managers can improve the strategic business value of information technology [19]. Also, as we said in Chapter 10, the problems of employee resistance and poor user interface design can only be solved by direct end user participation in systems development projects. Overseeing such involvement is another vital management task.

SECTION II Managing Global IT

The International Dimension

Whether they are in Berlin or Bombay, Kuala Lumpur or Kansas, San Francisco or Seoul, companies around the globe are developing new models to operate competitively in a digital economy. These models are structured, yet agile; global, yet local; and they concentrate on maximizing the risk-adjusted return from both knowledge and technology assets [10].

Thus, international dimensions have become a vital part of managing a business enterprise in the internetworked global economies and markets of today. Whether you become a manager in a large corporation or the owner of a small business, you will be affected by international business developments, and deal in some way with people, products, or services whose origin is not from your home country.

Analyzing Global Exchange Services and Allstate

Read the Real World Case on Global Exchange Services and Allstate on the next page. We can learn a lot about the benefits and challenges of offshore systems development from this case. See Figure 12.9.

Global Exchange Services and Allstate are among a small group of U.S. companies who are sending major parts of their systems development work offshore to software developers in other countries, but accomplishing the work by establishing and staffing their own IT development centers in these countries. In this way, the companies are getting the benefits of a major reduction in wage costs, while still retaining control of the software development process and the developers of its business application software. Thus GSX shifts a major amount of its software development to its development center in Bangalore, India, while Allstate depends heavily on the software development

FIGURE 12.9

Tasos Tsolakis is senior vice president of global technology for Global Exchange Services, and oversees the company's development centers in the United States and Bangalore, India.

Source: Chris Hartlove

REAL WORLD CASE 2

Global Exchange Services and Allstate: Challenges and Solutions in Offshore Systems Development

Cost pressures top just about every company's list of reasons for sending greater amounts of IT work offshore. IT labor rates in India, the Philippines, and elsewhere are as much as 70 percent lower than those in the United States. As such, they're simply too compelling to ignore, IT executives say. But equally compelling is the potential of losing control over foreign technology workers and the quality of IT projects based thousands of miles away. So Allstate Insurance Co. and Global Exchange Services Inc. (GXS) are among a small group of U.S.-based Fortune 500 companies that have set up and staffed their own IT centers in lower-cost countries like India, Ireland, India, and Hungary to address the twin issues of cost and control.

GXS. In this "offshore-insourcing" model, foreign IT workers aren't contractors but employees of the U.S.-based companies. They receive the same training, use the same software development tools, and adhere to the same business processes as their IT counterparts in the United States. The big difference is that they're paid a lot less. For example, for every $100 that GXS (www.gxs.com) spends on an IT employee in the U.S., it spends just $30 on an employee in Bangalore, India, where it employs 230 IT workers. "Manila is even less expensive—perhaps 30 to 40 percent less than India," says Tasos Tsolakis, senior vice president of global technology at GXS.

By shifting about 70 percent of GXS's internal IT projects and 40 percent of its IT work on customer-facing applications to offshore centers, Tsolakis estimates that he has saved about $16 million a year for the past three years. At the same time, he says, GXS has been able to ensure quality and meet software delivery deadlines, because the offshore employees and projects are managed using the same quality control processes that the company applies in the United States.

"Clearly, the labor rate is the big driver for hiring employees abroad, but you need to treat them like your regular U.S.-based teams. Every development tool and testing tool I have here, my resources in Bangalore have. It's critical that they feel a part of your team. They're first-class citizens like everyone else is," Tsolakis says, adding, "That's how you can really create synergies and optimize resources."

Allstate. Allstate (www.allstate.com) has 650 offshore IT employees who work in Belfast and Londonderry in Northern Ireland. The centers in those cities were set up in 1998 and 1999, respectively, as a result of the IT labor shortage in the United States caused largely by a crush of Y2K work and the then-thriving dot-com economy. "We had an additional issue in that we had a large number of software contractors working for us here in Chicago and they were extremely expensive. With the labor crunch and Y2K, we had a ratio of 50 percent of contractors who were constantly leaving for higher-paying jobs," recalls Mike Scardino, assistant vice

president for finance at Allstate. Cost savings was one of the big advantages of hiring offshore employees, and it remains so.

The company is also retaining critical business knowledge and intellectual capital that used to walk out the door with departing IT contractors. "In the insurance business, there's a tremendous amount of business knowledge that goes with programmers. You can't just bring somebody in who knows Cobol," Scardino says. "Now, the business knowledge stays with the employees. That's a huge benefit and a big driver in terms of our ability to maintain our existing applications and to develop new ones."

GXS. Keeping U.S.-based IT workers informed of the company's plans for distributing various IT projects is a critical component of managing onshore/offshore IT groups. "The U.S. teams ask, 'What's the future for me, and why should I stay if you're moving work offshore?' " says Tsolakis. "You need to give an overall direction and plan. It's important to address this upfront. If you don't do that, you end up losing some key resources that you don't want to lose."

Tsolakis also says that on-site management, preferably by a local national, works best at offshore regional IT centers. GXS's Bangalore facility is managed by an Indian executive who reports directly to Tsolakis. "We have a whole infrastructure, including an HR person in Bangalore helping with recruiting and a finance person. This is because it's important to mesh the local culture with the U.S. culture," he says.

Allstate. For IT executives considering setting up and staffing an offshore IT center, Scardino advises that they first make "sure the economics of the local environment are sustainable, that there's talent, that there's a quality workforce and that those things aren't going to change." For all of these reasons, Northern Ireland was an ideal location for Allstate, Scardino says. "And part of the success of being in Northern Ireland is also because people in the United States are willing and able to go there. Routinely, we have people on the ground over there and people from Northern Ireland are over here," he says.

Case Study Questions

1. What are the business benefits and limitations of sending software development offshore? Use the companies in this case as examples.

2. What is the business value and limitations of the insourcing model of offshore software development? Use GSX and Allstate as examples.

3. Should U.S companies send their software development and other IT functions offshore? Why or why not?

Sources: Adapted from Julia King, "The Best of Both Shores," *Computerworld*, April 21, 2003, pp. 37–38; and "IT's Global Itinerary," *Computerworld*, September 15, 2003, pp. 26–27.

FIGURE 12.10

The major dimensions of global e-business technology management.

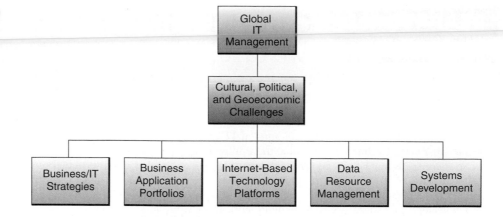

work of its development center that it established in Northern Ireland. Both companies emphasize involving both their U.S. and offshore developers in the management of the software development process through programs of communication, consultation, and professional travel.

Global IT Management

Figure 12.10 illustrates the major dimensions of the job of managing global information technology that we will cover in this section. Notice that all global IT activities must be adjusted to take into account the cultural, political, and geoeconomic challenges that exist in the international business community. Developing appropriate business and IT strategies for the global marketplace should be the first step in **global information technology management.** Once that is done, end user and IS managers can move on to developing the portfolio of business applications needed to support business/IT strategies; the hardware, software, and Internet-based technology platforms to support those applications; the data resource management methods to provide necessary databases; and finally the systems development projects that will produce the global information systems required.

Cendant Corp.: Global IT Management

Lawrence Kinder faced a typical kind of global challenge. He is executive vice president and CIO with global responsibility for IT at Cendant Corp., which recently acquired Avis Group holdings. His company, a service and information provider for automotive transportation and vehicle management in Garden City, New York, grew internationally in 1999 by acquiring the U.K.'s PHH Vehicle Management Services, the world's second-largest vehicle leasing and fleet management company, and Wright Express LLC, the world's largest credit card and information services provider.

"We grew organically in North America and built a solid and stable IT foundation that we have been able to leverage in Europe," Kinder says. The key is to take the time to understand the day-to-day workings of each local IT group, he says, and to put strategic IT planning on the back burner until all groups can focus on leveraging their cultures and talents.

Kinder says he regularly brings together company leaders with similar roles from the United States, Canada, and Europe to "give each other a shot of adrenaline." He says developing and supporting global businesses is more demanding than supporting time to do strategic planning. But, he says, "Giving my global IT leaders the opportunity to think more broadly about their applications and solve international business problems has created a true learning organization" [14].

Cultural, Political, and Geoeconomic Challenges

"Business as usual" is not good enough in global business operations. The same holds true for global e-business technology management. There are too many cultural, political, and geoeconomic (geographic and economic) realities that must be confronted in order for a business to succeed in global markets. As we have just said, global information technology management must focus on developing global business IT strategies and managing global e-business application portfolios, Internet technologies, platforms, databases, and systems development projects. But managers must also accomplish that from a perspective and through methods that take into account the cultural, political, and geoeconomic differences that exist when doing business internationally.

For example, a major **political challenge** is that many countries have rules regulating or prohibiting transfer of data across their national boundaries (transborder data flows), especially personal information such as personnel records. Others severely restrict, tax, or prohibit imports of hardware and software. Still others have local content laws that specify the portion of the value of a product that must be added in that country if it is to be sold there. Other countries have reciprocal trade agreements that require a business to spend part of the revenue they earn in a country in that nation's economy [17].

Geoeconomic challenges in global business and IT refer to the effects of geography on the economic realities of international business activities. The sheer physical distances involved are still a major problem, even in this day of Internet telecommunications and jet travel. For example, it may still take too long to fly in specialists when IT problems occur in a remote site. It is still difficult to communicate in real time across the world's 24 time zones. It is still difficult to get good-quality telephone and telecommunications service in many countries. There are still problems finding the job skills required in some countries, or enticing specialists from other countries to live and work there. Finally, there are still problems (and opportunities) in the great differences in the cost of living and labor costs in various countries. All of these geoeconomic challenges must be addressed when developing a company's global business and IT strategies.

Cultural challenges facing global business and IT managers include differences in languages, cultural interests, religions, customs, social attitudes, and political philosophies. Obviously, global IT managers must be trained and sensitized to such cultural differences before they are sent abroad or brought into a corporation's home country. Other cultural challenges include differences in work styles and business relationships. For example, should one take one's time to avoid mistakes, or hurry to get something done early? Should one go it alone or work cooperatively? Should the most experienced person lead, or should leadership be shared? The answers to such questions depend on the culture you are in and highlight the cultural differences that might exist in the global workplace. Let's take a look at a real world example involving the global IT talent pool.

Global Competition for IT Talent

Opportunity for professional growth is a major element of the competition between global businesses and governments for IT talent. Many IT workers understand that their résumé is their most important asset and seek out positions where they can work with modern or leading-edge technologies. While many countries offer opportunities to work in emerging technologies, the United States leads in the sheer number and variety of IT jobs working with résumé-enhancing technologies. The question that faces policy makers in other countries is where their nation has room to improve their competitiveness by attracting or retaining skilled IT talent.

Australia, for example, has a literate and affluent population, with higher Internet use than the United States, but lacks the market size and concentration of investment capital to compete with the United States in providing IT employment opportunities. As a result, there are thousands of Australians working in Silicon Valley despite a shortage of over 30,000 IT professionals at home. Some Latin American and many other countries suffer because of their limited telecommunications infrastructures. While countries like Chile have modern systems with competitive telecommunications pricing and Internet access, others have government-run telephone companies with service levels that don't support modern e-commerce development. For example, in some countries, dedicated Internet connections are not available and all telephone calls, including Internet connectivity, are priced by the duration of the connection.

With worldwide competition for IT professionals and unprecedented mobility in the IT workforce it seems that the best method for attracting or retaining IT workers involves the development of an overall program of economic, social, and technical opportunity. India and China, for example, seem to be experiencing a reverse brain drain as experienced IT professionals return home to take leadership roles in new ventures. Increased domestic demand, fueled by a combination of new domestic software needs, increased Internet connectivity, new e-commerce ventures, and local software shops developing for foreign customers, are all attracting experienced managers and entrepreneurs back home and providing rewarding employment for local entry-level technologists.

Canada, Japan, and even India have all taken recent steps to facilitate the entry of foreign professional workers, especially IT specialists. Australia and New Zealand recruit foreign professionals, including those from the United States, by promoting the natural beauty of their countries and the relaxed lifestyles. Australia has considered easing the immigration process for IT specialists and has already relaxed its rules for foreign students who wish to remain to work. Other countries are taking steps to address the outflow of companies and talented individuals.

Thus, Costa Rica has parlayed political stability, a growing educational infrastructure, and an aggressive program to recruit foreign firms such as Intel into an unemployment rate less than 5 percent and wage and job opportunities that tend to keep talented citizens at home. And Trinidad and Tobago have created a foreign investment zone aimed at high-tech industries and have eliminated import duties on computer equipment in an attempt to increase foreign investment and encourage a generation of domestic computer users [25].

Global Business/IT Strategies

Figure 12.11 illustrates that many firms are moving toward **transnational strategies** in which they integrate their global business/IT activities through close cooperation and interdependence among their international subsidiaries and their corporate headquarters [16]. Businesses are moving away from (1) multinational strategies where foreign subsidiaries operate autonomously; (2) international strategies in which foreign subsidiaries are autonomous but are dependent on headquarters for new processes, products, and ideas; or (3) global strategies, where a company's worldwide operations are closely managed by corporate headquarters.

In the transnational approach, a business depends heavily on its information systems and Internet technologies to help it integrate its global business activities. Instead of having independent IS units at its subsidiaries, or even a centralized IS operation directed from its headquarters, a transnational business tries to develop an integrated and cooperative worldwide hardware, software, and Internet-based architecture for its IT platform. Figure 12.12 illustrates how transnational business and IT strategies were implemented by global companies [24].

Global Business/IT Applications

The applications of information technology developed by global companies depend on their business and IT strategies and their expertise and experience in IT. However, their IT applications also depend on a variety of **global business drivers,** that is, business requirements caused by the nature of the industry and its competitive or environmental forces. One example would be companies like airlines or hotel chains that have

FIGURE 12.11 Companies operating internationally are moving toward transnational business and IT strategies. Note some of the chief differences between international, global, and transnational business and IT strategies.

Comparing Global Business/IT Strategies		
International	**Global**	**Transnational**
• Autonomous operations.	• Global sourcing.	• Virtual business operations via global alliances.
• Region specific.	• Multiregional.	• World markets and mass customization.
• Vertical integration.	• Horizontal integration.	
• Specific customers.	• Some transparency of customers and production.	• Global e-commerce and customer service.
• Captive manufacturing.	• Some cross regionalization.	• Transparent manufacturing.
• Customer segmentation and dedication by region and plant.		• Global supply chain and logistics.
		• Dynamic resource management.
Information Technology Characteristics		
• Stand-alone systems.	• Regional decentralization.	• Logically consolidated, physically distributed, Internet connected.
• Decentralized/no standards.	• Interface dependent.	• Common global data resources.
• Heavy reliance on interfaces.	• Some consolidation of applications and use of common systems.	• Integrated global enterprise systems.
• Multiple systems, high redundancy and duplication of services and operations.	• Reduced duplication of operations.	• Internet, intranet, extranet Web-based applications.
• Lack of common systems and data.	• Some worldwide IT standards.	• Transnational IT policies and standards.

FIGURE 12.12 Examples of how transnational business and IT strategies were implemented by global companies.

Tactic	Global Alliances	Global Sourcing and Logistics	Global Customer Service
Examples	British Airways / US Air KLM / Northwest Qantas / American	Benetton	American Express
IT Environment	Global network (online reservation system)	Global network, EPOS terminals in 4,000 stores, CAD/CAM in central manufacturing, robots and laser scanner in their automated warehouse	Global network linked from local branches and local merchants to the customer database and medical or legal referrals database
Results	○ Coordination of schedules ○ Code sharing ○ Coordination of flights ○ Co-ownership	○ Produce 2,000 sweaters per hour using CAD/CAM ○ Quick response (in stores in 10 days) ○ Reduced inventories (just-in-time)	○ Worldwide access to funds ○ "Global Assist" hotline ○ Emergency credit card replacement ○ 24-hour customer service

FIGURE 12.13

These are some of the business reasons driving global business applications.

Business Drivers for Global IT
● **Global customers.** Customers are people who may travel anywhere or companies with global operations. Global IT can help provide fast, convenient service.
● **Global products.** Products are the same throughout the world or are assembled by subsidiaries throughout the world. Global IT can help manage worldwide marketing and quality control.
● **Global operations.** Parts of a production or assembly process are assigned to subsidiaries based on changing economic or other conditions. Only global IT can support such geographic flexibility.
● **Global resources.** The use and cost of common equipment, facilities, and people are shared by subsidiaries of a global company. Global IT can keep track of such shared resources.
● **Global collaboration.** The knowledge and expertise of colleagues in a global company can be quickly accessed, shared, and organized to support individual or group efforts. Only global IT can support such enterprise collaboration.

global customers, that is, customers who travel widely or have global operations. Such companies will need global IT capabilities for online transaction processing so they can provide fast, convenient service to their customers or face losing them to their competitors. The economies of scale provided by global business operations are other business drivers that require the support of global IT applications. Figure 12.13 summarizes some of the business requirements that make global IT a competitive necessity [9].

Of course, many global IT applications, particularly finance, accounting, and office applications, have been in operation for many years. For example, most multinational companies have global financial budgeting and cash management systems, and office automation applications such as fax and e-mail systems. However, as global operations expand and global competition heats up, there is increasing pressure for companies to install global e-commerce and e-business applications for their customers and suppliers. Examples include global e-commerce websites and customer service systems for customers and global supply chain management systems for suppliers. In the past, such systems relied almost exclusively on privately constructed or government-owned telecommunications networks. But the explosive business use of the Internet, intranets, and extranets for electronic commerce has made such applications much more feasible for global companies.

TRW Inc: Global Business/IT Challenges

In the world of global IT operations, timing is everything. And so is knowing the ropes of the country you're in. Take, for example, Cleveland-based TRW Inc., a $17 billion technology, manufacturing, and services company with operations in 35 countries. When TRW's plant in Poland experiences a problem with its enterprise resource planning system or its global wide area network, the first wave of support comes from the local IT team. If that group is unsuccessful in righting the situation, backup is called in from a second team and even a third in the same time zone in either the U.K. or Germany.

Speed is of the essence, and local support means faster access to end users and resources, such as service providers, telephone companies, and equipment. This clustering of quick-response IT support team by time zones and proximity is just one of the lessons learned by Mostafa Mehrabani, who has served as vice president and CIO at TRW for three years and for the past two years has developed the company's global IT operations.

"For a while, we were trying to perform day-to-day support of LANs and IT development for our Asian operations from the U.S.," he says. "We came to the conclusion that while you can get someone on the phone, it isn't the same as being there and understanding the culture." So TRW developed centers of excellence, which are groups of subject-matter experts who assist employees throughout the company with their problems and requirements. "Often, we don't have the luxury of certain technical expertise in every part of the world, and we don't have the need for full-time experts in every region. Pooling resources to solve global IT issues is a major advantage." says Mehrabani [14].

Global IT Platforms

The management of technology platforms (also called the technology infrastructure) is another major dimension of global IT management—that is, managing the hardware, software, data resources, telecommunications networks, and computing facilities that support global business operations. The management of a global IT platform is not only technically complex but also has major political and cultural implications.

For example, hardware choices are difficult in some countries because of high prices, high tariffs, import restrictions, long lead times for government approvals, lack of local service or spare parts, and lack of documentation tailored to local conditions. Software choices can also present unique problems. Software packages developed in Europe may be incompatible with American or Asian versions, even when purchased from the same hardware vendor. Well-known U.S. software packages may be unavailable because there is no local distributor, or because the software publisher refuses to supply markets that disregard software licensing and copyright agreements [9].

Managing international data communications networks, including Internet, intranet, extranet, and other networks, is a key global IT challenge. Figure 12.14 outlines the top ten international data communications issues as reported by the IS executives at 300 Fortune 500 multinational companies. Notice how political issues dominate the top ten listing over technology issues, clearly emphasizing their importance in the management of global telecommunications.

FIGURE 12.14

The top ten issues in managing international data communications.

International Data Communications Issues
Network management issues
● Improving the operational efficiency of networks
● Dealing with different networks
● Controlling data communication security
Regulatory issues
● Dealing with transborder data flow restrictions
● Managing international telecommunication regulations
● Handling international politics
Technology issues
● Managing network infrastructure across countries
● Managing international integration of technologies
Country-oriented issues
● Reconciling national differences
● Dealing with international tariff structures

Source: Adapted from Vincent S. Lai and Wingyan Chung, "Managing International Data Communications," *Communications of the ACM*, March 2002, p. 91.

Establishing computing facilities internationally is another global challenge. Companies with global business operations usually establish or contract with systems integrators for additional data centers in their subsidiaries in other countries. These data centers meet local and regional computing needs, and even help balance global computing workloads through communications satellite links. However, offshore data centers can pose major problems in headquarter's support, hardware and software acquisition, maintenance, and security. That's why many global companies turn to application service providers or systems integrators like EDS or IBM to manage their overseas operations.

Citibank: Consolidating Global IT Platforms

A $100 million-plus global IT consolidation project is enabling Citibank (www.citibank.com) to replace a decades-old set of back-office corporate banking systems in all of its overseas corporate offices with a single global system with standard user interfaces and business processes. The New York–based bank has already completed changeover projects in the Asia-Pacific region, Western and Eastern Europe, and Latin America. The changeover, which began in early 2000, is expected to continue through 2004. There are still rollouts to be completed in more than 100 countries.

The bank said the project will pay for itself by letting the company avoid development costs related to a clunky legacy back-office system. Developed in-house in the 1970s, the old system has morphed into 58 disparate software applications, said Jeff Berg, executive director of program management at Citibank's parent, New York–based Citigroup Inc. "In the '70s, we were growing rapidly in countries around the world. To get up and running quickly, we'd use this system called Cosmos (Consolidated Online Modulated Operating System)," Berg said. "As the bank grew, we did make a mistake in that we released the source code to each of the countries, and they changed it."

Berg said Citibank now has a single system that's customized for each country it operates in, using each nation's language, regulatory rules, and business processes. Berg said Citibank plans to reduce the number of its data centers in Europe from 18 to about 4 by standardizing on the new banking software from i-Flex Solutions Inc. in Bangalore, India. The bank anticipates an 18-month return on investment, said Berg. The software, called Flexcube, is based on an Oracle database. It automates the general ledger as well as customer accounting, deposits and withdrawals, and interest on accounts, among other services. Citibank will be able to simply change parameters in the new software to incorporate a particular country's language, regulations, and currency conversions [15].

The Internet as a Global IT Platform

What makes the Internet and the World Wide Web so important for international business? This interconnected matrix of computers, information, and networks that reaches tens of millions of users in over one hundred countries is a business environment free of traditional boundaries and limits. Linking to an online global infrastructure offers companies unprecedented potential for expanding markets, reducing costs, and improving profit margins at a price that is typically a small percentage of the corporate communications budget. The Internet provides an interactive channel for direct communication and data exchange with customers, suppliers, distributors, manufacturers, product developers, financial backers, information providers—in fact, with all parties involved in a given business venture [3].

So the Internet and the World Wide Web have now become vital components in international business and commerce. Within a few years, the Internet, with its interconnected network of thousands of networks of computers and databases, has established itself as a technology platform free of many traditional international boundaries and limits. By connecting their businesses to this online global infrastructure, companies can expand their markets, reduce communications and distribution costs,

FIGURE 12.15

Key questions for companies establishing global Internet websites.

Key Questions for Global Websites
• Will you have to develop a new navigational logic to accommodate cultural preferences?
• What content will you translate, and what content will you create from scratch to address regional competitors or products that differ from those in the United States?
• Should your multilingual effort be an adjunct to your main site, or will you make it a separate site, perhaps with a country-specific domain name?
• What kinds of traditional and new media advertising will you have to do in each country to draw traffic to your site?
• Will your site get so many hits that you'll need to set up a server in a local country?
• What are the legal ramifications of having your website targeted at a particular country, such as laws on competitive behavior, treatment of children, or privacy?

and improve their profit margins without massive cost outlays for new telecommunications facilities. Figure 12.15 outlines key considerations for global e-commerce websites [13].

The Internet, along with its related intranet and extranet technologies, provides a low-cost interactive channel for communications and data exchange with employees, customers, suppliers, distributors, manufacturers, product developers, financial backers, information providers, and so on. In fact, all parties involved can use the Internet and other related networks to communicate and collaborate to bring a business venture to its successful completion. However, as Figure 12.16 illustrates, much work needs to be done to bring secure Internet access and electronic commerce to more people in more countries. But the trend is clearly on continued expansion of the Internet as it becomes a pervasive IT platform for global business.

Global Data Access Issues

Global data access issues have been a subject of political controversy and technology barriers in global business operations for many years, but have become more visible with the growth of the Internet and the pressures of e-commerce. A major example is the issue of **transborder data flows** (TDF), in which business data flow across international borders over the telecommunications networks of global information systems. Many countries view TDF as violating their national sovereignty because transborder data flows avoid customs duties and regulations for the import or export of goods and services. Others view transborder data flows as violating their laws to protect the local IT industry from competition, or their labor regulations for protecting local jobs. In

FIGURE 12.16 Current numbers of Internet users by world region.

World Regions	Population (2003)	Usage (Year 2000)	Usage (Year 2003)	(%) of Total	Growth (2000–2003)	% Populations (Penetration)
Africa	879,855,500	4,514,400	8,073,500	1.2%	78.8%	0.9%
America	864,854,400	126,157,000	228,768,058	35.1	81.3	26.5
Asia	3,590,196,700	114,303,000	200,319,063	30.7	75.3	5.6
Europe	722,509,070	103,075,900	190,297,994	29.2	84.6	26.3
Middle East	259,318,000	5,272,300	12,019,600	1.8	128.0	4.6
Oceania	31,528,840	7,619,500	13,069,832	2.0	71.3	41.4
World Total	6,348,262,510	360,942,100	652,527,047	100.0	80.8	10.3

Source: Adapted from www.internetworldstats.com

FIGURE 12.17	U.S. – EU Data Privacy Requirements

Key data privacy provisions of the agreement to protect the privacy of consumers in e-commerce transactions between the United States and the European Union.

- Notice of purpose and use of data collected
- Ability to opt out of third-party distribution of data
- Access for consumers to their information
- Adequate security, data integrity, and enforcement provisions

many cases, the data flow business issues that seem especially politically sensitive are those that affect the movement out of a country of personal data in e-commerce and human resource applications.

Many countries, especially those in the European Union, may view transborder data flows as a violation of their privacy legislation since, in many cases, data about individuals are being moved out of the country without stringent privacy safeguards. For example, Figure 12.17 outlines the key provisions of a data privacy agreement between the United States and the European Union [21]. The agreement exempts U.S. companies engaging in international e-commerce from EU data privacy sanctions if they join a self-regulatory program that provides EU consumers with basic information about, and control over, how their personal data are used. Thus, the agreement is said to provide a "safe harbor" for such companies from the requirements of the EU's Data Privacy Directive, which bans the transfer of personal information on EU citizens to countries that do not have adequate data privacy protection [21].

Council of Europe: Global Cybercrime Treaty

Some information technology managers fear that the Council of Europe's controversial cybercrime treaty, which was approved by 26 member states, plus the United States, Canada, Japan, and South Africa in November 2001, will affect their businesses from both a liability and a security perspective. But before getting all worked up over liability issues, American IT leaders need to remember that European nation-states are cooperating with the United States in terms of cyberlegislation and law enforcement, explains Martha Stansell-Gamm, chief of the Computer Crime and Intellectual Property Section at the U.S. Department of Justice (DOJ). Stansell-Gamm was the DOJ's representative in the drafting of the treaty. The United States participated because it has observer status within the Council of Europe.

"We already have many treaties—bilateral and multilateral—on law enforcement matters like extradition, mutual assistance, money laundering, and corruption," she says. "An awful lot of what's going into this treaty is not new; this just combines technology and criminal law and international law."

Just as in other international law enforcement pacts, the primary objective of the treaty is to break the bottlenecks in international cyberinvestigations, says Stansell-Gamm.

The new Convention on Cybercrime treaty contains provisions which regulate illegal access, illegal interception of electronic communications, data interference, system interference, misuse of devices, computer-related forgery and fraud, child pornography, copyright violations, and corporate liability. Treaty backers say it will serve as a foundation for legislation on such issues by the European Union and its member states, and for cooperative agreements with other countries [18].

Internet Access Issues

The Paris-based organization Reporters Without Borders (RSF) reports that there are 45 countries that "restrict their citizens' access to the Internet." At its most fundamental, the struggle between Internet censorship and openness at the national level

FIGURE 12.18

Countries that restrict or forbid Internet access by their citizens.

Global Government Restrictions on Internet Access

- **High Government Access Fees**
  Kazakhstan, Kyrgyzstan

- **Government Monitored Access**
  China, Iran, Saudi Arabia, Azerbaijan, Uzbekistan

- **Government Filtered Access**
  Belarus, Cuba, Iraq, Tunisia, Sierra Leone, Tajikistan, Turkmenistan, Vietnam

- **No Public Access Allowed**
  Burma, Libya, North Korea, Sudan, Syria

revolves around three main means: controlling the conduits, filtering the flows, and punishing the purveyors. In countries such as Burma, Libya, North Korea, Syria, and the countries of Central Asia and the Caucasus, Internet access is either banned or subject to tight limitations through government-controlled ISPs, says the RSF [22].

Figure 12.18 outlines the restrictions to public Internet access by the governments of 20 countries deemed most restrictive by the Paris-based Reporters Without Borders (RSF) [22]. See their website at www.rsf.fr.

So the Internet has become a global battleground over public access to data and information at business and private sites on the World Wide Web. Of course this becomes a business issue because restrictive access policies severely inhibit the growth of e-commerce with such countries. Most of the rest of the world has decided that restricting Internet access is not a viable policy, and in fact, would hurt their countries' opportunities for economic growth and prosperity. Instead, national and international efforts are being made to rate and filter Internet content deemed inappropriate or criminal, such as websites for child pornography or terrorism. In any event, countries that significantly restrict Internet access are also choosing to restrict their participation in the growth of electronic commerce [22].

To RSF and others, these countries' rulers face a lose-lose struggle against the Information Age. By denying or limiting Internet access, they stymie a major engine of economic growth. But by easing access, they expose their citizenry to ideas potentially destabilizing to the status quo. Either way, many people will get access to the electronic information they want. "In Syria, for example, people go to Lebanon for the weekend to retrieve their e-mail," says Virginie Locussol, RSF's desk officer for the Middle East and North Africa [22].

Global Systems Development

Just imagine the challenges of developing efficient, effective, and responsive applications for business end users domestically. Then multiply that by the number of countries and cultures that may use a global e-business system. That's the challenge of managing global systems development. Naturally, there are conflicts over local versus global system requirements, and difficulties in agreeing on common system features such as multilingual user interfaces and flexible design standards. And all of this effort must take place in an environment that promotes involvement and "ownership" of a system by local end users.

Other systems development issues arise from disturbances caused by systems implementation and maintenance activities. For example: "An interruption during a third shift in New York City will present midday service interruptions in Tokyo." Another major development issue relates to the trade-offs between developing one system that can run on multiple computer and operating system platforms, or letting each local site customize the software for its own platform [9].

Other important global systems development issues are concerned with global standardization of data definitions. Common data definitions are necessary for sharing data among the parts of an international business. Differences in language, culture, and technology platforms can make global data standardization quite difficult. For example, a sale may be called "an 'order booked' in the United Kingdom, an 'order scheduled' in Germany, and an 'order produced' in France" [17]. However, businesses are moving ahead to standardize data definitions and structures. By moving their subsidiaries into data modeling and database design, they hope to develop a global data architecture that supports their global business objectives.

Systems Development Strategies

Several strategies can be used to solve some of the systems development problems that arise in global IT. First is transforming an application used by the home office into a global application. However, often the system used by a subsidiary that has the best version of an application will be chosen for global use. Another approach is setting up a *multinational development team* with key people from several subsidiaries to ensure that the system design meets the needs of local sites as well as corporate headquarters.

A third approach is called *parallel development.* That's because parts of the system are assigned to different subsidiaries and the home office to develop at the same time, based on the expertise and experience at each site. Another approach is the concept of *centers of excellence.* In this approach, an entire system may be assigned for development to a particular subsidiary based on their expertise in the business or technical dimensions needed for successful development. A final approach that has rapidly become a major development option is to outsource the development work to global or *offshore* development companies who have the skills and experience required to develop global business/IT applications. Obviously, all of these approaches require development team collaboration and managerial oversight to meet the global needs of a business. So, global systems development teams are making heavy use of the Internet, intranets, groupware, and other electronic collaboration technologies [9]. See Figure 12.19.

FIGURE 12.19

An example of Internet-enabled collaboration in global IT systems development. Note the roles played by the client company, offshore outsource developer, global open-source community, and the just-in-time development team.

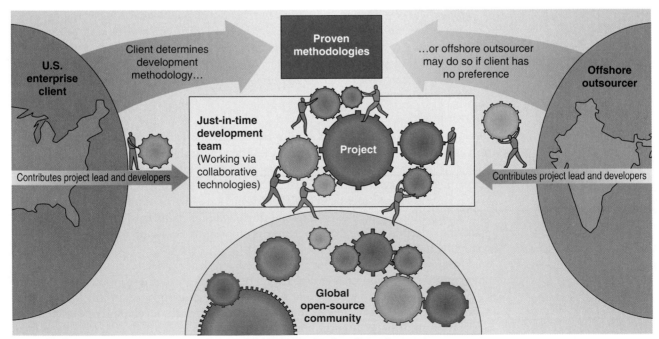

Source: Adapted from Jon Udell. "Leveraging a Global Advantage." *Infoworld*, April 21, 2003, p. 35.

DHL Worldwide: Global Systems Development	San Francisco–based DHL Worldwide Express Inc. has opened development centers in the U.K. and in Malaysia, India, and other parts of Asia. The international delivery giant is able to take advantage of time differences between these locations and California to create an extended workday.

"For us, large-scale development is not a hothouse environment, it's an everyday reality," says Colum Joyce, a global e-business strategy manager based in DHL's offices in Brussels. That means establishing development facilities around the world, as well as working with outsourcers where necessary, he says. These realities, combined with the lower turnover rates and salaries in many foreign countries—the average salary for a skilled programmer in India, for example, is about $30,000, according to Niven—are driving global companies to open offshore facilities.

DHL's offshore developers tailor e-business applications to country-specific requirements and even take lead roles in some development efforts, such as a wireless service applications project that's under way in Europe and Asia. Joyce says the company looks at several factors when hiring in these locations, including the technical and linguistic skills of local workers, long-term business viability, and knowledge transfer. "A mastery of English is a key skill set, as it is the operating language of all cross-group communication for all development, whether it be verbal, hard copy, or electronic communication," Joyce says.

"It is not so much the knowledge but the willingness and flexibility to learn that is important in hiring global IT workers," Joyce explains. "In an incredibly dynamic environment, it is the attitude, rather than gross development capability, that counts the most in recruitment." Nonetheless, Joyce acknowledges that success in such endeavors depends heavily on adopting market standards in technology infrastructures and on ensuring that there's continual communication among development teams in disparate locations. To that end, DHL puts a great deal of effort into developing what Joyce calls "hybrid managers" who are heavily immersed in both IT and business.

"This has been a process we have engaged in for over 15 years," Joyce says. "The boundaries are really transparent now, and managers and personnel are cross-comfortable with the global business and its supporting infrastructure" [6].

Summary

- **Managing Information Technology.** Managing IT can be viewed as having three major components: (1) managing the joint development and implementation of e-business and IT strategies, (2) managing the development of e-business applications and the research and implementation of new information technologies, and (3) managing IT processes, professionals, and subunits within a company's IT organization and IS function.

- **Failures in IT Management.** Information systems are not being used effectively or efficiently by many organizations. The experiences of successful organizations reveal that the basic ingredient of high-quality information system performance is extensive and meaningful management and user involvement in the governance and development of IT applications. Thus, managers may serve on executive IT groups and create IS management functions within their business units.

- **Managing Global IT.** The international dimensions of managing global information technologies include dealing with cultural, political, and geoeconomic challenges posed by various countries; developing appropriate business and IT strategies for the global marketplace; and developing a portfolio of global e-business and e-commerce applications and an Internet-based technology platform to support them. In addition, data access methods have to be developed and systems development projects managed to produce the global e-business applications that are required to compete successfully in the global marketplace.

- **Global Business and IT Strategies and Issues.** Many businesses are becoming global companies and moving toward transnational business strategies in which they integrate the global business activities of their subsidiaries and headquarters. This requires that they develop a global IT platform, that is, an integrated worldwide hardware, software, and Internet-based network architecture. Global companies are increasingly using the Internet and related technologies as a major component of this IT platform to develop and deliver global IT applications that meet their unique global business requirements. Global IT and end user managers must deal with limitations on the availability of hardware and software, restrictions on transborder data flows, Internet access, and movement of personal data, and difficulties with developing common data definitions and system requirements.

Key Terms and Concepts

These are the key terms and concepts of this chapter. The page number of their first explanation is in parentheses.

1. Application development management (427)
2. Centralization or decentralization of IT (425)
3. Chargeback systems (427)
4. Chief information officer (428)
5. Chief technology officer (428)
6. Cultural, political, and geoeconomic challenges (435)
7. Data center (427)
8. Downsizing (425)
9. Failures in IT management (429)
10. Global business drivers (436)

11. Global information technology management (434)
    a. Business/IT applications (436)
    b. Business/IT strategies (436)
    c. Data access issues (441)
    d. IT platforms (439)
    e. Systems development issues (443)
12. Human resource management of IT (428)
13. Internet access issues (442)
14. Internet as a global IT platform (440)
15. Management involvement in IT (430)

16. Managing information technology (422)
17. Managing the IS function (425)
18. Operations management (427)
19. Outsourcing IS operations (426)
20. System performance monitor (427)
21. Technology management (429)
22. Transborder data flows (441)
23. Transnational strategy (436)
24. User services (429)

Review Quiz

Match one of the key terms and concepts listed previously with one of the brief examples or definitions that follow. Try to find the best fit for the answers that seem to fit more than one term or concept. Defend your choices.

_____ 1. Information systems have not been used efficiently or effectively.

_____ 2. An executive IT council is an example.

_____ 3. Managing business/IT planning and the IS function within a company.

_____ 4. Managing application development, data center operations, and user services are examples.

_____ 5. Many IT organizations have centralized and decentralized units.

_____ 6. Managing the creation and implementation of new business applications.

_____ 7. End users need liaison, consulting, and training services.

_____ 8. Planning and controlling data center operations.

_____ 9. Corporate locations for computer system operations.

_____ 10. Rapidly changing technological developments must be anticipated, identified, and implemented.

_____ 11. Recruiting and developing IT professionals.

_____ 12. The executive responsible for strategic business/IT planning and management.

_____ 13. The executive in charge of researching and implementing new information technologies.

_____ 14. Software that helps monitor and control computer systems in a data center.

_____ 15. The cost of IS services may be allocated back to end users.

_____ 16. Many business firms are replacing their mainframe systems with networked PCs and servers.

_____ 17. Using outside contractors to provide and manage IS operations.

_____ 18. Managing IT to support a company's international business operations.

_____ 19. Integrating global business activities through cooperation among international subsidiaries and corporate headquarters.

_____ 20. Differences in customs, governmental regulations, and the cost of living are examples.

_____ 21. Global customers, products, operations, resources, and collaboration.

_____ 22. Applying IT to global e-commerce systems is an example.

_____ 23. The goal of some organizations is to develop integrated Internet-based networks for global electronic commerce.

_____ 24. Transborder data flows and security of personal databases are top concerns.

_____ 25. Standardizing global use of computer systems, software packages, telecommunications networks, and computing facilities is an example.

_____ 26. The Internet is a natural global networking choice.

_____ 27. Global telecommunications networks like the Internet move data across national boundaries.

_____ 28. Some countries deny or limit Internet access.

_____ 29. Agreement is needed on common user interfaces and website design features in global IT.

Discussion Questions

1. What has been the impact of information technologies on the work relationships, activities, and resources of managers?

2. What can business unit managers do about performance problems in the use of information technology and the development and operation of information systems in their business units?

3. Refer to the Real World Case on the Chicago Board of Trade in the chapter. What role should a company's executives and business unit managers play in managing the IT function in a business? Why?

4. How are Internet technologies affecting the structure and work roles of modern organizations? For example, will middle management wither away? Will companies consist primarily of self directed project teams of knowledge workers? Explain your answers.

5. Should the IS function in a business be centralized or decentralized? What recent developments support your answer?

6. Refer to the Real World Case on Global Exchange Services and Allstate in the chapter. What ethical and societal issues should the management of companies

consider when making offshore outsourcing or insourcing decisions? Give several examples to illustrate your answer.

7. How will the Internet, intranets, and extranets affect each of the components of global information technology management, as illustrated in Figure 12.10? Give several examples.

8. How might cultural, political, or geoeconomic challenges affect a global company's use of the Internet? Give several examples.

9. Will the increasing use of the Internet by firms with global business operations change their move toward a transnational business strategy? Explain.

10. How might the Internet, intranets, and extranets affect the business drivers or requirements responsible for a company's use of global IT, as shown in Figure 12.13? Give several examples to illustrate your answer.

Analysis Exercises

1. **CEO Express: Top-Rated Websites for Executives**
   Check out this top-rated site *(www.ceoexpress.com)* for busy executives. See Figure 12.20. Membership is free and open to students and professors, too. The site provides links to top U.S. and international newspapers, businesses and technology magazines, and news services. Hundreds of links to business and technology research sources and references are provided as well as travel services, online shopping, and recreational websites.

   a. Evaluate the CEO Express website as a source of useful links to business and technology news, analysis, and research sources for business executives and professionals.

   b. Compare CEO Express with Google News (news.google.com). What advantages does CEO Express provide?

   c. Report on one item of business or IT news, analysis, or research that might have value for your present or future career in business.

2. **The World Bank: Global Information & Communications Technology**
   The World Bank Group's Global Information & Communication Technologies Department (GICT) plays an important role in developing and promoting access to information and communications technologies (ICT) in developing countries. See Figure 12.21.

FIGURE 12.20

The CEO Express website.

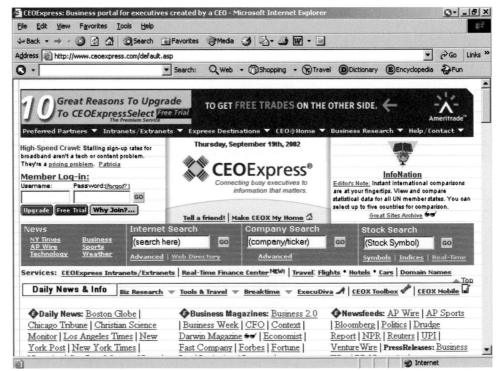

Source: Courtesy of CEO Express.

FIGURE 12.21

The website of the World Bank's Global Information and Communications Technologies Department.

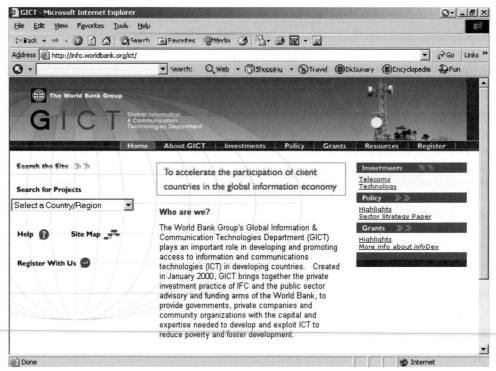

Source: Courtesy of info.worldbank.org/ict.

GICT brings together the private investment practice of the International Finance Corporation and the public sector advisory and funding arms of the World Bank to provide governments, private companies, and community organizations with the capital and expertise needed to develop and exploit information and communications technologies to accelerate the participation of all countries in the global information economy and thus reduce poverty and foster economic and social development.

a. Explore the World Bank's GICT website at *www.worldbank.org/ict* and investigate several of their projects to help countries participate in the global information economy.

b. Evaluate the effectiveness of two of the GICT's projects. Explain the reasons for your evaluations.

3. **U.S. Electronic Shopping and Mail-Order Houses**
The U.S. Census Bureau surveyed e-commerce and mail order shopping houses in its "Annual Retail Trade Survey" and made the data from 1999 through 2001 available online. The U.S. Census Bureau surveys many different facets of the U.S. economy and makes this information freely available. Knowledge workers can mine this data for useful information.

Download the original U.S. Census Bureau's spreadsheet from *www.census.gov* or the McGraw-Hill PowerWeb website for Management Information Systems. The "Total" columns represent retail sales in millions. The "e-commerce" columns represent the portion of retail sales generated through e-commerce in millions.

a. Using the spreadsheet and data provided calculate the growth rates for e-commerce-based trade and trade not based on e-commerce.

b. Prepare a one page paper analyzing e-commerce trends. In your paper, identify the merchandise line that is experiencing the largest growth in e-commerce sales. Using your own experience or additional research, speculate on what makes this merchandise line so different from the three merchandise lines experiencing the least growth.

Data source: U.S. Census Bureau, Annual Retail Trade Survey

4. **Quarterly Retail and e-Commerce Sales**
The U.S. Census Bureau has conducted quarterly retail and e-commerce sales surveys since 1999 and makes the data available online.

Download the original U.S. Census Bureau's data from *www.census.gov* or the McGraw-Hill PowerWeb website for Management Information Systems. The "Total" column represents retail sales in millions. The "e-commerce" column represents the portion of retails sales generated through e-commerce (also in millions). By using simple spreadsheet tools, one can gain some interesting insights from this data set.

a. Using spreadsheet software, plot the data sets for e-commerce sales and non-e-commerce retail sales. Make a line graph presenting both data sets together.

Be sure to subtract the e-commerce data from the retail sales data in order to calculate non-e-commerce sales amounts for each quarter. Briefly summarize what you notice just from looking at a graphical representation of this data.

b. Create linear regression models for both e-commerce and for non-e-commerce data sets. The function LINEST in MS Excel will provide the appropriate results. Using your models, create matching data sets and graph these together with your original data sets. Briefly summarize insights these tools helped you gain about the data.

c. Create exponential regression models for both e-commerce and for non-e-commerce data sets. The function LOGEST in MS Excel will provide the appropriate results. Using your models, create matching data sets and graph these together with your original data sets. Calculate the standard deviations for your original data sets. Briefly summarize insights these tools helped you gain about the data.

Data source: U.S. Census Bureau, Estimated Quarterly U.S. Retail Sales: Total and E-commerce

REAL WORLD CASE 3

Bio-ERA and Burlington Northern Santa Fe: The Business Case for Global Collaborative Development

When Stephen Aldridge, CEO of the Bio Economic Research Association (www.bioera.net), also known as Bio-ERA, needed help earlier this year developing a Web portal and its associated applications, he called on Assembla, a small software development company in Needham, Massachusetts. From Assembla, the call went out and a geographically dispersed team of developers came together almost immediately. Andy Singleton, Assembla founder, brought together and managed developers in Ekateringburg, Russia, who worked with Bio-ERA employees in the United States. The far-flung team collaborated by using the open-source portal development software XOOP (extensible Object Oriented Portal) in conjunction with the project management software tool PowerSteering, developing and launching the portal within weeks.

The project amounted to a radically different way to build software and foreshadows the future of a distributed global collaborative model of software development. Low-cost application development talent is located around the world, and with Internet-based, open-source tools available for collaborative application development, teams can now come together quickly to get a job done. Thus, Burlington Northern Santa Fe (www.bnsf.com), in Fort Worth, Texas, collaborates with offshore outsourcer Infosys Technologies in Bangalore, India. And Sun Microsystems, in Sunnyvale, California, is nurturing an open-source development project for its StarOffice suite with the help of Web-based collaborative development software from CollabNet, Inc.

For IT executives seeking to avoid the complex tasks of software development, the ability to form just-in-time teams using outsourced talent allows them to concentrate on running their core businesses. "As we generate more and more people educated in writing code, and as we see the practicality of using such software-capable people from around the world because of the capability of Internet-based collaborative networks, it seems apparent that the use of distributed application development is inevitable," says Christopher Myer, a former director at Cap Gemini Ernst & Young.

Bio-ERA. At Bio-ERA, a new Cambridge, Massachusetts-based life sciences research company, Aldridge says he needed a third party like Assembla that could locate, organize, and manage talent while his portal plans took shape. "You have to have an IT manager, someone who understands software development and has experience managing a distributed team and a platform," the CEO says. With the worldwide increase in the number of software developers and the establishment of outsourcing organizations "there's been a sea of change in the availability of development talent," Aldridge says. The team of Russian and Bio-ERA developers was assembled within days. "I had a business need. I needed to get a website portal built that had a certain number of features," Aldridge says. "I wanted it fast and cheap."

"We needed someone like Andy Singleton of Assembla, who was good at taking a business request and parsing it out into a software-development project and making it a work-managed project using a tool like PowerSteering, which has collaborative features and project management features," Aldridge adds. "And the guys in Russia and Andy, and me and my guys can go to it. And if we have an issue we can raise it."

Burlington Northern Santa Fe. Distributed application development—a component of the dynamic-development model—can also offer significant benefits to large enterprises, many of which look to offshore outsourcers to handle a major share of their development work. For example, at Burlington Northern Santa Fe, CIO Jeff Campbell says the railroad company began contracting in 2001 with offshore outsourcer Infosys Technologies. Infosys' work for BNSF includes as much as 40 percent of BNSF s application development initiatives and other computing needs. But as much as 25 percent of the Infosys workload is actually done stateside. The talent is in place for any ad-hoc jobs that may arise.

With just-in-time assembly of teams, Campbell turned to Infosys for help setting up an important IT management project soon after he was promoted from chief IT sourcing officer to CIO last October. "My pager was going off 24 hours a day with IT work requests. I had to worry about on-time delivery of services, budget, and management skills," Campbell says. "I decided I needed a Web-based balanced scorecard tool. I had a niche need and I was able to go out to an offshore developer and quickly start on the project."

Campbell met with his BNSF developers and with the Infosys developers from India to create a new distributed IT management component within weeks. "We invited the Infosys project leader to come in and we mapped out the features we needed, which included 14 performance metrics. We created an executive dashboard, or pulse point, for a CIO. I can bring it up and see all the metrics of how my IT organization is doing and drill down to find out how the organization is performing."

Case Study Questions

1. How is the open-source model affecting the development of application software for business?

2. What are the business benefits of the global or collaborative approach to software development? Use the companies in this case as examples.

3. What are several potential challenges or limitations that might arise when using a global collaborative approach to software development? How can companies address such challenges?

Source: *Building Apps on the Fly* by McCarthy, Jack. Copyright 2003 by Infoworld Media Group, Inc. Reproduced with permission of Infoworld Media Group, Inc. in the format Textbook via Copyright Clearance Center.

Avon Products and Guardian life Insurance: Successful Mangement of IT Projects

t's deja vu again at many companies when it comes to track records in using IT to help achieve business goals. Consider the following:

- At companies that aren't among the top 25 percent of IT users, three out of 10 IT projects fail on average.

- Less than 40 percent of IT managers say their staffs can react rapidly to changes in business goals or market conditions.

- Less than half of all companies bother to validate an IT project's business value after it has been completed.

Those are just a few of the findings from a survey of IT managers at about 2,000 companies, including more than 80 percent of the *Fortune* 1,000, released in June 2003 by the Hackett Group in Atlanta. However, top-tier IT leaders didn't reach the top of their professions by being softies.

Indeed, a vast majority of them regularly rely upon hard-dollar metrics to consistently demonstrate to top brass the business value IT investments are expected to yield. That's what sets them apart from so many of their colleagues. "Good business-case methodology leads to good project management, but it's amazing how many companies fall short here," says Stephen J. Andriole, a professor of business technolgy at Villanova University and consultant at Cutter Consortium. The lack of good project management at such companies may also lead to business units taking on IT development projects without the knowledge or oversight of a company's IT department. Business units may initiate such "rogue projects" because they see the IT department as too slow, or a source of too much red tape and extra costs.

Avon Products. "We apply all of the analytical rigor and financial ROI tools against each of our IT projects as well as other business projects, "says Harriet Edelman, senior vice president and CIO at Avon Products Inc. (www.avon.com) in New York. Those tools include payback, NPV, and IRR calculations, as well as risk analyses on every investment, she says.

The $6 billion cosmetics giant also monitors each IT project to gauge its efficiency and effectiveness during the course of development and applies a red/yellow/green coding system to reflect the current health of a project, says Edelman. A monthly report about the status of projects that are valued at more than $250,000 and deal with important strategic content is presented to senior line managers, the CEO, and the chief operating officer. In addition, Avon uses an investment-tracking database for every IT project to monitor project costs on a rolling basis. The approach makes it easier for the company's IT and business managers to quickly determine whether a project should be accelerated, delayed, or canceled and assists the finance organization in forecasting requirements.

Guardian Life Insurace. Dennis S. Callahan sys he has "put a strong emphasis on governance" since becoming CIO at The Guardian Life Insurance Company (www.glic.com) two years ago. Callahan has done so, in part, by applying NPV and IRR calulations to all IT projects with a five-year cash flow. "The potential fallout from inaction could result in loss of market share," says Callahan, who was promoted to executive vice president recently. So Guardian's approach to IT investments "is very hard-dollar-and metrics-oriented, with a bias toward action," he says. Still, Callahan and his team do have a process for incorporating "soft" costs and benefits into their calculations. They do that, Callahan says, by encouraging their business peers "to discuss how an investment can impact market share and estimate how those numbers are going to change. Same thing with cost avoidance—if we invest in a project that's expected to help us avoid hiring 10 operations staffers to handle gowing business transaction volumes."

Callahan also keeps close tabs on capital spending throughout the course of a project. New York-based Guardian has a project management office that continually monitors the scope, time, and cost of each project valued at more than $100,000, according to Callahan. Guardian also has monthly reviews of variances of scope, time, and costs on all projects costing more than $100,000.

Using return-on-investment calculations to cost-justify and demonstrate the value of IT investments to senior management is only one of the techniques top IT leaders use to win project approvals, say Callahan and others. "We approach everything that we do in terms of payback." President and CEO Dennis Manning and other board members "really relate to that kind of justification," Callahan says. "So we turn that into hard-dollar returns and benefits for application development and infrastructure investment." "One of the biggest things we do in demonstrating value to the CEO and the board is showing that everything we do reflects the company's business strategy," says Rick Omartian, chief financial officer for Guardian's IT department.

Case Study Questions

1. What are several possible solutions to the failures in IT project management at many companies described at the start of this case? Defend your proposals.

2. What are several key ways that Avon and Guardian assure that their IT projects are completed succesfully and support the goals of the business?

3. If you were the manager of a business unit at Avon or Guardian, what are several other things you would like to see their IT groups do to assure the success of an IT project for your business unit? Defend your suggestions.

Source: Adapted from Thomas Hoffman, "How Will You Prove IT Value?" *Computerworld*, January 6, 2003, p. 26; Julia King, "Survey Shows Common IT Woes Persist," *Computerworld*, June 23, 2003, p. 21; and Gary Anthes, "Dealing with Rogue IT," *Computerworld*, September 1, 2003, pp. 27–28.

Review Quiz Answers

Chapter 1

Foundations of Information Systems in Business

1. 21	7. 26c	13. 11	19. 4	25. 27a	31. 17d	37. 29
2. 22	8. 16	14. 28	20. 18	26. 27b	32. 17e	38. 20
3. 19	9. 1	15. 13	21. 14	27. 25	33. 30	39. 12
4. 26	10. 10	16. 2	22. 14a	28. 17a	34. 30c	40. 23a
5. 26a	11. 8	17. 3	23. 14b	29. 17b	35. 30b	41. 23
6. 26b	12. 9	18. 15	24. 27	30. 17c	36. 30a	42. 7

Competing with Information Technology

1. 3	4. 11	7. 6	10. 14	13. 17	15. 8	17. 7
2. 4	5. 5	8. 16	11. 2	14. 15	16. 9	
3. 12	6. 13	9. 10	12. 1			

Computer Hardware

1. 3	8. 23	15. 29	22. 41c	29. 37	36. 9	43. 35
2. 2	9. 22	16. 19	23. 38e	30. 26	37. 46	44. 34
3. 8	10. 1	17. 43	24. 30	31. 24	38. 39	45. 10
4. 7	11. 16	18. 21	25. 27	32. 11	39. 34b	46. 13
5. 31	12. 15	19. 20	26. 30a	33. 36	40. 34a	47. 25
6. 33	13. 17	20. 40	27. 42	34. 4	41. 45	48. 25d
7. 28	14. 14	21. 12	28. 32	35. 5	42. 6	

Computer Software

1. 31	7. 33	13. 18	19. 7	25. 12	31. 22	37. 20
2. 2	8. 11	14. 34	20. 38	26. 19	32. 27	38. 15
3. 24	9. 35	15. 10	21. 5	27. 4	33. 14	39. 37
4. 32	10. 21	16. 3	22. 25	28. 13	34. 39	
5. 28	11. 30	17. 36	23. 16	29. 9	35. 17	
6. 8	12. 26	18. 6	24. 29	30. 23	36. 1	

Chapter 5

Data Resource Management

1. 6	5. 1	9. 8d	13. 3	17. 11e	20. 8e	23. 15a
2. 9	6. 14	10. 15d	14. 11b	18. 10	21. 8b	24. 15c
3. 5	7. 7	11. 4	15. 11c	19. 8a	22. 15e	
4. 13	8. 15b	12. 2	16. 11d			

Chapter 6

Telecommunications and Networks

1. 35	7. 10	13. 11	19. 25	25. 20a	31. 21	37. 38
2. 4	8. 32	14. 5	20. 39	26. 20b	32. 27	38. 22
3. 2	9. 37	15. 33	21. 24	27. 26	33. 9	
4. 3	10. 17	16. 34	22. 36	28. 14	34. 16	
5. 12	11. 30	17. 18	23. 23	29. 13	35. 1	
6. 15	12. 31	18. 19	24. 28	30. 6	36. 29	

Chapter 7

Introduction to e-Business Systems

1. 9	7. 18	13. 29	19. 27	25. 14	31. 26	37. 13a
2. 7	8. 31	14. 20	20. 19	26. 21	32. 8	38. 33a
3. 15	9. 22	15. 17	21. 3	27. 34	33. 13	39. 8b
4. 10	10. 6	16. 25	22. 2	28. 35	34. 33	40. 13b
5. 11	11. 5	17. 1	23. 28	29. 4	35. 32	41. 33b
6. 23	12. 12	18. 24	24. 16	30. 30	36. 8a	

Chapter 8

Electronic Commerce Systems

1. 6	5. 5	9. 9d	13. 10	17. 3c	21. 9e	25. 12
2. 6b	6. 9	10. 9i	14. 3	18. 3b	22. 11	26. 7
3. 6a	7. 9a	11. 9f	15. 3d	19. 2	23. 1	
4. 6c	8. 9g	12. 9c	16. 3a	20. 8	24. 4	

Chapter 9

Decision Support Systems

1. 8	7. 28	13. 1c	19. 10	25. 30	31. 18	37. 19
2. 9	8. 7	14. 1a	20. 22	26. 17	32. 14	38. 16
3. 23	9. 3	15. 1b	21. 11	27. 13	33. 13d	
4. 6	10. 25	16. 27	22. 2	28. 13a	34. 21	
5. 12	11. 1	17. 4	23. 2a	29. 13b	35. 26	
6. 24	12. 1d	18. 5	24. 29	30. 20	36. 15	

Chapter 10

Developing Business/IT Solutions

1. 23	7. 32*a*	13. 33	19. 34	25. 9	31. 30	37. 7
2. 31	8. 14*a*	14. 15	20. 29	26. 13	32. 5	38. 1
3. 18	9. 25	15. 17	21. 26	27. 10*a*	33. 16	
4. 3	10. 27	16. 22	22. 28	28. 10*c*	34. 19	
5. 32*b*	11. 11	17. 12	23. 20	29. 10*b*	35. 4	
6. 14*b*	12. 6	18. 24	24. 21	30. 2	36. 8	

Chapter 11

Security and Ethical Challenges

1. 26	6. 3	11. 16	16. 15*b*	21. 9	26. 22	31. 14
2. 21	7. 2	12. 6	17. 15*d*	22. 11	27. 20	32. 25
3. 29	8. 5	13. 28	18. 15*e*	23. 7	28. 10	
4. 17	9. 12	14. 15*a*	19. 8	24. 30	29. 1	
5. 18	10. 13	15. 15*c*	20. 24	25. 27	30. 19	

Chapter 12

Enterprise and Global Management of Information Technology

1. 9	6. 1	11. 12	16. 8	21. 10	26. 14	28. 13
2. 15	7. 24	12. 4	17. 19	22. 11*a*	27. 22	29. 11*e*
3. 16	8. 18	13. 5	18. 11	23. 11*b*		
4. 17	9. 7	14. 20	19. 23	24. 11*c*		
5. 2	10. 21	15. 3	20. 6	25. 11*d*		

Selected References

Preface

1. Sawhney, Mohan, and Jeff Zabin. *The Seven Steps to Nirvana: Strategic Insights into e-Business Transformation.* New York: McGraw-Hill, 2001.

Chapter 1—Foundations of Information Systems in Business

1. Kalakota, Ravi, and Marcia Robinson. *E-Business 2.0: Roadmap for Success.* Reading, MA: Addison-Wesley, 2001.

2. Lee, Allen. "Inaugural Editor's Comments." *MIS Quarterly*, March 1999.

3. Leinfuss, Emily. "Making the Cut." *Computerworld*, September 20, 1999.

4. Norris, Grant; James Hurley; Kenneth Hartley; John Dunleavy; and John Balls. *E-Business and ERP: Transforming the Enterprise.* New York: John Wiley & Sons, 2000.

5. Radcliff, Deborah. "Aligning Marriott." *Computerworld*, April 20, 2000.

6. Steadman, Craig. "ERP Pioneers." *Computerworld*, January 18, 1999.

7. Steadman, Craig. "Failed ERP Gamble Haunts Hershey." *Computerworld*, November 1, 1999.

8. Vijayan, Jaikumar. "E-Procurement Talks Back." *Premiere 100 Best in Class* supplement, *Computerworld*, March 11, 2002.

9. Vijayan, Jaikumar. "Securing the Center." *Computerworld*, May 13, 2002.

10. Weiss, Todd. "Hershey Upgrades R/3 ERP System without Hitches." *Computerworld*, September 9, 2002.

Chapter 2—Competing with Information Technology

1. Applegate, Lynda; Robert D. Austin; and F. Warren McFarlan. *Corporate Information Systems Management: Text and Cases.* 6th ed. Burr Ridge, IL: Irwin/McGraw-Hill, 2003.

2. Bowles, Jerry. "Best Practices for Global Competitiveness." Special Advertising Section. *Fortune*, November 24, 1997.

3. Caron, J. Raymond; Sirkka Jarvenpaa; and Donna Stoddard. "Business Reengineering at CIGNA Corporation: Experiences and Lessons from the First Five Years." *MIS Quarterly*, September 1994.

4. Christensen, Clayton. *The Innovators Dilemma: When New Technologies Cause Great Firms to Fail.* Boston: Harvard Business School Press, 1997.

5. Cronin, Mary. *The Internet Strategy Handbook.* Boston: Harvard Business School Press, 1996.

6. Davenport, Thomas H. *Process Innovation: Reengineering Work through Information Technology.* Boston: Harvard Business School Press, 1993.

7. El Sawy, Omar, and Gene Bowles. "Redesigning the Customer Support Process for the Electronic Economy: Insights from Storage Dimensions." *MIS Quarterly*, December 1997.

8. El Sawy, Omar; Arvind Malhotra; Sanjay Gosain; and Kerry Young. "IT-Intensive Value Innovation in the Electronic Economy: Insights from Marshall Industries." *MIS Quarterly*, September 1999.

9. Ewing, Jack. "Sharing the Wealth." *Business Week e-biz*, March 19, 2001.

10. Frye, Colleen. "Imaging Proves Catalyst for Reengineering." *Client/Server Computing*, November 1994.

11. Garner, Rochelle. "Please Don't Call IT Knowledge Management!" *Computerworld*, August 9, 1999.

12. Goldman, Steven; Roger Nagel; and Kenneth Preis. *Agile Competitors and Virtual Organizations: Strategies for Enriching the Customer.* New York: Van Nostrand Reinhold, 1995.

13. Grover, Varun, and Pradipkumar Ramanlal. "Six Myths of Information and Markets: Information Technology Networks, Electronic Commerce, and the Battle for Consumer Surplus." *MIS Quarterly*, December 1999.

14. Hall, Mark. "Portal Hides Integration Complexity." *Computerworld*, July 22, 2002.

15. Hamm, Steve, and Marcia Stepaneck. "From Reengineering to E-Engineering." *Business Week e.biz*, March 22, 1999.

16. Jones, Kathryn. "The Dell Way." *Business 2.0*, February 2003.

17. Kalakota, Ravi, and Marcia Robinson. *E-Business 2.0: Roadmap for Success*. Reading, MA: Addison-Wesley, 2001.

18. Kettinger, William; Varun Grover; and Albert Segars. "Do Strategic Systems Really Pay Off? An Analysis of Classic Strategic IT Cases." *Information Systems Management*, Winter 1995.

19. Kettinger, William; James Teng; and Subashish Guha. "Business Process Change: A Study of Methodologies, Techniques, and Tools." *MIS Quarterly*, March 1997.

20. Kover, Amy. "Schwab Makes a Grand Play for the Rich." *Fortune*, February 7, 2000.

21. Neumann, Seev. *Strategic Information Systems: Competition through Information Technologies*. New York: Macmillan College Publishing Co., 1994.

22. Nonaka, Ikujiro. "The Knowledge Creating Company." *Harvard Business Review*, November–December 1991.

23. Porter, Michael, and Victor Millar. "How Information Gives You Competitive Advantage." *Harvard Business Review*, July–August 1985.

24. Prokesch, Steven. "Unleashing the Power of Learning: An Interview with British Petroleum's John Browne." *Harvard Business Review*, September–October 1997.

25. Sambamurthy, V.; Anandhi Bharadwaj; and Varun Grover. "Shaping Agility through Digital Options: Reconceptualizing the Role of Information Technology in Contemporary Firms." *MIS Quarterly*, June 2003.

26. Seybold, Patricia. *Customers.com: How to Create a Profitable Business Strategy for the Internet and Beyond*. New York: Times Books, 1998.

27. Shapiro, Carl, and Hal Varian. *Information Rules: A Strategic Guide to the Network Economy*. Boston: Harvard Business School Press, 1999.

28. Siekman, Philip. "Why Infotech Loves Its Giant Job Shops." *Fortune*, May 12, 1997.

29. Songini, Marc. "ERP Effort Sinks Agilent Revenue." *Computerworld*, August 26, 2002.

30. Weill, Peter, and Michael Vitale. *Place to Space: Migrating to E-Business Models*. Boston: Harvard Business School Press, 2001.

Chapter 3—Computer Hardware

1. *Computerworld*, *PC Week*, *PC Magazine*, and *PC World* are just a few examples of many good magazines for current information on computer systems hardware and its use in end user and enterprise applications.

2. The World Wide Web sites of computer manufacturers such as Apple Computer, Dell Computer, Gateway, IBM, Hewlett-Packard, Compaq, and Sun Microsystems are good sources of information on computer hardware developments.

3. Alexander, Steve. "Speech Recognition." *Computerworld*, November 8, 1999.

4. "Computing in the New Millennium." In Technology Buyers Guide, *Fortune*, Winter 2000.

5. DeJesus, Edmund. "Building PCs for the Enterprise." *Computerworld*, May 7, 2001.

6. Guyon, Janet. "Smart Plastic." *Fortune*, October 13, 1997.

7. "Hardware." In Technology Buyer's Guide, *Fortune*, Winter 1999.

8. Joch, Alan. "Fewer Servers, Better Service." *Computerworld*, June 4, 2001.

9. Kennedy, Ken, and others. "A Nationwide Parallel Computing Environment." *Communications of the ACM*, November 1997.

10. Messerschmitt, David. *Networked Applications: A Guide to the New Computing Infrastructure*. San Francisco: Morgan Kaufmann Publishers, 1999.

11. Ouellette, Tim. "Goodbye to the Glass House." *Computerworld*, May 26, 1997.

12. Ouellette, Tim. "Tape Storage Put to New Enterprise Uses." *Computerworld*, November 10, 1997.

13. Reimers, Barbara. "Blades Spin ROI Potential." *Computerworld*, February 11, 2002.

14. Simpson, David. "The Datamation 100." *Datamation*, July 1997.

15. "Top 500 Supercomputer Sites: ASCII White." www.top500.org, May 18, 2003.

Chapter 4—Computer Software

1. Examples of many good magazines for current information and reviews of computer software for business applications can be found at ZD Net, the website for ZD Publications (www.zdnet.com), including *PC Magazine, PC Week, PC Computing, Macworld, Inter@ctive Week,* and *Computer Shopper.*

2. The Web sites of companies like Microsoft, Sun Microsystems, Lotus, IBM, Apple Computer, and Oracle are good sources of information on computer software developments.

3. Caulfield, Brian. "What the Heck Are Web Services?" *Business 2.0,* April 2002.

4. Iyer, Bala; Jim Freedman; Mark Gaynor; and George Wyner; "Web Services: Enabling Dynamic Business Networks," *Communications of the Association for Information Systems,* Volume 11, 2003.

5. Mearian, Lucas. "Fidelity Makes Big XML Conversion." *Computerworld,* October 1, 2001.

6. Microsoft Corporation. "Introducing the Windows 2003 Family." www.microsoft.com, July 1, 2003.

7. Oracle Corporation. "Visa to Save Millions a Year by Automating Back-Office Processes with Oracle E-Business Suite." Customer Profile. www.oracle.com, September 13, 2002.

8. Salesforce.com. "Fujitsu Technology Solutions Sees 750% ROI with salesforce.com." www.salesforce.com, October 3, 2002.

9. Sliwa, Carol. ".Net vs. Java." *Computerworld,* May 20, 2002.

10. Thomas, Owen. "Websites Made Easier." *eCompany,* March 2001.

11. Vogelstein, Fred. "Servers with a Smile." *Fortune.* September 30, 2002.

12. Wainewright, Ivan. "An Introduction to Application Service Providers (ASPs)." TechSoup, May 1, 2000.

Chapter 5—Data Resource Management

1. Baer, Tony. "Object Databases." *Computerworld,* January 18, 1999.

2. Fayyad, Usama; Gregory Piatetsky-Shapiro; and Padraic Smith. "The KDD Process for Extracting Useful Knowledge from Volumes of Data." *Communications of the ACM,* November 1996.

3. Fox, Pimm. "Extracting Dollars from Data." *Computerworld,* April 15, 2002.

4. Fox, Pimm. "Insights Turn into Profits." *Computerworld,* February 18, 2002.

5. Jacobsen, Ivar; Maria Ericsson; and Ageneta Jacobsen. *The Object Advantage: Business Process Reengineering with Object Technology.* New York: ACM Press, 1995.

6. IBM Corporation. "Credit Union Central Alberta Upgrades MIS Reporting with DB2." Success stories, ibm.com, July 19, 2002.

7. IBM Corporation. "DB2 Business Intelligence." www.ibm.com, July 27, 2003.

8. Kalakota, Ravi, and Marcia Robinson. *E-Business 2.0: Roadmap for Success.* Reading, MA: Addison-Wesley, 2002.

9. Lorents, Alden, and James Morgan. *Database Systems: Concepts, Management and Applications.* Fort Worth: The Dryden Press, 1998.

10. Mannino, Michael. *Database Application Development and Design.* Burr Ridge, IL: McGraw-Hill/Irwin, 2001.

11. Nance, Barry. "Managing Tons of Data." *Computerworld,* April 23, 2001.

12. Nash, Kim. "Merging Data Silos." *Computerworld,* April 15, 2002.

Chapter 6—Telecommunications and Networks

1. Armor, Daniel. *The E-Business (R)Evolution: Living and Working in an Interconnected World.* Upper Saddle River, NJ: Prentice Hall, 2000.

2. Barksdale, Jim. "The Next Step: Extranets." *Netscape Columns: The Main Thing,* December 3, 1996.

3. Bresnick, Alan. "Verizon Turns Up Heat in Online Data Wars." *Cable Datacom News,* June 1, 2003.

4. "Cable Modem Info Center." www.cabledatacomnews.com, July 26, 2003.

5. Campbell, Ian. "The Intranet: Slashing the Cost of Doing Business." Research Report, International Data Corporation, 1996.

6. Chatterjee, Samir. "Requirements for Success in Gigabit Networking." *Communications of the ACM,* July 1997.

7. Cope, James. "Privacy for Hire." *Computerworld,* February 11, 2002.

8. Cronin, Mary. *Doing More Business on the Internet.* New York: Van Nostrand Reinhold, 1995.

9. CyberAtlas, Inc. "The Big Picture: Geographics: Population Explosion!" www.cyberatlas.internet.com, June 23, 2003.

10. Housel, Thomas, and Eric Skopec. *Global Telecommunications Revolution: The Business Perspective.* New York: McGraw-Hill/Irwin, 2001.

11. Kalakota, Ravi, and Marcia Robinson. *E-Business 2.0: Roadmap for Success.* Reading, MA: Addison-Wesley, 2001.

12. Lais, Sami, "Coping with Bandwidth Hogs." *Computerworld*, September 16, 2002.

13. Lais, Sami. "Satellites Link Bob Evans Farms." *Computerworld*, July 2, 2001.

14. Messerschmitt, David. *Network Applications: A Guide to the New Computing Infrastructure.* San Francisco: Morgan Kaufmann Publishers, 1999.

15. Murphy, Kate. "Cruising the Net in Hyperdrive." *Business Week*, January 24, 2000.

16. O'Brien, Atiye. "Friday Intranet Focus." *Upside.com: Hot Private Companies.* Upside Publishing Company, 1996.

17. Orenstein, David. "Price, Speed, Location All Part of Broadband Choice." *Computerworld*, July 26, 1999.

18. Papows, Jeff. "Endquotes." *NetReady Adviser*, Winter 1997.

19. Radding, Alan. "Leading the Way." *Computerworld ROI*, September/October 2001.

20. Stuart, Anne. "Cutting the Cord." *Inc. Tech*, 2001, No. 1.

Chapter 7—Electronic Business Systems

1. Betts, Mitch. "Kinks in the Chain." *Computerworld*, December 17, 2001.

2. Bylinsky, Gene. "The e-Factory Catches On." *Fortune*, August 13, 2001.

3. Caulfield, Brian. "Systems That Talk Together, Kick Butt Together." *eCompany*, January/February 2001.

4. Caulfield, Brian. "Facing Up to CRM." *Business 2.0*, August/September 2001.

5. "Communications Leader Becomes Customer-Focused E-Business." *Siebel.com*, March 12, 2001.

6. Davenport, Thomas. *Process Innovation: Reengineering Work through Information Technology.* Boston: Harvard Business School Press, 1993.

7. DeMeyer, Desiree, and Don Steinberg. "The Smart Business 50—General Electric." *Smart Business*, September 2001.

8. Diddlebock, Bob. "Share and Share Alike." *Context*, December 2001–January 2002.

9. Engardio, Pete. "Why the Supply Chain Broke Down." *Business Week*, March 19, 2001.

10. Gates, Bill. *Business @ the Speed of Thought.* New York: Warner Books, 1999.

11. Geoff, Leslie. "CRM: The Cutting Edge of Serving Customers." *Computerworld*, February 28, 2000.

12. Hamm, Steve, and Robert Hoff. "An Eagle Eye on Customers." *Business Week*, February 21, 2000.

13. Hoffman, Thomas. "Intranet Helps Workers Navigate Corporate Maze." *Computerworld*, June 4, 2001.

14. Johnson, Amy. "CRM Rises to the Top." *Computerworld*, August 16, 1999.

15. Kalakota, Ravi, and Marcia Robinson. *E-Business 2.0: Roadmap for Success.* Reading, MA: Addison-Wesley, 2001.

16. Keen, Peter, and Craigg Balance. *Online Profits: A Manager's Guide to Electronic Commerce.* Boston: Harvard Business School Press, 1997.

17. Keenan, Faith. "Opening the Spigot." *Business Week e.Biz*, June 4, 2001.

18. Martin, Chuck. *The Digital Estate: Strategies for Competing, Surviving, and Thriving in an Internetworked World.* New York: McGraw-Hill, 1997.

19. Mello, Adrian. "ERP Fundamentals." *Tech Update*, ZDNet.com, February 7, 2002.

20. Merian, Lucas. "Retailers Hit Installation Bumps with SAP Software." *Computerworld*, February 19, 2001.

21. Norris, Grant; James Hurley; Kenneth Hartley; John Dunleavy; and John Balls. *E-Business and ERP: Transforming the Enterprise.* New York: John Wiley & Sons, 2000.

22. Orenstein, David. "Enterprise Application Integration." *Computerworld*, October 4, 1999.

23. Rigby, Darrell; Frederich Reichheld; and Phil Schefter. "Avoid the Four Perils of CRM." *Harvard Business Review*, February 2002.

24. Robb, Drew. "Rediscovering Efficiency." *Computerworld*, July 16, 2001.

25. Salesforce.com. "Baker Tanks Leverages salesforce.com's Wireless Access to Extend Range of Customer Service." Salesforce.com, 2002.

26. Sawhney, Mohan, and Jeff Zabin. *The Seven Steps to Nirvana: Strategic Insights into e-Business Transformation.* New York: McGraw-Hill, 2001.

27. Siebel Systems. "eBusiness: Managing the Demand Chain." White Paper. Siebel.com, 2002.

28. Siebel Systems. "Communications Leader Becomes Customer-Focused E-Business." Siebel.com, March 12, 2001.

29. Songini, Marc. "Policing the Supply Chain." *Computerworld*, April 30, 2001.

30. Tucker, Jay. "The New Money: Transactions Pour across the Web." *Datamation*, April 1997.

31. Weill, Peter and Michael Vitale. Place to Space: *Migrating to E-Business Models.* Harvard Business School Press, 2001.

Chapter 8—Applications in Business and Management: Electronic Commerce Systems

1. Armor, Daniel. *The E-Business (R)Evolution: Living and Working in an Interconnected World.* Upper Saddle River, NJ: Prentice Hall, 2000.

2. Cross, Kim. "Need Options? Go Configure." *Business 2.0*, February 2000.

3. Davis, Jeffrey. "How IT Works." *Business 2.0*, February 2000.

4. Davis, Jeffrey. "Mall Rats." *Business 2.0*, January 1999.

5. Essex, David. "Betting on Win 2K." *Computerworld*, February 26, 2001.

6. Fellenstein, Craig, and Ron Wood. *Exploring E-Commerce, Global E-Business, and E-Societies.* Upper Saddle River, NJ: Prentice Hall, 2000.

7. Fingar, Peter; Harsha Kumar; and Tarun Sharma. *Enterprise E-Commerce.* Tampa, FL: Meghan-Kiffer Press, 2000.

8. Georgia, Bonnie. "Give Your E-Store an Edge." *Smart Business*, October 2001.

9. Gulati, Ranjay, and Jason Garino. "Get the Right Mix of Clicks and Bricks." *Harvard Business Review*, May–June 2000.

10. Hoque, Faisal. *E-Enterprise: Business Models, Architecture and Components.* Cambridge, UK: Cambridge University Press, 2000.

11. Kalakota, Ravi, and Marcia Robinson. *E-Business 2.0: Roadmap for Success.* Reading, MA: Addison-Wesley, 2001.

12. Kalakota, Ravi, and Andrew Whinston. *Electronic Commerce: A Manager's Guide.* Reading, MA: Addison-Wesley, 1997.

13. Keenan, Faith, and Timothy Mullaney. "Let's Get Back to Basics." *Business Week e.biz*, October 29, 2001.

14. Leon, Mark. "Trading Spaces." *Business 2.0*, February 2000.

15. May, Paul. *The Business of E-Commerce: From Corporate Strategy to Technology.* Cambridge, UK: Cambridge University Press, 2001.

16. Morgan, Cynthia. "Dead Set against SET?" *Computerworld*, March 29, 1999.

17. Rayport, Jeffry and Bernard Jaworski. *Introduction to e-Commerce*, New York: McGraw-Hill/Irwin, 2001.

18. Rosenoer, Jonathan; Douglas Armstrong; and J. Russell Gates. *The Clickable Corporation: Successful Strategies for Capturing the Internet Advantage.* New York: The Free Press, 1999.

19. "Servers with a Smile." In Technology Buyers Guide, *Fortune*, Summer 2000.

20. Seybold, Patricia, with Ronnie Marshak. *Customers.Com: How to Create a Profitable Business Strategy for the Internet and Beyond.* New York: Times Business, 1998.

21. Sliwa, Carol. "Users Cling to EDI for Critical Transactions." *Computerworld*, March 15, 1999.

22. "Tech Lifestyles: Shopping." *Fortune*, Technology Buyers Guide, Winter 2001.

23. "Telefónica Servicios Avanzados De Informació Leads Spain's Retail Industry into Global Electronic Commerce." At www.netscape.com/solutions/business/profiles, March 1999.

24. Young, Eric. "Web Marketplaces That Really Work." *Fortune/CNET Tech Review*, Winter 2002.

Chapter 9—Decision Support Systems

1. "AmeriKing." Customer Profile. Plumtree.com. October 25, 2002.

2. Ashline, Peter, and Vincent Lai. "Virtual Reality: An Emerging User-Interface Technology." *Information Systems Management*, Winter 1995.

3. Begley, Sharon. "Software au Naturel." *Newsweek*, May 8, 1995.

4. Belcher, Lloyd, and Hugh Watson. "Assessing the Value of Conoco's EIS." *MIS Quarterly*, September 1993.

5. Bose, Ranjit, and Vijayan Sugumaran. "Application of Intelligent Agent Technology for Managerial Data Analysis and Mining." *The Data Base for Advances in Information Systems*, Winter 1999.

6. Botchner, Ed. "Data Mining: Plumbing the Depths of Corporate Databases." Special Advertising Supplement. *Computerworld*, April 21, 1997.

7. Brown, Eryn. "Slow Road To Fast Data." *Fortune*, March 18, 2002.

8. Brown, Stuart. "Making Decisions in a Flood of Data." *Fortune*, August 13, 2001.

9. Bylinsky, Gene. "The e-Factory Catches On." *Fortune*, August 13, 2001.

10. Cox, Earl. "Relational Database Queries Using Fuzzy Logic." *AI Expert*, January 1995.

11. Darling, Charles. "Ease Implementation Woes with Packaged Datamarts." *Datamation*, March 1997.

12. Deck, Stewart. "Data Visualization." *Computerworld*, October 11, 1999.

13. Deck, Stewart. "Data Warehouse Project Starts Simply." *Computerworld*, February 15, 1999.

14. Deck, Stewart. "Early Users Give Nod to Analysis Package." *Computerworld*, February 22, 1999.

15. Deck, Stewart. "Mining Your Business." *Computerworld*, May 17, 1999.

16. Egan, Richard. "The Expert Within." *PC Today*, January 1995.

17. Freeman, Eva. "Desktop Reporting Tools." *Datamation*, June 1997.

18. Gantz, John. "The New World of Enterprise Reporting Is Here." *Computerworld*, February 1, 1999.

19. Gates, Bill. *Business @ the Speed of Thought.* New York: Warner Books, 1999.

20. Goldberg, David. "Genetic and Evolutionary Algorithms Come of Age." *Communications of the ACM*, March 1994.

21. Gorry, G. Anthony, and Michael Scott Morton. "A Framework for Management Information Systems." *Sloan Management Review*, Fall 1971; republished Spring 1989.

22. Hall, Mark. "Get Real." *Computerworld*, April 1, 2002.

23. Hall, Mark. "Supercomputing: From R&D to P&L." *Computerworld*, December 13, 1999.

24. Hoffman, Thomas. "In the Know." *Computerworld*, October 14, 2002.

25. Jablonowski, Mark. "Fuzzy Risk Analysis: Using AI Systems." *AI Expert*, December 1994.

26. Kalakota, Ravi, and Marcia Robinson. *E-Business 2.0: Roadmap for Success.* Reading, MA: Addison-Wesley, 2001.

27. Kalakota, Ravi, and Andrew Whinston. *Electronic Commerce: A Manager's Guide.* Reading, MA: Addison-Wesley, 1997.

28. King, Julia. "Sharing GIS Talent with the World." *Computerworld*, October 6, 1997.

29. Kurszweil, Raymond. *The Age of Intelligent Machines.* Cambridge, MA: The MIT Press, 1992.

30. Lundquist, Christopher. "Personalization in E-Commerce." *Computerworld*, March 22, 1999.

31. Machlis, Sharon. "Agent Technology." *Computerworld*, March 22, 1999.

32. Mailoux, Jacquiline. "New Menu at PepsiCo." *Computerworld*, May 6, 1996.

33. McNeill, F. Martin, and Ellen Thro. *Fuzzy Logic: A Practical Approach.* Boston: AP Professional, 1994.

34. Mitchell, Lori. "Enterprise Knowledge Portals Wise Up Your Business." *Infoworld.com*, December 2000.

35. Murray, Gerry. "Making Connections with Enterprise Knowledge Portals." White Paper. *Computerworld*, September 6, 1999.

36. Orenstein, David. "Corporate Portals." *Computerworld*, June 28, 1999.

37. Ouellette, Tim. "Opening Your Own Portal." *Computerworld*, August 9, 1999.

38. Pimentel, Ken, and Kevin Teixeira. *Virtual Reality through the New Looking Glass.* 2nd ed. New York: Intel/McGraw-Hill, 1995.

39. Roberts-Witt, Sarah. "Plumtree Helps Fast Food Firm Build Whopper of a Portal." *ZDNet Update*, February 19, 2002.

40. Rosenberg, Marc. *e-Learning: Strategies for Delivering Knowledge in the Digital Age.* New York: McGraw-Hill, 2001.

41. Scheier, Robert. "Finding Pearls in an Ocean of Data." *Computerworld*, July 23, 2001.

42. Turban, Efraim, and Jay Aronson. *Decision Support Systems and Intelligent Systems.* Upper Saddle River, NJ: Prentice Hall, 1998.

43. Vandenbosch, Betty, and Sid Huff. "Searching and Scanning: How Executives Obtain Information from Executive Information Systems." *MIS Quarterly*, March 1997.

44. Wagner, Mitch. "Engine Links Ads to Searches." *Computerworld*, June 2, 1997.

45. Wagner, Mitch. "Reality Check." *Computerworld*, February 26, 1997.

46. Watson, Hugh, and John Satzinger. "Guidelines for Designing EIS Interfaces." *Information Systems Management*, Fall 1994.

47. Watterson, Karen. "Parallel Tracks." *Datamation*, May 1997.

48. Winston, Patrick. "Rethinking Artificial Intelligence." Program Announcement, Massachusetts Institute of Technology, September 1997.

49. Wreden, Nick. "Enterprise Portals: Integrating Information to Drive Productivity." *Beyond Computing*, March 2000.

Chapter 10—Developing Business/IT Solutions

1. Anthes, Gary. "The Quest for IT E-Quality." *Computerworld*, December 13, 1999.

2. Clark, Charles; Nancy Cavanaugh; Carol Brown; and V. Sambamurthy. "Building Change-Readiness Capabilities in the IS Organization: Insights from the Bell Atlantic Experience." *MIS Quarterly*, December 1997.

3. Cole-Gomolski, Barbara. "Companies Turn to Web for ERP Training." *Computerworld*, February 8, 1999.

4. Cole-Gomolski, Barbara. "Users Loath to Share Their Know-How." *Computerworld*, November 17, 1997.

5. Cronin, Mary. *The Internet Strategy Handbook.* Boston: Harvard Business School Press, 1996.

6. Diese, Martin, Conrad Nowikow, Patrick King, and Amy Wright. *Executive's Guide to E-Business: From Tactics to Strategy.* New York: John Wiley & Sons, 2000.

7. "Design Matters." *Fortune*, Technology Buyers Guide, Winter 2001.

8. Hawson, James, and Jesse Beeler. "Effects of User Participation in Systems Development: A Longitudinal Field Experiment." *MIS Quarterly*, December 1997.

9. Hills, Melanie. *Intranet Business Strategies*. New York: John Wiley & Sons, 1997.

10. Kalakota, Ravi and Marcia Robinson. *E-Business 2.0: Roadmap for Success*. Reading, MA: Addison-Wesley, 2001.

11. King, Julia. "Back to Basics." *Computerworld*, April 22, 2002.

12. Lazar, Jonathan. *User-Centered Web Development*. Sudbury, MA: Jones and Bartlett Publishers, 2001.

13. McDonnel, Sharon. "Putting CRM to Work." *Computerworld*, March 12, 2001.

14. Melymuka, Kathleen. "An Expanding Universe." *Computerworld*, September 14, 1998.

15. Melymuka, Kathleen. "Energizing the Company." *Computerworld*, August 13, 2001.

16. Melymuka, Kathleen. "Profiting from Mistakes." *Computerworld*, April 20, 2001.

17. Morgan, James N. *Application Cases in MIS*. 4th ed. New York: Irwin/McGraw-Hill, 2002.

18. Neilsen, Jakob. "Better Data Brings Better Sales." *Business 2.0*, May 15, 2001.

19. Nielsen, Jakob. "Design for Process, Not for Products." *Business 2.0*, July 10, 2001.

20. Orenstein, David. "Software Is Too Hard to Use." *Computerworld*, August 23, 1999.

21. Ouellette, Tim. "Giving Users the Key to Their Web Content." *Computerworld*, July 26, 1999.

22. Ouellette, Tim. "Opening Your Own Portal." *Computerworld*, August 9, 1999.

23. Schwartz Matthew. "Time for a Makeover." *Computerworld*, August 19, 2002.

24. Senge, Peter. *The Fifth Discipline: The Art and Practice of the Learning Organization*. New York: Currency Doubleday, 1994.

25. Sliwa, Carol. "E-Commerce Solutions: How Real?" *Computerworld*, February 28, 2000.

26. Solomon, Melissa. "Filtering Out the Noise." *Computerworld*, February 25, 2002.

27. Songini, Marc. "GM Locomotive Unit Puts ERP Rollout Back on Track." *Computerworld*, February 11, 2002.

28. Whitten, Jeffrey, and Lonnie Bentley. *Systems Analysis and Design Methods*. 5th ed. New York: McGraw-Hill/Irwin, 2000.

Chapter 11—Security and Ethical Challenges

1. Alexander, Steve, and Matt Hamblen. "Top-Flight Technology." *Computerworld*, September 23, 2002.

2. Anthes, Gary. "Biometrics." *Computerworld*, October 12, 1998.

3. Anthes, Gary. "When Five 9s Aren't Enough." *Computerworld*, October 8, 2001.

4. Boutin, Paul. "Burn Baby Burn." *Wired*, December 2002.

5. Deckmyn, Dominique. "More Managers Monitor E-Mail." *Computerworld*, October 18, 1999.

6. Dejoie, Roy; George Fowler; and David Paradice, eds. *Ethical Issues in Information Systems*. Boston: Boyd & Fraser, 1991.

7. Donaldson, Thomas. "Values in Tension: Ethics Away from Home." *Harvard Business Review*, September–October 1996.

8. Dunlop, Charles, and Rob Kling, eds. *Computerization and Controversy: Value Conflicts and Social Choices*. San Diego: Academic Press, 1991.

9. Elias, Paul. "Paid Informant." *Red Herring*, January 16, 2001.

10. Harrison, Ann. "Virus Scanning Moving to ISPs." *Computerworld*, September 20, 1999.

11. "In Depth: Security." *Computerworld*, July 9, 2001.

12. Joy, Bill. "Report from the Cyberfront." *Newsweek*, February 21, 2000.

13. Johnson, Deborah. "Ethics Online." *Communications of the ACM*, January 1997.

14. Lardner, James. "Why Should Anyone Believe You?" *Business 2.0*, March 2002.

15. Levy, Stephen, and Brad Stone. "Hunting the Hackers." *Newsweek*, February 21, 2000.

16. Madsen, Peter, and Jay Shafritz, *Essentials of Business Ethics*, New York: Meridian, 1990.

17. McCarthy, Michael. "Keystroke Cops." *The Wall Street Journal*, March 7, 2000.

18. Nance, Barry. "Sending Firewalls Home." *Computerworld*, May 28, 2001.

19. Naughton, Keith. "CyberSlacking." *Newsweek*, November 29, 1999.

20. Neumann, Peter. *Computer-Related Risks*. New York: ACM Press, 1995.

21. Phillips, Robert. *Stakeholder Theory and Organizational Ethics*. San Francisco: Berrett-Koehler, 2003.

22. Radcliff, Deborah. "Cybersleuthing Solves the Case." *Computerworld*, January 14, 2002.

23. Robinson, Lori. "How It Works: Viruses." *Smart Computing*, March 2000.

24. Rothfeder, Jeffrey. "Hacked! Are Your Company Files Safe?" *PC World*, November 1996.

25. Rothfeder, Jeffrey. "No Privacy on the Net." *PC World*, February 1997.

26. Sager, Ira; Steve Hamm; Neil Gross; John Carey; and Robert Hoff. "Cyber Crime." *Business Week*, February 21, 2000.

27. Smith, H. Jefferson, and John Hasnas. "Debating the Stakeholder Theory." *Beyond Computing*, March–April 1994.

28. Smith, H. Jefferson, and John Hasnas. "Establishing an Ethical Framework." *Beyond Computing*, January–February 1994.

29. Solomon, Melissa, and Michael Meehan. "Enron Lesson: Tech Is for Support." *Computerworld*, February 18, 2002.

30. Spinello, Richard. *Cyberethics: Morality and Law in Cyberspace*. 2nd ed. Sudbury, MA: Jones and Bartlett Publishers, 2003.

31. Verton, Dan. "Insider Monitoring Seen as Next Wave in IT Security." *Computerworld*, March 19, 2001.

32. VanScoy, Kayte. "What Your Workers Are Really Up To." *Ziff Davis Smart Business*, September 2001.

33. Vijayan, Jaikumar. "Nimda Needs Harsh Disinfectant," *Computerworld*, September 24, 2001.

34. Vijayan, Jaikumar. "Securing the Center." *Computerworld*, May 13, 2002.

35. Willard, Nancy. *The Cyberethics Reader*. Burr Ridge, IL: Irwin/McGraw-Hill, 1997.

36. York, Thomas. "Invasion of Privacy? E-Mail Monitoring Is on the Rise." *Information Week Online*, February 21, 2000.

Chapter 12—Enterprise and Global Management of Information Technology

1. Bryan, Lowell; Jane Fraser; Jeremy Oppenheim; and Wilhelm Rall. *Race for the World: Strategies to Build a Great Global Firm*. Boston: Harvard Business School Press, 1999.

2. Christensen, Clayton. *The Innovators Dilemma: When New Technologies Cause Great Firms to Fail*. Boston: Harvard Business School Press, 1997.

3. Cronin, Mary. *Global Advantage on the Internet*. New York: Van Nostrand Reinhold, 1996.

4. El Sawy, Omar; Arvind Malhotra; Sanjay Gosain; and Kerry Young. "IT-Intensive Value Innovation in the Electronic Economy: Insights from Marshall Industries." *MIS Quarterly*, September 1999.

5. Fryer, Bronwyn. "Payroll Busters." *Computerworld*, March 6, 2000.

6. Gilhooly, Kym. "The Staff That Never Sleeps." *Computerworld*, June 25, 2001.

7. Grover, Varun; James Teng; and Kirk Fiedler. "IS Investment Opportunities in Contemporary Organizations." *Communications of the ACM*, February 1998.

8. Hall, Mark. "Service Providers Give Users More IT Options." *Computerworld*, February 7, 2000.

9. Ives, Blake, and Sirkka Jarvenpaa. "Applications of Global Information Technology: Key Issues for Management." *MIS Quarterly*, March 1991.

10. Kalakota, Ravi, and Marcia Robinson. *E-Business 2.0: Roadmap for Success*. Reading, MA: Addison-Wesley, 2001.

11. Kalin, Sari. "The Importance of Being Multiculturally Correct." Global Innovators Series, *Computerworld*, October 6, 1997.

12. Kirkpatrick, David. "Back to the Future with Centralized Computing." *Fortune*, November 10, 1997.

13. LaPlante, Alice. "Global Boundaries.com." Global Innovators Series, *Computerworld*, October 6, 1997.

14. Leinfuss, Emily. "Blend It, Mix It, Unify It." *Computerworld*, March 26, 2001.

15. Mearian, Lucas. "Citibank Overhauls Overseas Systems." *Computerworld*, February 4, 2002.

16. Mische, Michael. "Transnational Architecture: A Reengineering Approach." *Information Systems Management*, Winter 1995.

17. Palvia, Prashant; Shailendra Palvia; and Edward Roche, eds. *Global Information Technology and Systems Management*. Marietta, GA: Ivy League Publishing, 1996.

18. Radcliff, Deborah. "Playing by Europe's Rules." *Computerworld*, July 9, 2001.

19. Ross, Jeanne, and Peter Weill. "Six IT Decisions Your IT People Shouldn't Make." *Harvard Business Review*, November 2002.

20. Songini, Marc and Kim Nash. "Try, Try Again." *Computerworld*, February 18, 2002.

21. Thibodeau, Patrick, "Europe and U.S. Agree on Data Rules." *Computerworld*, March 20, 2000.

22. Taggart, Stewart. "Censor Census." *Business 2.0*, March 2000.

23. Vijayan, Jaikumar. "The Outsourcing Boom" *Computerworld*, March 18, 2002.

24. Vitalari, Nicholas, and James Wetherbe. "Emerging Best Practices in Global Systems Development." In *Global Information Technology and Systems Management*, ed. Prashant Palvia et al. Marietta, GA: Ivy League Publishing, 1996.

25. West, Lawrence, and Walter Bogumil. "Immigration and the Global IT Workforce." *Communications of the ACM*, July 2001.

Accounting Information Systems
Information systems that record and report business transactions, the flow of funds through an organization, and produce financial statements. These provide information for the planning and control of business operations, as well as for legal and historical record-keeping.

Ada
A programming language named after Augusta Ada Byron, considered the world's first computer programmer. Developed for the U.S. Department of Defense as a standard high-order language.

Ad Hoc Inquiries
Unique, unscheduled, situation-specific information requests.

Agile Competition
The ability of a company to profitably operate in a competitive environment of continual and unpredictable changes in customer preferences, market conditions, and business opportunities.

Algorithm
A set of well-defined rules or processes for the solution of a problem in a finite number of steps.

Analog Computer
A computer that operates on data by measuring changes in continuous physical variables such as voltage, resistance, and rotation. Contrast with Digital Computer.

Analytical Database
A database of data extracted from operational and external databases to provide data tailored to online analytical processing, decision support, and executive information systems.

Analytical Modeling
Interactive use of computer-based mathematical models to explore decision alternatives using what-if analysis, sensitivity analysis, goal-seeking analysis, and optimization analysis.

Applet
A small limited-purpose application program, or small independent module of a larger application program.

Application Development
See Systems Development.

Application Generator
A software package that supports the development of an application through an interactive terminal dialogue, where the programmer/analyst defines screens, reports, computations, and data structures.

Application Portfolio
A planning tool used to evaluate present and proposed information systems applications in terms of the amount of revenue or assets invested in information systems that support major business functions and processes.

Applications Architecture
A conceptual planning framework in which business applications of information technology are designed as an integrated architecture of enterprise systems that support strategic business initiatives and cross-functional business processes.

Application Server
System software that provides a middleware interface between an operating system and the application programs of users.

Application Software
Programs that specify the information processing activities required for the completion of specific tasks of computer users. Examples are electronic spreadsheet and word processing programs or inventory or payroll programs.

Application-Specific Programs
Application software packages that support specific applications of end users in business, science and engineering, and other areas.

Arithmetic-Logic Unit (ALU)
The unit of a computing system containing the circuits that perform arithmetic and logical operations.

Artificial Intelligence (AI)
A science and technology whose goal is to develop computers that can think, as well as see, hear, walk, talk, and feel. A major thrust is the development of computer functions normally associated with human intelligence, for example, reasoning, inference, learning, and problem solving.

ASCII: American Standard Code for Information Interchange
A standard code used for information interchange among data processing systems, communication systems, and associated equipment.

Assembler
A computer program that translates an assembler language into machine language.

Assembler Language
A programming language that utilizes symbols to represent operation codes and storage locations.

Asynchronous
Involving a sequence of operations without a regular or predictable time relationship. Thus operations do not happen at regular timed intervals, but an operation will begin only after a previous operation is completed. In data transmission, involves the use of start and stop bits with each character to indicate the beginning and end of the character being transmitted. Contrast with Synchronous.

Audit Trail
The presence of media and procedures that allow a transaction to be traced through all stages of information processing, beginning with its appearance on a source document and ending with its transformation into

information on a final output document.

Automated Teller Machine (ATM)
A special-purpose transaction terminal used to provide remote banking services.

Back-End Processor
Typically, a smaller general-purpose computer that is dedicated to database processing using a database management system (DBMS). Also called a database machine or server.

Background Processing
The automatic execution of lower-priority computer programs when higher-priority programs are not using the resources of the computer system. Contrast with Foreground Processing.

Backward-Chaining
An inference process that justifies a proposed conclusion by determining if it will result when rules are applied to the facts in a given situation.

Bandwidth
The frequency range of a telecommunications channel, which determines its maximum transmission rate. The speed and capacity of transmission rates are typically measured in bits per second (BPS). Bandwidth is a function of the telecommunications hardware, software, and media used by the telecommunications channel.

Bar Codes
Vertical marks or bars placed on merchandise tags or packaging that can be sensed and read by optical character-reading devices. The width and combination of vertical lines are used to represent data.

Barriers to Entry
Technological, financial, or legal requirements that deter firms from entering an industry.

BASIC: Beginner's All-Purpose Symbolic Instruction Code
A programming language developed at Dartmouth College designed for programming by end users.

Batch Processing
A category of data processing in which data are accumulated into batches and processed periodically. Contrast with Realtime Processing.

Baud
A unit of measurement used to specify data transmission speeds. It is a unit of signaling speed equal to the number of discrete conditions or signal events per second. In many data communications applications it represents one bit per second.

Binary
Pertaining to a characteristic or property involving a selection, choice, or condition in which there are two possibilities, or pertaining to the number system that utilizes a base of 2.

Biometric Controls
Computer-based security methods that measure physical traits and characteristics such as fingerprints, voice prints, retina scans, and so on.

Bit
A contraction of "binary digit." It can have the value of either 0 or 1.

Block
A grouping of contiguous data records or other data elements that are handled as a unit.

Branch
A transfer of control from one instruction to another in a computer program that is not part of the normal sequential execution of the instructions of the program.

Browser
See Web Browser.

Buffer
Temporary storage used when transmitting data from one device to another to compensate for a difference in rate of flow of data or time of occurrence of events.

Bug
A mistake or malfunction.

Bulletin Board System (BBS)
A service of online computer networks in which electronic messages, data files, or programs can be stored for other subscribers to read or copy.

Bundling
The inclusion of software, maintenance, training, and other products or services in the price of a computer system.

Bus
A set of conducting paths for movement of data and instructions that interconnects the various components of the CPU.

Business Ethics
An area of philosophy concerned with developing ethical principles and promoting ethical behavior and practices in the accomplishment of business tasks and decision making.

Business Intelligence (BI)
A term primarily used in industry that incorporates a range of analytical and decision support applications in business including data mining, decision support systems, knowledge management systems, and online analytical processing.

Business Process Reengineering (BPR)
Restructuring and transforming a business process by a fundamental rethinking and redesign to achieve dramatic improvements in cost, quality, speed, and so on.

Business/IT Planning
The process of developing a company's business vision, strategies, and goals, and how they will be supported by the company's information technology architecture and implemented by its business application development process.

Byte
A sequence of adjacent binary digits operated on as a unit and usually shorter than a computer word. In many computer systems, a byte is a grouping of eight bits that can represent one alphabetic or special character or can be packed with two decimal digits.

C
A low-level structured programming language that resembles a machine-independent assembler language.

C++
An object-oriented version of C that is widely used for software package development.

Cache Memory
A high-speed temporary storage area in the CPU for storing parts of a program or data during processing.

Capacity Management
The use of planning and control methods to forecast and control information processing job loads, hardware and software usage, and other computer system resource requirements.

Case-Based Reasoning
Representing knowledge in an expert system's knowledge base in the form of cases, that is, examples of past performance, occurrences, and experiences.

Cathode Ray Tube (CRT)
An electronic vacuum tube (television picture tube) that displays the output of a computer system.

CD-ROM
An optical disk technology for microcomputers featuring compact disks with a storage capacity of over 500 megabytes.

Cellular Phone Systems
A radio communications technology that divides a metropolitan area into a honeycomb of cells to greatly increase the number of frequencies and thus the users that can take advantage of mobile phone service.

Central Processing Unit (CPU)
The unit of a computer system that includes the circuits that control the interpretation and execution of instructions. In many computer systems, the CPU includes the arithmetic-logic unit, the control unit, and the primary storage unit.

Change Management
Managing the process of implementing major changes in information technology, business processes, organizational structures, and job assignments to reduce the risks and costs of change and optimize its benefits.

Channel
(1) A path along which signals can be sent. (2) A small special-purpose processor that controls the movement of data between the CPU and input/output devices.

Chargeback Systems
Methods of allocating costs to end user departments based on the information services rendered and information system resources utilized.

Chat Systems
Software that enables two or more users at networked PCs to carry on online, real-time text conversations.

Check Bit
A binary check digit; for example, a parity bit.

Check Digit
A digit in a data field that is utilized to check for errors or loss of characters in the data field as a result of data transfer operations.

Checkpoint
A place in a program where a check or a recording of data for restart purposes is performed.

Chief Information Officer
A senior management position that oversees all information technology for a firm concentrating on long-range information system planning and strategy.

Client
(1) An end user. (2) The end user's networked microcomputer in client/server networks. (3) The version of a software package designed to run on an end user's networked microcomputer, such as a Web browser client, a groupware client, and so on.

Client/Server Network
A computer network where end user workstations (clients) are connected via telecommunications links to network servers and possibly to mainframe superservers.

Clock
A device that generates periodic signals utilized to control the timing of a computer. Also, a register whose contents change at regular intervals in such a way as to measure time.

Coaxial Cable
A sturdy copper or aluminum wire wrapped with spacers to insulate and protect it. Groups of coaxial cables may also be bundled together in a bigger cable for ease of installation.

COBOL: COmmon Business Oriented Language
A widely used business data processing programming language.

Code
Computer instructions.

Cognitive Science
An area of artificial intelligence that focuses on researching how the human brain works and how humans think and learn, in order to apply such findings to the design of computer-based systems.

Cognitive Styles
Basic patterns in how people handle information and confront problems.

Cognitive Theory
Theories about how the human brain works and how humans think and learn.

Collaborative Work Management Tools
Software that helps people accomplish or manage joint work activities.

Communications Satellite
Earth satellites placed in stationary orbits above the equator that serve as relay stations for communications signals transmitted from earth stations.

Competitive Advantage
Developing products, services, processes, or capabilities that give a company a superior business position relative to its competitors and other competitive forces.

Competitive Forces
A firm must confront (1) rivalry of competitors within its industry, (2) threats of new entrants, (3) threats of substitutes, (4) the bargaining power of customers, and (5) the bargaining power of suppliers.

Competitive Strategies
A firm can develop cost leadership, product differentiation, and business innovation strategies to confront its competitive forces.

Compiler
A program that translates a high-level programming language into a machine-language program.

Computer
A device that has the ability to accept data; internally store and execute a program of instructions; perform mathematical, logical, and manipulative operations on data; and report the results.

Computer-Aided Design (CAD)
The use of computers and advanced graphics hardware and software to provide interactive design assistance for engineering and architectural design.

Computer-Aided Engineering (CAE)
The use of computers to simulate, analyze, and evaluate models of product designs and production processes developed using computer-aided design methods.

Computer-Aided Manufacturing (CAM)
The use of computers to automate the production process and operations of a manufacturing plant. Also called factory automation.

Computer-Aided Planning (CAP)
The use of software packages as tools to support the planning process.

Computer-Aided Software Engineering (CASE)
Same as Computer-Aided Systems Engineering, but emphasizing the importance of software development.

Computer-Aided Systems Engineering (CASE)
Using software packages to accomplish and automate many of the activities of information systems development, including software development or programming.

Computer Application
The use of a computer to solve a specific problem or to accomplish a particular job for an end user. For example, common business computer applications include sales order processing, inventory control, and payroll.

Computer-Assisted Instruction (CAI)
The use of computers to provide drills, practice exercises, and tutorial sequences to students.

Computer-Based Information System
An information system that uses computer hardware and software to perform its information processing activities.

Computer Crime
Criminal actions accomplished through the use of computer systems, especially with intent to defraud, destroy, or make

unauthorized use of computer system resources.

Computer Ethics
A system of principles governing the legal, professional, social, and moral responsibilities of computer specialists and end users.

Computer Generations
Major stages in the historical development of computing.

Computer Graphics
Using computer-generated images to analyze and interpret data, present information, and do computer-aided design and art.

Computer Industry
The industry composed of firms that supply computer hardware, software, and services.

Computer-Integrated Manufacturing (CIM)
An overall concept that stresses that the goals of computer use in factory automation should be to simplify, automate, and integrate production processes and other aspects of manufacturing.

Computer Matching
Using computers to screen and match data about individual characteristics provided by a variety of computer-based information systems and databases in order to identify individuals for business, government, or other purposes.

Computer Monitoring
Using computers to monitor the behavior and productivity of workers on the job and in the workplace.

Computer Program
A series of instructions or statements in a form acceptable to a computer, prepared in order to achieve a certain result.

Computer System
Computer hardware as a system of input, processing, output, storage, and control components. Thus a computer system consists of input and output devices, primary and secondary storage devices, the central processing unit, the control unit within the CPU, and other peripheral devices.

Computer Terminal
Any input/output device connected by telecommunications links to a computer.

Computer Virus or Worm
Program code that copies its destructive program routines into the computer systems of anyone who accesses computer systems that have used the program, or anyone who uses copies of data or programs taken from such computers. This spreads the destruction of data and programs among many computer users. Technically, a virus will not run unaided, but must be inserted into another program, while a worm is a distinct program that can run unaided.

Concurrent Processing
The generic term for the capability of computers to work on several tasks at the same time, that is, concurrently. This may involve specific capabilities such as overlapped processing, multiprocessing, multiprogramming, multitasking, parallel processing, and so on.

Connectivity
The degree to which hardware, software, and databases can be easily linked together in a telecommunications network.

Control
(1) The systems component that evaluates feedback to determine whether the system is moving toward the achievement of its goal and then makes any necessary adjustments to the input and processing components of the system to ensure that proper output is produced. (2) A management function that involves observing and measuring organizational performance and environmental activities and modifying the plans and activities of the organization when necessary.

Control Listing
A detailed report that describes each transaction occurring during a period.

Control Totals
Accumulating totals of data at multiple points in an information system to ensure correct information processing.

Control Unit
A subunit of the central processing unit that controls and directs the operations of the computer system. The control unit retrieves computer instructions in proper sequence, interprets each instruction, and then directs the other parts of the computer system in their implementation.

Conversion
The process in which the hardware, software, people, network, and data resources of an old information system must be converted to the requirements of a new information system. This usually involves a parallel, phased, pilot, or plunge conversion process from the old to the new system.

Cooperative Processing
Information processing that allows the computers in a distributed processing network to share the processing of parts of an end user's application.

Cost/Benefit Analysis
Identifying the advantages or benefits and the disadvantages or costs of a proposed solution.

Critical Success Factors
A small number of key factors that executives consider critical to the success of the enterprise. These are key areas where successful performance will assure the success of the organization and attainment of its goals.

Cross-Functional Information Systems
Information systems that are integrated combinations of business information systems, thus sharing information resources across the functional units of an organization.

Cursor
A movable point of light displayed on most video display screens to assist the user in the input of data.

Customer Relationship Management (CRM)
A cross-functional e-business application that integrates and automates many customer serving processes in sales, direct marketing, account and order management, and customer service and support.

Cybernetic System
A system that uses feedback and control components to achieve a self-regulating capability.

Cylinder
An imaginary vertical cylinder consisting of the vertical alignment of tracks on each surface of magnetic disks that are accessed simultaneously by the read/write heads of a disk drive.

Data
Facts or observations about physical phenomena or business transactions. More specifically, data are objective measurements of the attributes (characteristics) of entities such as people, places, things, and events.

Data Administration
A data resource management function that involves the establishment and enforcement of policies and procedures for managing data as a strategic corporate resource.

Data Conversion
Converting data into new data formats required by a new business application and its software and databases. Also includes correcting incorrect data, filtering out unwanted data, and consolidating data into new databases and other data subsets.

Database
An integrated collection of logically related data elements. A database consolidates many records previously stored in separate files so that a common pool of data serves many applications.

Database Administration
A data resource management function that includes responsibility for developing and maintaining the organization's data dictionary, designing and monitoring the performance of databases, and enforcing standards for database use and security.

Database Administrator
A specialist responsible for maintaining standards for the development, maintenance, and security of an organization's databases.

Database Maintenance
The activity of keeping a database up-to-date by adding, changing, or deleting data.

Database Management Approach
An approach to the storage and processing of data in which independent files are consolidated into a common pool, or database, of records available to different application programs and end users for processing and data retrieval.

Database Management System (DBMS)
A set of computer programs that controls the creation, maintenance, and utilization of the databases of an organization.

Database Processing
Utilizing a database for data processing activities such as maintenance, information retrieval, or report generation.

Data Center
An organizational unit that uses centralized computing resources to perform information processing activities for an organization. Also known as a computer center.

Data Conferencing
Users at networked PCs can view, mark up, revise, and save changes to a shared whiteboard of drawings, documents, and other material.

Data Design
The design of the logical structure of databases and files to be used by a proposed information system. This produces detailed descriptions of the entities, relationships, data elements, and integrity rules for system files and databases.

Data Dictionary
A software module and database containing descriptions and definitions concerning the structure, data elements, interrelationships, and other characteristics of a database.

Data Entry
The process of converting data into a form suitable for entry into a computer system. Also called data capture or input preparation.

Data Flow Diagram
A graphic diagramming tool that uses a few simple symbols to illustrate the flow of data among external entities, processing activities, and data storage elements.

Data Management
Control program functions that provide access to data sets, enforce data storage conventions, and regulate the use of input/output devices.

Data Mining
Using special-purpose software to analyze data from a data warehouse to find hidden patterns and trends.

Data Model
A conceptual framework that defines the logical relationships among the data elements needed to support a basic business or other process.

Data Modeling
A process where the relationships between data elements are identified and defined to develop data models.

Data Planning
A corporate planning and analysis function that focuses on data resource management. It includes the responsibility for developing an overall information policy and data architecture for the firm's data resources.

Data Processing
The execution of a systematic sequence of operations performed upon data to transform it into information.

Data Resource Management
A managerial activity that applies information systems technology and management tools to the task of managing an organization's data resources. Its three major components are database administration, data administration, and data planning.

Data Warehouse
An integrated collection of data extracted from operational, historical, and external databases, and cleaned, transformed, and cataloged for retrieval and analysis (*data mining*), to provide business intelligence for business decision making.

Debug
To detect, locate, and remove errors from a program or malfunctions from a computer.

Decision Support System (DSS)
An information system that utilizes decision models, a database, and a decision maker's own insights in an ad hoc, interactive analytical modeling process to reach a specific decision by a specific decision maker.

Demand Reports and Responses
Information provided whenever a manager or end user demands it.

Desktop Publishing
The use of microcomputers, laser printers, and page-makeup software to produce a variety of printed materials that were formerly produced only by professional printers.

Desktop Videoconferencing
The use of end user computer workstations to conduct two-way interactive video conferences.

Development Centers
Systems development consultant groups formed to serve as consultants to the professional programmers and systems analysts of an organization to improve their application development efforts.

Digital Computer
A computer that operates on digital data by performing arithmetic and logical operations on the data. Contrast with Analog Computer.

Digitizer
A device that is used to convert drawings and other graphic images on paper or other materials into digital data that are entered into a computer system.

Direct Access
A method of storage where each storage position has a unique address and can be individually accessed in approximately the same period of time without having to search through other storage positions. Same as Random Access. Contrast with Sequential Access.

Direct Access Storage Device (DASD)
A storage device that can directly access data to be stored or retrieved, for example, a magnetic disk unit.

Direct Data Organization
A method of data organization in which logical data elements are distributed randomly on or within the physical data medium. For example, logical data records distributed randomly on the surfaces of a magnetic disk file. Also called direct organization.

Direct Input/Output
Methods such as keyboard entry, voice input/output, and video displays that allow data to be input into or output from a computer system without the use of machine-readable media.

Disaster Recovery
Methods for ensuring that an organization recovers from natural and human-caused disasters that have affected its computer-based operations.

Discussion Forum
An online network discussion platform to encourage and manage online text discussions over a period of time among members of special interest groups or project teams.

Distributed Databases
The concept of distributing databases or portions of a database at remote sites where the data are most frequently referenced. Sharing of data is made possible through a network that interconnects the distributed databases.

Distributed Processing
A form of decentralization of information processing made possible by a network of computers dispersed throughout an organization. Processing of user applications is accomplished by several computers interconnected by a telecommunications network, rather than relying on one large centralized computer facility or on the decentralized operation of several independent computers.

Document
(1) A medium on which data have been recorded for human use, such as a report or invoice. (2) In word processing, a generic term for text material such as letters, memos, reports, and so on.

Documentation
A collection of documents or information that describes a computer program, information system, or required data processing operations.

Downsizing
Moving to smaller computing platforms, such as from mainframe systems to networks of personal computers and servers.

Downtime
The time interval during which a device is malfunctioning or inoperative.

DSS Generator
A software package for a decision support system that contains modules for database, model, and dialogue management.

Duplex
In communications, pertains to a simultaneous two-way independent transmission in both directions.

EBCDIC: Extended Binary Coded Decimal Interchange Code
An eight-bit code that is widely used by mainframe computers.

Echo Check
A method of checking the accuracy of transmission of data in which the received data are returned to the sending device for comparison with the original data.

e-Commerce Marketplaces
Internet, intranet, and extranet websites and portals hosted by individual companies, consortiums of organizations, or third-party intermediaries providing electronic catalog, exchange, and auction markets to unite buyers and sellers to accomplish e-commerce transactions.

Economic Feasibility
Whether expected cost savings, increased revenue, increased profits, and reductions in required investment exceed the costs of developing and operating a proposed system.

EDI: Electronic Data Interchange
The automatic electronic exchange of business documents between the computers of different organizations.

Edit
To modify the form or format of data. For example: to insert or delete characters such as page numbers or decimal points.

Edit Report
A report that describes errors detected during processing.

EFT: Electronic Funds Transfer
The development of banking and payment systems that transfer funds electronically instead of using cash or paper documents such as checks.

Electronic Business (e-Business)
The use of Internet technologies to internetwork and empower business processes, electronic commerce, and enterprise communication and collaboration within a company and with its customers, suppliers, and other business stakeholders.

Electronic Commerce (e-Commerce)
The buying and selling, marketing and servicing, and delivery and payment of products, services, and information over the Internet, intranets, extranets, and other networks, between an internetworked enterprise and its

prospects, customers, suppliers, and other business partners. Includes business-to-consumer (B2C), business-to-business (B2B), and consumer-to-consumer (C2C) e-commerce.

Electronic Communications Tools
Software that helps you communicate and collaborate with others by electronically sending messages, documents, and files in data, text, voice, or multimedia over the Internet, intranets, extranets, and other computer networks.

Electronic Conferencing Tools
Software that helps networked computer users share information and collaborate while working together on joint assignments, no matter where they are located.

Electronic Data Processing (EDP)
The use of electronic computers to process data automatically.

Electronic Document Management
An image processing technology in which an electronic document may consist of digitized voice notes and electronic graphics images, as well as digitized images of traditional documents.

Electronic Mail
Sending and receiving text messages between networked PCs over telecommunications networks. E-mail can also include data files, software, and multimedia messages and documents as attachments.

Electronic Meeting Systems (EMS)
Using a meeting room with networked PCs, a large-screen projector, and EMS software to facilitate communication, collaboration, and group decision making in business meetings.

Electronic Payment Systems
Alternative cash or credit payment methods using various electronic technologies to pay for products and services in electronic commerce.

Electronic Spreadsheet Package
An application program used as a computerized tool for analysis, planning, and modeling that allows users to enter and manipulate data into an electronic worksheet of rows and columns.

Emulation
To imitate one system with another so that the imitating system accepts the same data, executes the same programs, and achieves the same results as the imitated system.

Encryption
To scramble data or convert it, prior to transmission, to a secret code that masks the meaning of the data to unauthorized recipients. Similar to enciphering.

End User
Anyone who uses an information system or the information it produces.

End User Computing Systems
Computer-based information systems that directly support both the operational and managerial applications of end users.

Enterprise Application Integration (EAI)
A cross-functional e-business application that integrates front-office applications like customer relationship management with back-office applications like enterprise resource management.

Enterprise Collaboration Systems
The use of groupware tools and the Internet, intranets, extranets, and other computer networks to support and enhance communication, coordination, collaboration, and resource sharing among teams and workgroups in an internetworked enterprise.

Enterprise Information Portal
A customized and personalized Web-based interface for corporate intranets and extranets that gives qualified users access to a variety of internal and external e-business and e-commerce applications, databases, software tools, and information services.

Enterprise Knowledge Portal
An enterprise information portal that serves as a knowledge management system by providing users with access to enterprise knowledge bases.

Enterprise Model
A conceptual framework that defines the structures and relationships of business processes and data elements, as well as other planning structures, such as critical success factors, and organizational units.

Enterprise Resource Planning (ERP)
Integrated cross-functional software that reengineers manufacturing, distribution, finance, human resources and other basic business processes of a company to improve its efficiency, agility, and profitability.

Entity Relationship Diagram (ERD)
A data planning and systems development diagramming tool that models the relationships among the entities in a business process.

Entropy
The tendency of a system to lose a relatively stable state of equilibrium.

Ergonomics
The science and technology emphasizing the safety, comfort, and ease of use of human-operated machines such as computers. The goal of ergonomics is to produce systems that are user-friendly: safe, comfortable, and easy to use. Ergonomics is also called human factors engineering.

Exception Reports
Reports produced only when exceptional conditions occur, or reports produced periodically that contain information only about exceptional conditions.

Executive Information System (EIS)
An information system that provides strategic information tailored to the needs of executives and other decision makers.

Executive Support System (ESS)
An executive information system with additional capabilities, including data analysis, decision support, electronic mail, and personal productivity tools.

Expert System (ES)
A computer-based information system that uses its knowledge about a specific complex application area to act as an expert consultant to users. The system consists of a knowledge base and software modules that perform inferences on the knowledge and communicate answers to a user's questions.

Extranet
A network that links selected resources of a company with its customers, suppliers, and other business partners, using the Internet or private networks to link the organizations' intranets.

Facilities Management
The use of an external service organization to operate and manage the information processing facilities of an organization.

Fault Tolerant Systems
Computers that have multiple central processors, peripherals, and system software and that are able to continue operations even if there is a major hardware or software failure.

Faxing (Facsimile)
Transmitting and receiving images of documents over the telephone or computer networks using PCs or fax machines.

Feasibility Study
A preliminary study that investigates the information needs of end users and the objectives, constraints, basic resource requirements, cost/benefits, and feasibility of proposed projects.

Feedback
(1) Data or information concerning the components and operations of a system. (2) The use of part of the output of a system as input to the system.

Fiber Optics
The technology that uses cables consisting of very thin filaments of glass fibers that can conduct the light generated by lasers for high-speed telecommunications.

Field
A data element that consists of a grouping of characters that describe a particular attribute of an entity. For example: the name field or salary field of an employee.

Fifth Generation
The next generation of computers. Major advances in parallel processing, user interfaces, and artificial intelligence may provide computers that will be able to see, hear, talk, and think.

File
A collection of related data records treated as a unit. Sometimes called a data set.

File Management
Controlling the creation, deletion, access, and use of files of data and programs.

File Processing
Organizing data into specialized files of data records designed for processing only by specific application programs. Contrast with Database Management Approach.

Financial Management Systems
Information systems that support financial managers in the financing of a business and the allocation and control of financial resources. These include cash and securities management, capital budgeting, financial forecasting, and financial planning.

Firewall
Computers, communications processors, and software that protect computer networks from intrusion by screening all network traffic and serving as a safe transfer point for access to and from other networks.

Firmware
The use of microprogrammed read only memory circuits in place of

hard-wired logic circuitry. See also Microprogramming.

Floating Point
Pertaining to a number representation system in which each number is represented by two sets of digits. One set represents the significant digits or fixed-point "base" of the number, while the other set of digits represents the "exponent," which indicates the precision of the number.

Floppy Disk
A small plastic disk coated with iron oxide that resembles a small phonograph record enclosed in a protective envelope. It is a widely used form of magnetic disk media that provides a direct access storage capability for microcomputer systems.

Flowchart
A graphical representation in which symbols are used to represent operations, data, flow, logic, equipment, and so on. A program flowchart illustrates the structure and sequence of operations of a program, while a system flowchart illustrates the components and flows of information systems.

Foreground Processing
The automatic execution of the computer programs that have been designed to preempt the use of computing facilities. Contrast with Background Processing.

Format
The arrangement of data on a medium.

FORTRAN: FORmula TRANslation
A high-level programming language widely utilized to develop computer programs that perform mathematical computations for scientific, engineering, and selected business applications.

Forward Chaining
An inference strategy that reaches a conclusion by applying rules to facts to determine if any facts satisfy a rule's conditions in a particular situation.

Fourth-Generation Languages (4GL)
Programming languages that are easier to use than high-level languages like BASIC, COBOL, or FORTRAN. They are also known as nonprocedural, natural, or very-high-level languages.

Frame
A collection of knowledge about an entity or other concept consisting of a complex package of slots, that is, data values describing the characteristics or attributes of an entity.

Frame-Based Knowledge
Knowledge represented in the form of a hierarchy or network of frames.

Front-End Processor
Typically a smaller, general-purpose computer that is dedicated to handling data communications control functions in a communications network, thus relieving the host computer of these functions.

Functional Business Systems
Information systems within a business organization that support one of the traditional functions of business such as marketing, finance, or production. Functional business systems can be either operations or management information systems.

Functional Requirements
The information system capabilities required to meet the information needs of end users. Also called system requirements.

Fuzzy Logic Systems
Computer-based systems that can process data that are incomplete or only partially correct, that is, fuzzy data. Such systems can solve unstructured problems with incomplete knowledge, as humans do.

General-Purpose Application Programs
Programs that can perform information processing jobs for users from all application areas. For example, word processing programs, electronic spreadsheet programs, and graphics programs can be used by individuals for home, education, business, scientific, and many other purposes.

General-Purpose Computer
A computer that is designed to handle a wide variety of problems. Contrast with Special-Purpose Computer.

Generate
To produce a machine-language program for performing a specific data processing task based on parameters supplied by a programmer or user.

Genetic Algorithm
An application of artificial intelligence software that uses Darwinian (survival of the fittest) randomizing and other functions to simulate an evolutionary process that can yield increasingly better solutions to a problem.

Gigabyte
One billion bytes. More accurately, 2 to the 30th power, or 1,073,741,824 in decimal notation.

GIGO
A contraction of "Garbage In, Garbage Out," which emphasizes that information systems will produce erroneous and invalid output when provided with erroneous and invalid input data or instructions.

Global Company
A business that is driven by a global strategy so that all of its activities are planned and implemented in the context of a whole-world system.

Global e-Business Technology Management
Managing information technologies in a global e-business enterprise, amid the cultural, political, and geoeconomic challenges involved in developing e-business/IT strategies, global e-business and e-commerce applications portfolios, Internet-based technology platforms, and global data resource management policies.

Global Information Technology
The use of computer-based information systems and telecommunications networks using a variety of information technologies to support global business operations and management.

Globalization
Becoming a global enterprise by expanding into global markets, using global production facilities, forming alliances with global partners, and so on.

Goal-Seeking Analysis
Making repeated changes to selected variables until a chosen variable reaches a target value.

Graphical User Interface
A software interface that relies on icons, bars, buttons, boxes, and other images to initiate computer-based tasks for users.

Graphics
Pertaining to symbolic input or output from a computer system, such as lines, curves, and geometric shapes, using video display units or graphics plotters and printers.

Graphics Pen and Tablet
A device that allows an end user to draw or write on a pressure-sensitive tablet and have the handwriting or graphics digitized by the computer and accepted as input.

Graphics Software
A program that helps users generate graphics displays.

Group Decision Making
Decisions made by groups of people coming to an agreement on a particular issue.

Group Decision Support System (GDSS)
A decision support system that provides support for decision making by groups of people.

Group Support Systems (GSS)
An information system that enhances communication, coordination, collaboration, decision making, and group work activities of teams and workgroups.

Groupware
Software to support and enhance the communication, coordination, and collaboration among networked teams and workgroups, including software tools for electronic communications, electronic conferencing, and cooperative work management.

Hacking
(1) Obsessive use of a computer.
(2) The unauthorized access and use of computer systems.

Handshaking
Exchange of predetermined signals when a connection is established between two communications terminals.

Hard Copy
A data medium or data record that has a degree of permanence and that can be read by people or machines.

Hardware
(1) Machines and media. (2) Physical equipment, as opposed to computer programs or methods of use.
(3) Mechanical, magnetic, electrical, electronic, or optical devices. Contrast with Software.

Hash Total
The sum of numbers in a data field that are not normally added, such as account numbers or other identification numbers. It is utilized as a control total, especially during input/output operations of batch processing systems.

Header Label
A machine-readable record at the beginning of a file containing data for file identification and control.

Heuristic
Pertaining to exploratory methods of problem solving in which solutions are discovered by evaluation of the progress made toward the final result. It is an exploratory trial-and-error approach guided by rules of thumb. Opposite of algorithmic.

Hierarchical Data Structure
A logical data structure in which the relationships between records form a hierarchy or tree structure. The relationships among records are one to many, since each data element is related only to one element above it.

High-Level Language
A programming language that utilizes macro instructions and statements that closely resemble human language or mathematical notation to describe the problem to be solved or the procedure to be used. Also called a compiler language.

Homeostasis
A relatively stable state of equilibrium of a system.

Host Computer
Typically a larger central computer that performs the major data processing tasks in a computer network.

Human Factors
Hardware and software capabilities that can affect the comfort, safety, ease of use, and user customization of computer-based information systems.

Human Information Processing
A conceptual framework about the human cognitive process that uses an information processing context to explain how humans capture, process, and use information.

Human Resource Information Systems (HRIS)
Information systems that support human resource management activities such as recruitment, selection and hiring, job placement and performance appraisals, and training and development.

Hybrid AI Systems
Systems that integrate several AI technologies, such as expert systems and neural networks.

Hypermedia
Documents containing multiple forms of media, including text, graphics, video, and sound, that can be interactively searched, like Hypertext.

Hypertext
Text in electronic form that has been indexed and linked (hyperlinks) by software in a variety of ways so that it can be randomly and interactively searched by a user.

Hypertext Markup Language (HTML)
A popular page description language for creating hypertext and hypermedia documents for World Wide Web and intranet websites.

Icon
A small figure on a video display that looks like a familiar office or other device such as a file folder (for storing a file) or a wastebasket (for deleting a file).

Image Processing
A computer-based technology that allows end users to electronically capture, store, process, and retrieve images that may include numeric data, text, handwriting, graphics, documents, and photographs. Image processing makes heavy use of optical scanning and optical disk technologies.

Impact Printers
Printers that form images on paper through the pressing of a printing element and an inked ribbon or roller against the face of a sheet of paper.

Index
An ordered reference list of the contents of a file or document together with keys or reference notations for identification or location of those contents.

Index Sequential
A method of data organization in which records are organized in sequential order and also referenced by an index. When utilized with direct access file devices, it is known as index sequential access method, or ISAM.

Inference Engine
The software component of an expert system, which processes the rules and facts related to a specific problem and makes associations and inferences resulting in recommended courses of action.

Infomediaries
Third-party market-maker companies who serve as intermediaries to bring buyers and sellers together by developing and hosting electronic catalog, exchange, and auction markets to accomplish e-commerce transactions.

Information
Information is data placed in a meaningful and useful context for an end user.

Information Appliances
Small Web-enabled microcomputer devices with specialized functions, such as hand-held PDAs, TV set-top boxes, game consoles, cellular and PCS phones, wired telephone appliances, and other Web-enabled home appliances.

Information Architecture
A conceptual framework that defines the basic structure, content, and relationships of the organizational databases that provide the data needed to support the basic business processes of an organization.

Information Center
A support facility for the end users of an organization. It allows users to learn to develop their own application programs and to accomplish their own

information processing tasks. End users are provided with hardware support, software support, and people support (trained user consultants).

Information Float
The time when a document is in transit between the sender and receiver, and thus unavailable for any action or response.

Information Processing
A concept that covers both the traditional concept of processing numeric and alphabetic data, and the processing of text, images, and voices. It emphasizes that the production of information products for users should be the focus of processing activities.

Information Quality
The degree to which information has content, form, and time characteristics that give it value to specific end users.

Information Resource Management (IRM)
A management concept that views data, information, and computer resources (computer hardware, software, networks, and personnel) as valuable organizational resources that should be efficiently, economically, and effectively managed for the benefit of the entire organization.

Information Retrieval
The methods and procedures for recovering specific information from stored data.

Information Superhighway
An advanced high-speed Internet-like network that connects individuals, households, businesses, government agencies, libraries, schools, universities, and other institutions with interactive voice, video, data, and multimedia communications.

Information System
(1) A set of people, procedures, and resources that collects, transforms, and disseminates information in an organization. (2) A system that accepts data resources as input and processes them into information products as output.

Information System Model
A conceptual framework that views an information system as a system that uses the resources of hardware (machines and media), software (programs and procedures), people (users and specialists), and networks (communications media and network support) to perform input, processing, output, storage, and control activities that transform data resources (databases and knowledge bases) into information products.

Information Systems Development
See Systems Development.

Information System Specialist
A person whose occupation is related to the providing of information system services. For example: a systems analyst, programmer, or computer operator.

Information Technology (IT)
Hardware, software, telecommunications, database management, and other information processing technologies used in computer-based information systems.

Information Technology Architecture
A conceptual blueprint that specifies the components and interrelationships of a company's technology infrastructure, data resources, applications architecture, and IT organization.

Information Technology Management
Managing information technologies by (1) the joint development and implementation of business and IT strategies by business and IT executives, (2) managing the research and implementation of new information technologies and the development of business applications, and (3) managing the IT processes, professionals, subunits, and infrastructure within a company.

Information Theory
The branch of learning concerned with the likelihood of accurate transmission or communication of messages subject to transmission failure, distortion, and noise.

Input
Pertaining to a device, process, or channel involved in the insertion of data into a data processing system. Opposite of Output.

Input/Output (I/O)
Pertaining to either input or output, or both.

Input/Output Interface Hardware
Devices such as I/O ports, I/O buses, buffers, channels, and input/output control units, which assist the CPU in its input/output assignments. These devices make it possible for modern computer systems to perform input, output, and processing functions simultaneously.

Inquiry Processing
Computer processing that supports the real-time interrogation of online files and databases by end users.

Instruction
A grouping of characters that specifies the computer operation to be performed.

Intangible Benefits and Costs
The nonquantifiable benefits and costs of a proposed solution or system.

Integrated Circuit
A complex microelectronic circuit consisting of interconnected circuit elements that cannot be disassembled because they are placed on or within a "continuous substrate" such as a silicon chip.

Integrated Packages
Software that combines the ability to do several general-purpose applications (such as word processing, electronic spreadsheet, and graphics) into one program.

Intelligent Agent
A special-purpose knowledge-based system that serves as a software surrogate to accomplish specific tasks for end users.

Intelligent Terminal
A terminal with the capabilities of a microcomputer that can thus perform many data processing and other functions without accessing a larger computer.

Interactive Marketing
A dynamic collaborative process of creating, purchasing, and improving products and services that builds close relationships between a business and its customers, using a variety of services on the Internet, intranets, and extranets.

Interactive Processing
A type of real-time processing in which users can interact with a computer on a real-time basis.

Interactive Video
Computer-based systems that integrate image processing with text, audio, and video processing technologies, which makes interactive multimedia presentations possible.

Interface
A shared boundary, such as the boundary between two systems. For example, the boundary between a computer and its peripheral devices.

Internet
The Internet is a rapidly growing computer network of millions of business, educational, and governmental networks connecting hundreds of millions of computers and their users in over 200 countries.

Internetwork Processor
Communications processors used by local area networks to interconnect them with other local area and wide area networks. Examples include

switches, routers, hubs, and gateways.

Internetworks
Interconnected local area and wide area networks.

Interoperability
Being able to accomplish end user applications using different types of computer systems, operating systems, and application software, interconnected by different types of local and wide area networks.

Interorganizational Information Systems
Information systems that interconnect an organization with other organizations, such as a business and its customers and suppliers.

Interpreter
A computer program that translates and executes each source language statement before translating and executing the next one.

Interrupt
A condition that causes an interruption in a processing operation during which another task is performed. At the conclusion of this new assignment, control may be transferred back to the point where the original processing operation was interrupted or to other tasks with a higher priority.

Intranet
An Internet-like network within an organization. Web browser software provides easy access to internal websites established by business units, teams, and individuals, and other network resources and applications.

Inverted File
A file that references entities by their attributes.

IT Architecture
A conceptual design for the implementation of information technology in an organization, including its hardware, software, and network technology platforms, data resources, application portfolio, and IS organization.

Iterative
Pertaining to the repeated execution of a series of steps.

Java
An object-oriented programming language designed for programming real-time, interactive, Web-based applications in the form of applets for use on clients and servers on the Internet, intranets, and extranets.

Job
A specified group of tasks prescribed as a unit of work for a computer.

Job Control Language (JCL)
A language for communicating with the operating system of a computer to identify a job and describe its requirements.

Joystick
A small lever set in a box used to move the cursor on the computer's display screen.

K
An abbreviation for the prefix kilo-, which is 1,000 in decimal notation. When referring to storage capacity it is equivalent to 2 to the 10th power, or 1,024 in decimal notation.

Key
One or more fields within a data record that are used to identify it or control its use.

Keyboarding
Using the keyboard of a microcomputer or computer terminal.

Knowledge Base
A computer-accessible collection of knowledge about a subject in a variety of forms, such as facts and rules of inference, frames, and objects.

Knowledge-Based Information System
An information system that adds a knowledge base to the database and other components found in other types of computer-based information systems.

Knowledge Engineer
A specialist who works with experts to capture the knowledge they possess in order to develop a knowledge base for expert systems and other knowledge-based systems.

Knowledge Management
Organizing and sharing the diverse forms of business information created within an organization. Includes managing project and enterprise document libraries, discussion databases, intranet website databases, and other types of knowledge bases.

Knowledge Workers
People whose primary work activities include creating, using, and distributing information.

Language Translator Program
A program that converts the programming language instructions in a computer program into machine language code. Major types include assemblers, compilers, and interpreters.

Large-Scale Integration (LSI)
A method of constructing electronic circuits in which thousands of circuits can be placed on a single semiconductor chip.

Legacy Systems
The older, traditional mainframe-based business information systems of an organization.

Light Pen
A photoelectronic device that allows data to be entered or altered on the face of a video display terminal.

Liquid Crystal Displays (LCDs)
Electronic visual displays that form characters by applying an electrical charge to selected silicon crystals.

List Organization
A method of data organization that uses indexes and pointers to allow for nonsequential retrieval.

List Processing
A method of processing data in the form of lists.

Local Area Network (LAN)
A communications network that typically connects computers, terminals, and other computerized devices within a limited physical area such as an office, building, manufacturing plant, or other work site.

Locking in Customers and Suppliers
Building valuable relationships with customers and suppliers that deter them from abandoning a firm for its competitors or intimidating it into accepting less-profitable relationships.

Logical Data Elements
Data elements that are independent of the physical data media on which they are recorded.

Logical System Design
Developing general specifications for how basic information systems activities can meet end user requirements.

Loop
A sequence of instructions in a computer program that is executed repeatedly until a terminal condition prevails.

Machine Cycle
The timing of a basic CPU operation as determined by a fixed number of electrical pulses emitted by the CPU's timing circuitry or internal clock.

Machine Language
A programming language where instructions are expressed in the binary code of the computer.

Macro Instruction
An instruction in a source language that is equivalent to a specified sequence of machine instructions.

Magnetic Disk
A flat circular plate with a magnetic surface on which data can be stored by selective magnetization of portions of the curved surface.

Magnetic Ink
An ink that contains particles of iron oxide that can be magnetized and detected by magnetic sensors.

Magnetic Ink Character Recognition (MICR)
The machine recognition of characters printed with magnetic ink. Primarily used for check processing by the banking industry.

Magnetic Tape
A plastic tape with a magnetic surface on which data can be stored by selective magnetization of portions of the surface.

Mag Stripe Card
A plastic wallet-size card with a strip of magnetic tape on one surface; widely used for credit/debit cards.

Mainframe
A larger-size computer system, typically with a separate central processing unit, as distinguished from microcomputer and minicomputer systems.

Management Information System (MIS)
A management support system that produces prespecified reports, displays, and responses on a periodic, exception, demand, or push reporting basis.

Management Support System (MSS)
An information system that provides information to support managerial decision making. More specifically, an information-reporting system, executive information system, or decision support system.

Managerial End User
A manager, entrepreneur, or managerial-level professional who personally uses information systems. Also, the manager of the department or other organizational unit that relies on information systems.

Managerial Roles
Management as the performance of a variety of interpersonal, information, and decision roles.

Manual Data Processing
Data processing that requires continual human operation and intervention and that utilizes simple data processing tools such as paper forms, pencils, and filing cabinets.

Manufacturing Information Systems
Information systems that support the planning, control, and accomplishment of manufacturing processes. This includes concepts such as computer-integrated manufacturing (CIM) and technologies such as computer-aided manufacturing (CAM) or computer-aided design (CAD).

Marketing Information Systems
Information systems that support the planning, control, and transaction processing required for the accomplishment of marketing activities, such as sales management, advertising, and promotion.

Mass Storage
Secondary storage devices with extra-large storage capacities such as magnetic or optical disks.

Master File
A data file containing relatively permanent information that is utilized as an authoritative reference and is usually updated periodically. Contrast with Transaction File.

Mathematical Model
A mathematical representation of a process, device, or concept.

Media
All tangible objects on which data are recorded.

Megabyte
One million bytes. More accurately, 2 to the 20th power, or 1,048,576 in decimal notation.

Memory
Same as primary storage.

Menu
A displayed list of items (usually the names of alternative applications, files, or activities) from which an end user makes a selection.

Menu Driven
A characteristic of interactive computing systems that provides menu displays and operator prompting to assist an end user in performing a particular job.

Metadata
Data about data; data describing the structure, data elements, interrelationships, and other characteristics of a database.

Microcomputer
A very small computer, ranging in size from a "computer on a chip" to hand-held, laptop, and desktop units, and servers.

Micrographics
The use of microfilm, microfiche, and other microforms to record data in greatly reduced form.

Microprocessor
A microcomputer central processing unit (CPU) on a chip. Without input/output or primary storage capabilities in most types.

Microprogram
A small set of elementary control instructions called microinstructions or microcode.

Microprogramming
The use of special software (microprograms) to perform the functions of special hardware (electronic control circuitry). Microprograms stored in a read-only storage module of the control unit interpret the machine language instructions of a computer program and decode them into elementary microinstructions, which are then executed.

Microsecond
A millionth of a second.

Middleware
Software that helps diverse software programs and networked computer systems work together, thus promoting their interoperability.

Midrange Computer
A computer category between microcomputers and mainframes. Examples include minicomputers, network servers, and technical workstations.

Millisecond
A thousandth of a second.

Minicomputer
A type of midrange computer.

Model Base
An organized software collection of conceptual, mathematical, and logical models that express business relationships, computational routines, or analytical techniques.

Modem
(MOdulator-DEModulator) A device that converts the digital signals from input/output devices into appropriate frequencies at a transmission terminal and converts them back into digital signals at a receiving terminal.

Monitor
Software or hardware that observes, supervises, controls, or verifies the operations of a system.

Mouse
A small device that is electronically connected to a computer and is moved by hand on a flat surface in order to move the cursor on a video screen in the same direction. Buttons on the mouse allow users to issue commands and make responses or selections.

Multidimensional Structure
A database model that uses multidimensional structures (such as cubes or cubes within cubes) to store data and relationships between data.

Multimedia Presentations
Providing information using a variety of media, including text and graphics displays, voice and other audio, photographs, and video segments.

Multiplex
To interleave or simultaneously transmit two or more messages on a single channel.

Multiplexer
An electronic device that allows a single communications channel to carry simultaneous data transmissions from many terminals.

Multiprocessing
Pertaining to the simultaneous execution of two or more instructions by a computer or computer network.

Multiprocessor Computer Systems
Computer systems that use a multiprocessor architecture in the design of their central processing units. This includes the use of support microprocessors and multiple instruction processors, including parallel processor designs.

Multiprogramming
Pertaining to the concurrent execution of two or more programs by a computer by interleaving their execution.

Multitasking
The concurrent use of the same computer to accomplish several different information processing tasks. Each task may require the use of a different program, or the concurrent use of the same copy of a program by several users.

Nanosecond
One billionth of a second.

Natural Language
A programming language that is very close to human language. Also called very-high-level language.

Network
An interconnected system of computers, terminals, and communications channels and devices.

Network Architecture
A master plan designed to promote an open, simple, flexible, and efficient telecommunications environment through the use of standard protocols, standard communications hardware and software interfaces, and the design of a standard multilevel telecommunications interface between end users and computer systems.

Network Computer
A low-cost networked microcomputer with no or minimal disk storage, which depends on Internet or intranet servers for its operating system and Web browser, Java-enabled application software, and data access and storage.

Network Computing
A network-centric view of computing in which "the network is the

computer," that is, the view that computer networks are the central computing resource of any computing environment.

Network Data Structure
A logical data structure that allows many-to-many relationships among data records. It allows entry into a database at multiple points, because any data element or record can be related to many other data elements.

Neural Networks
Computer processors or software whose architecture is based on the human brain's meshlike neuron structure. Neural networks can process many pieces of information simultaneously and can learn to recognize patterns and programs themselves to solve related problems on their own.

Node
A terminal point in a communications network.

Nonprocedural Languages
Programming languages that allow users and professional programmers to specify the results they want without specifying how to solve the problem.

Numerical Control
Automatic control of a machine process by a computer that makes use of numerical data, generally introduced as the operation is in process. Also called machine control.

Object
A data element that includes both data and the methods or processes that act on those data.

Object-Based Knowledge
Knowledge represented as a network of objects.

Object-Oriented Language
An object-oriented programming (OOP) language used to develop programs that create and use objects to perform information processing tasks.

Object Program
A compiled or assembled program composed of executable machine instructions. Contrast with Source Program.

OEM: Original Equipment Manufacturer
A firm that manufactures and sells computers by assembling components produced by other hardware manufacturers.

Office Automation (OA)
The use of computer-based information systems that collect, process, store, and transmit electronic messages, documents, and other forms of office

communications among individuals, workgroups, and organizations.

Offline
Pertaining to equipment or devices not under control of the central processing unit.

Online
Pertaining to equipment or devices under control of the central processing unit.

Online Analytical Processing (OLAP)
A capability of some management, decision support, and executive information systems that supports interactive examination and manipulation of large amounts of data from many perspectives.

Online Transaction Processing (OLTP)
A real-time transaction processing system.

Open Systems
Information systems that use common standards for hardware, software, applications, and networking to create a computing environment that allows easy access by end users and their networked computer systems.

Operand
That which is operated upon. That part of a computer instruction that is identified by the address part of the instruction.

Operating Environment
Software packages or modules that add a graphics-based interface between end users, the operating system, and their application programs, and that may also provide a multitasking capability.

Operating System
The main control program of a computer system. It is a system of programs that controls the execution of computer programs and may provide scheduling, debugging, input/output control, system accounting, compilation, storage assignment, data management, and related services.

Operation Code
A code that represents specific operations to be performed upon the operands in a computer instruction.

Operational Feasibility
The willingness and ability of management, employees, customers, and suppliers to operate, use, and support a proposed system.

Operations Support System (OSS)
An information system that collects, processes, and stores data generated by the operations systems of an organization and produces data and

information for input into a management information system or for the control of an operations system.

Operations System
A basic subsystem of the business firm that constitutes its input, processing, and output components. Also called a physical system.

Optical Character Recognition (OCR)
The machine identification of printed characters through the use of light-sensitive devices.

Optical Disks
A secondary storage medium using CD (compact disk) and DVD (digital versatile disk) technologies to read tiny spots on plastic disks. The disks are currently capable of storing billions of characters of information.

Optical Scanner
A device that optically scans characters or images and generates their digital representations.

Optimization Analysis
Finding an optimum value for selected variables in a mathematical model, given certain constraints.

Organizational Feasibility
How well a proposed information-system supports the objectives of an organization's strategic plan for information systems.

Output
Pertaining to a device, process, or channel involved with the transfer of data or information out of an information processing system. Opposite of Input.

Outsourcing
Turning over all or part of an organization's information systems operation to outside contractors, known as systems integrators or service providers.

Packet
A group of data and control information in a specified format that is transmitted as an entity.

Packet Switching
A data transmission process that transmits addressed packets such that a channel is occupied only for the duration of transmission of the packet.

Page
A segment of a program or data, usually of fixed length.

Paging
A process that automatically and continually transfers pages of programs and data between primary storage and direct access storage devices. It provides computers with multiprogramming and virtual memory capabilities.

Parallel Processing
Executing many instructions at the same time, that is, in parallel. Performed by advanced computers using many instruction processors organized in clusters or networks.

Parity Bit
A check bit appended to an array of binary digits to make the sum of all the binary digits, including the check bit, always odd or always even.

Pascal
A high-level, general-purpose, structured programming language named after Blaise Pascal. It was developed by Niklaus Wirth of Zurich in 1968.

Pattern Recognition
The identification of shapes, forms, or configurations by automatic means.

PCM: Plug-Compatible Manufacturer
A firm that manufactures computer equipment that can be plugged into existing computer systems without requiring additional hardware or software interfaces.

Peer-to-Peer Network (P2P)
A computing environment where end user computers connect, communicate, and collaborate directly with each other via the Internet or other telecommunications network links.

Pen-Based Computers
Tablet-style microcomputers that recognize handwriting and hand drawing done by a pen-shaped device on their pressure-sensitive display screens.

Performance Monitor
A software package that monitors the processing of computer system jobs, helps develop a planned schedule of computer operations that can optimize computer system performance, and produces detailed statistics that are used for computer system capacity planning and control.

Periodic Reports
Providing information to managers using a prespecified format designed to provide information on a regularly scheduled basis.

Peripheral Devices
In a computer system, any unit of equipment, distinct from the central processing unit, that provides the system with input, output, or storage capabilities.

Personal Digital Assistant (PDA)
Hand-held microcomputer devices that enable you to manage information such as appointments, to-do lists, and sales contacts, send and receive e-mail, access the Web, and exchange such information with your desktop PC or network server.

Personal Information Manager (PIM)
A software package that helps end users store, organize, and retrieve text and numerical data in the form of notes, lists, memos, and a variety of other forms.

Physical System Design
Design of the user interface methods and products, database structures, and processing and control procedures for a proposed information system, including hardware, software, and personnel specifications.

Picosecond
One trillionth of a second.

Plasma Display
Output devices that generate a visual display with electrically charged particles of gas trapped between glass plates.

Plotter
A hard-copy output device that produces drawings and graphical displays on paper or other materials.

Pointer
A data element associated with an index, a record, or other set of data that contains the address of a related record.

Pointing Devices
Devices that allow end users to issue commands or make choices by moving a cursor on the display screen.

Pointing Stick
A small buttonlike device on a keyboard that moves the cursor on the screen in the direction of the pressure placed upon it.

Point-of-Sale (POS) Terminal
A computer terminal used in retail stores that serves the function of a cash register as well as collecting sales data and performing other data processing functions.

Port
(1) Electronic circuitry that provides a connection point between the CPU and input/output devices. (2) A connection point for a communications line on a CPU or other front-end device.

Postimplementation Review
Monitoring and evaluating the results of an implemented solution or system.

Presentation Graphics
Using computer-generated graphics to enhance the information presented in reports and other types of presentations.

Prespecified Reports
Reports whose format is specified in advance to provide managers with information periodically, on an exception basis, or on demand.

Private Branch Exchange (PBX)
A switching device that serves as an interface between the many telephone lines within a work area and the local telephone company's main telephone lines or trunks. Computerized PBXs can handle the switching of both voice and data.

Procedure-Oriented Language
A programming language designed for the convenient expression of procedures used in the solution of a wide class of problems.

Procedures
Sets of instructions used by people to complete a task.

Process Control
The use of a computer to control an ongoing physical process, such as petrochemical production.

Process Design
The design of the programs and procedures needed by a proposed information system, including detailed program specifications and procedures.

Processor
A hardware device or software system capable of performing operations upon data.

Program
A set of instructions that cause a computer to perform a particular task.

Programmed Decision
A decision that can be automated by basing it on a decision rule that outlines the steps to take when confronted with the need for a specific decision.

Programmer
A person mainly involved in designing, writing, and testing computer programs.

Programming
The design, writing, and testing of a program.

Programming Language
A language used to develop the instructions in computer programs.

Programming Tools
Software packages or modules that provide editing and diagnostic capabilities and other support facilities to assist the programming process.

Project Management
Managing the accomplishment of an information system development project according to a specific project plan, in order that a project is completed on time, and within its budget, and meets its design objectives.

Prompt
Messages that assist a user in performing a particular job. This would include error messages, correction suggestions, questions, and other messages that guide an end user.

Protocol
A set of rules and procedures for the control of communications in a communications network.

Prototype
A working model. In particular, a working model of an information system that includes tentative versions of user input and output, databases and files, control methods, and processing routines.

Prototyping
The rapid development and testing of working models, or prototypes, of new information system applications in an interactive, iterative process involving both systems analysts and end users.

Pseudocode
An informal design language of structured programming that expresses the processing logic of a program module in ordinary human language phrases.

Pull Marketing
Marketing methods that rely on the use of Web browsers by end users to access marketing materials and resources at Internet, intranet, and extranet websites.

Push Marketing
Marketing methods that rely on Web broadcasting software to push marketing information and other marketing materials to end users' computers.

Quality Assurance
Methods for ensuring that information systems are free from errors and fraud and provide information products of high quality.

Query Language
A high-level, humanlike language provided by a database management system that enables users to easily extract data and information from a database.

Queue
(1) A waiting line formed by items in a system waiting for service. (2) To arrange in or form a queue.

RAID
Redundant array of independent disks. Magnetic disk units that house many interconnected microcomputer hard disk drives, thus providing large, fault-tolerant storage capacities.

Random Access
Same as Direct Access. Contrast with Sequential Access.

Random Access Memory (RAM)
One of the basic types of semiconductor memory used for temporary storage of data or programs during processing. Each memory position can be directly sensed (read) or changed (write) in the same length of time, irrespective of its location on the storage medium.

Reach and Range Analysis
A planning framework that contrasts a firm's ability to use its IT platform to reach its stakeholders, with the range of information products and services that can be provided or shared through IT.

Read Only Memory (ROM)
A basic type of semiconductor memory used for permanent storage. Can only be read, not "written," that is, changed. Variations are Programmable Read Only Memory (PROM) and Erasable Programmable Read Only Memory (EPROM).

Real Time
Pertaining to the performance of data processing during the actual time a business or physical process transpires, in order that results of the data processing can be used to support the completion of the process.

Real-Time Processing
Data processing in which data are processed immediately rather than periodically. Also called online processing. Contrast with Batch Processing.

Record
A collection of related data fields treated as a unit.

Reduced Instruction Set Computer (RISC)
A CPU architecture that optimizes processing speed by the use of a smaller number of basic machine instructions than traditional CPU designs.

Redundancy
In information processing, the repetition of part or all of a message to increase the chance that the correct information will be understood by the recipient.

Register
A device capable of storing a specified amount of data such as one word.

Relational Data Structure
A logical data structure in which all data elements within the database are viewed as being stored in the form of simple tables. DBMS packages based

on the relational model can link data elements from various tables as long as the tables share common data elements.

Remote Access
Pertaining to communication with the data processing facility by one or more stations that are distant from that facility.

Remote Job Entry (RJE)
Entering jobs into a batch processing system from a remote facility.

Report Generator
A feature of database management system packages that allows an end user to quickly specify a report format for the display of information retrieved from a database.

Reprographics
Copying and duplicating technology and methods.

Resource Management
An operating system function that controls the use of computer system resources such as primary storage, secondary storage, CPU processing time, and input/output devices by other system software and application software packages.

Robotics
The technology of building machines (robots) with computer intelligence and humanlike physical capabilities.

Routine
An ordered set of instructions that may have some general or frequent use.

RPG: Report Program Generator
A problem-oriented language that utilizes a generator to construct programs that produce reports and perform other data processing tasks.

Rule
Statements that typically take the form of a premise and a conclusion such as If-Then rules: If (condition), Then (conclusion).

Rule-Based Knowledge
Knowledge represented in the form of rules and statements of fact.

Scalability
The ability of hardware or software to handle the processing demands of a wide range of end users, transactions, queries, and other information processing requirements.

Scenario Approach
A planning approach where managers, employees, and planners create scenarios of what an organization will be like three to five years or more into the future, and identify the role IT can play in those scenarios.

Schema
An overall conceptual or logical view of

the relationships between the data in a database.

Scientific Method
An analytical methodology that involves (1) recognizing phenomena, (2) formulating a hypothesis about the causes or effects of the phenomena, (3) testing the hypothesis through experimentation, (4) evaluating the results of such experiments, and (5) drawing conclusions about the hypothesis.

Secondary Storage
Storage that supplements the primary storage of a computer. Synonymous with auxiliary storage.

Sector
A subdivision of a track on a magnetic disk surface.

Security Codes
Passwords, identification codes, account codes, and other codes that limit the access and use of computer-based system resources to authorized users.

Security Management
Protecting the accuracy, integrity, and safety of the processes and resources of an internetworked e-business enterprise against computer crime, accidental or malicious destruction, and natural disasters, using security measures such as encryption, firewalls, antivirus software, fault-tolerant computers, and security monitors.

Security Monitor
A software package that monitors the use of a computer system and protects its resources from unauthorized use, fraud, and vandalism.

Semiconductor Memory
Microelectronic storage circuitry etched on tiny chips of silicon or other semiconducting material. The primary storage of most modern computers consists of microelectronic semiconductor storage chips for random access memory (RAM) and read only memory (ROM).

Semistructured Decisions
Decisions involving procedures that can be partially prespecified, but not enough to lead to a definite recommended decision.

Sensitivity Analysis
Observing how repeated changes to a single variable affect other variables in a mathematical model.

Sequential Access
A sequential method of storing and retrieving data from a file. Contrast with Random Access and Direct Access.

Sequential Data Organization
Organizing logical data elements according to a prescribed sequence.

Serial
Pertaining to the sequential or consecutive occurrence of two or more related activities in a single device or channel.

Server
(1) A computer that supports applications and telecommunications in a network, as well as the sharing of peripheral devices, software, and databases among the workstations in the network. (2) Versions of software for installation on network servers designed to control and support applications on client microcomputers in client/server networks. Examples include multiuser network operating systems and specialized software for running Internet, intranet, and extranet Web applications, such as electronic commerce and enterprise collaboration.

Service Bureau
A firm offering computer and data processing services. Also called a computer service center.

Smart Products
Industrial and consumer products, with "intelligence" provided by built-in microcomputers or microprocessors that significantly improve the performance and capabilities of such products.

Software
Computer programs and procedures concerned with the operation of an information system. Contrast with Hardware.

Software Package
A computer program supplied by computer manufacturers, independent software companies, or other computer users. Also known as canned programs, proprietary software, or packaged programs.

Software Piracy
Unauthorized copying of software.

Software Suites
A combination of individual software packages that share a common graphical user interface and are designed for easy transfer of data between applications.

Solid State
Pertaining to devices such as transistors and diodes whose operation depends on the control of electric or magnetic phenomena in solid materials.

Source Data Automation
The use of automated methods of data entry that attempt to reduce or eliminate many of the activities, people,

and data media required by traditional data entry methods.

Source Document
A document that is the original formal record of a transaction, such as a purchase order or sales invoice.

Source Program
A computer program written in a language that is subject to a translation process. Contrast with Object Program.

Special-Purpose Computer
A computer designed to handle a restricted class of problems. Contrast with General-Purpose Computer.

Speech Recognition
Direct conversion of spoken data into electronic form suitable for entry into a computer system. Also called voice data entry.

Spooling
Simultaneous peripheral operation online. Storing input data from low-speed devices temporarily on high-speed secondary storage units, which can be quickly accessed by the CPU. Also, writing output data at high speeds onto magnetic tape or disk units from which it can be transferred to slow-speed devices such as a printer.

Stage Analysis
A planning process in which the information system needs of an organization are based on an analysis of its current stage in the growth cycle of the organization and its use of information systems technology.

Standards
Measures of performance developed to evaluate the progress of a system toward its objectives.

Storage
Pertaining to a device into which data can be entered, in which they can be held, and from which they can be retrieved at a later time. Same as Memory.

Strategic Information Systems
Information systems that provide a firm with competitive products and services that give it a strategic advantage over its competitors in the marketplace. Also, information systems that promote business innovation, improve business processes, and build strategic information resources for a firm.

Strategic Opportunities Matrix
A planning framework that uses a matrix to help identify opportunities with strategic business potential, as well as a firm's ability to exploit such opportunities with IT.

Structure Chart
A design and documentation technique to show the purpose and relationships of the various modules in a program.

Structured Decisions
Decisions that are structured by the decision procedures or decision rules developed for them. They involve situations where the procedures to follow when a decision is needed can be specified in advance.

Structured Programming
A programming methodology that uses a top-down program design and a limited number of control structures in a program to create highly structured modules of program code.

Structured Query Language (SQL)
A query language that is becoming a standard for advanced database management system packages. A query's basic form is SELECT . . . FROM . . . WHERE.

Subroutine
A routine that can be part of another program routine.

Subschema
A subset or transformation of the logical view of the database schema that is required by a particular user application program.

Subsystem
A system that is a component of a larger system.

Supercomputer
A special category of large computer systems that are the most powerful available. They are designed to solve massive computational problems.

Superconductor
Materials that can conduct electricity with almost no resistance. This allows the development of extremely fast and small electronic circuits. Formerly only possible at supercold temperatures near absolute zero. Recent developments promise superconducting materials near room temperature.

Supply Chain
The network of business processes and interrelationships among businesses that are needed to build, sell, and deliver a product to its final customer.

Supply Chain Management
Integrating management practices and information technology to optimize information and product flows among the processes and business partners within a supply chain.

Switch
(1) A device or programming technique for making a selection. (2) A computer that controls message switching among the computers and terminals in a telecommunications network.

Switching Costs
The costs in time, money, effort, and inconvenience that it would take a customer or supplier to switch its business to a firm's competitors.

Synchronous
A characteristic in which each event, or the performance of any basic operation, is constrained to start on, and usually to keep in step with, signals from a timing clock. Contrast with Asynchronous.

System
(1) A group of interrelated or interacting elements forming a unified whole. (2) A group of interrelated components working together toward a common goal by accepting inputs and producing outputs in an organized transformation process. (3) An assembly of methods, procedures, or techniques unified by regulated interaction to form an organized whole. (4) An organized collection of people, machines, and methods required to accomplish a set of specific functions.

System Flowchart
A graphic diagramming tool used to show the flow of information processing activities as data are processed by people and devices.

Systems Analysis
(1) Analyzing in detail the components and requirements of a system. (2) Analyzing in detail the information needs of an organization, the characteristics and components of presently utilized information systems, and the functional requirements of proposed information systems.

Systems Approach
A systematic process of problem solving that defines problems and opportunities in a systems context. Data are gathered describing the problem or opportunity, and alternative solutions are identified and evaluated. Then the best solution is selected and implemented, and its success evaluated.

Systems Design
Deciding how a proposed information system will meet the information needs of end users. Includes logical and physical design activities, and user interface, data, and process design activities that produce system specifications that satisfy the system requirements developed in the systems analysis stage.

Systems Development
(1) Conceiving, designing, and implementing a system. (2) Developing information systems by a process of

investigation, analysis, design, implementation, and maintenance. Also called the systems development life cycle (SDLC), information systems development, or application development.

Systems Development Tools
Graphical, textual, and computer-aided tools and techniques used to help analyze, design, and document the development of an information system. Typically used to represent (1) the components and flows of a system, (2) the user interface, (3) data attributes and relationships, and (4) detailed system processes.

Systems Implementation
The stage of systems development in which hardware and software are acquired, developed, and installed; the system is tested and documented; people are trained to operate and use the system; and an organization converts to the use of a newly developed system.

Systems Investigation
The screening, selection, and preliminary study of a proposed information system solution to a business problem.

Systems Maintenance
The monitoring, evaluating, and modifying of a system to make desirable or necessary improvements.

System Software
Programs that control and support operations of a computer system. System software includes a variety of programs, such as operating systems, database management systems, communications control programs, service and utility programs, and programming language translators.

System Specifications
The product of the systems design stage. It consists of specifications for the hardware, software, facilities, personnel, databases, and the user interface of a proposed information system.

Systems Thinking
Recognizing systems, subsystems, components of systems, and system interrelationships in a situation. Also known as a systems context or a systemic view of a situation.

System Support Programs
Programs that support the operations, management, and users of a computer system by providing a variety of support services. Examples are system utilities and performance monitors.

Tangible Benefits and Costs
The quantifiable benefits and costs of a proposed solution or system.

Task and Project Management
Managing team and workgroup projects by scheduling, tracking, and charting the completion status of tasks within a project.

Task Management
A basic operating system function that manages the accomplishment of the computing tasks of users by a computer system.

TCP/IP
Transmission control protocol/Internet protocol. A suite of telecommunications network protocols used by the Internet, intranets, and extranets that has become a de facto network architecture standard for many companies.

Technical Feasibility
Whether reliable hardware and software capable of meeting the needs of a proposed system can be acquired or developed by an organization in the required time.

Technology Management
The organizational responsibility to identify, introduce, and monitor the assimilation of new information system technologies into organizations.

Telecommunications
Pertaining to the transmission of signals over long distances, including not only data communications but also the transmission of images and voices using radio, television, and other communications technologies.

Telecommunications Channel
The part of a telecommunications network that connects the message source with the message receiver. It includes the hardware, software, and media used to connect one network location to another for the purpose of transmitting and receiving information.

Telecommunications Control Program
A computer program that controls and supports the communications between the computers and terminals in a telecommunications network.

Telecommunications Controller
A data communications interface device (frequently a special-purpose mini- or microcomputer) that can control a telecommunications network containing many terminals.

Telecommunications Monitors
Computer programs that control and support the communications between the computers and terminals in a telecommunications network.

Telecommunications Processors
Internetwork processors such as switches and routers, and other devices such as

multiplexers and communications controllers that allow a communications channel to carry simultaneous data transmissions from many terminals. They may also perform error monitoring, diagnostics and correction, modulation-demodulation, data compression, data coding and decoding, message switching, port contention, and buffer storage.

Telecommuting
The use of telecommunications to replace commuting to work from one's home.

Teleconferencing
The use of video communications to allow business conferences to be held with participants who are scattered across a country, continent, or the world.

Telephone Tag
The process that occurs when two people who wish to contact each other by telephone repeatedly miss each other's phone calls.

Teleprocessing
Using telecommunications for computer-based information processing.

Terabyte
One trillion bytes. More accurately, 2 to the 40th power, or 1,009,511,627,776 in decimal notation.

Text Data
Words, phrases, sentences, and paragraphs used in documents and other forms of communication.

Throughput
The total amount of useful work performed by a data processing system during a given period of time.

Time Sharing
Providing computer services to many users simultaneously while providing rapid responses to each.

Total Quality Management
Planning and implementing programs of continuous quality improvement, where quality is defined as meeting or exceeding the requirements and expectations of customers for a product or service.

Touch-Sensitive Screen
An input device that accepts data input by the placement of a finger on or close to the CRT screen.

Track
The portion of a moving storage medium, such as a drum, tape, or disk, that is accessible to a given reading head position.

Trackball
A rollerball device set in a case used to move the cursor on a computer's display screen.

Transaction
An event that occurs as part of doing business, such as a sale, purchase, deposit, withdrawal, refund, transfer, payment, and so on.

Transaction Document
A document produced as part of a business transaction. For instance: a purchase order, paycheck, sales receipt, or customer invoice.

Transaction File
A data file containing relatively transient data to be processed in combination with a master file. Contrast with Master File.

Transaction Processing Cycle
A cycle of basic transaction processing activities including data entry, transaction processing, database maintenance, document and report generation, and inquiry processing.

Transaction Processing System (TPS)
An information system that processes data arising from the occurrence of business transactions.

Transaction Terminals
Terminals used in banks, retail stores, factories, and other work sites that are used to capture transaction data at their point of origin. Examples are point-of-sale (POS) terminals and automated teller machines (ATMs).

Transborder Data Flows (TDF)
The flow of business data over telecommunications networks across international borders.

Transform Algorithm
Performing an arithmetic computation on a record key and using the result of the calculation as an address for that record. Also known as key transformation or hashing.

Transnational Strategy
A management approach in which an organization integrates its global business activities through close cooperation and interdependence among its headquarters, operations, and international subsidiaries, and its use of appropriate global information technologies.

Turnaround Document
Output of a computer system (such as customer invoices and statements) that is designed to be returned to the organization as machine-readable input.

Turnaround Time
The elapsed time between submission of a job to a computing center and the return of the results.

Turnkey Systems
Computer systems where all of the hardware, software, and systems

development needed by a user are provided.

Unbundling
The separate pricing of hardware, software, and other related services.

Uniform Resource Locator (URL)
An access code (such as http://www.sun.com) for identifying and locating hypermedia document files, databases, and other resources at websites and other locations on the Internet, intranets, and extranets.

Universal Product Code (UPC)
A standard identification code using bar coding, printed on products that can be read by the optical supermarket scanners of the grocery industry.

Unstructured Decisions
Decisions that must be made in situations where it is not possible to specify in advance most of the decision procedures to follow.

User Friendly
A characteristic of human-operated equipment and systems that makes them safe, comfortable, and easy to use.

User Interface
That part of an operating system or other program that allows users to communicate with it to load programs, access files, and accomplish other computing tasks.

User Interface Design
Designing the interactions between end users and computer systems, including input/output methods and the conversion of data between human-readable and machine-readable forms.

Utility Program
A standard set of routines that assists in the operation of a computer system by performing some frequently required process such as copying, sorting, or merging.

Value-Added Carriers
Third-party vendors who lease telecommunications lines from common carriers and offer a variety of telecommunications services to customers.

Value-Added Resellers (VARs)
Companies that provide industry-specific software for use with the computer systems of selected manufacturers.

Value Chain
Viewing a firm as a series, chain, or network of basic activities that adds value to its products and services and thus adds a margin of value to the firm.

Videoconferencing
Real-time video and audio conferencing (1) among users at

networked PCs (desktop videoconferencing), or (2) among participants in conference rooms or auditoriums in different locations (teleconferencing). Videoconferencing can also include whiteboarding and document sharing.

Virtual Communities
Groups of people with similar interests who meet and share ideas on the Internet and online services and develop a feeling of belonging to a community.

Virtual Company
A form of organization that uses telecommunications networks and other information technologies to link the people, assets, and ideas of a variety of business partners, no matter where they may be located, in order to exploit a business opportunity.

Virtual Machine
Pertaining to the simulation of one type of computer system by another computer system.

Virtual Mall
An online multimedia simulation of a shopping mall with many different interlinked retail websites.

Virtual Memory
The use of secondary storage devices as an extension of the primary storage of the computer, thus giving the appearance of a larger main memory than actually exists.

Virtual Private Network
A secure network that uses the Internet as its main backbone network to connect the intranets of a company's different locations, or to establish extranet links between a company and its customers, suppliers, or other business partners.

Virtual Reality
The use of multisensory human/computer interfaces that enable human users to experience computer-simulated objects, entities, spaces, and "worlds" as if they actually existed.

Virtual Storefront
An online multimedia simulation of a retail store shopping experience on the Web.

Virtual Team
A team whose members use the Internet, intranets, extranets, and other networks to communicate, coordinate, and collaborate with each other on tasks and projects, even though they may work in different geographic locations and for different organizations.

VLSI: Very-Large-Scale Integration
Semiconductor chips containing hundreds of thousands of circuits.

Voice Conferencing
Telephone conversations shared among several participants via speaker phones or networked PCs with Internet telephone software.

Voice Mail
Unanswered telephone messages are digitized, stored, and played back to the recipient by a voice messaging computer.

Volatile Memory
Memory (such as electronic semiconductor memory) that loses its contents when electrical power is interrupted.

Wand
A hand-held optical character recognition device used for data entry by many transaction terminals.

Web Browser
A software package that provides the user interface for accessing Internet, intranet, and extranet websites. Browsers are becoming multifunction universal clients for sending and receiving e-mail, downloading files, accessing Java applets, participating in discussion groups, developing Web pages, and other Internet, intranet, and extranet applications.

Web Publishing
Creating, converting, and storing hyperlinked documents and other material on Internet or intranet Web servers so they can easily be shared via Web browsers with teams, workgroups, or the enterprise.

Web Services
A collection of Web and object-oriented technologies for linking Web-based applications running on different hardware, software, database, or network platforms. For example, Web services could link key business functions within the applications a business shares with its customers, suppliers, and business partners.

What-If Analysis
Observing how changes to selected variables affect other variables in a mathematical model.

Whiteboarding
See Data Conferencing.

Wide Area Network (WAN)
A data communications network covering a large geographic area.

Window
One section of a computer's multiple-section display screen, each of which can have a different display.

Wireless LANs
Using radio or infrared transmissions to link devices in a local area network.

Wireless Technologies
Using radio wave, microwave, infrared, and laser technologies to transport digital communications without wires between communications devices. Examples include terrestrial microwave, communications satellites, cellular and PCS phone and pager systems, mobile data radio, and various wireless Internet technologies.

Word
(1) A string of characters considered as a unit.
(2) An ordered set of bits (usually larger than a byte) handled as a unit by the central processing unit.

Word Processing
The automation of the transformation of ideas and information into a readable form of communication. It involves the use of computers to manipulate text data in order to produce office communications in the form of documents.

Workgroup Computing
Members of a networked workgroup may use groupware tools to communicate, coordinate, and collaborate, and to share hardware, software, and databases to accomplish group assignments.

Workstation
(1) A computer system designed to support the work of one person. (2) A high-powered computer to support the work of professionals in engineering, science, and other areas that require extensive computing power and graphics capabilities.

World Wide Web (WWW)
A global network of multimedia Internet sites for information, education, entertainment, e-business, and e-commerce.

XML (Extensible Markup Language)
A Web document content description language that describes the content of Web pages by applying hidden identifying tags or contextual labels to the data in Web documents. By categorizing and classifying Web data this way, XML makes Web content easier to identify, search, analyze, and selectively exchange between computers.

Name Index

Abbott, Dean, 154
Ackerman, Joe, 345–346
Adams, Chuck, 417
Admire, Ellis, 209
Ahlberg, Christopher, 303
Aiello, Wayne, 268, 269
Alexander, Steve, 35, 290, R–2, R–7
Alien, Ray, 136
Alvarez, Gene, 290
Amirian, Brian, 404–405
Anderson, Debra, 208
Andersson, Curt J., 242
Andriole, Stephen J., 452
Anthes, Gary, 269, 315, 336, 452, R–6, R–7
Applegate, Lynda, R–1
Armor, Daniel, R–3, R–5
Armstrong, Douglas, 270, R–5
Armstrong, Lance, 39
Arndt, Michael, 315
Aronson, Jay, R–6
Arthur, W. Brian, 257
Ashline, Peter, R–5
Asnin, Marc, 212
Athitakis, Mark, 289
Austin, Robert D., R–1

Bacon, Allison, 357
Baer, Tony, R–3
Baier, Bruce, 253
Balance, Craigg, R–4
Balls, John, R–1
Barksdale, Jim, R–3
Barnholt, Ned, 52
Barr, Anne, 243–244
Barrett, Craig R., 208
Bates, Christine, 167
Baxter, Amy, 369
Bearden, Keith, 17
Beckwith, Larry, 192
Beeler, Jesse, R–7
Begley, Sharon, R–5
Belcher, Lloyd, R–5
Benioff, Marc, 212–214
Bennet, Steve, 102–103
Bennett, Chip, 421
Bentley, Lonnie, R–7
Berg, Jeff, 440
Berlow, Marc, 138, 420

Betts, Mitch, 384, R–4
Bezos, Jeff, 4, 5, 6, 375
Bharadwaj, Anandhi, 53, R–2
Biagini, Larry, 232
Biggs, Dee, 253
Blitch, Bruce, 417
Boehme, Alan, 136, 235
Bogumil, Walter, R–8
Bonifacius, Bradley, 257
Bose, Ranjit, R–5
Botchner, Ed, R–5
Boutin, Paul, R–7
Bowles, Gene, R–1
Bowles, Jerry, R–1
Boylan, Jo Ann, 308
Boyle, Matthew, 208
Branscom, Michael, 398
Bresnick, Alan, R–3
Brown, Carol, R–6
Brown, Eryn, R–5
Brown, Stuart, R–5
Bryan, Lowell, R–8
Burke, Carol, 421
Burke, Doug, 301
Bush, Steve, 369
Bylinsky, Gene, R–4, R–5

Cahanin, Patti, 312
Callahan, Dennis S., 452
Calloway, D. Wayne, 300
Campbell, Frank C., 328
Campbell, Ian, R–3
Campbell, Jeff, 451
Cantrell, Scott, 341
Carey, John, 315, R–8
Caron, J. Raymond, R–1
Carr, Nicholas, 39
Carrara, Chris, 70
Carson, Randy, 329
Castaldi, Carty, 404
Caulfield, Brian, R–3, R–4
Cavanaugh, Nancy, R–6
Chandrasekher, Anand, 208
Chatham, Bob, 63
Chatterjee, Samir, R–3
Childress, Mike, 78, 79
Christensen, Clayton, R–1, R–8
Chung, Wingyan, 439
Ciancio, Tony, 337

Clark, Charles, R–6
Cohen, Jackie, 205
Cohen, Michael D., 254
Cole-Gomolski, Barbara, R–6
Collette, Stacy, 171, 341, 357
Collica, Randy, 315
Comeau, Michael, 269
Conlin, John, 405–406
Connerty, William, 314, 315
Connors, Bob, 308
Consilvio, Jean, 167, 168
Cook, Scott, 103
Cooper, Russ, 406, 417
Cope, James, R–3
Cox, Earl, R–5
Craig, Mary, 389
Craver, Barry, 99
Creese, Guy, 159
Cronin, Mary, R–1, R–3, R–6, R–8
Cross, Kim, R–5
Curry, Bill, 5

Dalzell, Rick, 375
Daneri, Julio, 47
Darling, Charles, R–5
Davenport, Thomas H., R–1, R–4
Davies, Dave, 369
Davis, Jeffrey, R–5
DeBoever, Larry, 35
Deck, Stewart, R–5
Deckmyn, Dominique, R–7
DeJesus, Edmund, R–2
Dejoie, Roy, R–7
Dell, Michael, 38, 39
Dell'Antonia, Jon, 362
DeMeyer, Desiree, R–4
Dickson, Randy, 406
Diddlebock, Bob, R–4
Diese, Martin, R–6
Distefano, John, 341
Donaldson, Thomas, R–7
Doring, Joachim, 57
Dukes, Trevor, 152
Duncan, Mike, 366
Dunleavy, John, R–1
Dunlop, Charles, R–7
Dunn, Joan, 168
Duseja, Sweta, 418

Earls, Alan, 139
Edelman, Harriet, 452
Edwards, Cliff, 379
Egan, Richard, R–6
Ehr, Mark, 235
Eisenfeld, Beth, 213
Eldridge, Dan, 20, 21
Eldridge, Stephen, 451
Elias, Paul, R–7
Ellis, Steve, 115–116, 289
Ellison, Larry, 213
El Sawy, Omar, R–1, R–8
Engardio, Pete, R–4
Engle, Michael, 418
Ennen, Dave, 100
Ericsson, Maria, 158, R–3
Essex, David, R–5
Estes, Kirk, 263
Ewing, Jack, R–1

Fanning, Shawn, 389
Farrow, Bill, 420, 421
Fayyad, Usama, R–3
Fellenstein, Craig, R–5
Ferra, Joe, 171
Ferraro, Lou, 167
Fiedler, Kirk, R–8
Fingar, Peter, R–5
Fishman, Charles, 183
Fitzgerald, Charles, 39
Flynn, Ed, 426
Fodor, Mark, 116
Fortenberry, Jason, 138–139
Fowler, George, R–7
Fox, Pimm, 67, R–3
Fraser, Jane, R–8
Freedman, Jim, 129, R–3
Freeman, Eva, R–6
Friendman, Amanda, 182
Frye, Colleen, R–1
Fryer, Bronwyn, R–8

Gantz, John, R–6
Garino, Jason, R–5
Garner, Rochelle, R–1
Garrison, Sara, 410
Gates, Bill, R–4, R–6
Gates, Russell, 270, R–5
Gaynor, Mark, 129, R–3
Geoff, Leslie, R–4
Georgia, Bonnie, R–5
Gilhooly, Kym, R–8
Girard, Greg, 218
Gius, Richard, 357
Gnenz, Bill, 148
Goldberg, David, R–6
Goldman, Steven, R–1
Good, Tom, 398, 399
Gorchokov, Vasili, 385
Gordon, Jason, 103
Gorry, G. Anthony, R–6
Gosain, Sanjay, R–1, R–8
Graham, Patricia, 168
Gralla, Preston, 116

Gray, John, 136
Gray, Roger, 36
Green, Heather, 62, 208
Greene, Jay, 135, 379
Greenway, Hellen, 67
Griffith, James W., 242
Gross, Neil, R–8
Grossman, Mark, 415
Grove, Andy, 39
Grover, Varun, 53, R–2, R–8
Gualda, George, 18, 187
Guha, Subashish, R–2
Gulati, Ranjay, R–5
Gullotto, Vincent, 379
Guyon, Janet, R–2

Hagerty, John, 144
Hall, Mark, R–2, R–6, R–8
Halphide, David, 253
Hamblen, Matt, R–7
Hamm, Steve, 379, R–2, R–4, R–8
Hance, Chris, 183
Harding, Jim, 167
Harizal, Tracy, 36
Harniman, Brian, 352
Harris, Lisa, 223
Harrison, Ann, R–7
Hartley, Kenneth, R–1, R–4
Hartlove, Chris, 432
Hasnas, John, R–8
Havenstein, Heather, 253
Hawk, Keith, 306
Hawson, James, R–7
Hedley, Mark, 375
Helbach, Morris, 168
Heller, Matt, 70
Henry, Elizabeth, 369
Herhold, Scott, 121
Hill, Tom, 21, 29
Hills, Melanie, R–7
Hof, Robert D., 257
Hoff, Robert, 39, R–4, R–8
Hoffman, Thomas, 36, 375, 452, R–4, R–6
Hoque, Faisal, R–5
Housel, Thomas, R–3
Huber, Ray L., 328, 329
Hudson, Dick, 383
Huels, Holger, 337
Huera, Frank, 386
Huff, Sid, R–6
Humphreys, John, 73
Hurley, James, R–1, R–4
Hypponen, Mikko, 378, 379

Immelt, Jeff, 38, 39
Ivanov, Alexey, 385
Ivar, Jacobsen, 158
Ives, Blake, R–8
Iyer, Bala, 129, R–3

Jablonowski, Mark, R–6
Jacobsen, Ageneta, 158, R–3
Jacobsen, Ivar, R–3
Jahne, Dave, 417

Jarvenpaa, Sirkka, R–1, R–8
Jaworski, Bernard, R–5
Joch, Alan, R–2
Joel, David, 314
Johnson, Amy, 357, R–4
Johnson, Deborah, R–7
Jones, Kathryn, R–2
Jorgenson, Bob, 70
Joy, Bill, R–7
Joyce, Colum, 445

Kalakota, Ravi, R–1, R–2, R–3, R–4, R–5, R–6, R–7, R–8
Kalin, Sari, R–8
Kauppila, Ken, 159
Kavanaugh, Steven R., 328
Keen, Peter, R–4
Keenan, Faith, R–4, R–5
Kellam, Larry, 336
Kelly, Daryll, 167
Keng Fiona Fui-Hoon Nah, 387
Kennedy, Ken, R–2
Kerstetter, Jim, 379
Kettinger, William, R–2
Kheradpir, Shaygan, 379
Kimball, Ralph, 167
Kinder, Lawrence, 434
King, Julia, 21, 433, 452, R–6, R–7
King, Patrick, R–6
Kirby, Jim, 208
Kirkpatrick, David, 39, R–8
Klein, Terry, 227
Kling, Rob, R–7
Knight, Richard L., 410
Knoll, Christian, 336
Koeper, Jeff, 368
Kogel, John, 100
Kornicker, Peter, 69
Kothanek, John, 384–385
Kovacevich, Richard M., 289
Kover, Amy, R–2
Kuhn, Chris, 122–123
Kumar, Harsha, R–5
Kundra, Vivek, 417
Kurszweil, Raymond, R–6

Lacik, Joseph, Jr., 35
Laduke, Kelly, 340
Laff, Steven, 262
Lai, Vincent S., 439, R–5
Lais, Sami, R–4
Lambert, Katherine, 153
Lambert, Russ, 10
LaPlante, Alice, R–8
Lardner, James, R–7
Lashinsky, Adam, 257
Lay, Ken, 383
Lazar, Jonathan, R–7
Lee, Allen, R–1
Lefkowitz, Robert M., 135
Leinfuss, Emily, R–1, R–8
Lengyel, Randy, 100
Lennon, Kevin, 421
Lenza, Al, 79

Leon, Mark, 63
Leposky, Mark, 225
Lesyna, Michael, 183
Leveille, Edward N., 290
Levin, Vladimir, 385–386
Levine, Josh, 121
Levy, Rena, 167
Levy, Stephen, R–7
Lewis, W. Douglas, 357
Lidz, Larry, 391
Liew, Roger, 121
Locussol, Virginie, 443
Long, Micah, 66
Lopez, Jose A., 176
Lopez, Kevin, 209
Lorents, Alden, R–3
Lundquist, Christopher, R–6
Lynas, Robin, 136

McArthur, Hugh, 418
McBride, Geraldine, 218
McCarter, Bill, 426
McCarthy, Jack, 451
McCarthy, Michael, R–7
McCoy, Gretchen, 105
McDonnel, Sharon, R–7
McEwan, Bill, 218, 219
McFarlan, F. Warren, R–1
Machlis, Sharon, R–6
McIniss, Bret, 268, 269
McKenzie, Ray, 368
McKinley, John A., Jr., 135
McNamee, Roger, 213
McNeill, F. Martin, R–6
Madera, John, 170
Madsen, Peter, R–7
Mailoux, Jacquiline, R–6
Malhotra, Arvind, R–1, R–8
Manning, Dennis, 452
Mannino, Michael, 141, 150, R–3
Manrique, Hernando, 311–312
Manter, Tom, 73
Marchand, Catherine, 374
Marino, Mike, 345
Mark, Leon, R–5
Marsh, Andy, 340, 341
Marshak, Ronnie, R–5
Martin, Chuck, R–4
Maruster, Rob, 79
Mason, Ken, 114
Mathias, Michael, 162
Maughan, Deryck C., 283
May, Paul, R–5
Mearian, Lucas, R–3, R–8
Meehan, Michael, R–8
Mehrabani, Mostafa, 438–439
Mello, Adrian, R–4
Melymuka, Kathleen, 47, 254, 421, R–7
Merager, David, 154
Merian, Lucas, R–4
Messerschmitt, David, R–2, R–4
Millar, Victor, R–2
Miller, Andy, 234, 235
Miller, Ken, 385
Mills, Steven A., 135

Mische, Michael, R–8
Mitchell, Curtis, 168
Mitchell, Lori, R–6
Monahan, Grace, 167
Morgan, Cynthia, R–5
Morgan, James, 353, 372, R–3, R–7
Morton, Michael Scott, R–6
Mucha, Thomas, 289
Mullaney, Timothy, R–5
Mullinax, A.R., 369
Murphy, Kate, R–4
Murray, Gerry, R–6
Mutch, Steve, 144–145
Myer, Christopher, 451

Nagel, Roger, R–1
Nance, Barry, 403–404, R–3, R–7
Narang, Anne, 369
Nash, Kim, R–3, R–8
Nash, Mike, 379
Naughton, Keith, R–7
Nee, Eric, 103
Neilson, Paul, 70
Nelson, Roger, 33
Neumann, Peter, R–7
Neumann, Seev, R–2
Nielsen, Jakob, 349, R–7
Nonaka, Ikujiro, R–2
Norrington, Lorrie, 102–103
Norris, Grant, R–1, R–4
Nowikow, Conrad, R–6
Nowitz, Richard T., 69
Null, Christopher, 67

O'Brien, Atiye, R–4
Omartian, Rick, 452
Omidyar, Pierre, 256
Oppenheim, Jeremy, R–8
Orenstein, David, R–4, R–6, R–7
Orenstein, Susan, 121
Ort, Sheldon, 304
Osbourne, Peter, 129
Ott, Kevin, 417
Ouellette, Tim, R–2, R–6, R–7
Ounjian, John, 341

Paglio, Peter, 99
Palmer, Nathaniel, 374
Palvia, Prashant, R–8
Palvia, Shailendra, R–8
Papows, Jeff, R–4
Paradice, David, R–7
Paris, Alexander P., 62
Patterson, Dave, 358
Pavlick, Dan, 253
Peltz, Danny, 289
Peters, Lisa, 269
Phillips, Robert, R–7
Piatetsky-Shapiro, Gregory, R–3
Picton, Bill, 290
Pimentel, Ken, R–6
Port, Otis, 315
Porter, Michael, 44, R–2
Potter, Michelle, 183

Preis, Kenneth, R–1
Prevo, Jim, 218
Price, Ken, 279
Prokesch, Steven, R–2

Quirk, Cate, 154

Rabbinovitch, Edward, 401
Raby, David, 47
Radcliff, Deborah, R–1, R–7, R–8
Radding, Alan, R–4
Rall, Wilhelm, R–8
Ramanlal, Pradipkumar, R–2
Rasmussen, Michael, 154
Rayport, Jeffry, R–5
Reagin, Mike, 116
Reichheld, Frederich, R–4
Reimers, Barbara DePompa, 209, R–2
Richards, Frank M., 399
Richards, Mark, 378
Riddoch, Ross, 222
Riesmeyer, Barbara J., 328
Rigby, Darrell, R–4
Rightmer, Jerry, 136
Robb, Drew, R–4
Roberts-Witt, Sarah, R–6
Robinson, Lori, R–7
Robinson, Marcia, R–1, R–3, R–4, R–5, R–6, R–7, R–8
Roche, Edward, R–8
Rogers, Gary, 293
Rosenberg, Bruce, 48–49
Rosenberg, Marc, 56, R–6
Rosencrance, Linda, 79
Rosenoer, Jonathan, 270, R–5
Ross, Jeanne W., 431, R–8
Ross, Kim, 197–198
Rothfeder, Jeffrey, R–8
Rothman, Simon, 257
Russom, Philip, 139
Rymal, David, 400–401

Saffo, Paul, 379
Sager, Ira, R–8
Salzman, 194
Sambamurthy, V., 53, R–2, R–6
Samuel, Craig, 254
Samuels, John, 63
Sanford, James, 21
Sargent, Erik, 355
Satzinger, John, R–6
Sawhney, Mohan, R–1, R–4
Sayles, Rodger, 154
Scardino, Mike, 433
Schaller, Denise, 421
Schatt, Stan, 208
Schefter, Phil, R–4
Scheier, Robert, 100, 341, R–6
Schlosser, Julie, 293
Schmitt, Bill, 171
Schonfeld, Erick, 121, 213
Schoonover, Ethan, 254
Schultz, Eugene, 386
Schultz, Ted, 369

Schwartz, Mathew, 399, R–7
Schwieder, Wylie, 205
Scott, David, 366
Scott, Stuart, 232
Segars, Albert, R–2
Seltzer, Bill, 281
Senge, Peter, 342, R–7
Seral, John, 292, 293
Seybold, Patricia, R–2, R–5
Shafritz, Jay, R–7
Shahnam, Liz, 368
Shapiro, Carl, R–2
Sharma, Tarun, R–5
Shpak, Danny, 198
Siebel, Tom, 213
Siekman, Philip, R–2
Simpson, David, R–2
Simpson, Sheda, 374
Singleton, Andy, 451
Skopec, Eric, R–3
Sliwa, Carol, 136, R–3, R–5, R–7
Slusar, Bettina, 213
Smallwood, Trisha, 269
Smith, Cecil, 369
Smith, H. Jefferson, R–8
Smith, Padraic, R–3
Smith, Richard, 257
Solomon, Melissa, R–7, R–8
Songini, Marc, 168, 337, R–2, R–4, R–7,
      R–8
Spinello, Richard, R–8
Spooler, Sharon, 430
Stangel, Bill, 128
Stanley, Tim, 63
Stansell-Gamm, Martha, 442
States, Ann, 292
Steadman, Craig, R–1
Steele, Fran, 46, 47
Steele, Jim, 213
Steinberg, Don, R–4
Stem, Manfred, 100
Stepaneck, Marcia, R–2
Stewart, Barrie, 152
Stewart, Howard, 388
Stoddard, Donna, R–1
Stoller, Don, 153, 154
Stone, Brad, R–7

Strassman, Paul, 39
Stuart, Anne, R–4
Sugumaran, Vijayan, R–5
Sumic, Zarko, 36
Sun, Dawen, 167
Swanson, Carol, 312
Szygenda, Ralph, 379

Taggart, Stewart, R–8
Tedeschi, Bob, 293
Teixeira, Kevin, R–6
Tenenbaum, Bernard H., 257
Teng, James, R–2, R–8
Teng, Limei, 387
Thibodeau, Patrick, R–8
Thomas, Owen, 375, R–3
Thro, Ellen, R–6
Timmermans, Willem, 47
Torvald, Linus, 120
Treacy, Michael, 213
Trombly, Maria, 235
Tsolakis, Tasos, 432, 433
Tucker, Jay, R–4
Turban, Efraim, R–6
Turing, Alan, 316

Uddin, Jamil, 167
Udell, Jon, 444
Ulfelder, Steve, 99

Valentine, Brian, 379
Vandenbosch, Betty, R–6
VanScoy, Kayte, R–8
Varian, Hal, R–2
Ved, Nitin, 418
Verton, Dan, 399, R–8
Vijayan, Jaikumar, 136, 417, 418, R–1, R–8
Violino, Bob, 235, 341
Vitalari, Nicholas, R–8
Vitale, Michael, R–2, R–4
Vizzini, Kelly, 253
Vlastelca, John, 19
Vogelstein, Fred, 5, 135, R–3
Volkman, Henry, 357

Wagner, Jan, 208
Wagner, Mitch, R–6
Wainewright, Ivan, R–3
Waraniak, John, 51
Watkins, Harry, 63
Watson, Hugh, R–5, R–6
Watterson, Karen, R–6
Weill, Peter, 431, R–2, R–4, R–8
Weill, Sandy, 283
Weiss, Todd, R–1
Welch, Jack, 39
West, Lawrence, R–8
West, Richard, 319
Wetherbe, James, R–8
Wetzel, Kevin, 209
Whinston, Andrew, R–5, R–6
White, Pete, 418
Whitford, Scott, 239
Whitman, Meg, 256, 257, 258
Whitten, Jeffrey, R–7
Wildstrom, Stephen, 415
Wilke, Jeff, 5
Willard, Nancy, R–8
Willebeek-LeMair, Marc, 417
Wilson, Carl, 6
Winkler, Connie, 374
Winston, Patrick, R–6
Wohl, Ron, 253
Wood, Dennis, 369
Wood, Ron, R–5
Wreden, Nick, R–6
Wright, Amy, R–6
Wright, Dan, 47
Wyner, George, 129, R–3

York, Edward, 406
York, Thomas, R–8
Yoshinaga, Darrell, 239
Young, Eric, R–5
Young, Kerry, R–1, R–8

Zabin, Jeff, R–1, R–4
Zakutney, Joe, 16
Zetlin, Minda, 135
Zill, Mike, 297–298
Zollars, William D., 62

Company Index

Abbott Consulting, 154
Aberdeen Group, Inc., 63, 73, 159
Acquired Intellup, 330
Acxiom Inc., 392
A-DEC Inc., 17, 50, 218
Adobe, 109
Aether Systems, 99
Aetna Inc., 162
Age fotostock, 81
Agilent Technologies, 51, 52
AGM Container Controls, 388
Air Canada, 379
Air Liquide America LP, 336
Air2Web, Inc., 194
Alberta Central, 148
Allstate Insurance Co., 121, 432–434
Amazon.com, 4–6, 19, 42, 121, 228, 265, 269,
    271, 273–274, 275, 276, 325, 335, 375
American Airlines, 60, 177, 437
American Chemical Council, 279
American Express, 206, 437
American Mobile Satellite, 192
America Online (AOL), 73, 108, 243, 251,
    393
AmeriKing Inc., 311–312
Amersham Biosciences, 20–22, 29
AMR Research Inc., 144, 154, 218, 357
Anadarko Petroleum Corp., 168
Anderson Cancer Center, 418
Apple Computer Co., 106, 120
Aptex Software, 320
Arby's, 303
Argosy Gaming Co., 138–140
Ariba Inc., 235, 265, 269, 278
Ark Asset Management Co., 198
Arlington County, VA, 417
AskJeeves, Inc., 107, 324
AskMe Corp., 47
Assembla, 451
AT&T Corp., 99, 120, 278
AT&T Wireless Services, 340–342
Audiogalaxy, 389
Auerbach, 360
Autobytel.com, 287
AutoNation, 257
Autonomy Corp., 319
AutoTrader.com LLC, 257
Avaya Inc., 209
Aventail Corp., 426

Aviall Inc., 35
Avis Group, 434
Avnet Inc., 59, 197
Avnet Marshall, 42, 423, 424–426
Avon Products Inc., 452

Baan Co., 16
BAE Systems PLC, 318
Baker Tanks, 238–240
BancOne, 44
BankFinancial, 314–316
Bank of America (BofA), 146, 206
Bank of London, 386
Banner Health System, 417
Barnes and Noble, 264, 282
Barnesandnoble.com, 262, 282
Barrington Research Associates, Inc., 62
BEA Systems, 121, 122, 129
Be Free, 261–262
Benetton, 437
Ben & Jerry's, 292–293
Bertelsmann, 262
Best Software Inc., 67, 136, 235
Bio Economic Research Association, 451
BiosGroup, 336
BizRate.com, 334
BlackBerry, 171, 293
Blackboard Inc., 73
Blue Cross-Blue Shield of Minnesota,
    340–341
Bob Evans Farms, Inc., 192
Boehringer Ingelheim, 337
Boeing, 70, 321
Boise Cascade, 264, 312
Bowstreet, 374
BP PLC, 47
BrainPlay.com, 282
British Aerospace, 318
British Airways, 437
BroadVision, 35
Buick, 171
Burger King, 311, 312
Burlington Northern Santa Fe, 451
Business Applications and Solutions, 312
Business Data & Intelligence, 312
Business Objects SA, 154
BuyerZone, 349–350
Bynari InsightServer, 100

Cadence Design Systems, 180
Cadillac, 171
Caldera, 120
Candle Corporation of America, 100
Cap Gemini Ernst & Young, 341, 451
Capital One Financial Corp., 205, 289
Cardinal Health Inc., 356–357
Carnegie Mellon University, 391
Catalyst Manufacturing Services, 35
CDW Corp., 63
Celanese Chemicals Ltd., 170–171
Cendant Corp., 434
CEO Express, 448
Cervalis Inc., 401
CGI Group Inc., 426
Charles Gupton Photography, 394
Charles Schwab & Co., 42, 44, 243–244
Check Point Software, 418
ChemConnect, 278–279
ChevronTexaco Corp., 47
Chicago Board of Trade, 420–422
Cisco Systems, 42, 55, 209, 226, 262, 277,
    278, 297–298
Citibank, 283, 385–386, 440
Citicorp, 42, 392
Citigroup, 206, 283, 341, 440
CitiStreet, 340–342
Clarke American Checks, Inc., 363–364
Clark Martire & Bartolomeo, 383
CleverPath, 158
CNF, 183
CNN, 243, 418
Cognos Inc., 337
Cole National Corp., 116
Colgate-Palmolive Co., 216–217
CollabNet, Inc., 451
Commerce One, 235, 265, 269, 278
CompuBank, 206
Computer Associates (CA), 122, 158, 280,
    303, 310, 408
Computer Associates International,
    Inc., 427
Computer Economics Inc., 379, 390
Computerworld, 290
Comsat, 192
Comshare, 14, 154, 247, 301
Connecticut General, 218
Conoco, Inc., 309
Consolidated Freightways, 42

Consolidated Rail, 303
Con-Way NOW, 182–183
Corbis, 69, 74, 82, 91, 170, 322, 356, 394
Corbis Saba, 212
CorDaptix, 36
Corel, 106, 109, 111, 149
Corporate Express Inc., 234–235, 268–270
Countrywide Home Loans, 181
Covisint, 278
Crane Engineering, 368
Credit Union National Association, 315
CSX Corp., 379
Cutler-Hammer, 327–329
Cutter Consortium, 452
CyberAtlas, Inc., R–3

DaimlerChrysler, 135
Datapro, 360
Dean Stallings Ford, 257
Dell Computer, 38–40, 42, 54, 62, 70, 93,
    135, 227–228, 262, 278, 280
Deloitte Touche Tohmatsu, 384
The Delphi Group, 374
Delta Air Lines Inc., 78–79
Del Taco Inc., 356–357
Delta Technology Inc., 79
DHL Worldwide Express Inc., 445
Digex Inc., 426
Digital Vision, 234
DMR Consulting, 368
Dollar Rent A Car Inc., 73, 128–129
DoubleClick, 392
Dow Jones & Co., 325
Drugstore.com, 282
Duke Energy, 369
DuPont, 374, 398–400

EarthLink, 262
Eastman Kodak Co., 20–22, 29
eAuto, 289
eBay, 5, 42, 60, 256–258, 271, 275, 278, 384,
    388, 404
Eddie Bauer, 271
EDS, 440
eLance.com, 251
Eli Lilly, 303–304
Eloquent Inc., 21, 29
Enron Corp., 383
Enterprise Management Associates, 235
Entrabase.com, 286
Entuity Ltd., 198
eOn Communications Corp., 209
Epiphany, 219
Epson, 135
Ericsson, 191, 226
eSniff, 405–406
eToys, 289
E*Trade Financial Corp., 44, 121, 289
Evolutionary Technologies, 159
eWorkExchange, 251
Excite, 325, 334
Experian Automotive, 159–160
Experio Solutions Corp., 35
ExxonMobil Corp., 47

Fast Search, 176
FedEx, 39, 42, 303
Fidelity Investments, 127–128, 170–172
Fireman's Fund Insurance Co., 426
FMC Corp., 426
Ford Motor Co., 183, 286, 336
Forrester Research, Inc., 63
Fortune, 452
FonMeyer Drugs, 210
FreeMarkets Inc., 258, 259, 265, 278, 279
Freemerchant, 275–276
Frito-Lay Inc., 345–346
F-Secure Corp., 378–379
Fujitsu Technology Solutions Inc., 114

The Gap, 375
Gartner Inc., 213, 341, 389, 430
Geisinger Health Systems, 398–400
General Electric (GE), 5, 38–40, 103, 136,
    176, 232, 235, 278, 293, 321, 433
GE Global Exchange Services, 280
GE Industrial Systems, 232
GE Plastics, 292–294
GE Power Systems, 136, 234–235
General Foods, 39
General Mills, 341
General Motors (GM), 208, 286, 378–379
GM Locomotive Group, 365–366
Gentex, 62
Genuity Inc., 426
Getty Images, 85, 234
Gevity HR, 223
Giga Information Group, 139, 154
Global Exchange Services, 432–434
Global Marine Inc., 383
Globalstar, 192
Gnutella, 389
Go.com, 320
Google, 107, 176, 262
GoTo.com Inc., 70
Grant Thornton Inc., 209
Great Plains Software, 103
Green Mountain Coffee Roasters, Inc., 218
Grokster, 198
Groove Networks, 254
Guardian Life Insurance Co., 452
GUS PLC, 159

Hackett Group, 452
Haht Commerce Inc., 290
Hamilton Standard, 55
Hannaford, 201
Harley-Davidson, 262
Harrah's Entertainment Inc., 63
H.B. Fuller Co., 209
Henry Schein Inc., 167
Heritage Services, 278, 279–280
Hershey Foods Corp., 16, 50, 218
Hewlett-Packard (HP), 20–22, 29, 52, 67,
    69, 73, 74, 83, 86, 121, 135, 136, 144,
    171, 254, 277, 314–316, 375
HP Enterprise Systems, 315
HP Services, 254
Hilton Hotels, 48–49, 59

Hitachi, 321
Home Depot, 136, 257
HotJobs.com, 242
Hudson & Associates, 383
Hummingbird Ltd., 139
Hyperion Solutions Corp., 246, 298, 301,
    309
HYPERparallel, 146

IBM, 33, 36, 61, 72, 73, 74, 75, 83, 99, 100,
    116, 120, 121, 122, 129, 135, 136, 148,
    158, 159, 160, 196, 215, 257, 267, 277,
    301, 308, 325, 327, 359, 426, 440, R–3
IDC, 73, 135
i-Flex Solutions Inc., 440
iManage, 61
Index Stock, 86
Informatica Corp., 167
Information Advantage, 303
Informix, 63
Infosys Technologies, 451
Infravio, Inc., 116
Ingram Micro, 298
Inovant, Inc., 410
Institute for the Future, 379
Intec Engineering Partnership Ltd., 46–47
Intel Corp., 38–40, 39, 72, 76, 135, 208,
    280, 436
Intellsat, 192
InterContinental Hotels Group, 356–357
International Rectifier Corp., 301
Internet Society, 175
Internetworldstats.com, 441
Intuit, 102–103, 251
iPaq, 67

Jabil Circuit, 55
J.D. Edwards, 259
JetBlue Airways Corp., 62
Jo-Ann Stores, Inc., 218
Jobweb.org, 242
Johnson Controls, 51
Johnson & Johnson, 153, 154

Kalido Ltd., 144
KaZaA, 198, 389
KB Online Holdings LLC, 282
KB Toys, 282
KBtoys.com, 282
KeyCorp, 308, 309
Key Technology Service, 308
Kinetics Inc., 79
KLM, 437
Kodak, 20–22, 29
KPMG, 105
Krispy Kreme, 103
Kroger Co., 269
Kruse International, 257

Lands' End, 271
Lawrence Berkeley National
    Laboratory, 386
Lawson Software, 35

Lehman Brothers Holdings Inc., 418
Levi Strauss, 303
Lexis-Nexis, 306 307
Lillian Vernon Corp., 209
Link Staffing Services Inc., 18, 187
Linux, 120, 196, 209
Lone Star Doughnuts, 102–103
Look Smart, 107
Lotus Development Corp., 106, 109, 111,
    112, 113, 121, 126, 149, 160, 192, 232,
    233, 244, 401
Lowe & Partners Worldwide, 254
Lucent, 226
Lycos, 107, 334

McAfee, 251, 406, 407
McGraw-Hill Companies, 32
McKesson Drugs, 218
MacMillan Bloedel Corp., 330
Mark's Work Wearhouse, 136
Marriott, 6, 208, 264
MasterCard, 266, 267
Mazu Networks Inc., 404–405
MBNA America, 205
Mercer Management Consulting, 430
Merrill Lynch, 44, 121, 135
Meta Group, Inc., 36, 290, 366, 368
Microsoft Corp., 21, 39, 61, 83, 102–103,
    106, 107, 108, 109, 110, 111, 112, 116,
    118, 119–120, 121, 122, 126, 127, 129,
    135, 136, 142, 149, 151, 152, 154, 160,
    175, 196, 251, 263–264, 267, 275, 286,
    299, 301, 323, 354, 355, 356, 357, 375,
    378–379, 390–391, 401, 417, R–3
Microsoft Network, 393
MicroStrategy Inc., 152, 167, 307
Mikasa, 121
Moen Inc., 42, 224–225
Monster.com, 70, 223, 242, 252
Morgan Stanley & Co., 323
Morpheus, 198, 389
Motorola Inc., 257
MSN, 334
MTV Networks, 404–405
MultiLogic Inc., 330
Murnet Technologies, 354
MySimon, 325
MySQL.com, 149, 150

Nappi Distributors, 99
Napster, 389
Navigator Systems, 345
NBC Universal Games Inc., 153–154
NCR Corp., 63, 303, 306
NetForensics, 418
Netscape Communications, 107, 108, 175,
    266, 267, 275
NetSolve Inc., 417
Network Associates Inc., 379
The New York Times, 387
Nielsen Media Research, 197–198
Nielsen Norman Group, 349
Nike, 218
Nordstrom, 375

Northwest Airlines, 78–79, 341, 437
Novell, 112, 196, 208, 401, 417
NTT/Verio Inc., 276–277
Nu Tech Solutions Inc., 336

Office Depot, 281–282
OfficeMax, 349–350
Office Products Corp., 34
Old Dominion Freight Line, 99
OneChannel Inc., 297, 298
1-800 Flowers, 115–116
Online Resources Corp., 418
OpenReach Inc., 18, 187
Oracle Corp., 21, 52, 102–103, 105, 121,
    149, 153, 154, 158, 159, 160, 212, 213,
    214, 219, 223, 235, 253, 269, 277, 293,
    337, 421, 440, R–3
Orbitz Inc., 120
OshKosh B'Gosh, 362
Overture, 107
Owens & Minor Inc., 153–154

Pacific Gas and Electric Co., 36
Palisade Software, 306, 322
Palm, 99
Pantellos, 278
PayPal, Inc., 265, 266, 384–385
Pella, 253
People First Finance LLC, 430
Peoples Bank & Trust Co., 308
PeopleSoft, 214, 218, 219, 235, 253, 263,
    277
PepsiCo, 300, 303
Petsmart Inc., 218
Pfizer, 39
PHH Vehicle Management Services, 434
PhotoDisc, 94
Picture Quest, 86
Pinnacle Manufacturing, 60
Plantronics, Inc., 83
Plumtree, 312
Prada, 171
Prescient Systems, 253
Priceline.com, 42, 352
Procter & Gamble, 42–43, 293, 336
Prodigy Biz, 275–276, 286
Progressive Corp., 62
Progressive Insurance, 66–67
Providence Health Systems, 115–116, 355,
    400–401
Providence Washington Insurance, 290
Prudential Financial, 168

Qantas Airlines, 437
Qualcomm. Inc., 182, 183
Quantum, 91
Quark, 109
Qwest Communications, 313–314

Rack Room Shoes, 201
Recourse Technologies Inc., 386–387
Red Hat, 120
REI, 121

REI.com, 272
Reliable Tools Inc., 257
Requisite Technology, 262
Retail Technology Products, 222
Retek Inc., 136
Rite-Aid, 282
RNT Productions, 82
Rolls-Royce PLC, 35
RSA Data Security, 401

SABRE Decision Technologies, 303
Sabre Holdings, 60
Salesforce.com, 113, 114, 212–214, 239, R–3
SalesLogix, 67
Salomon Smith Barney, 283
SAP AG, 16, 100, 102–103, 212, 213, 217,
    218–219, 235, 253, 290, 336, 337,
    363–366
SAP America, 214, 218, 277
Sartorious AG, 70
SAS Institute Inc., 315
SCO, 135
Sears Roebuck & Co., 201, 257
Sedgwick James Inc., 303
Sephora, 121
7-Eleven, 201
724 Inc., 406
Shell Exploration and Production, 144–145
Shop at Home Network, 162
Siebel Systems, 35, 212, 213, 219, 221–222,
    259, R–4
Siemens AG, 57
Silicon Graphics, 74, 323
Silver Lake Partners, 213
Skydive Chicago, 33
Skyworks Solutions, 253
Snap-on Inc., 181
Sobeys Inc., 218–219
Solectron Corp., 226
Sonalysts, Inc., 405–406
Sony, 135
Southwest Airlines, 62, 121, 336
Southwire Co., 374
Spacenet Inc., 192
SPL WorldGroup, 36
Spotfire, 303–304
Sprint, 193
SPSS Inc., 315
Staples, Inc., 42
State Farm Insurance Co., 351–352
State Street Corp., 341
Straightline, 253
Strategic Business Solutions, 388
Strategic Systems Inc., 253
SunGard Data Systems, 213
Sun Microsystems Inc., 71, 106, 120, 121, 122,
    127, 130, 135, 277, 323, 375, 421, 451
Supergo Bike Shops, 261–262
SurfControl, 388
Sybase, Inc., 35, 128, 374
Sygma, 322
Symantec, 406
Symbol Technologies Inc., 99, 171
Syntellect Interactive Services, 229
Synygy Inc., 21

T. Rowe Price, 121
Target Corp., 171, 341
TaylorMade Golf Co., 224–225
Technology Solutions Co., 366
Telebanc Financial, 289
Telecom Malaysia, 57
Telstra Corp., 221–222
Terra Lycos, 277
Terra Nova Trading LLC, 417
Tessenderlo Kerley Inc., 417
Tharco Inc., 290
Things Remembered, Inc., 115–116
3M, 153, 154
360 Commerce, 136
Time Inc., 121
Timken Co., 242
TippingPoint Technologies, 417
TiVo, 135
Tommy Hilfiger, 135
Toshiba, 321
Toys "R" Us, 5, 42
Trading Solutions, 320
Travelers Insurance, 283
TravelNow, 122
Travelocity, 60, 262
Trend Micro, 406
Trimble Navigation, 182–183
TruSecure Corp., 379, 406, 417
TRW Inc., 438–439

UniFirst Corp., 66–67
Unilever, 293

Unisys, 303
United Parcel Service (UPS), 194, 208
U.S. Bancorp, 315
U.S. Steel, 253
United Technologies Corp., 55
University of Chicago, 390–391
UNIX, 196
Unocal Corp., 269
US Air, 437

Vaultus Mobil Technologies, 67
Verio, 276–277
VeriSign Inc., 267
Verizon Communications, 378–379
Vermont Information Processing, 99
VerticalNet, 278
Viacom International, 404
VISA, 44, 266, 267, 410
Visa International, 105, 410
Visible Decisions, 323
Visual Insights, Inc., 304

Wachovia Bank, 315
Walker Information, Inc., 63
Wal-Mart, 39, 42–43, 135, 171, 280,
    314–316, 375, 392
Walt Disney Co., 257
Wang Global, 400
Washington Post, 121
WebMD.com, 116
WebMethods, 116, 227–228, 235, 269

Welch Foods Inc., 253
Wells' Dairy, 208
Wells Fargo & Co., 115–116, 206, 289
WESCO International, Inc., 10
Western Chemical Corp., 34
WH Smith PLC, 152
Wingspan, 206
Winnebago Industries Inc., 100
Wisconsin Physicians Service Insurance
    Corp. (WPS), 100
Works.com, 278
World Bank, 448–449
World Wide Web Consortium, 175
Wright Express LLC, 434
W.W. Grainger & Co., 262
Wyndham International Inc., 375

Xelus, 35
Xerox, 39, 388

Yahoo!, 108, 175, 243, 275, 404
Yellow Corp., 62

Zurich North America, 358

Subject Index

Acceptance phase, development, 345
Access control, 260–261
Accessibility, for IS services evaluation, 362
Access speed, 88
Accounting systems, 236, 244–246
Accounts payable systems, 236, 245
Accounts receivable systems, 236, 245
Accuracy, of information, 295
Acquisition, implementation and, 367, 370
Active data dictionaries, 160–161
Active matrix LCD displays, 86–87
Adaptive learning systems, 317
Adaptive systems, 23, 317
Addition, data processing and, 28
Administrative coordination, 44
Advertising
  incentives and e-commerce, 272
  the Internet used for, 177–178
  systems, 237
Aesthetics, corporate websites and, 351
Agents, intelligent. see Intelligent agents
Agile companies, 52–54
  ERP and, 218
Agile manufacturing, 240
Agile systems development, 344
Agility, 52–54, 240, 344
Algorithms, 321
Alliances
  global, 437
  strategies for, 40–42, 55
Always-on Internet connection, 402
Analysis/design phase, 17, 344
Analytical data store, 144
Analytical modeling, 304–308
Anonymous remailers, 392
Antivirus software, 384, 390
Applets, 127, 130, 188
  malicious, 386
Application development, 340, 344–345. see
    also Information systems (IS) develop-
    ment; System development
  analysis/design phase, 344
  databases, 150, 151–152
  design/implementation phase, 344
  implementation/maintenance
    phase, 344
  investigation/analysis phase, 344
  management of, 422, 427

Application(s). see also Application develop-
    ment; Application software
  fault-tolerant, 409
  global business/IT, 436–439
  servers, 121, 122–123
  software. see Application software
  trends, 172, 174
Application service providers, 73, 112–114,
    426
Application software, 26, 102–114
  alternatives for, 112–114
  application-specific programs, 104–105
  business application software, 104–105
  desktop publishing, 109
  electronic spreadsheets, 109–110, 247
  e-mail, 106–107
  for end users, 104
  general purpose programs, 104
  groupware, 104, 112
  instant messaging, 108
  integrated packages, 106
  personal information managers, 111–112
  presentation graphics, 110–111
  productivity packages, 104
  service providers (ASPs), 73, 112–114,
    426
  for small businesses, 103
  software suites, 103, 104
  Web browsers, 107
  word processing, 109
Architecture(s)
  applications, business/IT, 424
  e-commerce processes, 260
  enterprise application, 214–215
  network, 199–200
  telecommunications, 184
Archival storage, 141
Arithmetic-logic unit, 75
Artificial intelligence (AI), 124, 314–330. see
    also Expert systems
  application areas, 317
  business value of, 314–316
  cognitive science, 316–317
  commercial applications, 318
  defined, 316
  domains of, 316–318
  fuzzy logic systems, 317, 320–321
  genetic algorithms, 321
  for information retrieval, 318
  intelligent agents. see Intelligent agents

  intelligent behavior, attributes of, 316
  for knowledge management, 318–319
  natural interfaces, 317–318
  neural networks, 319–320
  risk optimizer software, 322
  robotics, 317, 318
  virtual reality. see Virtual reality
ASCII, 88–89
Assemblers, 123–124, 130
Association of IT Professionals, 382, 384
Attributes, 26, 140–141, 316
Auctioning/bidding, 260, 278
Auction websites, 278
Auditing business systems, 410–412
Audit trail, 411–412
Authentication, 260
Automated JIT warehousing, 44
Automated teller machines, 72, 201, 265
Automation, 240–241, 270
Availability criteria, ES, 329
Awareness in buying, Web vs. traditional, 273

Backbone network, 186–187
Back doors, 386
Background mode, 119
Backup
  files, for security, 407
  IS services evaluation and, 362
  systems, 80
Bandwidth, 197–198, 200, 201
Banners, 238
Bar coding, 84
Bargaining power of customers, 40–42
Bargaining power of suppliers, 40–42
Barriers to entry, 43
Batch processing, 12, 230
Baud rate, 200
Behavior tracking, 260
Benefit preference analysis, 243
Benefits administration, 243
Bibliographic databases, 143
Bidding/auctioning, 260
Billing, 245
Binary data, 88, 320
Binary representation, 88
Biometrics, 384, 408, 409
Bit (binary digit), 88
Blade servers, 73
Bloatware, 106
Bluetooth wireless technology, 193

Bots (software robots), 323
Bottom line focus, for decisions, 305
Broadband channels, 200
Broadband content, 351
Brochureware, 268, 270
Browsers, 185
Browsing Internet sites, 175
Buffer overflow, 386
Bugs, 130
Building Web stores, 274
Build-to-order manufacturing, 240
Bulletin board systems, 175
Burners, CD, 92
Buses, 77
Business applications, 7, 210–337. *see also*
    Application(s)
    EAI, 122, 227–228
    e-business. *see* e-Business
    of the Internet, 175–178
    software, 104–105
    trends, telecommunications, 174
    of Web services, 116
    wireless, 171
Business decision making. *see* Decision
    support systems
Business drivers, for global IT, 436–438
Business ethics, 380–381
Business improvement, 50
Business intelligence, 154
    business value of, 292–293
    tools, 297
Business/IT planning, 423–425
    applications architecture, 424
    data resources, 424
    e-business planning, 424–425
    IT architecture, 424
    IT organization, 424
    major components, 423–424
    resource management, 423
    strategy development. *see* Strategic IT
    technology architecture, 424
    technology platform, 424
Business operations. *see also* Operations/
    Operations management
    business processes and, 8
    intranets and, 179–180
    support of, 12–13
Business position, IS services and, 362
Business processes
    operations and, 8
    reengineering, 50–52
    supporting, 8
    value chains and, 44
Business systems. *see* Information systems
    (IS) development; System
Business-to-business (B2B) e-commerce,
    258, 259, 260, 268, 277
    B2B portals, 270
    CRM and, 270
    private B2B exchanges, 279–280
    public B2B exchanges, 278–279
    SCM and, 270
    trends in, 270
Business-to-consumer (B2C) e-commerce,
    258–259, 265, 268
    advertising/incentives and, 272
    buying process, 273

community and, 272, 273
CRM and, 270
customer service, 274, 276
look and feel factors, 272
performance/service factors, 272
and personal attention, 272–273
Portal, B2C, 270
SCM and, 270
security/reliability and, 272, 273
selection/value and, 272
success factors, 271–273
top retail websites, 271
trends in, 270
Web store. *see* Web stores
Business-to-government (B2G) e-com-
    merce, 258
Business use of the Internet. *see* The Internet
Bus network, 198–199
Buying/selling
    automation of, 260
    B2C e-commerce and, 273
    e-commerce and, 258, 273
    using the Internet, 176
Byte, 88

C++, 124–125, 127
Cable modem, 196, 402
Cache memory, 77
Call center software, 221
Capacity planning, 241
    networks, 197, 274
Capital budgeting, 236, 246–247
Career matching, 243
CASE, 117
Case-based reasoning, ES, 325, 326
Case managers, 50
Cash disbursements, 245
Cash management systems, 246
Cash receipts, 245
Catalogs
    dynamic multimedia, 274
    e-commerce, 278
    generation of, 260
    management of, 260, 262, 264, 270
    search engines, 274
Cathode ray tube, 86
CD drives, 80
    CD burners, 92
    CD-R, 92–94
    CD-ROM, 92–94
    CD-RW, 92–94
    CD-RW/DVD, 93–94
Cell switching technologies, 201
Cellular phones, 174, 193
Censorship, 393
Centers of excellence, 444
Centralization of IT, 425
Central processing unit, 75–76
Change
    action plan, 368
    management, 366–369
    sponsors, 368
    teams, 368
Channels, 184
    clicks and bricks, 281–283, 289
    telecommunications, 184–185

Character, 140
Chargeback systems, 427–428
Chat rooms, 175, 176, 274
Chief Executive Officer, 422, 423, 428
Chief Information Officer, 422, 423, 428
Chief Technology Officer, 422, 428, 429
Child files, 407
CICS, 196
Circuit switching, 200–201
Clarity, of information, 295
Classification, data processing, 28
Clicks and bricks, 281–283, 289
Clients, 188
    client/server applications, 214
    client/server networks, 188
    client services, 429
    universal, 107
    very thin, 193
Clip art, 109
Clock speed, 77
Co-adaptation, planning and, 423
Coaxial cable, 190
Code Red Worm, 390
Cognitive science, 316–317
Collaboration, 51. *see also* Enterprise collab-
    oration systems
    buying, collaborative, 260
    e-commerce and, 260, 265
    global, 438, 451
    intranets and communications, 178–179
    manufacturing, collaborative, 240
    swarming, 254
    tools for, 121, 232
    work management tools, 121, 232
Command-driven user interfaces, 117–118
Commercial applications
    of AI, 318. *see also* Business applications
Communications
    of international data, 439
    intranets and collaboration, 178–179
    media, 27
    network, 184
    satellites, 174, 191–192
    telecom. *see* Telecommunications
Communities of interest, 238, 265
Community-based target marketing, 237–238
Community relationships, 272, 273
Comparisons, data processing and, 28
Compatibility, as hardware evaluation
    factor, 360
Compensation administration, 242–243
Compensation analysis systems, 236
Compensation effectiveness/equity, 243
Competing with IT. *see* Strategic IT
Competitive advantage, 8
Competitive forces, 40–41
Competitive strategy concepts, 40–42
Competitors, rivalry of, 40–42
Compilers, 124, 130
Completeness, of information, 295
Completion phase, development, 345
Complex data types, 157
Complexity, ES suitability and, 329
Components of IS, 20–29
    IS activities, 27–28, 29
    adaptive system, 23
    data resources, 6, 24–27

environment, 23
feedback and control, 22–23
hardware. *see* Computer hardware
information systems model, 24–25
input, 22–23
interface, 23
network resources, 24–25, 27
open system, 23
output, 22–23
people resources, 24–25
processing, 22–23
software resources, 24–25, 26. *see also*
    Software
subsystem, 23
system concepts, 20–24
system defined, 22
Computer-aided design, 240–241, 323
Computer-aided engineering, 240–241, 363
Computer-aided manufacturing, 44–45, 241
Computer-aided process planning, 241
Computer-assisted instruction, 397
Computer-based information systems, 6
Computer-based training, 397
Computer codes, 88–89
Computer crime, 383–391. *see also* Security
    management
    antivirus software, 384, 390
    biometrics, 384
    content filtering, 384
    cyber theft, 385–386
    defenses, 412
    defined, 384
    hacking, 385, 386
    on the Internet, 384–385
    Internet workplace abuses, 387
    intrusion detection systems, 384
    piracy of intellectual property, 389
    public-key infrastructure, 384
    smart cards, 384
    software piracy, 389
    time and resource theft, 387–388
    unauthorized use at work, 387–388
    virtual private networks, 384
    viruses/worms. *see* Computer
        viruses/worms
Computer failure controls, 408–409
Computer Fraud and Abuse Act, 393
Computer hardware, 6, 65–100
    blade servers, 73
    evaluation of, 359, 360–361
    as IS component, 24–26
    for IS services evaluation, 362
    mainframe computers, 73–75, 100
    microcomputer systems. *see* Microcom-
        puter systems
    midrange systems, 72–73
    minicomputers, 72–73
    mobile computing systems, 67
    as software evaluation factor, 361
    supercomputer systems, 74–75
    system concept, 75–77
    technologies, 6
    types of computer systems, 68–75
    view of data, 140
Computer hardware view of data, 140
Computer-integrated manufacturing, 240–241
Computer libel and censorship, 393

Computer matching, 392–393
Computer monitoring, 394–395
Computer peripherals, 26, 78–94
    backup systems, 80
    CD drives, 80
    defined, 80
    DVD drives, 80
    hard disk drives, 80
    input technologies. *see* Input
    monitors, 80
    output technologies, 86–87
    printers, 80
    scanners, 80
Computer processing speeds, 77
Computer profiling, 392–393
Computer software. *see* Software
Computer Software Piracy and Counterfeit-
    ing Amendment, 389
Computer systems, 25
    concept, 75–77
    defined, 75
    fault tolerant, 92, 230
    Internet access to, 176
    mainframe, 73–75, 100
    microcomputers. *see* Microcomputer
        systems
    minicomputers, 72–73
    supercomputers, 74–75
    types of, 68–75
Computer terminals, 71–72
Computer viruses/worms, 384
    business challenges of, 379
    Code Red Worm, 390
    defenses against, 406–407
    Nimda Worm, 390–391
Conceptual design, databases, 161
Conciseness, of information, 295
Confidential data, transmission of, 387
Configuration, e-commerce, 262–263
Connectivity, 173, 360–361
Consideration step, in buying process, 273
Consolidation, 300, 440
Consultants, extranets and, 181
Consultation phase, development, 345
Consumers
    B2C e-commerce. *see* Business-to-
        consumer (B2C) e-commerce
    consumer privacy. *see* Privacy
    consumer-to-consumer (C2C)
        e-commerce, 260
    extranets and, 181
Contact management, using CRM, 219–220
Content-based search, 260
Content-based target marketing, 237–238
Content dimension, information quality, 295
Content filtering/monitoring, 384
Content management, 260, 262, 264, 384
Context-based target marketing, 237–238
Contextual labels, 126
Continuous speech recognition, 82–83
Contract costing, 243
Contract manufacturing, 240
Contractors, extranets and, 181
Contract programming, 112
Control(s), 77
    access, 260–261
    computer failure, 408–409

on costs, 218, 241
e-commerce access, 260–261
end user development and, 354
failure. *see* Failure/Failure controls
feedback and, 22–23
information systems, 410–412
inventory systems, 236, 245
machine, 241
numerical, 241
payroll, 243
process control. *see* Process control
of quality, 241
requirements, system development, 350
robotics, 241
shop floor, 241
of system performance, 27–28
systems and audits, 410–412
Conversion
    data, 363
    for IS services evaluation, 362
    systems implementation, 370
        challenges of, 367
        methods for, 364–365
Cookie files, 238, 276
Copyright infringement, 387
Core business systems, upgrading, 357
Corporate intranets. *see* Intranets
Corporate PC criteria, 70
Corporate Websites, 351
Cost(s)
    barriers, overcoming, 174
    contract costing, 243
    controlling, 218, 241
    cost leadership strategy, 40–42
    as hardware evaluation factor, 360
    intangible, 347
    of labor, budgeting and, 243
    production cost control, 241
    reducing, 177–178, 218
    of shipping, 274
    switching, 43
    system feasibility studies and, 347
    tangible, 347
    total cost of ownership, 70
Country-orientation, data communication
    and, 439
Create function, DBMS, 149
Creativity, Web development and, 355
Credit card processing, 274
Credit management systems, 236
Crisp data, 320
Critical success factors, 308
Cross-functional applications, 14, 214–216
Crossover, genetic algorithms, 321
Cultural challenges, for global IT, 435
Currency, of information, 295
Customer(s). *see also* Customer relationship
    management; Customer service
    account management, 274
    agility of, 53
    attracting, using the Internet, 177–178
    awareness, corporate websites and, 351
    bargaining power of, 40–42
    customer-focused businesses, 48–49, 63
    databases, 148
    extranets and, 181
    global, 438

Customer(s). —*cont.*
  locking in, 42
  loyalty systems, 63, 177–178
  self-service kiosks, 79, 270
  value of, 48
  Website experiences of, 349–350
Customer relationship management, 48, 67,
    212–215, 366–367
  application components, 220
  B2B e-commerce, 270
  B2C e-commerce, 270
  benefits and challenges of, 222–223
  as business focus, 219–223
  business value of, 221–222
  contact/account management, 219–220
  customer service and support, 221
  failures of, 222–223
  marketing and fulfillment, 221
  retention and loyalty programs, 221
  sales management, 220
  systems, 236, 237
  user resistance to, 368
  value chains and, 44
Customer service
  B2C e-commerce and, 274, 276
  global, 437
  systems, 36
  using CRM, 221
  using e-mail, 274
  using the Internet, 177–178
  value chains and, 44
  Web stores and, 274, 349–350
Custom website design services, 274
Cybercrime. *see also* Computer crime
  global treaty on, 442
Cybernetic system, 22
Cyber theft, 385–386

Data
  access, global, 441–443
  concepts, fundamental, 140–141
  confidential, transmission of, 387
  conversion, 363
  defined, 26
  fuzzy, 317, 320
  information vs., 26–27
Database, 26, 141–143
  accessed via Internet, 175
  defined, 150
  distributed, 142–143
  external, 143
  fault-tolerant, 409
  hypermedia, 143
  operational, 141–142
Database administrators, 160
Database design/development, 149,
    160–163
  application development, 149, 151–152
  conceptual design, 161
  data planning, 161–162
  logical design, 161–163
  physical design, 161–163
  requirements, specification of, 161
Database interrogation, 149–151, 152
Database maintenance, 149, 151, 230
Database management approach, 148

Database management systems/software
    (DBMS), 121, 149–152, 359
  application development, 150, 151–152
  components of, 150
  database defined, 150
  database interrogation, 149–151, 152
  database maintenance, 149, 151, 230
  database management approach, 148
  database tuning, 150
  defined, 149
  functions of, 149
  graphical queries, 151
  natural language queries, 151, 152
  nonprocedural access, 150
  procedural language interface, 150
  SQL queries, 150–151, 152
  strategic data, protecting, 154
  structures. *see* Database structures
  transaction processing, 150–152
Database structures, 155–160
  evaluation of, 158–159
  hierarchical, 155–156
  multidimensional, 156
  network, 155, 156
  object-oriented, 157–158
  relational, 155, 156, 159–160
Database tuning, 150
Data centers, 427
Data conversion, 363, 370
Data definition language, 160
Data dependence, 148
Data dictionary, 160
Data entry, 27–28, 230
Data file, 141
Data glove, 322
Data integration, 147
Data items, 140
Data link layer, 200
Data manipulation language, 152
Data marts, 143
Data mining, 145–146, 297, 307–308
Data modeling, 162
Data planning, 161–162
Data privacy, international, 442
Data processing, 27
Data redundancy, 147
Data repository, 260
Data resource management, 137–168
  challenges, 168
  database. *see* Database; Database manage-
      ment systems/software (DBMS)
  data concepts, 140–141
  data mining, 145–146
  data warehouses, 143–145, 167
  defined, 138
  file processing, 146–148
  technologies, 6
Data resources, 6. *see also* Data resource
      management
  as IS component, 24–27
  security of. *see* Security management
Data visualization systems, 303–304
Data warehouses, 143–145
  business value of, 167
Datum, 26. *see also* Data
DDN (digital data network), 201
Dead links, 351

Debuggers, 130
Decentralization of IT, 425
Decision rooms, 232
Decision structure, 294–296
Decision support systems, 8, 10–11, 13–14,
    291–337
  AI. *see* Artificial intelligence (AI)
  business intelligence, 292–293, 297
  components of, 302
  data mining and, 307–308
  data visualization, 303–304
  decision structure, 294, 295–296
  defined, 301
  enterprise information portals. *see* Enter-
      prise information portals
  enterprise resource planning. *see* Enter-
      prise resource planning
  executive information systems, 308–309
  expert systems. *see* Expert systems
  geographic information systems, 303
  goal-seeking analysis, 305–306
  information quality, 294–295
  knowledge management, 312–313
  level of decision making, 294
  management information systems. *see*
      Management information systems
  model bases and, 302
  online analytical processing. *see* Online
      analytical processing
  operational management, 294, 296
  optimization analysis, 305, 306
  semistructured decisions, 294, 295–296
  sensitivity analysis, 305
  strategic management, 294, 296
  structured decisions, 294, 295–296
  tactical management, 294, 296
  trends in, 296–297
  unstructured decisions, 294, 295–296
  using, 304–308
  Web-based financials, 337
  Web-enabled, 302–303, 306–307, 337
  what-if analysis, 305
Demand reports and responses, 299
Demodulation, 194
Demographic target marketing, 237–238
Denial of service, 386, 404–405
Dense wave division multiplexing, 191
Design/Design phase
  application development, 344
  computer-aided, 240–241, 323
  conceptual, 161
  database. *see* Database design/development
  expert systems for, 328
  IS solutions, developing, 17
  logical, 161–163
  physical, 161–163
  prototyping, 344
  systems design, 343, 350–353
  user interfaces, 351–352
  Website design tools, 274
Desktop publishing, 109
Desktops, 69, 109
Development. *see* Information systems (IS)
      development
Diagnostics applications, ES, 328
Differentiation strategy, 40–42
Digital camcorders, 85

Digital cameras, 85
Digital dashboard, 310
Digital network technologies, 173
Digital wallet payment system, 266
Digitizer pen, 82
Direct access memories, 89, 90
Direct access storage devices, 89, 90
Direct cutover conversion, 364–365
Disaster recovery, 409–410
Discrete speech recognition, 82–83
Discussion groups, 176, 274
Distributed databases, 142–143
Distributed denial of service, 404
Distributed shared memory, 74
Distribution channels, Internet creating, 178
Distributors, extranets and, 181
Documentation, 361, 363, 367, 370
Document file, 141
Document management, 84, 260
Document/report generation, 230
Documents, 109
Domain suitability criteria, ES, 329
Dotcom companies, 271
Downloads, 176
    non-work-related, 307
    of software, 175
Downsizing, 188, 294, 425
Drag and drop, 125
Drill-down data, 300, 308
DSL (digital subscriber line), 192, 196, 402
DSS software, 247
Dual scan LCD displays, 86–87
Dumb terminals, 71–72
Dumpster diving, 386
DVD drives, 80
    DVD, 93–94
    DVD-R, 93
    DVD-ROM, 93
    DVD-RW/R with CD-RW, 93
Dynamic content generation, 260
Dynamic multimedia catalogs, 274
Dynamic signature verification, 408, 409
Dynamic system, 22

e-Business, 11, 211–254
    applications, 8–10
    defined, 9
    empowerment, 270
    enterprise business systems. *see* Enterprise business systems
    functional business systems. *see* Functional business systems
    planning, 424–425
    role in business, 8–10
    software suite, 105
    technology management, 434
e-Catalog, 260, 262, 264, 270
e-Commerce, 9, 11, 212. *see also* Business-to-business (B2B) e-commerce; Business-to-consumer (B2C) e-commerce
    application trends, 268–270
    business-to-government (B2G), 258
    buying process, 258
    clicks and bricks in

business case for, 289
    channel choices, 281–283
    e-commerce integration, 281–283
consumer-to-consumer (C2C), 260
electronic payment. *see* Electronic payment systems
exchanges, 278–280
    marketing/discovery phase, 258
    marketplaces, 278–281
        auction, 278
        catalog, 278
        EDI and, 280–281
        exchange, 278
        many to many, 278
        many to one, 278
        many to some, 278
        one to many, 278
        portal, 278
        some to many, 278
    online marketplaces, 257, 290
    process architecture, 260
    processes. *see* e-Commerce processes
    scope of, 258–260
    selling process, 258
    service and support, 258
    success factors, 271–273
    technologies, 258
    transaction processing, 258
    trends, 268–270
e-Commerce architect, 428
e-Commerce channel, 282–283
e-Commerce portals, 278
e-Commerce process architecture, 260
e-Commerce processes, 260–265
    access control, 260–261
    catalog management, 260, 262, 264, 270
    collaboration and trading, 260, 265
    configuration of, 262–263
    content management, 260, 262, 264
    electronic payment. *see* Electronic payment systems
    event notification, 260, 264–265
    profiling and personalizing, 260, 261–262
    purchasing, 263–264
    search management, 260, 262
    security measures, 260–261
    workflow management, 260, 263, 264
Economic feasibility, 346–347
Effectiveness, of IT, 16
Effective use, of IT, 430
Efficiency
    benefits, from ERP, 217
    of IS, 16
    in using IT, 430
    as software evaluation factor, 361
e-Government, 258
Electronic audit trail, 411–412
Electronic billboards, 238
Electronic breaking and entering, 385
Electronic business systems, 211–254
    enterprise. *see* Enterprise business systems
    functional. *see* Functional business systems
Electronic commerce. *see* e-Commerce
Electronic Communications Privacy Act, 393
Electronic communication tools, 231
Electronic conferencing tools, 231–232

Electronic data interchange, 116, 259, 280–281
Electronic data processing, 10, 11
Electronic discussion forums, 175
Electronic funds transfer, 265–266
Electronic mail (e-mail), 106–107, 175, 176
    abuses of, 387
    customer service via, 274
    event notification sent to, 260
    monitoring, as security defense, 405–406
    network security and, 18, 405–406
    order notification, 274
    promotions, 274
Electronic meeting systems, 232
Electronic mouse, 80–81
Electronic payment systems, 265–267
    electronic funds transfer, 265–266
    secure payments, 266–267
    Web payments, 265
Electronic spreadsheets, 109–110, 247
e-Mail. *see* Electronic mail (e-mail)
Employee(s). *see also* Personnel
    requirements forecasting, 236
    resource, as IS component, 24–25
    self-service (ESS), 243
    skills inventory systems, 236
Employment challenges, of IT, 393–394, 435–436
Encapsulation capability, 157
Encryption of data, 266, 392
    network security and, 401–402
    order processing and, 274
    password encryption, 407
    website administration and, 274
End-to-end supply chain visibility, 240
End user involvement, 25
    application software, 104
    computing and, 10–11
    development and, 353–355
    managing change, 366–368
    and managing the IS function, 429–430
    resistance to change, 366–368
    web development, 355
Enterprise agility, ERP and, 218
Enterprise application architecture, 214–215
Enterprise application integration, 122, 227–228, 235
Enterprise business systems, 212–233
    application architecture, 214–215
    application integration, 122, 227–228, 235
    collaboration. *see* Enterprise collaboration systems
    cross-functional applications, 214–216
    customer relationship marketing. *see* Customer relationship management
    enterprise resource planning. *see* Enterprise resource planning
    supply chain management. *see* Supply chain management
    transaction processing. *see* Transaction processing
Enterprise collaboration systems, 9, 12–13, 121, 231–233
    electronic communication, 231
    electronic conferencing, 231–232

Enterprise collaboration systems —*cont.*
  swarming collaboration, 254
  work management, 232
Enterprise information portals, 178–180,
    310–312
  business value of, 310–312
  implementing, 374
Enterprise information systems, 308
Enterprise knowledge portals, 312
Enterprise management of IT, 419–452
  domestic. *see* Managing IT
  global. *see* Global IT management
Enterprise model, 161
Enterprise resource management, 161
Enterprise resource planning, 50, 52, 136,
    144, 214, 215
  agility and, 218
  application components, 216
  benefits of, 217–218
  cost reduction and, 218
  decision support and, 218
  efficiency improvements using, 217
  failures, 218–219
  quality benefits from, 217
  Web-based, 363–364
Entities, 26, 140–141, 161
Entity relationship diagrams, 161
Entry, barriers to, 43
Environment, as system concept, 23
EPROM, 90
Equity, 381
Ergonomics, 360, 396
ERP. *see* Enterprise resource planning
e-tailing, 271
Ethernet, 193, 201
Ethics, 18, 380–383
  business ethics, 380–381
  equity, 381
  exercise of corporate power, 381
  failures in, 383
  guidelines for, 382–383
  honesty, 381
  informed consent principle, 382
  justice principle, 382
  minimized risk principle, 382
  proportionality principle, 382
  rights, 381
  social contract theory, 381
  stakeholder theory, 381
  stockholder theory, 381
  technology ethics, 381–382
Evaluation factors
  defined, 359
  hardware, software, services, 358–362
Event-driven systems, 260, 264
Event-driven transaction messaging, 260
Event notification, 260, 264–265
Exception reports, 298
Exchanges, e-commerce, 278–280
Executive class information delivery, 297
Executive information systems, 11, 13, 14,
    308–309
Executives, IT, 428–429
Executive support systems, 308
Exercise of corporate power, 381
Expertise suitability criteria, ES, 329

Expert systems, 11, 14–15, 317, 325–330
  AI. *see* Artificial intelligence (AI)
  applications/categories, 325–327, 328
  availability suitability criteria, 329
  benefits of, 327
  case-based reasoning, 325, 326
  complexity suitability criteria, 329
  components of, 325, 326
  criteria (suitability) for use of, 329
  decision management, 328
  design/configuration, 328
  development of, 325, 329–330
  diagnostics/troubleshooting, 328
  domain suitability criteria, 329
  expertise suitability criteria, 329
  expert system shell, 325, 329
  frame-based knowledge, 325, 326
  knowledge base component, 325
  knowledge engineering, 330
  limitations of, 329
  modules, 428
  object-based knowledge, 325, 326
  process monitoring/control, 328
  rule-based knowledge, 325, 326
  selection/classification, 328
  software resources component, 325
  strategic, 327–329
  structure suitability criteria, 329
  suitability criteria for, 329
Expert system shell, 325, 329
Explicit knowledge, 56
eXtensible Markup Language, 126–128,
    136, 143, 193
  Web services based on, 281
External databases, 143
External ISPs, used at work, 387
Extract, transform and load (ETL), 139
Extranets, 9, 45, 178, 296, 297
  business value of, 180–181
  exchanges and, 270

Face recognition systems, 408, 409
Failure/Failure controls, 408–409
  ERP, 218–219
  fail-over capabilities, 409
  fail-safe capabilities, 409
  fail-soft capabilities, 409
  in IT management, 16, 421, 429–431
Fault tolerant capacity (RAID), 92
Fault tolerant systems, 92, 230, 409–410
FDDI, 201
Feasibility studies, 346–348
Federal Copyright Act, 389
Feedback, 22–23, 345
Fiber channel LANs, 92
Fiber distributed data interface, 201
Field, 140
Fifth discipline, 342
Fifth-generation languages, 124
File processing. *see also* Database; Database
    management systems/software (DBMS);
    File(s)
  traditional, 146–148

File(s), 141
  data dependence problem, 148
  data integration, lack of, 147
  data redundancy problem, 147
  fault-tolerant, 409
  file server, 185
  file sharing software, 389
  maintenance programs, 147
  management, 118–119
  retention measures, 407
Filter software, 193
Finance industry, 171
Finance systems, 236
Financial analysts, 247
Financial forecasting, 236, 337
Financial management systems, 246–247
Financial models, 247
Financial planning systems, 246, 247
Financial reporting, 245
Fingerprint verification systems, 408, 409
Firewalls, 274, 402–404
First-generation languages, 123
Fixed-length records, 141
Flame mail, 393
Flaming, 393
Flatbed scanners, 84
Flattened organizations, 294
Flexible manufacturing systems, 240
Flexible order processing, 274
Flexible software, 361
Floppy disks, 91
Formats, of data files, 148
Form dimension, of information, 295
Foundation concepts, IS, 7
Fourth-generation languages, 123, 124, 151
Frame-based knowledge, 325, 326
Frame relay network, 201
Frequency, of information, 295
Frequency division multiplexing, 195
Front-end processors, 185
Fulfillment, using CRM, 221
Full text databases, 143
Functional business systems, 14–15,
    234–247
  accounting. *see* Accounting systems
  financial management, 246–247
  human resources. *see* Human resource
    systems
  manufacturing. *see* Manufacturing systems
  marketing. *see* Marketing/Marketing
    systems
Functional requirements, 348, 350
Fuzzy data, 317, 320
Fuzzy logic, 317, 320–321
Fuzzy rules, 320

Garbage in, garbage out, 410–411
Gatekeeper, 402
Gateway, 196
General e-mail abuses, 387
General ledger systems, 236, 245
General purpose application software, 104
Genetic algorithms, 317, 321
Genetic pattern analysis, 408, 409
Geoeconomic challenges, for global IT, 435

Geographic barriers, overcoming, 174
Geographic databases, 303
Geographic information systems, 303
Gigabytes, 89
Gigaflops, 74
Gigahertz, 77
Global alliances, 437
Global business drivers, 436–438
Global collaboration, 438, 451
Global customers, 437, 438
Global customer service, 437
Global cybercrime treaty, 442
Global IT management, 432–445
    applications, 436–439
    business drivers, 436–438
    cultural challenges, 435
    data access issues, 441–443
    data communications issues, 439
    geoeconomic challenges, 435
    global cybercrime treaty, 442
    international dimension of, 432–434
    Internet access issues, 442–443
    Internet platform issues, 439–441
    key questions for global websites, 441
    offshore systems development, 433
    platforms, 439–441
    political challenges, 435
    strategies, 436
    systems development issues, 443–445
    technology management, 434
    transnational strategies, 436–437
    U.S.-EU data privacy, 442
Global knowledge management, 57
Global operations, 438
Global positioning systems, 303
Global products, 438
Global resources, 438
Global sourcing and logistics, 437
Global strategy, global e-business, 437
Global systems development, 443–445
Global websites, 441
Goal-seeking analysis, 305–306
Governance structures, 429–430
GPS satellite networks, 182–183
Grandparent files, 407
Graphical image file, 141
Graphical programming interfaces, 130
Graphical queries, 151
Graphical user interface (GUI), 80, 106,
    117–118, 125
Graphics tablet, 82
Group support systems, 232
Groupware, 104, 112, 247
Growth strategy, 40–42

Hacking, 385, 386, 387
Hand geometry verification, 408, 409
Handheld wireless computers, 99
Hard disk drives, 80, 91–92
Hardware. *see* Computer hardware
Health issues, 395–396
Help desk software, 221
Hierarchical databases, 155–156
High-earth orbit satellites, 191–192
High-level languages, 123, 124

High-speed Ethernet, 201
History file, 141
Home satellite, 196
Honesty, 381
Host computers, 185
Host-host transport layer, 200
Hosting, website, 274
Hub, 196
Human factors engineering, 396
Human information processing, 317
Human resource management, 236, 242, 428
    value chains and, 44
Human resource planning, 243
Human resource systems, 242–244
    compensation administration, 242–243
    and corporate intranets, 242–243
    the Internet and, 242
    operational systems, 243
    staffing, 242–243
    strategic systems, 243
    tactical systems, 243
    training and development, 242–243
    web-based, 243–244
Hyperlinks, 125–126
Hypermedia databases, 143
Hypertext markup language (HTML),
    125–126, 143, 193
    hypermedia publishing, 178

Image processing, 93
Implementation. *see* Systems implementation
Inbound logistics, value chains and, 44
Incentives, for e-commerce success, 272
Incompatibilities, websites and, 351
Inconsistencies, in file processing, 148
Individuality, challenges to, 395
Industry trends. *see* Trends
Inference engine, 325
Infomediaries, 278
Information, defined, 27
Information appliances, 71
Information-based products, 178
Information brokers, 324
Information centers, 425, 429
Information filters, 324
Information management agents, 324
Information overload, 298
Information processing, 27
Information products, 28, 29
Information quality, 294–295
Information retrieval, AI, 318
Information superhighway, 175
Information system activities, 27–28, 29
Information systems (IS). *see also* Informa-
    tion systems (IS) development
    activities. *see* Information system activities
    business applications. *see* Business
        applications
    business process support, 8
    components of. *see* Components of IS
    decision support. *see* Decision support
        systems
    defined, 6
    efficiency of, 16
    foundation concepts, 7

framework, 7
function, 19
knowledge of, required, 7
maintenance. *see* Maintenance/
    Maintenance phase
managing. *see* Managerial challenges of IS;
    Managing the IS function
model of IS, 24–25
recognizing, 29
resources, 6, 24–27, 29
roles of, 8. *see also* Business applications
services, 359, 361–362
specialists, 25
subsidiaries, 426
success with, 5
trends in, 10–12
types of, 12–15
Information systems (IS) development,
    340–355. *see also* Application develop-
    ment; System development
business/IT solutions, 17
development centers, 427
development processes, 7
development tools, 121
end user development, 353–355
feasibility studies, 346–348
parallel, 444
prototyping, 343–346
self-service Web systems, 340–342
systems analysis. *see* Systems analysis
systems approach, 340, 342–343
systems concepts and, 20
systems design. *see* Systems design
systems development cycle, 343
systems development process, 346–348
systems implementation phase, 343
systems investigation phase, 343
systems maintenance phase, 343
systems thinking, 342–343
Web store, 274–275
Information systems (IS) resources, 6,
    24–27, 29
Information technologies (IT), 6, 7. *see also*
    Technology
architecture, 424
careers, 18–19
competing with. *see* Strategic IT
data management. *see* Data resource
    management
effectiveness of, 16
hardware. *see* Computer hardware
infrastructure management, 422
managing. *see* Managing IT
platforms, global, 439–441
software. *see* Computer software
successes and failures, 16, 35
telecom. *see* Telecommunications
Informed consent principle, 382
Inheritance, 157
Inkjet printers, 87
Innovation strategy, 40–42
Input, 22–23, 27–28, 75–76
    digital camcorders, 85
    digital cameras, 85
    end user development and, 353–354
    magnetic stripe technology, 85

Input —*cont.*
  MICR, 85
  optical scanning, 84–85
  pen-based computing, 81–82
  pointing devices, 80–81
  reader-sorters, 85
  smart cards, 85
  speech recognition, 82–83
  technologies, 80–85
Inquiry processing, 230–231
Installation phase, systems, 345
Instant messaging, 108, 175
Insurance industry, DSS systems in, 303
Intangible benefits, 347–348
Intangible costs, 347
Integrated packages, 106
Integrated shopping carts, 274
Integrated Web store, 270
Integration, clicks and bricks, 281–283
Integration goal, manufacturing, 240–241
Integrity problems, file processing, 148
Intellectual property piracy, 389
Intelligent agents, 317, 323–325
Intelligent behavior, attributes of, 316
Intelligent terminals, 71–72
Interactive marketing, 236–237, 270
Interenterprise information systems, 43, 55
Interfaces, 23
  command-driven, 117–118
  fiber distributed data, 201
  graphical, 130. *see also* Graphical user
    interface (GUI)
  interface tutors, 324
  natural, 80, 317–318
  network interface card, 185
  network interface layer, 200
  online customer, 257, 290
  operating systems, 117–118
  procedural language, 150
  software, 115, 163
  user. *see* User interface
Interface tutors, 324
Internal view of data, 162
International data communication, 439, 442
International IT. *see* Global IT management
International Standards Organization (ISO),
  199
The Internet. *see also* Web-based systems
  abuses, workplace, 387
  access, global IT and, 442–443
  business use of, 176–177
  business value of, 177–178
  e-business. *see* e-Business
  e-commerce. *see* e-Commerce
  global IT platform, 440–441
  human resources and, 242
  Internet protocol layer, TCP/IP, 200
  Internet revolution, 175–178
  Internet service providers, 175
  Internet Society, 175
  leisure use at work, 387
  networking technologies, 173
  phone systems, 209
  retailing, 271
  technologies, 173–174
  telecom networks, 175–178

  terminals, 72
  usage
    popular uses, 176
    privacy issues, 391–392
    by region, 441
    unauthorized, 387
Internetworked security defenses, 401–407,
  418
  denial of service, 404–405
  e-mail monitoring, 405–406
  encryption, 401–402
  firewalls, 402–404
  managing network security systems, 418
  password encryption, 407
  virus defenses, 406–407
Internetwork processors, 195–196
Interoperability, 173
Interpreters, 124, 130
Intranets, 9, 44, 296, 297
  business operations and, 179–180
  business value of, 178–180
  for collaboration, 178–179
  for communication, 178–179
  human resource systems and, 242–243
  role of, 178–180
  Web publishing and, 179
Intrusion detection, 384
Invasion of privacy, 394–395
Inventory control systems, 236, 245
Inventory e-commerce reports, 274
Inventory file, 141
Investigation phase
  application development, 344
  IS development, 17
  prototyping, 344
  systems, 17, 343, 346, 347
Investment industry, 171
Investment management, 236, 246
ISDN, 192, 196, 201

Java, 124–125, 127, 136
Junk e-mail, 393
Justice principle, 382
Just-in-time warehousing, 44

Keyboards, 80
Keystroke analysis verification, 408, 409
Kilobytes, 89
Knowledge, 56
  bases, 11, 26, 312, 317, 325
  discovery, 307
  engineer, 330
  engineering, 330
  explicit, 56
  frame-based, 325, 326
  of IS, required, 7
  management. *see* Knowledge management
    systems
  object-based, 325, 326
  portals, 312
  rule-based, 325, 326
  tacit, 56
  workers, 25
Knowledge-based information system, 325
Knowledge-based systems, 11, 317, 325

Knowledge-creating companies, 56–57
Knowledge management systems, 14–15,
  56–57, 215, 312–313
  business intelligence tools, 297
  global, 57
  obstacles to, 367
  strategic uses of IT and, 47

Labor cost analyses, 243
Labor force tracking, 243
Language processors, 130
Language translator programs, 130
LANs. *see* Local area networks
Laptop computer, 69
Large-capacity storage media, 88
Laser printers, 87
Lasers, 87, 190
Learning curve, 365
Learning organization, 56
Legacy systems, 136, 188, 214, 223
Leisure use of the Internet, at work, 387
Level of management decision making, 294
Leveraging IT, for strategic advantage, 43
Libel, computer, 393
"Lights out" data centers, 428
Limits, Web development and, 355
Linux operating system, 100, 120, 135
Liquid crystal display (LCD) screen, 82, 86
Local area networks, 185–186
  fiber channel, 92
  wireless, 70, 193
Local microwave, 196
Locking in customers, 42
Locking in suppliers, 42
Logical data elements, 140–141
Logical design, 161–163
Logical view of data, 140, 162–163
Logic bombs, 386
Look and feel factor, e-commerce, 272
Low-earth orbit satellites, 192
Loyalty, 221, 273

Machine control, 241
Machine languages, 123
Machines, 25
Mac OS X operating systems, 120
Macroinstructions, 124
Magnetic disks, 88, 90–92
Magnetic ink character recognition, 85
Magnetic stripe technology, 85
Magnetic tape, 88, 92
Mainframe computer systems, 73–75, 100
Main microprocessor, 75
Maintain function, DBMS, 149
Maintenance/Maintenance phase
  application development, 344
  business systems development, 343
  database, 149, 151, 230
  developing IS solutions, 17
  of IS, 362, 365
  programs, 147, 148
  prototypes/prototyping and, 344
  as software evaluation factor, 361
Malicious applets, 386

Management information systems, 10–14, 298–299
  business intelligence tools for, 297
  demand reports/responses, 299
  exception reports, 298
  periodic scheduled reports, 298
  push reporting, 299
  reporting alternatives, 298–299
Management involvement, in IT, 429–430
Management support systems, 13–14. *see also*
    Management information systems;
    Managing IT; Managing the IS function
Managerial challenges of IS, 15–19. *see also*
    Managing IT; Managing the IS function
Managerial pyramid, 294
Managers, Web development and, 355
Managing IT, 420–452. *see also* Managing
    the IS function
  application development, 422
  business and IT strategy, 422
  business/IT planning. *see* Business/IT
    planning
  conventional vs. e-business, 426
  failures in, 421, 429–431
  global. *see* Global IT management
  IT organization and infrastructure, 422
  major components of, 422
  successful projects, case study, 452
Managing organizational change, 366–369
  change management defined, 368
  end user involvement, 366–367
  end user resistance, 366–368
Managing the IS function, 425–429
  application development, 427
  end user involvement, 429–430
  human resource management of IT, 428
  IS operations, 427–428
  IT executives, 428–429
  management involvement and, 429–430
  organizing IT, 425–426
  technology management, 429
  user services, 429
Manufacturing alliances, 55
Manufacturing execution systems, 236, 241
Manufacturing resource planning, 236, 241
Manufacturing systems, 236, 240–242
  automation goal, 240–241
  computer-aided, 241
  computer-integrated, 240–241
  execution systems, 241
  integration goal, 240–241
  machine control, 241
  resource planning, 236, 241
  simplification goal, 240–241
Many-to-many e-commerce, 278
Many-to-many relationship, 156
Many-to-one e-commerce, 278
Many-to-some e-commerce, 278
Marketing/Marketing systems, 236, 240
  CRM and, 221
  discovery phase, e-commerce, 258
  sales force automation, 236–239
  targeted marketing, 44, 237–238
  value chains and, 44
  Web marketing, 177–178
  Web stores and, 274
Market research/forecasting, 237

Markets/Marketplaces, 178. *see also*
    e Commerce
Mass customization, 52, 262
Massively parallel processing, 74
Master file, 141
Material requirements planning, 241
Media
  communications, 27
  data, 25
  dynamic multimedia catalogs, 274
  hypermedia, 143, 178
  information presentation and, 295
  large-capacity storage, 88
  storage tradeoffs, 87–89
  telecommunications, 184, 185, 190–191
Mediation, 260
Medium, 184
Medium-band channels, 200
Megabytes, 89
Megahertz, 77
Memory, 76
Menu-driven user interfaces, 117–118
Mesh network, 198–199
Message boards, 260
Metadata, 144, 160, 168
Metadata repository, 144, 160
Metropolitan area networks, 185
Microcomputer systems, 68–72
  computer terminals, 71–72
  connectivity and, 70
  corporate PC criteria, 70
  defined, 68
  information appliances, 71
  network computers, 71
  operating systems, upgrading, 70
  performance/value equation, 70
  recommended features, 70
Microprocessors, 75, 119
Microseconds, 77
Microsoft Windows, 72, 119–120, 417
Middleware, 122, 173, 196, 227, 359
Midrange computer systems, 72–73
Milliseconds, 77
Minicomputers, 72–73
Minimized risk principle, 382
Minisupercomputers, 74
MIPS, 73, 77
Mnemonics, 123
Mobile computing systems, 67
Mobile radio systems, 174
Models/Modeling
  analytical, 304–308
  data modeling, 162
  enterprise model, 161
  financial models, 247
  information systems model, 24–25
  intelligent agent based, for SCM, 336
  model bases, DSS and, 302
  OSI model, 199–200
  telecommunications network, 184–185
  three-tier client/server, 188
Modems, 194–195, 196
Modulation, 194
Monitors, 80
Moonlighting, 387
Mouse, 80–81
Multidimensional database structures, 156

Multifunction units, 84
Multinational development team, 444
Multiplexers, 195
Multiprogramming, 119
Multitasking capabilities, 119
Mutation, genetic algorithms, 321

Nanosecond, 77
Narrow-band channels, 200
Natural interfaces, 317–318
Natural language(s), 124, 317
  queries, 151, 152
Natural user interface, 80
Navigation ease, websites, 351
Negotiation, 260
Network, 6. *see also* Network alternatives;
    Network security
  business value, 174–175
  computers, 71
  database structure, 155, 156
  defined, 184
  fault-tolerant, 409
  firewalls, 274
  management, 121, 439
  monitoring, 388. *see also* Sniffers
  navigation agents, 324
  neural, 317, 319–320
  resources, 24–25, 27
  security. *see* Network security
  servers, 69, 72
  sniffers, 266, 385–388
  support, 27
  terminals, 71–72, 184–185
Network alternatives, 182–201
  architectures/protocols, 199–200
  backbone network, 186–187
  bandwidth management, 197–198
  channels, 184–185
  client/server networks, 188
  coaxial cable, 190
  components of networks, 184
  computing concept, 188
  dense wave division multiplexing, 191
  fiber optics, 190–191
  interface card, 185
  interface layers, 200
  local area networks. *see* Local area networks
  management, 197
  media, 184, 190–191
  metropolitan area networks, 185
  model, 184–185
  monitoring, 197
  network-centric computing concept, 188
  network computers, 184–185, 188
  network computing concept, 188
  network model, 184–185
  networks defined, 184
  operating system, 185, 196
  peer-to-peer networks, 188–190
  processors, 184–185
  servers, 185
  software, 184–185
  topologies, 184, 198–199
  twisted-pair wire, 190
  types of networks, 185–190
  virtual private networks, 186–187

Network alternatives —*cont.*
  wide area networks, 185
  wireless. *see* Wireless technologies
Network security. *see also* Internetworked
    security defenses
  e-mail and, 18, 405–406
  encryption of data, 401–402
  ethics and, 18
  managing, 418
  security monitors, 122, 274, 408
  for VPNs, 384
Neural networks, 317, 319–320
Neurons, 319
New entrants, threat of, 40–42
Newsgroups, 175, 260, 387
Nimda Worm, 390–391
Nonhierarchical organizations, 294
Nonprocedural access, DBMS, 150
Nonprocedural languages, 124
Non-work-related downloads/uploads, 387
Numerical control, 241

Object, 157
Object-based knowledge, 325, 326
Objective C programming languages, 127
Object-oriented databases, 157–158
Object-oriented DBMS, 157
Object-oriented programming, 124–125
Objects, 125
Office automation systems, 13
Officers, corporate, 422, 423, 428, 429
Offline devices, 80
Offshore development companies, 444
Offshore software, 112
Offshore systems development, 433
Off state, 88
One's (binary), 88
One-to-many e-commerce, 278
One-to-many relationship, 156
One-to-one marketing, 261, 273
Online accounting systems, 245–246
Online analytical processing, 156, 300–301
  business intelligence tools for, 297
  consolidation of data, 300
  drill-down data, 300
  slicing and dicing of databases, 300
Online behavior target marketing, 237–238
Online community, 260
Online customer interface, 257, 290
Online devices, 80
Online help, 274
Online HRM systems, 242
Online marketplaces, 257, 290
Online point-of-sale, value chains and, 44
Online processing, 12
Online sales, 177–178
Online tech support, 274
Online transaction processing, 228–229
ON state, 88
On-the-fly applet execution, 130
Open-source software, 120
Open system, 23, 173
Operating systems, 117–121
  file management, 118–119
  functions, 117–119
  Linux, 100, 120, 135

Mac OS X, 120
Microsoft Windows, 72, 119–120, 417
  performance monitors, 121–122
  resource management, 118–119
  task management, 118–119
  UNIX, 120–121
  upgrading, 70
  user interfaces, 117–118
  utilities in, 118–119, 121
Operational agility, 53
Operational databases, 141–142
Operational feasibility, 347
Operations/Operations management,
    427–428. *see also* Business operations
  DSS and, 294
  global, 438
  human resource systems and, 243
  intranets and, 179–180
  operations support systems, 12
  value chains and, 44
Optical character recognition, 84
Optical disks, 88, 92–94
Optical routers, 191
Optical scanning, 84–85
Optimization analysis, 305, 306
Orders
  information and, 295
  management process for, 51–52
  notification of, via e-mail, 274
  processing, 245
  flexible, 274
  systems, 236
  value chains and, 44
Organizational analysis, 348
Organizational change. *see* Managing orga-
    nizational change
Organizational feasibility, 346, 347
Organizational redesign, 50
Organizing IT, 425–426
OSI model, 199–200
Outbound logistics, 44
Output
  of an application, 353–354
  of computer systems, 76, 86–87
  of information products, 27–28
  printed output, 87
  of a system, 22
  voice response systems, 86
Outsourcing, 112, 426

Packet switching, 201
Pagers, 193
Parallel conversion, 364–365
Parallel development, 444
Parallel processing, 74
Parametric-based search, 260
Parent files, 407
Parent objects, 157
Partnering agility, 53
Partner relationship management, 215
Partners, extranets and, 181
Passive data dictionaries, 160–161
Passive iris scan, 409
Password crackers, 386
Password encryption, 407

Password protection, 274
Password systems, 407
Payment method support, 260
Payment verification, 260
Payroll, 245
Payroll control, 243
Payroll file, 141
Payroll systems, 236
Payroll transaction processing, 245
PCS phone systems, 174, 193
PDAs. *see* Personal digital assistants
Peers, 189
Peer-to-peer connection, 189, 389
Peer-to-peer networking, 188–190, 389
Pen-based computing, 81–82
Performance
  e-commerce success factor, 272
  as hardware evaluation factor, 360
  for IS services evaluation, 362
Performance appraisal planning, 243
Performance evaluations, 243
Performance measurement, 295
Performance monitors, 121–122, 427
Performance/value equation, 70
Periodic scheduled reports, 298
Peripherals. *see* Computer peripherals
Personal attention, 272–273
Personal computers, 68. *see also* Microcom-
    puter systems
Personal digital assistants, 66, 71, 82,
    239–240
Personal information managers, 111–112
Personalization, 260–262
Personalized Web pages, 274
Personnel. *see also* Employee(s)
  as IS component, 24–25
  requirements forecasting, 236
Petabyte, 89
Phased conversion, 364–365
Photons, 190
Physical design, databases, 161–163
Physical layer, 200
Physical view of data, 162–163
Picosecond, 77
Pilot conversion, 364–365
Piracy of software/intellectual property, 389
Plagiarism, 387
Plasma displays, 87
Platforms, 424, 439–441
Plunge conversion, 364–365
Point and click, 125
Pointing devices, 80–81
Pointing stick, 81
Point-of-sale, 12–13, 72
Political challenges, for global IT, 435
Pornography, on the Internet, 387
Portals
  B2B, 270
  B2C, 270
  e-commerce, 270, 278
  enterprise information. *see* Enterprise
    information portals
  enterprise knowledge, 312
Ports, 196
Postimplementation review, 365
Power supplies, redundant, 274

Practice manager, 429
Preference step, buying processes, 273
Presentation
    agents, 324
    graphics, 110–111
    of information, 295
    layer, OSI model, 200
    phase, systems development, 345
Present system, analysis of, 348–349
Pricing calculation, 260
Primary business processes, 44
Primary storage unit, 76, 88
Printed output, 87
Printers, 80, 87
Privacy, 391–393
    anonymous remailers, 392
    computer libel/censorship, 393
    computer matching, 392–393
    computer monitoring and, 394–395
    computer profiling, 392–393
    consumer privacy challenges, 392
    Electronic Communications Privacy
        Act, 393
    encryption, 392
    flame mail, 393
    flaming, 393
    international data privacy, 442
    Internet use and, 391–392
    invasion of, 394–395
    junk e-mail, 393
    laws, 393
    right to, 391
    spam/spamming, 393
    of U.S.-EU data, 442
Private B2B exchanges, 279–280
Private key, 401–402
Procedural language interface, 150
Procedural programming languages, 125, 150
Procedures, 26
Process, fault-tolerant, 409
Process architecture, 260
Process control, 328, 399, 428
    ES application, 328
    security management for, 399
    systems, 12–13, 236, 241
Processing
    CPU and, 75–76
    of input into output, 22–23
    as IS activity, 27–28
    requirements, 350, 354
    speeds, 77
Processors
    fault-tolerant, 409
    telecommunications, 194–196
Process teams, 50
Procurement of resources
    automation of, 270
    integration of, business value, 269
    value chains and, 44
    Web-based, 264, 269
Product configuration, 260, 262
Production cost control, 241
Production databases, 141
Production forecasting, 241
Production information systems, 236, 240.
    see also Manufacturing systems

Production scheduling, 241
Productivity packages, 104
Product management systems, 237
Products, global, 438
Product simulation and prototyping, 241
Professional workstations, 68
Profile management, 260
Profiling, 260, 261–262
Program maintenance, 148
Programming editors, 130
Programming languages, 123–129
    assembler languages, 123–124
    fifth-generation, 124
    first-generation, 123
    fourth-generation, 123, 124, 151
    high-level languages, 123, 124
    machine languages, 123
    natural, 124
    nonprocedural, 124
    object-oriented, 124–125
    procedural, 125
    second-generation, 123
    third-generation, 124
    Web languages, 125–129
Programming software, 130–131
Programming tools, 130–131
Programs, 26
Project management, 358
PROM, 90
Proportionality principle, 382
Protocols, 196, 199–200
Prototypes/Prototyping, 241, 343–346, 351,
    363
    analysis/design phase, 344
    with application development, 344–345
    design/implementation phase, 344
    implementation/maintenance phase, 344
    investigation/analysis phase, 344
    phase, of systems development, 345
    prototyping process, 344–345
Proxy software, 193
Psychographic target marketing, 237–238
Public B2B exchanges, 278–279
Public domain software, 389
Public key, 384, 401–402
Purchases/Purchasing, 245
    e-commerce and, 263–264
    purchasing transaction processing, 245
    traditional vs. Web buying processes, 273
Pure peer-to-peer network, 190
Push reporting, 299

Quality
    as benefit of ERP, 217
    quality control, 241
    as software evaluation factor, 361
    of working conditions, 395
Query/Query language, 149–151

Radio frequency identification, 171
RAID, 92
Raising barriers to entry, 43
RAM, 88–90
Rapid application development, 344
Reader-sorters, 85
Real-time processing, 12, 229, 230

Receiver, 184
Recognizing information systems, 29
Records, 141
Recruiting, 243
Redundancy
    data, 147
    RAID, 92
    of servers and power, 274
Reengineering business processes, 50–52
Registers, 75, 77
Registration forms, 351
Regulatory issues, international data, 439
Reiteration phase, 345
Relational databases, 155, 156, 159–160
Relations, tables, 156
Relevance, of information, 295
Reliability
    as e-commerce success factor, 272, 273
    as hardware evaluation factor, 360
Report generator, 149–151
Reporting alternatives, MIS, 298–299
Request for proposal, 359
Request for quotation, 359
Requirements
    control, 350
    database specifications, 161
    functional, 348, 350
    material requirements planning, 241
    personnel, forecasting, 236
    processing capacity, 350, 354
    storage, 350
    Web store, 274–277
Resources/Resource management
    acquisition strategies, 375
    in business/IT planning, 423
    global, 438
    information systems, 6, 24–27, 29
    as operating system function, 118–119
    procurement of, 44, 264, 269, 270
Responsible end user, 18
Responsible professional, 382–383
Retail industry, 171, 303
Retention/loyalty programs, 221
Retina scanning, 408, 409
Revenue generation, Internet, 177–178
Rights, ethical issues and, 381
Right to privacy, 391
Ring network, 198–199
Risk optimizer software, 322
Rivalry of competitors, 40–42
Robotics
    commercial applications, 318
    control, 241
    as domain of AI, 317
    software robots, 323
Role-based content routing, 260
Role-based search, 260
Role of IT, 50–51
Role-playing agents, 324
Roles of IS, 8
ROM, 90, 92–94
Root record, 155–156
Router, 196, 402
Rule-based content routing, 260
Rule-based knowledge, 325, 326
Rule-based search, 260

Salary forecasting, 243
Sales
  analysis, 245
  management, 220, 237
  online, 177–178
  order processing, 245
  records, updates to, 28
  reports, e-commerce and, 274
  sales force automation, 236–239
  transaction processing system, 245
  value chains and, 44
Satellites, 174, 182–183, 191–192, 196
Scalability, 274, 360
Scanners (input), 80
Scans (hacking), 385, 386
Schemas, 162
Schematic phase, development, 345
Scope, 258–260, 295
Scoring system, for systems implementation, 359
Searchability, of websites, 351
Search agents, 324
Search engines, 175, 274
Search management, 260, 262
Secondary storage, 77, 88
Second-generation languages, 123
Secure electronic payments, 266–267
Secure Electronic Transaction, 266–267
Secure Socket Layer, 266
Security codes, 407
Security management, 260, 398–412
  audits, 410–412
  backup files, 407
  biometric security, 408
  computer crime. *see* Computer crime
  computer failure controls, 408–409
  computer viruses/worms. *see* Computer
    viruses/worms
  for data resources, 399
  disaster recovery, 409–410
  e-commerce and, 260–261, 272, 273
  employment challenges, 435–436
  ethics. *see* Ethics
  fault tolerant systems, 409–410
  goal of, 400
  internetworked security. *see* Internet-
    worked security defenses
  networks, 197
  privacy issues. *see* Privacy
  for process control networks, 399
  security codes, 407
  security monitors, 122, 274, 408
  as software evaluation factor, 361
  systems controls/audits, 410–412
  tools of the trade, 400–407
  of *Windows* software, 417
Selection
  and classification, ES application, 328
  as e-commerce success factor, 272
  genetic algorithms, 321
Self-service kiosks, 79
Self-service Web sales, 270
Self-service Web systems, 270, 340–342
Selling process, e-commerce and, 258
Semantics, 124
Semiconductor memory, 88–90
Semistructured decisions, 294–296

Sender, 184
Sensitivity analysis, 305
Sequential access devices, 89
Servers, 178, 188
  application, 121, 122–123
  blade, 73
  client/server applications, 188, 214
  file, 185
  network, 69, 72, 185
  redundant, 274
  superservers, 73–74
  Web server software, 359
Service and support, e-commerce, 258, 272
Services, IS, 359, 361–362
Session layer, OSI model, 200
Shareware, 120, 389, 390
Shipping costs, calculating, 274
Shop floor control, 241
Shop floor scheduling, 241
Shopping carts, 260, 265, 274
Signature dynamics verification, 408, 409
Simplification, of manufacturing, 240–241
Simulation, 241
Site licenses, 389
Skill assessment, 243
Slave computers, 404
Slicing and dicing of databases, 300
Slide shows, 111
Small businesses software, 103
Smart cards, 85, 384, 407
Smart telephones, 193
Sniffers, 266, 385–388
SOAP Web service protocol, 128–129
Social contract theory, 381
Social engineering, 386
Societal solutions, 397
Software, 6, 101–136
  application. *see* Application software
  database. *see* Database management
    systems/software (DBMS)
  development of, 367, 370
  evaluation of, 359, 361
  as hardware evaluation factor, 360
  for IS services evaluation, 362
  piracy of, 389
  resources, 24–26, 325
  software interface, 115, 163
  software robots, 323
  software suites, 103, 104
  software surrogates, 323
  system software. *see* System software
  technologies, 6
  telecommunications, 184–185, 196–198
Software Publishers Association, 389
Some-to-many e-commerce, 278
SONET network, 201
Sorting, data processing and, 28
Source document, 28, 80
Sourcing and logistics, global, 437
Spam, 393
Spamming, 393
Speaker-independent voice recognition, 83
Speech recognition systems, 82–83
Spoofing, 386
Spreadsheets. *see* Electronic spreadsheets
Spread spectrum technology, 193
SQL queries, 150–152

Staffing, 242–243. *see also* Employee(s);
    Personnel
Stakeholder theory, of business ethics, 381
Star network, 198–199
Statements (programming instructions), 124
Statistical data banks, 143
Stockholder theory, of business ethics, 381
Stockless inventory replenishment, 43
Storage, 27–28, 76–77, 87–94
  access speed, 88
  binary digit (bit), 88
  binary representation, 88
  byte, 88
  direct access memories, 89, 90
  end user development and, 354
  floppy disks, 91
  hard disk drives, 91–92
  IS activity, 28
  large-capacity storage media, 88
  magnetic disks, 88, 90–92
  magnetic tape, 88, 92
  media tradeoffs, 87–89
  optical disks, 88, 92, 93–94
  primary storage unit, 88
  RAID, 91
  read only memory, 90
  requirements, systems development, 350
  secondary storage, 88
  semiconductor memory, 88, 89–90
  sequential access devices, 89
  storage area networks, 92
  tradeoffs, 87–89
  volatility of, 90
  WORM, 93
Storefront software, 359
Strategic IT
  agile companies and, 52–54
  alliance strategy, 40–42
  bargaining power of customers, 40–42
  bargaining power of suppliers, 40–42
  barriers to entry, 43
  business processes reengineering, 50–52
  competitive forces, 40–41
  competitive strategy concepts, 40–42
  cost leadership strategy, 40–42
  customer-focused businesses, 48–49, 63
  customer loyalty systems, 63
  data resources, protecting, 154
  development of, 423
  differentiation strategy, 40–42
  growth strategy, 40–42
  human resource systems and, 243
  innovation strategy, 40–42
  Internet technologies and, 48–49, 54–55
  knowledge-creating companies, 56–57
  knowledge management, 14–15, 47, 56–57
  leveraging IT investment, 43
  locking in customers, 42
  locking in suppliers, 42
  manufacturing alliances, 55
  order management process, 51
  rivalry of competitors, 40–42
  for strategic advantage, 38–45
  strategic expert systems, 327–329
  strategic IS, 11, 14–15, 40–44
  strategic management, 294
  strategic uses of IT, 41–44

strategy development, 423
strategy management, 422
switching costs and, 43
threat of new entrants, 40–42
threat of substitutes, 40–42
value chain and, 44–45
virtual companies, 54–55
Structural barriers, overcoming, 174
Structured decisions, 294, 295–296
Structure suitability criteria, ES, 329
Subject area databases, 141
Subschemas, 162
Substitutes, threat of, 40–42
Subsystem, 23
Succession planning, 243
Suitability criteria, expert systems, 329
Summarization, data processing and, 28
Supercomputer systems, 74–75
Superservers, 73–74
Suppliers
    bargaining power of, 40–42
    extranets and, 181
    locking in, 42
Supply chain, 224
Supply chain management, 144, 161, 214,
    215, 223–226
    application components, 225
    B2B e-commerce and, 270
    B2C e-commerce and, 270
    benefits/challenges of, 225–226
    business value of, 253
    end-to-end visibility, 240
    failures, 225
    supply chain life cycle, 224, 225
    Web-enabled, 224–225
Support
    using CRM, 221
    as hardware evaluation factor, 360
    value chains and, 44
Surfing the Web, 176
Swarming collaboration, 254
Switch (communications processor),
    195–196, 199
Switching alternatives, telecom, 200–201
Switching costs, for customers, 43
Symmetric multiprocessing, 74
Syntax, 124
System
    analysis phase. *see* Systems analysis
    controls and audits, 410–412
    defined, 22, 75
    design. *see* Systems design
    development. *see* System development
    fault-tolerant, 409
    implementation. *see* Systems
        implementation
    integrators, 361, 426
    investigation, 343, 346, 347
    maintenance, 343, 365
    management programs, 104, 115–117,
        121–122
    performance monitors, 121–122, 427
    programmers, 124
    repository, 363
    security monitors, 122, 274, 408
    software. *see* System software
    specifications, 353

systemic view, 342
systems context, 342
systems thinking, 342–343
testing, 363
System development. *see also* Application
    development; Information systems (IS)
    development
    of global systems, 443–445
    for IS services evaluation, 362
    life cycle, 343
    process, 346–348
    programs, 104, 117
Systems analysis, 343, 348–350
    control requirements, 350
    functional requirements analysis, 350
    organizational analysis, 348
    present system, analysis of, 348–349
    processing requirements, 350
    storage requirements, 350
    user interface requirements, 350
Systems approach, 340, 342–343
Systems design, 350–353
    business system development, 343
    expert systems for, 328
    system specifications, 353
    user interface design, 351–352
Systems implementation, 343, 356–370
    application development, 344
    challenges, ten greatest, 367
    conversion methods, 364–365
    core business systems, upgrading, 357
    data conversion and, 363
    defined, 356–357
    developing IS solutions, 17
    direct cutover conversion, 364–365
    documentation and, 363
    failure in, 365–366
    hardware evaluation, 359, 360–361
    IS maintenance, 365
    overview, 370
    parallel conversion, 364–365
    phased conversion, 364–365
    pilot conversion, 364–365
    plunge conversion, 364–365
    project management, 358
    prototyping, development and, 344
    services evaluation, 359, 361–362
    software evaluation, 359, 361
    testing and, 363, 367, 370
    timeline, 359
    training and, 363–364
    upgrading core systems, 357
System software, 26, 102–103, 115–130
    application servers, 121, 122–123
    collaboration tools, 121
    database manager, 121
    development tools, 121
    enterprise application integration, 122,
        227–228, 235
    language translator programs, 130
    middleware, 122
    network management, 121
    operating systems. *see* Operating systems
    programming languages. *see* Programming
        languages
    programming tools/software, 130–131
    security monitors, 122, 274, 408

system development programs, 104, 117
system management programs, 104,
    115–117, 121–122

Table, 141, 156
Tablet PCs, 82
Tacit knowledge, 56
Tactical management, 294
Tactical systems, 243
Tangible benefits, 347–348
Tangible costs, 347
Targeted marketing, 44, 237–238
Task management function, 118–119
Taxes, calculating, 274
TCP/IP network protocols, 178, 199–200
Team phase, systems development, 345
Technical feasibility, 347
Technical team leader, 429
Technology. *see also* Information
    technologies (IT)
    architecture, 424
    development, 44
    e-commerce, 258
    ethics, 381–382
    as hardware evaluation factor, 360
    for international data communications, 439
    management, 429
    systems concepts and, 20
    trends, Telecom industry, 172, 173–174
Telecommunications, 169–209
    application trends, 172, 174
    bandwidth alternatives, 200, 201
    business application trends, 174
    business value of, 174–175
    channels, 184–185
    decision support systems and, 303
    defined, 172
    extranets, role of, 180–181
    industry trends, 172–173, 303
    the Internet revolution. *see* The Internet
    internetwork processors, 195–196
    intranets. *see* Intranets
    media, 184, 185, 190–191
    modems, 194–195, 196
    monitors, 185, 196
    multiplexers, 195
    network. *see* Network; Network alternatives
    processors, 194–196
    software for, 196–198
    switching alternatives, 200–201
    technologies, 6, 27, 172, 173–174
    telecommunications software, 184–185
    wireless business applications, 171
Telepresence, 322, 323
Teleprocessing monitors, 196
Templates, 111, 274
Terabytes, 89
Teraflops, 74, 77
Terminals, 71–72, 184–185
    VSAT, 192, 201
Terrestrial microwave systems, 191
Testing, systems, 363, 367, 370
Text data, 109
Thin clients, 188
Third-generation languages, 124
Third-generation wireless technology,
    193–194

Threat of new entrants, 40–42
Threat of substitutes, 40–42
Three-tier client/server model, 188
Throughput, 77
Time and resource theft, 387–388
Time barriers, overcoming, 174
Time dimension, of information, 295
Time division multiplexing, 195
Time elements, 77
Timeline, systems implementation, 359
Timeliness, of information, 295
Time period, of information, 295
Time-sharing, 119
Token ring, 201
Topologies, 184, 198–199
Total cost of ownership, 70
Total quality management, 240
Touchpad, 81
Touch screens, 81
Trackball, 81
Trackpoint, 81
Traditional marketing, 273
Traffic management, 197
Training
    effectiveness of, 243
    human resource systems and, 242–243
    for IS services evaluation, 362
    systems implementation and, 363–364,
        367, 370
Transaction, 72, 228, 274, 359
Transaction databases, 141
Transaction file, 141
Transaction processing, 12–13, 150–152
    cycles, 229–231
    database management software, 150–152
    e-commerce and, 258
    online, 228–229
    systems, 228–231
    transactions, defined, 228
Transaction services software, 359
Transaction terminals, 72
Transborder data flows, 441
Transmission of confidential data, 387
Transnational strategies, 436–437
Transport layer, OSI model, 200
Trends
    B2B e-commerce, 270
    B2C e-commerce, 270
    DSS, 296–297
    e-commerce applications, 268–270
    information systems, 10–12
    in telecom networks, 172–174
Trojan horse, 386
Troubleshooting function, 365
Turnover analysis, 243
24x7 website hosting, 274
Twisted-pair wire, 190
Two-tier client/server architecture, 188
Types of databases, 141–143
Types of information systems, 12–15

UDDI Web service, 128–129
Unauthorized use, at work, 387–388
Universal client, 107
Universal Product Code, 84
UNIX operating system, 120–121
Unstructured decisions, 294, 295–296

Updates, to sales records, 28
Upgrading core business systems, 357
Uploads, non-work-related, 387
U.S. Computer Matching and Privacy Act,
    393
U.S.-EU data privacy, 442
Usage, Internet, unauthorized, 387
Use function, DBMS, 149
User interface, 28, 349
    agents, 324
    design, 351–352
    operating systems, 117–118
    requirements, 350
User password protection, 274
User services, managing, 429
Utilities, operating systems, 118–119, 121

Value, e-commerce success and, 272
Value-added carriers, 201
Value-added network companies, 280
Value-added resellers, 361–362
Value chains, 44–45, 224
Variable-length records, 141
Very-large-scale integration, 87–89
Very-small-aperture terminal, 192, 201
Very thin clients, 193
Video monitors, 86
Video output, 86–87
Virtual communities, 238
Virtual companies, 54–55
Virtual corporation, 54–55
Virtual machines, 119
Virtual manufacturing, 55
Virtual memory, 118–119
Virtual organization, 54–55
Virtual private networks, 18, 180, 186–187,
    280
    computer security for, 384
Virtual reality, 317–318, 321–323
Virtual teams, 9, 112
Viruses. *see* Computer viruses/worms
Visual Basic, 124–125
Visual programming, 125
Voice-messaging computers, 83
Voice print verification, 408, 409
Voice response systems, 86
Voice verification (voice print), 408, 409
Volatility, 90

Walker (movement monitor), 322
Wands, 84
War dialing, 386
Web-based systems. *see also* The Internet
    advertising, 177–178, 274
    brochures, 268, 270
    browsers, 107, 178, 185
    development, end user, 355
    DSS, 302–303, 306–307, 337
    ERP training, 363–364
    financial analysis/reporting, 337
    human resources, 243–244
    intelligent agents, 325
    knowledge management, 312–313
    manufacturing, 242
    marketing, 177–178
    marketing communications, 273
    payment, 265. *see also* Electronic payment
        systems

publishing, 126, 179
sales force automation, 238–240
SCM, 224–225
self-service data analysis, 297
server software, 359
services. *see* Web services
stores. *see* Web stores
tools for decision support, 306–307
Web clipping technologies, 193–194
Web hosting company, 274
websites. *see* Website/Web page
Web languages
    HTML, 125–126, 178, 193
    Java, 124–125, 127, 136
    XML, 126–128, 136, 143, 193
Web services, 116, 128–129
    SOAP protocol, 128–129
    UDDI directory, 128–129
Website/Web page
    advertising on, 274
    corporate, 351
    customer experiences with, 349–350
    design tools, 274
    hosting, 274
    online help, 274
    usage statistics, e-commerce and, 274
Web stores, 270, 359
    customer service and, 274, 349–350
    developing, 274–275
    managing, 274, 276–277
    storefront software, 359
What-if analysis, 110, 305
Wide area networks, 185
Wi-Fi, 193, 201
    business value of, 208
Windows, 72, 119–120, 417
Wireless application protocol, 193–194
Wireless business applications, 171
Wireless computers, 99
Wireless LANs, 70, 193
Wireless markup language, 193
Wireless technologies, 174, 191–194
    bluetooth, 193
    cellular phones, 193
    communications satellites, 191–192
    pagers, 193
    PCS phone systems, 193
    terrestrial microwave systems, 191
    Wi-Fi, 193, 201
    wireless Web, 193–194
Wizards (software), 323
Word processing software, 109
Workflow management, 260, 263, 264
Workflow software engine, 263
Workforce planning/scheduling, 243
Working conditions, IT and, 395
Work management tools, 121, 232
Workstation computers, 69
World Wide Web Consortium, 175
Worms. *see* Computer viruses/worms
WORM storage, 93

XML (eXtensible Markup Language),
    126–129, 136, 143, 193
    Web services based on, 281

Zero (binary), 88
Zombie computers, 404, 405